FUNDAMENTALS OF
COURT INTERPRETATION

University of Arizona
Summer Institute for
Court Interpretation Series

FUNDAMENTALS OF COURT INTERPRETATION
Theory, Policy, and Practice

Roseann Dueñas González
University of Arizona

Victoria F. Vásquez
University of Arizona

Holly Mikkelson
Monterey Institute for International Studies

In consultation with:

Sofia Zahler
Former Director of Court Interpreter Services
U.S. District Court, Los Angeles

Frank M. Almeida
Director of Court Interpreter Services
U.S. District Court, Los Angeles

Linda Haughton
Staff Interpreter, U.S. District Court, El Paso

CAROLINA
ACADEMIC
PRESS
700 KENT ST.
DURHAM, NC
27701

International Standard Book Number: 0-89089-414-0
Library of Congress Card Catalog Number: 92-71353

Carolina Academic Press
700 Kent Street
Durham, North Carolina 27701
(919) 489-7486

Printed in the United States of America

Contents

Foreword

There are several reasons why I am delighted to encourage the reader to explore Professor González's *Fundamentals of Court Interpretation*, but among them are two such strictly personal considerations as the fact that I was interested in witness testimony (Unit 5, Chapter 22) even before I became actively involved in sociolinguistics and the further fact that I was interested in interpreting even long, long before that.

I could not have been more than three or four years old, still spending many hours in the crib every day just to be out of harm's way, when my mother began leaving me with her mother when she herself left the house to do the weekly shopping. Bobbe (grandma) Beyle may have been a somewhat sad or depressed person, but she was easy for me to be with because, on the one hand, she let me do whatever I wanted to and, on the other hand, she fed me chocolates at the slightest provocation. We all have our limitations, however, and bobbe's was that after more than half a dozen years in the USA she still knew virtually no English and, therefore, couldn't communicate at all with the cleaning woman who invariably also came on the same day that mother did her weekly shopping.

The interpreter role and its potential for abuse

I remember not only translating from English to Yiddish and from Yiddish to English as a mere child (and not only for the cleaning woman and bobbe, but for many others in our sizable immigrant neighborhood), but I also remember the sense of power that I experienced in that connection, because not only was I a crucial link in the communication chain but because I could subtly influence the outcomes of communicative interactions by emphases and modifications that I myself introduced into the ongoing flow of communication. Almost three decades later, I came to recognize, as does Professor González now, that translating and interpreting are not at all identical processes and that the latter is fraught with many more dangers of "third party influence" (less euphemistically put, interpreter influence) than is the former. The professionalization, regulation and certification of the interpreter role constitutes a modern bureaucratic effort to overcome the potential abuses of the interpreter role of which I had already become dimly aware at the tender age of three or four. The abuses of which I speak are societally patterned, of course, and have to do with the inherent exploitability of the societally weak by the societally strong. As a result, they are all the more in need of societal supervision and correction.

Influencing witness testimony

More than a quarter century later, in the mid fifties, I had my second naive encounter with another potential area for miscarriage of justice within the interactive process that constitutes the very heart of our legal system. This occurred in the time of McCarthyism, when days and weeks were spent glued to televised hearings in which witnesses were taunted and badgered and put under all kinds of stress, within the hearing chamber and in the "real world" as well. It came to the point that even claiming one's constitutional rights to invoke the Fifth Amendment protection against potential self-incrimination was interpreted as a sign of treasonable guilt, punishable by blacklisting, dismissal and shunning, regardless of what the hearings themselves might recommend.

It was then that I, a just-completed Ph.D. in hand, and an older colleague, Rudolf Morris (then a sociologist at Marquette University and deeply imbued with the highest principle of Catholic morality) decided to convene a panel of forensic experts (social scientists and legal specialists) to discuss orally, and then in print, the issue of witness performance under stress. The issue of the *Journal of Social Issues* (1957, 13, no. 2), that constituted the ultimate fruit of our labors, was subsequently often cited as an intellectual contribution to overcoming the anti-constitutional hysteria among some defenders of the "American way of life."

An intellectual contribution to the pursuit of justice for the non-English speaking

Professor González's work is a further contribution along just these lines, reminding us all that the non-English speaking are entitled to and, unfortunately, often require protection if the very best that American justice promises and is capable of is actually obtainable in practice. Like all genuinely intellectual contributions, her work is both theoretical and practical. Its practical worth is derived not only directly, from the very nature of some of the topics considered, but also indirectly, from her theoretical interests as well. "There is nothing as practical as a good theory" the brilliant American social psychologist Kurt Lewin (himself a refugee from Nazi terror) was wont to say. Professor González demonstrates this truth over and over again. I may be forgiven for seeing this most clearly in her linguistic unit (Unit 5) and in her unit on interpretation theory (Unit 6), but many others will perhaps more easily do so in her historical and legal units.

In sum, this is a very useful and stimulating work. It combines theory and practice, insight and experience, linguistics and law, social science and history, all of the foregoing being brought together with the prophet's call "Justice, justice shall thou pursue!" Accordingly, I am delighted to introduce it to the worlds of scholarship and legal practice, in the certainty that both will be grateful to Professor González for her contribution to their improved functioning insofar as our non-English speaking brethren are concerned. Ultimately, we are judged—as individuals, as societies and as nations—for the help we give to those that cannot help themselves. González has helped us make sure that we will not be found wanting in that connection as heretofore, a connection in which, unfortunately, we not only cannot do enough, but one in which we still do not usually do even that which is required by law.

Joshua A. Fishman
Distinguished University Research Professor,
Social Sciences Emeritus
Ferkauf Graduate School of Psychology
Yeshiva University

July 1990

Acknowledgments

There are many to thank for their help and support in bringing *Fundamentals of Court Interpretation* to fruition. However, this book would not have been possible without the major funding and personal support of Agnese Nelms Haury, whose interest in the fair and even administration of justice has spurred, at critical moments, the development of the field of court interpreting. Agnese Haury's support of the initial Summer Institute for Court Interpreting at the University of Arizona in 1983 marked a milestone in court interpreter training. Her underwriting of the first Training of Trainers of Court Interpreters in 1984 and her sponsorship of the University of Arizona Summer Institute for Court Interpretation at Montclair State College in New Jersey in 1985 demonstrate an unparalleled commitment to this important emerging area. Words cannot sufficiently express our gratitude to her. *Fundamentals* is a tribute to the visionary and pioneer spirit of Agnese Nelms Haury.

We are grateful also to the University of Arizona Foundation for its support of this volume and for its early joint sponsorship with Agnese Haury to offer quality training where there was none—efforts that have given the Summer Institute for Court Interpreting and the Training of Trainers Institute at the University of Arizona the opportunity to influence a growing field of professionals, to shape standards of practice, and to provide a foundation for intellectual inquiry.

Agnese Nelms Haury and the University of Arizona Foundation, through their sponsorship of these early efforts, are also due credit for influencing an entire generation of scholars, academicians, and professionals who have either attended the Institutes as students or have been associated with the Institute as associate faculty. Researchers such as Susan Berk-Seligson, University of Pittsburgh, and Nancy Schweda-Nicholson, University of Delaware, attended the Institute. Court interpreting professionals who later became associate faculty include: Dr. Linda Haughton, Staff Interpreter of the United States District Court in El Paso; Laura Murphy and Lauren García, staff interpreters of the United States District Court in Tucson. Also among the students of the Institute are court interpreting specialists and professionals such as Fritz Hensey, Federally Certified Interpreter and Associate Professor of Spanish at the University of Texas at Austin; Patricia Michelsen-Whitley, Chief Interpreter of the United States District Court, Southern District of New York; Susana Sawrey, Federally Certified Interpreter, Washington State; Donna Whitman, Head Interpreter, Pima County Superior Court, and many other notable persons in the field.

Others influenced by these student and teacher training efforts of the Summer Institute at the University of Arizona are teaching and administrative associates of the Institute such as Marilyn Tayler of Montclair State College and the New Jersey Consortium; Joanne Engelbert of Montclair State College; Edward Rock, Supervisory Interpreter, Federal District Court in Tucson; Rosa Olivera, Supervisory Interpreter of the United States District Court, Central District of New York; Holly Mikkelson, Director of the Court Interpreting Program at the Monterey Institute of International Studies; Sara Krauthamer, former California Court Interpreter Association President; and our most recent associate, Mr. Sam Adelo, J.D., Federally Certified Interpreter.

To our consultants, the late Dr. Sofia Zahler, Federally Certified Interpreter and former Director of Court Interpreter Services, United States District Court, Central District of California, Los Angeles; Mr. Frank M. Almeida, Federally Certified Interpreter and Director of Interpreter Services, United States District Court, Central District of California, Los Angeles; and Dr. Linda Haughton, Federally Certified Staff Interpreter, United States District Court, Central District of Texas, El Paso, we extend our most heartfelt appreciation and admiration for their generous sharing of information. They spent countless hours reading the manuscript, editing, and discussing with us the myriad issues presented in this work. Their willingness to share their profound knowledge and vast experience through this work distinguishes their extraordinary professionalism.

We are deeply honored that Professor Emeritus Joshua Fishman of Yeshiva University took precious time during an especially difficult period to both read a portion of the manuscript and write a Foreword for our book. We are also grateful to colleagues who have kindly read various portions of the manuscript at various stages in the process: Jon A. Leeth, former Chief, Programs Branch, Court Administration Division of the Administrative Office of the United States Courts, currently Director of Training, The Peace Corps; Professor David Marshall, University of South Dakota; Dr. Charles Stansfield, Director of Research, Center for Applied Linguistics; and various members of the Department of English, University of Arizona.

We also wish to thank those interpreters and researchers who have come before and from whom we have learned so much: the late Ely Weinstein, Federally Certified Interpreter and core faculty member of the Summer Institute for Court Interpretation at the University of Arizona and past president of the California Court Interpreters Association; the late Theodore Fagan, Former Chief Interpreter of the United Nations and core faculty member of the Summer Institute for Court Interpretation at the University of Arizona; the late David Gerver, Professor of Psychology, University of Stirling, Scotland, psycholinguist and interpreting researcher; and the late Sara Neiman, Federally Certified Interpreter and past president of the California Court Interpreters' Association.

Our sincere appreciation is extended to the many members of the federal judiciary who have been instrumental in ensuring justice for non-English speakers. Our special thanks go to the Honorable Richard Bilby, United States District Court of Tucson, Arizona for many years of help and support for all Summer Institute activities, his open-door policy to Summer Institute students, and most of all for his judicial insight, which has informed much of the policy in this book. And our thanks to state court jurists and numerous attorneys for interest, insight, information, and encouragement.

We are grateful to everyone who has aided us in our research and in the word-processing of the seemingly countless drafts. Our first thanks are to John Bichsel of the University of Arizona, who managed the word processing and databases and edited and proofread copy. His commitment to this project was selfless, and he worked weekends, holidays, and vacations to ensure that we met our most critical deadlines. We are also immensely appreciative of the fine work of Heshim Jung, our research assistant and assistant bibliographer, whose hundreds of hours of tedious work will never be forgotten; of the comprehensive work and input of our legal research assistant Adele Drumlevitch, J.D., City Public Defender, City of Tucson; and of the dedicated and hard work of University of Arizona student Ed Muldowney for his careful word-processing of thousands of edits. Our thanks also to Jonathan Hale, Carmela Mezquita, and Carolina Melara Katz, all University of Arizona students who assisted. We also acknowledge the invaluable assistance of Mr. Ron Cherry, J.D., Head Librarian, University of Arizona College of Law.

We appreciate the overall support of Dr. Henry Koffler, former President of the University of Arizona; the help of Richard B. Kinkade, former Dean of the Faculty of Humanities, who enthusiastically supported this project from the outset; and our many thanks to Bill Wright, Manager of Business and Finance of the College of Arts and Sciences of the University of Arizona who has over the years consistently facilitated the smooth running of the Summer Institute and related projects.

We thank our editor at Carolina Academic Press, Mayapriya Long, for her belief in this project, her patient extension of deadlines, her enthusiasm, and assistance.

And finally, we thank our families—the Gonzálezes, the Vásquezes, and the Willises. To Bob González we give special and hearty thanks for his substantive and moral support, encouragement, technical advice of all kinds, and assistance with numerous tasks such as entertaining various children, transporting authors and consultants, reading, proofreading, word processing, copying, running errands, and various and sundry tasks. His patience was unending as was his willingness to do whatever was necessary to get the job done. Greater love hath no man shown! To the González family—Marisa Camille and Roberto J. González and to Gloria, Gilbert, and Oralia, thanks for the patience, love, support, and help of all kinds.

To the Vásquez family and many friends, thanks for their love, support, patience, and understanding. And we extend special appreciation to the late Benjamin V. Vásquez and Frances E. Vásquez, whose examples have inspired this work. A special acknowledgment is also extended to Professor Bruce Sales, Director, Law-Psychology and Policy Program of the University of Arizona for his unwavering support and superb teaching.

To Jim Willis, we are grateful for the technical assistance with the development of diagrams and for his patience and support. To Gahan and Ned Mikkelson, thanks for patience and understanding. A special note of gratitude to Etilvia Arjona Chang, Director of the Translation and Interpretation Program at the University of Hawaii, for inspiration and encouragement.

And most of all, to the hundreds of students who have attended the University of Arizona Summer Institute for Court Interpretation and the Court Interpreting Program at the Monterey Institute of International Studies, we are grateful for all that we have learned from them.

Roseann Dueñas González
Victoria Félice Vásquez
Holly Mikkelson

SPECIAL NOTE: Our sincerest apologies to anyone who finds the term "speech and hearing impaired" offensive. We now realize the accepted term is "deaf." We hope that this error will not prevent the reader from finding the information in this book helpful.

FUNDAMENTALS OF
COURT INTERPRETATION

Introduction

Chapter 1

Dilemmas in Due Process

1. Statement of the Problem

The United States has always been a linguistically diverse country in which English is the indisputable language of public life (Fishman, Nahirny, Hofman, & Hayden, 1966). This linguistic feature of the United States invariably affects how we conduct our businesses, run our government, and interact among ourselves. Bridging the language barrier between public language and the home languages of community members, either formally or informally, has become a prominent issue in our daily lives.

Nowhere is this fact more apparent than in our legal system. Language services have historically, although not systematically, been provided non-English-speaking participants in the criminal justice system when deemed necessary by the trial judge. From the earliest recorded time in United States legal history, cases have been heard that involved interpreters or the services they render (*Amory v. Fellowes*, 1809; *In re Norberg*, 1808; *Meyer v. Foster*, 1862). Moreover, legislation affecting the appointment and compensation of interpreters appeared as early as the middle of the nineteenth century (California Code of Civil Procedures §1884; New York Laws, 1869; Pennsylvania Act of March 27, 1865).

Unfortunately, because of a general lack of understanding among the judiciary and the public concerning the consequences of not providing appropriate language services, interpreters have never been subject to uniform professional or legal regulation. Consequently, through the years, the use of unqualified, untested, and untrained individuals as interpreters has led to a serious abridgment of due process rights for many United States citizens.

It is not surprising then, that anecdotal evidence, congressional testimony, and governmentally commissioned studies attest to the inadequacy of interpretation as practiced in the courts (Astiz, 1980, 1986; Berk-Seligson, 1987, 1988; Comptroller General of the United States, 1977; Gonzalez, 1976, 1977; Judicial Council of California, 1977; Lopez, 1975; New Jersey Supreme Court Task Force on Interpreter and Translation Services, 1985; *Senate Bill No. 1724*; *Senate Bill No. 565*; *Senate Bill No. 1853*). A plethora of cases illustrate these injustices and violations of due process (*Arizona v. Natividad*, 1974; *United States ex rel. Negron v. New York*, 1970; *United States v. Carrin*, 1973). What is clear from this brief glimpse of the legal literature is that the problem has been enduring and pervasive.

To this day, limited- or non-English speakers who come before the courts have no guarantee that their stories will be told or that they will understand what the court is telling them. Moreover, when they do tell their stories, it is more likely than not that significant portions of their testimony will be distorted by the interpreter omitting information present in the original testimony, adding information not present, or by stylistically altering the tone and intent of the speaker. Judges and juries are not given the opportunity to "hear" the testimony as it was originally spoken, and defendants and witnesses cannot fully comprehend the questions asked of them. This linguistic distortion compromises the fact-finding process, and, as a result, the fundamental right of non-English speakers to participate in the legal system is violated.

Because the accommodation of non-English speakers in the justice system has evolved primarily on a case-by-case basis in courtrooms outside the public arena, there is little public awareness of the inequality caused by inadequate language services; these dilemmas in due process are vast, yet go largely unnoticed. However, several recent cases reported in the media highlight the inequities witnesses, defendants, and attorneys suffer as the result of the use of unqualified and untested interpreters (Davis, 1980; Goldner, 1987a, 1987b, 1987c; *People v. Nguyen*, 1989; testimony of T. Kamiyama to the Grand Jury in the matter of the Rev. Sun Myoung Moon, 1981; Zavala, 1977). Because interpreted hearings are not regularly recorded (in audio), few documented examples of the problem exist. However, some striking examples can be found. Recently, Ewell and Schrieberg (1989) of the *San Jose Mercury News,* a California newspaper, conducted an intensive nine-month investigation that included monitoring by an independent federally certified or professionally qualified interpreter who recorded inaccurate interpretations made by the court-appointed interpreter. These investigative reporters approached the interpreting issue quite methodically and conducted extensive interviews with national, state, and local interpreting and language experts including: Jon A. Leeth, formerly of the Administrative Office of the United States Courts; Robert Joe Lee, of the Administrative Office of the New Jersey Courts; Carlos Astiz, professor at State University of New York, Buffalo; Eugene Briere, Professor Emeritus of the University of Southern California; and the authors of this volume. Also interviewed were members of the California judiciary and other legal personnel, court administrators, state testing officials, officers of the California Court Interpreters Association, and federally and state certified interpreters. In an effort to discover the condition of interpreting practice in California, the *San Jose Mercury News* surveyed 509 working interpreters. Ewell and Schrieberg's conclusion is clear: poor interpreting practices in California state courts are pervasive.

One case that illustrates well the poor quality of interpretation services these reporters found is *People v. Nguyen*, 1989 (Ewell & Schrieberg, 1989). In this case, a Vietnamese defendant, Nguyen, was accused of murdering Hai Tang but convicted of the lesser charge of manslaughter after a jury heard the testimony of the victim's wife, Be Le, through the court-appointed interpreter, Tran. According to the investigative reporter, "There was no doubt about it. Quang Nguyen sneaked into Be Le's home with an assault rifle, waited for Be and her husband, Hai Tang, to come home and then killed him" (p. 16A). Yet throughout the two-day trial, the facts of the case were consistently skewed by the interpreter's rendition of the state witness's testimony. It was noted that:

> A court interpreter is sworn to truthfully interpret the testimony word for word. Instead, Tran omitted words, phrases and whole sentences, mistranslated frequently, and spoke in pidgin English. Sometimes, the question was interpreted incorrectly, leading to a confusing exchange that forced the deputy district attorney to ask Be the same question repeatedly. The effect was to batter the credibility of his own star witness.... (p. 16A)

A sample of the interpreter's alleged inaccuracies in the Nguyen trial is taken from the transcription as published in the newspaper account. Below is an illustration first of what the jury heard, including the attorney's questions where pertinent, followed by what the independent interpreter hired by the *San Jose Mercury News* transcribed while listening to the same witness.

Jury Heard: . . . He said that if that day he had a gun, then he **could kill** [emphasis ours] the policeman. . . .

Mercury News: . . . He said if he had a gun he **would have killed** [emphasis ours] the policeman. . . .

[Author's analysis: The use of the modal *could*, as opposed to *would*, denotes the difference between the ability to do something and the will or intention to do something.]

Jury Heard: . . . He may have some kind of a reprisal action against us. . . .

Mercury News: . . . I was afraid that he would think that we looked down on him. I did not want to create feelings of hatred and vengeance. . . .

[Author's analysis: The interpreter omitted an entire sentence and summarized incorrectly the main ideas in the witness's testimony. He made the jury think the victim and witness may have had something to fear from the defendant because of their own actions, rather than letting them understand that the witness was trying to diffuse a deteriorating situation.]

Attorney: . . . When you saw somebody inside the bedroom there, did you say anything? . . .

Jury Heard: . . . I just scream. I say, "Who is there?" . . .

Mercury News: . . . I screamed: "Oh, God! Who is there?" . . .

[Author's analysis: By leaving out the phrase "Oh, God!, the interpreter misrepresented the witness's fearful state of mind.]

Attorney: . . . Did you see him making motions with his finger on the trigger as if he's pulling back on the trigger? . . .

Jury Heard: . . . I only saw him moving like this (interpreter made gesture with his hand) and then I saw him pulling things back. . . .

Mercury News: . . . I saw him pull or squeeze the rifle with his finger as if there was something stuck in the rifle. . . .

[Author's analysis: Interpreter summarized incorrectly, omitting specific, significant details.]

Attorney:	...Did he say anything in response?...
Jury Heard:	...I was confused that moment, but I only knew that he took the handle of the rifle and beat me....
Mercury News:	...At that time my ears were buzzing because he turned the handle of the rifle and hit me. (p. 16A)

[Author's analysis: Interpreter overtranslated the statement about the "ears buzzing" and made the witness seem inconsistent and inaccurate by saying she was confused and beaten. The interpreter changed the important "he turned the handle of the rifle," making the witness seem less precise.]

The interpreter for this case unintentionally garbled the source message and spoke in a kind of creolized English, marked with heavy interference from Vietnamese pronunciation, word sense, grammar, and world view. Viewed separately, each linguistic distortion does not always seem consequential. When the number and frequency of interpretation distortions is pervasive in a trial, however, it may lead the jury to judge witnesses as hesitant, evasive, and unsure of themselves. Undetected and/or uncorrected interpreter errors make clear answers appear non-responsive, muddled, and evasive. Ultimately, as is true in this case, an accurate assessment of the veracity of the witness is virtually impossible. In fact when questioned by the reporter, the jury maintained that "their conclusion that the prosecution's star witness, Be, was evasive under questioning" (p. 16A) was crucial to their verdict—a verdict that allows Nguyen to be released in as little as eight years.

The transcripts make it obvious that the English-speaking members of the court and the non-English-speaking witnesses were not at the same trial. The true facts and circumstances, as well as the intent of the parties involved, never surfaced in this trial, and justice was thwarted. Had the court used a well-qualified interpreter, though, its fairness and trustworthiness as a social arbitrator would be beyond reproach. For an extended discussion of the violations of the legal rights of defendants, see Unit 3, Chapter 12.

In another recent case, the results of poor interpretation in a United States grand jury proceeding threatened international repercussions (Testimony of T. Kamiyama to the Grand Jury in the Matter of the Rev. Sun Myoung Moon, 1981). In 1981, a Japanese accountant, who was an employee of the Rev. Sun Myoung Moon, was called to testify before a New York grand jury in connection with pending tax evasion charges against his employer. Because of his apparently inconsistent statements, Mr. Kamiyama was later indicted and convicted of perjury and served a four and one-half month sentence in the federal penitentiary (p. 106). Members of the Japanese Diet (the Japanese parliament) and others considered the substandard interpreter services "a grave miscarriage of justice, carried out against a Japanese citizen solely because of his lack of proficiency with the English language" (p. 109).

This high-powered lobby requested not only a continued investigation into the circumstances surrounding Mr. Kamiyama's conviction, but also urged a reversal of the conviction and protection against similar problems in the future. The lobby presented into the record a "Declaration of Takeru Kamiyama," which served as a record of the errors committed by the prosecution interpreter. Selected passages of the defendant's testimony are presented below with comments from an independent Japanese translator, who was employed by the lobby to transcribe the proceedings. Note that the transcript excerpts follow a question-answer format. The first Q and A set reflect the actual grand jury transcript and what the English-speaking court heard. The second set, Q′ and A′, reflect the Japanese translator's rendition of the taped grand jury proceeding, which reveals what was actually said by the interpreter and Mr. Kamiyama. Each set of questions and answers is followed by the translator's comments about the appropriateness of the interpretation.

QUESTION

Q **Prosecutor's Question**
You carried the checkbook with you from the very beginning of the account?

Q′ **Prosecution Interpreter's Version of the Question as Heard by Mr. Kamiyama**
So then, from the very beginning—that's after opening the account—from the beginning, (you) Mr. Kamiyama [verb missing] the checkbook . . . [sentence unfinished].

Comments on Question

1. The interpreter did not finish his rendering of the question asked in Q.

ANSWER

A **Prosecution Interpreter's Version of Mr. Kamiyama's Answer**
Yes, I kept it myself from the beginning.

A′ **Mr. Kamiyama's Answer as Correctly Translated**
As for that, I kept it [English word "keep" in Japanized [sic] form is used].

Comments on Answer

1. Mr. Kamiyama says nothing that can be translated as "Yes," "from the beginning," or "myself." These words make A appear to be a response to Q.

2. Mr. Kamiyama begins his answer without hearing the missing verb in Q′; so it is not clear whether or not he is responding to the "you carried" in Q.

3. The Japanized [sic] English word "keep" used in A′ does not necessarily imply physical possession. (p. 155)

QUESTION	ANSWER
Q **Prosecutor's Question** And did Reverend Moon write out the other portions of the check, other than his signature?	A **Prosecution Interpreter's Version of Mr. Kamiyama's Answer** No. No, he didn't do it.
Q' **Prosecution Interpreter's Version of the Question as Heard by Mr. Kamiyama** So then . . . er . . . were there ever occasions when the Reverend personally would write, in addition to (his) signature, the amount and various other places?	A' **Mr. Kamiyama's Answer as Correctly Translated** There were not. There were not.

Comments on Question	**Comments on Answer**
No comments.	No comments. (p. 156)

QUESTION	ANSWER
Q **Prosecutor's Question** You prepared all the checks for him?	A **Prosecution Interpreter's Version of Mr. Kamiyama's Answer** That's correct.
Q' **Prosecution Interpreter's Version of the Question as Heard by Mr. Kamiyama** What you are saying . . . are saying that (you or someone), in order to be able to have the Reverend sign, wrote in beforehand all the other places, and then requested the signature?	A' **Mr. Kamiyama's Answer as Correctly Translated** Yes.

Comments on Question

1. It is never explicitly made clear in Q' whether the question is about Mr. Kamiyama's actions or someone else's

2. Q' does not ask "all the checks" but "all the other places." It does not, therefore, correspond to Q. (p. 157)

Comments on Answer

No comments.

QUESTION

Q **Prosecutor's Question**
Did you discuss with him the reason why you were buying stock in Tong Il?

Q' **Prosecution Interpreter's Version of the Question as Heard by Mr. Kamiyama**
Er...did you speak with the Reverend about anything (concerning) the reason for buying stock in Tong Il?

ANSWER

A **Prosecution Interpreter's Version of Mr. Kamiyama's Answer**
I don't dare consult with him on such matters.

A' **Mr. Kamiyama's Answer as Correctly Translated**
[As if to himself] How many times are they asking this? [In a louder voice] I don't consult (with him) about such matters.

Comments on Question

1. It is not clear in Q' who is doing the buying: Q says "the reason why you were buying" and Q' says "the reason for buying."

Comments on Answer

1. A' does not provide a yes-no answer to a question that requires one. Therefore, A' is not a direct response to Q'.

2. The rendering "don't dare consult" in A is erroneous. (p. 165)

As was the case in *People v. Nguyen* (1989), cited above, the use of interpreters who have not been certified as competent for work in judicial proceedings results in costly challenges, unjustly convicted defendants, and can, as in this instance, impugn the international image of the United States system of law as fair and just.

Many cases involving poor interpretation are not appealed, and because the legal reporter system only publishes appellate decisions, it is impossible to estimate the number of cases in state courts which are affected by this issue. However, the 1978 Court Interpreters Act (see Unit 1, Chapter 5) now requires federal court systems to compile yearly the number of hearings which involve the use of interpreters. In 1988, 49,850 hearings or docketable events required an interpreter. Of these, 46,000 or 92.5 percent were Spanish/English (Administrative Office of the United States Courts, 1989a). In spite of the court system's failure to provide empirical evidence of such hearings, interpreters across the nation can easily relate case after case in which gross injustices were caused by poor interpretation.

A legendary case of injustice resulting from substandard interpretation is that of Gregorio Cortez. This case, which occurred in Texas in 1906, was chronicled in a film which has garnered much critical acclaim, *The Ballad of Gregorio Cortez* (Esparza & Young, 1983). Gregorio was a borderman who endured seven trials and twelve years of prison because of an inept interpreter. The incident began when a sheriff went to investigate a report of a stolen horse at the home of Gregorio, who did not speak any English. The sheriff, accompanied by a Texas Ranger who acted as an interpreter, asked Gregorio if he had traded a horse that day. Gregorio answered, *No he cambiado un caballo . . . pero una yegua sí.* The interpreter told the sheriff that Gregorio wasn't going to answer him. The sheriff, who believed that Gregorio had in fact traded a horse, told the interpreter that Gregorio was lying. Then the sheriff said, I'll have to arrest you then, to which Gregorio answered, *No me pueden arrestar por nada,* which the interpreter translated as "No man can arrest me," when it should have been, "You can't arrest me for nothing ('no reason')."

When Gregorio made this response, the sheriff was ready to draw, and Gregorio's brother tried to stop him by approaching and attempting to explain what had transpired. Misunderstanding the intentions of the brother, the sheriff shot him; and, in defense of his brother, Gregorio pulled a gun and shot the sheriff. It was found later in the trial that the confusion originated from the interpreter's unfamiliarity with the word *yegua.* What Gregorio truthfully answered was that he had not traded a *caballo* (in Spanish a "stallion") but a *yegua* ("a mare"). Thus, a law official's feeble knowledge of Spanish (which he called Mexican) caused the death of a rancher, initiated the single largest manhunt ever conducted by the Texas Rangers, and resulted in the death of two sheriffs. In addition, Gregorio's family suffered severe humiliation and abuse during the trial, and he endured twelve years of unjust imprisonment. Gregorio Cortez, who died shortly after his release from prison, became a famous folk hero and was immortalized in numerous *corridos* (traditional ballads) about this travesty, and in the narrative *"With His Pistol in His Hand": A Border Ballad and Its Hero* (1958) by folklorist Américo Paredes.

A more current example is that of the 1977-80 Hanigan Trials in Arizona. Three undocumented Mexican men—en route to an Arizona ranch where they had been promised work—were kidnapped and tortured by three Douglas ranchers—a father and his two sons. Although the state case clearly involved undeniable wrongdoing on the part of the Hanigan family, they were exonerated after having been brought to trial. The state's witnesses, the three young Mexican men, spoke no English and depended entirely upon the services of an interpreter who regrettably did not have the depth and breadth of knowledge to represent their voices. The trial was replete with both gross and subtle inaccuracies and misinterpretations. For example, *me encadenaron a una taza* was interpreted as "they chained me to a cup," when quite clearly, in that particular context, *taza* referred to a toilet bowl, not a cup (Gonzalez, 1983).

Because the first proceeding was never deemed a mistrial, a second trial based on the same charges (double jeopardy) could not be brought against the Hanigans. However, the proceedings were so patently unfair that the local and national Hispanic community protested until the Justice Department filed a federal charge under the Hobbs Act against the Hanigans for interfering in interstate commerce.

Former United States attorney, and lead counsel on the Hanigan trial, Michael Hawkins, reported that many inconsistencies revealed at the federal trial stemmed from poor interpretation of the testimony at the state level (personal communication, March 12, 1990). One particular issue puzzled the jury. Why hadn't the three young men tried to escape when they were left alone in a pickup truck with a camper shell? At the state trial the interpreter's rendition of the Mexicans' response to that question referred to the camper as having a **latch inside the door**. This issue damaged the witnesses's credibility because the jury couldn't understand why, if there were a latch inside the camper, the three young Mexican men had not simply opened it and escaped. In reality, the facts indicated the correct interpretation should have been that there was a **lock** that had been bolted from the outside.

There were other language problems, too. Whenever the young men answered any question concerning time, dimension, or distance with the Spanish phrase *más o menos* ("more or less" literally, but "approximately" in its idiomatic sense), the interpreter related *más o menos* as "more or less" instead of "approximately." This led the examining attorneys down a confusing and often damaging (for the government's case) line of questioning: "Was it more or less?," "How much more?," "How much less?"

Seemingly trivial differences in meaning caused problems of inordinate dimensions. Testimony such as the following was repeatedly twisted by inadequate interpretation, negatively affecting the outcome of the trial:

Context: Were you burned?

Original: *A mí me quemaron con una varilla porque cuando pusieron el fuego, lo . . . pues pusieron la varilla ahí. Luego, lo pasaron a los tres . . . así, por todo el cuerpo, y nosotros nos retorcíamos.*

Interpreter: Uh, I was burned because they put a, a like a—a stick, some sort of, uh, a, thing, and . . . they put that in the fire, and then they put it on our bodies, and we kept moving around trying to get away. (Zavala, 1977, pp. 33-34)

[Interpreter omitted "the three of us" and used "stick" instead of iron rod, thus diminishing the seriousness of the action described.]

Should be: They burned me with a rod because when they made the fire, it . . . , well they put the rod there. Then they ran it over the three of us— over our entire body like that, and we were writhing.

*   *   *

Original: And did you go back the same way that you had approached the windmill earlier that morning?

Interpreter: *¿Y se fue él, a, a la misma—la misma parte, uh, como habían llegado al papalote esa mañana?* (Zavala, 1977, p. 37)

[And did he go to the same, the same place as they had arrived at the windmill that morning?]

[Interpreter distorted "approached the windmill" and distorted "and did you go back the same way?" The witness responded to a significantly different question from the one originally asked.]

Should be: *¿Y regresaron por el mismo camino por el que ya se habían acercado al papalote esa mañana?*

*   *   *

Context: The question is, "Isn't it true that they didn't put the iron on any other part of the body except for the feet?"

Original: *Más que en los pies no le pusieron.*

Interpreter: They didn't put anywhere else than on my feet/Only on my feet they put it. (p. 35)

[Object is omitted in first; second is a literal translation that diminishes the force of the witness's statement.]

Should be: They didn't put it anywhere but on my feet.

According to Michael Hawkins, Linda Davis, and José Rivera, prosecutors for the two federal trials, misinterpretations like these at the state trial dominated the subject matter of the federal trial (personal communication, March 12, 1990).

According to Alex Gaynes, the defense attorney for one of the Hanigans, the interpretation process itself—not specifically misinterpretation—played a significant part in the lack of credence attributed to the plaintiffs' stories. Gaynes contends that "translation is an inherently difficult process. If the lawyers are smart enough to take advantage of the salient meaning differences between languages, they can exploit the translation for their own ends" (personal communication, March 16, 1990). Gaynes did just that. He capitalized on what little he knew about Spanish to the defendant's advantage. He noticed that English was particularly rich in extremely specific verbs denoting forms of physical abuse: strike, punch, beat, beat up, hit, sock, knock out, flatten, cream, knock flat, knock cold, rap, smash, jab, hammer, bang, whack, thump, pound. He also observed that these verbs could be rendered by the Spanish verb *golpear,* which generally means "to strike" or "to hit."

Gaynes realized that he could greatly weaken the government's case by making it appear that the complaining witness was merely "touched" by the defendant's hand as he made a motion to strike him. In other words, Gaynes used the broad set of meanings connoted by *golpear* and sophisticated questioning techniques to debilitate the government's strongest evidence. The following are approximations of the line of questioning that took place in the trial (personal communication, March 16, 1990).

1. Isn't it true that you told Mr. Polley that the North American **smashed** you right in the face?
   (*¿No es verdad que Ud. le dijo al Sr. Polley que el norteamericano le **golpeó** en la mera cara?*)

2. Isn't it true that you testified at a previous hearing that the man **hit** you in the face?
   (*¿No es cierto que Ud. atestiguó en una audiencia previa que el hombre le **golpeó** en la cara?*)

3. Didn't you tell Mr. Smith that you were **beaten up**?
   (*¿No le dijo Ud. al Sr. Smith que Ud. fue **golpeado**?*)

4. Isn't it true that you later told Mr. Polley that he just **touched** you with his fist when he raised his hand to strike you?

(*¿No es cierto que después Ud. le dijo al Sr. Polley que el nada más le tocó a Ud. con el puño cuando levantó la mano para* **golpearlo***?*)

Other issues that were problematic and that severely confused witness testimony were questions phrased in the double negative. The question, "Is it not true that you never did receive any money at all?," presents problems of ambiguity to English speakers and comprehension problems for speakers of other languages. The Spanish rendition is *¿No es cierto que Ud. nunca recibió dinero alguno?* The question is very often confusing to the Spanish speaker, who may respond to it with another question such as "Are you asking if I received money?" or "Could you repeat the question please; I didn't quite understand."

For this reason, Gaynes also believes that translation in the courts is an area that should be studied by aspiring and practicing lawyers because of the pitfalls and opportunities this communication device presents. Only one of the Hanigans was later convicted on the federal indictment (Davis, 1980; Miller, 1981). At the first trial it was evident that had a competent interpreter been present, the case would never have had to be retried in a federal court. It was also clear that the use of a certified interpreter at the federal proceeding was the major difference between the facts uncovered in the two trials. Undeniably, there is a significant problem in courtrooms when limited- or non-English-speaking populations present themselves. This text addresses the various aspects of the use of interpreter services to solve this legal dilemma.

2. Background

Court interpretation is the fastest growing field of specialization in translation and interpretation inside and outside the United States. Accordingly, it is also one of the most active areas of language policy and planning (Arjona, 1983; Marshall, 1986; Rubin, 1985; Schweda-Nicholson, 1986). As minority language populations are assimilated into various world societies, these societies become increasingly aware of the barriers language differences present to the administration of justice and other government services. Language policies have evolved that mandate language services in all legal contexts (Arjona, 1983; Carr, 1988; Marshall, 1986; Repa, 1988; Roy-Nicklen, 1988; Rubin, 1985; Task Force on Aboriginal Languages, 1986). In the past two decades in the United States, a growing concern for due process and access rights of limited- and non-English-speaking persons has attached more formal status to interpretation in both court and quasi-legal forums (Adams, 1973; Bergenfield, 1978; Blaine, 1974; Callejo, 1968; Chang & Araujo, 1975; Conley, 1979; Cronheim & Schwartz, 1976; Flaherty, 1983; Grabau & Williamson, 1985; Ilich, 1986; Rydstrom, 1971; Safford, 1977). Following the lead of the federal judicial system's language policy and implementation plan, set into motion by the Court Interpreters Act of 1978, several states are contemplating similar programs (Court Interpreter Task Force of the State of Washington, 1986; Gonzalez, 1988; Leeth, 1985; New Jersey Supreme Court Task Force on Interpreter and Translation Services, 1985; *Senate Bill No. 1853*; Valdés & Wilcox, 1986). In point of fact, court interpretation is the newest and most vital form of interpretation in the United States (Sanders, 1989).

Because this is an emerging field, little is known about the highly precise and demanding work done by court interpreters. A misunderstanding persists among some judicial system administrators about the quality of interpretation required to bridge the linguistic gap faced by non-English-speaking individuals (Astiz, 1986). There is also a chronic belief that court interpreting is a role that any bilingual can fill—including university professors, secretaries, court librarians, officers of the law, friends, relatives, lawyers, or any untested interpreter. This pervasive myth is illuminated by Jon A. Leeth of the Administrative Office of the United States Courts: "Most people believe that if you are bilingual you can interpret. That's about as true as saying that if you have two hands you can automatically be a concert pianist" (Sanders, 1989, p. 25). Once it is recognized that a stringent language proficiency is required as a starting point for the interpreter, the minimalist "seat of the pants" interpreting standard that is currently sanctioned in many agencies and in some courthouses will be seriously questioned, scrutinized, and changed. Because professionals and laypersons alike misconstrue the nature and purpose of court interpreting, it is necessary to examine it in the broader domain of legal interpretation.

2.1. The Goal of Court Interpreting: Legal Equivalence

The goal of court interpreting is to produce a **legal equivalent** (Gonzalez, 1989c), a linguistically true and legally appropriate interpretation of statements spoken or read in court, from the second language into English or vice versa. Legal equivalence (Gonzalez, 1989c) is the distinguishing characteristic of court interpreting, and sets it apart from all other branches of interpretation. "Interpreters must be able to translate with exactitude ... while accurately reflecting a speaker's nuances and level of formality. .... The interpretation cannot be summary or convey only the gist of the original source message" (Federal Judicial Center, 1989, p. 7). Instead of a summary, then, the court interpreter is required to interpret the original source material without editing, summarizing, deleting, or adding while conserving the language level, style, tone, and intent of the speaker or to render what may be termed the **legal equivalence** of the source message (Gonzalez, 1989c).

Thus, court interpreters are primarily charged with delivering to the court and to a non-English-speaking defendant the linguistic equivalent of all spoken and written communications. They are obliged to mirror the "voice" of the defendant or witness by transferring the message from the source language (SL) into the target language (TL) exactly as it was originally spoken—or as exactly as the target language allows. It is important to remember that from the beginnings of judicial proceedings triers of fact (the judge or jury) have to determine the veracity of a witness's message on the basis of an impression conveyed through the speaker's demeanor. The true message is often in **how** something is said rather than in **what** is said; therefore, the style of a message is as important as its content.

The interpreter is required to render in a **verbatim manner** the form and content of the linguistic and paralinguistic elements of a discourse, including all of the pauses, hedges, self-corrections, hesitations, and emotion as they are conveyed through tone of voice, word choice, and intonation; this concept is called **conservation** (Gonzalez, 1986, 1987b; Gonzalez & Arjona, 1989).

It is interesting to note that legal equivalence (Gonzalez, 1989c) shares a common feature with the concept of **dynamic equivalence** as developed by Nida and Taber (1974)—the notion that the message should have the same **effect** on the TL audience as the message had on the SL audience. As Nida and Taber (1974) put it, dynamic equivalence is "the degree to which the receptors of the message in the receptor language respond to it in substantially the same manner as the receptors in the source language" (p. 24). Legal equivalence goes one step further, however, in that the **form** and **style** of the message are regarded as equally important elements of meaning.

2.2. The Goal of the Court Interpreter

The goal of a court interpreter is to enable the judge and jury to react in the same manner to a non-English-speaking witness as they do with one who speaks English. Also, the legal equivalent provided by the court interpreter **is the record.** It serves as the basis for any potential appeal. For the court interpreter, protecting the record is accomplished through disciplined and rigorous attention to transferring the conceptual message and style from the SL to the TL. Through the interpreter the judge and jury are given the opportunity to make judgments about the general socioeconomic, educational, and cultural background of the witness on the basis of the speaker's linguistic style and choice of words. The latter point is especially important in terms of its legal implications. As O'Barr (1982) notes:

> the social organization of the court requires that individual decisions (about who is telling the truth, what really happened, who is right or wrong, and so on) be reconciled into a single shared decision by members of the jury. At least two issues are therefore critical in understanding the legal process that takes place in the courtroom—understanding the way individual decisions are made (e.g., how speech style conveys messages about truthfulness, competence, intelligence, and trustworthiness) and understanding how individual decisions are affected by the context or social structure within which they are made. (p. 97)

Many statutes and rules of court require that the transcript reflect a verbatim record of the proceedings (*Corpus Juris Secundum,* 1988). Because the interpreter's version becomes the record, the interpreter must uphold the verbatim standard. But since it is often impossible to find in the TL a direct equivalent for each word uttered in the SL, a truly verbatim interpretation is literally impossible. It is, therefore, the interpreter's task to mediate between these two extremes: the verbatim requirement of the legal record and the need to convey a meaningful message in the TL. These requirements—to account for every word of the SL message without compromising the syntactic and semantic structure of the TL—are seemingly mutually exclusive. However, the dichotomy is resolved by focusing on conceptual units that must be conserved, not word-by-word, but concept-by-concept. To be true to the global SL message, paralinguistic elements such as hesitations, false starts, hedges, and repetitions must be conserved in a verbatim style and inserted in the corresponding points of the TL message.

Also, the limited- or non-English-speaking defendant should be enabled to hear everything that an English speaker has the privilege to hear. Due process considerations require that the defendant be privy to everything that is said—including any comments said in jest, supposed "off the record" comments, and other exchanges that occur in the course of a courtroom proceeding. The conservation of the complete message as spoken by a witness, judge, or attorney allows the non-English-speaking defendant to make critical judgments about any factual aspects of his or her case. This is the same opportunity offered the English speaker—nothing more and nothing less. Conversely, the interpreter provides nothing more than is provided for the English speaker—no explanations and no elaborations.

For the examining attorney, it is imperative that a witness hear the questions he or she poses in their entirety. Language is a tool used by the attorney for presenting the most credible and persuasive case for the client. As Philbrick (1949) observes:

> Lawyers are students of language by profession. . . . They exercise their power in court by manipulating the thoughts and opinions of others, whether by making speeches or questioning witnesses. In these arts the most successful lawyers reveal (to those who can appreciate their performance) a highly developed skill. (p. vi)

Language is also the tool used to probe for and discover the truth; therefore, the form of a question is as important as its content. The attorney who calculates each word in every question, in order to elicit a particular response, must in essence delegate this delicate linguistic task to the interpreter. The attorney has no recourse but to depend on the interpreter to capture every bit of meaning as originally articulated. Whether the attorney is accusatory, cynical, straightforward, or heckling, the rhetorical stance must be conserved, not only for the attorney's sake but for maintenance of the fidelity of the legal process. The presentation of testimony through the question-and-answer process between the attorney and the witness is the very crux of the United States adversarial system of law. Therefore, it is of the utmost importance that the interpreter proceed with linguistic exactitude.

2.2.1. The Adaptation Role

Interpreters must not adapt their rendition to suit the level of language, educational background, interests, or preferences of the TL receptor. According to the research of Carlos Astiz (1986), **adaptation** is erroneously considered a necessary activity by a great number of interpreters:

> they simplify and outline court proceedings for individuals who in the interpreters' judgment, would not understand an accurate rendering . . . and to explain to the individuals in question . . . what was going on, particularly in Court, in the hope of putting them more at ease. (p. 34)

Astiz contends that this **adaptation role** is "outright and without qualification" beyond the role of the court interpreter and contradicts the goals of accuracy and precision; the duty of the interpreter is to make the legal situation "as similar as humanly possible to that faced by the same individual but without the linguistic disability" (Astiz, 1986, p. 34).

Adaptation is, however, still a controversial issue for some interpreters. Astiz's research revealed that some courts condone this practice, arguing that explaining and putting the concepts into words the non-English speaker can understand (by changing the register of the original) is necessary to "make up for the language barrier and the total ignorance of the individual" of the legal procedures and hearings involved (Astiz, 1986, p. 34). This notion is strongly opposed by attorneys and judges who voice the concern that in the process of "adapting" and changing information, an interpreter would "provide erroneous [legal and other linguistic] information" (Astiz, 1986, p. 34). According to Chief Judge Richard Bilby (1983) of the United States District Court of the Southern District of Arizona:

The interpreter is only a medium; everything that goes in has to come out exactly as it was said. This is a two-way proposition—not just for the judge and the jury, but for the witness or defendant to hear everything as it was said. This guarantees the legal process.

Conservation, rather than adaptation, has become the trend for members of the federal judiciary and many state court judges.

In general, then, the duty of the court interpreter is to serve as a conduit between non-English speakers and English-speaking officials in legal and quasi-legal forums. As they convert one language into another, interpreters play a critical role in the administration of justice and make it possible to ensure the rights of due process and participation in the court system for all those involved—limited- and non-English speakers as well as English speakers.

2.2.2. Prerequisites for Court Interpreting

A court interpreter must have a superior, unquestionable command of two languages and must be able to manipulate registers from the most formal varieties to the most casual forms, including slang. The interpreter's vocabulary must be of considerable depth and breadth to support the wide variety of subjects that typically arise in the judicial process. At the same time, the interpreter must have the ability to orchestrate all of these linguistic tasks while interpreting in the simultaneous and consecutive and interpretation modes for persons speaking at rates of 200 words or more per minute.

These cognitively complex tasks demand acute memory, concentration, and analysis skills. Court interpreters must possess a wide general knowledge of the world and a graduate-level educational background or commensurate life and reading experiences. Prior to the Federal Court Interpreter Examination, no objective standard existed to measure court interpreting competence. Whereas the Foreign Service Institute (FSI) Test measures language proficiency, that criterion alone was insufficient for determining interpreting ability—a level 55 score on the FSI represents minimal language skills required for court interpreting. Existing court interpreting tests were insufficient because they did not test legal equivalence (Gonzalez, 1989c) and, most importantly, were not objective measures. Unfortunately, these high-level interpreting skills are difficult to find, and the demand for qualified court interpreters has not been satisfied (Sanders, 1989).

3. Growth of a Profession

Although court interpreters have been used in the United States since *In re Norberg* (1808), regulations governing their use have been generally nonexistent, the quality of language services generally suspect. For decades, due process, as guaranteed by the Fourth, Fifth, Sixth, Eighth, and Fourteenth Amendments to the Constitution, was violated by federal, state, and local courts, by not recognizing the need for linguistic services to limited- and non-English-speaking and other linguistically disabled populations. The case law is replete with examples of the injustices and violation of due process that have occurred in our courts.

The Civil Rights Movement brought increased attention to minority rights and the demand for the rights of linguistically handicapped populations, including the speech- and hearing-impaired. By 1977, the need for interpreters was recognized as a nationwide problem; a total of forty-nine states and the federal government had rules of procedure, judicial rules, case law, and statutes protecting the rights of the linguistically disadvantaged (Comptroller General of the United States, 1977). However, the demand for interpretation in many instances was filled by individuals whose bilingual and interpreting capabilities had not been measured, which precluded the courts from determining the quality of interpretation.

In 1978, years of hard work by language minority populations and members of the federal judiciary brought about the enactment of the 1978 Court Interpreters Act, which mandated the services of an interpreter for any person "who does not have the ability to comprehend the language of the proceedings or the charge involved in any crime or civil case brought by the United States government" (Gonzalez, 1986). The Act also mandated that interpreters be qualified through a certification examination, and for the first time in the United States language minority persons appearing in federal court were assured of the basic right to due process.

Until the development and administration of the Federal Court Interpreter Spanish/English Examination in 1979, few practitioners of this exacting task had their interpreting skills assessed. Out of the 12,122 administrations of this examination from 1980 through 1989, only 388 candidates have met the requisite minimal competencies (Gonzalez, 1989c). In state and municipal courts, the majority of court interpreters have also not had their skills validly tested. Many interpreters, in both state and federal courts, have not received formal training of any kind and do not abide by a common professional standard. In short, the use of underprepared or nonproficient persons as interpreters is pervasive (Astiz, 1980, 1986; Berk-Seligson, 1987; Chang & Araujo, 1975; Gonzalez, 1988; Leeth, 1985; Sanders, 1989).

Policy, practices, and performance are inconsistent from state to state, city to city, and courthouse to courthouse. The result of a major ethnographic study of interpreted hearings reveals that there is much to be desired in the fidelity and accuracy of practicing interpreters (Berk-Seligson, 1988). With the exception of the federal court system, which is, for the most part, in the vanguard of court interpreting policy and practice, the language needs of limited- and non-English speakers in the judicial process have not been addressed uniformly in the United States.

This distressing lack of quality and standardized practice in the courts demands the development and implementation of a set of basic policies about court interpreting and fundamental linguistic, professional, and legal principles that can guide the courts and the interpreter profession. Most importantly, this body of policies should emanate from the most informed research and practice in the field. Because of its relatively new status as a profession and field of investigation, there is a dearth of academic research and professional literature. Ideally, any examination of court interpreting must take into account the legal, ethical, linguistic, sociological, and psychological underpinnings. *Fundamentals of Court Interpretation* addresses these concerns and others.

The growth of court interpretation as a profession can be measured by a number of significant indices. One of these is the number of persons—approximately 7,000—who have applied for the Federal Court Interpreter Certification Examination during the last nine years (Gonzalez, 1989c). Other indicators of growth include the approximately 700 persons who are members of the California Court Interpreters Association, and the nearly 500 members of the National Association of Judiciary Interpreters and Translators. Also significant is the founding and growth of the Court Interpreting Section of the American Translators Association, the court interpreter associations of Arizona, Massachusetts, New Jersey, New Mexico, Texas, the Translators and Interpreters Education Society, and the nearly 500 students a year who take translating and interpreting courses and programs at the following institutions, among others: Arizona State University, California State University at Los Angeles, City University of New York, Florida International University, Georgetown University, John Jay College of Criminal Justice, Montclair State College (along with a variety of two-year colleges in New Jersey that work with the Consortium on Higher Education and the Training of Court Interpreters), Monterey Institute of International Studies, New York University, Northern Arizona University, University of Arizona, University of California at Los Angeles, University of Delaware, and the University of Hawaii.

4. The Increased Demand for Interpreting Services in the Courts and Quasi-Judicial Forums

Demographic trends in the United States strongly indicate the likelihood of a continuing, growing demand for language services in the courts. The number of limited- or non-English-speaking persons in the United States will reach 50,000,000 by the year 2020 (Waggoner, 1988). This means that one out of every three school-age children in the United States will be from a limited- or non-English-speaking background. The language needs of this population are on the increase, even in light of the negative sentiments expressed by many "English-only" proponents.

As the demographics of the United States shift in the next two decades, race, ethnic background, and language will present the courts with an increasingly difficult set of problems. Logically, one of the most direct approaches is to expand and upgrade court interpreter services and ensure their formalization into the United States judicial system. According to Paul Siegel, director of the Education Division of the United States Census Bureau, in the year 2000, one out of every three Americans will hail from a non-English-speaking or culturally different home (personal communication, May 1987).

This issue has become a prominent concern of the courts and other quasi-judicial agencies and has received recent professional attention. In 1988, an issue of *The Court Manager,* a widely distributed journal for court administrators, focused on linguistic, ethical, and administrative aspects of court interpreting. Also, the American Society of American Judicature featured a panel on the courts and changing demographics; the National Center for State Courts has featured a number of panels specifically dedicated to court interpreting services at several 1988 and 1989 regional and national meetings. These panels and meetings point to the increased recognition of members of the judiciary and the bar regarding the complexities presented by interlingual and cross-cultural communication. Furthermore, in less professional circles, evidence of rising public awareness and interest in language policy in the courts is evidenced in numerous articles published in many popular magazines and newspapers during the last decade (Adelo, 1986a, 1986b, 1989; Berreby, 1982; Deitch, 1985; Ewell & Schrieberg, 1989; Farmer, 1983; Garland, 1981a, 1981b; Henshaw, 1986; Negri, 1984; Reinhold, 1987; Sanders, 1989; Schrieberg, 1989; Schrieberg & Ewell, 1989; Silva, 1981).

This current popular interest is reflected more and more in the professional domain. The American Bar Association and state court systems are seriously studying the complexities the new demographics present to the courts, and are contemplating several solutions. One such solution involves the establishment of curricular requirements in law schools to sensitize lawyers to the cultural and linguistic aspects of dealing with limited- and non-English-speaking clients and their language intermediaries—court interpreters (Hansen, Dator, Frye, Nudelman, & O'Neill, 1988).

Other solutions include legislation mandating court interpreter certification that has been approved in three states: California, New Mexico, and Washington. The New Jersey legislature is currently considering a court interpreter act, modeled on the Federal Court Interpreters Act yet more comprehensive. New York already has administrative procedures which test court interpreters for approved job positions. Arizona, Massachusetts, Texas, Iowa, and many other states have in the past or are now considering procedures, either by legislative action, administrative rule, or professional organization, to certify court interpreters.

A number of federal and state agencies are also considering the use of bilingual personnel or interpreters or the establishment of interpreter or bilingual personnel positions and certification in such diverse settings as the Immigration and Naturalization Service, the Drug Enforcement Agency, the Social Security Administration, a few municipalities in the Southwest, the Texas Employment Commission, every public agency in California, and most recently the social services agencies of the state of Oregon.

The recent decision by the Administrative Office of the United States Courts (AO) to certify interpreters in Haitian Creole and Navajo (Gonzalez, 1989a, 1989b; Gonzalez and Vasquez, 1990) reflects the general trend toward the expansion of language services in the federal courts. In addition, in response to the growing demand for Asian language interpreters in the federal courts, the AO has formally requested that Congress designate Korean the next language for a certification program (J. A. Leeth, personal communication, August 11, 1989). Also under consideration by the AO, in response to the needs of federal districts, is the future certification of Mandarin, Cantonese, and the Southeast Asian languages of Thai and Vietnamese (personal communication, August, 11, 1989).

5. Professional Problems

Many professional problems are directly related to the underestimation of the linguistic and bilingual proficiency court interpreting requires and the cognitive demands it makes on the individual interpreter. Once the exigency of the court interpreter's tasks and the direct relationship between the quality of the completion of those tasks and the quality of the record are comprehended, then court interpreting will rise to a higher level of professionalism, as it has done to a large degree in the federal court system.

In some settings, interpreters are much in demand, and "the court system has difficulty competing with private business and other government agencies in attracting and retaining qualified interpreters" (Federal Judicial Center, 1989, p. 7). In other settings, however, regardless of the demand for interpreters and the rigor of the work they perform, court interpreters are often "relegated to clerical status, with low pay, and asked to work without time to prepare" (Sanders, 1989, p. 65).

Appreciation for the full value of the court interpreter's role in the judicial process is still evolving. Compare, for example, the relative difference in status between the court reporter and the court interpreter. Although the role, function, tasks, and preparation of the court reporter are of unquestioned value to the legal community, court interpreters are not accorded the same merit, even though they must do all that a court reporter does in addition to numerous additional cognitive and linguistic tasks (Mikkelson, 1984). Consider the following: a court reporter must listen and transcribe and engage in a number of complex listening and comprehension tasks in order to transcribe the source message into the record verbatim (Walker, 1987). During that same period of time, the court interpreter must listen, comprehend, abstract the message from the words and word order of the message, store the ideas into memory, and then set about searching for conceptual and semantic matches to reconstruct the message in the other language, all this within the cultural and linguistic constraints and operating rules of that language. This takes place while the interpreter is listening for the next "language chunk" to process while simultaneously monitoring his or her own output (Gerver, 1971).

A primary goal of this volume is to elaborate these processes and tasks in the hope of bringing about a realistic view and better understanding of this complex activity.

Chapter 2

Definitions, Scope, and Limitations

This chapter outlines the field of translation and interpretation and illustrates its relationship to the court interpreting profession. It then proceeds to explain the overall scope and structure of the text. First though, this chapter introduces the reader to the basic definitions of the most common terms used in this text.

1. Legal Interpretation

Legal interpretation refers to interpretation that takes place in a legal setting such as a courtroom or an attorney's office, wherein some proceeding or activity related to law is conducted. Legal interpretation is subdivided according to the legal setting into (1) quasi-judicial and (2) judicial interpreting or what is normally referred to as **court interpreting**.

1.1. Quasi-Judicial Interpreting

Quasi-judicial interpreting refers to the interpretation of interviews and hearings that typically occur in out-of-court settings (extra-judicial) but may have a bearing on in-court proceedings. These interviews and hearings include, but are not limited to, attorney-client interviews and interviews between other criminal justice or law enforcement personnel and the defendant or arrestee (see Unit 3, Chapter 13). Another quasi-judicial setting is administrative hearings, such as those conducted by the Immigration and Naturalization Service, the Social Security Administration, the National Labor Relations Board, and state and local agencies having jurisdiction over juvenile matters, employment, motor vehicles, industrial accidents, and public assistance. These quasi-judicial hearings are critical because final determinations made by the administrative agencies rely on their records, and they may form the basis for an appeal to a state or federal district court. For this reason, the interpretation in out-of-court hearings and interviews must be of the same quality and precision as that rendered in a courtroom.

1.2. Judicial Interpreting

Judicial interpreting or **court interpreting** relates specifically to interpretation which takes place in a courtroom. Court interpreting encompasses numerous hearings, including initial appearances, arraignment on the indictment, bail hearings, the trial proper, sentencing, and any other necessary judicial proceedings (see Unit 2, Chapter 10). Depositions, although conducted outside the courtroom, are included in the

25

category of judicial interpreting because testimony given in a deposition is taken under oath; it is, therefore, treated identically to testimony related in court.

2. Categories of Interpretation

All branches of interpretation share common concerns, and it is worthwhile to consider their similarities and differences. Legal interpreting, of which court interpreting is a subdivision, is one of six following branches: (1) conference, (2) escort, (3) seminar, (4) business, (5) medical/mental health, and (6) legal.

2.1. Conference Interpretation

Of all branches, conference interpreting is the best understood, most thoroughly studied, and has an established body of scholarly research and professional guidelines. The most comprehensive study is the work contained in Gerver and Sinaiko (1978) and Seleskovitch (1978a, 1978b). To gain a more informed perspective on court interpreting, conference interpreting will first be defined and then compared in its goals and procedures to court interpretation. The standards applied to conference interpreting offer us a well-known point of reference with which to contrast court interpretation. This contrast will clarify the parameters of this relatively new professional domain and allow the reader to better comprehend the unique legal assumptions, policies, and procedures explored in this text.

Conference interpretation refers to language services performed in order to facilitate communication among speakers of various languages attending a given meeting or conference. To provide a continuous high-quality interpretation, conference interpreters work in teams, often in booths, and their interpretation is broadcast to participants wearing headphones. To aid them in simultaneously or consecutively interpreting speeches and lectures, conference interpreters are generally provided in advance with texts of the speeches when they are available. Because of the highly technical subject matter that may be encountered in a conference setting, interpreters study the areas of knowledge and correlate terminology beforehand in order to prepare themselves as thoroughly as possible for the interpreting task.

2.2. Conference Interpretation versus Court Interpretation

The role of the conference interpreter as a language intermediary in an international, political, or business setting has been traditionally regarded as the highest standard in interpreting. In contrast, the work of court interpreters is thought to be less precise. The greatest misconception is the gross underestimation of the cognitive, linguistic, and interpreting complexity of court interpreting. Additionally, there is little appreciation for the tremendous increase in the demand for court interpreters, a need that was not foreseen two decades ago. In fact, the shortage of court interpreters has far surpassed the call for conference interpreters. Moreover, in cases involving limited- and non-English-speaking defendants, the role of the court interpreter has become as vital as that of the prosecuting and defense counsel. Whereas conference interpreters regarded court interpreters with some skepticism, recently that view has shifted dramatically, and many conference interpreters are beginning to embrace this rapidly expanding field.

The late Theodore Fagan, former Chief Interpreter of the United Nations, attributed this change of perspective to the fact that many conference interpreters did not at first understand the legal requirements and strict standards of court interpretation. When a number of conference interpreters presented themselves for the Federal Court Interpreter Certification Examination in 1980, they were surprised by the test's scrupulous attention to the conservation of register, paralinguistic elements, and style. Court interpreters, they discovered, had to possess not only the formal registers of the language but also the informal and idiomatic styles (personal communication, February 18, 1980).

Clearly the demands of legal equivalence (Gonzalez, 1989c) in court interpretation have cast judicial interpretation into the same sphere of challenge and complexity as conference interpreting. To many conference interpreters and other observers, court interpreting is in some respects more demanding. Leeth (1985), former director of the Court Interpreting and Reporting Division of the Administrative Office of the United States Courts (AO), and a pioneer in the implementation of judicial language policy, compares court interpreting and conference interpreting in this manner:

> Court interpreters must conserve the tone of the language, the timbre of the vocabulary with a fidelity to the original source that distinguishes the truly great literary translations. Conference interpreting is first draft translating: Court interpreting is polished translation. (p. 8)

2.2.1. The Goal of Conference Interpreting: Conceptual Transfer

The interpreting literature reveals that conference interpreters may often deliberately improve a speaker's delivery and condense the TL rendition of an original source message (Seleskovitch, 1978a, 1978b; Weber, 1984). They polish usage and syntax; edit faulty logic and predication; omit repetition, hedges, hesitations, and false starts; illuminate the subject for the listener; and make speakers sound more articulate and lucid than they sound in their own language. This interpreting style is appropriate to the conference setting, where the impetus is to share ideas. The goal of the conference interpreter is to facilitate communication in as elegant and unobtrusive a manner as possible. The conference is a setting in which life and liberty are not generally at stake, the misrepresentation of one word or fact will not alter a critical legal decision. Although precision and accuracy are facets of conference interpreting, the goal is to communicate on the macro or global level rather than on the micro level as do court interpreters. Relaying the conceptual message in conference interpretation is sufficient, while court interpretation demands that all facets of the original message be mirrored, thus realizing the legal equivalent (Gonzalez, 1989c).

3. Other Related Branches of Interpretation

Now that an analysis of court interpreting and conference interpreting has been presented, it may be helpful to examine the other three basic branches of interpretation as well. **Seminar interpreting** is often thought of as a subdivision of conference interpretation and refers to the interpretation of formal addresses and roundtable discussions at meetings and small conferences. The basic difference between conference interpreting and seminar interpreting is the size of the meeting.

Escort or **liaison interpreting** is a term primarily utilized by the State Department to define the role of interpreters who "escort" visiting political, business, or civic dignitaries from other countries on official travels throughout the United States. Escort interpretation is marked by the spontaneity and the broad spectrum of situations interpreters may find themselves in, from formal meetings to tours of factories to cocktail parties. The mode most often used in this type of interpretation is consecutive, and is usually limited to a few sentences at a time.

Business interpreting is a branch of the profession that is growing steadily as the private sector of the United States economy becomes more internationally oriented and as more persons of varied linguistic backgrounds in the United States enter into business agreements. Interpreters in this field, who are often hired as translators/ interpreters, negotiate the language of contracts, brochures, advertising, customer support materials, technical manuals, bargaining and negotiations, and of meetings for individuals in the private sector or in corporations. Employing organizations include banks, multinational corporations, import-export businesses, real estate firms, agri-business, and many others. Many aspects of business interpreting are quite different from court interpreting, such as the translation of advertising and promotional materials, in which a great deal of cultural adaptation may be required to reach the target audience. However, there are situations in business interpreting that require the same attention to detail as court interpreting; the alteration of the language in a bid proposal or contract, for example, could lead to gross misunderstandings and an eventual loss of revenue. The common denominator of business interpreting and court interpreting, then, is the legal aspect.

Medical/mental health interpreting typically takes place in three major settings: hospitals, offices of professional health care providers, and emergency care units. This branch of interpretation is often perceived by those unfamiliar with the process as a relatively simple task in which most of the meaning is conveyed through gestures. However, medical interpreting is analogous to court interpreting in a number of ways; it provides a communication bridge between sophisticated and unsophisticated users of language. In the legal domain the interpreter serves to protect the life and liberty of the defendant and ensures the maximum potential for justice. In the medical/mental health domain the interpreter serves to protect the quality of life of the patient. Medical/mental health interpretation is similar to interpreting witness testimony in that the client may be in a very emotional state, and the interpreter is his or her only voice; regardless, the interpreter has an ethical obligation to remain neutral.

The medical interpreter must have a full command of technical medical terms in both languages to assist the doctor in taking a medical history and informing the patient of the diagnosis as well as specific instructions for treatment. As in court interpreting, there is a need for conveying subtlety of meaning such as the precise degree of pain or other very specific symptoms. Because the information garnered from doctor-patient interviews will be used to render a diagnosis or to submit a report to a specialist, the interpreted answer to any question may have major consequences for patients. Interest is growing in this area (Abril, 1987; Gish, 1988; Marcos, 1980; Putsch, 1985).

Thoroughness and precision are critical in mental health interpreting since psychologists and psychiatrists pay particular attention to **how** a person expresses his or her feelings and under what circumstances these feelings are triggered in order to discern the mental state of the patient. Therefore, in this setting, it is imperative that the interpreter employ the same standards of conservation and accuracy that prevail when interpreting testimony for the record in a court of law.

In mental health interpreting the interpreter must often act as a cultural expert to a much greater degree than in court interpreting. It is possible for even a well-trained mental health professional to misconstrue verbal responses or physical actions that are culture-bound behaviors. For example, if a patient reports that upon feeling disoriented, he proceeded to crack an egg, place it under the bed, and utter a ritualistic statement to ward off evil, the interpreter should inform the mental health professional—after the interview and the patient has departed—that such behavior is part of traditional folk medicine practiced in some cultures.

Because there is great potential for misunderstandings and erroneous conclusions and perhaps even loss of life or liberty, and because of the critical decisions involved in both the medical and mental health fields, it is important for professionals in these fields to familiarize themselves with the use of interpreters. Finally, it is advisable that summary interpretation be avoided and that the standards of court interpretation be adopted for all medical/mental health interpretations.

Community interpreting refers to any interpretation provided by non-professional interpreters. Amateur interpreters provide services in hospitals, public meetings, medical offices, stores, social service agencies, schools, churches, parent organizations, police departments, real estate offices, and a legion of other agencies both public and private. Their dedication and interest is to be commended, but often the standard for interpretation is set by their linguistic limitations rather than by the language needs of the client.

Generally, community interpreters have no formal training. Interpreting as a profession did not emerge until the early twentieth century, and formal training in interpretation did not begin until after World War II. Interpretation is indeed seen as a community duty by many, and the interpreting profession has drawn on this pool of individuals who have been interpreting all their lives for friends, family, and even complete strangers.

However, tragedies have resulted from the use of untrained interpreters who are not competent to deal with serious matters of law, business, and medicine. It is now recognized that in criminal matters far too much is at stake to rely on non-professional, albeit well-meaning, interpreters. It is time to recognize the possible dangers in other critical areas of public concern as well. For example, someone facing the loss of social security benefits may have to rely on a friend or relative to interpret in what amounts to a quasi-legal meeting; or an eight-year-old may be given the task of explaining a complex set of instructions about medication to a parent. It is clear that much work is needed to bring professional standards and/or professional services to many areas of public concern. And as the public understands more of the nature of court interpreting, it is possible that the professional standards and ethics of this branch of interpreting might offer a model for other areas of interpretation.

4. Fundamentals of Court Interpretation: Scope

It is this multitude of needs and concerns that *Fundamentals of Court Interpretation* addresses. The text not only attempts to synthesize the evolving knowledge in the field and to set professional standards, but also represents the first multidisciplinary effort to inform a variety of audiences about the theoretical and practical issues involved in court interpreting. Although court interpreters have been a part of the judicial process since the late 1800s, significant professional and scholarly activity has emerged only in the last ten years. The intended audience for this book is a diverse one: practicing and aspiring interpreters, members of the state and federal judiciary, attorneys, court clerks, heads of interpreter services, and other court personnel who may find this work helpful as a reference for the administration of court interpreter services. The text will also be of value to linguists and researchers from a variety of disciplines interested in the linguistic, psycholinguistic, and rhetorical dimensions of court interpreting.

Fundamentals poses the following questions:

- What is the role of the interpreter in the judicial context and other quasi-legal forums, and what are the parameters of his or her duties and responsibilities?

- What constitutes the appropriate use of the interpreter in the judicial setting?

- What are the cognitive and linguistic processes involved in the complex task of interpreting, and what language obstacles does the interpreter encounter in transferring meaning from one language to another?

- What are the theoretical and pragmatic features of simultaneous interpretation, consecutive interpretation, and sight translation as practiced in the judicial context?

- What are the linguistic, ethical, and professional problems an interpreter encounters and how can they be most efficaciously resolved within the judicial setting?

As it is designed, *Fundamentals* endeavors to be as valuable to the judiciary as it is to students, practitioners, supervisory interpreters/clerks, and scholars in a host of disciplines who wish to investigate theoretical phenomena related to court interpretation. The fields directly or tangentially concerned with court interpreting include such diverse areas as law, linguistics, psychology, cognitive psychology, law and social science, social psychology, legal anthropology, psychometrics, English as a Second Language, foreign languages and literature, and translation and interpretation.

Unit 1 presents the history of court interpretation from a language policy point of view. An overview of interpretation case law highlights the inequities suffered by language minorities—in particular Hispanics—and underscores the pressing need for court interpreters. A description of these events reveals how inadequate interpretation violated defendants' rights and served as a catalyst for the 1978 Court Interpreters

Act, which mandated the provision of certified court interpreters for limited- or non-English speakers involved in the judicial process. Finally, the unit briefly summarizes the status of interpretation outside the United States.

Unit 2 presents an overview of the United States legal system and the interrelationship between the judicial, legislative, and executive branches of the United States government. The unit also introduces the interpreter to the United States criminal justice system, with some attention paid to the differences between civil and criminal law. Additionally, the unit presents a brief discussion of comparative legal traditions, focusing primarily on the common law and civil law traditions. It is important for interpreters to have a basic understanding of both systems and their procedural and substantive differences, so that they will be able to interpret legal terms or concepts correctly even when there is no equivalent in the target system.

Unit 3 focuses on the effective use of interpreter services. The unit provides definitions of the role of the interpreter, including that of expert witness and officer of the court. It also discusses preferred modes of interpretation within specified settings, and implications for legal and quasi-legal settings outside the courtroom such as juvenile matters and immigration hearings. This unit concentrates on the logistics of performing simultaneous and consecutive interpretation and sight translation modes in the legal/courtroom setting. These sections do not reflect current practice, but rather offer the preferred forms and techniques given the needs of the judiciary, the defendant/client, and the ethical and professional duties of the court interpreter. The intent of the unit is to standardize practice and to aid courts struggling with these practical issues of interpreter utilization. The unit also presents a discussion of the ways judges and other actors in the court can facilitate and support the interpreter's role, and looks at cultural issues and challenges to interpretations by other actors in the courtroom. Finally the appropriate use of interpreters with multiple defendants is addressed from a managerial perspective.

Unit 4 addresses the court administration of interpreter services. The main objective of this unit is to forward a set of recommended strategies, policies, and practices that are intended to ameliorate management and utilization problems, and to facilitate standardization of policy. Recruitment, in-service training, and assignment of both certified and uncertified interpreters are the specific foci of this unit. Furthermore, the unit examines the management of interpreter services provided in Spanish as well as other, less frequently encountered languages. Finally, the unit discusses emergency interpreter services, including recommended strategies for meeting language service needs on short notice. This unit not only responds to the needs of administrators of court interpreter services, but also formulates policy for use of court interpreters in diverse legal settings.

Unit 5 concentrates on handling the vast intrinsic complexities of language that an interpreter must grasp, such as the nuance of words, the effect of culture on the transfer of ideas from one language to another, problems with idiomatic usage, and linguistic tolerance for diverse varieties of language.

Another primary focus of this unit is an analysis of the features of legal language that describes the register of courtroom English as measured by readability analysis, word frequency, and various syntactic analyses. In addition, this unit discusses how court interpretation relates to the findings of legal anthropologists and other linguists on the effect of various language styles (specifically powerless and powerful speech) on the legal process and in particular in light of the intrusion of interpreters. Chapters 22 and 23 present taxonomies of interpreter error and their probable origin.

Unit 6 focuses on the theory and practice of consecutive interpretation, simultaneous interpretation, and sight translation—the three primary modes of interpretation in the courtroom setting. After a discussion in Chapter 24 of the interpreting process, from both the theoretical and the practical points of view, Chapter 25 reviews prevailing theories of interpretation and introduces Simultaneous Human Information Processing (SHIP), a comprehensive model of human information processing developed by the authors. Based on current theories of memory, unconscious processing, and whole-brain models of cognitive processing (ACT* and PDP), SHIP endeavors to efficiently account for the tremendous volume of information processing involved in court interpreting. The remaining chapters are devoted to the three modes of interpreting: simultaneous interpretation, consecutive interpretation, and sight translation. Each chapter describes the mode from a psycholinguistic standpoint and discusses its application in the judicial setting. In addition, strategies and exercises are suggested to improve technique in each of the three modes.

Unit 7 focuses on the practical considerations and tasks of court interpreting. The unit begins with an introduction to the courtroom and legal actors and is followed by a logistical, sequential explanation of the court interpreter's actions from the moment of assignment through the proceeding to trial. Finally, ethical and procedural recommendations are made for interpreting done outside the courtroom.

Also examined are procedures which must be incorporated into the interpreter's behavior—from carrying a pad and pencil to the use of electronic equipment along with other related tasks such as tape transcription and translation, and document translation. The final chapter in this unit describes in detail how the interpreter can access a wealth of published and unpublished glossaries. The chapter also emphasizes the need to compile personal glossaries and a comprehensive reference library and explains how the interpreter can use the latest developments in computer technology to build personal data banks of terms.

Unit 8 focuses on professional issues affecting the interpreter: ethics and responsibilities, standards of practice, and professional conduct. Like other professionals, court interpreters adhere to a code of ethics. Ethical considerations such as confidentiality are elucidated to orient interpreters as to the appropriate behavior. An expanded discussion of specific ethical dilemmas and their most appropriate resolution will hopefully offer guidelines for interpreters and the courts which use their services. Additionally, the role of the professional association is emphasized, with information provided on professional organizations, newsletters, and journals. The interpreter's continuing education is another topic covered in this unit. There is also a survey of the universities, colleges, and professional institutions that offer courses, degree programs, concentrations, or certificates directly and indirectly related to court interpretation.

A major feature of this unit is a discussion of current federal, state, and administrative certification and examination procedures. The essential concepts of "conservation of meaning," "register," and "legal equivalent" (Gonzalez, 1989c) are highlighted. In addition, this unit examines the administrative procedures and purposes of certification testing. The testing information includes an examination of the intent of testing and its content validity and reliability as well as the research that forms the basis of certification examinations.

Unit 9, A Look to the Future, concentrates on the future of this relatively new field of professional endeavor. It covers legal topics such as multiple defendants, multiple interpreters, and the effect of English language amendments on interpreter services.

Professional issues such as recertification, malpractice, certification of legal translators, and machine translation and interpretation are discussed. The last chapter also elucidates the need for a national professional organization, and for degree programs in court interpreting at institutions of higher learning. The possibility of instituting certification programs to regulate and standardize interpreter services for other areas where interpretation is practiced, such as administrative agencies and the medical field, is another topic covered in this chapter. Mechanisms are proposed for the pooling of resources by various national and regional entities in order to accomplish this task.

The **appendices** include a list of professional organizations of court interpreters and related professions, as well as the 1978 Court Interpreters Act, its 1988 Amendment, and other pertinent statutes and regulations.

5. Limitations of *Fundamentals*

Although *Fundamentals of Court Interpretation* concentrates on the theoretical, legal, administrative, and practical aspects of court or judicial interpreting, the principles forwarded apply to any quasi-judicial setting, though such settings are only tangentially discussed in the text. Most significantly, this volume is directed to the practitioners of court interpreting in any language. Many of the language examples are in Spanish, only because Spanish is the language most in demand for court services in the United States. However, the authors are well aware of the demand for at least sixty-five other languages in the federal court system and the equal or greater demand in the state courts for these other languages as well. It is important to note that the interpreting principles, theories, ethical, and linguistic considerations are universal and apply to any language.

Fundamentals is not a comprehensive legal reference. Although an overview of the United States criminal justice process is presented, it is by no means exhaustive. It is intended to give the novice an understanding of basic criminal procedure and to serve as one of many sources for novices and practicing interpreters. Topics such as bankruptcy, divorce, and contract law are beyond the scope of this text. Furthermore, the law-related appendices are compiled with the judiciary, counsel, scholars, and interested students of court interpretation in mind. These appendices are not intended as exhaustive compendiums, but rather as a starting point to stimulate further research on court interpreting.

The term **translation**, in its general and most frequently used sense, refers to the mental and physical processes involved in transferring meaning from one language to another—whether in spoken or written form. Because of this generic meaning, "translation" is used interchangeably with the term "interpretation" throughout this text.

Fundamentals focuses on **court interpretation** and not **translation** in the formal sense. **Interpretation** almost universally refers to the transfer of meaning from one language into another for the purpose of **oral** communication between two persons who do not share the same language. Although **translation**—the transference of a written text from one language to another—of legal documents is briefly reviewed as one of the many tasks of the court interpreter, **legal translation** or **general translation** in the formal sense of the theoretical, stylistic, and pragmatic issues involved in converting a written text from one language to another will not be discussed. Treatises on translation such as the works of Newmark (1981), Brislin (1976), Nida (1964, 1976), Nida and Rayburn (1982), and Nida and Taber (1974) are recommended for practitioners and students of interpretation who are interested in the formal study of this ancient and fascinating field of scholarship and practice. Legal translation can be best studied by consulting the work of Engelbert (1982). For pragmatic works for Spanish-English translators, see Bayley (1973), Rivera-Garcia (1974), and Vásquez-Ayora (1977).

Sign language interpretation, research, practice, and history will not be treated in *Fundamentals,* although court interpretation among sign language interpreters is a long-standing profession. In fact, sign language interpretation has been theoretically and pragmatically analyzed in great detail over a period of many years, and sign interpreters are a politically astute, professionally organized community. A recent work by Frishberg (1986), published by the Registry of Interpreters for the Deaf (RID), captures the distinctive linguistic, pragmatic, and cultural aspects of sign language interpretation. Sign language interpreting, in research and professional materials, shares many assumptions with court interpretation, but differs from the goals and the verbatim standard of performance of spoken language court interpreters.

Fundamentals is dedicated to reporting and proposing theoretical models of court interpreting, and to improving performance through the synthesis of theory and enlightened practice. The intention of this work is not so much to document current reality as to suggest policies and procedures in keeping with current insightful practice, theory, and research.

Foremost, the authors of *Fundamentals* see this work as a clearinghouse of information, a compilation of informed theory and practice, and the initiation of a dialogue among scholars, members of the judiciary and the bar, court administrators, practitioners of interpreting, student interpreters, teachers of court interpretation, and teacher trainers. Out of this dialogue we hope will come an understanding of the fact that court interpreting is indispensable to the fair and even-handed administration of justice for all limited- and non-English-speaking persons in the United States.

Unit 1
Historical Antecedents

Chapter 3
Movement Toward Equal Access

The dual focus of this chapter is the prevailing attitudes in the United States concerning the use of non-English languages and the legislative action taken to guarantee equal access for all citizens to educational, political, employment, and legal institutions. The chapter first discusses the evolution of attitudes toward foreign languages and linguistic minorities throughout United States history, and analyzes the equal access legislation passed in the 1960s and 1970s that extended full constitutional guarantees to language minorities. This chapter culminates with a discussion of the 1978 Court Interpreters Act.

1. Introduction

The advancement of constitutional guarantees for language minorities closely parallels the struggle for civil rights. Like civil rights, language has been a source of heated debate throughout much of United States history, debate that has taken the form of demonstration, litigation, and legislation. Like civil rights initiatives, policies and laws that promote and enforce the rights of language minorities have confronted institutional obstructions and ethnocentric detractors (Gonzalez, Schott, & Vasquez, 1988; Heath, 1981; Judd, 1987; Marshall, 1986). The opposition faced by language minorities revolves around the controversy over whether the use of languages other than English will enhance or impede their social progress—and whether it is pragmatic or even patriotic. This controversy should not obscure the fact that limited- or non-English-speaking persons are denied access to certain rights guaranteed to all United States citizens (Gonzalez, Vasquez, & Bichsel, 1991). A non-English speaker's right to a court interpreter during his or her trial is not a language right, but simply guarantees the right to equal access to the legal system. The court interpreter allows the non-English-speaking individual to enjoy due process and equal protection under the law.

It is ironic that access to the legal system through the provision of court interpretation has in the past met with substantial resistance from the courts, the same institution that is thought to ultimately guarantee both language-related access and civil rights. Only recently, as a result of the Court Interpreters Act of 1978, has the right to a court interpreter been firmly established in **federal** courts.

2. History of Attitudes Toward Foreign Languages in the United States

The following discussion provides an overview of the historical attitudes toward what has popularly been termed "language rights" in the United States. The following subsections cover the eighteenth and nineteenth centuries, the "English-only" movement in the early twentieth century, and the changing attitudes in the early 1960s and 1970s.

2.1. The Eighteenth and Nineteenth Centuries

The framers of the Constitution consciously avoided declaring English the official language of the United States. This decision was most likely based on two considerations: to protect the freedom of individual choice of religion and language and to encourage immigrants to join the new enterprise (Heath, 1977). For at least 100 years after the founding of the United States, a relatively tolerant attitude toward other languages prevailed. Various ethnic groups conducted their organizations and schools bilingually, and state constitutions were either written bilingually or provisions were made for the protection of native languages (Hakuta, 1986).

As the nation expanded and immigration increased, intolerance toward other languages and cultures escalated. In the middle of the nineteenth century, statutory laws prescribing English began to appear. These "English-only" sentiments were most likely due to a changing ethnic composition brought about by (1) the substantial increase in the number of non-English-speaking immigrants from Ireland and central, southern, and eastern Europe; (2) the conquest of Mexican territory, causing thousands of Spanish-speaking Mexicans to become United States citizens; and (3) the recruitment of thousands of Asians for work on the railroads. Many Americans who descended from English settlers or identified with them were resentful of the newcomers and instituted "Language policies ... that were primarily designed to discriminate against ... [them] and limit their political, economic, and social power" (San Miguel, 1986, p. 2). For example, provisions of the Treaty of Guadalupe Hidalgo (1848) which could have been construed to include "language rights" for Mexican-Americans were ignored. By 1903, thirty-nine states had legislated constitutional provisions that undermined non-English public and private schools. Similar proscriptions occurred in many situations despite provisions protecting the use of languages other than English. For example, various measures prohibited Chinese immigrants from testifying in court, denied the Japanese the right to own land, segregated Mexican children into special schools, and prohibited the teaching of the German language in public and private schools (Acuña, 1972; Combs & Trasviña, 1986; Hakuta, 1986; San Miguel, 1986).

2.2. Increasing "English-Only" Sentiments in the Twentieth Century

An increased need for cheap labor and a rapid rise in immigration followed the outbreak of World War I. Fueled by attitudes of racial and cultural superiority, well-developed exclusionary behavior toward immigrant populations escalated into pervasive xenophobia, reaching a zenith in the 1920s (Madrid, 1986). During 1913-23 the role of education as the agent for "Americanization" was formulated and set firmly in place. Much educational policy legislation during this period focused on the regulation of language in the schools. By 1923, thirty-four states had passed legislation mandating English as the language of school instruction to the exclusion of other languages (San Miguel, 1986). Nebraska, for example, prohibited teaching in any language other than English in both public and private schools.

This law was challenged in *Meyer v. Nebraska* (1923), where the Supreme Court ruled that a state law requiring English as the sole medium of instruction violated the liberty guaranteed by the Fourteenth Amendment. Justice Reynolds wrote the following in the *Meyer* decision:

> The protection of the Constitution extends to all, to those who speak other languages as well as to those born with English on the tongue. Perhaps it would be highly advantageous if all had ready understanding of our ordinary speech, but this cannot be coerced by methods which conflict with the Constitution— a desirable end cannot be promoted by prohibited means. (p. 401)

This decision, in effect, made statutes in twenty states voidable; however, it was a highly controversial ruling. Sporadic attempts to curtail the public and private use of other languages continued and "English-only" sentiments escalated, especially in the 1950s, when they were spurred on by the Cold War and McCarthyism. Fears of the English-speaking majority further increased when large numbers of Mexicans were brought into the United States under the auspices of the Bracero program, a farm labor plan that compensated for the lack of manpower available in the United States during and after World War II and the Korean War. At this time the legal proscription against Spanish began, most evident in an anti-Spanish campaign mounted in the schools. Corporal and other forms of punishment were administered to children caught speaking Spanish. Teachers, administrators, and school board members were threatened with the loss of their jobs if they allowed students to speak any language other than English in the schools (San Miguel, 1986).

2.3. Changes in Attitude: The Sixties and Seventies

It was not until the 1960s and 1970s that the concept popularly referred to as language rights developed in the collective conscience of America. With this growing consciousness came laws that allowed, and in some instances required, the use of non-English languages for certain public functions. Language rights, however, is a misnomer; those laws which include "language" as a remedy in actuality were enacted to ensure "access rights." Laws that arose out of this period identified language as a tool for promoting equal access to basic institutions in the United States: They were designed to ensure political, legal, educational, and employment access for tradition- ally powerless minority groups (Macías, 1979). These laws are not "language right" policies; they simply guarantee access to privileges which all citizens enjoy. This "language rights" versus "access rights" confusion may be responsible for some of the negative sentiment attached to access laws:

> Conflating access rights with "language rights" obscures the original intent and ultimate goal of this body of legislation, making it appear that Mexican Amer- icans and other minority groups possess something that they do not have. The clarification of these terms is essential to the intelligent resolution of the language rights controversy.... Mexican Americans have no language rights. What they do have is equal access rights to specific American institutions, rights now jeop- ardized by widespread acceptance of an argument founded on illogic. (Gonzalez et al., 1991)

The political climate of the sixties and seventies fostered the recognition and protection of minority or underprivileged classes in society. This trend was evident in the Civil Rights Movement, which demanded rights for all minorities and linguistically handicapped populations, namely the hearing- and speaking-impaired and limited- and non-English-speaking persons.

During this period non-English-speaking minority groups recognized that the inability to communicate in English denied them equal access to public institutions. Minority groups, in particular Spanish speakers, began lobbying for policies to permit them fuller participation in society. Dedicated work by civil rights activists and others engendered the Civil Rights Act of 1964 (specifically Titles VI and VII), the Voting Rights Act of 1965, the Bilingual Education Act of 1968, the Equal Employment Opportunity Act of 1972, the Voting Rights Act Amendment of 1975, and the Court Interpreters Act of 1978. These acts helped to bridge the linguistic gap between language-handicapped persons and government agencies, thereby affording access to services to people who had previously been denied them. These laws do not supplant the primacy of English, but they do protect the rights of access and, ultimately, encourage an understanding of and respect for United States social and legal systems by limited- and non-English-speaking persons who may in the past have had reasonable cause to doubt that our systems welcomed them. When minorities are granted access to education, employment, voting, and justice, they adhere to and participate in the national civic culture (Karst, 1986).

3. Civil Rights Legislation: Access Laws

With the changing attitudes came an understanding that access to specific institutions was guaranteed by the United States Constitution. The four major institutions that were affected by this change in attitude were the educational, political, employment, and legal systems. In each of these areas landmark federal legislation addressed and guaranteed access to these privileges for all.

3.1. Educational Access

The Bilingual Education Act of 1968 (Title VII, Amendment to the 1965 Elementary and Secondary Education Act) was the first federal legislation to recognize and meet "the special educational needs of children of limited-English-speaking ability in schools having a high concentration of children from families ... with incomes below $3,000 per year" (Bilingual Education Act, 1968). In 1974, largely as a result of the Lau Remedies (below), amendments to the Act eliminated the $3,000 per year prerequisite and broadened protections to all children of limited English proficiency. This bilingual education legislation was enacted following the outcry of parents of Hispanic children who were failing in "English-only" schools (Blanco, 1978). The intent of the Act was to stimulate innovative programs, often utilizing the native language as a medium of instruction, in order to facilitate the education of limited- and non-English-speaking children. The programs were to be supported eventually through local and state funds. Although any school that met the stipulations of the Act could apply for funds by creating bilingual programs to serve its non-English-speaking children, local school systems were, regrettably, under no legal obligation to do so and many did not. In addition, many schools that did implement programs under the auspices of the Bilingual Education Act aimed only at attaining English proficiency, with no emphasis on developing the child's native language skills (Hakuta, 1986).

A more rigorous effort at bilingual education was set into motion by the landmark Supreme Court decision *Lau v. Nichols* (1974). In a class-action suit brought by parents of Chinese public school students against the San Francisco Unified School District, the students complained that because there were no special programs to meet their specific linguistic needs they could not benefit from instruction in English. The case was argued and won on the basis of Title VI of the Civil Rights Act of 1964, which mandated that "no person in the United States shall, on the ground of race, color, or national origin, be excluded from participation in, be denied the benefits of, or be subjected to discrimination under any programs or activity receiving federal financial assistance" (Teitelbaum & Hiller, 1977, p. 6).

The Supreme Court held that "there is no equality of treatment merely by providing students with the same facilities, textbooks, teachers and curriculum; for students who do not understand English are effectively foreclosed from any meaningful education" (Teitelbaum & Hiller, 1977, p. 7). The Supreme Court further stated, "it seems obvious that the Chinese-speaking minority receives fewer benefits than the English-speaking majority which denies them a meaningful opportunity to participate in the educational program—all earmarks of discrimination banned by the regulations" (p. 8). There were three significant outcomes of the *Lau* decision: (1) It favorably influenced a number of other cases that resulted in court-mandated bilingual programs; (2) it mandated transitional bilingual education and disallowed English as a Second Language programs without a native language instruction component for elementary limited- and non-English-speaking children; and (3) it directly influenced federal policy when the United States Office of Education formed a task force to create guidelines for school districts judged to be out of compliance with Title VI and the *Lau* decision.

These guidelines, best known as the "Lau Remedies," directed school boards to identify students with a primary or home language other than English, and to implement transitional bilingual programs under specified conditions. *Lau* paved the way for other policies using language remedies, such as the Court Interpreters Act of 1978.

3.2. Political Access

The Civil Rights Act of 1964 clearly had an enormous effect in advancing the rights of minorities; however, the Voting Rights Act did not have as immediately efficacious an outcome for language minorities as did the Bilingual Education Act and the Lau Remedies. While the Voting Rights Act, by outlawing gerrymandering, did allow minorities the opportunity to cast a meaningful vote, that opportunity was an empty legal gesture since limited- and non-English-speaking persons could not understand the language of the ballot.

It was not until the 1975 Amendments to the 1968 Voting Rights Act that language minorities were granted equal access to the right to vote. This legislation mandated the use of bilingual or multilingual ballots where there were large concentrations of language minorities. By passing this legislation, Congress affirmed the existence of inequality based on language, thus marking an important step in the history of political access rights based on language remedies.

3.3. Employment Access

Title VII of the Civil Rights Act of 1964 was enacted by Congress to prohibit private employment discrimination. As amended by the 1972 Equal Employment Opportunity Act, Title VII offers protection to all state and local government and educational institution employees. Employment discrimination based on sex, race, color, religion, or national origin is proscribed. Although this Act, like the others, does not specifically include language as a vehicle for insuring protection under the law, it prohibits the speaking of native languages as a basis for discriminating against employees by employers.

3.4. Legal Access

While equal access to the political process, education, and employment were guaranteed by the Voting Rights Act, the Bilingual Education Act, and the Equal Employment Opportunity Act, a vacuum of access rights remained. On a daily basis in the legal system non-English-speaking persons were denied due process under the law (*Arredondo & Tapia*, 1971-72). A report by the United States Commission on Civil Rights (1970) revealed widespread evidence that legal protection in the administration of justice had been withheld from Mexican Americans and other language minority groups. The "inability to communicate between Spanish-speaking United States citizens and English-speaking officials" (p. iii) exacerbated the inequities, including unduly harsh treatment, arrest on insufficient grounds, physical and verbal abuse, and disproportionately severe penalties.

Chapter 4

Bridging the Language Gap: Access to Due Process

This chapter presents an overview of measures taken within the judicial sphere to ensure equal access to justice, specifically through court interpreter services. It first reviews the federal rules governing court interpretation and explains the constitutional basis for the underlying statutory right to an interpreter. The following section also presents major decisions that affected non-English speakers in the courts and discusses the practical implications of these rulings for the provision of interpreter services. The final section analyzes the inadequacies that resulted from the deficient interpreting provided in the United States justice system prior to the 1978 Court Interpreters Act.

1. Federal Rules of Procedure

As previously discussed, in the sixties and seventies the nation began moving slowly toward recognizing that language barriers negatively affected the quality of life for language minorities. Before 1978, few rules, regulations, or statutes existed that addressed any aspect of the use of interpreters in federal proceedings. Those in existence included the Criminal Justice Act of 1964; Rule 43(f) of the *Federal Rules of Civil Procedure and Appellate Procedure* (1968); Rule 604 of the *Federal Rules of Evidence* (1966); and Rule 28(b) of the *Federal Rules of Civil-Appellate-Criminal Procedure* (1968). Prior to the enactment of these rules federal courts were providing interpreters through the Justice Department to aid in the prosecution of criminal cases, particularly in those districts where the talent of government lawyers was directed to the prosecution of the illicit drug trade and immigration offenses endemic to the United States-Mexico border (Real, 1973, p. 34).

Until 1978, appointment of interpreters was limited to cases involving indigents. Three statutes were of particular importance:

(a) 28(b) in *Federal Rules of Civil-Appellate-Criminal Procedure* (1968) provided the following:

> The Court may appoint an interpreter of its own selection and may fix the reasonable compensation of such interpreter. Such compensation shall be paid out of funds provided by law or by the government, as the court may direct.

This rule left the appointment of an interpreter to the court's discretion and, furthermore, allowed the court to select its own interpreter without guidelines on competency. This rule eventually became Rule 41—Interpreters and Experts, and also Rule 604—Interpreters (Federal Criminal Code, 1989). This rule stands essentially the same as cited above and has been adopted with each new version of the *Federal Rules of Criminal Procedure,* which is published every year for use in federal courts.

43

(b) Rule 43(f) of the *Federal Rules of Civil Procedure* (Federal Rules of Civil, 1968) as amended in 1966 stated that:

> The court may appoint an interpreter of its own selection and may fix his reasonable compensation. The compensation shall be paid out of funds provided by law or by one or more of the parties as the court may direct, and may be taxed ultimately as costs, in the discretion of the court.

Rule 43(f) can now be found in *Federal Rules of Civil Procedure* (Federal Civil Judicial, 1989), and is considered an appointment rule. Its related Rule 604 for the qualifications of interpreter as expert witness is discussed later (see Unit 3, Chapter 12). Civil proceedings involve private parties and do not involve criminal sanctions imposed by the state; therefore, this rule allowed the court to appoint its own interpreter for the benefit of an indigent non-English-speaking or language-handicapped defendant embroiled in a controversy.

(c) The Criminal Justice Act of 1964 allowed for payment of services, other than counsel, which are "necessary to an adequate defense." Payment is made through the United States Treasury. This Act is still in force today.

These statutes did not directly mandate that an interpreter be appointed by the federal courts to defendants who were non-English speakers. Rather, it allowed discretion in the hiring and payment of interpreters by the court. More importantly, these statutes did not address numerous problems which plagued interpreter services, such as the poor quality of interpretation found in the courts, lack of training for interpreters, the lack of interpreter ethics, and the lack of certification examinations, to name a few.

The right of a defendant to be present at trial had long been established, beginning with *Lewis v. United States* (1892). The right to assistance of counsel and the right to confront witnesses under the Sixth Amendment have been construed by the Court of Appeals of Alabama in *Terry v. State* (1925; see also Morris, 1967), to mean:

> The accused must not only be accorded all necessary means to know and understand the testimony given by said witnesses. . . . Mere confrontation of the witnesses would be useless, bordering upon the farcical, if the accused could not hear or understand their testimony. (p. 387)

The additional requirement that a defendant have "sufficient . . . ability to consult with his lawyer with a reasonable degree of rational understanding" was recognized in a case dealing with the issue of competency to stand trial, *Dusky v. United States* (1960). And a defendant's ability to exercise his or her right to be confronted with adverse witnesses, applicable to the states through the Fourteenth Amendment, had been guaranteed in *Pointer v. Texas* (1965). These particular cases laid the groundwork for the holding in *United States ex rel. Negron v. New York* (1970), where the Second Circuit Court of Appeals found that a defendant must be able to comprehend and participate meaningfully in the proceedings.

Previously, judges and attorneys had a mistaken impression that the interpreter's role was not an objective one, and that appointment of interpreters unfairly aided the defendant (Gonzalez, 1988). This suspicion was compounded by the fact that many *ad hoc* interpreters lacked professional training. The combination of misunderstanding, misinformation, and bias may have contributed to the reluctance of many courts to utilize their services.

Prior to 1978, an interpreter was never mandatory, even in a trial situation where a defendant or witness clearly did not speak English. Additionally, when an interpreter was utilized, there were no mandated judicial or even extra-judicial means of confirming his or her language ability. Theoretically, and very often in practice, interpretation could be completely dismissed, despite a specific request or an obvious necessity. Even if interpretation was stipulated, it is very likely that a non-proficient interpreter's poor performance may have abridged the defendant's rights. As Pousada (1979) points out, these provisions had an additional weakness: "The implementation of these guidelines is subject to the discretion of the judge, and abuse of that discretion is rarely proven" (p. 192). As Schweda-Nicholson (1985) points out, however, the courts at least made the important observation that interpreters possess an arcane skill. Therefore, the judge had the sole power to determine who had these skills and who would be the court interpreter.

In the only case it has heard on the issue of appointment of interpreters, *Perovich v. United States* (1907), the Supreme Court of the United States established that it was within the discretion of the court whether or not to appoint an interpreter. Since the issue of whether the defendant has a constitutional right to a state-provided interpreter had not been raised in *Perovich,* the issue was not decided by the Supreme Court. As a general rule, the Supreme Court will not rule upon issues which are not squarely presented before it; therefore, since that particular issue was not raised, the court was silent and will undoubtedly remain so unless it is presented in another case.

Prior to 1978, only one federal decision stated that if the federal court is notified that a defendant has a language problem, then the court must clearly inform the defendant of his or her right to an interpreter, at the expense of the state if indigent and throughout the proceedings (*United States v. Carrin,* 1973). These rules and decisions were written predominantly for the indigent defendant, and did not recognize the right of **every** limited- or non-English-speaking defendant to interpreted proceedings.

2. Precursors to the Federal Court Interpreters Act

The three federal rules paved the way for the introduction of an enactment which would affect the federal courts. In May of 1973, California Senator John V. Tunney introduced Senate Bill 1724, The Bilingual Courts Act, which set into motion a legislative effort that did not come to fruition until 1978. During the hearings on S. 1724 Tunney stated before the Subcommittee on Improvements in Judicial Machinery of the Committee on the Judiciary of the United States Senate that he had introduced the bill to "remedy a long-standing deficiency in our Federal Judicial System—the inability of thousands of non-English-speaking Americans to defend themselves adequately in proceedings conducted in a language alien to them" (Tunney, 1973, p. 14). Senator Tunney clearly defined the issue of court interpreter before the Senate subcommittee:

The cornerstone of our legal system is the equality of treatment that it guarantees to every citizen, rich or poor, old or young, black, brown or white. We cannot permit the circumstances of birth to decide the right of redress in a courtroom. The long strides which we made throughout the 1960's in extending civil rights protection to minority groups should not be taken as evidence that our task is completed. If persons must still come before our courts unable to comprehend fully the nature of the testimony or the charges that have been made against them, then they are suffering a handicap which is impermissible under our laws and our Constitution. (Tunney, 1973, p. 14)

The year after S. 1724 failed to pass the scrutiny of the Senate subcommittee, a slightly revised version, Senate Bill 565 (1974), was introduced. The intent of both bills, among other goals, was to amend Rule 28(b) of the *Federal Rules of Criminal Procedure* (Federal Rules of Civil-Appellate, 1968) by requiring the use of certified interpreters. The 1975 version of the legislation also provided for the electronic recording of proceedings for interpretation verification. Although the 1975 effort passed in the Senate (*Congressional Record*, 1975a), it was defeated in the House (*Congressional Record*, 1975b). Despite this failure, these early attempts were important precursors of the Court Interpreters Act, as will be discussed in Chapter 6 of this unit.

3. Protection of Constitutional Rights by Interpreter

There is no explicit constitutional right to an interpreter; however, the Constitution specifically provides individual rights and liberties to all United States citizens, and for the Fourth, Fifth, Sixth, Eighth, and Fourteenth Amendments to have any legal meaning, provision of interpreter services must be offered to limited- and non-English speakers. But for decades due process rights as guaranteed by these amendments were regularly violated by federal, state, and local courts that failed to recognize the need for and to provide interpreting services for limited- and non-English-speaking persons and other linguistically disabled populations. These members of our society, therefore, did not enjoy their rights for the obvious reason: they could not understand or communicate in the language of the judicial system—English.

The statutory remedy attempted by Senator Tunney was proposed in response to the history of frustration and neglect that language minorities faced in the courtroom. This struggle is most evident in case law, which is replete with examples of inattention to the plight of limited- and non-English-speaking persons in the legal process, often brought about by a procedural rather than ethical approach to providing access. The case law also documents the actions of forward-looking jurists who recognized the linguistic barrier and sought thoughtful solutions to the unequal treatment of language minorities. In his testimony before Congress in 1973, Senator Joseph Montoya stated that "It is tragic to have to admit...that there exists...unequal protection under [the] law, and unequal opportunity for justice, or an unequal provision in defense of personal or property rights of [some] American citizens" (Montoya, 1973, p. 167). Because some limited- and non-English-speaking defendants do speak some English, it was sometimes difficult for courts to believe their failure to offer interpreter services violated their constitutional rights. In fact, withholding an interpreter from a non-English-speaking defendant during court proceedings abridges the right to cross-examination provided by the Sixth Amendment. An attorney cannot adequately cross-examine without the assistance of the client (Chang & Araujo, 1975). Moreover, no defense testimony or argument is adequate when attorneys cannot confer with their clients. The client is essentially not allowed to participate in the preparation of his or her own defense. Furthermore, any court denying a limited- or non-English-speaking defendant an interpreter discriminates against that person and the population or class of persons he or she represents; in other words, that defendant is denied equal protection under the law (Chang & Araujo, 1975).

4. Early State Cases Concerning Interpreters

Early judicial rulings concerning the non-English speaker's right to an interpreter are often contradictory. The earliest recorded case involving interpretation is *In re Norberg* (1808), in which a witness unfamiliar with the English language needed an interpreter. The Massachusetts Supreme Court held that when an interpreter is utilized, he or she must be sworn in, and under oath attest to the fact that he or she is acquainted with the language to be interpreted. *Norberg* illustrates an early example of a court concerned with the quality of interpretation, and court interpretation in general. However, judges and court administrators seemed to "underestimate the complexity and far-reaching ramifications of bridging or rather failing to bridge the language gap" (Gonzalez, 1988, p. 3).

In addressing interpreter issues, states looked to federal case law and in particular to the single United States Supreme Court case—*Perovich v. United States* (1907). In *Perovich* the Supreme Court ruling avoided the issue of a right to a court interpreter by addressing the problem on procedural rather than constitutional grounds. Many cases originating in the states were taken on appeal by federal district courts. In general, because United States district courts are required to follow federal precedent, cases accepted on appeal were not overturned. Thereby the provision and right to a court interpreter was set back for over seventy years by the decision's translation into judicial practice. By not recognizing the critical connection between court interpretation and protecting constitutional rights the court prolonged the denial of access rights for limited- or non-English-speaking populations.

5. Court Interpretation Before 1978 in State Courts

A wide array of approaches to the procurement of interpreting services filled the vacuum created by the absence of an effective judicial answer. These approaches can be grouped into four major areas: (1) the discretion of the court to appoint an interpreter; (2) the concept of linguistic "presence" and the right of confrontation; (3) the waiver of the right to an interpreter; and (4) the use and selection of *ad hoc* interpreters. However, because the courts justified the denial of interpreter services under these same rationales, they became a double-edged sword.

5.1. Discretion of the Court as to the Need for Interpreters

Traditionally, most trial courts following *Perovich* have demonstrated a casual attitude and even a marked reluctance to provide interpreters for defendants, as evidenced by *Escobar v. State* (1926), *Viliborghi v. State* (1935), *In re Muraviov* (1961), *Cervantes v. Cox* (1965), *People v. Annett* (1967), and *U.S. ex rel. Ortiz v. Sielaff* (1976), among others. In general, an interpreter was provided to a limited- or non-English speaker only in cases where it was grossly apparent that the defendant understood little or no English, and "if the record indicated that a failure to provide an interpreter had in any manner hampered the defendant in presenting his case to the jury" (*Escobar v. State*, 1926, p. 169).

Escobar v. State (1926) illustrates a narrow but important application of this justification (Gonzalez, 1977). In this case, although the defendant was accused of murder and his counsel had requested an interpreter before the trial, the court held that the denial of an interpreter did not deprive him of a fair trial due to the nature of the evidence presented. In the court's view, the defendant's testimony in Spanish did not represent a significant burden to presenting proof to deny the murder. The court also observed that three witnesses used Spanish to render their testimony and that testimony in Spanish proved only minor points (Lopez, 1975). This oft-cited case exemplifies a common presumption that long-time citizens of the United States understand English despite indications to the contrary (Chang & Araujo, 1975; Gonzalez, 1977).

Viliborghi v. State (1935) is yet another example of the application of a narrow standard used to deny interpreter services. After deciding that the defendant's testimony was not hampered by his lack of English proficiency, the court proclaimed he did not require an interpreter. In this case, as in many others, the accused *may* have appeared to be able to speak English well enough to testify, but he undoubtedly did not understand the entire proceedings and may not have understood the linguistic intricacies and ramifications of his own limited English testimony. While some limited-English speakers can communicate in home language, they cannot function in the complex register of English used in the courtroom (Gonzalez, 1977). This language variety may be wholly out of the linguistic proficiency and cultural experience of limited-English speakers.

Many courts have denied requests for an interpreter after perfunctory examinations of a defendant's English, the results of which often exhibited that the accused only had a minimal ability to understand the proceedings. In *People v. Annett* (1967), a court assessed a defendant's ability to speak and understand English after posing eleven questions, each of which received a monosyllabic "yes" response. Only four questions, resulting in either a "yes" or "no" answer, were necessary before a California trial court determined that a defendant's English competency was adequate (Chang & Araujo, 1975; *In re Muraviov*, 1961).

A United States court of appeals judged a defense attorney's performance as adequate, even though the attorney denied his own client's request for an interpreter (*U.S. ex rel. Ortiz v. Sielaff*, 1976). Another United States court of appeals characterized interpretation as something that may be necessary for an attorney to effectively communicate with his or her client only in extreme circumstances (*Cervantes v. Cox*, 1965).

5.2. Concept of "Presence" and Right of Confrontation

The ruling in *Perovich* (1907) held firm, and refusal by the courts to appoint interpreters for non-English-speaking persons became the rule rather than the exception. As Pousada (1979) states, "the rights accorded by the Sixth Amendment of confrontation and assistance of counsel are empty when the defendant is not 'linguistically present' at his own trial" (p. 191). In a dissenting opinion Justice Tobriner stated in *Jara v. Municipal Court* (1978) that without an interpreter, the limited- or non-English speaker takes part in "a Kafka-esque ritual deemed by the majority to constitute...a fair trial," (p. 188); the majority held that courts are not constitutionally required to appoint interpreters at public expense in civil cases.

The distinction between physical presence and "linguistic" presence is legally the same distinction made by the courts on the issue of mental incompetency in the *Dusky v. United States* (1960) ruling. The court essentially decided that a defendant must be present in both mind and body if due process rights are to be met. For all individuals, then, understanding the proceeding includes linguistic comprehension. The physical presence of the defendant in the courtroom may satisfy the letter of the law, but not the spirit of the law.

Beyond legal arguments, it is a fair and just presumption that in court a person should be allowed to understand the proceedings and be given the opportunity to communicate in his or her preferred mode of discourse, or be provided with an intermediary who can facilitate that communication. Chang and Araujo (1975) summarize this precept: "we are confronted with the absurdity of a system which grants an attorney to the indigent defendant but refuses to provide an interpreter so he can effectively communicate with counsel" (p. 820).

Arizona v. Natividad (1974) represents a turning point in the case law regarding the court's discretion in determining the need for an interpreter. It was the first decision to perceive the issue as one of "linguistic presence," meaning that without an interpreter, many limited- or non-English-speaking persons are not legally present in the courtroom. The defendant's right to due process was the issue in *Arizona v. Natividad* (1974). The court recognized the

> affirmative duty of the trial court to determine when an interpreter is required in order to protect the constitutional guarantees of right to counsel, the right of confrontation, and the right to be informed of the charges. (Lopez, 1975, p. 9)

In this case, Justice Lockwood held that

> the inability of a defendant to understand the proceedings would be not only fundamentally unfair but particularly unjust in a state where a significant minority of the population is burdened with the handicap of being unable to effectively communicate in our national language. (*Arizona v. Natividad,* 1974, p. 733)

Justice Lockwood further stated that the defendant's inability to understand spontaneous testimony would not only limit his counsel's effectiveness but would also reduce his trial to a situation similar to one in which

> a defendant was forced to observe the proceedings from a soundproof booth or seated out of hearing at the rear of the courtroom, being able to observe but not

comprehend the criminal processes, whereby the state had put his freedom in jeopardy. (p. 733)

Justice Lockwood went so far as to say that "such a trial comes close to being an invective against an insensible object, possibly infringing upon the accused's basic right to be present in the court room at the very stage of his trial" (p. 733). This landmark decision set a precedent and offered a clear directive to the judicial system:

> the trial court . . . is in the best position to determine whether a defendant possesses the requisite degree of fluency in the English language, so that his right to confront witnesses, right to cross-examine those witnesses, and the right to competent counsel will not be abridged. (p. 733)

5.3. The Waiver of the Right to an Interpreter

In addition to determining the level of a defendant's fluency in English and whether an interpreter is warranted, it was within the court's discretion to determine that the defendant waived the right to an interpreter in a situation where neither the defendant nor the attorney requests interpreting services. In *Black's Law Dictionary* (1979), a waiver is defined as "the intentional or voluntary relinquishment of a *known* [emphasis added] right" (p. 1417). Many courts held that failure to request an interpreter constituted a waiver of that right, which in effect unfairly placed the burden of knowing the extent of one's legal rights upon the non-English-speaking defendant or his unknowing counsel (*Gonzalez v. People of Virgin Islands*, 1940; *People v. Estany*, 1962; *People v. Hernandez*, 1960; *People v. Ramos*, 1970; *Suarez v. U.S.*, 1962).

In *People v. Ramos* (1970), a New York court of appeals found that the court did not have a duty to appoint an interpreter where the defense failed to assert that the defendant was a limited- or non-English speaker, and where there were no "obvious manifestations" of the defendant's inability to speak English (Chang & Araujo, 1975). Occurrences such as this were numerous until a United States court of appeals ruled in the landmark case of *United States ex rel. Negron v. New York* (1970) that the right to an interpreter is not forfeited by a mere failure to request one. The court held that

> an indigent, poorly educated Puerto Rican thrown into a criminal trial as his initiation to our trial system cannot be expected to come to that trial with a comprehension that the nature of our adversary processes is such that he is in peril of forfeiting even the rudiments of a fair proceeding unless he insists upon them. (p. 388)

In this particular case, the defendant did not speak English and his court-appointed attorney did not speak Spanish. The defendant was afforded only periodic translation summaries provided by an interpreter for the prosecution. The defendant won his appeal on the grounds of inadequate translation for those portions of his trial conducted in English. The rationale offered by the court was that "considerations of fairness, the integrity of the fact-finding process, and the potency of our adversarial system of justice forbid that the state should prosecute a defendant who is not present at his own trial" (p. 388). The court recognized the affirmative duty of the trial court to determine when an interpreter is required. This responsibility had to be met for the protection of the constitutional guarantees of right to counsel, the right of confrontation, the right to be informed of the charges, and the right to understand the nature of the proceedings brought against the defendant by the state.

A few years after *Negron*, in *United States v. Carrion* (1973), the court held that it was the responsibility of the trial court to investigate a defendant's proficiency in English and, based upon this, to determine whether an interpreter was necessary; thus the burden of responsibility for requesting an interpreter shifted to the court. A concern similar to that of *Negron* was also expressed by the *Carrion* court regarding the idea of fairness and the right to an interpreter.

or interpretation are similar in severity ial of interpretation. Historically the who had interpreted or were willing to e who was presumed to be bilingual," h interpreting ability" (Gonzalez, 1988, fendants or witnesses, court personnel, rarians, bilingual attorneys, attorneys' reters were coerced into service in spite ncy and understanding of courtroom McCarter, 1978). Anecdotal evidence omical situations involving faulty ren- d, 1830; *Gee Long v. State*, 1928; *Gonzales v. State*, 1977; *People v. Chavez*, 1981; Valdés, 1982).

5.4.1. Using Bilingual Attorneys as Interpreters

Courts quite often met their interpreting service needs by appointing Spanish-speaking attorneys for Spanish-speaking defendants and witnesses. The attorney, while performing the duties of an interpreter, cannot at the same time effectively represent the legal interests of a defendant, for "it is a combination of tasks which unfortunately cannot be simultaneously implemented" (Gonzalez, 1988, p. 23). An interpreter focuses on the meaning of a spoken message, then discards the words from the source language (SL) and searches for the ones that best express the same meaning in the target language (TL), while simultaneously listening to the continuing source language message. Interpreters serve as conduits and do not assimilate the information long enough to allow for a great deal of analysis, at least not at a legal level. Although analysis is a key element of the interpreting process, it is a linguistic analysis that the interpreter performs. An attorney, on the other hand, listens, takes notes, and undertakes a legal analysis in order to (1) evaluate the opposing counsel's evidence, (2) formulate new questions to correct flaws of various kinds in testimony, (3) highlight or diminish a fact, (4) gather further information to support or counter an argument, and (5) monitor whether all of the legal elements of a law have been introduced. It is cognitively impossible to perform both the role of the interpreter and attorney simultaneously and competently (Gonzalez, 1988).

When a bilingual attorney also serves as the interpreter, the client's right to both competent interpretation and legal counsel is essentially forfeited. A California state appeals court, in *People v. Chavez* (1981), decided that the constitutional rights of a defendant are denied when the defense attorney must also act as an interpreter. According to Frankenthaler and McCarter (1978), an attorney may be prohibited from functioning as an interpreter by the legal Canons of Professional Ethics. To act as an interpreter, the attorney must also qualify as an expert witness. The attorney may be in jeopardy of entering into a conflict of interest if the interpretation is for his or her client at the witness stand. The authors point out that it is "a serious misconception to somehow equate legal expertise with linguistic expertise" (p. 132).

5.4.2. Appointment of Friends, Relatives, or Adversaries of the Defendant

Another group of interpreters the courts traditionally relied on were friends and relatives of defendants or witnesses. In these instances the defendant had the burden of providing an interpreter in a hearing which the state initiated. *Ad hoc* interpreters could unwittingly or intentionally misrepresent both sides of the communication process (*Doucette v. State*, 1983; *Kay v. State*, 1976; *State v. Burns*, 1899). Friends or relatives may feel compelled to modify testimony or queries by the officer of the court in order to hide facts and responses that they believe might be damaging to the defendant. They may add, subtract, embellish, or ignore parts of the discourse, depending on their own internal rationale as to what might be helpful or harmful to their friend or family member. The potential lack of objectivity on the part of the friend or relative can result in a biased interpretation.

It is not only perilous for ethical reasons to hire a friend or relative, it is linguistically hazardous. Often these *ad hoc* interpreters are not native speakers of English. In addition, the ability to speak two languages does not, in itself, constitute the interpreting proficiency required to render a comprehensive and precise interpretation. The speed with which the interpreter must process the message and construct a translation demands a full command of the techniques of interpretation and an understanding of the legal language, jargon, and procedure of the legal process.

In an effort to keep their dockets at manageable levels, courts have even used *ad hoc* interpreters who are potentially detrimental to the defendant, such as arresting police officers or co-defendants. In *Gee Long v. State* (1928), a Chinese-speaking defendant was accused of murdering a member of a *tong*—a Chinese association historically opposed to his own; his court-appointed interpreter was a professed member of that *tong*.

A more recent example of the use of an *ad hoc* interpreter who was potentially prejudicial is found in the New Jersey grand jury's second consideration of *State v. Sung J. Lee* (1986). In this case Lee Kim, the victim, complaining witness, and sister of the defendant, had testified against her brother. Later in the session an alleged eyewitness, Ok Kyu Kim, testified, and Lee Kim was asked to interpret. The prosecutor's rationale for using Lee Kim to interpret for Ok Kyu Kim was that he did not know where else to find a Korean interpreter. As illustrated in this case, the use of *ad hoc* rather than professionally certified interpreters compromises the court's ability to ensure fair, just, and equitable treatment of those who come before it.

6. Deficient Interpreting Skills

Each of these *ad hoc* solutions has a potentially disastrous legal consequence, but the most serious problem with such solutions involves the untested interpreting abilities of those providing the interpretation. One of the primary findings in the report by the United States Commission on Civil Rights (1970) concerned the lack of adequate interpretation afforded Mexican Americans in the judicial system; interpreters were not readily available, and, when they were, the interpreters were often untrained and unqualified. Often, their bilingual and interpreting capabilities had not been measured and their abilities ranged from excellent proficiency in one language and limited proficiency in the other to a variety of home language vocabulary limited to topics germane to the home in both languages.

Few court officers possessed the linguistic and testing insight and training necessary to recognize that justice was compromised on a regular basis by the lack of competent interpretation. Even with the utilization of full-time staff and free-lance interpreters that practice in federal, state, and local courts, the dispensation of justice by the courts was likely just as erratic as it was when *ad hoc* interpreters were previously used (Astiz, 1986; Comptroller General, 1977). The misinterpretation or negligent interpretation by an unqualified interpreter could easily have distorted crucial testimony or eliminated determinative evidence.

In the early 1970s, a number of studies commissioned primarily by the court systems began to investigate the parameters of non-English speakers' problems in dealing with the justice system (Lopez, 1973, 1975; United States Commission on Civil Rights, 1970). Although these studies addressed the inadequacies of local courts or jurisdictions within a narrow and often parochial context, they represent seminal attempts to both describe the problem of access to the judicial system for non-English-speaking populations and recommend policy and management plans as possible solutions (Lopez, 1975). A study commissioned by the Judicial Council of California entitled *A Report to the Judicial Council [of California] on the Language Needs of Non-English-Speaking Persons in Relation to the State's Justice System,* (1977), conducted by Arthur Young and Company, is just one example of a state's serious effort to examine this issue and propose solutions.

A careful review of these studies reveals an almost universally applicable set of problems and conclusions about the inconsistent, arbitrary, and sometimes non-existent interpreter services for the non-English-speaking and hearing- and speech-impaired populations. These local studies were corroborated by national surveys such as that conducted by the Comptroller General of the United States (1977), *Use of Interpreters for Language-Disabled Persons Involved in Federal, State, and Local Judicial Proceedings,* at the request of the Subcommittee on Civil and Constitutional Rights of the Committee on the Judiciary. Both the local studies and national surveys disclosed an almost *laissez-faire* attitude by the judicial system toward the special needs of non-English speakers. The research indicated that awareness of the problem by the courts was so poor that in many cases no data about the demand for and provision of interpreter services were kept.

7. Recognizing the Pervasiveness of Inadequate Interpretation

The results of these reviews reflected the courts' mixed decisions regarding their erratic use of interpreters. Specific problems were identified, including a reliance on *ad hoc* interpreters and the uneven skills among official interpreters in local, state, and federal courts.

Basing his conclusions on numerous court observations and interviews, Carlos Astiz (1980) reported that there were great variations in interpreting technique, as well as an almost universal disregard for accuracy. He also noted that some interpreters had short memory spans and that they interrupted the speakers, asked for repetitions, or omitted part of the questions or answers regularly. More recently, Berk-Seligson (1988) made similar observations during a seven-month study of English-Spanish/ Spanish-English interpretation in federal, state, and local courts and ultimately questioned the courts' ability to guarantee limited- or non-English-speaking people their rights: "In fact, one comes away with a sense of alarm over the general state of affairs in most courts" (p. 10). Berk-Seligson's findings corroborated Astiz's (1986) contention that there is no "legal difference in terms of meeting the constitutional guarantees of non-English-speaking individuals between refusal to provide interpreting services and use of incompetent interpreters" (p. 33).

Yet the courts have traditionally not addressed the issue of incompetent interpretation, even when cognizant of its occurrence. Courts have often reversed cases involving unqualified interpreters, but have based their reversals on other unrelated factors, as noted by Astiz (1980) in connection with a case, *U.S. v. Vera* (1975): "While the decision was based on a general understanding of the facts to which the defendants pleaded guilty, the exchanges quoted by the Circuit Court point to evidence of inadequate interpretation" (p. 11).

In cases where the courts either noticed or were informed of faulty interpretation, they have been reluctant to make conclusive statements or decisions to that effect, as evidenced in *U.S. v. Pena* (1976). In this case, the court denied the appeal based on the fact that the "defendant was repeatedly warned of his rights in Spanish as well as English" (p. 294), even though the defendant complained of having difficulties when the agent who arrested him used a Disney World interpreter to translate his rights to him from a standard form.

Other courts have simply been unaware that misinterpretation or lack of proper interpretation has occurred and that the defendant has suffered as a result. The problem of misinterpretation in the courtroom arises because the defendant must blindly rely on a court-appointed interpreter and is consequently in communicative isolation from the proceedings. This problem is compounded by the fact that most trial transcripts include only the English version of a defendant's or witness's testimony, leaving no opportunity for a court or a defendant's attorney to review the validity of the interpretation against the original source language (Astiz, 1980). Because of this fact, cases remanded or reversed on the basis of poor translation or misinterpretation are few (Astiz, 1980; *Torres v. U. S.*, 1974; *U.S. v. Diharce-Estrada*, 1976). The *Diharce* court reversed the conviction partially because the "defendant's pretrial statements were not transcribed even though Diharce spoke only broken English and it was not unlikely that, without the aid of an interpreter, misunderstandings could result" (p. 639). In *Torres* (1974), the Fifth Circuit reversed a guilty plea because "The record shows that the statement of the factual basis for the plea was not translated for Torres..." (p. 958).

Eventually bilingual judges, magistrates, and attorneys recognized the inadequacies of interpretation in the courtroom, and began to take local and national action to correct the situation. Bilingual judges and attorneys who recognized the many gross inequities arising from the lack of adequate interpretation were heavily represented at the hearings conducted for the proposed Bilingual Courts Act of 1973 (*Senate Bill No. 1724,* 1973) and the congressional hearings (U.S. Senate Judiciary Committee, 1977) in 1978 for the Court Interpreters Act. Their collective testimony played a critical role in the establishment of certification. But for their concern the problem might have gone unnoticed, for "it is impossible for the accused to show by specific evidence that his interpreter, either by reason of bias or incompetency, was incorrectly interpreting the testimony of the English-speaking witnesses" ("The Right to," 1970-71, p. 164).

The importance of proper interpretation cannot be overstated as Chang and Araujo (1975) suggest, "Since language is the principal medium of communication in all legal proceedings, the ability to understand the language used in them is critical to the fairness of those proceedings" (p. 801). One misinterpreted word, phrase, or tone could mean the difference between a fair trial or a grave incident of injustice. As a Utah court pointed out in *State v. Vasquez* (1942), a question by a defendant or witness "may bring forth an answer that might turn the scales from innocence to guilt or from guilt to innocence" (p. 905). Yet the competency question and the affirmation of non-English-speaking persons' rights to a court interpreter were never squarely addressed at the federal level in legislation until the enactment of Public Law 95-539, the Court Interpreters Act of 1978.

Chapter 5

The Court Interpreters Act

This chapter presents a detailed analysis of the Court Interpreters Act of 1978. It first enumerates the Act's provisions, and continues with a discussion of its benefits and shortcomings. The next section explains how enforcement of the Act was assessed by the Federal Court Interpreter Advisory Board. Finally, the chapter discusses the amendments made to the Court Interpreters Act in 1988.

1. Introduction

On October 29, 1978, Public Law 95-539, the Court Interpreters Act (Appendix A), was passed by the Senate and the House of Representatives and signed into law by President Carter. This bill mandates the use of qualified interpreters in any criminal or civil action initiated by the United States in which a defendant or witness "... speaks only or primarily a language other than the English language ... so as to inhibit such [a] party's comprehension of the proceedings or communication with counsel or the presiding judicial officer, or so as to inhibit such witness' comprehension of questions and the presentation of such testimony" (Court Interpreters Act, 1978, §1827(d)1-2).

Most importantly, the Act prescribes the availability of **certified** interpreters to populations that are unable to comprehend the language of the proceedings or the charges in any criminal or civil case brought by the United States Government. This legislation also provides interpreters for *writs of habeas corpus* petitions initiated in the name of the United States.

2. Provisions of the Court Interpreters Act

This landmark access legislation sets an exemplary standard that forthrightly addresses the three most important points surrounding the issue of language services in the courts:

(1) It recognizes for the first time the defendant's need and right to comprehend the entire proceedings and to communicate with the attorney, thereby allowing full participation in his or her own defense.

(2) It mandates the use of interpreters in bankruptcy courts and federal court settings.

(3) It recognizes the need for quality interpretation and calls for the certification of interpreters by objective testing, helping to increase the awareness of the importance of the court interpreter's role to the administration of justice for

limited- and non-English-speaking and hearing-impaired populations. The law also provides for fee schedules for interpreting services.

2.1. Recognition of Defendant's Needs

The Court Interpreters Act represents the first time legislation has acknowledged the defendant's need to comprehend everything that is stated in a courtroom in connection with his or her case, and to communicate with his or her attorney during the preparation of his or her defense. It specifies the use of simultaneous as well as consecutive and summary interpretation, thereby reflecting practices developed prior to 1978 in courtrooms out of necessity and preference, sometimes with little regard for their communicative impact or compliance with the legal requirements of preserving the record or presenting a full and precise rendition. While some scholars have speculated about the reasons for the inclusion of these three modes (Pousada, 1979), the 1978 Act merely chronicles practices that had developed in the courts by tradition rather than principle. Both the consecutive and simultaneous modes have their proper places in the courtroom; however, the summary mode violates the stated purpose of the law—that is, to ensure the full and consistent communicative participation of the defendant or witness. Of course, when the law was written, neither court interpreters nor judicial officers fully understood the objectives of interpretation in the courts and the preferred methods by which to reach those aims. In addition to naming the three modes, the law also stipulates that "special interpretation services," such as simultaneous interpretation in multidefendant criminal or civil actions, may be provided if the presiding judicial officer determines them to be necessary. The appropriate uses of the consecutive and simultaneous modes are described in detail in Unit 3, Chapter 13.

2.2. Recognition of the Need for Quality

The Court Interpreters Act established the first federal law that focused not only on the right to court interpreters but also on the competency level that interpreters must possess to perform language services. The establishment of a program to facilitate the use of court interpreters was placed under the auspices of the director of the Administrative Office of the United States Courts (AO), who was specifically directed to "... prescribe, determine, and certify the qualifications of persons who may serve as certified interpreters in courts of the United States ... and in so doing, the Director shall consider the education, training, and experience of those persons" (Court Interpreters Act, 1978, §1827(b)). The Federal Court Interpreter Certification Examination process will be covered in Unit 8, Chapter 36.

This legislation emphasizes that if a limited- or non-English-speaking person is to receive equal access to the legal system, the caliber of interpretation must be high enough to ensure that that person can completely understand the proceedings. It is also the director's responsibility to prescribe a fee schedule for services rendered by interpreters; such fees, costs, and salaries are to be paid by the Attorney General's office from sums appropriated to the Department of Justice.

2.3. Mandating Interpreters

Judges, magistrates, or referees in bankruptcy proceedings who preside over any criminal or civil action initiated by the United States in district courts are directed to utilize the services of the most available certified court interpreters, or when none is available, an otherwise competent interpreter, whenever it is such an officer's determination that an involved party or a witness may have an *inhibited* comprehension of the proceedings or communications with counsel or the presiding judicial officer. If an interpreter is not appointed by a judicial officer, an individual who required such services may seek the assistance of the court clerk or the AO to obtain a court interpreter. With the exception of witnesses, individuals may waive the provision of interpreter services after consultation with counsel and after explanation by the judge of the nature of the waiver. The Act also specifies that a witness or defendant may choose his or her own non-certified interpreter, except in special cases where such a substitution is found to potentially endanger the reliability or sincerity of the interpretation.

3. Benefits of the Court Interpreters Act

The immediate beneficiaries of the Court Interpreters Act were the many groups previously excluded from legal proceedings. As elucidated by Leeth (1985):

> The legislation was truly historic... it finally put the non-English speaker on the same footing as the English speaker. At least it was clear that a person who could not hear the proceedings in his own language could not be said to be present at his own trial—could not be said to have had the opportunity to confront witnesses against him. (p. 2)

Passage of the Court Interpreters Act signaled a new era in court interpretation. It has led to significant improvement in the quality of interpretation in the federal court system and inaugurated the accommodation of the interpreter as a new courtroom actor who, in conjunction with other officers of the court, works to implement and assure the integrity of the fact-finding adversarial system of law (Gonzalez, 1988).

3.1. Improved and Standardized Pay Scales

The federal judiciary recognized both the importance of the interpreter to the fair administration of justice for limited- and non-English speakers, and the complexity of the linguistic and interpreting tasks that define minimal competency for the interpreter. From these two insights came a notable advancement in the professional status of the court interpreter, as well as a significant improvement in the salary structures for staff and per diem interpreters. Five years after its passage, for example, Arjona (1983) reported the impressive effects of the Act: standardized pay scales in federal courts for certified and non-certified interpreters, an increase in full-time positions and salaries, and new technology utilized in the courts for simultaneous interpretation. The overall positive effect was revealed in the heightened awareness of the plight of the non-English-speaking litigant and of the court's need for accurate interpretation in languages other than English. "Thus, judges, lawyers, and litigants are becoming aware of improved communication alternatives available to them. The profession, as a whole, is restructuring itself because of the law. . . . Lawyers and judges are increasingly wary of using non-certified interpreters" (p. 4).

The impact of certification on the professional status of court interpreters in an area highly resistant to change has been remarkable. The Government Service (GS) level of court interpreters prior to 1978 was 5–7, which translated approximately to $10,000-$14,000 per annum. This pay level doubled after the implementation of Public Law 95-539, when the starting salary for certified staff interpreters became GS 10, or $26,261-$34,136 per year. A pay raise was instituted in 1985, which increased significantly both per diem rates—to $210 from $175 per day—and staff rates—to an entry level of GS 10-13.

Figure 1. 1985 Entry Level Pay
Grade 10: no experience
Grade 11: 1 year's experience
Grade 12: 2 years' experience
Grade 13: supervisory entry level

In 1988, the Federal Court Interpreter Advisory Board recommended an increment (Administrative Office of the United States Courts, 1987), which went into effect in July 1989. As market demands increase, the federal courts have found it necessary to compete with state courts for the limited available qualified interpreters. In 1989, the AO recommended to the Federal Judicial Conference a salary increase for both staff and per diem interpreters. The revised salary schedule, when approved by the Federal Judicial Conference and Congress, will be GS grades 12-14 ($34,580-$48,592 per annum). According to the AO the entry level for supervisory interpreters will be grade 15, starting at $57,158 per year (Ed Baca, personal communication, March 9, 1990).

3.2. The Ripple Effect

More important, however, is the ripple effect stimulated by the Court Interpreters Act. The Act not only set new policy in the federal court system, it also became a model for state and municipal courts, as well as for administrative law agencies. This ripple effect has been slow but steady. Since 1978, at least ten states have begun to seriously contemplate upgrading interpreting services through certification; the states of California, New Mexico, and Washington, have embarked upon certification programs, while New Jersey has a comprehensive testing, training, and certification program. The overall effect of the Act is discussed briefly in the next section of this unit and the certification testing section in Unit 8, Chapters 36 and 37.

4. Shortcomings of the Court Interpreters Act

4.1. Determining Linguistic Competency

While it is unquestionable that the Court Interpreters Act has significantly improved the quality of court interpretation in the federal court system (Administrative Office of the United States Courts, 1987), some scholars feel that several issues that have a bearing on its implementation in the courtroom remain unaddressed. For example, once an initial request for the appointment of a court interpreter has been made by the judge, counsel, or an interested party, it is left to the discretion of the judge to determine whether a person is communicatively impaired. It is a contentious point among many scholars that judges are expected to decide upon linguistic competency. Although specific responsibilities to guarantee the qualifications of court interpreters are delegated to the Director of the AO, no specific provisions are made to guide a judge in determining the linguistic competency of a witness or defendant. Frankenthaler (1980) warns that:

> If we ask for predictability and administrability in the carrying out of the laws and in the protection of the rights of the citizens of our country, there must be standards to guide judicial officers in the judgements exercised in such hearings. Judicial officers are not necessarily trained linguists. Nor is it appropriate that we ask them to be so. Yet they must decide upon the linguistic competency of parties and witnesses. (pp. 53-54)

Frankenthaler calls for standardization to determine the need for court interpreters. This standardization, she believes, will begin to solve the "discretion dilemma" (p. 54).

Frankenthaler (1980) and Pousada (1979), who see this issue as a problem, may be using federal case law and current practice in state and municipal courts as a point of reference. In practice, since 1978, the appointment of the interpreter for those who request one in the federal courts has proven to be a non-issue, with the quality issue having been addressed by certification. According to Jon Leeth, former Chief of the Programs Branch, Court Administration Division of the AO, the awareness of the judiciary and attorneys since the passage of the 1978 Act makes it difficult for the request for an interpreter to go unheeded (personal communication, March 3, 1989). In practice, according to an informal survey of interpreter supervisors in major federal courts as reported at a 1988 meeting of the Federal Court Advisory Board at which R. Gonzalez was present, an interpreter is provided if anyone—the attorney, witness, or any court official—makes a request (private meeting, 1988). Furthermore, since the passage of Public Law 95-539, no cases have been appealed in federal court on the grounds of denial of an interpreter.

4.2. Training, Testing, and the Lack of Competent Interpreters

The problem of appointing court interpreters based on the judge's discretion seems *de minimis* in comparison to the major dilemma plaguing state and federal courts: the lack of objectively tested, competent interpreters. In the federal court, this problem exists only with other-than-Spanish interpreters especially in jurisdictions where Spanish/English certified interpreters are on staff or are otherwise readily available as per diem interpreters. The quandary of judging the competency of interpreters for languages other than Spanish is pervasive. The dearth of competent interpreters is most critical in cases where other-than-Spanish languages are not offered by traditional language service providers such as the United Nations or the State Department, or not represented in the standard international conference interpretation societies such as the *Association Internationale d'Interprètes de Conférence* (AIIC) [International Association of Conference Interpreters].

Another area in need of improvement is the training of court interpreters. Although all federally certified interpreters must pass a rigorous standardized written language proficiency and oral-skills performance examination, there is no such standardization for the orientation of interpreters, nor are there guidelines for the uniform practice of court interpretation in federal courts. Since 1978, the Federal Court Interpreter Spanish/English Certification Examination has been offered seven times. The Federal Court Interpreter Certification Program has administered 12,122 written and oral examinations. Out of 9,750 candidates, 2,015 have passed the written portion of the examination, making them eligible to take the oral portion. Out of 2,372 oral administrations, 388 candidates have successfully completed the oral examination and are now certified federal court interpreters (Gonzalez, 1989c). These statistics translate into an overall success rate of 3.9 percent, or 16 percent of those taking the oral (includes candidates who have re-taken the written and/or oral portions of the examination). One factor contributing to this low pass rate is that, to date, the federal government has not developed any training programs for aspiring interpreters. Despite the lack of pre-testing education programs, 388 federally certified Spanish/English interpreters have demonstrated their ability to serve as a medium of communication between the court and limited- or non-English speakers. It is highly probable that there would be a higher success rate in the certification testing and consequently more competent interpreters available if there were government-sponsored pre-certification training programs.

Another major reason for the low pass rate is that many bilinguals in this country who present themselves as viable candidates discover that their language skills do not meet the performance standards set by the examination, either in language proficiency or in interpreting ability. This rude awakening suffered by many bilingual candidates is symptomatic of a deeper problem in the United States as a whole, and one that is a major concern to language planners: bilinguals in this country have no opportunity to develop their mother tongues, nor, as Snyder (1988) has pointed out, is the learning of a second or even a third language considered a prerequisite for basic education, as is the case in most foreign countries. Without the reinforcement and expansion brought about by more formal study of a language, language loss begins to occur on the individual and group level. On the individual level, the tragedy is that some lose the language altogether; many "bilinguals" barely maintain the limited variety of language they acquired as children, while others never have the opportunity to expand their limited repertoires through more formal study (Crawford, 1989; Cummins, 1976, 1989; Hakuta, 1986). This unfortunate phenomenon occurs because there are few bilingual programs, and only a handful in the entire country practice the **maintenance model,** a curriculum designed to teach elementary and secondary students in two languages that are on par with each other (Hakuta, 1986). Under such programs students study the formal aspects of both languages, read the great literature, and learn other semantic domains and registers besides "home Spanish." As a result, the United States has lost the potential language resources of entire minority language groups (Fishman, Nahirny, Hofman, & Hayden, 1966).

5. Monitoring the Court Interpreters Act

One of the most positive features of this model access legislation is the fact that the planners included a system for reporting how the interpreting needs of the court are met. The law states that "...the Director...shall report annually on the frequency of requests for, and the use and effectiveness of, interpreters" (Court Interpreters Act, 1978, §1827(b)). This wording implies a decided "monitoring" function of the law, to gather information about future needs and other issues. From this ongoing needs assessment, two important actions by the AO have ensued: (1) the establishment of the Federal Court Interpreters Advisory Board in 1987, and (2) the sponsorship of an amendment to the original Act, the Court Interpreters Amendment of 1988, to be discussed in Section 6 of this unit.

5.1. Federal Court Interpreters Advisory Board

In 1987, the Federal Court Interpreters Advisory Board was established to assess the state of interpreting services in the federal court system from an administrative, judicial, linguistic, and legal viewpoint and to recommend improvements and solutions to problems. The preamble to the report (Administrative Office of the United States Courts, 1987) states the Board's five tasks:

> Establish criteria which would trigger certification of interpreters in languages other than Spanish; Establish guidelines for "Professionally Qualified Interpreters" who may be used if no certified interpreter is reasonably available; Propose pay schedules for freelance interpreters; Propose orientation programs for professionally qualified interpreters; and Develop a code of professional responsibility of the official interpreters working in the United States Courts. (p. i)

The five areas specified in the preamble will be discussed here in terms of the scope of the issue and the subsequent recommendations by the Federal Court Interpreters Advisory Board.

5.1.1. Establish Criteria to Trigger Certification

One of the most misunderstood aspects of the Federal Court Interpreter Certification Program is its decision to certify interpreters in high-demand languages. For example, in 1988, out of 49,933 federal court appearances requiring an interpreter, 46,064 (93 percent) involved Spanish-language witnesses and defendants (Administrative Office of the United States Courts, 1989a). This number has fluctuated from 90 percent to 96 percent since 1980.

Although frequency of demand is the primary criterion used to determine which languages will be certified, the Advisory Board contemplated criteria by which languages other than those in significant demand would be certified. In the Advisory Board's research into the current state of interpretation at the federal level, it was found that only four courts mentioned a need for interpreters in a language other than Spanish: New Mexico urged certification in Navajo, and California Central mentioned a need for Cantonese, Mandarin, and Thai interpreters. New York Southern District Court recommended certification in additional languages, but failed to specify. Additionally, Florida Southern District Court responded that some judges had requested certification in Haitian Creole. Only New Mexico's request for Navajo certification was an official recommendation by the court. The Advisory Board suggested that, given the region-specific problems raised by the use of Navajo and Haitian Creole in federal district courts, it might be reasonable to certify interpreters in those languages based on the uniqueness of the district court's situation and not on a statistically governed need. Administration of such a program would be limited to specific geographic areas and would not require a costly, nationwide testing system (Administrative Office of the United States Courts, 1987, p. I-3).

The triggering criterion in this case would be a formal request from the court to solve a sustained problem of such proportion that the court, over a four-to-five-year period, would be otherwise unable to resolve. An alternative triggering criterion for certification of region-specific languages could be a bipartite or tripartite agreement entered into by the AO and the federal branch executive agencies and/or the state court systems to share the costs of developing and administering certification instruments. If this were the case, federal judiciary standards would need to be met. In instances where the AO and the federal or state interests are compatible, the Advisory Board strongly recommended collaboration (Administrative Office of the United States Courts, 1987, p. I-3).

The Navajo and the Haitian populations represent regional language service problems for the courts that cannot be served through traditional means or by reliance on agencies such as the State Department. Both populations are isolated from mainstream United States culture. Geographically, the Navajo are isolated in New Mexico and Arizona, and Haitian Creole speakers are mainly located in Florida, New York City, Boston, and Washington, D.C.

For both of these languages there have been substantial problems finding qualified interpreters for court proceedings and the critical need for interpreters has extended past the minimum five-year period established as a criterion by the Federal Advisory Board. The federal courts are now in the process of certification testing for court interpreters for these two languages.

5.1.2. Establish Guidelines for "Professionally or Otherwise Qualified Interpreters"

The 1978 Court Interpreters Act states that if no certified interpreter is reasonably available, the courts can call upon "otherwise competent interpreters," also known as "otherwise qualified interpreters," who may be permitted to participate in United States judicial proceedings if they meet the prerequisites set forth by the Federal Court Interpreter Advisory Board (Administrative Office of the United States Courts, 1987, p. II-1). Other languages that pose special problems for the courts because of the general unavailability of qualified interpreters from traditional sources such as the

State Department or universities are Asian languages such as Korean, Vietnamese, Thai, certain Chinese dialects, and others.

This category applies to non-Spanish interpreters who do not have the opportunity to take a federal examination to qualify for certification. Most larger federal court districts utilize from twenty to twenty-five languages every year, and not necessarily the same languages from year to year. This poses a problem for the courts, because even if a given language is seldom required, a proceeding cannot take place without an interpreter. Therefore, the Advisory Board proposed that "otherwise qualified interpreters" be divided into two categories: professionally qualified interpreters (PQ) and language skilled interpreters (LS). "Professionally qualified" interpreters are those interpreters who are highly qualified but who speak a language for which the federal government has no certification examination available. Particularly noteworthy is the fact that PQ interpreters' compensation is commensurate with certified interpreters.

According to the Advisory Board Report (Administrative Office of the United States Courts, 1987):

1. *Professionally Qualified Interpreters* are those who meet the following two requirements jointly:

   a. they either work as freelance *conference level interpreters* [emphasis in original], under contract, for the Office of Language Services of the U.S. Department of State, or for the United Nations and related or similar agencies, (or were employed by such agencies) which have examined them for relevant interpretation skills . . . ; or

   b. they are members in good standing of professional interpreters' associations whose by-laws and practice at a minimum require the following for admission to active membership:

      i. an application containing the statement of the number of days of successful experience in the conference setting, which must be at least 50 days;

      ii. an indication of the languages from which and into which the applicant is able to interpret and which he speaks as a native;

      iii. the sponsorship of three active members in good standing who have been members of the same association for at least two years, whose languages are the same as the applicant's and who attest to having witnessed the performance of the applicant, as well as attest to the accuracy of the statements required in the preceding paragraphs number i and ii (pp. II-10-11).

Interpreters who do not meet the professional qualifications are classified as language skilled interpreters. This category of interpreters is paid on a different scale than certified or PQ interpreters. The other category of interpreters named in this report are language skilled interpreters, who do not meet the prerequisites delineated for PQ interpreters, "but who can show to the satisfaction of the court, their ability to interpret from English into another language and from another language into English" (Administrative Office of the United States Courts, 1987, p. II-12).

These guidelines represent the most expedient solution to a vexing problem which the federal judiciary and other agencies have the responsibility to resolve. If states, regions, federal courts, and other federal agencies were to form consortia to certify a certain set of languages or to make available telephone assessment, these considerable language problems could be more efficiently solved. Recommended assessment procedures to ascertain the competency of language skilled individuals are covered in Unit 4, Chapter 15, Section 3.

5.1.3. Proposed Pay Schedules for Freelance Interpreters

A pay schedule for freelance interpreters was devised, taking into consideration the professional standing of the interpreter and a standard of fairness in contracting. Compensation per hour and for half and whole days is delineated for freelance interpreters. Travel and other fees, including overtime and cancellations, are discussed in this section of the Advisory Board report and then repeated almost in their entirety in the interim regulations promulgated pursuant to the Amendments to the Federal Court Interpreters Act. (Appendix B, Interim Regulations for Federal Court Interpreters).

5.1.4. Orientation Program for "Professionally Qualified/ Language Skilled Interpreters"

As mentioned previously, over the past ten years, 90 to 96 percent of all federal proceedings requiring interpretation call for interpreters of Spanish. The remaining 5 percent of interpreter services for low-demand languages in federal courts have been provided by PQ or LS interpreters. These interpreters pose a special problem for the federal courts. Many PQ interpreters are highly-skilled, exemplary conference interpreters, but they are often unfamiliar with the specifics of legal language, judicial procedure, interpreting techniques used in courts, and the judicial and ethical considerations that differentiate court interpretation from conference/escort or other nonlegal interpretation forms.

In order to better prepare PQ interpreters for the more formal legal situations of the federal courts, the Federal Court Interpreters Advisory Board (Administrative Office of the United States Courts, 1987), has made recommendations designed to enhance the skills of PQ/LS interpreters in the federal court system:

> The recommendations of the Advisory Board encompass both the ideal orientation programs, as well as the minimum effort that should be expended to enhance the quality of due process through interpretation of proceedings.... [Although it is recognized that no statutes currently provide for the training of nongovernmental employees], the Advisory Board, nevertheless, is aware that legislation has been introduced in the Congress which would permit the FJC [Federal Judicial Center] to give limited training for specific purposes to nonfederal employees when in the interest of the administration of justice. (pp. IV-2-4)

The Advisory Board's recommendations were made in keeping with the spirit of pending FJC legislation by Congress. The Advisory Board recommended the establishment of a required Federal Court Interpreters National Orientation Seminar for candidates wishing to receive PQ or LS interpreter status; it noted that this orientation should not exclude already certified Spanish/English interpreters who wish to continue or augment their professional training.

The Advisory Board recommended that this campaign to orient PQ and LS candidates be aggressively instituted without delay. It stated that the orientation should be conducted in a seminar format and that various materials should be developed, namely, a Federal Court Interpreters manual and videotape. Manuals should be distributed to all federal district judges, court executives, clerks of court, and public defenders; videotapes should be distributed to all clerks of court in every district court in the country. The Advisory Board recommended that the FJC implement this program nationwide, for the purpose of standardizing practice and orientation.

5.1.5. Develop a Code of Professional Conduct

The Code of Conduct (Appendix C-Code of Professional Responsibility of the Official Interpreters of the United States Courts) developed by the Advisory Board and later modified for inclusion in the *Federal Court Interpreters Manual and Procedures* (Administrative Office of the United States Courts, 1990) is intended to govern the professional conduct of federal court interpreters but can certainly be used as a governing code applicable to all court interpreters, regardless of the context. Adoption of a federal code of professional conduct will not only further the professionalization of the interpreting profession, but will also offer minimum guidelines for the conduct of interpreters as officers of the court.

6. The Court Interpreters Amendments Act, 1988

As a part of the monitoring function of the Court Interpreters Act and the ongoing reporting structure to assess the effects of certification, it became apparent to the federal judiciary, interpreters, and other specialists that the original bill should be amended and improved. Therefore, after a three-year process, the Court Interpreters Amendments Act of 1988 (Appendix C) was enacted. One of the contentious points during the debate about this Amendment and its unsuccessful precursor, Senate Bill No. 1853, revolved around which additional languages should be required and upon what discernible criteria such a decision should be based. The 1988 Act clearly gives the Director of the AO the discretion to certify languages, and also allows the federal Judicial Conference to do the same. On the subject of certification, the Act stipulates the following:

> The Director may certify interpreters for any language if the Director determines that there is a need for certified interpreters in that language. Upon the request of the Judicial Conference of the United States for certified interpreters in a language, the Director shall certify interpreters in that language. Upon such a request from the judicial council of a circuit and the approval of the Judicial Conference, the Director shall certify interpreters for that circuit in the language requested. (Court Interpreter Amendments Act, 1988, §1827(b)(1)).

The Federal Advisory Board has also recommended that the Director of the AO undertake certification for special region-specific requests if they are of such duration and proportion that no other recourse exists.

Another enduring problem relates to the use of specialists in languages for which certification does not exist. The law specifies the use of "otherwise qualified interpreters," and the criteria to be used to determine whether a language specialist or bilingual is "otherwise qualified" is as follows:

> The Director shall provide guidelines to the courts for the selection of otherwise qualified interpreters, in order to ensure that the highest standards of accuracy are maintained in all judicial proceedings subject to the provisions of this chapter. (§1827(b)(2))

The Act furthermore instructs the director to "maintain a current master list of all certified interpreters and otherwise qualified interpreters" (§1827(b)(3)); the Amendment also authorizes the Director to "report periodically on the use and performance of both certified and otherwise qualified interpreters in judicial proceedings... and on the languages for which interpreters have been certified" (§1827(b)(3)). This amendment clearly mandates periodic reports on the "use" and "performance" of both certified and professionally qualified interpreters.

A unique and forward-looking aspect of this Act is its attention to the issue of sound recordings of the interpreted testimony. It mandates:

> Upon the motion of a party, the presiding judicial officer shall determine whether to require the electronic sound recording of a judicial proceeding... [considering] the qualifications of the interpreter and prior experience... whether the language to be interpreted is not one of the languages for which the Director has certified interpreters, and the complexity or length of the proceeding. (§704, 1827(d)(2))

This affords a defendant the opportunity to request a recording of the proceeding and allows for an appeal on the basis of incompetent interpretation. The provision protects the due process rights of non-English speakers in the event of inaccurate interpretation.

Two other very important improvements to the Court Interpreters Act were also mandated: (1) the extension of certified court interpreter services to grand jury proceedings, and (2) the specification of the interpretation modes to be used in the courtroom. "The interpretation provided... shall be in the simultaneous mode for any party... and in the consecutive mode for witnesses" (§709, 1827(k)). This prescription corrects the inadequate provisions made in Public Law 95-539, which mandated simultaneous, consecutive, and summary modes, and did not specify preferred uses of simultaneous and consecutive, or caution against the use of the summary mode.

The Amendment has omitted the summary mode altogether, in essence declaring it inappropriate for judicial interpretation and reinforcing the basic principle of the original Act: to allow the defendant, through the simultaneous interpretation of the proceedings, to be linguistically, cognitively, and physically present at his or her own trial and to participate in his or her own defense. This represents an important step towards uniformity of policy and practice in the federal courts. Most importantly, it sets a clear standard for state and municipal courts. Furthermore, administrative law agencies and other quasi-judicial forums which do not systematically provide for full participation of non-English-speaking claimants or respondents at the federal or state level, may also find guidance in these thoughtful pronouncements.

7. The Court Interpreters Act as Amended— Interim Regulations

Pursuant to the 1988 Amendments of the Court Interpreters Act, Interim Court Interpreter Regulations (Administrative Office of the United States Courts, 1989b) have been enumerated for use in the District Courts. Some recommendations set forth by the 1987 Federal Court Interpreter Advisory Board have been integrated into the interim regulations. For example, the category of "otherwise qualified" interpreters has been redefined to include PQ and LS interpreters, as described in the report to the director (Administrative Office of the United States Courts, 1987). Also included is the criteria which a court clerk or other employing officer must use in order to decide if a non-certified interpreter qualifies as a PQ or LS interpreter. These interim regulations reflect the positive, proactive stance of the federal courts on the importance of due process for the non-English speaker. These explicit guidelines will serve not only to further standardize policy and practice, but will become important criteria for assessing successful interpreting performance. These, and other administrative issues relevant to compensation, are dealt with in the interim regulations. They represent a milestone in the professional regard accorded interpreters by the federal courts and can easily serve as models for other agencies wishing to improve their policy and practice guidelines pertaining to court interpreter services (see Appendix B, Interim Court Interpreter Regulations).

Chapter 6

Court Interpretation at the State and Local Court Level

This chapter examines the development of the legislative initiatives taken to guarantee quality interpretation for non-English speakers in the state courts. It discusses the merits and shortcomings of interpretation in California, New Mexico, New Jersey, and Washington, states in which legislation has passed or is being strongly considered. As a result of the 1978 Act, it became a statutory right for non-English-speaking and hearing-impaired persons to have an interpreter in an action initiated by the federal government. As Pousada (1979) points out, however, P.L. 95-539 is limited in that it has "no jurisdiction over any state or municipal court and does not include administrative boards; for example, immigration or social security hearings" (p. 188).

Despite the "ripple effect" of the Court Interpreters Act in terms of the increased professionalism of the field, the quality of interpretation in state and local courts remains inconsistent and poor in many areas. When federal certification was first introduced, its effect on state courts was most potent. In 1983, Arjona reported that "judges are increasingly willing to allow for the use of federally certified interpreters at the state level" (p. 4). This trend appears to have been short-lived, and federal certification has not been automatically required in most states; only New Mexico, the Texas State Employment Agency, and New Jersey have accepted federal certification as an official credential.

Since 1985, thirteen states and municipalities have created task forces to study interpreting issues, including Oregon, Utah, Iowa, Delaware, Washington, D.C., Washington, Florida, Texas, and Arizona. With the exception of Washington and New Jersey, none of these task forces has moved toward resolution. As was so aptly stated by Jon Leeth (1985), former Chief, Programs Branch, Court Administration Division of the AO: "Some state court systems will have to be brought kicking and screaming into the fold of equal justice before the law" (p. 10).

State and local court interpretation practices and policies vary widely, both among and within states. Astiz's (1980) extensive research on the quality of Spanish-English court interpretation in several states revealed a general misunderstanding of the role of the interpreter by both interpreters and court officials, and a pervasive lack of quality interpreting. In a later study of the quality of court interpreting in two federal, three state, two municipal, and two justice of the peace courts, Berk-Seligson (1988) revealed "that some court-appointed interpreters are doing an abysmal job, [and] some are consistently superb in the fidelity with which they render their interpretations" (p. 11).

The most overwhelming problem in the state and municipal courts has been the general lack of qualified, competent interpreters and the lack of valid and reliable mechanisms by which competent interpreters can be identified and tested. According to Astiz (1980): "Most states . . . have made no formal attempt to identify competent interpreters" (p. 21). Although made nearly a decade ago, this observation remains valid for the majority of state and municipal courts. The problem is pronounced, primarily because of the lack of certification and training programs, and it affects all languages including Spanish. Even in states that recognize interpretation as a right and credential interpreters by examination—such as California, New Jersey, New Mexico, and New York—there is an absence of quality interpreter services in all languages, including Spanish. Thus, the need for competency testing and training to improve proficiency is especially great at the state and city court levels.

In state and local courts that require no certification or any kind of testing to demonstrate competence in interpretation, individuals who present themselves as proficient bilingual interpreters may be neither bilingual nor proficient. This state of affairs is attributable to three factors: (1) the non-competitive salary schedule accorded interpreters in most cities and states, making these positions unattractive to persons who possess well-developed language and interpreting skills (see Unit 4, Management of Court Interpreter Services); (2) the lack of training available in two-year and four-year colleges and universities; and (3) the limited attention paid in the public school system, including two-year and four-year institutions of higher learning, to native language maintenance, second language proficiency development, and professional training for those skills required before entering the interpreting field or any other professional-level profession requiring the use of foreign language and interpreting skills.

Although in some states Spanish poses what seems to be an insurmountable language services problem, languages other than Spanish also present tremendous difficulty to private and government entities wishing to communicate with their non-English-speaking clientele. However, this problem stems from a fundamental lack of second language emphasis in our schools, from kindergarten to college. In this country there is a lamentable dearth of specialists in a number of languages deemed critical by the State Department for the defense and commercial prosperity of the United States (Lambert, 1987; *Strength through Wisdom*, 1979). The Federal Court Interpreter Advisory Board addressed this issue by recommending that state and federal agencies form a consortium to plan and develop certification examinations for the languages identified as critical (Administrative Office of the United States Courts, 1987). However, as of this writing, no efforts in this regard are under way.

As of September 1989, only three states have legislative acts providing for interpreter services and for assessing the competency of the interpreter: California, New Mexico, and Washington. Two of these states, California and New Mexico, have constitutional provisions which make the right to an interpreter a supreme law. New Jersey has introduced a bill that is still pending.

1. California

California took the lead on May 24, 1978, by passing Assembly Bill No. 2400 (1978), mandating court interpreter services and competency testing of interpreters. This premiere law was preceded by the comprehensive Dymally-Alatorre Bilingual Services Act of 1973, which mandated the use of bilingual personnel in all state agencies. The 1973 Act was designed to provide for effective communication between all levels of government and clients who had been precluded from utilizing public services because of language barriers. Following the passage of the 1973 Bilingual Services Act a number of assembly bills were introduced in hopes of alleviating the language barrier for non-English-speaking Californians in all aspects of public life and services—such as voting, contractual agreements, and summons (Blaine, 1974).

On November 5, 1974, prompted by the landmark 1973 Act, a constitutional amendment was passed in California to guarantee access to the courts for limited- and non-English-speaking citizens. The California Constitution of 1974 (article 1, section 14) states that "a person who is unable to understand English who is charged with a crime has a right to an interpreter throughout the proceedings." Four years after this constitutional right to an interpreter was established, steps were taken to ensure limited- and non-English-speaking Californians a fair opportunity to participate in their own trials and proceedings. Before the court interpreting act was passed in California in 1977, the Los Angeles County Superior Court took a leadership role and became the first court to test the competency of interpreters (Gonzalez, 1985).

Signed into law on May 24, 1978, five months before the federal Court Interpreters Act passed, Assembly Bill 2400 provides for "equal justice under the law to all California citizens and residents and the special needs of non-English-speaking persons in their relations with the judicial system" (§68560(d)). This Act mandates programs to ensure adequate interpretation services and to compile statistics on the use of interpreters statewide.

This bill leaves the standards for certification in the hands of the Judicial Council of California. It also mandates that the Judicial Council of California establish standards for professional conduct, certification, and recertification, and for determining the need for court interpreters in a trial. The Act declares that "provision of competent interpreter services in courts and judicial agencies would be facilitated by a coordinated effort to provide testing programs and to assure adequate interpreter services . . . " (§68560(e)). When the bill was passed, a certification program was initiated and entrusted to the Cooperative Personnel Services of the California State Personnel Board. This credentialing examination is discussed in Unit 8, Chapter 37.

The institutionalization of court interpreting services in California occurred in a fashion parallel to that of the federal level. California has positively influenced the field of court interpreting by developing a credentialing examination for employment in state courts and administrative agencies; the relative professional value of court interpreting has also increased through the dedication of pioneer interpreters in the California Court Interpreters Association (Gonzalez, 1985). While there are doubts about the rigor and validity of the California state credentialing examination, there is no doubt that California was the first state to recognize the necessity of language intermediaries in the administration of justice and to establish standards for qualifying court interpreters.

Because of the dubious comprehensiveness and validity of the credentialing examination that was initially administered in California, the adequacy of interpreter services in the entire state has been questioned. According to Astiz (1980), "The few attempts made by states such as California and New York to select criminal court interpreters through examination have, in my professional opinion, been worthless . . . [and] have failed to discriminate between competent and incompetent interpreters" (p. 21). Jon Leeth (1985) has said that the California examination is dangerous because the state has put its stamp of approval on certified interpreters, leading judges, and attorneys to relax their vigilance on the assumption that interpreters who have passed the state test are qualified. "I continue to believe that that is a dangerous situation because it lulls the users . . . into a false sense of security. They believe they are getting accurate and complete interpretations when in fact they are not" (p. 10). Since these comments were made in the early 1980s, the California certification examination has reportedly been improved. There has, however, been no empirical validation to substantiate these reports.

These concerns are currently being subjected to closer scrutiny. Interestingly enough, the bill provides for recertification: "a requirement for periodic review of each recommended court interpreter's skills and for removal from the recommended list of those court interpreters who fail to maintain their skills" (§68564(d)). Appropriate solutions can be elaborated with the cooperation of the state personnel and linguistic and court interpretation experts. Minimum competency standards can be established through thoughtful research on data obtained from the judiciary, master interpreters, and other experts (Gonzalez, 1988). A certification examination can then be developed that reflects those minimum standards. Finally, training and recertification can be authorized for previously certified individuals who do not meet the new standard.

2. New Mexico

Although the right to an interpreter has been guaranteed by New Mexico's constitution since 1911, no specific legislation governed this matter until the Court Interpreters Act of 1985 (see New Mexico, 1985) was passed by the legislature on April 4. This Act defined an interpreter as

> a person who has a sufficient range of formal and informal language skills in English and another language so that he is readily able to interpret, translate and communicate simultaneously and consecutively in either direction between a non-English speaking person and other parties. (§38-10-2(B))

It mandates the provision of certified interpreters for any non-English-speaking person who is a witness or a principal party to a case. The Act specifically provides for the certification of interpreters and establishes a court interpreters advisory committee to develop and oversee a certification examination. It also specifies that the New Mexico Administrative Office of the Courts should provide for the development and administration of all examinations, courses, and training required for certification of interpreters.

This statute is not exceptional in its approach, yet it does make adequate provisions for its implementation by calling for the creation of an advisory committee to aid in the establishment of certification standards and develop general guidelines for the training and management of court interpreters. In fulfillment of these objectives, the advisory committee published a comprehensive guide, *The Use of Court Interpreters in New Mexico: A Handbook for Judges, Attorneys, and Interpreters* (Valdés & Wilcox, 1986). This handbook provides for the certification of interpreters of Spanish, indigenous languages, and the languages of the speech- and hearing-impaired. According to the handbook, New Mexico certification treats Spanish, indigenous languages, and sign language interpretation separately. These certification provisions and a description of the examination procedure will be discussed in Unit 8, Chapter 37. The validity and caliber of the New Mexico credentialing examination have been disputed, placing into question the adequacy of the interpreting services provided in the state of New Mexico. The state of New Mexico initiated brief training workshops to help interpreters meet the required competency level, but has not embarked on any extensive preparatory or in-service programs.

3. New Jersey

According to the Administrative Office of the Courts of the State of New Jersey, almost one-fifth of the state's population speaks a language other than English at home (New Jersey Supreme Court Task Force on Interpreter and Translation Services, 1985). In the New Jersey state court system, this linguistic diversity results in an estimated 8,000 court proceedings per month that involve a non-English language or an American Sign Language or Signed English interpreter (New Jersey Consortium of Educators, 1988). To meet the state courts' need for interpreters, New Jersey has taken the national lead among states in addressing issues of professional competence for legal interpreters and equal access to justice for linguistic minorities (Hippchen, 1977). A combination of government and private groups have cooperated to establish and fund a court interpreter training program in institutions of higher education in New Jersey.

The goals of the New Jersey Consortium of Educators in Legal Interpretation and Translation (1988) are

> to provide currently practicing bilingual interpreters with educational opportunities which have never before existed as well as to produce a cadre of highly skilled professionals to meet the future needs of the State's linguistic minorities. (p. ii)

The state of New Jersey recognizes that in order to provide equal access to the legal system for linguistic minorities and to keep the court calendar efficient, steps must be taken to increase the awareness of judges and court personnel of the need and proper utilization of legal interpreters and translators and to enhance their professionalization.

The most distinctive feature of the New Jersey movement is the involvement of the Supreme Court of New Jersey and its desire to model its actions on those of the federal court system. The supreme court appointed a task force that specifically and carefully addressed a series of background questions before deciding on a set of recommendations to include in its final report, *Equal Access to the Courts for Linguistic Minorities* (New Jersey Supreme Court Task Force on Interpreter and Translation Services, 1985). This comprehensive report set the stage for a chain of further studies, including a pilot certification examination based on carefully researched minimal competency standards, and an objective scoring mechanism.

A state Court Interpreters Act has been proposed but is still pending in the New Jersey legislature. Assembly Bill No. 2089 (Administrative Office of the New Jersey Courts, Assembly Bill No. 2089) contains comprehensive proposals " ... concerning the selection, qualification, employment, and supervision of legal interpreters and making an appropriation therefor [sic]" (p. 1, ln. 1). Assembly Bill No. 2089 represents a modified version of a bill that was originally submitted in 1985. As of May 1990, this legal access law has not passed. The bill states that:

> it shall be the policy of this State to secure the rights of persons who are unable to understand readily or to communicate readily in the English language and who consequently cannot be fully protected in legal proceedings unless qualified interpreters are available to assist them. (p. 1, ln. 7)

The bill is remarkably comprehensive and specifies precisely the goal of what we have termed "legal equivalence:" "Legal interpreters and translators shall faithfully and accurately reproduce in the receptor language the closest natural equivalent of the source-language message, primarily in terms of meaning and secondarily in terms of style, without embellishment, omission or explanation" (p. 6, ln. 16). The bill further elaborates the definition of a legal equivalent:

> When interpreting during the questioning of a witness, legal interpreters and translators shall convey the speaker's emphasis and emotional tone only to the degree necessary to convey the speaker's messages, without reenacting or mimicking the speaker's messages, without reenacting or mimicking the speaker's tone, emotions or dramatic gestures. (p. 7, ln. 11)

Although some of this "legal equivalent" stylistic advice is objectionable, it does make clear the duties of the interpreter and offers a point of departure for any court administrator or judge from which to ascertain quality of interpretation.

In addition to this accurate delineation of the function of a court interpreter, the bill also specifies in detail a number of ethical boundaries and responsibilities, not just for the interpreter, but for the judiciary and legal counsel as well. The bill also contains some provisions that are unprecedented in statutes on interpreting, including (1) the appropriation of $300,000 to "develop curriculum, materials, and programs for the education of legal interpreters and legal translators under the coordination of an institution of higher education" (p. 11, ln. 3); and (2) a monitoring function which requires that a full report on the implementation plan be submitted within twenty-four months after the effective date of the Act.

Assembly Bill No. 2089 (Administrative Office of the New Jersey Courts, Assembly Bill No. 2089) presents, in form and substance, an ideal access policy that uses language as a remedy; its shortcomings are minuscule. One large area of contention for attorneys is the fact that any witness whose English language skills are suspect may be subjected to a communicative competence test. This removes the issue from the discretion of the judge and essentially from the control of the attorney. Some attorneys believe the use of an interpreter is a black mark against their clients who come before juries. There are two sensitive provisions in the bill that may force it to submit to prolonged consideration. The first is the communicative competence instrument under advisement by the New Jersey Task Force on Interpreter and Translation Services—one developed explicitly for that purpose but which has never been implemented. Additionally, the provision prohibiting judges and legal counsel from acting as interpreters may not be accepted by some members of the judiciary and members of the bar.

4. Washington State

For the past five years the state of Washington has been intently moving toward creating legislation, certification, and professional standards for interpreters. The number of limited- and non-English-speaking persons in the state of Washington is relatively large; it is one of three states with the largest number of Asian Americans in the nation, the other two being California and Texas (Waggoner, 1988). In 1985, in response to numerous inquiries from members of the Washington State Legislature, the judiciary, interpreters, and other concerned individuals, a Court Interpreter Task Force was formed by the Office of the Administrator for the Courts. In its October 1986 initial report, the Task Force recommended that the Supreme Court of Washington: (1) adopt a code of ethics, (2) prescribe minimum qualifications of and certify interpreters, (3) adopt standard interpretation of judicial forms in several languages, and (4) support in-service training and continuing professional education for court interpreters and translators (Court Interpreter Task Force of the State of Washington, 1986).

A notable achievement for the state of Washington is the production of a series of videotapes on interpretation by the Office of the Administrator of the Courts. Produced in June of 1985, these professional-quality videotapes give examples of substandard ethical and linguistic interpreter practices and suggest correct standards. The issues are representative in terms of their commonality among untrained interpreters; the suggested solutions are also valid and well illustrated. Other films produced for interpreters by the Office of the Administrator of the Courts are "Interpreting as a Recognized Profession," "Cultural Factors," "Methodology," and "Interpreters in the Courtroom." All these videotapes are available from the Washington State Film Library (Court Interpreter Task Force of the State of Washington, 1986).

On April 17, 1989, the Washington State Legislature passed substitute Senate Bill No. 5474, "An Act Relating to Interpreters in Legal Proceedings." This Act proposes the following:

> It is hereby declared to be the policy of this state to secure the rights, constitutional or otherwise, of persons, who because of a non-English-speaking cultural background, are unable to readily understand or communicate in the English language, and who consequently cannot be fully protected in legal proceedings unless qualified interpreters are available to assist them. (p. 1)

The most important provision in this new language policy is the requirement that the courts appoint certified interpreters:

> Whenever an interpreter is appointed to assist a non-English speaking person in a legal proceeding, the appointing authority shall, in the absence of a written waiver by a person, appoint a certified or a qualified interpreter to assist the person throughout the proceedings. (p. 2)

This Act also orders the Office of the Administrator of the Courts to establish and administer a comprehensive testing and certification program for interpreters. It also directs the establishment of a "certification preparation equivalent and suitable training programs to ensure the availability of certified interpreters" (p. 3). Interestingly, this law patterns itself on the federal courts' policy and implementation program and includes a provision stating that "the office of the administrator for the courts may charge reasonable fees for testing, training, and certification" (p. 4). Charging a fee for training is an innovation at the state level, and represents a viable approach to raising revenue to support a comprehensive program of training and testing.

Section 9 of this law would have empowered the Office of the Administrator for the Courts to create a committee to study the certification issue, to recommend performance standards, and to establish priorities among various language groups in their search for due process under the law. However, in May of 1989, this section was vetoed by the Governor because the committee's membership was restrictive and did not appear to include "state agency and city and town participation in the adoption of standards and procedures for certification" (Governor B. Gardner, personal communication, May 12, 1989). In the letter vetoing Section 9 of the proposed bill, Governor Gardner authorizes the administrator of the courts to create an advisory group that is more representative of all interested and affected parties.

The passage of this law places Washington in a leading role in state court interpretation policy and implementation. The training and certification component will allow Washington to create adequate standards of performance and prepare its staff and free-lance pool of interpreters to meet the established goals. The state of Washington's provision of certification and performance standards for interpreters may be the impetus to bring about a more professional status for court interpreters in other states as well.

5. New York

Even though New York State has one of the largest and most diverse ethnic populations in the United States, it does not have a court interpreter law among its statutes. As noted in Table 1 of the Development and Validation of Written Examinations for Court Interpreter—Spanish-Speaking (Ferrara & Minter, 1986, p. 1), New York courts use interpreters 250 times per day, with Spanish being the language most in demand. Because the tasks and goals of court interpreters were not understood, a job analysis was conducted in 1980 in which personnel experts observed court interpreters performing in court settings (p. 1). From these observations a general job description for court interpreters was derived. A standard work analysis survey asked practicing interpreters to list the most difficult aspects of their jobs, as well as other questions. Based on this analysis, the New York State Unified Court System subsequently established a civil service examination for the position of court interpreter in Spanish. This examination is discussed later in Unit 8, Chapter 37.

As of 1985, there were 110 staff interpreters in New York State distributed among the family, civil, district, and criminal courts in the various counties and boroughs of New York City—three of them in the senior interpreter rank (Ferrara & Minter, 1986, p. 2). This civil-service "job" rather than "professional" classification and the lack of a legislative-based mandate to certify denies court interpreters in New York the opportunity to be measured by stringent performance-based standards. Unfortunately, this practice has had three negative effects: (1) no quality control for the state court system, (2) no increase in professional standing for interpreters, and (3) no guarantee or check on the quality of interpretation for limited- and non-English-speaking persons. As David Fellmeth, Senior Court Interpreter in New York City, observed, "Everybody gets a piece of due process.... But how big a piece depends on the interpreter" (Sanders, 1989, p. 25). New York is now attempting to improve its credentialing techniques and to provide the training that will allow staff interpreters to improve their language and interpreting abilities (D. Fellmeth, personal communication, August 17, 1989).

6. Conclusions

There are a number of reasons that states other than California, New Jersey, New Mexico, and Washington have not significantly improved the condition of interpretation in their state. After a comprehensive study of court interpreting in a variety of court systems, Astiz (1986) concludes that many state and local court officials do not feel:

> they have the obligation to bridge the linguistic barrier faced by non-English speaking individuals that come into contact with their agencies; (2) that having been required to ... they have done so in a highly formalistic fashion, committing as little of their time, effort, and budget as possible.... (p. 56)

On the same note, after years of discussion with state judicial administrators, Leeth (1985) blames the reticence of states to move toward certification on four factors:

> 1. State governments do not want to spend the money to attract and retain highly skilled people.
>
> 2. State governments do not want to develop training programs to help their employees master and perfect their skills.
>
> 3. States do not know how to develop valid tests.
>
> 4. Some state court systems have not recognized that there is a problem, and sad to say ... some court systems probably truly believe in equal justice for everybody but the foreign-born. (p. 11)

Leeth also suggests that many state certification and training problems could be resolved if states acted in concert, and if states entered into cooperative agreements for training and testing with the federal government and with other federal and state agencies requiring interpreter services. See Unit 8, Chapter 37, for a further discussion of state certification.

Chapter 7

Court Interpretation Outside the United States

This chapter focuses on the status of the court interpreting profession and the regulation of language services in Canada and Australia, countries with legal systems similar to that of the United States. These countries are of particular interest because of the innovative solutions they have applied toward the problem of ensuring fair treatment for all members of their ethnically and linguistically diverse immigrant and indigenous populations.

1. Introduction

As world societies learn to deal with increasing colonial and immigrant language minority populations, language services have by necessity become a basic staple of government. Of all government institutions, the legal/judicial domain is one of the most critical when contemplated in terms of the potential loss of liberty and property. Legal or court interpreters and translators constitute one of the largest subgroups of the interpreting profession. Some countries have developed far more elaborate constitutional and human-rights-oriented judicial interpreter programs, complete with orientation/education programs for clients of court interpreters. However, other agencies and organizations have not concentrated as much on the quality of interpretation as has the federal judiciary of the United States. There is, undoubtedly, national and international respect for the United States federal certification procedure (Coughlin, 1984; Ewell & Schrieberg, 1989; Schrieberg & Ewell, 1989). As of this writing, judicial performance and professional interpreting standards in many countries contrast significantly with those in place in United States federal courts, and in general do not approach the quality of language services and professional status established through this rigorous examination. However, it is beneficial to examine these systems for features that are adaptable to the United States context, and to understand the contribution others have made under even more difficult circumstances.

2. Canada

Language services and interpreters have been commonplace for many years in Canada because the country has two official languages as well as several Native American tribes that have managed to keep their cultures and languages intact because of geographic and cultural isolation and constitutional protections. Measured in terms of salary, Canada appears to lag behind the United States in the professionalization of court interpreting. This is often symptomatic of the "back door method" with which interpreters have been integrated into government service, and an indication that its complexities are not understood.

In Canada, the federal government is directly involved with court interpreting in immigration, a few administrative boards, and a handful of federal courts. Most provincial governments currently have no formalized certification, training, or selection process operant in their court systems (Repa, 1988). Judging from the reports of Carr (1988) and Repa (1988), court interpreting has made the greatest gains in Ontario, where bilingual policies promote the use of interpreters, competency testing, training, and accreditation models. Gains have also been made on an individual basis by such educators as Roberts, who has published a manual, *Interpretation in the Courts* (1981), and sponsored some legal interpreter training at the University of Ottawa. Two other Canadian entities solve their language service problems in unique ways, with varying degrees of success: the Province of British Columbia and the Northwest Territories.

2.1. British Columbia

Although the Province of British Columbia is not commonly regarded as a multicultural set of communities, it has many different ethnic groups, and the fabric of its society daily becomes more diverse. For instance, the influx of limited- and non-English-speaking children into the Vancouver school system was significant in the academic year 1987-88, when 10,000 of the city's 50,000 students were enrolled in ESL classes, and more than half of all students had a mother tongue that was neither English nor French (Carr, 1988). The ethnic population of Vancouver, once heavily Chinese and Japanese, has become extremely diversified. Persons of different linguistic and cultural backgrounds in a virtually monolingual English-speaking society such as British Columbia naturally face difficulties in all phases of their existence, but most critically in the legal system, and particularly in the courtroom.

According to a report by the Task Group on Court Interpreting in British Columbia (1985) titled *Toward a Court Interpreting System in British Columbia,* the *ad hoc* methods of training and selecting court interpreters are inadequate in British Columbia and, in particular, Vancouver. The goal of the Task Group was to comprehensively survey:

(1) existing services, human resources, and training opportunities;

(2) models of delivery of interpreting services in other provinces and selected English-speaking countries; and

(3) solutions most compatible with conditions and requirements in the courts of British Columbia.

A history of problems much like those documented in United States case law (see Chapter 3 of this unit) was presented in the report. Many of the same legal issues were in dispute, including legal presence in court, fundamental justice (due process of law), and the misuse of family, friends, and attorneys as interpreters. It is an interesting replay of the United States legal arguments and the judicial responses to the needs of limited- and non-English speakers, in a country that recognizes and shares both common law and civil law traditions. (See Unit 2, Chapter 11 for a discussion of common and civil law.) Accordingly, the conclusions reached by the task group were almost identical to the conclusions of many reports written in the United States in the Seventies. The overwhelming conclusion was that a defendant's right to an interpreter is nullified if a poor quality interpreter is employed (Task Group on Court Interpreting in British Columbia, 1985).

Because the Charter of Rights and Freedoms guarantees the right to an interpreter, it is surprising that Canada disregards the competency of those interpreters as an essential component of their use. Section 14 of the Canadian Charter of Rights and Freedoms (1982) states that "a party or witness in any proceeding who does not understand or speak the language in which the proceedings are conducted or who is deaf has the right of the assistance of an interpreter."

It is unfortunate that, even though interpreters have been used in the Canadian judicial system since the founding of the country, the need for competency standards and proof of proficiency has been only recently addressed (Task Group on Court Interpreting in British Columbia, 1985). The authors cite an observation made in a report of the Commission on Bilingualism and Biculturalism (1970), titled *The Law of Languages in Canada*:

> It seems difficult to accept the fact that interpreters, on whose competence and fidelity the property or freedom of an individual may depend, are not given any special training and are not required to establish their qualifications by means of an official examination. If court stenographers are tested, why not interpreters? (p. 24)

Although this work has been a major catalyst in the improvement of court interpreter services in some provinces, the authors of this report assert that in 1985 the situation in British Columbia was unchanged; according to Carr (1988), the following recommendations have not been acted on:

(1) The formulation and institutionalization of a system of accreditation. Skills to be tested included language proficiency in English and the language in question, legal procedures, terminologies, and interpreting skills.

(2) The creation of a training program at an institution of higher learning in British Columbia.

(3) The establishment of a central register of accredited interpreters in British Columbia.

(4) The elucidation of the interpreter's role in the legal process to be delineated through court interpreting legislation.

It seems that without the force of a statute such as the federal Court Interpreters Act of 1978, court interpreting policy in Canada has generally gone unaddressed, even though the right to interpretation is constitutionally guaranteed. According to Repa (1988), in a paper read before the Annual Meeting of the American Translators Association entitled "Professional Status Today and Tomorrow: Case of Court Interpreters in Canada," the situation in Canada has not improved radically, although he cites improvement in court interpreting services in some jurisdictions because of training and accreditation. Carr (1988) states that some goals in training interpreters have been achieved, and refers to the program at Vancouver Community College, established in 1979, as "the only fully-operational multi-lingual training program . . . in Canada" (p. 418). This program offers training in twenty languages and has graduated ninety students since its inception. The curriculum and materials for this program have been published in a *Manual for Court Interpreters* (Carr, 1984). This 150-hour pioneer court interpreting program focuses on instruction in legal procedure and terminology, interpreting techniques and practice (not including simultaneous interpretation), and professional skills such as public speaking. Students are admitted to the program upon passing a written and oral entrance examination. Any language a student is interested in pursuing becomes an instructional part of the curriculum.

The problems with such a curriculum are predictable; finding competent instructors and developing materials in various languages are the first of many. Students who graduate from this program, as well as anyone else who desires, can take the Society for Translators and Interpreters of British Columbia (STIBC) examination, established in 1982. This accrediting procedure consists of a mock trial to test the candidate's interpreting skills and a written examination to test the candidate's proficiency in English and the language of specialty, as well as knowledge of legal procedures and terminologies (Carr, 1988).

The STIBC has currently proposed that this accreditation be established nationally for court interpreters, administered under the aegis of the Canadian Translators and Interpreters Council. The examination has been compared to the Federal Court Interpreter Certification Examination, but it cannot be compared in terms of complexity or criterion-referenced standards; notwithstanding, it is a beginning. The primary difference between certification in the United States and Canada is that in the United States the employing agency is the Administrative Office of the United States Courts (AO) or various state governments, while in Canada certification efforts have been undertaken by a professional organization.

2.2. The Northwest Territories

The government of the Northwest Territories has become a model for developing a court interpreting program with limited linguistic or fiscal resources. The Government Language Bureau of the Northwest Territories initiated a successful training program, which it is currently transferring to an educational institution. The Northwest Territories is an example of a government becoming a language planner and policy implementer for its growing and linguistically diverse population.

The Northwest Territories (NWT) has made formidable efforts to maintain aborigine languages and to develop a plan to serve their legal and political interpreting and translating needs. These territories, not yet an official province of Canada, have a population of 50,000 Inuit, Dene, Metis, and Euro-Canadian people, a relatively small population spread out over an immense land mass—much larger than most countries, and, at 3,244,608 square kilometers, larger than the top one-third of Canada (Roy-Nicklen, 1988, p. 429). Dene (Athabaskan) languages in the NWT include Dogrib, Chipewyan, Loucheux, and North and South Slavey with some dialects. Inuit (Eskimo) includes three dialects: Inukitut, Innuinaktun, and Inurialuktun. Another language family, Algonquian, is represented by Cree (Devine, 1983). This culturally, linguistically, and geographically rich area is struggling simultaneously to keep its precious heritage and to obtain government services from a federal government that is officially English- and French-speaking. The territorial government asserts that the Canadian Charter of Rights and Freedoms (1982)(§35) recognizes and affirms aboriginal rights (Roy-Nicklen, 1988, p. 430). The federal Official Languages Act

·gal rights reduced. Whereas
s, the Canadian equivalent
h that tradition, in 1984,
·ial Language Act (1969),
Chipwyan, North Slavey,
T Interpreter/Translator
providing interpreting
, it is part of the De-
role is to interpret for
ie Language Bureau staff
·e major dialects of Inuit,
Fr   ιage Bureau, see *Aboriginal*
La   *Territories* (Biscaye & Howard,

.. strengthened by the Ordinance to
Recog   υι the Aboriginal Languages and to Establish the
Offici   ιne Northwest Territories (1984) and the subsequent federal-
territor... ιunding agreement to which the government committed $16,000,000 to
fund indigenous language development from 1984 to 1989. A principal study by the
Northwest Territories Department of Justice (1987) titled *Breaking the Silence: A
Special Report on Interpreting in the Northwest Territories Courts* made twenty-three
recommendations to improve the judicial system for unilingual speakers. A primary
recommendation of this report called for legislating the right to interpretation and
translation within the courts (Task Force on Aboriginal Languages, 1986). Another
of these recommendations was to initiate a long-term training program. However,
because of fiscal and time constraints, and the pressing needs of the courts, a short-
term training program was implemented instead. This six-week legal interpreter training program began in the summer of 1986 in Yellowknife, NWT, and was followed
by an accreditation examination conducted by a panel of court interpreting specialists
and jurists. The examination consisted of a mock-trial in which the candidates were
asked to interpret in simultaneous, consecutive, and sight translation modes. The
report of the Task Force on Aboriginal Languages (1986), written in five major
aboriginal languages, states that court interpreters/translators in the NWT:

- provide written translation as well as oral interpretation;
- provide interpretation in a legislature;
- perform simultaneous interpreting in a native language;
- perform interpreting or translating in every subject area;
- interpret and translate both ways: from a native language to English and English
  to a native language;
- develop audio-visual materials, including script-writing;
- use computers to translate or record terminology;
- provide language services to multiple groups at once: Legislative Assembly, Executive, all government departments, courts... and any other organization,
  board, group, agency, council, or individual. (p. 45)

The interpreting and translating tasks in legal/bureaucratic settings are complex, and another recommendation and ultimate goal of the Task Force is to bring about wider recognition and adequate compensation for these specialists.

Despite the fact that the interpreting/translating project in the NWT is a comprehensive one—not solely dedicated to court interpreting—the legal-bureaucratic domain is foremost in priority, thereby making the effort to train and examine the proficiency of these aboriginal language interpreters a complex procedure. As for its direct relevance to the United States context, it should be remembered that few Native American groups in our nation are as isolated geographically, culturally, and linguistically as the Native groups in the NWT. However, the Navajo people have somewhat similar histories in the United States (Ortiz, 1983).

In 1986, Arctic College was mandated to create a one-year formal interpreter/ translator certificate training program for aboriginal languages. This program was to begin in 1988 and was to train ten students who had completed grade 10 or above, in addition to possessing native proficiency in their mother tongues (Roy-Nicklen, 1988). The stated goal of this program is not unrealistic; it is not to produce highly skilled interpreters and translators but to produce individuals who can facilitate interlingual communication to some degree. These goals, while understandable within the context of the NWT, are not sufficient for interpreters in the United States federal or state court systems. The model formulated by the NWT can be adopted in form and spirit, although the goals should be modified to meet the demanding minimal competency requirements of judicial interpretation in the United States and to ensure legal equivalence (Gonzalez, 1989c).

As Repa (1988) states, "Court interpreting in Canada is well established as an activity but has a long way to go yet to become a profession" (p. 441). The criterion-referenced performance standards set for a certification or accreditation procedure can affect professional advancement collectively and individually more than any other single factor. Once the appropriate accreditation program has been established and promulgated, court interpreting in Canada may begin to make the same professional strides made by federal and some state interpreters in the United States. An important element in the United States for increasing professionalization for interpreters is the passage of certification legislation at the federal and state levels. Pursuing similar goals at the federal and provincial levels in Canada, not only to mandate interpreter services but also to define the interpreter's role in the judicial process and prescribe certification and the funding necessary to bring it about, may serve Canadian interpreters well. For the most part, language services in the Canadian courts are further behind those in the United States in terms of the effect of planning and policy on the federal level, and to a lesser degree on the provincial levels except, possibly, for Ontario. However, Canada is much further ahead of the United States in recognizing the need to certify aborigine languages because of the special problems that members of native language groups face without interpreting and language services.

3. Australia

Australia is a country where one-third of the population is foreign born, and is a multicultural and multilingual society, although its views are often highly monocultural (Cunliffe, 1984). The community contains some eighty distinct ethnic groups, speaking more than sixty different languages. Some individuals have not and may never attain fluency in English, and, "For these people the communication barrier and cultural difference between Australia and their country of origin prevent them from fully exercising their legal rights, duties and entitlements" (Legal Services Commission of New South Wales & The Law Society of New South Wales, 1984, p. 1). Many aborigines share this problem, as they do not speak English at a level requisite to understanding the formal register and legal terminology in the Australian system of law.

The Australian court interpreting situation is both similar and dissimilar to that of the United States. It is a common law, adversarial system of law, and its problems regarding the establishment of a right to an interpreter mirror those encountered in the United States in both the case law and the experiences of limited- and non-English-speaking persons in everyday public life. The major difference is that Australia has not yet established this right at a constitutional or statutory level. According to Vickovich (1984), in recent years great inroads have been made in serving the non-English-speaking members of the community as a result of the efforts of the Ethnic Affairs Commission at the state level in the training of police officers, prison officers, and probation and parole officers. This equals and may even surpass similar efforts at the state level in the United States. However, because immigrants are unaware of legal procedures and basic civil rights, injustices continue. Vickovich describes the conditions in New South Wales as a number of injustices that beset the entire criminal justice system, from the limited-English speaker's initial encounter with the law to a court proceeding. She declares that the functioning of the judicial process is often impeded by inadequate interpreting services in trials and hearings, as well as pre-trial procedures.

The right to an interpreter in court remains a largely unresolved issue in the Australian legal justice system. Cunliffe (1984), of the Australian Law Reform Commission, in a seminar on Interpreter Usage in the Legal System proposed the following reform:

(1) *Recognising a 'right'*: In place of the current law in Australia under which the witness does not have a right to use an interpreter but may do so only with leave of the court, it will be a legal right for a witness to give evidence through an interpreter unless the court is satisfied that the witness can speak and understand the English language to a sufficient degree.

(2) *Recognising particular needs*: In place of the assumption that people are *either* 'English speaking' or [emphasis in original] 'non-English speaking', the law should recognise specifically the problem of a witness who can cope to some extent but not completely. The right to an interpreter should extend to cases where particular questions and answers cannot be satisfactorily dealt with, except through an interpreter.

(3) *Adopting a new criterion*: The criterion to be used by the courts in permitting an interpreter should not be, as at present, the vague test of the 'interests of justice'. Instead, it should be whether it is necessary to permit an interpreter to enable the witness to understand and answer the questions put to him.

(4) *Changing professional attitudes*: In addition to the changes in the letter of the law, it will be necessary to bring about changes in professional attitudes,

changes in the understanding by judges, magistrates and lawyers of the subtleties of interpretation in practice; and greater awareness amongst people not fluent in the English language of the sensitivity of the Australian system to their needs. (pp. 8-9)

It appears that the only legally accepted right to an interpreter is enjoyed by defendants who know no English and are unrepresented. This situation only pertains to a small number of cases. No right to an interpreter exists for witnesses (Vickovich, 1984), and there is heated dispute over the proficiency necessary for a limited-English speaker to stand trial in English.

Vickovich (1984) sees as a solution to these problems the hiring of interpreters as staff members and the presence of more bilingual officials in administrative positions. She also recommends in-service training for the judiciary and magistrates on the linguistic and cultural problems of the limited- and non-English-speaking defendant. In addition, she calls for a greater emphasis on pre-service education for lawyers. Her final recommendation is the formation of a standing committee, representing the legal profession, the judiciary, police interpreters, and other administrative entities to join forces to "monitor abuses and push for reform" (p. 11).

The picture that Vickovich paints is similar to conditions in the United States before the 1970s. Australia has many hurdles to overcome before it realizes the goal of providing access to legal justice for its language minorities. For all its shortcomings, Australia has made two worthwhile contributions to the field:

(1) efforts toward a national accreditation system for interpreters; and

(2) efforts to educate the users of interpretation.

3.1. National Accreditation

The National Accreditation Authority for Translators and Interpreters was established by the Minister for Immigration and Ethnic Affairs. The purpose of NAATI was to establish professional standards and provide accreditation for the certification of translators and interpreters at a professional level (National Accreditation Authority for Translators and Interpreters, 1978). This organization was initially established in 1977 by the Commonwealth government, and on July 1, 1983, NAATI was re-established as an independent body, jointly funded by the Commonwealth, the States, and the Northern Territory. This agency's primary goal is to establish professional standards for interpreters and translators and to develop the methods by which interpreters and translators could be accredited at various levels of competency. The impressive aspect of this accreditation examination is that it is available in aboriginal languages, sign language, Arabic, Chinese, Serbo-Croatian, and at least twenty other languages (NAATI, 1987). Accreditation through NAATI is possible in three ways:

(1) by passing an NAATI test;

(2) by completing a course of studies approved by NAATI . . . and

(3) providing evidence of specialized qualifications in interpreting/translating gained overseas which are judged by the authority to be equivalent to the standards required by it, primarily at Levels 4 and 5. (p. 3)

The levels of accreditation available for court interpreters range from Level 1, which represents low and incidental use of language, to Levels 4 and 5, which represent the standards required, for instance, at international conferences. The levels of accreditation are described as follows:

Level 1: Elementary level, in which "persons are accredited *not* [emphasis in original] as interpreters and/or translators, but as 'language aides' ... appropriate for persons ... capable of using a minimal knowledge of a language for ... simple communication." Their ability may be helpful in performing their primary job duties.

Level 2: "[R]epresents a level of ability for ordinary purposes of general business conversation, reading and writing." A category "suitable for those who use a second language as part of their principle duties." Candidates who meet this proficiency level or higher levels will be categorized as "Interpreters, Translators, or both." (p. 4)

Level 3: " ... [F]irst professional level for ... *general purpose* [emphasis in original] tasks of interpreting ... in a wide range of ... subjects. [P]ractitioners may specialize in particular areas or subjects." (p. 4)

Level 4: "[F]irst professional level for *specialist*" [emphasis in original] translators and interpreters. Interpreters who meet this level of proficiency are "capable of both consecutive and simultaneous interpreting at *international* [emphasis in original] economic, scientific and political meetings and conferences." (p. 4)

Level 5: "[P]innacle of the profession," represented by a "small and select group" of interpreters, translators, and interpreter/translators. (pp. 4-5)

One of the problems with categorization is that the criteria for meeting accreditation standards are not performance based. To label this accreditation test an interpreting or translating proficiency examination is very misleading, considering that Levels 1 and 2 describe individuals who do not have interpreting ability, but merely possess some degree of bilingual competence. The levels progress rather sharply from basic bilingual competency to professional interpretation ability between Levels 2 and 3. It is also quite significant that court or judicial interpretation is only mentioned in the performance description of Level 5, as a possible area of specialization, even though judicial interpretation is certainly on par with, if not more demanding in some aspects than, conference interpretation. It is also noteworthy that the superior level of interpretation—Level 5—is not conferred on the basis of an examination. These "master" interpreters should be meeting the highest performance standards based on objective criteria to meet the needs of the agency engaging their services. It would be a more valid accreditation if Level 5 were conferred on the basis of objective testing, performance evaluations, and other criteria deemed significant by the accrediting authority.

It is heartening to see that Level 3, which is regarded as the first professional level, assumes a high standard of general education and specialized training in order to meet basic competence. In fact, the eligibility requirements for the various levels all require a certain general education background. For instance, Level 1 requires four to six years of Australian secondary education; Level 2 requires the same educational background plus NAATI accreditation at Level 1 in the testing language. As the expectations for interpreting performance increase, so does the corresponding required educational level. Level 3 candidates must have a general education at the degree or diploma level. Level 4 candidates must hold a degree—in any subject—from a recognized institution of higher education. The degree requirement may be waived for those who, in the judgment of the authority, demonstrate equivalent professional knowledge and experience.

The NAATI examination is designed to reflect the performance criteria enunciated in the levels of accreditation and consists of a written and oral examination at Level 1; an interpreting test, a cultural and social aspects test, and an ethics test at Level 2; and an interpreting test and a dialogue interpreting test at Level 3, similar to the testing format commonly called consecutive mode testing in the United States—a dialogue between two speakers. Each dialogue contains approximately 400 words and is divided into suitable segments, not to exceed sixty words. Level 3 candidates are not tested in simultaneous interpretation.

Level 4 represents a definite demarcation in the performance levels of this examination. One important difference is that accreditation is always one-way; it measures the ability to go from one language into another. Candidates who seek two-way accreditation are required to take a separate test in each language. To satisfy the prerequisite of job experience, candidates are required to provide an employer's certificate to prove that they have practiced as an interpreter for a minimum of two years. Level 4 examinations include:

> (1) *Interpreting test*—Candidates are required to interpret three 1,500-word speeches, two simultaneous (one "seen" text given a week in advance for preparation, on a scientific or medical topic, and one "unseen") and one consecutive. The rate of delivery of speeches is approximately ninety (90) words per minute.

> (2) *Consecutive test*—Candidates are tested on three- to five-minute conference-style consecutive passages.

Evaluation of the performance at Level 4 is based on the following criteria: it should reflect the register, tone, style, and content of the source text, and it must be fluent, with few stylistic or idiomatic errors and no grammatical lapses.

Level 5 represents the pinnacle of interpretation performance and requires the candidate to demonstrate an oral and aural proficiency equivalent to that of a graduate-level native speaker with an excellent command of all registers of the target language. Persons at this level are expected to have areas of specialty such as legal or medical language proficiency (NAATI, 1987).

This examination has much to offer with regard to the comprehensiveness of testing under one authority; however, its standards do not compare favorably with those of the United States Federal Court Interpreter Certification Examination (FCICE). For example, simultaneous interpreting examinations used by NAATI test a person's ability at 90 words per minute, while the FCICE tests an interpreter's ability at 120 through 160 words per minute and asks candidates to meet the challenge of interpreting a simultaneous text sight unseen. This standard reflects the salient quality of judicial interpreting—spontaneity. In addition, the NAATI does not test the examination of a witness by an attorney, which is a very different kind of communication from that of an ordinary interchange between two speakers, one of whom is seeking information or confirmation. It is interesting to note that the longest segments of NAATI's "dialogue" exercise compare favorably with the longest segment of the FCICE in the "consecutive" portion (see Unit 8, Chapter 36, for more information about the FCICE). Furthermore, sight translation, a mode often used in legal and judicial interpreting, is omitted from these examinations. Since objective scoring procedures are not mentioned, it is logical to assume that none have been devised.

On the whole, the NAATI represents an ambitious undertaking. It does have, as previously mentioned, the drawback of being a bilingual proficiency test rather than an interpreting test at Levels 1 and 2, and one can only guess at how well those examining procedures reflect the functional aspects of any job in which language use is an important part. Specifically, the test should not be used to examine court interpreters for three reasons: (1) it does not reflect the rigorous demands of the three modes used in judicial interpreting: simultaneous (unseen or spontaneous), legal consecutive, and sight translation; (2) it does not test for mastery of all the linguistic registers encountered in the legal context, from formal, frozen language to the language of some lay witnesses—slang, argot, highly idiomatic language—to the language of expert witnesses; and (3) it would not be a valid instrument to determine ability in judicial interpretation because its format, content, and assessment methods are not sufficiently refined to measure the unique elements of court interpreting.

3.2. Educating the Users of Interpretation

One remarkable and avant-garde element of the Australian court interpreting sphere is the fact that the courts and affiliated agencies print instructional materials in a variety of languages. One brochure from the New South Wales Attorney General's Department entitled *Information About Local Courts* is written in English and contains a message in Arabic, Chinese, Croatian, Greek, Italian, Maltese, Serbian, Spanish, and Vietnamese, advising non-English speakers how to obtain interpreter assistance. The brochure also gives information about how to obtain the services of a lawyer, and other pertinent information.

Another brochure offers legal and other advice in Spanish (Legal Aid Commission of New South Wales, 1984). A key section of the brochure explains to the individual how to request an interpreter in both Spanish and English. Another brochure written in Spanish and published by the Legal Aid Commission of New South Wales (1987) is titled *¿Quién es quien en los tribunales? [Who's Who in the Courts?]*. This brochure presents an illustration of a courtroom and introduces the courtroom actors, including the Spanish interpreter to the Spanish-speaking client. Phone numbers for other forms of assistance are included. Yet another brochure, published by the Legal Service Commission of New South Wales and the Law Society of New South Wales (1984), titled *Interpreters in the Legal System,* explains why and under what conditions one should request an interpreter. It also lists a number of dos and don'ts to aid lawyers, magistrates, judges, court officials, doctors, police officers, and public servants in the proper utilization of the interpreter, defining the role of the interpreter and distinguishing him or her from other officers of the court. These and other educational materials should be developed and used in the United States to help clients and court personnel understand the role of the interpreter. Brochures for the judiciary and other court personnel could also be developed and distributed. Materials, which are official bilingual documents of the Office of Court Interpreting, should be distributed by the interpreter or by the clerk of court to new users of interpreter services.

Unit 2
Legal Overview

Chapter 8

Overview of the United States Government

1. Introduction

A basic tenet of interpretation and translation is that one cannot translate what one does not understand. Although strong bilingual and interpreting skills are prerequisite to the ability to transfer meaning from one language into another, this alone cannot guarantee that an individual will be able to accomplish the task of court interpretation. By definition, court interpretation is the transference of meaning from one language to another performed in a legal setting. Not unpredictably then, for court interpreters to carry out their task competently they must be aware of how the legal system works. Without the ability to comprehend what is happening in a court of law, or in any legal setting, a court interpreter cannot possibly hope to convey the meaning to the court and all its attaches, or to "make present" the non-English-speaking participants who rely upon the interpreter as their single means of communication (Zahler, 1989a).

The purpose of this unit is to provide the novice interpreter with a general outline of the United States legal system, and the criminal justice system in particular. Within that system, the federal and state structures parallel one another. Because there are fifty individual states and several "territories," all may differ radically on specific points of law, structure, personnel, or systems (Baum, 1986; Furcolo, 1977; Keefe & Ogul, 1981). The interpreter who encounters a system that varies from that presented here should follow the local procedures and laws. An axiom with which attorneys and judges are intimately familiar is that for every rule there is an exception, and for every exception, there is yet another exception; interpreters who have worked in the legal system will also find this to be true. It should be noted that this unit covers material which was in force as of the date of publication of this work.

2. Definition of Law

Law is as old as humanity. Very often, law summarizes a set of rules that may be explicit or implicit. Sometimes the law is written, while in other instances it may be the oral tradition, custom, habit, or tacit agreement among members of a society. Even the smallest society, which is the family, cannot subsist without some rules (Zahler, 1989a). Over time many rules have become systematized and formalized or written. Because laws are an expression of the morals and values of a given society, and because both morals and values change over time, the law itself is constantly changing (Cataldo, Kempin, Stockton, & Weber, 1980; Ehrmann, 1976; Harris,

1984). As has been noted by *Wells v. Kansas City Life Ins. Co.* (1943), "The law is a living thing that must keep [pace] with the people and conditions it regulates" (p. 758).

There are many concepts of what "the law" is. In its broad meaning, law is a body of rules of action or conduct prescribed by a controlling authority and having binding legal force. Law can mean, in a narrow sense, the manifestation of the sovereign power to command, forbid, or permit actions or behaviors as provided in a constitution. These specific "laws" are often called statutes or acts. However, there are many intermediary meanings of law which are the focus of much scholarly debate (Cataldo et al., 1980; Ehrmann, 1976; Harris, 1984; Liebesny, 1981; Zahler, 1989a).

The law serves many purposes in a society (Harris, 1984). Some examples of the functions of law are to settle disputes, maintain order, secure efficient government, and protect citizens from unfair governmental power or regulation. For a more exhaustive treatment of the philosophical and functional divisions of law, see *Law and the Legal System: An Introduction* (Mermin, 1982). Generally, there are five sources of law: constitutions, statutes, administrative rules and regulations, local ordinances, and case law (Cataldo et al., 1980; Ehrmann, 1976; Liebesny, 1981; Mermin, 1982). How the laws of a nation are administered depends upon the structure of the government that has the responsibility to enact and execute them; a brief overview of the United States government is the subject of this chapter.

3. Overview of the United States Government

In the United States power is distributed among a central authority called the federal government, fifty independent states, the District of Columbia, the Commonwealth of Puerto Rico, and the territories of Guam and the Virgin Islands. (Throughout this text we will refer to the federal and state governments but will assume that the reader will include the other legal domains within the discussion.) The distribution and delegation of power among the federal government and the states derive from the United States Constitution and its amendments (Cataldo et al., 1980; Furcolo, 1977; Pritchett, 1977). Therefore, all laws in the United States, regardless of whether they originate from the federal government or the states, ultimately stem from or must be in accordance with the United States Constitution. The authority of the federal government over the states derives from auxiliary powers set forth in the Constitution, including power over treaties, coinage of money, immigration and naturalization, postal services, and others. All powers not delegated to the federal government, and not otherwise prohibited from being delegated, are reserved for the states. These powers include but are not limited to promulgation and enforcement of laws governing record-keeping of births and deaths, and laws relating to marriage and divorce. Some powers are concurrent in the federal government and the states, such as law enforcement and public health and welfare (Zahler, 1989a).

The government is divided into three branches: the executive, legislative, and judicial branches (Cataldo et al., 1980; Hay, 1976). Although these branches are independent, there is much interaction among them. Similar tripartite structures exist in the states, and interaction among the three branches of government applies at that level as well.

The function of the legislative branch of government is the making or enactment of laws. The federal legislature is called the Congress, which is composed of the House of Representatives and the Senate. At the state level the bicameral names are similar; however, sometimes the equivalent of the House of Representatives is called the Assembly or the House of Assembly (Zahler, 1989a).

The executive branch is charged with carrying out or executing the laws. In the federal system the executive branch is composed of the President of the United States and his cabinet. The cabinet is composed of secretaries of specified departments such as Education, State, Defense, Treasury, State and others (Pritchett, 1977). At the State level the functions of the executive branch are carried out by the Governor and his or her secretaries.

The judicial branch interprets and applies the laws. This branch is composed of a hierarchy of courts which have the responsibility of trying cases and/or reviewing the decisions of other courts. In most court systems there are three levels: (1) lower, (2) trial, and (3) appellate courts that include the supreme courts (Baum, 1986; Hay, 1976). Many of the distinctions among different courts come about because of their varying jurisdictional powers (see Jurisdiction, below, in Chapter 9).

The theory and practice of separation of powers between the states and the central authority, or federal government, is called federalism (Hay, 1976). An underlying assumption of the Constitution is that liberty and freedom are dependent upon dividing power into the legislative, executive, and judicial branches so that a checks-and-balances relationship is established. The concepts of separation of powers and checks and balances are specifically defined in the Constitution. Law-making, administrative, and judicial powers are thus shared by the three branches of the federal government (Pritchett, 1977). This means that each branch of government is not necessarily restricted to its own type of power. For example, Congress has some judicial power because it may create federal courts, and by the same token the United States Supreme Court has some legislative power when it declares unconstitutional a statute enacted by the legislative branch. Similarly, the executive branch has some overlap in legislative and judicial powers that it may exercise, such as veto power and the ability to grant amnesty.

No single branch—executive, judicial, or legislative—has any more power than the other. Moreover, each branch has the responsibility and duty to review the actions of the other branches. Since each branch has legislative, executive, and judicial powers, each has the ability to review and complement the other's power. This tripartite operation of government is the United States system of checks and balances.

Before reviewing the United States judicial system, the important concept of federal supremacy (Cataldo et al., 1980; Pritchett, 1977) must be mentioned. Article VI, paragraph 2 of the Constitution states: "This Constitution, and the Laws of the United States which shall be made in Pursuance thereof; and all Treaties made, or which shall be made, under the Authority of the United States, shall be the Supreme Law of the Land." Consequently, if provisions of state constitutions or state laws are inconsistent with the federal constitution, such provisions are voidable and, when challenged, may be declared so by the United States Supreme Court. Our primary interest from the standpoint of court interpretation is to understand the United States justice system (Zahler, 1989a), a description of which follows in Chapter 9.

Chapter 9

Overview of the United States Criminal Justice System

1. Introduction

As mentioned before, the United States justice system, like those of most countries in the world, among other purposes is designed to help resolve disputes. It is important to distinguish between the administration of justice by the courts and proceedings conducted by administrative agencies that are mandated or created by law. According to Schwartz (1984):

> Administrative law itself is that branch of the law that controls the administrative operations of government. It sets forth the powers that may be exercised by administrative agencies, lays down the principles governing the exercise of those powers, and provides legal remedies to those aggrieved by administrative action. (p. 2)

Some examples of administrative agencies are the National Labor Relations Board (NLRB), Immigration and Naturalization Service (INS), Internal Revenue Service (IRS), Social Security (SS), and the Department of Motor Vehicles (DMV). Generally, administrative agencies are delegated power by state or federal legislatures to create rules and regulations that may have the force of law, and in some cases are given the police power to enforce those regulations. These agencies often have both legislative and judicial powers and may also conduct trial-like hearings (Hay, 1976). Although these hearings are not judicial proceedings themselves, the decisions made therein may be subject to judicial review. In spite of the fact that approximately 90 percent of all cases between governmental entities and private citizens are heard and decided by administrative agencies, this text will concern itself primarily with the administration of justice in the field of criminal law, where approximately 70 to 90 percent of all working court interpreters are recognized as judicial personnel or court attaches (Zahler, 1989a).

2. The Constitution and Its Amendments

The Constitution of the United States and its twenty-six amendments specifically provide guarantees to individuals who are criminally prosecuted by a state or federal government. The Constitution is the supreme law of the land, and when the states joined the union each specifically agreed to the supremacy of the federal government and its laws, pursuant to the supremacy clause. Expressly, article VI provides that no state law shall be supreme to federal laws or the Constitution. The Fourteenth Amendment guarantees full constitutional protections to all citizens in the states, including the right to due process of law. The following amendments are the most important to the criminal law system.

The first ten amendments to the Constitution of the United States are known collectively as the Bill of Rights (Pritchett, 1977). Among their provisions is the basis for several freedoms enjoyed by United States citizens: the freedoms of speech, religion, and assembly. In the administration of justice, the Fourth Amendment places restrictions on governmental rights of search and seizure and other rights of persons accused of crimes. The Fourth Amendment, introduced in 1791, reads:

> The right of the people to be secure in their persons, houses, papers, and effects, against unreasonable searches and seizures, shall not be violated, and no Warrants shall issue but upon probable cause, supported by Oath or affirmation, and particularly describing the place to be searched, and the persons or things to be seized.

This amendment and all the rights contained therein are referred to as the Fourth Amendment rights of search and seizure. An attorney will often refer to how a defendant's Fourth Amendment rights have been violated (Furcolo, 1977). Typically this involves a case in which the arrest or search warrant has not been properly obtained. The specialized criminal terminology introduced in this chapter will be discussed more fully in Chapter 10 (see Chapter 10, Criminal Procedure).

The Fifth Amendment, also introduced in 1791, reads:

> No person shall be held to answer for a capital, or otherwise infamous crime, unless on a presentment or indictment of a Grand Jury, except in cases arising in the land or naval forces, or in the Militia, when in actual service in time of War or public danger; nor shall any person be subject for the same offence to be twice put in jeopardy of life or limb; nor shall be compelled in any criminal case to be a witness against himself, nor be deprived of life, liberty or property, without due process of law; nor shall private property be taken for public use, without just compensation of law.

This very important amendment imparts many rights to the criminal defendant, including the right to be publicly charged with a crime in what is called an indictment (see Chapter 10, Criminal Procedure); not to be prosecuted twice for the same offense, popularly referred to as double jeopardy; not to be denied life, liberty, or property without due process under the law, referred to as due process; and to be compensated for private land which has been condemned by the government for its own use, otherwise known as indemnity (Pritchett, 1977). This amendment is especially prominent in the criminal justice process, and is of particular importance as it is one of the legal bases that justify the use of interpreters in the legal setting (Zahler, 1989b). For example, if the state does not use an interpreter when it criminally prosecutes a defendant who is a non-English speaker, that defendant will most probably be denied life, liberty, or property without due process of law (see Unit 1, Chapter 3).

The Sixth Amendment, introduced in 1791, reads:

> In all criminal prosecutions, the accused shall enjoy the right to a speedy and public trial, by an impartial jury of the State and district wherein the crime shall have been committed, which district shall have been previously ascertained by

law, and to be informed of the nature and cause of the accusation; to be confronted with the witnesses against him; to have compulsory process for obtaining witnesses in his favor; and to have the assistance of counsel for his defense.

This amendment guarantees the right to a speedy trial by jury, unless waived by the defendant; to understand the charges brought against him by the government; to confront the witnesses accusing him of a crime; to be able to subpoena witnesses on his own behalf; and to have an attorney assist him in presenting a defense (Cataldo et al., 1980; Pritchett, 1977). The most important clause of this amendment for the non-English-speaking defendant or witness is the right to be informed of and to understand the nature of the charges lodged against him by the government. Without an interpreter, receiving and exercising this minimal constitutional protection would be impossible for a limited- or non-English speaker (Zahler, 1989c).

The Eighth Amendment, introduced in 1791, reads:

Excessive bail shall not be required, nor excessive fines imposed, nor cruel and unusual punishments inflicted.

The right to bail, when the issue may be raised, and how it is dispensed is discussed in Chapter 10. The excessive fines provision is often referred to as the cruel and unusual punishment clause, and has been the cornerstone of the controversial topic of capital punishment. A discussion of this debate is beyond the scope of this text; suffice it to say that interpreters will encounter arguments about excessive punishment during the sentencing phase of the criminal trial and must be able to interpret them to the defendant (Zahler, 1989c).

The Fourteenth Amendment, section 1, introduced in 1868, reads, in part:

All persons born or naturalized in the United States, and subject to the jurisdiction thereof, are citizens of the United States and of the State wherein they reside. No State shall make or enforce any law which shall abridge the privileges or immunities of citizens of the United States; nor shall any State deprive any person of life, liberty, or property, without due process of law; nor deny to any person within each jurisdiction the equal protections of the laws.

At the heart of the Fourteenth Amendment is the idea that all the enumerated constitutional rights are extended to citizens in every state of the union. It reiterates the right to due process and equal protection of the law for all citizens. Historically, due process has come to mean all of the procedural protections typically associated with the Constitution, including the Fourth, Fifth, Sixth, and Eighth Amendments. Another distinction made under the Fourteenth Amendment is that of substantive due process; a discussion of this complex field of law is beyond the scope of this text; however, the interpreter should be aware that this distinction is made. Equal protection refers to the idea that there will be an equal application of United States laws to all persons regardless of their race, color, national origin, gender, or religious beliefs (Pritchett, 1977). Of course, these terms are presented in an attempt to acquaint the interpreter with the relevant terminology and is by no means intended as a full legal discussion of these topics.

3. Criminal Law

Within the administration of justice, there is a major distinction between criminal and civil law. Similarities and differences between these two types of law will be explained in Chapter 11. A **criminal offense** is any act or omission punishable by law. Criminal law declares what conduct falls under the definition of criminal offense and also prescribes the punishment to be imposed for such conduct (Zahler, 1989b). For example, the state may declare that crossing a public street in a place that is neither an intersection nor a demarcated crosswalk is punishable by a fine and may set the amount of that fine. The sources of criminal law are chiefly in the penal code or its equivalent, in health and safety codes, business and professional codes, the vehicle code, welfare and institutions codes, and many other special statutes and ordinances (Hay, 1976). Because of the guarantees provided by the Constitution through its amendments, the United States government has the burden of proving the guilt of the alleged offender; more conventionally, these rights are interpreted as meaning that the defendant is presumed innocent until proven guilty.

4. Burden of Proof

Burden of proof is used to mean either the necessity of establishing a fact, that is, the burden of persuasion, or the necessity of producing or going forward with evidence (burden of production). Almost always, the burden of proof or persuasion in a criminal case is on the prosecution; it has the duty of proving the accusations by presenting enough evidence to establish that the facts they assert are true (Berger, Mitchell, & Clark, 1989; Mauet, 1988; Waltz, 1983). Almost always, the prosecution also has the burden of production—that of producing and presenting the evidence to the **trier of fact** (judge or jury). The only exception is when the defendant claims an affirmative defense which works to shift the burden of going forward with the evidence from the prosecution to the defense. One example is the use of the insanity defense. The defense asserts that the defendant was insane at the time of the crime and, therefore, must produce evidence which would tend to prove this claim.

Two distinctions can be made within the concept of burden of proof: (1) burden of production (going forward with producing evidence) and (2) burden of persuasion (convincing the trier of fact that you have proven the case) (Mauet, 1988). Most commonly, the state is charged with meeting the burden of persuasion. In a criminal prosecution, the state or federal government has the burden of proving guilt beyond a reasonable doubt. However, there exist three standards of proof: (1) preponderance of the evidence, (2) clear and convincing evidence, and (3) evidence beyond a reasonable doubt (Mauet, 1988; Waltz, 1983). **Preponderance of the evidence** is a general standard of proof most often used in civil cases; it is the evidence which is more believable or convincing to the trier of fact than the evidence presented in opposition. It is often said that the weight of the evidence or proof must be only a bit more than 50 percent to meet this standard. The preponderance of the evidence standard sometimes applies in the granting of motions in the criminal procedure area (see Chapter 10, Criminal Procedure). The next higher standard is **clear and convincing evidence.** This standard requires the trier of fact to be persuaded that there is a high probability that the fact in question exists. It applies to some civil cases and in the criminal arena to some lesser crimes (Zahler, 1989e).

Beyond a reasonable doubt is the highest standard of proof and applies to most criminal cases. Beyond a reasonable doubt is a special standard or quantum of proof. It is not a mere possibility of doubt, because everything relating to human affairs and depending on moral evidence is open to some possible or imaginary doubt (Zahler,

1989c). Reasonable doubt is that state of the mind, which after the entire comparison and consideration of all the evidence, leaves the minds of the jurors in such a condition that they cannot say they feel an abiding conviction—to a moral certainty—of the truth of the charges asserted. Another definition often used in federal court is as follows:

> Reasonable doubt does not require that the prosecution prove guilt beyond all possible doubt. The test is one of reasonable doubt. A reasonable doubt is one based on reason and common sense. Proof beyond a reasonable doubt must be of such a convincing character that a reasonable person would not hesitate to act and rely upon it in the most important and vital of his own affairs. (Zahler, 1989c)

5. Punishment

If the prosecution has met its burden of proving the charges against the defendant, the defendant is declared guilty and then punishment is administered (see Chapter 10, Criminal Procedure). In modern criminal law, punishment is justified in order to achieve one or more of the following purposes: incapacitation, deterrence, retribution, or rehabilitation (Carr, 1989; Harris, 1984; Zahler, 1989a).

Incapacitation in general consists of depriving somebody of the normal capacity of knowing, doing, or performing something. Applied to criminal law, this means that the offender's freedom would be limited, making it impossible for more harm to be caused. **Deterrence,** on the other hand, consists in coercing the defendant or others in society from committing unlawful acts; that is, the state through threat of incarceration, fines, or loss of liberty discourages potential criminal offenders through fear, anxiety, or doubt from doing something harmful to others or their property.

Retribution, which means "just punishment," is defined as society's right to administer punishment for a bad act. If a person violates a law and guilt has been established, then imprisonment for a certain time will be the price that the offender must pay society for performing that bad act. Finally, **rehabilitation** seeks to make the offender a useful member of society after incarceration. The rehabilitation of a prisoner may consist of participation in a variety of educational, vocational, psychological, and anti-addiction programs during the time of incarceration. Recently there has appeared a trend toward the retributive and deterrent models of punishment leading the United States away from a rehabilitation model (Zahler, 1989b).

6. The Judicial Setting

From the perspective of the lay person, most of what is thought of as "justice" is administered in a courtroom. Despite this perception, the judicial setting is not necessarily limited to the courtroom; court interpreters must be prepared to work in different environments related to ongoing criminal cases. Whether interpreting interviews, translating documents, or transcribing tapes, the interpreter must be prepared to work in holding tanks or in jails; in attorneys' offices or in courtrooms; in agency offices such as pre-trial services, probation, or the parole board, or in the interpreter's home or in any other location where the interpreter provides services.

The major distinction in the judicial setting is between criminal and civil cases. Civil cases typically involve private interests, a subject that will be discussed in more detail later in this chapter. Court interpreters in the United States work primarily in criminal matters, although there is a growing trend for their use in civil trials and administrative agency hearings (*Gardiana v. Small Claims*, 1976; Groisser, 1981; *Jara v. Municipal Court*, 1978).

The administration of criminal justice in the United States relies heavily upon an intricate, cooperative network of law enforcement agencies. There are myriad agencies which have the responsibility of enforcing the law and are authorized to collect information, perform investigations, report offenses, and to arrest those who violate criminal laws. Cooperating with the courts are the four major groups largely responsible for the primary stages in the administration of justice: law enforcement agencies, prosecuting authorities, defense counsel, and corrections officials. Police and law enforcement agencies principally investigate crimes and apprehend suspected offenders. Prosecutors and defense counsel are attorney adversaries in a process wherein the guilt or innocence of the suspected offender is determined. Corrections officials are charged with carrying out the punishments imposed by the courts. Although these definitions greatly simplify these groups, they are fundamentally accurate (Zahler, 1989b). Each of these actors plays a vital role in a specific part of the criminal justice process. This process can be divided into distinct stages: (1) investigation and arrest; (2) pre-trial processes; (3) the trial; and (4) sentencing and rehabilitation (Hay, 1976). These stages will be elaborated upon in the next chapter.

In the criminal justice system, the courts are unique in that they are involved in all stages of the process. Because the United States is divided into independent states that are members of a federal union, there are two court systems: state and federal (Cataldo et al., 1980; Hay, 1976). The latter are usually called United States courts. Although most courts carry out similar procedures in their hearings and trials, there are several philosophical or functional groups into which most courts can be divided. After the differences between these courts are delineated, a review of the state and federal hierarchies and their judicial officers will follow.

7. Distinctions among Courts

Most courts can be divided into three distinct types: lower or inferior, trial, and appellate courts. This distinction has nothing to do with the legal importance of the courts, but describes their jurisdictional power—the legal right to hear and decide a case (Hay, 1976). Lower courts are typically responsible for the resolution of "petty" matters, for example, cases in which small monetary amounts are in controversy, or a person has violated a law with minor penalties such as traffic fines. In usual practice, no permanent record of lower court proceedings is kept (Zahler, 1989a).

Trial courts handle cases of a more serious nature and also hear appeals from the lower courts. These appeals are usually concerned with questions of law rather than questions of fact. However, because opinions of cases from lower courts are not cited, the appeal may be heard *de novo* and a new trial is conducted where evidence is taken and a record is made. To a limited extent these courts may also exercise appellate jurisdiction, the power of the court to hear and decide a case from another legal or quasi-legal entity. For instance, they may be authorized to review decisions made in administrative hearings at which a transcript is made. The existence of a record eliminates the need for a trial *de novo*. Trial courts are courts of record and general jurisdiction; they can hear every type of matter unless the issues are reserved for other courts, i.e., only the federal district courts may hear issues arising under the federal laws or the United States Constitution (Pritchett, 1977). If it is warranted, the decision of the trial court can be appealed.

First in the hierarchy are the appellate courts which hear appeals from the courts of general jurisdiction. Judgments from courts of general jurisdiction are upheld, reversed, or modified by the appellate courts if the request for an appeal is granted. There may be several appeals to different courts, and when the highest court in the string of appellate courts hears the matter, the decision is final, unless the court remands the matter back to the previous court for further findings. Generally, these distinctions apply to both the federal and state court systems. In a later section those distinctions, of which the interpreter must be aware, will be discussed.

8. Jurisdiction

There are many meanings of the word "jurisdiction" in the law. Commonly, it is an area whose boundary is defined either geographically or by law, in which a specified agency has authority to carry out its primary responsibilities. In connection with courts, jurisdiction is the legal authority by which judicial officers take cognizance of and decide cases (Hay, 1976; Pritchett, 1977). A judge may have jurisdiction or the legal right to exercise his or her authority over the legal outcome of the case; more specifically, this type of jurisdiction refers to the scope of authority or types of matters a court can properly hear—often called subject matter jurisdiction. For instance, a bankruptcy court judge may not properly hear a criminal case because the charges exceed the jurisdictional reach of the court.

Courts may have their jurisdiction legally narrowed or defined. Federal courts have jurisdiction over matters that meet specific constitutional requirements, while state statutes often delineate which state courts may hear traffic matters, homicides, or appeals. Some courts are specialized and hear only one topic, such as admiralty, administrative, or bankruptcy matters. Many state trial courts are general jurisdiction courts, and they may hear a range of matters which are both criminal and civil (Cataldo et al., 1980).

Finally, jurisdiction can also refer to the geographic area in which the case is brought. Most often this final type of jurisdiction is called venue. The venue of a court may be changed if, for example, there is publicity adverse to the defendant and proof is offered which would tend to show that the jury selected in that area would be irreparably biased against the alleged offender.

9. State Courts

Inferior or lower courts in the states are generally called either municipal or justice of the peace courts. Municipal courts usually have criminal jurisdiction over misdemeanors and infractions, corresponding to that of police courts in other countries. In some cases, they also have jurisdiction in civil matters over small monetary concerns. They often also handle the initial stages in felony matters. These courts can be specialized, for example, hearing only small claims or traffic matters. In municipal courts, often known as city courts, the presiding judicial officer is either referred to as a municipal court judge or a magistrate. Justice of the peace courts have similar jurisdiction, either in rural or small urban areas like towns. The presiding officers in these courts are called justices of the peace. The next level of court in the states is the trial courts or courts of general jurisdiction, often called superior courts, county courts, or courts of common pleas. The judicial officers who administer justice in these courts are called judges (Zahler, 1989b).

In most states, the highest appellate court is called the state supreme court, and its members are called justices. In approximately two-thirds of the states, there is only one level of appeal, and that court is known as the state supreme court. In the remainder of the states, however, there are two levels of appellate courts, called state courts of appeals or state appellate divisions. Depending on the state, the judicial officer of the court is referred to either as a justice or judge (Baum, 1986). New York is a major exception to this rule: the trial court is referred to as the supreme court; the appellate court is referred to as the New York Appellate Court with divisions specified; and the highest court of appeals is called the New York Appeals Court (Zahler, 1989b).

10. Federal Courts

Lower or inferior courts in the federal system are usually called magistrate courts. Similar to lower state courts, particularly municipal courts, magistrate courts are authorized to try misdemeanor cases, but only with the consent of the defendant. The judicial officer in charge of the court is called the magistrate.

The next level of courts are the United States district courts, which are basic trial courts of general jurisdiction and can hear any matter not reserved for any other higher or specialized court, such as bankruptcy, customs courts, or the United States Supreme Court among others (Pritchett, 1977). In a few instances, the United States district court will also provide the first level of appellate review for matters initially heard in magistrate's court. The judicial officer in charge of these courts is called a judge.

The highest appellate court in the federal system is the United States Supreme Court, often called the U.S. Supreme Court or the Supreme Court of the United States. The members of this court are referred to as justices. The court is composed of one Chief Justice and eight Associate Justices. The United States Supreme Court may review decisions of the highest state appellate courts and the federal courts of appeals, also called circuit courts of appeals. The Supreme Court of the United States has original but not necessarily exclusive jurisdiction over some matters. Original jurisdiction is the power to consider a cause of action (lawsuit), at its inception, in the Supreme Court; for example, the Court hears matters concerning ambassadors and public ministers, and cases in which states are parties.

The Supreme Court may judicially review cases involving the decision of a lower court, primarily to inspect the record for irregularities, regardless of whether the case is based on a federal or state statute, a federal treaty, or a state constitutional provision that may be in conflict with the United States Constitution. The Court reserves the right to determine which cases it will hear and may accept a case on a writ of *certiorari*. **Certiorari** is a Latin word which means "to be informed of," and the Supreme Court in its discretion may grant "*cert.*," which requires the lower court to send a certified copy of the transcript of the case to be reviewed (*Black's Law,* 1979).

11. Other Agencies and Officials

Because there are parallel systems at the state and federal levels, the courts in the United States can be described as a bifurcated system. There are parallel criminal justice agencies and personnel at both the federal and state levels whose primary responsibility is the enforcement of laws throughout the jurisdiction over which they have authority (Kamisar, LaFave, & Israel, 1986). At the state level there are usually general police agencies such as state police departments or the state highway patrol. Among the local police agencies there is usually at least one at the county level—the sheriff's department, for example—and almost all cities and many townships have their own police departments.

In the federal system, the Federal Bureau of Investigation (FBI) serves as the general police agency. It is responsible for enforcing all federal laws other than those which are within the purview of other specialized police agencies, such as the Drug Enforcement Administration (DEA), Customs, the Alcohol, Tobacco, and Firearms Department (ATF), and the Department of the Treasury.

Each state has prosecutors who are responsible for the prosecution of individuals under its jurisdiction's laws. Within the state system the authority is divided among local prosecutors, each of whom has primary control over prosecutions for offenses committed within the prosecutorial district. They are commonly known as prosecuting attorneys, county prosecutors, or state, district, and city attorneys. Typically, there is one attorney in charge of a political division or unit such as a county or city and that person is referred to as the prosecuting attorney. The head of each prosecutorial office has the ability to appoint assistant or deputy prosecuting attorneys. For example, the district attorney (D.A.) appoints deputy district attorneys and the city attorney appoints assistant city attorneys. However, in courtroom practice, this titular distinction is often not made. Thus, every attorney in the D.A.'s office is called a "D.A." (Kamisar et al., 1986; Zahler, 1989b).

Each state has a chief legal officer called the state attorney general, who represents the state in all legal matters. Often the governor or a state department may request that he or she issue an opinion on a given matter. The primary responsibility for federal prosecution rests with United States attorneys, who are appointed by the President with the consent of the Senate. There is one United States attorney for each judicial district. Each United States attorney hires assistant United States attorneys to aid in carrying out responsibilities of the office, but the number that can be hired is established by the Attorney General of the United States (Kamisar et al., 1986).

The Attorney General is the head of the Department of Justice and is the chief legal officer for the federal government. He or she represents the United States in legal matters generally, and gives advice and opinions to the President and to departments of the federal government when requested. The Attorney General is not to be confused with the Solicitor General of the United States, who is in charge of representing the government before the Supreme Court of the United States. However, the Attorney General is not precluded from appearing in person before the Supreme Court in cases of exceptional gravity or importance. Since most court proceedings are adversarial in nature, there is a parallel system of defense attorneys on the state and federal levels.

Defense attorneys may be retained privately or as public sector attorneys, that is, public defenders or court-appointed attorneys. All defense attorneys who are employed at public expense to represent defendants are called public defenders, but as with prosecuting attorneys, there is a chief public defender of each political unit. If the office is funded by the state, the head public defender is appointed either by the state supreme court or a nonpartisan board appointed by the court. When the office is funded locally, the chief public defender is likely to be selected by the legislative body that funds the agency. Like the chief prosecutor, the chief public defender appoints assistants or deputies, called assistant or deputy public defenders (Zahler, 1989a).

On the federal level, each district has one chief public defender (FPD) who has the authority to hire as many deputies as is legally permissible. These assistants are called deputy federal public defenders (DFPD). It is the responsibility of the FPD to provide defense for all defendants in felony cases who are financially unable to retain counsel, and also in misdemeanor cases if so ordered. The public defender's office cannot represent more than one defendant per case, nor can it represent a defendant if it has previously represented a co-defendant or relative, or has been connected with the same or a similar case related to the defendant.

In this instance, the public defender declares a conflict and a "conflict attorney," usually a court-appointed attorney, is retained by the presiding judicial officer. The name of the attorney appears on a list of attorneys who have offered their services and are retained on the condition of accepting such appointments. In federal court those lists are called Indigent Defendants Panels. In state court the lists may be called the Court Appointed List or Court Rolls.

12. Civil Law

Although the majority of cases heard by courts in the United States justice system are of a criminal nature, the number of civil law cases is also substantial. It is important not to confuse the distinction between civil law and criminal law, on the one hand, and the differences between the civil law system and the common law system on the other hand. Similarities and differences between common law systems and civil law systems will be explained in Chapter 11.

In contrast to criminal law, which defends society against an individual's unacceptable and punishable conduct, civil law deals with controversies between two private parties, or between a private party and a government agency (Cataldo et al., 1980; Harris, 1984; Hay, 1976). For example, if Party A contracts with Party B to sell a specific car and then does not do so, Party B has the right to sue Party A for specific performance (to fulfill the contract as written). This typifies the private nature of the interests in a civil law suit.

The party who sues, the **plaintiff**, most commonly seeks legal remedies such as (a) monetary compensation or damages; (b) injunction(s)—petitions to permit or forbid a particular action, such as ordering Party A to sell the car to Party B, as in the above example; (c) declaration of the party's rights alleged in a formal written statement of the illegal actions or complaint, such as the right of Party B in the example above to buy the car specified in the contract; or (d) all of the above (Cataldo et al., 1980; Hay, 1976).

Parties to a civil suit allege civil wrongs, not criminal acts. That is why the result of the civil case will not be criminal punishment, but will be the redress of a wrong, a payment of damages, the acknowledgment of one or more rights, or other similar consequences. In general, courts place the parties in the same or similar position as before they were wronged, i.e., before they were injured or financially harmed. In civil actions, the party that is being sued is called the **defendant**. In some actions, however, the party who brings the action is called the **petitioner** and the party against whom the action is brought is called the **respondent**; these referents are used most often in administrative law hearings, marriage dissolutions (no-fault divorces), and in non-controversial estate matters (Zahler, 1989e).

Civil matters may be heard and settled in both state courts and federal courts; but federal civil matters can only be heard and settled in federal courts (Pritchett, 1977). Some examples of federal matters are violations of titles of the Civil Rights Act or the Fair Labor Standards Act; contracts relating to insurance, maritime, financial, or other matters which meet the diversity of citizenship requirements; interstate or international transportation clauses; and/or other legal claims established by Congress such as patent and copyright matters and torts (French for "harms" such as personal injury or defamation) that are interstate and/or international in nature.

Because of the great variety of civil matters, it is important for an interpreter to prepare as much as possible before interpreting in a civil case. The cases may often be very technical in nature and involve complex concepts such as the engineering integrity of a mechanical device or structure, international monetary issues, or complex medical problems, among others. Interpreters prepare by familiarizing themselves with the nature of the matter and by requesting a copy of the formal complaint, the answer (formal written document which disputes the allegations), and any other relevant documents from the party hiring the interpreter (Zahler, 1989e). He or she may also request an interview with the attorney handling the case in order to receive a general outline of the case and any specialized or technical vocabulary that might be needed. The interpreter would do well to read and understand specialized terminology of experts who will testify in the case and to study the basic subject matter. Just as is true in a criminal matter, it is important to interview witnesses or parties prior to the beginning of civil proceedings.

The government in a civil law action has the same rights, duties, and responsibilities as a private individual. For example, if a government-owned car collides with a private citizen's property and causes damage to it, the private citizen may sue the government for recovery of the value of the damaged property. A corporation is also considered a private individual for purposes of lodging a civil suit (Merman, 1982).

Public Law 95-539, the Court Interpreters Act, enacted in October, 1978 at the federal level, guarantees interpreter services in civil matters when the government initiates an action against an individual in a United States district court, including writs of habeas corpus. **Habeas corpus** (literally, "you have the body") is a civil petition that is typically begun by prisoners who believe they are being wrongfully imprisoned. In a civil matter, Federal Rules of Civil Procedure (*Federal Civil Judicial,*

1989), Rule 604 designates the interpreter as an expert witness, and the interpreter has all the rights, duties, and responsibilities of this class of witness. The provision of interpreters for civil cases varies from state to state and is typically a private procurement by privately retained counsel. However, the cost of interpreting services is often recoverable as a court cost that is charged against the losing party as part of a damage award. A majority of the states have adopted the *Federal Civil Judicial Procedure and Rules* (1989); see also Landers, Martin, & Yeazell (1988); for specific details, each state's rules of civil procedure should be consulted.

13. The Adversarial System

The process of conducting trials and presenting evidence in United States courts is often characterized as being adversarial, as opposed to inquisitorial (Auerbach, Hurst, Garrison, & Mermin, 1985). In an adversarial system, two sides—the prosecution and the defense—present their version of the events at issue after which the judge or jury must choose what seems to them to be the most plausible version, weighing the competing evidence and attributing one side with more credibility than the other. Unlike the adversarial system, in which the lawyers do the bulk of the questioning, in an inquisitorial process lay and professional judges question and listen to accounts of an alleged criminal event from witnesses.

Judges in the adversarial system only occasionally ask questions and, in most jurisdictions in the United States (Glendon, Gordon, & Osakwe, 1982), the jury is virtually precluded from asking questions. Although these fact finders must determine which side is more truthful, they have little or no control over what facts they learn. Hence, in at least one aspect, lawyers have more control over witnesses and the flow of information than do judges (Zahler, 1989f).

Chapter 10

Criminal Procedure

This chapter generally delineates the criminal justice process in the United States, using state criminal procedure as the basis of the discussion. Where applicable, comparisons will be drawn with the federal system. Because there is some overlap in the stages (e.g., the concept of bail appears from arrest through trial), certain concepts will be treated in separate sections.

Criminal procedure is the combination of laws and rules which govern the different stages in the administration of the criminal justice system: investigation, arrest, arraignment, trial, sentencing, and imposition of penalties (Kamisar, LaFave, & Israel, 1986). This chapter will progress in a chronological manner, beginning with the pre- and post-arrest investigation phase.

1. Pre- and Post-Arrest Investigations

Once law enforcement agencies, most often the police, become aware of the commission of a crime, they must determine whether the alleged crime actually was committed. If it was, they must also determine whether there is sufficient information that points to the guilt of a particular person prior to arresting and charging that person with the violation. In order to answer these questions the law enforcement agency must collect evidence that may justify the arrest of a particular person or be helpful in establishing the alleged offender's guilt at trial (Kamisar et al., 1986).

The scope of the pre-arrest investigation will vary considerably with the nature of the crime. For example, in a case involving money laundering to support illicit drug activities, the pre-arrest investigation may last for several years. The prosecutor also may conduct investigations of offenses with the aid of a grand jury. Most commonly, investigation of the facts surrounding the commission of a crime will be conducted in a post-arrest investigation (Carr, 1989; Hay, 1976).

2. Arrest

Once a law enforcement agency has gathered enough information, it can make an arrest. The definition of an **arrest** is taking a person into custody for the purpose of charging him with the commission of a criminal offense. **Custody** may mean the physical detention of a person; in its broadest sense it is the restraint of liberty. However, depending on the situation, there may be many different elements which define custody. For example, whether the person believes he or she is free to go, whether handcuffs are used, whether the person is allowed to physically leave a police station, and so on, compose the elements of custody. In state matters, depending on

111

the nature of the charged offense, a **citation** may be issued instead of arresting the suspected offender. In federal matters the equivalent document is called a **summons** (Zahler, 1989b).

An arrest may be made with or without a warrant. The word "warrant" also has many meanings, but for the purpose of this overview we shall refer only to arrest and search warrants. The **arrest warrant** is a court order made on behalf of a state or federal government that commands a law enforcement officer to arrest a person and bring him or her before a magistrate. Often issued at the same time is a **search warrant**, which commands the arresting officer to examine a person, place, or thing for any evidence of participation in a criminal offense (Carr, 1989; Kamisar et al., 1986).

Traditionally, criminal offenses are divided into infractions, misdemeanors, and felonies. The different categories of criminal offense are determined by the kind and gravity of the punishment: fine, fine and imprisonment, short or long imprisonment, and life sentence or death (Zahler, 1989b). **Infractions** are minor offenses consisting of a violation of a statute or ordinance only punishable with a fine and expressly designated within the law in question as an infraction. This distinction is not found in all state penal codes; however, at the federal level such distinctions are made. In some penal codes the infraction has been subsumed as a "class C misdemeanor," and although it is not called an infraction, for all intents and purposes it is equivalent. An arrest is rarely made if the violation is simply an infraction (Criminal Code, 1988).

Misdemeanors are offenses punishable by fine and/or imprisonment for up to but not exceeding one year. **Felonies** are more serious offenses which are punishable, in most states and the federal system, by fines and/or imprisonment for more than one year, life imprisonment, or death (Criminal Code, 1988). A law enforcement officer may make an arrest without a warrant, also called a **warrantless arrest,** if he or she has probable cause to believe that the person arrested has committed a felony, or, if the person has committed a misdemeanor in the officer's presence—*in flagrante delicto,* or in the criminal act (Zahler, 1989d).

At the time of arrest, the arresting officer will usually make a cursory search, or **frisk** of the arrestee's person, and will remove any contraband, weapons, or evidence relating to a crime (Kamisar et al., 1986). Then the officer will transport the arrestee to the police station, a detention center, or some similar **holding facility**. At the holding facility the suspect is booked.

Booking is a clerical process consisting of the registration of the name, address, crime for which a person is arrested, and description—height, weight, eye color, and any other characteristics useful in identifying the arrestee. In many states and federal districts the arrestee is also fingerprinted and photographed. The suspect will also be informed of the charge or charges on which he or she has been booked and will be allowed to make at least one phone call. Usually before, and sometimes after the booking, but always before any custodial interrogation, the arrestee is advised of his or her Miranda rights. Typically, the Miranda warnings are given in a form similar to the following:

- You have the right to remain silent. Anything you say can and will be used against you in a court of law.

- You have the right to consult an attorney and to have the attorney present during interrogation. If you cannot afford an attorney, one will be provided for you free of charge.
- Do you understand each of the rights I have explained to you?
- Do you wish to waive your right to remain silent and your right to have an attorney present and do you wish to answer my questions now?

The arresting officer usually is the same person who fills out the booking information and a police or arrest report on the incident (Kamisar et al., 1986). If the arrestee was booked on a minor offense, he or she may be able to obtain his or her release on payment of cash bail, promising to appear before a magistrate at a specified date and time. In some jurisdictions, if the arrestee is unable to post such bail, the officer in charge may release him or her upon issuance of a citation (Zahler, 1989b). The topic of bail will be discussed further later in this chapter.

Persons arrested for serious offenses, and those who are arrested on minor offenses but are unable to obtain their release, will be held until they can be brought before a magistrate. Before entering the detention center they will be subjected to a second search, more thorough than the first one. This search is designed primarily to inventory the arrestee's personal belongings and to prevent the introduction of weapons or contraband into the detention center (Kamisar et al., 1986).

After the arrest and booking is completed, the police report is reviewed by a higher-ranking police officer who has the power to determine whether a person should be charged with the crime for which he or she has been arrested, or with a lower charge if appropriate. If there is a decision not to prosecute, the arrestee may be released from the police station or other detention center at the discretion of the higher ranking police officer. In some departments if the person was arrested for a felony, it is generally accepted that approval to dismiss the charge may only be obtained from the prosecuting agency (Zahler, 1989a).

The second step in determining whether to press charges is usually the review of the case by an assistant prosecutor. In some jurisdictions, this screening occurs some time after charges have been brought, while in others prosecutors review all felony and misdemeanor cases before filing charges. In still other jurisdictions, prosecutors prefer screening felony cases only. Among the many factors that prosecutors will consider, the most important are the strength of the evidence, the arrestee's criminal record, and the gravity of the charge. If the prosecution decides to press charges, the next step in the criminal justice process is filing a complaint with the magistrate court (Zahler, 1989b).

A **complaint** is a formal written statement of the charge(s) presented before a magistrate having jurisdiction. It indicates that a specified (or unknown) person has committed a particular offense, and makes an offer to prove the facts underlying the charge for the purpose of initiating a prosecution. The complaint ordinarily includes a brief description of the offense and is sworn to by a complainant, typically a law enforcement official. In some instances, especially in traffic matters, the police report may serve as the complaint. In misdemeanor cases, the complaint will serve as the charging instrument throughout the proceedings. In felony cases, on the other hand, the complaint serves to put forth the charges only before the magistrate court: an **information** or **indictment** will replace the complaint as the charging instrument when the case reaches the trial court (Zahler, 1989b).

There may be one or more **superseding informations** or **indictments.** A superseding information or indictment is filed when further investigations have revealed either that more defendants than were originally charged committed the criminal offense, or that more offenses have been committed; in other words, the superseding indictment may increase the number of defendants or the number of criminal charges contained in the original complaint. The previous or original information or indictment is called the **underlying indictment** or **information,** and may be replaced either in whole or in part by the superseding indictment or information.

3. First Appearance

Once the complaint has been filed and reviewed, the arrestee, who is now formally a **defendant,** is presented before the magistrate (Kamisar et al., 1986). In state matters, this step in the proceedings is usually called the **arraignment** or **arraignment on the complaint.** The arraignment typically takes place in the municipal, justice, or magistrate court. In federal court, this step is referred to as the **initial appearance** or **arraignment on the complaint**; it takes place before a United States magistrate. According to Zahler (1989b) arraignment is difficult to define and interpret because it has many meanings; a better approach is to indicate its purposes:

(1) to identify the defendant and verify his or her true name.

(2) to inform the defendant of his or her constitutional rights. These rights typically include:

- The right to an attorney of the defendant's own choosing at all stages of the proceedings. If the defendant cannot afford an attorney, the court will appoint an attorney to represent him or her, at no initial cost to the defendant, but with the possibility of total or partial reimbursement at the end of the proceedings.

- The right to be released on reasonable bail pending trial.

- The right to a speedy and public trial, by jury or judge.

- The right against self-incrimination, or not to have to testify against himself or herself.

- The right to confront and cross-examine witnesses who are testifying against him or her.

- The right to subpoena witnesses on the defendant's own behalf.

(3) to inform the defendant of the charges against him or her and ask him or her to plead either guilty, not guilty, or in some states **nolo contendere** or no contest. In certain instances a defendant in criminal court may wish to resolve proceedings against him or her by accepting responsibility for having violated a law, while not wanting this plea in criminal court to be used against him or her in a subsequent civil action arising from the facts in the instant case. A *nolo contendere* plea is equivalent to a no contest plea in the criminal action and cannot be used as evidence against the defendant in a subsequent civil suit. A plea of guilty would offer no such protection. In federal court, the defendant is also informed of the charges against him or her at this point, but he or she is not required to plead.

(4) to set bail; to reduce the bail upon which the bailee has been released; to increase bail; or to release on own recognizance (O.R., promise to appear). In federal court, a bail hearing may be held. If bail is granted, its amount and conditions are set at the same time. On the federal level, the Comprehensive Crime Control Act of 1984 has introduced the concept of detention and provides rules that govern the defendant's detention pending trial. A detention hearing may be held at the initial appearance upon the request of the prosecution. Amendments to the Comprehensive Crime Control Act of 1984 provide for the imposition of additional types of release conditions not found in the previous legislation.

(5) To set a date for trial if the outcome of the proceeding makes it necessary (in state as well as in federal court). If a defendant pleads not guilty to a misdemeanor, the next stage will be the trial. If the defendant consents, he or she may be tried by a municipal court judge or a magistrate, but he or she has a right to be tried by a superior court judge if the case is in state court, or by a United States district judge if it is a federal matter. If the defendant pleads not guilty to a felony, the magistrate will advise him or her that the next step in the procedure is the preliminary hearing, and a date is set for that hearing unless the defendant chooses to waive that right. (Zahler, 1989b)

4. Preliminary Hearing or Grand Jury Proceedings

The **preliminary hearing**, also called **preliminary examination**, is a court proceeding with the purpose of

(1) determining if a crime has been committed, and

(2) determining if there are reasonable grounds to believe that the defendant has committed that crime; in other words, if there are reasonable grounds to prosecute.

Defendants appear in court with counsel, unless acting as their own attorneys (**in propria persona**), and are confronted with evidence the prosecuting attorney deems sufficient in order to prove there are reasonable grounds to prosecute. The prosecution need not meet the beyond a reasonable doubt standard of proof, for at this stage a lesser standard is sufficient.

The preliminary hearing is an adversary proceeding where the defendant may challenge the prosecution's evidence and present contradictory evidence (Carr, 1989; Mauet, 1988). However, since a defendant is presumed innocent until proven guilty, the defense usually presents contradictory evidence during the preliminary hearing. Typically, the government will present its case through witness testimony. The defense will limit itself to cross-examining the prosecution's witnesses in order to discover as much of the government's case (theories and evidence) as is possible. In turn, this information will be used in preparing the client's case (defense).

At the end of the hearing the magistrate may:

(1) dismiss the case and release the defendant if the magistrate finds that:
- the prosecution's evidence was insufficient; or
- there are other legal grounds for release, including a lack of **probable cause** for search and/or seizure and/or arrest. Probable cause or reasonable grounds means that the prosecution has succeeded in presenting sufficient evidence to prove the existence of the facts warranting the proceedings against the defendant. The legal test to prove the reasonableness of such charges is that the evidence must be such that it would induce a reasonable, intelligent and prudent man to believe that the accused person committed the crime charged. (Zahler, 1989b)

(2) hold the defendant to answer to the charges if he believes that the evidence produced was sufficient. In this case, the judge will **bind over** the case and order the defendant to be arraigned in superior court or in the United States district court and to be tried there at a later date.

If the magistrate finds that the prosecution's evidence only supports a misdemeanor charge, the magistrate will reject the felony charge and allow the prosecutor to substitute the lesser one. The lesser charge will then be set for trial in the magistrate court. In federal cases, however, the preliminary hearing will only take place if there is no indictment (information) before the date set for the preliminary hearing (Zahler, 1989b).

In some states and in the federal system, felony prosecutions must be based on a grand jury's indictment, unless there is a waiver by the defense. The **grand jury** or **charging grand jury** is composed of a body of citizens who are selected from the community to investigate crimes and determine whether there is enough evidence to bring a person to trial for the violation of a law. Some prosecutors ordinarily bring cases directly before the grand jury, while others present their cases only after holding a preliminary hearing. If there has been a preliminary hearing, the decision on that hearing is not binding on the grand jury. There are some jurisdictions where it is permissible to have only a preliminary hearing, others require grand jury indictments or accusations, and others permit both. If the charging jury determines there is probable cause to prosecute, it returns an indictment known as a **true bill**.

There are also **special** or **investigating grand juries** that are used in almost all jurisdictions. Such juries investigate, often of their own accord, criminal activity in the particular jurisdiction and can initiate criminal cases by bringing indictments. A third type of jury is the **petty** or **trial jury**. This jury is a group of citizens from the local community who are selected at random and sworn in by a court of general jurisdiction (Zahler, 1989b). They determine any question or issue of fact in a civil or criminal action in accordance with the controlling law in the case and the evidence introduced at the trial.

5. Arraignments in Courts of General Jurisdiction

The next step in criminal procedure is the **arraignment** of the defendant before the court of general jurisdiction (trial court), also called **arraignment on the infor-**

mation or **indictment** (Berger, Mitchell, & Clark, 1989). In state courts, the defendant is brought before the trial court, informed of the final charges, and asked to enter a plea of either guilty, not guilty, or *nolo contendere* (if permitted). Actually there are more pleas available to the defendant, but they are seldom used at this stage of the case; the most important is double jeopardy. Under the Fifth Amendment, a person may not be tried twice for the same offense, and as a result, this defense may be invoked at the arraignment. In state court, a date is set for pre-trial conferences, for motions if necessary, and sometimes also for the trial itself.

In federal court, this kind of arraignment is called a **post-indictment arraignment**. This proceeding, defined in the local rules of each district, is not conducted in the same manner in all district courts. In some federal districts the magistrate advises the defendant of his or her constitutional rights (see First Appearance, above) and informs the defendant of the charges lodged after the indictment is read; the defendant is requested to plead either guilty, not guilty, or *nolo contendere*. The judge who is to preside at the trial is then drawn by lot, a date is scheduled for the trial, and deadlines are set for the filing of pre-trial motions. The judge who is assigned to the case is responsible for it until proceedings terminate.

In other districts, the entire indictment arraignment is conducted by a United States district judge rather than a magistrate. In still other districts, this proceeding is divided between a magistrate and a judge. For example, in the Central District of California, a United States magistrate advises defendents of their constitutional rights, informs them of the charges brought and orders them to plead before a United States district judge, usually on the same day. In such courts the first part of the proceedings before the magistrate is referred to as the **post-indictment arraignment** and the second phase before the judge is called **plea and trial setting** (P&T), where a date is scheduled for the trial and deadlines are announced for the filing of pre-trial motions (Zahler, 1989b).

6. Pre-Trial Procedures

All proceedings before trial, in misdemeanor as well as felony cases, are pre-trial procedures. Starting from the day of the first appearance, either for arraignment on the complaint or initial appearance, many different kinds of motions may be made by both the prosecution and the defense. There are conferences also, called status, pre-trial, or omnibus conferences or hearings, at which the parties attempt to dispose of a case without a trial, or to stipulate or agree to the evidence to be introduced, the amount of bail to be set, and other similar matters.

6.1. Pre-Trial Motions

In state and federal proceedings, many motions are likely to be filed before trial commences by parties seeking various actions or rulings by the court. The most common types of motions include: discovery and inspection of evidence, dismissal of the case, suppression of evidence, severance of parties and charges, consolidation of parties and charges, change of venue, appointment of experts, bill of particulars (in federal court), requests for continuances, and bail and/or modifications of conditions of release. Motions are applications to the court requesting an order or a ruling in favor of the applicant; generally, they are filed in a pending action and they may be made, either orally or formally, in writing (Berger et al., 1989).

Discovery motions or motions for discovery and inspection are, as indicated by their names, requests to produce certain types of information that a party may want to use at trial. Either side has the right to file this type of motion; however, the defense utilizes the discovery motion more often than the prosecution. The most commonly discoverable items are:

(1) the names, addresses, and relevant written or recorded statements of all intended prosecution witnesses;

(2) the defendant's and defense witnesses' prior felony convictions that the prosecution intends to use at trial;

(3) the arrest record of the victim or complaining witness in violent crimes (**rap sheet**) where self-defense is an issue;

(4) the identity and information as to the whereabouts of any **informants** (persons who give accusatory information to the police) if their testimony would bear upon the issue of guilt, and probable cause;

(5) the names, addresses, and all written reports and statements made by expert witnesses in connection with the case, and the results of any mental or physical examinations, or scientific tests or comparisons;

(6) a list of all papers, documents, photographs, or tangible objects intended to be used at trial or which were obtained from and supposedly belong to the defendant;

(7) a list of all prior acts of the defendant which the prosecution intends to use in order to prove motive, intent, knowledge, or other similar states of mind;

(8) all material or information which tends to mitigate, lessen, or negate a defendant's guilt, or which would help to reduce the defendant's sentence.

A **motion for discovery** must be made in writing prior to the hearing. Time periods allowed for the discovery of items vary from state to state, but are typically about ten days. The motion must state the items sought to be discovered and the purposes for which they are needed, and must claim that the information is not readily available without discovery (Berger et al., 1989; Mauet, 1988).

A **bill of particulars** is a request for more specific details of offenses charged in the complaint, indictment, or information, and is designed to advise the court, and more particularly the defendant, of what evidence will be presented. The motion for a bill of particulars is usually initiated by the defense and is used most often in federal courts (Zahler, 1989b).

Often two or more charges, called **counts**, are ordered together in the same indictment or information if they are of the same or similar character, based on the same behavior, connected together in their commission, or are alleged to have been part of a common scheme or plan. Similarly, two or more defendants may be charged together in the same indictment if each defendant is accused of the same offense, the several offenses are a part of a common conspiracy, plan, or scheme, or the offenses are so closely intertwined that it would be difficult to separate proof of one from proof of the other. The trial court has discretionary authority, upon motion by the parties or the court, to **sever defendants, offenses**, or both. For the same reasons, if it is more convenient for either party to have alleged offenders and charges tried together, a motion to **consolidate** may be filed.

The motion for **change of venue** is a request for the court to have a trial moved to another county or district, thereby changing the court or place of trial. If the moving party establishes that a fair and impartial trial cannot be obtained in the jurisdiction in which trial would otherwise be held, a change of venue is requested. One of the most common grounds for a change of venue is if the crime is particularly heinous and the local community is inflamed and an impartial jury cannot be found in the city, county, or state where the offense allegedly occurred (Mermin, 1982).

Motions for the **appointment of experts** can be filed at any time of the proceedings (see Testimonial Evidence, 7.3.1.2 Expert Witnesses below). Experts testify about a specialized field of knowledge which is beyond the experience of the lay person. This testimony helps the trier of fact (judge or jury) to understand a particular fact or facts of the case (Mauet, 1988).

Probably the most frequently used motion is a **continuance**. This motion can be made either orally or in writing to postpone a hearing for which a party is not prepared. An extension of time is often granted when there is a conflict in the counsel's or court's calendar, when a key witness is not available on the date set for the proceeding, or when the judge grants more time for the preparation of the proceedings.

A **motion to suppress** is used to eliminate from a criminal trial any evidence that has been illegally seized in violation of the Fourth Amendment search and seizure provisions, the Fifth Amendment privilege against self-incrimination, or the Sixth Amendment right to counsel (see Unit 2, Chapter 8). The bases for granting a motion to suppress evidence include: (a) insufficiency of the warrant as written and presented; (b) failure to describe the property to be seized in the warrant; (c) lack of probable cause for the issuance of the warrant; and (d) violation of constitutional standards by law enforcement officials (Kamisar et al., 1986).

Several motions may be made before or after the beginning of a jury trial (see Jury Trial, below). One of the most important is the **motion *in limine***, which is a written motion asking the court not to permit presentation at trial of matters that are irrelevant, inadmissible, or whose probative value is less than the damage they may cause to the defendant in the minds of the jurors. In other words, it is a motion for a protective order against prejudicial questions and statements made or to be made in court where those statements would not help the trier of fact determine the issue. For example, a photograph of the mangled body of a victim may be more inflammatory to the jury than helpful in proving the victim was murdered; therefore, there would be a motion *in limine* to prohibit the prosecution from presenting it in court. When the motion refers to statements made by the defendant, it is sometimes called a **Beagle motion** (Zahler, 1989b). The prosecution must prove by the preponderance of the evidence that all the evidence which it seeks to use at trial, and which has been challenged by the defendant, has been acquired legally. If evidence is suppressed by granting the motion, it is possible that the prosecution might ask to dismiss the case if it has no additional evidence to convict. If there is other evidence, the case may still proceed to trial. The **motion to suppress** is the one most likely to culminate in the dismissal of a case.

A **motion to dismiss** is not as common as a pre-trial motion, but can be filed on the grounds of failure to provide due process or a speedy trial (Sixth Amendment), or insufficiency of the evidence, or any other legal reason that would justify dismissal. Usually, the defense attorney will introduce the motion to dismiss. Once the motion is granted, the defendant is released and bail, if any, is exonerated. This motion is used more commonly in the trial itself where the defense believes the prosecution has not proven all the elements of a charge and asks the court to dismiss the case because of insufficient evidence.

The use of pre-trial motions varies with the nature of the case. Motions may be hearings of short duration or very long proceedings, and frequently may involve the testimony of eyewitnesses and expert witnesses. The standard of proof in motion hearings is always lower than beyond a reasonable doubt and can be met by a preponderance of the evidence.

6.2. Disposition of Cases Other Than by Trial

A criminal case may be disposed of at almost any stage of the process in a variety of ways other than by trial. The most common is by change of plea wherein the defendant agrees to enter a plea of guilty. This decision may come as a result of a plea bargain; there is also the possibility of dismissal, diversion, or compromise.

6.2.1. Plea Bargains

A **plea bargain** is the disposition of criminal charges by agreement between the accused and the prosecutor. Plea bargains were not traditionally a legal part of the criminal justice system; recently, there has been some formal incorporation of this process into court rules at the state level (Arizona Rules of Court, 1988).

Negotiations for a plea bargain begin with the prosecutor and the defense attorney. A plea bargain usually consists of allowing the defendant to plead guilty, or in some instances *nolo contendere,* to only one or some of several counts in a multi-count complaint, information, or indictment. It may also involve a guilty plea or *nolo contendere* to a lesser offense; in exchange, at the time of sentencing, the prosecution may agree to dismiss the remaining charges, if any, and may even enter into a stipulation as to the type and length of the sentence or probation to be imposed. The defense attorney then explains to the defendant the bargain or agreement. The court is never a party to the negotiations (Zahler, 1989b).

One alternative to the plea bargain is the **Alford plea,** which originated in *North Carolina v. Alford* (1970). This plea permits a defendant to change the plea from not guilty to guilty without a concurring confession of guilt to the crime because personal circumstances would make engaging in a trial a hardship. Work, health, or family emergencies may qualify a defendant for this particular type of plea bargain.

After the parties have entered into a plea agreement, the following procedure may take place, with some local variations: some states require the submission of a written plea agreement which contains the terms of the bargain and is signed by the defendant, the counsel (if any), and the prosecutor. This negotiated agreement may be revoked by any party prior to its acceptance by the court. In other states, the agreement is not reduced to writing by the parties but is put on the record at the corresponding hearing.

The hearing may be a statute conference, a pre-trial status conference, or an omnibus hearing, or it may be specifically convened for the purpose of allowing the defendant to change the former plea of not guilty or *nolo contendere* pursuant to the agreement. Many states now require that all plea bargains be placed on the record at the time the guilty plea is entered. Usually, the prosecutor states the terms of the written or oral agreement reached between the prosecution and the defense. The judge asks the defense attorney if he or she agrees to the terms as announced by the prosecutor. The court thereafter will ascertain whether the defendant is aware of the minimum and maximum sentences possible, and the effect on immigration status if the defendant is not a United States citizen. The court will then certify that the plea is intelligently and voluntarily made.

The court takes the defendant's waiver of the following rights:

- the right to a jury trial or court trial;
- the right to confront and cross-examine witnesses;
- the right to put on a defense—for instance, to subpoena witnesses through the power of the court at no cost; and
- the right against self-incrimination.

If the defendant knowingly, understandingly, and voluntarily gives up the rights explained, and is not pleading guilty because of duress or promises except those contained in the plea bargain, and if there is a factual basis for the plea, the court will proceed to accept or reject the proposed negotiated plea (Zahler, 1989b).

Even after the court has accepted the plea agreement, and if the pre-sentence report does not justify the plea and sentencing agreement, the court is not bound by any provision in it. However, in such a situation the defendant is usually given the opportunity to withdraw the plea of guilty or *nolo contendere* and the case then reverts to the pre-trial stage. The plea bargain and the record regarding the change of plea may not be used against the defendant as proof of guilt at trial (Zahler, 1989b).

In federal court the change of plea procedure is similar to that used in state courts, but the agreement does not contain any reference as to terms or conditions of sentencing and/or probation. The judge explains to the defendant that sentencing is entirely within the judge's discretion. However, since September 1, 1987, federal judges must follow the Sentencing Guidelines and Policy Statements established by the United States Sentencing Commission (1987), pursuant to Chapter 2 of the Comprehensive Crime Control Act of 1984. This chapter is also known as the Sentencing Reform Act of 1984. The judge may depart from the guidelines only under exceptional circumstances (see Sentencing, below).

6.2.2. Pre-Trial Diversion

Pre-trial diversion is a recent system where certain defendants in criminal cases are referred to community agencies while their complaints or indictments are held in abeyance. The case is diverted from the criminal justice process if certain conditions are met. For example, the defendant may enter a work, educational, or counseling program under the supervision of the probation department. The period of diversion is usually no less than six months and no longer than two years. Upon completion of all the conditions of the program(s), if the defendant is not involved in the commission of other criminal violations, the defendant is entitled to have the case dismissed. Diversion programs are not available for all offenses (Zahler, 1989b).

6.2.3. Compromise

Compromise, also called **civil compromise**, usually involves some mutual concessions between the victim and the defendant. Compromise is only available in misdemeanor cases, and the offense must be of a type that gives the victim a civil remedy. Prior to trial the victim must appear before the court and acknowledge that he or she has received full satisfaction for the damages or injuries. The court may then exercise its discretion to either dismiss the case or assess costs or both. The parties involved distinguish a compromise from a plea bargain: a plea bargain involves the prosecution and the defendant, whereas in a compromise the victim and the defendant bargain.

6.3. Pre-Trial or Status Conferences

Pre-trial or **status conferences** and **omnibus hearings** are procedural devices used before trial to consider all matters that will promote an expeditious and fair trial (Zahler, 1989b). At the conclusion of the pre-trial conference the court prepares and files a memorandum of the matters agreed upon. No admissions made by the attorney or the defendant may be used against the defendant unless the admissions are reduced to writing and the defendant and attorney sign them at the conclusion of such conferences or hearings.

Very often changes in plea will take place in such conferences. In both state and federal proceedings, these conferences are usually the last steps of the pre-trial procedure. The term pre-trial conference has typically been used at the state level, whereas status conference has historically been used at the federal level. However, these terminological distinctions are now blurring; both terms may be used interchangeably. An omnibus hearing is a new term appearing at the state level, and although there may be some variations in what takes place in omnibus hearings, they are more or less procedurally equivalent to pre-trial conferences.

A **stipulation** is a voluntary agreement made between opposing counsel regarding the disposition of some obvious point, obviating the need for further proof or narrowing the issues to be litigated. It can also be an agreement, admission, or confession made in a judicial proceeding by the parties thereto or their attorneys. For example, the continuance of a hearing or of the trial itself can be made by stipulation during any hearing, and it is not uncommon for it to be made in the status conference. Trial date continuances must be within the deadlines provided for within state statutes or, in federal matters, by the Speedy Trial Act of 1974.

6.4. Bail

In general, **bail** is the means of procuring the release from custody of persons charged with a criminal offense by pledging money or property to guarantee their future appearance in court and compel them to remain within the jurisdiction. The issue of bail may arise at any time during the criminal justice process, from arrest until the moment of sentencing, and perhaps even after sentencing pending an appeal. The object of bail is to relieve the accused of imprisonment and the state or federal government of the expense of maintenance pending trial or hearing, and at the same time to secure the defendant's appearance at all stages of the proceedings. In some circumstances the defendant may also be released on a promise to appear, or "**on the individual's own recognizance**" or "**personal recognizance**," popularly referred to as O.R or R.O.R. (Zahler, 1984).

In the United States the right of the defendant to be granted bail derives from the Eighth Amendment to the United States Constitution, which in part reads: "Excessive bail shall not be required. . . ." The constitutions of most states have adopted this principle or a similar one. After much judicial interpretation, the prevailing construction is that the Eighth Amendment does not grant a universal "right" to bail. There are times when bail is not granted, for instance, in situations where violations are punishable by life imprisonment or death.

The first opportunity for an arrestee to be released is immediately following booking at the police station or detention center. At this point the arrestee may be able to obtain release after posting cash bail, promising to appear before a magistrate at a specified date and time. In some jurisdictions, if the arrestee is unable to post such **station house bail**, the officer in charge may release the arrestee upon issuance of a citation (Kamisar et al., 1986). This form of release applies only to minor offenses such as traffic matters and some types of misdemeanors.

Persons arrested on serious offenses, and those arrested on minor offenses who are unable to obtain their release at the holding facility, will remain in custody until they are ready to be presented before a magistrate. At the first or initial appearance (arraignment on the complaint) before the magistrate, the defendant may also be able to obtain release with conditions set for bail at the same time. Pre-trial release may be granted to a person on R.O.R. or by posting bail.

Several concepts must be explained before a full understanding of bail can be achieved: security, surety, and bail bond (Zahler, 1984). **Security** is the money or property pledged to the court or actually deposited in the court to effect the release of a person from legal custody and ensure future appearances. However, the term **surety** may refer to the bail proper or to the person posting the bail. A surety can be either a professional bail bondsman, a corporation, or a private individual. The **bail bond** is a document guaranteeing the appearance of the defendant in court as required, and recording the pledge of money or property to be relinquished to the court if the defendant fails to appear.

The court may or may not require that the pledge of money or property be **secured**. Pledges may be secured in several ways. The most common way is to employ a bail bondsman to whom a non-refundable fee is paid. In other cases, the court may require that a deposit of money be made before the person is released (usually a ten percent cash equivalent of the bail posted) and that the balance be fully justified or secured.

In the federal judicial system, the court may admit the defendant to bail by use of any of the following methods:

(1) Personal Recognizance Bond with only the defendant's signature—no money need be posted.

(2) Appearance Bond without Surety, also called Unsecured Appearance Bond, with a certain amount of money to be posted.

(3) Appearance Bond with a certain amount of cash to be posted.

(4) Appearance Bond for a certain amount with surety or affidavit of surety, not justified. Technically, justification means proof of solvency; in practice, it means that the defendant or surety(ies) have enough money to pay in case of forfeiture of the bond. However, justification is often used in court with the meaning of full security.

(5) Appearance Bond for a certain amount with surety or affidavit of surety or justification.

(6) Cash or Other Collateral Appearance Bond for a certain amount.

(7) Corporate Surety Bond in a certain amount (also known as the bail bondsman).

The amounts to be paid for each of the listed methods will vary and are set by the court after the bail hearing. In the state system there are similar methods of admitting a defendant to bail, although with different names.

Bail revocation is a court decision withdrawing the status of release on bail previously conferred upon the defendant. Bail may be revoked when the defendant is arrested for another crime or violates a condition of the bail release, such as a requirement that the defendant remain within a certain jurisdiction. **Bail forfeiture** is also a court determination that the defendant or the surety has lost the right to the money or property pledged because of failure to appear or because the defendant failed to fulfill other conditions of bail. Forfeiture may also entail the loss of the right to the sum of money deposited as security for the pledge. In this case, the court will retain it or the government will receive it. In most cases upon revocation of bail the defendant is remanded into custody.

In federal court there is no need to revoke bail prior to forfeiture because Federal Rules of Criminal Procedure (*Federal Criminal Code*, 1989), Rule 46 provides that "if there is a breach of condition of a bond, the district court shall declare a forfeiture of the bail" ((e)(1)). Willful failure to appear is a separate punishable criminal offense in the federal system (Comprehensive Crime Control Act, 1984). Neither revocation nor forfeiture of a bail is automatic upon failure to appear. Each is a court decision requiring a hearing. Bail forfeiture may be set aside (vacated) or remitted (pardoned) in whole or part by the court.

Bail exoneration occurs in accordance with Federal Rules of Criminal Procedure (*Federal Criminal Code*, 1989),

> when the condition of the bond has been satisfied or the forfeiture thereof has been set aside or remitted the court shall exonerate the obligors and release any bail. A surety may be exonerated by a deposit in cash in the amount of the bond or by the timely surrender of the defendant into custody. (46(f))

Furthermore, the Comprehensive Crime Control Act (1984), Chapter 1, permits the rejection of bail money if it has been illegally obtained; this Act applies only to the federal system.

7. The Trial

If a case has not been disposed of at any phase of the pre-trial procedure, it proceeds to trial. Trials are conducted in basically the same manner in municipal, state, and United States magistrate and district courts. Procedurally, there are very few distinctions between civil and criminal cases. The differences that do exist will be discussed later in this chapter. All criminal trials, regardless of whether they are heard in state or federal court, are public trials. This means that the defendant is never tried in secret. There is a constitutional guarantee to a public trial, and it is at trial that the defendant has an opportunity to exercise his Fourth, Fifth, Sixth, and Eighth Amendment rights. Essentially, these rights exist to check governmental abuses of authority and give every person the opportunity to be heard by a jury of peers before being pronounced guilty and punished. Without these full guarantees, modern due process could not be achieved; for the non-English speaker the enjoyment of these rights hinges on the use of interpreters during all phases of the criminal justice process, but particularly at trial (Zahler, 1989c).

There are two permutations of the basic criminal trial: the **court** or **bench trial** and the **jury trial**. In criminal cases the defendant is entitled to a trial by jury in all felonies, but not in all misdemeanors; waiver or the right to give up a jury trial is also possible (Kamisar et al., 1986). In some states, waiver of a jury trial can only be granted if the prosecution consents and if the judge accepts the waiver. Sometimes the judge will not allow the defendant to waive the jury trial if there is a possibility that the defendant cannot sufficiently understand the charges or the consequences of waiving a jury trial.

During a court trial only the judge hears evidence, renders judgment, and imposes sentence or discharges the defendant. Whereas in court trials the judge alone decides facts and applies the law, in jury trials the jury decides the facts and the judge applies the law. The analysis presented in this chapter concerning the production of evidence applies to both jury and court trials.

Court trials are regularly used in all types of offenses. In some states there are also court trials in the form of a **submission on the transcript** of the preliminary hearing, but this is true only in felony cases; as noted elsewhere, there is no preliminary hearing in misdemeanor cases. If this form of trial is used, either party may submit additional evidence if it so wishes. Submission on the transcript requires the same waivers as in a guilty plea. In infractions and misdemeanor cases, there may be a submission on the police report, with or without additional evidence. On the federal level, in addition to court trials there are **court trials on stipulated facts**, similar to the state trials called submission on the transcript, but in this instance the facts of the case are agreed upon, one by one, by both parties (Zahler, 1989c).

7.1. Impaneling of the Jury

The criminal jury trial begins with the **impaneling of the jury** (Berger et al., 1989; Mauet, 1988). Impaneling the jury consists of several steps:

(1) A jury panel is called. It is usually composed of forty or more people, typically randomly selected from local voter and/or motor vehicle registration lists.

(2) The judge briefly informs the panel of the charges contained in the complaint, information, or indictment.

(3) Twelve names of prospective jurors are randomly chosen by the court clerk from among the jury panel seated in the courtroom. The number of jurors in federal criminal trials is twelve, but this number is mandated by statute and is not constitutionally required (*Federal Criminal Code,* 1989). State rules allowing use of fewer than twelve jurors in non-capital cases have been upheld, *Williams v. Florida* (1970).

(4) Prospective jurors are submitted to a *voir dire* (to speak the truth), which is a process whereby jurors are questioned to determine their qualifications to serve as fair and impartial triers of fact. Administration of the *voir dire* allows both the prosecution and the defense to select jurors who will render a decision that is fair to the defendant and to society. In state courts the questioning is done alternately by the prosecutor and the defense attorney, whereas in the federal courts it is most often conducted by the judge, who usually determines the relevant questions in a conference with the prosecutor and defense counsel prior to impanelment. During the *voir dire* two types of challenges are permitted, peremptory challenges and challenges for cause. A **peremptory challenge** is a request from a party that the judge not allow a certain prospective juror to be a member of the jury, without having to indicate any reason or cause (Berger et al., 1989). Either side may excuse a prospective juror for any reason, real or imagined, based on any factor: age, sex, occupation, suspected bias, or simple intuition. The number of peremptory challenges which each party can use is ordinarily determined by statute or court rule.

A **challenge for cause** is the same request based on one or more specified cause or legal prerequisite (Mauet, 1988). For example, if a prospective juror has been convicted of a felony or is a close blood relative of the defendant, the juror may be excused for cause. Any statement of bias or prejudice made by a prospective juror during the *voir dire* may result in a challenge for cause. Since these challenges are always for a legal cause, they are not limited in number; however, each must be approved by the judge. Peremptory challenges are used more frequently than challenges for cause because the latter must be proven, whereas the former do not require any proof or formality. Prospective jurors are excused one by one, and new potential jurors are called by the court clerk.

(5) After both parties accept the jury, it is sworn in to try the case truly and impartially according to the evidence produced and the law. At this point the judge or the court clerk reads the indictment or information and the plea given by the defendant.

(6) It is customary to select one or more **alternates,** or replacement jurors. The number of alternates depends on the anticipated length of the trial. The alternate jurors must be present at all hearings, and must listen carefully to testimony and other proceedings, because at any moment they may be called to replace a juror who becomes incapacitated or for any reason cannot remain as a member of the jury. The alternate jurors are not relieved of their duty until the jury has returned after deliberating and has rendered its verdict.

7.2. Opening Statements

The prosecution opens the proceedings by offering an opening statement. The **opening statement** is a summary of the witnesses and evidence the prosecution will present for the purpose of proving the guilt of the accused (Mauet, 1988). The prosecution will not engage in legal arguments, but will enumerate the facts to be proved or issues involved in order to give the jury an orientation or overview of the case so that they will be better able to understand the evidence. The defendant or the defendant's attorney may make an opening statement if authorized by the law of the jurisdiction. It is very common for the defense to waive its right to make an opening statement, or to reserve it for later.

7.3. Presentation of Evidence

The prosecution presents its evidence first because it carries the burden of proof. In state court the prosecution's case is called the "people's case" or the "people's burden," and in federal court it is called the "government's case" or the "government's burden." The prosecution presents two types of evidence to prove its case: testimonial and tangible (Berger et al., 1989).

7.3.1. Testimonial Evidence

Basically, the first and most common form of evidence involves calling persons who reveal under oath their firsthand knowledge, what they have seen or know about the matter under adjudication. This form of evidence is called **testimonial evidence**. There are two subcategories of witnesses who present testimonial evidence: percipient witnesses and expert witnesses (Mauet, 1988).

7.3.1.1. Percipient Witnesses. In general, a **percipient witness** or **eyewitness** is one who is present, personally sees, perceives, or has direct knowledge of an act, event, or object, and who testifies under oath as to what has been seen, heard, or otherwise observed. The witness, also referred to as a lay witness, takes an oath to tell the truth, and the prosecutor who has called the witness conducts a direct examination. A **direct examination** is a series of specific questions put to the witness by a party to the action or counsel for the purpose of bringing before the court and jury, in legal form, the witness's knowledge of the facts of the matter or matters in dispute (Mauet, 1988).

Thereafter, opposing counsel—the defense attorney—may either cross-examine the witness or waive the client's right to cross-examination. The purpose of a **cross-examination** is to find out what the witness did not see or does not know, to reveal gaps and inconsistencies, or to persuade the jury not to believe the testimony of the witness. In other words, the defense attorney challenges the **credibility** of the witness. The more flawed the testimony, the less **weight** the trier of fact will give to the witness's rendition of the facts. When there is cross-examination, the prosecutor has the right to a **redirect examination**—that is, to again query the witness—and the defense attorney also has the right to **re-cross-examine** the witness.

Impeachment refers to the calling into question of a witness's veracity (Mauet, 1988). In general, though there are variations in many states, counsel impeaches a witness with respect to character, prior inconsistent statements, contradiction of facts, bias, or faulty personal character. The witness may be impeached either by cross-examination, usually preceded by a *voir dire,* or by extrinsic evidence—putting other witnesses on the stand or submit documents that introduce facts that tend to discredit the witness's testimony. A witness once impeached may be **rehabilitated** with evidence showing his or her credibility (Mauet, 1988). Any witness called to testify may be impeached. Historically, the party calling the witness could not impeach him or her unless the witness proved to be hostile or uncooperative. However, federal rules now allow impeachment of a witness by any party; the use of this rule is also on the rise in jurisdictions which have not as yet adopted the federal rules of evidence (Zahler, 1989c).

7.3.1.2. Expert Witnesses.   **Experts** are witnesses who have special knowledge of the topic about which they testify. That knowledge must generally be such that the average person does not possess it. Before being pronounced as an expert, the witness must be qualified. To qualify an expert witness, the examining attorney must establish a foundation using the witness's background that would show expertise on the particular subject in question. This expertise may be derived from education, personal experience, or observation. **Expert testimony** is the rendering of an opinion on a specialized topic of scientific, technical, or professional interest that may assist the trier of fact, be it judge or jury, in determining a fact at issue (Waltz, 1983). A classic example of this type of testimony involves a forensic pathologist who renders an opinion about the way in which a person died.

Although it would not be permissible to ask a lay witness to assume certain stated facts and express an opinion on that basis, in expert witness testimony such hypothetical questions are admissible as a way of informing the trier of fact of the expert's knowledge or experience. For example, in a drug-related matter a doctor may be properly asked: "If the defendant took a double dose of this medication, could he or she possibly have been conscious at the time of the act?" However, expert witness testimony is subject to the same objections as those that have been outlined for percipient witnesses. The credibility and opinion of the expert witness may also be questioned.

7.3.2. Tangible Evidence

Tangible evidence encompasses other kinds of evidence that are not testimonial, and includes **exhibits**, which may be either physical objects or documents, site visits, demonstrations, or reenactments. Tangible evidence consists of objects—anything that the trier of fact may see, feel, hear, or otherwise perceive—as distinguished from assertions made by witnesses about those same objects (Berger et al., 1989). Examples of tangible evidence include weapons, audio and videotape recordings, jewelry, maps, and so forth. **Documents** include all types of writings such as confessions, contracts, receipts, accounting books, personal notes or diaries, transcripts from prior proceedings, and other texts.

Exhibits can only be admitted into evidence after a foundation is laid. For this purpose, a **foundation** is a recognition, identification, or acknowledgment by a party or a witness that the object is authentic (Mauet, 1988). The admission of evidence is a legal decision made by the judge either at the pre-trial phase (motion to suppress evidence) or at trial itself (objections preserved for appeal). However, there are many exceptions to the admission of evidence which are beyond the scope of this text (Cleary, 1984).

7.4. Objections

An **objection** is a verbal statement of opposition against something to be said or done because the objecting party believes that the evidence is improper or illegal. Basically, there are three kinds of objections to introduction of evidence: (1) objections to questions asked by opposing counsel, (2) objections to answers given by witnesses, and (3) objections to the introduction of exhibits (Mauet, 1988). For example, an objection to a question posed a witness is a request that the court not permit the witness to answer. The objection must be made immediately after the question is asked, the response is made, or the exhibit is offered as proof.

Objections should contain the underlying legal basis, if it is not obvious (*Federal Criminal Code*, 1989), and should be expressed in as brief a form as possible. Counsel usually state the legal basis and are prepared to argue the point if necessary. They say, for example, "Objection, Your Honor, the question calls for a conclusion." Attorneys use objections to preserve a matter on the record for purposes of appeal. Objections are then placed in the transcript of the proceedings and a record is made; hence counsel has "protected the record" (Waltz, 1983). The failure of an attorney to raise a timely objection on the record usually causes the loss of the right to raise the issue before an appellate court.

Usually the judge will rule on the objection immediately, but sometimes will consider the validity of an objection or take it "under advisement," and the trial will proceed. Some time later in the trial the judge will make a ruling on the previous objection to complete the record. When a judge **sustains** an objection, the proposing party prevails. To wit, if the objection is to an improper question, the witness will be instructed not to answer. When the objection is to a witness's answer, counsel's request will result in a **motion to strike**. If the objection is to the introduction of an exhibit and it is sustained, the exhibit will not be admitted into evidence and will not be shown to the jury. If the objection is **overruled** or denied, objecting counsel may make an offer of proof, which may be necessary for two reasons: (1) it may convince a trial judge to reverse the ruling, and (2) the reviewing appellate court may eventually determine whether the exclusion was improper and, therefore, reverse the trial court's judgment (the ruling or holding of the trial court will be designated as **reversible error**—invalid).

In practice, the offer of proof must be made out of the presence of the jury. This can be achieved in one of two ways: (1) in the presence of the jury, counsel can request permission to approach the judge's bench for a side bar conference; or (2) if counsel believes that the offer of proof will be lengthy, a request at the side bar that the court excuse the jury for a short period of time can be made. A **side bar** conference is a meeting held at the side of the judge's bench, called the bar, conducted in a whisper so that the jury, defendant, and audience cannot hear what is being said. The conference is conducted by the judge in the presence of counsel, the court reporter or recorder, and any other necessary court attache for the purpose of resolving a legal issue or determining whether a particular line of questioning will be allowed.

Objections are most commonly raised during the testimony of either percipient or expert witnesses. They are also made if controversial documents or other tangible evidence (**exhibits**) is offered to prove the facts. The most common objections lodged against questions include the following: irrelevancy, immateriality, calling for conclusion, hearsay, leading, repetitive, beyond the scope, assuming facts not in evidence, vague, compound question, and argumentative (Lilly, 1978; Mauet, 1988). Those objections which are most often heard in practice will be reviewed in the next section.

7.4.1. Objections to Questions

In producing testimonial evidence, attorneys are attempting to elicit specific information which would tend to prove their case. However, there are many specific rules about how that inquiry should be conducted. Any question an attorney asks can be objected to if it is in a form which does not meet minimal standards of fair play. Some of the most important of those objections follow:

(1) A **leading question** is a question which suggests the desired answer. The form of the question would be: "Isn't it true you saw a red car driven by the defendant run down the victim?" The form of the objection would be: "Objection, your honor, the question is leading." Leading questions are almost always admissible in cross-examination and are sometimes admissible in direct examination (Lilly, 1978). There is an exception. Cross-examination is designed to show what the witness does not know, and leading questions are appropriate for this type of questioning. Also, a leading question will be allowed if a witness is very young or mentally handicapped.

(2) The Federal Rules of Evidence (*Federal Criminal Code*, 1989) define **hearsay** as "a statement, other than the one made by the declarant [witness] while testifying at the trial or hearing, offered in evidence to prove the truth of the matter asserted" (Rule 801(c)). The primary elements of hearsay are: (a) an assertion (statement or assertive conduct); (b) made or done out of court (meaning not at the instant trial or hearing); and (c) offered to prove the fact of the matter asserted in court. The latter is the most important or crucial aspect of hearsay; it requires an inquiry into the reasons why the statement is offered and to what issues it is meant to elucidate. The philosophical rationale for excluding hearsay evidence is that the opposing party is denied the opportunity to cross-examine the declarant, that is, the person who made the statement is not the witness in court on the stand.

An example of hearsay is the statement, "Tommy told me [Ben] that Jack said he was going to kill him," which is a statement made by Tommy's best friend Ben at the stand. Most often, the attorney will say: "Objection, your honor, hearsay." The statement will not be admitted into evidence because the parties cannot cross-examine the out-of-court declarant, Tommy. As with all rules, there are exceptions; the hearsay rule is not exempt. If a witness is repeating the out-of-court declarant's statement and the statement is not offered for its truth but only to prove that it has been uttered, it will be admissible as an exception to the hearsay rule. If a statement is hearsay and no exception to the rule applies, the evidence must be excluded upon appropriate objection. Exceptions to the hearsay rule are too numerous to include in this text; for more details, see the Federal Rules of Evidence (*Federal Criminal Code*, 1989; Mauet, 1988).

(3) A question is **vague** if it is imprecise or too broad; in a murder case a vague question would be: "Did you see the victim?" This question is vague as to place and time. The question is **irrelevant** if it does not relate to the matter at issue. A question is also considered irrelevant if it lacks probative weight, that is, if it is unlikely to resolve the issue before the court. For example, it is now generally accepted that querying a rape victim about her prior sexual experiences is a line of questioning not

relevant to the rape; it asks for information that does not support a fact in question. On the other hand, a question is **immaterial** if it is not pertinent, or if it is not important to the issue before the court. An example of this type of question would be the prosecution inquiring about the defendant's unrelated business matters during a murder trial. Vague, irrelevant, or immaterial questions are commonly objected to by opposing counsel, and such objections are usually sustained by the court (Mauet, 1988).

(4) **Argumentative** questions, in contrast, are those questions which do not elicit new information but simply restate facts and arrive at conclusions, and then ask the witness to affirm or deny the conclusion. For example, in a situation where a waitress testified about a stabbing in the bar where she worked, the following question would be argumentative: "You have testified that the bar was quite dark and you were at the counter about twenty feet away from the table where the incident occurred, so you really could not recognize the people involved, could you?" The question actually provokes an argument with the witness rather than bringing out new information not yet in evidence (Lilly, 1978).

(5) A question is considered **repetitive** if it has been asked and answered during the previous testimony of the same witness. For example, first the witness is asked if he or she was at the scene of the crime on the night in question. The next question asks if he or she could be mistaken and could he or she really have been elsewhere. The objection would be: "Objection, Your Honor, asked and answered."

(6) A **conclusion** is a deduction drawn from a fact or series of facts. In general, witnesses can only testify to facts; conclusions based on those facts are the responsibility of the jury. For example, if the defendant claims the insanity defense, only the judge or jury may legally find him or her to be insane at the time of the crime. If an expert witness is asked the question, "Was he or she insane at that time of the crime?" this asks the expert to draw the ultimate legal conclusion rather than asking about the defendant's specific behavior at the time the act was committed. Opposing counsel would state: "Objection, Your Honor, calls for a conclusion." Of course, experts may be asked hypothetical questions which they may answer (see Expert Witnesses, above).

(7) A question should not be asked that is **beyond the scope** of the direct, cross, or redirect examination. A question is beyond the scope when cross-examining counsel attempts to elicit facts from the witness about areas not previously covered during the direct examination (Mauet, 1988). Direct testimony in a hit-and-run trial, for example, covers the whereabouts of the defendant, the make and model of the car driven, whether the defendant had been under the influence of alcohol, and any alibi the defendant puts forth. If the defense then attempts to introduce evidence that the defendant is an excellent driver, there may be an objection that the line of questioning is beyond the scope of the inquiry.

(8) **Assumption of facts not in evidence** means asking a question which contains information that has not yet been uncovered and is, therefore, not on the record; its existence is still in dispute. If the question "When you got to the house that night, who was there when you arrived?" is asked before any evidence or testimony is offered to indicate that the defendant was ever at the house, an objection is in order (Lilly, 1978).

(9) A **compound question** is one that contains two or more separate facts within one question. Such an objection is sustainable because the answer will probably be

unclear. For example, consider the question, "Did you hear the defendant threaten the victim and did you see the defendant shoot him?" If one of the two facts in the question is false, neither a positive nor negative answer will be accurate (Mauet, 1988).

7.4.2. Objections to Answers

Objections to answers usually include irrelevancy, immateriality, conclusion, and hearsay, among others. The definitions of these types of objections are the same as those offered in the above Section 7.4.1., Objections to Questions. The primary distinction is that the witness has already answered a permissible question, so that sequence of time is the distinguishing characteristic in this type of objection. Two more kinds of objections to answers are discussed because they are very frequently used: privileged communication and unresponsiveness.

(10) **Privileged communications** are those made in confidence between parties having certain protected relations. The privilege is based on the policy that communications within certain intimate relationships must be protected from revelation at trial. The most traditional are attorney/client, doctor/patient, priest/penitent and husband/wife (Waltz, 1983). However, there has been a recent trend eroding the classic protection offered to participants in these relationships. The attorney/client privilege still survives, although there have been attacks on its validity in actual practice. Any communication, especially questions by the defendant to the attorney concerning the planning of the defense, enjoys special protection in the courtroom. This kind of objection will be raised, for example, if the defendant chooses to take the stand and the prosecutor asks: "Did your attorney tell you to claim self-defense after you murdered the victim or you wouldn't have a chance to win your case?"

(11) An answer which does not directly respond to a question is objectionable as **unresponsive**. If the answer goes beyond what is needed to respond to the question, the addition to the answer is considered volunteered and is also objectionable. For example, if the response to "Did you see the defendant run over the victim?" is: "Well, I actually saw a red car that I thought belonged to the defendant because it has a dent on the right side," it is not only unresponsive but is also filled with volunteered information that the opposing attorney will ask to have stricken from the record. Unresponsive questions can be corrected with a simple yes or no answer, and the judge may instruct the witness to answer in that style (Mauet, 1988).

7.4.3. Objections to Exhibits

Objections to exhibits include irrelevancy, immateriality, and hearsay, and have the same philosophical underpinnings as those made in connection with questions or answers (Lilly, 1978). The only difference here is that the introduction of a **tangible object** is being objected to by opposing counsel. There are two other specific objections relating to tangible objects that deserve mention: lack of foundation or authentication, and prejudice outweighing probative value.

(12) An objection for **lack of foundation** contends that opposing counsel is attempting to submit in evidence a tangible object without any showing that there is a basis for introducing that evidence. An example would be trying to introduce a gun

of the same model as the murder weapon without proof that it is the same weapon. An **authentication** objection, on the other hand, allows counsel to challenge the admission of an exhibit for lack of proof of veracity or originality. To overcome this objection, the offering counsel would try to prove its originality or veracity by calling witnesses who could prove the defendant signed a contract (Mauet, 1988).

(13) The exercise of the right to object to an exhibit for **prejudice outweighing probative value**, that is, on the grounds that its evidentiary value is less than the prejudice it may cause, is also called a motion *in limine* (see Pre-Trial Motions, above), and in some state jurisdictions, when it concerns the defendant's own statements, this motion is called a **Beagle motion** (Zahler, 1989b, 1989c). An example of this type of proof is when the prosecution, in an attempt to inflame the jury, tries to show pictures of injuries the victim sustained that were not the cause of death.

7.5. Resting the Case

After the prosecution has completed the presentation of its evidence—testimonial and other kinds—the prosecutor announces, "Your Honor, the People rest." In federal court, the prosecutor states, "Your Honor, the Government rests." At this point, the prosecutor believes that he or she has met the burden of proof and that enough evidence has been presented to prove beyond a reasonable doubt that the defendant is guilty of the charge brought by the state or federal government (Mauet, 1988).

7.6. The Defense

The case of the defense unfolds in the same way as that of the prosecution: presentation of lay and expert witnesses and other types of evidence. Defense witnesses may be cross-examined and any of the objections mentioned previously in this chapter may also be raised, if they are appropriate. It must be noted that the defendant may or may not take the stand. If the defendant chooses to do so, he or she may be cross-examined by the prosecutor. When taking the stand, the defendant is advised by his or her attorney that for all practical purposes he or she is waiving his or her Fifth Amendment right against self-incrimination. When the defense has finished presenting its evidence, the attorney issues the statement, "Your Honor, the Defense rests." Since the burden to prove guilt lies with the prosecutor, the defense need only present enough evidence to create a reasonable doubt in the mind of the trier of fact that the defendant committed the crime with which he or she is charged (Zahler, 1989c).

7.7. Rebuttals

After the prosecution and defense have both finished or rested their cases, there is an opportunity to present **rebuttal evidence**, which is testimony or tangible objects introduced in order to contradict the opponent's evidence (Mauet, 1988). For example, if a child four years of age witnesses a murder, there is a presumption that such a young witness will be unreliable. Evidence can be presented to overcome the presumption of a fact or a *prima facie* (on its face) case of guilt. A **presumption** is an assumption of fact resulting from statutory or judicial law or rule requiring such fact to be deduced from another fact or facts established in the case. In other words, a presumption requires that a particular inference be drawn from an ascertained group of facts. In effect, once a presumptive fact is introduced, the burden to disprove or rebut that fact lies with the opposing party, since the burden of proof has shifted by means of a presumption.

Presumptions are divided between conclusive presumptions and rebuttal presumptions. A **conclusive presumption** is one in which proof of the basic fact renders the existence of the presumed fact conclusive and irrefutable; most often these types of presumptions can be found in civil law. In other words, a conclusive presumption does not permit any proof to be admitted for the purpose of invalidating it. Most of these irrefutable presumptions come in the form of substantive law. For example, if a driver collides with an oncoming car while in a fog because the lights failed or were in disrepair, the driver is irrefutably liable for the accident. Drivers have a duty to keep their headlights repaired at all times, and are liable for any accidents resulting from defective conditions.

However, a rebuttal presumption, as its name suggests, can be rebutted or refuted by proving the invalidity of the fact. An example is a case in which a man is struck by a barrel and is rendered unconscious. **Prima facie** liability rests on the owner of the pickle factory whose warehouse the plaintiff was passing at the time he was struck; no other business on that block uses barrels, so the barrel must have come from the defendant's factory. The burden shifts to the owner of the pickle factory to show it was not his barrel which struck the plaintiff (Hay, 1976).

All the rules followed in the case in chief, or primary case, apply to the rebuttal phase. Both parties have an opportunity to present rebuttal evidence. Additionally, any rebuttal evidence may be refuted in a **surrebuttal** or **answer to the rebuttal** (Mauet, 1988). After all rebuttal evidence has been presented by one or both parties, the next stage of the proceedings is the presentation of closing arguments. It is very likely that neither counsel will choose to present rebuttal evidence; hence, the rebuttal phase of the trial occurs only if new evidence comes to light or other circumstances call for its use.

7.8. Closing Arguments

The **closing argument** or **summation** is a speech made by counsel, addressed to the trier of fact—either the judge or jury—in which each attorney analyzes the evidence in light of the law (Berger et al., 1989; Mauet, 1988). Each attorney, within the parameters of the law, will try to persuade the jury that his or her party must prevail. Defense counsel will suggest the meaning of the facts and how much weight the evidence should be given by the jury. The prosecutor has the right to speak first. The defense attorney thereafter presents arguments; this is the sole opportunity to address the jury on the merits of the defendant's case. Because the prosecutor has the burden of proving the guilt of the defendant, he or she has an opportunity to rebut after termination of defense counsel's argument.

7.9. Final Jury Instructions

Final **jury instructions** are given by the judge in a process called **charging the jury**. Instructions are the rules of law applicable to the case (Carr, 1989). The judge reads them to the jurors and admonishes them that they must follow these rules during their deliberations. The jury receives instructions of two types: general and special.

7.9.1. General Instructions

General instructions are those which are applicable to every case. Most general instructions are printed in form or pattern books (District Judges Association, 1985a, 1985b; Judicial Conference of the United States, 1988; LaFave & Israel, 1985). The general instructions which are most prevalent include, but are not limited to: explanation of direct and circumstantial evidence, burden of proof, conduct of jurors in the jury room, difference between admissions and confessions, explanation of general and specific intent, explanation of lesser included offense, distinction between malice and negligence, the concepts of unlawfulness, wantonness and willfulness, rules for deliberation, and the need for a unanimous verdict (Zahler, 1989b, 1989c).

Direct evidence can be explained in two manners to the jury: (a) evidence that directly proves a fact, i.e., that which is personally perceived by use of the five senses; and (b) evidence that takes the form of testimony by a person who claims to have personal knowledge of the commission of the crime, as a percipient witness or eyewitness. An example of direct evidence is a witness who testified to seeing the defendant approach the house at the time the crime was committed.

The jury is also instructed that **circumstantial evidence**, also called indirect evidence, is the confirmation of facts or circumstances from which the existence or non-existence of other facts or circumstances may be inferred or drawn. The showing of secondary facts from which a principal fact may be rationally inferred is circumstantial evidence. It can also be the proof of a chain of facts and circumstances which tend to show whether the defendant is guilty or not guilty. For example, imagine that immediately after the commission of a crime the police find a trail of muddy shoe prints leading from the yard to the house. This one lone circumstance may not be enough to prove guilt. More circumstantial evidence, such as the fact that the victim knew the defendant, proof that the defendant owed the victim money, together with a muddy shoe print which matches footwear owned by the defendant, may be enough to prove that the defendant was in the home of the victim at the time of the crime, but not necessarily that the defendant killed the victim. The judge will instruct the jury that both direct and circumstantial evidence are legal means of proof, except that circumstantial evidence must comply with certain legal conditions which are beyond the scope of this text.

Another general instruction to the jury is the definition of **burden of proof** and how it is to be evaluated. Often it is defined as the duty of the prosecution to prove a fact by presenting enough evidence to establish it as true. This burden must be met by proving the fact beyond a reasonable doubt (see Burden of Proof in Chapter 9).

The judge instructs the jury that it is important for a juror to understand the legal difference between admissions and confessions. An **admission** is defined as voluntary oral or written statements made by a person or lawyer that certain facts or circumstances from which guilt may be inferred do exist or are true. An example might be the statement, "Yes, I did break into her apartment the night she was killed." An admission only tends to prove the offense charged; it is not a confession of guilt. On the other hand, a **confession** is an admission of guilt by the accused or an admission of making other incriminating statements, either orally or in writing, that unconditionally admit commission of the act (Mauet, 1988), for example, "Yes, I killed her," or "Yes, I told the police I killed her."

In the United States it is generally true that to prove someone has committed a crime, two basic elements must always be present: *mens rea* and *actus rea* (Bartol, 1983). The prosecution must prove not only that the person committed the act (*actus rea*) but also that the defendant had the intent to commit the act (*mens rea*). **Intent** is a state of mind in which a person knows and desires the consequences of the act. For purposes of criminal liability, this state of mind must exist at the time the crime is committed. **Intent** is usually the most difficult part of the charge to prove, and the judge will give the jury special instructions in that regard.

Typically the judge will instruct that intent can be either general or specific. **General intent** means an intention to do that which the law prohibits; it is not necessary for the prosecution to prove that the defendant intended the precise harm or the precise results which actually came about. For example, when two men argue in a bar, the situation escalates and ends in someone's death. There was no specific plan to kill, but there is a general understanding that it is wrong to take somebody's life under any circumstances. **Specific intent** is the intent to accomplish the precise act which the law prohibits. For example, if a murder is planned it is a specific intent crime, usually first-degree murder with malice aforethought. The murder under these circumstances is considered to be intentional, willful, premeditated, and malicious.

Depending on whether the trial is criminal or civil, the judge may also instruct the jury on the difference between malice and negligence. **Malice** is a state of mind that accompanies an intentional commission of an evil or wrongful act without legal justification or excuse. **Negligence**, on the other hand, is the failure to exercise that degree of care that a person of ordinary prudence (**a reasonable man**) would exercise under the same circumstances. In other words, a negligent act is the failure to do something that a reasonable person would do; or the doing of something which a reasonable person would not do. It is usually an accidental act or omission which results in injury to another. Negligence is the pertinent legal standard of intent in personal injury claims.

The judge also instructs the jury on the second element which must be proven, that is, the commission of an unlawful act. An **unlawful act** is a behavior which is contrary, unauthorized, or prohibited by law. The extent to which the law has been disregarded varies and there are many subdivisions of this indifference, such as will-fulness and wantonness. A **willful act** generally means an act done with a bad purpose without justifiable cause, even without the intent to disregard or disobey a specific law. **Wantonness** means gross negligence or carelessness; it is sometimes considered a synonym for extreme recklessness. Its primary feature is that an act is committed with full knowledge that it will result in injury or damage to one or more persons, and it is committed despite that awareness. These modifiers are always connected to the primary charge for which the defendant is on trial.

However, a defendant need not be formally on trial for all charges that could be brought. In this instance, the judge would instruct the jury regarding lesser included offenses. A **lesser included offense** is necessarily established by offering proof of the more serious offense that is properly submitted to the jury. Should the prosecution's proof fail to establish guilt of the greater offense charged, then the jury is instructed to find the defendant guilty of the lesser included charge without the need for formal or multiple indictments (Zahler, 1989c). For example, attempted robbery is a lesser included offense in the crime of robbery, just as assault is ordinarily a lesser included offense in murder.

Among the general rules given by the judge to the jury is the instruction to elect a **foreperson**, that is, the presiding member who speaks for the jury. The judge advises the jury that it is not good policy for jurors to state opinions about guilt or innocence of the defendant in the early stages of the deliberation. It is assumed that such anticipatory statements may prevent jurors from changing their opinions even after listening to the evidence and the opinions of co-jurors; it is more fruitful to wait until after there has been an exchange of opinions (Zahler, 1989c). The judge also advises the jury to study the elements of each offense one by one before deciding if all of the elements were present at the time of the commission of the crime. The judge orders the jury to observe utmost secrecy and to avoid discussing the facts of the case with anyone other than members of the jury, to only start deliberations if all are present, and to send a note to the judge if the jury needs clarification regarding any jury instructions or legal issues, or if it desires a rereading of any portion of the testimony, or any other similar request.

7.9.2. Special Instructions

Special instructions are those given for specific offenses tried in the case which may or may not be applicable in other cases. The judge explains to the jury the elements of each offense that must be present in the case in their entirety in order to constitute the offense charged. Under most penal codes, to establish the crime of burglary, four elements must be present: (a) the defendant entered or remained unlawfully in (b) a certain structure with (c) the intent to (d) commit a theft or a felony (Criminal Code, 1988). If all four elements have not been proved by the government, then the defendant will either be acquitted or found guilty of the lesser included offense of theft (see Verdict, below).

Either party is permitted to request any instructions it wishes to be included in the charge to the jury. Most often they are submitted in writing, and a copy is given to the opposing party. For instructions which emanate from codified pattern books in use in the jurisdiction, there may be a special request for modification of the instruction before it is read to the jury. Modification of a standard jury instruction would allow the special circumstances of the particular case to come before the jury.

7.10. Bailiff's Oath

Once the judge has finished instructing the jury, a court officer, typically the bailiff, is sworn to take charge of the jury and **sequester** or secure them in a special deliberation room. The bailiff is also sworn to maintain the jury's privacy. At this time, the defendant and counsel are excused but requested to be ready and available on very short notice; the judge may specify the length of time. As soon as the jury leaves the courtroom to start deliberations, the judge declares a recess, unless there are other pending matters (Zahler, 1989c).

7.11. Jury Deliberations

When the jury convenes to begin deliberations, the jurors follow the instructions given them by the judge. During deliberations, if the jury has doubt as to an instruction or a definition used by the judge, the foreperson sends a note to the judge. The jury and the parties and counsel are then recalled to the courtroom, and usually the judge clarifies the ambiguity or gives additional instructions.

According to United States law, the verdict or decision of the jury must be unanimous; in other words, all members of the jury must agree on the verdict. If the jury appears to have some difficulty in reaching a unanimous verdict, it sends a note to the judge stating that there is a problem. The court then requests that the jury return to the courtroom in the presence of all parties involved and asks the foreperson whether a continuation of the deliberations might be fruitful and lead to a unanimous verdict. If the answer is negative, the judge may or may not give them the **Allen charge**. This charge or instruction is for the jury to make a renewed effort to arrive at a verdict; the name of the instruction derives from the case *Allen v. U.S.* (1896).

7.12. Hung Jury

When no unanimous verdict can be reached by the jury, it is said to be a **hung jury**. In such situations the jury informs the judge in a note that deliberations have reached a deadlock. The jury is then called back to the courtroom with all parties present. At this point the foreperson of the jury is asked in open court whether the jury has reached a verdict. The answer will be negative, and the judge declares a mistrial and discharges the jury (Zahler, 1989c). Depending upon the division of the vote, the prosecution will indicate whether a new trial will be set. If the vote is heavily in favor of acquittal, the prosecutor may ask the judge to dismiss the case or ask for a period of time to consult with superiors.

7.13. Verdict

The **verdict** is the formal decision or finding made by a jury impaneled and sworn for the trial at hand, upon matters duly submitted to it. The law requires that the verdict be returned and reported to the judge in open court. The verdict may be for **acquittal** (not guilty) or for **conviction** (guilty). If the verdict returned is not guilty, the judge dismisses the defendant and bail is exonerated. The judge also dismisses the jury after thanking them for their services and instructing them that they may now, if they wish, answer questions that counsel may pose about the reasons for their decisions, but they also have the right to refuse to do so. At this point, they are asked to return to the jury assembly room, where there may be more assignments for them.

If the verdict is for conviction, the jury is discharged with the same instructions that the judge gives after an acquittal. If the verdict is unanimously for conviction, the defense attorney usually requests a **polling** of the jury, which means each juror is individually asked whether he or she voted for conviction (Mauet, 1988). By the same token, if the unanimous verdict is for acquittal, the right to poll may be exercised by the prosecutor. In multi-count cases there may be acquittals as to some charges, and there may be convictions as to other charges in the complaint or information.

The court continues in session without the presence of the jury. Usually the defendant is then referred to the probation department and a date is set for the sentencing hearing, which in state matters usually takes place within four weeks. In federal matters sentencing takes place within two months according to the Sentencing

Guidelines established by the United States Sentencing Commission (1987), appointed pursuant to Chapter II of the Comprehensive Crime Control Act of 1984.

8. Sentencing

Ordinarily the last step in the judicial criminal justice process is sentencing the defendant. The structure of the sentence and the discretion of the judge in choosing among alternative sentences is controlled by statute. In misdemeanor cases, for example, the judge ordinarily has the discretion to impose fines, probation, a suspended sentence, or a term in jail not to exceed statutorial limits. For felonies, on the other hand, the judge usually chooses between imprisonment and probation. Sometimes there are offenses for which probation is forbidden in the statute. If probation is part or all of the sentence imposed on the defendant, the judge may set conditions of probation such as enrollment in an anti-drug abuse program, work in community service agencies, admission to educational programs, or any other program the judge deems desirable (Zahler, 1989c).

8.1. Pre-Sentencing Report

Sentencing commences with a **pre-sentence investigation**, conducted by a probation officer for the purpose of preparing a pre-sentence report for the court. While the trial informs the judge about the offenses committed and the facts of the case itself, the pre-sentence report provides information about the human being about to be sentenced (Zahler, 1989a, 1989c). First, the probation officer conducts an in-depth personal interview with the defendant to obtain his or her version of the events that gave rise to the prosecution, and inquires about the defendant's personal background, family status, education, income, work status, health, and so on. The probation officer also contacts the prosecutor and law enforcement agents connected with the offense to request any information they may have concerning the defendant's activities.

By using law enforcement agency **rap sheets**, the probation officer ascertains the defendant's prior criminal record. Additional information is gathered through other agencies such as former and current employers, financial, educational, medical, military, and other institutions that the defendant has had previous contact with, and the defendant's family relations. At times a second interview with the defendant is required to clarify the information gathered by the probation officer. Traditionally in state courts, pre-sentence reports could not be disclosed before the day of sentencing; recently, however, the majority of the states have established mandatory disclosure of portions or all of the pre-sentence report. Some states make this matter discretionary with the court (Zahler, 1989c).

8.2. Sentencing at the State Level

On the date set for sentencing the judge in state court declares that the probation report has been read and considered and asks whether the defense or prosecution would like to comment on it. After hearing the comments, the judge asks whether there is any legal cause why sentence should not be imposed. If the answer is in the negative, the judge may either grant probation under certain terms and conditions or may impose a straight or split sentence. **Straight sentence** usually refers to a term of imprisonment, whereas **split sentence** refers to a certain term of imprisonment and a prescribed period of probation, also called flat and soft time, respectively (Zahler, 1989c). In either case, the judge often follows the recommendations of the probation department; however, he or she has the discretion to vary from them as well. Finally, in both state and federal court, the defendant is advised of the right to appeal the trial court's conviction, the sentence, or both.

8.3. Sentencing at the Federal Level

In the United States district courts disclosure of pre-sentence reports was regularly required before the establishment of the Sentencing Guidelines (United States Sentencing Commission, 1987). The principal purpose of the guidelines is to establish sentencing policies and practices for the federal judicial system that will ensure the ends of justice by promulgating detailed guidelines prescribing the appropriate sentences for offenders convicted of federal crimes. A key feature of the legislation is the **determinate sentence model**, in which punishment is fixed by statute if certain preconditions are met.

The nature of the sentence is dictated by the severity of the offense and the offender characteristics explained in the guidelines. Some examples of offense categories include: bank robbery committed with a gun and theft of $2,500, fraud and deceit by means of a scheme to defraud more than one victim, and prohibited transactions in or shipment of firearms and weapons involving more than five weapons.

Each of these offenses would carry a sentence within a range of possible sentences depending on offender characteristics. Examples of offender characteristics are: an offender with one prior conviction who was not sentenced to imprisonment, an offender with one prior conviction who completed a period of incarceration, and a first-time offender. Under the new Sentencing Guidelines the range of sentencing for a person who is convicted for a level 28 offense and is a first-time offender would be between 78 and 97 months. However, if that same defendant had six previous convictions, the range of sentencing would be between 97 and 121 months.

According to the guidelines, the judge must select a sentence from within the guideline range; any departures must be on the record. The Sentencing Reform Act (Comprehensive Crime Control Act, 1984) also requires the offender to serve virtually all of any prison sentence imposed, and for that reason it abolishes parole and substantially restructures good behavior adjustments. By its nature, the new process establishes an adversary model of sentencing. Both prosecution and defense counsel play a more active role in sentencing than they did under the previous law. Additionally, the pre-sentence report will be subject to greater scrutiny (Zahler, 1989c).

To facilitate sentencing under the new law, the Judicial Conference Committee on the Administration of the Probation System has developed model local rules for consideration by the United States district courts. In the absence of adoption of the new rules by the court, the procedures set forth in the model rules may be considered by individual judges for use in their courtrooms.

The primary purpose of the procedures in the model rules is to provide for resolution of disagreements about material facts and about the application of the guidelines to the case in advance of the sentencing hearing. A second purpose is to ensure that those disagreements that cannot be resolved are identified for the sentencing judge. These primary goals of the Sentencing Act of 1987 are achieved by requiring that the prosecution and the defense first communicate any objections concerning the pre-sentence report to the probation officer so that there is an opportunity to respond to those objections and, if possible, to resolve them before forwarding the report to the sentencing judge.

In furtherance of those purposes, the model rule recommends that not less than twenty days prior to the date set for sentencing, the probation officer "shall" (must) disclose the pre-sentence investigation report to the defendant and to counsel for the defendant and the government. Within ten days thereafter counsel "shall" communicate to the probation officer any objections they may have as to any material information, sentencing classifications, sentencing guideline ranges, and policy statements contained in or omitted from the report. The model rule covers many details concerning the use of the objections and their possible solutions (United States Sentencing Commission, 1987).

The sentencing hearing will be much longer—and very possibly it will be an evidentiary hearing—if the judge so determines. It has been held that contested facts in sentencing proceedings are to be established by a preponderance of the evidence. As of this writing there are no cases challenging the Sentencing Reform Act, and it is believed that this will remain the appropriate standard (Zahler, 1989c). However, when resolution of an issue would have a great impact on the sentence, it may be argued that a higher standard of proof should be applied. The same procedural steps are followed in the federal courts as in the state courts: the judge declares having read the report, asks counsel for comments and recommendations, and then proceeds to sentence the defendant and advises the defendant of the right to appeal.

9. Appeals

An **appeal** is a request to a higher court to review the decision of a lower or inferior court (the final determination of a trial court or administrative agency). There are typically two stages of appeal in the federal system and in many state court systems. These stages are the appeal from the trial court to the intermediate appellate court, and possibly an appeal from the intermediate court to a supreme court. If provided by law, the prosecution or the defense may resort to this remedy if either believes the trial court has made an error. However, the prosecution is seldom entitled to resort to this course of action (Zahler, 1989c).

When the court of appeals renders its decision, either affirming or reversing the judgment, then an appeal to the highest appellate court can proceed. However, if the first appellate court either affirms, reverses, or modifies the judgment of the trial court in part, the case may be remanded to the trial court for further proceedings. At this point, the trial court judge will call a hearing in order to inform the defendant about the decision of the court of appeals. In federal matters this hearing is usually called **filing and spreading,** meaning the judgment of the court of appeals is filed or is entered on the docket of the trial court (Zahler, 1989c). Spreading signifies the publication or announcement of the judgment in open court to the defendant. The presence of the defendant is not always required at such hearings (Zahler, 1989c).

Chapter 11

Principles of Comparative Law

1. Introduction

This unit has thus far focused on a review of the United States legal system; however, because many offenders who appear in United States courts come from countries that employ other legal traditions, it is advisable for the interpreter to have a cursory knowledge and an appreciation of other legal systems. Interpreters will also benefit if they can determine whether parallel proceedings exist in other legal systems, and can identify them when they hear them discussed.

This chapter is not a comprehensive comparison between the United States and other countries' legal systems; rather, it is meant to give the interpreter a basic understanding of the major differences between two dominant legal systems: the common law and civil law traditions. Many times there is no correspondence between two legal concepts because the legal systems from which they stem are so distinct. The knowledge presented in this chapter, it is hoped, will facilitate the interpreter's task of providing comprehensive language services and conserving the underlying meaning of testimony.

2. Comparative Law Defined

Comparative law is a modern expression first used during the nineteenth century when it became clear that the various legal institutions of the world should be systematically investigated and compared. The term is synonymous, and can be used interchangeably, with the terms comparative legal systems, comparative legal traditions, or comparative legal families (Ehrmann, 1976; Liebesny, 1981).

There are many legal systems, and traditions or families but, in the modern Western world three are the most common: (a) the **civil law** or **Romano-Germanic** family (sometimes called the Romanistic family); (b) the **common law** or **Anglo-American law** tradition; and (c) the **socialist law** family or tradition (Liebesny, 1981). An in-depth comparison of the three major legal traditions can be found in *Comparative Legal Traditions in a Nutshell* (Glendon, Gordon, & Osakwe, 1982). Other legal traditions, such as the Nordic or Scandinavian legal family, are worth mentioning but will not be discussed here. The Nordic legal family encompasses Denmark, Finland, Iceland, Norway, and Sweden. Within their own legal systems the members of this family have incorporated some of the features of civil and common law traditions (Zahler, 1989f).

The final major distinction which deserves mention is composed of the philosophical, and religious or traditional systems. These systems do not constitute families

143

in and of themselves because they are entirely independent of each other. For example, the Muslim or Islamic, Jewish, Chinese, Japanese, and Korean traditions, and African customary tribal laws are all systems which serve the specific ethnic groups for which they are named, but they are not in and of themselves widely adopted, and, therefore, do not qualify as legal families or traditions (Glendon et al., 1982; Liebesny, 1981; Zahler, 1989f).

3. The Civil Law or Romano-Germanic Family

This family is usually traced back to the year 450 B.C., which is the presumed creation date of the Twelve Tables of Rome. However, the crucial event, as far as the development of civil law tradition is concerned, was the Justinian compilation of law around A.D. 534. It is today the dominant legal tradition in most parts of Western Europe, all of Central and South America, many parts of Asia and Africa, and even in a few enclaves in the common law world—the state of Louisiana and the Commonwealth of Puerto Rico in the United States, and Quebec, Canada (Liebesny, 1981; Zahler, 1989f). Until the end of the first third of this century, it was the dominant legal tradition in the countries of Eastern Europe, including the Soviet Union, which have since become socialist law countries. It has also influenced the law of international organizations (the United Nations and the World Court) and international law as well. Within the civil law tradition it is possible to identify Romanistic, Germanic, or Latin American legal subcultures. However, development of these fine distinctions are beyond the scope of this text.

A portion of contemporary civil law tradition has been extensively influenced by two nineteenth-century legal codes: the French Civil Code of 1804, known as the Code Napoleon, and the German Civil Code of 1896. The German Civil Code came into effect on the 1st of January, 1900, and along with the Code Napoleon, has served as a model for most of the other modern civil law codes. Napoleon is also credited with having ordered the writing and enactment of four other codes besides the Civil Code: the Penal, Commercial, Civil, and Criminal Procedure Codes (Glendon et al., 1982; Liebesny, 1981). The French Civil Code of 1804 is based on three legal theories: private property, freedom of contract, and the patriarchal family, which were concepts also known to the Romans. A few provisions, such as those on adoption and divorce by mutual consent, are attributable to the Code Napoleon (Liebesny, 1981). Napoleon's legislative influences were extended outside of France to the territories he conquered, such as Italy, Poland, what is now known as the Netherlands, and the ruins of the Hapsburg Empire.

4. The Common Law or Anglo-American Family

Of the three traditions, the common law family is the second oldest. The date commonly used to mark its inception is 1066, the year of the Battle of Hastings. However, 1215, the year the Magna Carta was signed, seems more appropriate to some legal scholars. Today, it is the legal tradition in force in Great Britain, Ireland, the United States, Canada, Australia, and New Zealand, and has had substantial influence on the law of many nations in Asia and Africa (Zahler, 1989f). The United States common law system has been covered extensively in preceding chapters.

Interestingly, in England the police have a judicial function and authority to try crimes, hence the name police courts, a term which is still used in the United States for magistrate courts. It should be apparent from previous discussion that in the United States the police have no judicial functions. As a point of interest, it should be noted that Germany, a prominent civil law country which is also a federal system, has a criminal procedure process that is more similar to the one in the United States than that of any other civil law country in the world (Liebesny, 1981).

5. The Socialist Law Tradition or Socialist Law Family

It is generally believed that this system originated at the time of the October 1917 revolution in Russia. The system did not become an identifiably different legal tradition until the mid-1930s. Prior to the Russian Revolution, the dominant legal tradition in the Russian Empire and in those other states of Eastern Europe, and other countries such as Cuba that have since adopted socialism, was the civil law tradition. Even though the external form, the internal division, and the system's attitude toward the sources of law differ significantly from the common law tradition, the role of the judiciary and judicial procedure in socialist law is essentially in the civil law mode (Glendon et al., 1982; Zahler, 1989f). The substantive rules of socialist law heavily reflect the principles of Marxism-Leninism, and are inspired by the indigenous culture of the individual countries where it has been adopted (Glendon et al., 1982). The Soviet system is the oldest national legal system within the socialist legal tradition. Its model has since been adopted in different parts of the world, ranging from Eastern Europe to Central and Southeast Asia to the Caribbean region and some parts of Africa.

The socialist criminal procedure system is essentially inquisitorial in nature, but it is not totally devoid of elements that are traditionally associated with the adversarial system. It is most analogous to the court-centered approach in which the judge directs the majority of the questioning and attorneys assist in uncovering the true actions of the accused. The socialist system recognizes the distinctions between criminal and civil law and allows adjudication of related matters at the same time. There is an extensive trial system that contains many of the same elements as civil and common law countries—pre-trial investigation, trial, and sentencing—however, its structure and chronological sequence differ from other systems. For example, socialist judges have available to them the personal background of the accused prior to trial to aid them in determining the guilt or innocence of the alleged offender.

Essentially, the similarities among the civil, common, and socialist law traditions are primarily of form rather than substance (Zahler, 1989b, 1989d, 1989e). Remarkably, the common law tradition has had virtually no impact on the development of socialist law. Although an understanding of the socialist legal tradition is of rising importance in the Western world, the scope of this text does not permit further comparison between this and the common law system of the United States. It must be noted that with the recent international developments in the Soviet block, democratic influences may lead to major reforms in existing legal systems.

Because many of the defendants in need of interpreters in the United States criminal justice system come from civil law countries, we will briefly focus on the major distinctions between these two systems, their assumptions, and procedures. The following sections of this chapter presuppose an understanding of the United States legal system as outlined in Chapters 9 and 10.

6. Comparison of Civil and Common Law Families

The legal systems of the different nations constituting each of these families are not the same, but they do have some elements in common and some elements that differentiate them from the legal systems of other families. It is also true that there are interrelationships between the different legal systems that should not be overlooked. Judges and attorneys, as a case in point, play similar roles in both systems.

It is often said that civil law is shaped by universities and scholars, and that it is a law of principles, whereas common law is shaped by proceduralists and practitioners, and is a law of judges (Glendon et al., 1982; Liebesny, 1981). This explains in part the different legal thinking of jurists in the different families. For example, resolutions of legal problems in civil law countries are guided by general principles, in contrast to common law countries, where they are resolved on a case-by-case basis. This primary difference results in different sources of law and legal authority (Zahler, 1989f). However, the dominant role of legal scholars in civil law countries has slowly diminished so that at present the emerging influence is by way of legislative mandate.

The impact of legal scholarship on English common law, historically, has been negligible. This tradition, originally designed by lawyers and judges, has been changing throughout the years, and the preeminence of judges has suffered considerable diminution in favor of the rising importance of codification and legislation in the legal arena. As a result, both the civil and common law systems are beginning to resemble each other and have interesting interrelationships in the sources and construction of basic laws.

Another important difference between civil and common law systems can be found in the sources of the law (Ehrmann, 1976). In civil law theories, a fundamental distinction is made between primary sources, which are binding on the judge, and secondary sources, sometimes called authorities, which are not. The primary sources in all civil law systems are enacted law and custom, and of the two, the former is vastly more important. Sometimes "general principles of law" are also listed as a primary source. Authorities may have weight when laws in the primary source are absent or incomplete, but their use is neither binding, necessary, nor sufficient as a basis for a judicial decision. Case law and the writings of legal scholars are considered to be secondary sources.

Stare decisis, or the principle of abiding by decided cases and not deviating from those decisions, is almost non-existent in civil law countries, where a judgment is only binding on the parties in the case in which it is pronounced (Glendon et al., 1982). In common law countries judgments pronounced by previous courts are very often binding on all succeeding similar cases. As a consequence of these systemic differences there is, in theory, more predictability and certainty in civil law countries and more flexibility and adaptability in common law countries.

Obviously, in any legal system, whatever a judge has said in earlier disputes is likely to be of interest in later cases with similar facts. The theoretical usefulness of prior case law should not be any less in a legal system where judges do not have to follow earlier decisions than in systems where judges are compelled to follow them. Even when the rules denominating sources of law in a system exclude precedent (**case law**) as a primary source of law, it nonetheless retains value. Precedent is often considered a teaching tool in civil law countries, and can be used before a case arises to instruct how statutory law is most wisely interpreted. In the common law system, precedent is a primary source of law, meaning the prior case does more than simply teach judges something; it exists separately, as law that must be recognized and followed. Failing that, it must be demonstrated how the precedent differs from the case that produced the rule, a process referred to as **distinguishing** cases from each other. Even in the common law system, judges have the latitude to vary from precedent because of new circumstances, changed technology, or even because of the adoption of new attitudes of ways of thinking in the country in question (Zahler, 1989f).

7. Public and Private Law

The fundamental legal distinction in all civil law countries is the difference between public and private law (Zahler, 1989f). Public law is concerned with matters of fundamental social interest, such as constitutional, criminal, and health law, among others. Private law, on the other hand, is designed to give rules and decide cases where the interests of one or more individuals or groups are at stake, for example, commercial, civil, contract, and insurance law. There are overlaps between the public and private law in civil law countries, and the divisions identified here are not absolute. A case in point is family law. In some civil law countries, like Chile, family law began as a private law system. Recently however, there has been an erosion of that system, and there is now a heavy emphasis on public interests and, therefore, a growing influence of public law (Zahler, 1989f).

In common law countries the distinction between private and public law is almost never made except perhaps in scholarly writings. An illustration in the common law tradition is administrative law; it has a mix of both public and private law characteristics (Schwartz, 1984). In contrast, legal scholars consider the bulk of public law to be administrative in civil law countries.

8. Notary Public

A notable distinction between civil and common law systems is the position occupied by the **notary** or **notary public**. The notary public in the civil law system is an important legal figure. In most civil law countries, a notary must be an attorney or have a law degree, and serves three major functions: (a) drafting certain documents such as pre-nuptial agreements and marriage contracts, wills, mortgages, and conveyances; (b) certifying these documents, which then will be admitted in court as true copies (this gives the documents filed by a notary a special evidentiary status in court proceedings); and (c) serving as a depository for the original copies of wills and other similar documents. Part of the uniqueness of the notary's position stems from the fact that the notary is a public official with a state-protected monopoly over many of the above-mentioned functions (Zahler, 1989c).

An attorney will draft a will, for example, and then the original is certified and put on file for life with a notary. There are a limited number of notarial offices established by law, and unlike the court-centered or adversarial lawyer, notaries are expected to be impartial and to instruct and advise equally all parties involved in the transactions they handle as to the laws applicable in their case. Because of the nature of these transactions, the notary often becomes a trusted family legal adviser whose assistance is needed in connection with the property aspects of such major events as marriage, divorce, and death of a family member.

In the United States, the notary public has neither the importance nor the status of a civil law system notary. No special training is required to become a notary public; however, an interested party must obtain a license from the state after proving good standing and character. The sole function of the notary is to attest that the person who signs the document is in fact the person referred to in that document, and that the document in question was signed in the notary's presence. This distinction between the civil law notary public and the notary public in the United States is often unknown to recent immigrants from a civil law system. At times new immigrants, especially those undergoing immigration and naturalization procedures, will naively pay unjustifiably large fees for the services of an unscrupulous notary public. They believe that the notary has rendered competent legal services and that the signed documents stamped with an official seal have a special legal value and are admissible in court.

9. Criminal Process Differences

In common law countries there are three widely held yet erroneous beliefs about criminal procedure in civil law countries: (1) that the accused is presumed guilty until proven innocent; (2) that there is no jury trial; and (3) that the trial is conducted in an inquisitorial or non-adversarial fashion. As a consequence, most people in common law countries believe that the civil law system treats the accused unfairly (Zahler, 1989f).

The first assumption has no basis in fact. By way of illustration, consider the Latin expression *in dubio pro reo* (Zahler, 1989d), which means when in doubt decide in favor of the defendant. This term is a legal equivalent for the concepts of "reasonable doubt" and the "presumption of innocence." This is a common standard in civil law countries, just as the presumption of innocence is an aspect of common law systems.

The second belief is erroneous because in certain systems particular juries do exist; in others, lay judges who participate in mixed courts with professional judges are analogous to the system offering the accused a jury. A lay judge is usually a person who is a recognized member of the community and does not have legal training but is appointed to sit on the bench to help professional judges resolve disputes in their community (Glendon et al., 1982; Zahler, 1989f).

The third misassumption, that the court-centered trial process resembles an inquisition, is also in error, and among legal scholars this approach is but one variation of judicial proceedings in general. Although the structure and progression of the proceeding differs from the adversarial system in the United States, there nonetheless exists an emphasis on the judicial resolution of a dispute that is regulated by governmental, constitutional, and legislative mandates.

Basically, in civil law countries the criminal justice process can be clearly divided into two phases: summary and plenary proceedings—*sumario* and *plenario* in Spanish-speaking countries (Mayagoitia, 1976; Zahler, 1989d). The first phase of a criminal proceeding is an extensive pre-trial investigation, conducted in some countries by the public prosecutor and in others by a judge, often called the examining magistrate. In Spanish-speaking countries this official is known as the *juez instructor* or *juez de instrucción* (Zahler, 1989d). Either the judge or the public prosecutor decides whether there is sufficient evidence to warrant charges. After interrogating the witnesses, collecting other evidence, and questioning the suspect, the charges are filed. Under modern codes of criminal procedure in some countries, the accused has the right to be represented or assisted by counsel during the interrogation and the right to remain silent.

If the examining magistrate or prosecutor determines there is reason to do so (in common law countries this would be called probable cause), the file compiled during the preliminary investigation is forwarded to the criminal court. This single phase, in Spanish-speaking civil law countries like Spain and most of the Latin American countries, is called *sumario* (Zahler, 1989d). The phase ends with a decision, similar to one made by common law judges in state courts after a preliminary hearing, to dismiss the case or bind the defendant over to the second part of the proceeding, called *plenario* (Zahler, 1989d). In Mexico, however, there are three distinct phases: the pre-trial investigation, the procedures conducted by and before the examining magistrate (also called *sumarios*) and, if the case continues to its trial phase, the *plenario*.

If the case is dismissed at the end of the investigatory phase, the dismissal (*sobreseimiento*) can be temporary or final (Zahler, 1989d). It is final if the judge is fully convinced that the accused has not committed the offense charged; it is temporary when there is doubt as to the guilt of the accused but not sufficient proof to justify continuing prosecution. The prosecution may then reopen or refile the complaint with new evidence within a five-year period, otherwise the temporary *sobreseimiento* becomes final. However, the decision is susceptible to appeal by either party.

In serious matters, the accused in civil law countries is usually held in preventive custody pending trial. Bail is usually available in common law countries as a matter of right under the Eighth Amendment, whereas in civil law countries it is offered to the defendant by the court as a matter of leniency. In some civil law countries, bail is a right for certain minor offenses not punishable by more than short jail time, fine, probation, or any combination thereof. In the United States federal court system, the notion of bail as a right has changed significantly since the enactment of the Comprehensive Crime Control Act of 1984, Chapter I, which provides for new concepts that make "permissible" the denial of bail in serious offense for federal crimes (see Bail, in Chapter 10).

During the trial in civil law systems, the presiding judge takes the adversarial lead in examining the witnesses and accused. Two major differences between these systems are that the judge is a less passive arbiter between the parties, and the prosecutor is a less partisan adversary to the defendant. This approach has been aptly termed the court-centered or "inquisitorial" approach. Another interesting feature of criminal procedure in the civil law system is the role accorded the victim. In some countries, if the same wrongful act gives rise to both criminal and civil liability, the injured person is permitted to intervene directly in the criminal action rather than being obligated to bring a separate civil suit (Glendon et al., 1982). If the victim chooses to become a party to the criminal suit and is successful, the court may order civil damages to be paid to the victim at the conclusion of the proceedings. It is worthwhile to mention that in West Germany and some other countries, if there is probable cause to believe that the defendant has committed a serious offense, the prosecutor has no discretion and cannot decide against prosecution and, consequently, has no power or authority to enter into a plea bargain.

Most civil law countries have both private and public prosecutors, as does England. Private prosecutors are employed by citizens who wish to file a lawsuit, for example, to punish an offender for forging the citizen's name on a check. In the common law system, however, the victim is a mere witness, also called the complaining witness, which is a very passive role. In common law countries the state or federal government becomes the aggrieved party and proceeds against the offender using the witness as part of its proof. In a separate and often later civil case, the victim may bring an independent action for monetary compensation and may use a criminal conviction as part of the evidence, not necessarily unqualified, of injury.

The second stage of the civil law criminal procedure is analogous to the criminal trial or the trial proper in the common law tradition. There are several differences between the procedures in the civil and common law systems. In the latter, the defendant has the right to full discovery and can use motions within wide yet discretionary bounds. In the former, there is no real "trial" in the common law sense of a single culminating event. Rather a continuous series of meetings, hearings, and written communications take place during which evidence is introduced, testimony is taken, and motions are made and decided. Everything, in essence, is reduced to writing, including witness testimony that is taken under oath and under penalty of perjury. The impeachment of witnesses and of judges is also possible in civil law countries, although the rules on the impeachment of judges are somewhat more limited—it may be done only once. This phase is essentially an evidence-gathering period (Glendon et al., 1982).

Questions asked of a witness may be objected to in civil law countries, just as in common law countries. Among the more important substantive differences in the two systems is the concept of hearsay. As discussed earlier, in a common law system anything that is said out of court by persons other than the witness testifying in court is objectionable as hearsay. In civil law countries, however, witnesses may testify to anything they directly heard or observed out of court. Hearsay in the civil law system is reserved for statements told to the witness by a second source—who told the witness what they heard or saw a third person do—but which the witness in court did not have an opportunity to see or hear directly. The statement, "He told me that he killed the bank guard" would be admissible, whereas the statement, "His girlfriend told me that he told her he had killed the bank guard" would not.

Another important difference between the two systems is the fact that under the civil law tradition neither the defendant nor the immediate family may testify under oath. This practice is adhered to in order to avoid the anguish of being forced to choose between testifying against oneself or committing a perjury and having close relatives make the same choices. Although it is said that there is no right against self-incrimination in civil law countries, the practice of not allowing the defendant to testify under oath for all intents and purpose serves the same function. In public law the defendant may not do what is not permitted, therefore waiver of the right to not testify is not allowed. However, the defendant may be questioned by the court as the subject of the investigation.

Confessions are admissions of guilt and admissions are voluntary statements about facts adduced by the opposing party without an admission of guilt; both concepts exist in civil and common law countries. However, in a civil law country, criminal conviction cannot be based on a confession alone without proving supporting circumstances, whereas in a common law country a confession alone is enough to bring a conviction. The concepts of probable cause—*motivo fundado, motivo plausible,* or *prueba semi-plena* in Argentina, meaning half evidence (Zahler, 1989d)—and direct and circumstantial evidence, are similar to the common law concepts and also exist in most civil law systems.

The general rule in civil law countries is that in the course of a criminal proceeding the judge or jury is only permitted to consider that which is on the record. Matters not in the record are non-existent. However, there is a trend toward permitting judges and jurors to listen to their "inner convictions" sustained by the notion of *in dubio pro reo.* In other words, if there is no abiding conviction in the minds of the judge or jurors, which at its heart means that they are not convinced beyond a reasonable doubt of the defendant's guilt, they must rule in his or her favor because the presumption of innocence has not been overcome. This, of course, is the exact parallel to the standard of proof required in criminal law in common law countries.

The composition of the criminal court varies from country to country, and even within the same country. Usually one to three professional judges sit with a number of lay judges on the bench. Both the professional and lay judges participate in decisions on all factual and legal issues relating to the determination of guilt and sentencing. Recall that in the common law system the jury is the ultimate trier of fact, whereas the judge determines legal issues and imposes sentences. As an exception, in Spain and in other Latin American countries, there is only one judge throughout the second phase of the criminal procedure, whereas in Germany, Austria, and some other European countries that belong to the civil law system, the court has the standard composition of one to three professional judges and a number of lay judges (Glendon et al., 1982).

After the plenary or trial phase, judgments of the criminal and civil trial courts may as a general rule be appealed to an intermediary court. In criminal cases, the prosecution as well as the defense has the right to appeal. Unlike a common law appeal of a trial court's decision, the proceeding in this intermediate court may involve a full review *de novo* of the facts as well as of the law in the case. The panel of appellate judges initially will make its independent determination of the facts on the basis of the original record. In addition, the appellate court may question the witnesses again, or even take new evidence or request expert opinions. A party dissatisfied with the results of the appeal may seek review by the highest court, which, like a common law appellate court, in theory considers only questions of law. Some of these high courts follow the French system of *cassation,* while others follow the West German system of "revision" (Liebesny, 1981). **Cassation** means invalidation of a decision because there has been a procedural or substantive violation of law (Zahler, 1989d); **revision,** on the other hand, means review or examination for purposes of possible correction of the sentence. The latter system is practiced in Austria and Switzerland (Liebesny, 1981).

In some civil law countries appellate procedure in criminal cases does not follow the above pattern of *de novo* review. In Germany, for example, decisions of the trial court in cases of serious crimes are subject to appeal only on points of law, and such appeals are not heard by intermediate courts but by a court of last resort. This is true in the highest German court on the federal level, the *Bundesgericht* (Liebesny, 1981), which is similar to the United States Supreme Court. The right to appeal *de novo* does exist, however, for minor criminal offenses which are first heard before a single judge or a local court. In most civil law countries, the highest court is called the supreme court, although there are some exceptions. In France, for example, it is called *Cour de Cassation* (Zahler, 1989d).

Unit 3
Utilization of Interpreter Services

Chapter 12

The Role of the Court Interpreter in the United States Legal System

Unit 1 has given the reader a general introduction to the field of court interpreting, and Unit 2 to the criminal justice process in the United States. Unit 3 is designed to broaden the reader's understanding of the legal underpinnings for the use of interpreters in the United States, the proper use of interpreters in the criminal justice process, and the legal and philosophical rationales for the particular modes and settings that are inherent to the interpreting task. This chapter begins with a definition of the role of the court interpreter, and proceeds to offer the legal rationale for the use of interpreters in the United States legal system, especially in relation to the guarantees provided in the Fourth, Fifth, Sixth, Eighth, and Fourteenth Amendments. The still controversial legal status of court interpreters is also considered in this chapter.

1. The Court Interpreter Defined

An interpreter is a bilingual person who has the duty to act as the medium between the court and the non-English-speaking person. According to Gonzalez (1986), the interpreter is required

> to transfer all of the meaning he or she hears from the source language into the target language, not editing, summarizing, adding meaning, or omitting. The court interpreter is required to transfer the message into the other language exactly, or as close to exactly, as originally spoken. (p. 5)

This task demands conserving the language level, style, tone, and intent of the speaker. Specifically, the court interpreter is a language mediator who through interpretation allows the defendant to be linguistically and cognitively present in a legal setting. Without an interpreter it would be impossible for a non-English-speaking witness or defendant to "be present" in the courtroom, to understand what is happening, or to testify or aid in his or her own defense. Furthermore, without an interpreter the non-English-speaking defendant could not properly utilize an attorney to prepare his or her defense. Essentially, the defendant would be tried and convicted in a United States courtroom without being offered the opportunity to hear and speak (*Arizona v. Natividad*, 1974; Chang & Araujo, 1975; *United States ex rel. Negron v. New York*, 1970).

The proper role of the interpreter is to place the non-English speaker, as closely as is linguistically possible, in the same situation as an English speaker in a legal setting. In doing so the interpreter does not give any advantage or disadvantage to the non-English-speaking witness or defendant. In past practice, the interpreter was often expected to explain the legal process, procedure, and terminology, as well as to fill out legal documents for the non-English speaker. To accept this role was undeniably to render legal services, and in so doing placed the interpreter in a legal mine field.

Interpreters are not practicing attorneys, nor do they possess any specialized training—beyond a superficial understanding of legal procedure and terminology—which would qualify them to offer non-English speakers legal services. Moreover, there are often legal consequences associated with advising an alleged offender to take a certain plea, explaining what kind of sentence the person is to receive or how to fill out a form which will affect eligibility for bail. Unfortunately, in some courts, interpreters are regularly called upon to render these services, and if they comply, they do so without legal training, access to an offender's complete legal history, or any understanding of the ramifications of their actions (Zahler, 1989a).

A clear understanding of the court interpreter's role as a linguistic conduit through which all parties may understand one another will prevent this invalid encroachment upon the legal responsibilities of counsel. The interpreter becomes a tool of justice, allowing the process to work for non-English speakers just as it works for English speakers. More importantly, the interpreter allows the court to communicate with non-English-speaking witnesses and defendants and helps the adversary process take its natural course: to produce evidence which would tend to prove or disprove the charges lodged against the defendant by the state or federal government.

2. Rationales for the Use of Interpreters in the United States Legal System

The United States legal system is based upon the Constitution and all of the substantive and due process guarantees that it provides (Carr, 1989; Furcolo, 1977; Pritchett, 1977). A mainstay of the United States common law tradition has been the stringent protection of those individual rights within the judicial process. The strong belief that government should not intrude upon the privacy of the individual derives from the historical struggle to overcome the injustices suffered during the British domination of the Colonies. As was mentioned in Unit 1 of this volume, the civil rights era evoked sharp concern that this protection be extended to *all* individuals in the legal process, including the language-handicapped. During this era gross violations of the legal protections guaranteed in the Constitution were common, and a movement to offer equal protections for the language-handicapped developed at the state level (Gonzalez, 1986). Through construction of the supremacy clause at the federal level, Fourteenth Amendment guarantees of due process and equal protection of the law were extended to the language-handicapped with passage of Public Law 95-539, the Court Interpreters Act of 1978.

The innovation which helped to guarantee Fourth, Fifth, Sixth, and Eighth Amendment rights for non-English speakers was the mandated use of court interpreters. To understand how the court interpreter specifically helps to protect these guarantees requires, first, an analysis of the constitutional rights and how they are defined and implemented, and second, an extrapolation of the direct role that a court interpreter can play in providing these rights.

2.1. The Fourth Amendment

The Fourth Amendment (see Unit 2, Chapter 9) right of individuals to be secure against unreasonable governmental search and seizure is protected by the requirement of the issuance of arrest and search warrants based upon probable cause (Carr, 1989; Waltz, 1983). The warrant must be supported by an oath that the underlying cause is based on verifiable facts. An additional protection is added with the requisite that warrants expressly describe the places to be searched and the persons or things to be seized (Kamisar et al., 1986). Many of the statements or facts which police offer magistrates in order to obtain warrants are based upon investigative work involving the gathering of non-English-language documents that must be translated, the transcription and translation of non-English-language audiotape recordings, and the use of bilingual agents to engage in undercover operations.

If a court interpreter is not used to transcribe and translate the information, the resulting warrants may be replete with linguistic inaccuracies. As a result, a defense attorney may argue that the arrest or search warrant has not been properly obtained. Later, in court, the warrants may be found to be tainted or inaccurate, and the entire basis of the case will be invalidated and the charges dismissed (Zahler, 1989a).

Use of court interpreters, especially certified court interpreters, will help police agencies accurately assess the evidence gathered to procure warrants. As a result, there will be a greater likelihood of arresting and proceeding against the correct offender. The courts, in turn, will be able to rely on the information that forms the basis of the warrants, and there will be a more efficient use of limited law enforcement and judicial resources. Furthermore, if certified court interpreters are used, the criminal justice process will not become a battle of linguistic experts, and neither prosecution nor defense attorneys will feel compelled to lodge appeals based on bad translations or poor interpretation.

2.2. The Fifth Amendment

The Fifth Amendment also provides individuals with protections against illegal detention and having to unnecessarily stand trial by requiring the government to put forth an information, complaint, or indictment by a grand jury. During the period following the first arraignment or initial appearance, the magistrate must determine whether the government is justified in further detaining the individual (Carr, 1989; Pritchett, 1977; Waltz, 1983). It is during this initial proceeding that the interpreter can truly bridge the gap between the non-English speaker and the court by ensuring that the defendant understands the charges in the information, complaint, or indictment. The interpreter aids the court in determining whether the non-English speaker is being subjected to additional charges for the same offense, which would allow the individual to assert the double jeopardy plea (Carr, 1989), and whether there is a right to bail (Zahler, 1989b) or the defendant is in need of counsel (Pritchett, 1977).

It is an accepted legal precept that, theoretically, every act a person commits is testimony against himself and can be used as evidence in a court of law. The English-speaking individual whose actions and statements are challenged may speak for himself or communicate directly with his attorney in an attempt to counter the facts and charges lodged against him. The English-speaking individual has the ability to testify on his own behalf; in the same way, because he has the ability to comprehend the proceedings, the English-speaking defendant may also choose not to testify. Without a court interpreter, the non-English speaker is not only unable to explain his acts, but is powerless to testify on his own behalf if he so chooses. Without a court interpreter the non-English speaker is forced to "testify" against himself when not given the opportunity to clarify his actions. Thus, the use of certified court interpreters enables the non-English speaker to truly exercise his rights, the same rights that an English speaker, by virtue of understanding and speaking English, can claim.

Essentially, the alleged offender is guaranteed that he or she will not be deprived of "life, liberty or property," without due process of law according to the Fourteenth Amendment. Due process has come to mean that the defendant will have a fair hearing before an impartial jury of peers, or before a judge in a bench trial. In order to present a defense, the non-English-speaking defendant must have access to the same procedural rights as an English speaker. This requires that he be able to avail himself of all the rights guaranteed by other constitutional amendments.

2.3. The Sixth Amendment

The Sixth Amendment right to counsel is of such importance to the individual charged with a crime that even the offering of bilingual counsel in lieu of an interpreter would in effect be a violation of due process. The attorney has the duty and responsibility of providing the most competent legal services possible to clients; if the attorney is engaged in delivering interpreting services as well, legal and ethical responsibilities to the client cannot be met. The complexity of legal process and procedure would make a trial without an attorney tantamount to a trial without a defense (Carr, 1989; *Jara v. Municipal Court,* 1978; Pritchett, 1977). Therefore, providing the defendant with a competent court interpreter, as well as counsel, guarantees adequate legal assistance.

The right to a speedy trial, of course, protects against prolonged detention by the government without cause (Pritchett, 1977; Speedy Trial Act, 1974). The failure of a court to provide an interpreter, or the requirement that a non-English-speaking defendant be required to wait until an interpreter is available, may infringe upon the right to a speedy trial. Furthermore, if the defendant cannot understand counsel, the right of the government to hold the defendant lessens as time elapses during the search for a competent interpreter. Either the government must eventually let the defendant go, or the non-English speaker is prejudiced in presenting a defense. Neither alternative is acceptable, and either the public sensibilities, or the Constitution is affronted, or both.

The jury trial, guaranteed by the Sixth Amendment, is also a procedural device used to ensure that the government is not acting outside the wishes of those it governs; it thus reifies the role of law and the involvement of the public. Most importantly, the courts have long held that in order to present a defense the defendant must be informed of the nature and cause of the accusation (Carr, 1989; Pritchett, 1977). In the case of a language-handicapped individual who is charged with a crime, an interpreter facilitates the exercise of Sixth Amendment rights by enabling the defendant to confront adverse witnesses, to subpoena defense witnesses, and to assist communication with his or her attorney in calling witnesses and cross-examining the prosecution's witnesses (Carr, 1989; Pritchett, 1977).

Another Sixth Amendment clause that is crucial to the criminal justice process is the right of the defendant to be informed of and to understand the nature of the charges lodged. Achieving this minimal constitutional standard would be impossible without an interpreter. If a person is barred from comprehending the proceedings because of the lack of an interpreter, it violates our sense of justice and fair play which distinguishes our system of jurisprudence. Similar arguments have been advanced and accepted in the area of mental health law when a defendant's competency to stand trial or sanity at the time of the crime is an issue (Wexler, 1990). The rationale behind these arguments has not been that the mentally incompetent defendant was without knowledge of the facts of the alleged crime, but rather that he or she was unable to communicate with his or her attorney in order to participate in his own defense (*Dusky v. United States*, 1960).

The interpreter allows the defendant to comprehend the crime with which he or she has been publicly charged. When the court provides an interpreter, it erects a cultural and linguistic bridge whereby the non-English speaker has the ability to communicate with counsel and the court, to participate in his own defense, to understand the charges and any testimony against him, and to communicate at crucial points with counsel (Carr, 1989; Pritchett, 1977; Zahler, 1989b).

2.4. The Eighth Amendment

The court interpreter also allows the defendant to claim the Eighth Amendment right to be released on reasonable bail—by aiding the court in assessing the defendant's eligibility for release—and the right against cruel and unusual punishment at the time of sentencing—by guaranteeing that the court has accurate information on which to base sentencing decisions (Carr, 1989; Pritchett, 1977). In the final analysis, individuals who appear before the court in the United States should have these basic constitutional guarantees protected; for non-English speakers this protection is easily offered by the utilization of court interpreters for the court's language service needs. As stated in the Fourteenth Amendment of the United States Constitution, "no **person** [emphasis added] shall be deprived of life, liberty or property without due process of law." Analogous to the Fifth Amendment rights, this reiteration of individual rights was made to prevent infringement by the states of guarantees made to every individual under the Constitution.

3. Legal Status of the Court Interpreter

The status of the court interpreter in the legal system is still controversial. What is the interpreter when functioning in the courtroom? Is the interpreter an expert witness available to the court throughout the proceedings, or an officer of the court? The interpreter is perhaps the only "officer of the court" who is rendering "expert" services, i.e., the interpretation of a source language into a target language. This rare conjunction of roles has given rise to much legal debate. Independent of the debate, there are several rules which apply to court interpreters, such as Rule 604, *Federal Criminal Code and Rules* (1989).

This rule, which has been adopted in most states, provides that: "An interpreter is subject to the provisions of these rules relating to qualifications as an expert and the administration of an oath or affirmation to make a true translation." Depending upon how this rule is read, the interpreter *may* or *must* be considered as an expert witness. The language of Rule 604 is not clear as to the determination of the legal status of the court interpreter, specifically, whether the interpreter is an expert witness at the start of proceedings, or only if there is a challenge to an interpretation. Rather than deciding the issue, this rule refers to other federal rules of evidence (Federal Criminal Code, 1989); specifically, it implies that Rule 702 applies, which reads:

> Testimony of Expert: If scientific, technical, or other specialized knowledge will assist the trier of fact to understand the evidence or to determine a fact in issue, a witness qualified as an expert by knowledge, skill, experience, and training, or education, may testify thereto in the form of an opinion or otherwise.

The language of this rule indicates that the court interpreter is assisting the trier of fact to understand portions of the evidence consisting of testimony given in a language other than English. If this rule is invoked, the court interpreter is then treated just as any other expert witness called by the court.

Counsel or the court has the right to submit the court interpreter to a foundational *voir dire,* asking the court interpreter about professional background. This usually means the general background, including education, degrees, certifications, and employment history. They may also ask about the expert's specific background which includes the special training related to the issue at hand, any publications, or particular work experience that directly bears upon the issue about which the interpreter is testifying (Zahler, 1989c). The *voir dire* of a court interpreter places special emphasis on the way the target language was acquired, how long the interpreter has worked in court, and any exceptional qualifications possessed. Court interpreters will probably be asked to indicate whether they hold a federal, state, or county certification as an important element for judging competency. See Unit 8, Chapters 36 and 37 for further information on federal and state certification.

Interpreters are in a special position because they can be considered both experts and officers of the court at the same time. Officers of the court or court attachés are broad terms applicable to employees who work in the courtroom, judge's chambers, or offices belonging to a specific court. Employees who are officers of the court include the clerk of court, deputy clerks, courtroom deputies, law clerks, court stenographers or recorders, and secretaries. Upon entrance to the profession, attorneys and judges are administered oaths which make them officers of the court, regardless of whether they are working in a court or not. If court interpreters are deemed to be officers of the court, they must fulfill all the duties and responsibilities associated with that position (Zahler, 1989b).

Officers of the court have the duty to comport themselves in a dignified manner in all interactions with judges, counsel, other court officers, defendants, and witnesses (see Unit 8, Chapter 35). One responsibility officers have is that they must reveal anything that could affect their fairness and impartiality. Above all, the court officer is sworn to uphold the truth and never to perpetrate a fraud upon the court. Officers must also be candid with the court at all times. Court officers must never accept payment for services other than by the court or pertinent agencies. Typically, under this same oath officers of the court are sworn to uphold the laws and the Constitution of the United States. The underlying rationale for officers of the court to comply with these rules is to uphold the reputation and credibility of the court as an impartial place where justice can be imparted fairly.

Regardless of whether the court interpreter is considered an expert witness or an officer of the court, adoption of this attitude and compliance with these rules of behavior are required. Even contract interpreters should abide with all ethical and legal rules when they serve the courts, without regard to how often they are retained (Zahler, 1989a). These rules apply along with any and all professional codes of behavior that govern interpreters.

The legal status of court interpreters is a gray area because interpreters are employees who are undoubtedly officers of the court; yet, because of Federal Rules 604 and 702 and similar provisions in state courts, they can be challenged as can any expert witness. Returning to the focal legal issue, when specifically during the legal process does the court interpreter become an expert witness and how should the court proceed? There are several approaches to this issue. One is to accept the common practice of treating the interpreter as an officer of the court until such time as there is a challenge to any interpretation; then the interpreter switches roles and becomes an expert witness. Challenging counsel may then proceed with a foundational *voir dire* and offer a different version of the interpretation in dispute.

A second approach is to appoint the interpreter as the court's expert for the day, or for as long as the interpreter works on the case. This appointed court interpreter will then be presumed to have competence in the languages being used. For purposes of judicial economy, it would be possible for counsel to dispense with or reserve for later the administration of the foundational *voir dire*, and the interpreter as the court's expert. By appointing the court interpreter as an expert at the beginning of the proceedings, this status is recorded in the transcript, and the court as well as counsel can challenge the interpreter's expertise if problems arise later in the trial.

Another possibility for the courts to consider in determining linguistic issues is to treat the interpreter as a court officer, accept his or her rendition, and allow challenging counsel to preserve the issue for appeal. This procedure may be the only one available to courts that operate with but a single interpreter. Yet another possibility is if there are two or more interpreters in the courtroom, the judge, out of the hearing of the jury, may ask the second interpreter's opinion. If both court interpreters' opinions of the interpretation coincide, the judge can declare that the challenged interpretation stands. If it differs, however, then a third interpreter, such as a supervisory interpreter, should be brought in whose opinion can aid the judge in making a decision. In any event, no matter which solution is adopted, the practical effect is to preserve the matter on record for purposes of appeal.

Beyond the question of the legal status of the court interpreter is how the actual challenge to the interpretation should proceed. The Administrative Office of the United States Courts (1988) in draft regulations of the Court Interpreter Amendments Act tentatively recommended the following procedure for challenges to interpretation:

(a) If a party or counsel to a proceeding concludes that an interpreter has made a mistake in interpretation that might materially alter the understanding of the words or phrases interpreted, they shall call the matter to the attention of the presiding judicial officer. The presiding judicial officer shall conduct an inquiry out of the hearing of the jury, if any, as to the materiality of the alleged error. If the presiding judicial officer finds that the error might affect the understanding of the finder of fact, they shall:

(1) request that the question and answer at issue be read back;

(2) obtain from the challenger a specification of the alleged error and the interpretation advanced by the challenger as the correct interpretation of the challenged material; and

(3) inquire of the interpreter if the alternative proposed by the challenger is acceptable to the interpreter.

(b) If the dispute cannot be resolved by agreement, the presiding judicial officer shall decide after hearing both sides of the question which interpretation is the proper one under the circumstances. In making such determination, the version offered by the assigned interpreter shall be presumed correct, and the burden of proof shall be upon the party or counsel challenging the interpreter. (pp. 8-9)

It was apparent that the Administrative Office in these regulations avoided the issue of determining whether the interpreter is an expert or an officer of the court. It chose instead to adopt the method of presumption of expertise, thereby placing the burden of proving that the court interpreter is in error on the challenging party. There was, nonetheless, an implicit assumption that the court interpreter was an expert.

Although these regulations did not survive after the first draft, in accordance with the Court Interpreter Amendments Act of 1988, interim regulations have been issued by the Administrative Office of the United States Courts (1989b). Subsection 16 of the regulations states that, "unless stipulated by all parties, the interpreter shall be **qualified as an expert** [emphasis added] in accordance with Rule 604 of the Federal Rules of Evidence." It is now clear that the federal courts have chosen to formalize the role of interpreter as an expert in the proceedings.

This choice offers defendants the maximum protections: (1) they may challenge the interpreter's knowledge base; (2) preserve language issues on the record for purposes of appeal; and (3) in extreme instances seek to replace an interpreter whose abilities are consistently poor. The decision to follow the federal rules of evidence also frees the court to "presume" the competence of the court-appointed interpreter. This presumption, which at first glance seems to prejudice the defendant, in actuality serves many purposes including granting the defendant a speedy trial; it allows courts to proceed with trials without lengthy *voir dire* examinations, and it renders moot the issue of "apparent bias" by making the interpreter **the court's expert** rather than the defendant's or state's expert. Because it strikes such a fine balance of interests, it is recommended as the preferred method when courts are confronted with resolving this issue.

Chapter 13

The Use of Interpreters at Specific Stages of the Criminal Legal Process

The use of interpreters in the criminal justice process is often an impromptu procedure following legal customs that have evolved without planning and with no understanding of the interpreter's role. Often there are no guidelines or rationale to indicate whether a court interpreter at the witness stand is to utilize the consecutive or simultaneous mode of interpretation. This chapter specifically addresses the question of when an interpreter should be used, how many interpreters are needed to carry out the tasks, and which legal rights are protected by their use. This chapter also compares and contrasts the use of consecutive and simultaneous interpretation in the legal setting, and recommends the appropriate mode that the interpreter should use in each setting to conserve and deliver a legal equivalent of the language.

1. Pros and Cons of Consecutive Interpretation (CI) and Simultaneous Interpretation (SI) in the Judicial Setting

In deciding whether to use the consecutive or the simultaneous mode of interpreting in the judicial setting, interpreters and the users of interpreter service must recognize the impact of these modes on the administration of justice. The most important consideration is the conservation of meaning and protection of the record. Current thinking in the field of judicial interpreting leans toward the use of CI when testimony or statements by non-English speakers are interpreted into English for the record, and SI when the proceeding is taking place in English and needs to be interpreted for the benefit of non-English speakers. At times, however, judges or attorneys will decide to deviate from this pattern for reasons of expediency, such as to enhance understanding, to accommodate a hearing-impaired defendant, or for other reasons.

The advent of specialized equipment has made simultaneous interpreting more prevalent. Grusky (1988) reports that such equipment is now in regular use in some Los Angeles courts. She points out the advantages of using SI for witness testimony and concludes that it is preferable to use this mode at the witness stand:

> It saves valuable court time. As soon as counsel finishes asking a question, the witness's answer is forthcoming. It is more accurate than relying on the interpreter retaining long passages of oftentimes disjointed information, as is needed for

consecutive interpreting. This method makes it unnecessary for the interpreter to request that a question be repeated. Everyone wearing a headset can hear the witness's answer clearly, in spite of sometimes unfavorable courtroom acoustics. Interpreter fatigue is kept at a minimum, as the tension of trying to accurately retain long passages is reduced. The result is higher-quality interpretation. (p. 13)

However, this is a short-sighted examination that does not take into account the requirements of conservation, legal equivalence, or the research of the shortcomings of simultaneous interpretation.

The use of SI equipment also makes it possible to use a single interpreter in multiple-defendant cases, although interpreters still should work in teams to prevent fatigue and to enable defendants to confer with counsel (the state of California requires a separate interpreter for each defendant in order to guarantee this right). In some jurisdictions, precedent mandates certain modes of interpretation, making its use a legal requirement, and the interpreter should follow the law in these matters at all times. It is urged, however, that judges, counsel, and interpreters adopt the preferred mode whenever possible.

The first point that is always made about SI, whether it is used for witness testimony or for proceedings, is that it saves time. With the crowded court calendars that are the norm in every part of this country, time is indeed a major consideration. For example, imagine how cumbersome it would be for everyone to stop after every sentence for the defendant to be given a consecutive interpretation during a preliminary hearing, which is a practice a competent interpreter would not engage in. A competent interpreter can give the defendant a precise consecutive version of what is being said during such a proceeding, permitting the proceeding to continue as usual, undisturbed by the interpretation process. Even if time is of the essence and another mode seems more attractive, the preferred mode should be used.

In the past, summary interpretation (informing the defendant of the gist of testimony or arguments at the trial) was occasionally provided when interpreters were untrained non-professionals who were unable to keep up with the rapid pace of courtroom discourse; and, therefore, this mode is not recommended for use during witness testimony into either language.

The question of accuracy as an advantage of SI is far less clear-cut. Many interpreters (Seleskovitch, 1978a; Weber, 1984) contend that CI is preferred over SI when a high degree of accuracy is required. The main reason for this assertion is that the interpreter has heard the entire message before having to interpret it, and thus has the benefit of "thought-wholeness." The interpreter has time to organize the target language (TL) version and put it in proper form, correctly applying all the rules of grammar, style, and syntax in the TL, so there is less likelihood of awkward constructions or false cognates. This also allows more time to search long-term memory for the proper terminology without losing any of the source language (SL) input. In addition, the interpreter has the opportunity to take notes, and to consult those notes, and even a dictionary should it be necessary, before rendering the TL version. And, finally, the other parties involved have more time to organize their thoughts while the interpreter is at work, so they can formulate their questions and answers more concisely. In that regard, CI may actually save time.

In CI interpreters have more control over the situation: They can clarify ambiguities, ask for repetitions, or determine the meaning of problem terms. Moreover, they can see the reactions of the audience; they can see when the audience does not understand something, and they can adjust their interpretation accordingly (speaking more loudly, for example, correcting their own errors, or making different word choices, as long as they remain true to the register and content of the original). Finally, in CI interpreters may have the witness pause periodically so that they can intervene and interpret segments of lengthy testimony, thereby ensuring the utmost accuracy. This practice should be kept to a minimum, however, because of the negative impact it has on witness credibility. Interpreters practicing SI have less control over the situation; they have less rapport with the individual they are interpreting for, and are less able to monitor themselves for errors. Thus, there is greater potential for mistakes to be made in SI, and very little time to correct them.

Another advantage of CI is that it enables the judge and jury to assess the verbal and non-verbal behavior of the witness, which is particularly important for their evaluation on the issue of credibility. When SI is performed, everyone must focus on the interpreter, and important cues from the witness are missed. Moreover, because everyone in the room can hear both the SL and the TL versions, any inadvertent mistakes made by the interpreter may be caught by other bilingual individuals, attorneys, the judge, or even the witness who knows some English. This adds to the stress under which the interpreter is operating, of course, but it does make for greater accuracy, and a true professional appreciates the opportunity to correct legitimate errors.

The fatigue factor mentioned by Grusky (1988) is a significant consideration. Although CI looks simple, it is very taxing mentally. Interpreters are under a great deal of pressure to retain every single element of the SL message, and though their powers of recall can be supplemented by taking notes, they must rely primarily on their memory. If they ask for a repetition, the witness may not give the same answer the second time, and vital testimony may be lost. SI can also be very taxing if it is performed for long periods of time. Regardless of the mode of interpreting they are performing, interpreters should work in teams and spell each other periodically to prevent fatigue.

Another disadvantage of CI is that people are sometimes impatient and do not wait for the interpreter to complete the rendition. This happens when a witness who knows some English answers the question without waiting for the interpretation, or when an attorney picks up a few words of the witness's answer and launches right in to the follow-up question without waiting for the answer to be interpreted for the record. A great deal of misunderstanding and backtracking can result from this tendency. Moreover, there is no record of exactly what was said. Whenever a witness testifies through an interpreter, the court should adopt the instructions recommended in Unit 8, Chapter 34, Section 4.4, to make the parties aware of this potential problem and to protect the record.

During the examination of witnesses, it is standard practice for interpreters to use CI to interpret questions and switch to SI when objections arise. The problem with this procedure is that attorneys rarely wait until the question has been fully interpreted before beginning their objections. The interpreter does not have an opportunity to interpret the question before the objection to that question, and the witness may be confused.

There are two more reasons for choosing this mode: (1) It is a general rule in the courtroom that only one person speaks aloud at a time. This not only contributes to an orderly discussion, but also solves a very practical problem for the court reporter, whose duty it is to record every word uttered. If more than one person is speaking at once, the task for the court reporter is greatly complicated. (2) More importantly, defendants sitting at counsel table without an interpreter by their side now still have the right to hear both the question and the answer in their own language. The interpreter's CI of the questions and answers at the stand should be in a loud and clear voice so that all in the courtroom, including the defendant, may hear the complete interpretation. Not only is the defendant's right to hear the testimony important, but of course the English rendition is being entered into the record and must be well articulated so that there is no question or ambiguity in the minds of the judge, jury, legal counsel, audience, or the court reporter.

If the interpreter utilizes the simultaneous mode of interpretation, the interpreter will, of necessity, be speaking at the same time as another speaker and, even if whispering into the ear of the witness, will deprive the defendant of the opportunity to hear the question posed by the prosecution. In some courts that are equipped with an electronic system for simultaneous interpretation, testimony is interpreted in that mode. However, for the above articulated reasons, it is recommended that this practice not be adopted. A competent, experienced interpreter should be able to interpret in any mode and to solve the difficulties mentioned. As stated at the beginning of this discussion, the primary concerns should always be conservation of meaning, rendering of a legal equivalent, and the protection of the record.

The following sections are a chronological presentation of the interpreter at each stage of the criminal procedure process. Recommendations for the use of CI and SI during specific court proceedings and the legal rationales for their preference are also presented.

2. Arrest

Ideally, an interpreter should be present at every stage of the criminal justice process, from arrest through final release. In practice, however, there is almost never an interpreter present at the arrest. Problems may arise from this practice: often the arrestee does not understand the Miranda warnings, believing instead that he or she must consent to a custodial interrogation without having an attorney present, or must waive his or her rights. Mirandas are rules developed pursuant to judicial decision which, like the right to an interpreter, are important safeguards of constitutional guarantees. For example, many police officers say in Spanish to the arrestee, *Si Ud. no puede afrontar un abogado, la corte le va a dar uno sin pago.* In English this rendition may mean: "If you cannot confront an attorney, the court will give you one without payment." As can be seen, the police officer's rendition does not preserve the intent of the Miranda warning: "If you cannot afford an attorney, the court will appoint one to assist you at no cost." If there is doubt that the most important admonition referring to the waiver of the defendant's Miranda rights was given properly, the defense will file a suppression motion that, if granted, culminates in the dismissal of the entire case.

After giving the Miranda rights, the officer asks, "Do you waive the rights I have read to you and are you willing to talk to me?" This is often translated into Spanish as, *¿Quiére Ud. ceder los derechos y hablar conmigo?* which in English means, "Do you want to cede the rights and talk with me?" "Waive" in this technical sense really means to give up, and the appropriate Spanish word is *renunciar*. *¿Renuncia Ud. a sus derechos que le he explicado y quiere hablar conmigo?* is not only the best interpretation, but conserves the intent of this Miranda warning. The term "cede" may imply to the non-English speaker the ability to later reclaim the rights just waived.

Because of the recent erosion of the Miranda rights, it has now become common practice for police officers to administer the Miranda warnings during the booking phase of arrest rather than in the field (Zahler, 1989a). The use of interpreters at the detention center would help to eradicate the problems associated with misadministered Mirandas by allegedly bilingual police officers.

It is recommended that administration of Miranda warnings be done using the consecutive mode. The absence of a good interpreter at this phase has led to misunderstandings, which in turn have led to the arrest and prosecution of innocent persons. Moreover, prosecuting attorneys often have their cases frustrated by technicalities which lead to dismissal of charges when Miranda warnings are not properly interpreted. The use of interpreters thereby reduces the number of unnecessary and perhaps even illegal arrests, and enables further protection of victims' rights by reducing the number of charges dropped because of bad interpretations. Following are the Miranda warnings in both English and Spanish:

(a) You have the right to remain silent. Anything you say can and will be used against you in a court of law.

Ud. tiene el derecho de guardar silencio. Cualquier cosa que Ud. diga pueda usarse, y se usará, en su contra en un tribunal.

(b) You have the right to consult an attorney and to have the attorney present during interrogation. If you cannot afford an attorney, one will provided for you free of charge.

Ud. tiene el derecho de consultar a un abogado, y (el derecho de) ser acompañado del abogado durante el interrogatorio. Si Ud. no tiene los recursos/ medios para (pagar a) un abogado, se le designará uno sin costo alguno a Ud.

(c) Do you understand each of these rights I have explained to you?

¿Entiende Ud. cada uno de los derechos que le he explicado?

(d) Do you wish to waive your right to remain silent and your right to have an attorney present and do you wish to answer my questions now?

¿Desea Ud. renunciar a / desistir de su derecho de guardar silencio y su derecho de ser acompañado de un abogado, y desea contestar a mis preguntas ahora (mismo)?

3. Interviews

In current practice, the first opportunity for a court interpreter to participate in the criminal justice process usually comes when there is a call for interpreter services in an interview. There are two types of interviews. The first is between a public defender, or private counsel, and the arrestee. As a rule this type of interview is relatively short. The second type of interview can take place between a pre-trial service officer, or equivalent, and the alleged offender. An interview with the pre-trial services officer is conducted in order to find out the defendant's true name, address, educational level, health conditions, and other pertinent information. In both cases, the consecutive mode is recommended because this is a situation where questions are being asked and answered.

The interpreter may also be requested to assist with the completion of financial statements and bail information forms, usually at the interview with the attorney. Interpreters should not fill out these forms or any others without the presence of the attorney. Nor should they write in their interpretations of information given by the defendant. Both documents are signed under penalty of perjury, so it is the attorney's duty to alert the defendant to the consequences of misrepresenting information. Interpreters simply have the duty to give the most accurate and complete interpretation possible, and they should never do anything which could be considered the attorney's responsibility.

4. Initial Appearance

At the initial appearance or arraignment on the complaint, the interpreter is needed throughout the hearing to interpret the admonition of rights and everything said by the judge, counsel, and the defendant, whose answers are then preserved in English for the court transcript (Zahler, 1989a, 1989b). The services of the interpreter at this point help preserve the defendant's Fifth Amendment rights which allow him or her to understand the nature of the charges and to participate in his or her own defense. The interpreter should use the simultaneous mode to interpret for the defendant the running dialogue among the judge, prosecutor, and defense counsel. Whenever the judge questions the defendant, or if the defendant needs to communicate with the attorney, the consecutive interpretation mode should be used. Without the interpreter the court record would not be complete because the answers given by the defendant in his or her own language could not possibly be preserved by the court reporter (Zahler, 1989c).

In felony cases, if the defendant is indicted or an information is submitted, the next step would be the arraignment of the trial, also called the arraignment on the information in state courts, or post-indictment arraignment or arraignment on the indictment in federal courts. Here again, the court interpreter will interpret in the simultaneous mode everything said at the hearing by the judge and counsel; the consecutive mode will be used for any questions the judge may ask of the defendant, or any communication between the defendant and counsel. The use of the court interpreter at this phase serves to protect the court record as well as the defendant's Fifth and Sixth Amendment rights.

Between the initial appearance and the post-indictment arraignment, one or more bail review hearings may be requested by the defense, or the prosecution may request detention. The role of the interpreter is to simultaneously and consecutively interpret when necessary. Sometimes witness testimony is given at these hearings, and a second interpreter may be needed to interpret for the witnesses at the stand, using the consecutive mode. The use of a second interpreter allows the first to continue simultaneously interpreting the proceedings for the defendant, while being available should there be a need for the defendant to disclose information to counsel. If this is the case, then the consecutive mode should be employed.

In those federal courts where the post-indictment arraignment is conducted in part by a federal magistrate (admonishment of rights, information on charges, possible bail motions) and a United States district judge (plea and trial setting), the interpreter serves during both hearings in the same capacity as described in the preceding paragraph. At any time during the judicial process, there may be interviews between counsel and client, at which time an interpreter should be present to interpret in the consecutive mode. Even if the attorney is bilingual, the presence of the interpreter frees the attorney from having to perform the duties of interpretation while trying to render legal services. This practice ensures that the defendant has true assistance of counsel while at the same time allowing counsel to abide by ethical obligations to deliver the best defense possible.

5. Pre-Trial Motions and Status Conferences

A series of motions and conferences may take place upon request of one of the parties and sometimes upon the court's own motion. Throughout such hearings the role of the interpreter is to render the necessary language services, either consecutively if there are questions and answers, or simultaneously if there is an exchange between counsel and the court. If a motion requires witness testimony, again a second interpreter must be called to interpret in the consecutive mode for the witness at the stand.

The interpreter who is simultaneously interpreting for the defendant has the duty to interpret everything that is said in court, as is true in all other proceedings. Motions pose special problems for the interpreter, as counsel may cite a string of cases in support of the motion, refer to criminal statutes by number, or use obscure legal terms or even Latin expressions. It is the duty of the interpreter to render this especially dense language as accurately as possible.

The interpreter should direct specific questions from the defendant about cases or statutes to the defendant's counsel. When counsel uses a technical, Latin, or other non-English term and the defendant would like to know its meaning, it is not up to the interpreter to define the term; the interpreter should inform counsel of the client's question about meaning, and then interpret the answer given by the attorney (see Unit 8, Chapter 34). Defining the law, legal procedure, or even legal terms is the responsibility of the defendant's attorney. If the interpreter were to define terms, this practice might be viewed as improperly giving legal advice or practicing law. If the interpreter does not convey all of the information contained in motions, the non-English-speaking defendant is placed in an inferior position to that of an English-speaking defendant who would otherwise have had the opportunity to hear *all* of the proceeding.

6. Trials

In court or bench trials, as well as in jury trials, it is the responsibility of the interpreter to interpret to the defendant everything that is being said. The same degree of thoroughness is required for interpreting witness testimony, so a second interpreter must be called to interpret in the consecutive mode at the witness stand for non-English-speaking witnesses. For the special logistical considerations involved in interpreting at trial, see Unit 4. If the non-English-speaking defendant intends to present a defense, the trial is the last opportunity to put one forth; therefore, a very accurate interpretation of witness testimony, other kinds of evidence, and even objections and their rulings becomes crucial. At the same time, the services of the interpreter provide the only assurance in the criminal prosecution that the defendant's Fifth and Sixth Amendment rights will be preserved.

7. Post-Trial Procedures

Whenever a verdict is for conviction and the defendant is referred to the probation department in order to have a pre-sentence report prepared, the services of the court interpreter are crucial, especially during the interview conducted by the probation officer. In this phase, the cultural knowledge of the court interpreter, in addition to interpreting skills, comes into play. The probation officer often asks questions about the socioeconomic background of the defendant. Since there is a little more leeway during this type of interview, the probation officer may ask the interpreter if the statements made by the defendant are consistent with the customs of the defendant's native country. The interpreter should inform the probation officer of his or her opinion at the conclusion of the interview, out of the hearing of the defendant (see Unit 8, Chapter 34). As in other situations where questions and answers are involved, those interviews must be interpreted in the consecutive mode.

Prior to sentencing, the pre-sentence report must be sight translated to the defendant. If the attorney is not present for the sight translation, the interpreter should make note of any remarks or objections made by the defendant and communicate them to defense counsel as soon as possible. The rationale for reading the pre-sentence report is to grant the defendant the right to be informed of the facts ascertained by the probation officer, to evaluate their accuracy, and to be apprised of the recommendations included in the report.

8. Appeals

If any party files an appeal based on inaccurate interpretation, the only means by which the appellate court can determine the issue is to have at its disposal a record of the original testimony. This can be accomplished by recording all proceedings in which interpreters are utilized at the time the hearing originally takes place. The best method is to make an electronic sound recording of the proceeding. The record must be of both the source and target languages. Transcriptions of such recordings should follow guidelines for the translation of non-English-language documents as delineated in Unit 7, Chapter 32.

9. The Special Case of Multi-Defendants

Because it is so important for interpreters to be completely impartial and without bias, the appearance of a conflict of interest should be scrupulously avoided. Conflict of interest can manifest itself in many ways. For example, the interpreter may be related to one of the parties, may have an interest in the outcome of the trial, or may favor the party who has retained the interpreter's services. These situations must be disclosed to court and counsel at the beginning of each hearing. See Unit 8, Chapter 34, for further discussion of this issue.

A conflict of interest also exists if the defenses of co-defendants are contrary to one another in a multiple defendant case. Just as both defendants are afforded separate counsel, so should they be afforded separate interpreters. Doing so ensures that privileged attorney-client communications are kept confidential. The best procedure is to use two interpreters in multi-defendant proceedings with an electronic sound system. Thus, one interpreter interprets the proceedings through a closed circuit electronic transmission system, and all the defendants listen by means of individual headphones. This procedure also ensures a uniform interpretation. The other interpreter, who should be seated at counsel table, will assist in communication between client and counsel during the proceedings (see Unit 7).

Good practice dictates the appointment of separate interpreters for prosecution and defense. The rationale is that an interpreter who has had prior exposure to the case may be inadvertently influenced by information previously acquired. In United States district courts it is common practice that prosecution witness interpreters are hired by the Department of Justice through the Office of the United States Attorney, while interpreters who work for the court are hired by the Judiciary Branch by the Court Clerk pursuant to the Court Interpreters Act of 1978. Not only are two different interpreters appointed, but payment by two different employers eliminates any possible conflict of interest.

10. Other Legal Settings

There are many settings outside of the courtroom where interviews are conducted to lay the groundwork for certain procedures such as bail or detention hearings. Such procedures may precede court trials, and take place during the post-conviction and pre-sentence period as well. These interviews are not typically held in the courtroom proper but are administered in different locations where there are special facilities for attorney/client interviews such as detention centers, jails, and halfway houses, or any location within the courthouse including the holding tank, the hallways outside of the courtroom and the judge's chambers. If the defendant is released on bond pending trial, the interviews can take place in the lawyer's office. The most common interviews include attorney/client, pre-trial services, probation, physician, psychiatric, psychological, fingerprint, handwriting exemplar, and, in jurisdictions where they are admitted as evidence, polygraph examinations.

At times in the criminal justice process, depositions may be taken from material witnesses whose presence for trial and testimony cannot be assured, or from those who would face hardship if they remain available to the court. Depositions in civil matters are very frequent. Information obtained at depositions is treated as courtroom testimony, and the threat of perjury attaches after the witness takes an oath to truthfully answer questions. The transcript of the deposition, after having been read, approved, and signed by attending counsel and deposed witnesses, is then treated as if the testimony had been taken in court. The consecutive mode of interpretation should be used in all these interpersonal interviews, and as in all other interviews, the requirement of confidentiality and impartiality of the interpreter is essential. Because these other settings are still "judicial," the interpreter is bound to render an accurate and true interpretation to the best of his or her ability. In essence, the interpreter should adopt the attitude that he or she is for all intents and purposes still in a courtroom.

Facts, conversations, and anything revealed in these other settings could materially affect the outcome of the case or the sentencing of the defendant. All of the ethical considerations, protocol, duties, and responsibilities discussed in later chapters of this book apply to the interpreter who renders services in quasi- or non-judicial settings.

11. Juvenile Courts

The use of interpreters in administrative proceedings such as those conducted by the Immigration and Naturalization Service (see Chapter 38) and in quasi-legal settings such as family courts require special consideration. A host of issues arise in other settings; a discussion of the general parameters that emerge may serve the interpreter well in understanding the requirements of such alternative settings. The legal, ethical, and practical considerations which are affected must be made clear to the interpreter and those who use such services. Much of what is said about the use of interpreters in this setting can be applied to other proceedings of a like nature.

Juvenile proceedings represent another increasing market for court interpreter services. Juvenile courts are created by statute and have the specific responsibility to decide matters affecting minors. Juveniles are defined as youths under a specific age, usually sixteen to eighteen years, but this age varies from state to state. If a youth commits a crime after reaching this statutorily determined age, the juvenile is treated as an adult, and may be tried in a criminal court of general jurisdiction. At times a youth under the statutory age will be tried as an adult if the crime is of an especially heinous nature. The major function of the juvenile system is to prevent juvenile crime and to rehabilitate juvenile offenders.

There are two basic types of juvenile cases: (1) those concerning neglected and dependent children, in which the action is aimed at protecting children by ordering a separation from persons whose custody they are in; and (2) those concerning delinquent children who commit violations of law, are incorrigible, or are truants. There are many differences between the concepts and procedures in juvenile courts and those used to try adult criminals. For example, it was long accepted that the right to an attorney was not absolute for juveniles; hearsay testimony inadmissible in criminal trials was admissible in the adjudication of juvenile offenders; verdicts were often based on a preponderance of the evidence, but now are based on the standard of beyond a reasonable doubt. Many of the rights that criminal defendants had did not attach to juveniles, such as the right to a jury trial, the right to confront and cross-examine witnesses, the right to appointed counsel, and the right against self-incrimination. In 1967, *In re Gault* assured juveniles of due process rights in the adjudication of criminal offenses and the right to counsel at trial. This case is considered the most important development in the juvenile court system since the inception of the system.

Instead of complaints, informations, or indictments, **petitions** are filed against juveniles. The juvenile is not called the defendant, but rather the **minor** or sometimes the **respondent**. His last name is always omitted when the case is recorded; for instance, instead of *People v. John Henry*, the case will be *In re John* (read as "in the matter of John"). The trial is called an **adjudication** and the sentencing is called the **disposition**.

Juvenile courts can be established as lower courts of limited jurisdiction, or juvenile cases may be submitted to the highest court of general jurisdiction. Some states have independent juvenile court systems (Siegel & Senna, 1988). Their jurisdiction is determined by state statutes and constitutional amendments. The concept of **family courts** has been very important in the development of the jurisdiction of juvenile courts. In recent years, state legislatures concerned about serious juvenile crime have passed laws that automatically exclude serious crimes from the jurisdiction of juvenile courts, and have transferred them to the criminal courts even if committed by children under the legal age limit, provided that they are above a lower age limit (fifteen in most cases).

Like the criminal defendant, the juvenile may be arrested and detained in custodial facilities pending the adjudicatory hearing (Hahn, 1984). In addition to detention, even if for only a short period, the juvenile, the family, and the attorney must also consider the alternatives of diversion, bail, plea bargaining, and in serious cases, transfer of the minor to an adult court. While in custody, the minor may be placed in a variety of environments designed to provide sheltered care. Some of these environments include foster homes, residential facilities, rehabilitation homes, detention boarding homes, and programs of neighborhood supervision. These programs enable youths to live in private or public homes while the courts dispose of their cases.

The interpreter does not necessarily interpret for the juveniles themselves, but primarily for older witnesses and parents. Very often the minor is fluent in English but relations or other witnesses involved in the case do not speak or understand English. Therefore, the interpreter usually sits between the minor's parents and/or other relatives and simultaneously interprets all of the proceedings. Often questions posed by the judge or by relatives, as well as the admonishments of the court to parties concerning the minor, must be consecutively interpreted. If there are non-English-speaking witnesses during the hearing, a second interpreter should be called to interpret consecutively for witnesses at the stand, leaving the first interpreter with the parents, relatives, and attorney.

The juvenile court judge has more alternatives for sentencing than the ordinary trial court judge. The judge may elect to impose probation or might even impose home detention (Hahn, 1984). Rules regarding regular school attendance and curfew, abstention from alcohol and drugs, or twenty-four-hour notification to social workers of the juvenile's whereabouts may be required. Truancy cases often culminate in the judge specifically ordering school attendance. The juvenile may be instructed to make financial restitution to the victim; in most states, this is one of the conditions of probation. Fines or community service may be imposed, and even outpatient psychotherapy is available if the judge deems it necessary. If the youth has a problem with drugs or alcohol, the judge may also assign the youth to drug and alcohol treatment programs, with or without commitment into a specified facility. Finally, the minor may be committed to a special community rehabilitation program or placed in a foster home. The most severe punishment that a judge may order is the institutionalization of a juvenile in a facility called a youth camp, a special bureaucratic unit which supervises the institutionalization of youths. In Texas, for example, this unit is called the Texas Youth Council, and in California it is called the California Youth Authority.

12. Non-Judicial Settings

The number of non-English-speaking persons in the United States is growing geometrically. As this trend continues, clients or patients in hospitals, banks, or other businesses will require the use of interpreters. As noted in the introduction to this work, interpreters are being used in a wide variety of settings in every aspect of daily life: hospitals and other medical facilities, banks, real estate offices, multinational corporations, travel agencies, import-export businesses, and so on.

The common denominator in the use of interpreters among these areas is that in each case the life, liberty, or property of the client is at stake. In the medical field poor interpretation or misunderstanding of the true physical state of the patient could lead to a misdiagnosis and misadministration of medication, possibly resulting in death. In the mental health area, an incorrect diagnosis could lead to unwarranted medication with unforeseen side effects. If individuals are found to be dangerous to themselves or to others, their liberties may be restricted or deprived (hospitalization is tantamount to incarceration) when that determination rests upon an erroneous interpretation. For someone in a commercial business setting, a misinterpretation could result in decisions that lead to a loss of potential or actual property, earnings, or goodwill.

Adherence to the techniques and the parameters enunciated in this text will allow the interpreter working in non-judicial settings to provide accurate and meaningful interpretations. Precisely interpreted information will allow the professional relying on the interpretation to render better quality services to non-English-speaking clients. Another benefit of following the court interpreter model of interpretation is a greatly reduced risk of liability from inaccuracies and incomplete information. Any professional who delivers services which affect the client's life, liberty, or property may be sued for malpractice; and, if those actions are based upon information supplied by interpreters, the interpreter may be jointly liable. Interpreters working in settings other than the legal one are well advised to become familiar with the parameters of court interpretation. In a world that is growing increasingly complex and litigious, there is a need for more accuracy and precision in interpreting in all spheres of professional life. Society as a whole benefits from the use of interpreters, especially those interpreters whose skills have been demonstrated.

Chapter 14

Principles of the Proper Utilization of Interpreters in the Courtroom

As with all legal actors in the courtroom, interpreters face numerous limitations which can hamper their effectiveness. Many limitations come about because of physical and cultural factors that are beyond the interpreter's immediate control. However, these limitations can be remedied if other legal actors in the courtroom understand the proper role of the interpreter (see Unit 8, Chapters 34 and 35). Mutual cooperation and professional courtesy will culminate in the fair administration of justice and protection of the record of the proceedings. This chapter focuses on three dominant actors who have the ability to control the environment where the interpreter must perform professional functions—the judge, court clerk, and attorney—and suggests ways in which they can ensure the proper utilization of interpreter services. The chapter concludes with a discussion of the cultural problems that commonly arise in judicial interpreting, and recommends solutions to those problems.

1. Judges

The judge is the final arbiter in the courtroom proper of all legal disputes. Moreover, judges can set their own court rules about the way proceedings will be conducted (Judicial Council of California, 1979; Superior Court, 1985). Herein lies the potential for guaranteeing the proper utilization of court interpreters in individual courtrooms. Judges should understand that there are five major factors which can aid interpreters in the performance of their functions: (1) ability to hear every legal actor in the courtroom and close physical proximity to the witness, defendant, or attorney in order to speak without interrupting the proceedings; (2) provision for periodic breaks and teamwork with other interpreters to avoid fatigue; (3) access to important documents before the commencement of a proceeding; (4) provision of an administrative structure within the court to support their functions; and (5) aid from judges and attorneys to overcome culture-bound linguistic problems.

1.1. Hearing and Speaking, Physical Proximity

An interpreter who cannot hear cannot interpret. At the same time, if interpreters are not allowed to sit, stand, or otherwise position themselves wherever it is most efficient to speak to the witness or defendant, then their voices will be so loud that the proceedings will actually be hampered by what may seem to the court an unnecessary third voice. More importantly, if the interpreter cannot be heard by the defendant, due process is violated; if the interpreter cannot be heard by the witness, the reception and accuracy of testimony heard may be tainted.

Fortunately, there are several solutions to these problems. The judge may instruct the court to follow the guidelines listed below in order to alleviate the aural/oral limitations under which the interpreter labors. The judge has the ultimate responsibility of protecting the record of the proceedings; through assisting interpreters in their work, the judge will be able to fulfill his or her responsibility more efficiently. Two incipient problems, hearing and speaking, will be addressed first.

(1) If the interpreter cannot hear the person speaking, the judge may order counsel and witnesses to speak in audible voices, either upon the judge's own request, or upon the request of the interpreter.

(2) The judge can require microphones to be used whenever interpreters are utilized in the courtroom to ensure the audibility of anyone whose testimony should appear in the transcript. This practice also ensures that the court reporter will hear every word uttered in court.

(3) If the interpreter is having trouble hearing or is speaking in too loud a voice, the judge may permit the interpreter to sit wherever hearing is best facilitated. Usually the ideal acoustical situation for interpreters is beside the witness or defendant. However, if interpreters use sound equipment, they are not compelled to sit at the defendant's side at counsel table. In this instance, the interpreter may best be able to hear seated on the opposite side of the railing behind the defense table. The interpreter may request to change positions, or the judge who is aware of the interpreter's need to hear can instruct the interpreter to move into an advantageous position at the start of the proceedings. If the interpreter is in a courtroom that was not designed to accommodate interpreters at the witness stand, the judge can have the court provide a seat in the witness box high enough to place the interpreter at the level of the witness's ear.

(4) If attorneys or witnesses are speaking too rapidly for the interpreter to keep up, the judge can instruct all those persons who speak in the course of proceedings to slow their speech. Speech in the courtroom has been timed upwards of 220 words per minute. It is virtually impossible for an interpreter to keep pace with that rate of speech. Additionally, the abilities of interpreters vary greatly; some will be more able than others to match speeds with the speaker.

1.2. Fatigue

It is a well-known and much practiced policy for judges to allow their court reporters to take breaks whenever necessary in order to protect the court record. The judge understands in this situation that the court reporter can perform only so long before fatigue will begin to affect the accuracy of the transcript being recorded.

As explained elsewhere in this volume (see Unit 6), there are at least twenty-two cognitive skills which the interpreter is employing at all times during the rendition of the interpretation. This work is so taxing that conference interpreters employed by the United Nations are replaced every forty-five minutes by a co-interpreter. Interpreting in court is an even more demanding endeavor because interpreters frequently do not work in pairs. Moreover, they are typically unable to prepare in advance, as conference interpreters can, because they do not have access to documents containing pertinent information before the beginning of proceedings. Often there are many new concepts or spontaneous testimony which cannot be anticipated even with documents. The courts are working under heavy scheduling problems, so the interpreter may not even know the subject matter of a trial before beginning to interpret. All of these factors add to the stress under which the court interpreter operates, and thus contribute to interpreter fatigue. Nonetheless, the judge can make a difference.

(1) The judge can remember that, when a non-English speaker is before the court, the interpreter's rendition is the most important tool for preserving a record of the proceedings in the courtroom. When coupling this information with the idea that the interpreter is doing a strenuous task, and cannot work with great efficiency for more than forty-five minutes at a time, the judge may give the interpreter periodic recesses or ask the supervisory interpreter or court clerk for two interpreters to relieve one another.

(2) The judge can take note of the fatigue factor and limit the interpreter to an eight-hour day, excluding an hour for lunch.

(3) The judge can also accommodate the interpreter's needs, and will have a refreshed interpreter for afternoon proceedings, if the interpreter is given adequate time for lunch, not less than one hour. Protecting the interpreter's lunch hour by prohibiting counsel from enlisting the interpreter's assistance for lunchtime interviews will eliminate early fatigue.

1.3. Providing Information for Preparation

Just as a competent attorney would not appear in court without first having reviewed the client's file, so the interpreter should not be expected to interpret in a case without having an opportunity to read the complaint, information, or indictment. If the court has ordered any special reports or interviews with mental health experts or physicians, the court can aid the expected interpretation by providing the interpreter with as much material as possible. The judge can order the clerk of court to make copies of the following to give to the interpreter prior to the day of the trial, if at all possible: (1) complaints, informations, or indictments, (2) expert reports, (3) jury instructions, and (4) pre-sentence reports.

By providing the interpreter with as much documentary information as possible, and doing so well in advance of the proceedings, the judge is assured that the interpreter will have less reason to require a break in the proceedings to research obscure terminology. Furthermore, the accuracy of the interpretation of testimony will be much greater when the interpreter is given an opportunity to study and prepare for the proceedings. If at any time the judge is in doubt about a policy for the courtroom concerning the role, duties, and responsibilities of the interpreter, the judge may call upon the supervisory interpreter for recommendations.

2. Clerk of Court/Chief Judge

There are additional administrative/support services that can be provided for the interpreter by the clerk of court or the chief judge, depending on the division of functions, to aid the court in ensuring fairness and justice for non-English-speaking witnesses and defendants. For example, many times interpreters must work in multi-defendant cases. Technology is now available to make the interpretation of such cases more efficient. Providing the interpreter with sound equipment (see Unit 8, Chapter 17) can greatly facilitate interpretation, and for more than one defendant at a time. Although some courts do have sound equipment available, with the increase in the number of non-English-speaking witnesses and defendants, the amount of equipment available often falls short of the need. It would be wise for the clerk to estimate the highest number of non-English-language cases possible in one calendar day and then to purchase and have the necessary equipment available.

Interpreters often have duties out of court, such as translating non-English-language documents into English so that they may be offered into evidence. In this case, the clerk of court should provide typewriters or computers with the appropriate language keyboards, if available, so that interpreters may utilize them when doing their translations. In addition, the court should have basic language resources available or allow space for the storage of personal references, such as dictionaries and glossaries, in the courthouse.

If extra equipment for translation is not available, then the clerk may make available to the interpreter a secretary or a secretarial pool to produce a hard copy of a translated document. Access to clerical staff to help the interpreter process payroll documents or other statistical paperwork would help the interpreter concentrate on the task of interpreting rather than trying to seek support services or equipment elsewhere.

Many courts do not have translated forms available for non-English speakers, and, therefore, the forms must be interpreted separately for each defendant. The clerk can make extra copies of these forms available so that the interpreter may prepare translations to keep on file. Filling in the forms then becomes a much more efficient process. After the forms have been translated, the clerk could develop a file where they may be kept and used by other interpreters.

Because the courtroom deputies or court clerks are under the supervision of the clerk of court, the clerk is in a position to instruct courtroom deputies to inform supervisory interpreters of any calendar changes to help reschedule per diem interpreters. Since the supervisory interpreter, if there is one, cannot possibly attend all the hearings scheduled each day, the procedure for apprising that office of changes in calendars should be formalized. Finally, the clerk of court often may be the first and only person an interpreter has contact with prior to entering the courtroom. If this is the case, then the clerk can facilitate the process by making available copies of complaints, informations, or indictments prior to proceedings.

3. Attorneys

Both the prosecution and the defense can help the interpreter provide an accurate interpretation. It is to the advantage of defense counsel to aid the interpreter so that clients may have the benefit of a fair hearing before the court. It behooves the prosecution to aid the interpreter because the government has invested much time, energy, and funds in the prosecution of the defendant. The prosecutor can reduce the chances for a mistrial on the grounds of a poor interpretation by allowing the interpreter access to as much material as is permissible. Any complaints, informations or indictments, expert reports, summaries, case histories, pre-sentence reports, jury instructions, or other pertinent documents which may be released to any other officer of the court, and which would not infringe upon a privilege, should be given to the interpreter as far in advance of the proceeding as is possible. This includes any reports which counsel may wish to have the interpreter read to the defendant. If feasible, the interpreter should be given time to read the report and research terminology—one-half hour minimum or more depending on the length of the report—before being required to interpret it to the defendant.

Often interpreters are engaged by the defense or the prosecution through a supervisory interpreter. Since most interpreters work on a per diem basis, there often are not enough interpreters immediately available to meet the demand. Few staff interpreters are available for conferences because they are typically busy working trials or regular proceedings such as arraignments. If counsel keeps in mind that the supervisory interpreter or clerk of court needs advance notice of the need for interpreting services, then the appropriate per diem interpreters can be contracted.

In a similar vein, if counsel no longer needs the services of an interpreter, timely notice of the cancellation will allow for efficient rescheduling of contracted per diem interpreters, either for a later date or to another task. If the scheduled interview does take place, interpreters are greatly aided if they are allowed a short pre-appearance interview with the defendant in the presence of the attorney. If the defendant or any other non-English-speaking witness is to take the stand, it is first necessary to ascertain whether the interpreter can understand the specific language variety (dialect) of the witness in question.

There have been many instances of interpreters not being given an opportunity to speak to the witness in the attorney's presence so as to ascertain the register, level of education, or regional or social variety of language, and as a result the interview or proceedings was cancelled when the problem was discovered. There may be many dialects within one language which are mutually unintelligible to speakers of the same base language. For example, within Chinese there are five major varieties and countless other local variations that are spoken only in small areas in China, and sometimes in just one village. Therefore, to contribute to a better interpretation in court and during interviews with clients, the attorney would be well advised to discern which language is needed and, when possible, to allow the defendant and the assigned interpreter to speak casually for a few moments before the start of proceedings.

As was noted above in reference to the judge, the attorney should be aware of his or her form of speech at all times when utilizing interpreter services. The attorney should remember not to speak too rapidly, and to make questions to witnesses brief and as unambiguous as possible. Although interpreters often have phenomenal short-term memories, there are limits. If the question the attorney poses or the answer the witness is expected to supply is overly long, the attorney can facilitate the interpreter's task by allowing for pauses or asking more specific questions to break the testimony into shorter responses.

The attorney should remember to speak loudly enough for the interpreter to hear at all times. Furthermore, attorneys often turn their backs to the interpreter when making their opening or closing statements, thus limiting the audibility of their speech to those in front of them. Although the interpreter strives at all times to be in the best position possible to hear the proceedings, the attorney can facilitate the interpreter's aural reception by remembering to face the interpreter as much as possible.

4. Culturally Bound References

Possibly the thorniest problems for the interpreter are those posed by cultural and linguistic limitations. If, however, judges, attorneys, and other legal actors are aware of the limits of language, they can often help interpreters solve these problems efficiently. Each culture is separate and individual, and brings with it certain ideas, concepts, technologies, customs, habits, and systems which do not necessarily mirror the United States culture, and therefore the language of the court. For a thorough discussion and a series of examples, see Unit 8, Chapter 34, Subsection 1.4.8.

Many of these informational problems can be solved by having the judge or counsel announce and spell out names and addresses when it becomes apparent that the witnesses are unable to provide the needed information, or seem lost because they believe they have already supplied the court with the required information. This would free the interpreter from having to do the spelling or interrupting the proceedings to explain the cultural and linguistic difficulty the witness is experiencing.

Use of culturally bound concepts pose even bigger problems for the interpreter. Depending on the language, there are a variety of problems the interpreter encounters. If the interpreter understands the meaning of the source language and there is no equivalent in the target language and culture, then the interpreter must inform the judge that there is a problem expressing the idea in the second language. There are two solutions to this particular problem:

(1) The judge may instruct the attorney to rephrase the question using less culture-bound terms or to use terms which the witness can understand. If the attorney used a football field as a unit of measure and the game is not played in the witness's country, the attorney can use more common units such as meters.

(2) The judge can also instruct the witness to demonstrate the length or indicate something in the courtroom which is as tall or would weigh as much. The attorney can then estimate the measurement for the record. If the problem involves a concept or idea, then the judge can instruct the attorney to ask more specific questions.

With few exceptions, it is almost always possible to resolve culturally and language-bound interpreting problems. Given the importance of making an accurate record and ensuring that the interpreter does not usurp the duties and responsibilities of the attorney or perhaps the judge, the judiciary and legal personnel must be aware of the problems which impinge upon the interpreter in the course of interpreting. If the judge and attorneys do not give adequate attention to the resolution of these problems, the loss of precious judicial resources or a miscarriage of justice could result.

Unit 4

Management of
Court Interpreter Services

Chapter 15

Recruitment and Assessment of Interpreters

The ever-increasing number of matters involving limited and non-English-speaking defendants and witnesses in recent years has resulted in a burgeoning demand for interpreter services. The introduction of the court interpreter position into the justice system has created a concomitant rise in administrative duties such as record-keeping, statistical histories, payroll, recruitment, training, supervision, and assignment of court interpreters. These administrative functions must not be relegated to diverse departments and/or existing personnel. Instead, the profusion of these duties justifies the establishment of a supervisory position. This unit will examine those duties and responsibilities in detail. The focus of this chapter is the duties specifically related to the recruitment and assessment of interpreters. First, however, a discussion of the vital role of the supervising interpreter is in order.

If the volume of court interpreter matters reaches such a proportion that it impinges upon the workload of existing court personnel and jeopardizes the orderly management of the court or the clerk's office, the court administrator would be well advised to seriously consider the creation of an office of court interpreting with an administrator in charge. In local courts with such a low frequency of interpreter-related matters that an office is not warranted, all language service requests should, at the very least, be directed to one officer of the court.

The effective utilization of court interpreter services will necessitate an administrator who ultimately will be the administrative clearinghouse and liaison for all matters relating to interpreters and the services they perform. Accordingly, no administrative detail pertaining to interpreters should bypass this supervisor. Effective utilization of this office will ensure orderly and timely language services to the court.

1. Ideal Supervising Interpreter

As in many other administrative systems, two positions can be argued: (1) that the administrator in charge must be a practicing member of that profession or (2) that the supervisor's function will be primarily administrative and will not be dependent upon membership in the profession. In the field of public education a long-established philosophy holds that supervisory personnel (superintendents, principals) be teachers first, whereas in the field of public health administration, administrators need not be medical doctors.

The ideal interpreting supervisor is a person who has experience in interpretation, as it relates to the administration of justice, formal training in linguistics and/or advanced language studies, and preferably, formal education and/or experience in the field of administration. This comprehensive background would give the supervisor an appreciation for the problems and duties of the court interpreter and qualify the individual to oversee the clerical personnel who would fulfill numerous administrative responsibilities. A language-related background would give the supervisor an understanding of the linguistic aspects of court interpretation. The language and interpretation experience of the supervisor will be useful in the selection and training of interpreters as well as in monitoring their performance during the course of their service to the court. Also, the supervisory officer may be asked to participate in personnel committee meetings for the purpose of developing job descriptions, or to sit on test development panels and/or certification task forces.

Administrative background is essential to execute the duties of the administrator in charge of court interpreter services. This experience would also serve the supervisor well in the tasks related to the orderly functioning of the office, i.e., the daily assignments, statistical analyses, daily record-keeping, and a host of other administrative duties.

1.1. Desirable Personal Characteristics

The question of the personal characteristics of the supervisor is just as important as the educational and professional background. The court interpreter supervisor should possess qualities that will enable him or her to work well with others. Not only should the supervisor be able to supervise court interpreters successfully and effectively, but also be able to relate well to judges, attorneys, and other court personnel. The supervisor's dossier should reveal a history of successful professional interpersonal relationships. These will prove to be useful in helping to resolve professional and ethical problems relating to conflicts of interest, confidentiality, and other similar questions.

1.2. Assignment and Supervision Functions

The administration of court interpreter matters involves two functions: (1) selection, supervision, and training; and (2) assignment and payroll. It is recommended that these functions be handled by a single office rather than two separate ones. In jurisdictions where these functions are carried out by different offices, the functions of the interpreter assignment office are purely administrative and clerical in nature. They include receiving requests for interpreter services by date, case name, case number, courtroom, and the language that will be required, and for maintaining records of those requests and the corresponding assignments. The assignment officer contacts per diem interpreters on a daily contract basis and assigns them to the cases, or in some instances to certain courthouses, to act as court interpreter for the day. The assignment office also maintains records relating to payroll, and processes all requests from court interpreters regarding professional remuneration for services rendered. Because these functions are strictly administrative, it has been assumed that assignment personnel need not be interpreters or have any knowledge of a foreign language. However, if the assignment officer is unaware of the unique problems of court interpreting, the officer may inadvertently assign the wrong interpreter to a case, such as assigning an interpreter of a different dialect, or assigning an inexperienced interpreter to a serious criminal trial. Therefore, it is imperative that assignment functions be carried out under the direction of a supervisor who has full knowledge of the court interpreting profession.

1.3. Model of Court Interpreting Services Office

In a model court interpreting services office, the director assumes the comprehensive responsibilities of attending to all matters that pertain to the rendering of quality language services. In this model, the office of court interpreting services may or may not be a formal part of the clerk's office. In current practice in some jurisdictions, the office of court interpreting occupies a separate and distinct administrative office under the clerk's authority, yet is autonomous in function. In other jurisdictions, the office of court interpreting is a formal and integral part of the clerk's office.

Whatever the hierarchical configuration, the court interpreting office should consist of a director of interpreter services and a staff of administrative and clerical assistants who can reasonably handle the clerical and payroll responsibilities. This will free the director to hire, assign, orient, and train interpreters, as well as to monitor the quality of language services provided to the court. Before discussing the practical, clerical, and logistical considerations of operating the interpreting services office, those duties for which the director or supervisor of court interpreting is principally responsible will be discussed: (1) recruitment and assessment of certified, non-certified, and non-professionally qualified interpreters; (2) orientation and training; and (3) monitoring and supervision.

2. Recruitment

One of the foremost responsibilities of the supervisory interpreter is the recruitment of certified and non-certified—but otherwise qualified—per diem and staff interpreters. In essence this officer is responsible for the hiring of any person who interprets in the court. The responsibility for recruitment is further complicated by the question of competence. In the case of those languages for which government agencies have devised procedures—such as the Federal Court Interpreter Certification Examination—to evaluate the qualifications of court interpreters, it can be assumed that interpreters are linguistically (not necessarily professionally) competent. The question becomes more difficult for languages that are not tested in this manner.

Recruitment is further complicated by the dearth of available interpreters or proficient bilinguals in a given language. Another factor affecting the recruitment process is the urgency of the need for interpreter services in non-certified languages. All of these variables impinge on the recruitment process.

2.1. The Recruitment Process

For purposes of this discussion it is assumed that a roster of available interpreters by languages does not yet exist. In such cases, the director of court interpreting services must aggressively and systematically locate potential candidates, interview them, and establish a list of available interpreters by language, including everything from Arabic to Zulu. The priority given to the various languages should be determined by local demand.

2.2. Certified Languages

In the case of certified languages such as Spanish, the list of certified interpreters is available from the government agency that issued the certification. For federally certified court interpreters, the list is available from the Administrative Office of the United States Courts (AO). As of 1990, the AO certifies in three languages: Spanish, Haitian Creole, and Navajo. English language proficiency is requisite for all interpreter certifications. As of this writing, California, New Mexico, and Washington State are the only states that certify in languages other than Spanish (see Unit 8, Chapters 36 and 37). Accordingly, lists are available from city, county, state, and administrative agencies in those states which have certification procedures in place. If for any reason these lists are not available or not forthcoming, a copy may be obtained from a neighboring court. If a court interpreter whose name originally appeared on the list of interpreters cannot be located, a series of investigating strategies can be pursued, such as placing phone calls or writing to the Division of Motor Vehicles, translating and interpreting agencies, the office of the local postmaster, and local courts where the interpreter previously worked.

2.3. Non-Certified Languages

The recruitment of interpreters of non-certified languages presents a greater problem to the supervisor of court interpreting services. Although there may be candidates who will approach the court for employment, the need for court interpreting services in these less common languages demands a careful and determined mode of recruitment. The nationwide demand for interpreters for languages other than Spanish constitutes only five percent of the need in federal courts (Administrative Office of the United States Courts, 1987). Even if a given language is seldom required, the proceeding cannot take place without a qualified interpreter.

In larger federal court districts, at least twenty to twenty-five different languages are used every year, and they are not always the same languages. The federal Interpreter Utilization by Language Survey for the year 1988 reports the number of languages used in all federal district courts to be seventy, including such languages as Spanish, Haitian Creole, Ibo, Tagalog, Hindi, Persian (Farsi), Serbo-Croatian, Navajo, Apache, Korean, and French Creole (Administrative Office of the United States Courts, 1989a). In some state courts, the need for languages other than Spanish is much greater than in federal district courts because of demographics. For example, the number of per diem interpreters working for the Los Angeles Superior Court in languages other than Spanish has grown from 155 to 196 in the past five years (Mikkelson, 1989a). The Los Angeles Superior Court employs interpreters in over fifty languages (H. Mintz, personal communication, August 4, 1989). Throughout the country, there is almost no court that has not at some point faced the need for the services of a non-certified-language interpreter.

In order to meet the need for non-certified-language interpreters, the supervisor of interpreter services must by necessity be creative and resourceful in tracking the potential interpreter. It is important to remember that the person may be rarely called, but nonetheless should possess the best language and interpreting skills possible so as to afford the non-English speaker the fairest access to the court system. The supervisor should proceed with caution, for in the main, non-certified interpreters of any language bring with them no documentation as to their language or interpreting competence. Therefore, the interpreter supervisor should bear in mind that some assessment of that competence must be made (see Section 3 of this chapter). In those languages for which there are no certification or examination programs, the local court—namely, the director of interpreting services—will be responsible for establishing the procedures to determine competence.

The immediate place to begin the search for interpreters is locally situated government agencies that have similar language service needs: neighboring courts, local offices of federal investigatory agencies, and other administrative law agencies. Non-governmental agencies and institutions that are in contact with speakers of the desired language, such as ethnic churches and community organizations, foreign language departments in colleges and universities, local hospitals that use interpreters, and private language schools, represent a rich source of potential interpreters.

Not to be overlooked are the numerous national and international agencies such as the State Department, the United Nations, and the Red Cross that have similar needs for language services and often have available a list of interpreters that could be supplied to the courts. In an effort to solve purely local language problems, calling upon any agencies that are located far away or are entirely unrelated to the courts may seem inappropriate to the court administrator. In truth, these agencies can prove to be a most worthwhile resource for providing language service.

The supervising interpreter may communicate with the director of language services at any one of these agencies and request the names of local interpreters. In an emergency, or any situation where time is critical, the supervising interpreter may wish to telephone the agencies listed below if only to get the name of a single interpreter. The following agencies, institutions, and organizations are valuable sources for non-certified language interpreters.

2.4. Local Agencies

2.4.1. Municipal, State, and Federal Courts

The prime source of non-certified-language interpreters is neighboring courts, specifically the supervisory interpreter or person responsible for hiring non-certified-language interpreters. Many courts have on file the names of non-certified-language interpreters who have previously been interviewed and have appeared in court. However, supervising interpreters in these other courts may not always be in a position to evaluate the competence of potential interpreters.

The frequency of interpreter-related matters is greatest at the state court level; the state courts utilize interpreters in a wide variety of languages. As a consequence, state courts, especially those in large metropolitan areas, may be in a position to provide the names of appropriate individuals. Very few states have certification or qualifying examination programs for court interpreters like those implemented by California, New Jersey, New Mexico, New York, and Washington State. California and Washington are at present the only states to test interpreters in languages other than Spanish. However, many untested but experienced interpreters have acquired knowledge, skills, and experience on the job that may make them useful. Depending upon geographic location, the United States district courts also employ a large number of non-certified-language court interpreters.

2.4.2. Other Government Agencies

Local offices of either state or federal government agencies frequently utilize outside providers for interpreter services. These interpreter consultants are private practitioners who provide interpreting or translating services to agencies and normally work on a free-lance basis. In many cases, contract interpreters bring with them an extensive background relating to the case for which they are being sought. For example, the Drug Enforcement Agency (DEA) may have a Finnish interpreter under contract in a drug-related matter, and the case in the local court may have to do with precisely that topic.

These offices may be called upon to make referrals to the court. The prudent court administrator should be aware that many law enforcement agencies such as the Federal Bureau of Investigation (FBI), the DEA, the Immigration and Naturalization Service (INS), and the local police frequently utilize their own personnel to satisfy interpreting needs. These bilingual personnel should not be utilized in a criminal matter as interpreters because of the potential for conflict of interest and bias, and because many of them have never had their language or interpreting abilities measured by their own agencies.

2.4.3. National and International Agencies

2.4.3.1. The Office of Language Services of the United States Department of State. This office is responsible for all official translating and interpreting services for the Department of State. The Department's interpreters are called upon to interpret from English into one or more other languages or from one or more other languages into English at official talks, conferences, or during escort assignments. Both simultaneous and consecutive interpretation are used. Since subject matter may be widely divergent, Department of State interpreters and translators must have a good general educational background, supplemented, if possible, by practical experience in several fields.

The office employs a full-time staff of qualified linguists, and at the same time maintains a roster of contractors who may reside anywhere in the country. The full-time staff provides interpreter services in Arabic, Chinese, French, German, Italian, Japanese, Russian, and Spanish. Independent contractors also provide service in these languages, in addition to Bulgarian, Danish, Finnish, Greek, Hebrew, Hungarian, Icelandic, Indonesian, Korean, Laotian, Norwegian, Persian, Polish, Portuguese, Romanian, Serbo-Croatian, Swedish, Taiwanese, Thai, Turkish, and Vietnamese. Contractors are called upon to assist the Department as the need arises, during periods of peak workload, or in less common languages that the regular employees are not equipped to handle. The Department's interpreters and translators are hired and/or contracted after passing a test administered by a panel of examiners. Conference and seminar interpreters are required to pass a test in simultaneous interpretation; escort interpreters are required to pass a test in consecutive interpretation (Department of State, Interpreting Office, personal communication, June 10, 1989).

2.4.3.2. The Interpreter Services of the United Nations and Other International Agencies.   The United Nations tests applicants for the positions of interpreter and translator. Some are hired as full-time employees and many work full- or part-time on a free-lance basis under contract. The United Nations' full-time staff interprets Arabic, Chinese, English, French, Russian, and Spanish, and contracts with free-lance interpreters, when necessary, for the above languages only (United Nations, Interpretation Service Office, personal communication, June 10, 1989). The performance of both employees and free-lance interpreters is monitored. Other international organizations—many of them agencies of the United Nations—that have interpreters and translators working as full-time employees as well as on a free-lance basis include: the World Bank, the International Monetary Fund (IMF), the Inter-American Development Bank (IDB), the Economic Commission for Latin America (ECLA), the Pan American Health Organization (PAHO), the Inter-American Defense Board, Intelsat, and the Organization of American States (OAS).

2.5. Institutions of Higher Education

Traditionally, language departments of colleges and universities have not trained interpreters, although some of them have trained translators. Literature study has always been emphasized over linguistic study. Georgetown University represents an exception in that it has offered courses for translators and interpreters since 1949. In California, the Monterey Institute of International Studies has had an M.A. program in conference interpretation and translation for two decades, and court interpretation is also included in its curriculum.

In the last decade, the University of Delaware, among others, has developed similar courses of study. The University of California, Los Angeles (UCLA), has an advanced course on court interpretation and some translation courses in its Continuing Education Department. California State University, Los Angeles, and its Continuing Education Division in San Diego State University have a basic program for court interpretation and translation. The University of Arizona has had a Summer Institute for Court Interpretation since 1983. Montclair State College in New Jersey, John Jay College in New York, and City University of New York are establishing academic programs. In Miami, Florida International University has had translation programs for many years and it now also has a program for court interpretation, as does Miami-Dade Community College. There is a growing interest in providing training for court interpreters, but such training is mostly limited to Spanish/English and a few other European languages.

However, the supervisory interpreter can call on local two-year and four-year institutions to solve language service problems. The majority of institutions of higher learning offer some foreign language study. Commonly taught languages such as Spanish, French, German, and Italian are generally offered at most of these institutions. Larger universities may offer a wide array of languages, including those that are less commonly taught such as Eastern European, Middle Eastern, and Asian languages. Even if the language sought is not formally taught at the local university, language professors are often well aware of language proficient individuals in the community.

The interpreter supervisor should not be surprised to discover that a potential interpreter who has completed advanced language studies may not possess the interpreting skills necessary for successful performance in the court of law. Many students of foreign languages possess great knowledge of the language without necessarily having developed oral proficiency. Rarely will a language student have a full command of legal terminology in the foreign language. There will always be the need for an orientation session prior to introducing the neophyte interpreter into the legal arena.

2.6. Professional Associations

The supervisory interpreter should be aware that there are professional translator and interpreter associations that publish newsletters, membership directories, and journals and that sponsor conferences and training sessions. A relationship can be developed with the officers of these organizations in order to establish a network with practicing interpreters. These professional associations can then be of assistance in locating interpreters that are needed by the court. A supervisory interpreter, for example, can ask the membership chair, publications officer, or any officer of the organization to announce the need for a particular language interpreter or translator at the next meeting, or ask that it be publicized in the association newsletter. The supervisory interpreter should encourage the court to become an institutional member of these societies in order to obtain a membership directory, receive the association newsletter or journal, and enjoy any other privileges of membership that are helpful in the recruitment of interpreters (see Appendix E, Directory of Professional Associations).

The supervisory interpreter must be aware that membership in a professional association does not in and of itself provide evidence of interpreting skills, although some associations admit members on the basis of proficiency. For example, the Association Internationale d'Interprètes de Conférence (AIIC) [International Association of Conference Interpreters], The American Association of Language Specialists (TAALS), and the American Society of Interpreters (ASI) have rules for the admission of members to promote professional standards of language proficiency and interpreting skills. The American Translators Association (ATA) has only recently required an accreditation examination as a requisite for membership; however, the examination accredits only translators and not interpreters.

Although the National Association of Judiciary Interpreters and Translators (NAJIT) and California Court Interpreters Association (CCIA) have among their members highly qualified interpreters and translators, neither organization requires any test or proof of skills before granting membership. They require only a statement that the applicants have a professional interest in the field of interpretation and are currently a practicing interpreter.

The national and international organizations mentioned above have primarily conference interpreters on their lists. Some conference interpreters, though they possess excellent interpreting skills, might be totally unfamiliar with the techniques, legal language, procedures, and protocol of the courts. The *Federal Court Interpreters Advisory Board: Report to the Director* (Administrative Office of the United States Courts, 1987) describes how some conference interpreters, who were provided by the Office of Language Services of the Department of State to work at the federal court in the Central District of California, showed a great eagerness to learn legal terminology and court procedure, which were new fields for them. The Advisory Board addressed the issue of using conference interpreters in court, and reached the conclusion that good conference interpreters are easily trainable and are aware of the need to prepare themselves. Most of them adjust quickly to the court system and make good judicial interpreters.

2.7. Commercial Interpreting Agencies

Although commercial interpreting agencies seldom rigorously test the interpreters whom they place on their lists, they are frequently successful at finding interpreters with at least marginal skills in unusual languages. Occasionally courts have been able to fill a pressing need with the help of such agencies. In some jurisdictions the courts are the greatest consumer of services provided by these agencies, and they rely on such agencies to meet all of their interpreting needs. In these jurisdictions, the court often does not have an office of court interpreting services or a structure that maintains a cadre of staff or per diem interpreters.

Nonetheless, those courts that do maintain an office of court interpreting services can also utilize commercial interpreter agencies as resources. The supervisory interpreter may enter into a reciprocal relationship with the commercial agency. This entails a cooperative exchange of names of potential interpreters whenever the court or the commercial agency faces a particular language need and find they have no one to call.

The supervisory interpreter should request the name of the non-certified-language interpreter from the commercial agency so that the court may directly contract with the interpreter. The commercial agency should provide the information requested as a public service and out of professional courtesy to the court. In return, the commercial agency may call on the supervisory interpreter for the names of interpreters the agency needs and cannot find. The court should provide this service to the commercial agency to promote goodwill. If this reciprocal relationship cannot be arranged with a commercial agency, the court should seek other sources. Of course, this relationship with commercial agencies may be more feasible in large metropolitan areas than in small municipalities.

2.8. Community Organizations

Many community organizations are often established by diverse language groups. Examples include a German club, a Korean society, a Vietnamese service organization, or ethnically oriented churches like a Ukrainian Catholic Church or Bulgarian Orthodox Church. The supervising interpreter should be cognizant of the fact that these untested interpreters generally have little knowledge of courtroom protocol and procedures and lack a clear concept of interpreter duties and functions. Therefore, assuming that their language skills are found to be acceptable, these novices will need a structured orientation program that will introduce them to court protocol and the ethical responsibilities and restrictions placed upon the interpreter.

2.9. Conclusion

From all of these sources the supervisory interpreter will build a roster of names of interpreters representing numerous languages. After a period of months or years, the supervisory interpreter can anticipate the most frequently used languages in a particular jurisdiction and be prepared for whatever language services are needed in the court. As the demand for court interpreter services increases, the supervisory interpreter will in turn become an important link in the court interpreter informational network. However, these are short-term measures to address language services problems which should be solved through rigorous federal- and state-level certification procedures on the most frequently used and demographically justifiable languages.

3. Assessment Procedures

In the process of recruitment, the supervisory interpreter must fully ascertain the language proficiency and interpreting skills of the prospective interpreter. In the case of interpreters who have passed certification examinations, the supervisory interpreter will not be required to assess competency. The problem lies in assessing the language proficiency of prospective interpreters who have not passed an examination or been certified by any agency, and in some rare instances where certification exams are so questionable that they cannot be said to be a valid measure of performance. See Unit 8, Chapters 36 and 37 for more information on assessment procedures.

The interpreter performs two critical functions in the court: (1) to accurately interpret the proceedings of the court, that is, each and every word uttered by witnesses and all the members of the legal arena for the benefit of the defendant in the defendant's native language; and (2) to precisely interpret for the record the words of the non-English-speaking witness from the foreign language into English. It is, therefore, incumbent upon the supervisory interpreter to ascertain the interpreter candidate's language abilities; the supervisor must be satisfied fully that the prospective interpreter can accomplish these tasks.

For any supervisory interpreter, the task of testing language and interpreting skills in a number of languages is impossible. Except for the language or languages in which the supervisory interpreter is proficient, it is impossible to validly assess proficiency in all languages. Unfortunately, in the face of the seemingly impossible task of evaluating interpreting skills in a host of non-certified languages, standard practice has been to employ an appropriately surnamed person and, in a leap of faith, introduce that person into a court of law with no prior determination as to language competence. This untested interpreter is then expected to provide interpretation services for either a non-English-speaking defendant or a witness. The results have been less than satisfactory. In the absence of valid testing instruments administered by language specialists, the court and the defendant cannot be guaranteed a "true and accurate" interpretation of the proceedings.

Considering present restricted governmental budgets and the lack of awareness of language needs of non-English speakers by some courts, there is little hope that certification programs will be available in more than a few languages. Therefore, it falls to the office of court interpreting services to construct a set of strategies that will indicate bilingual proficiency and interpreting skills. To be sure, the task of evaluating interpreting skills is a challenge for the supervisor. However, there are strategies that can be employed to determine basic language skills in English and to some degree in the other language. Using the strategies outlined below, it is possible to come to a conclusion based on indirect evidence as to the prospective interpreter's language proficiency and perhaps even interpreting skills.

3.1. Interview

The supervisory interpreter can assess the background of the prospective interpreter through a structured interview process. This interview allows the supervisor to establish the language, educational, and professional background of the candidate, and at the same time affords the interviewer the opportunity to assess the English proficiency of the candidate. The interviewer must be satisfied that the candidate's English comprehension and verbal production skills are at a level commensurate with the demands of the court. An important consideration is the candidate's comprehensibility; although it may be accented, the candidate's speech must nonetheless be easily understood by the court reporter and all the participants in court.

During the course of the interview, questions should be organized so that the content and complexity progress from simple, casual chatting to a discussion of more linguistically and intellectually complex issues. This sequence of questions should put the candidates at ease and allow them to speak on the topic with which they are most familiar—namely, personal background and opinions. Questions that may be utilized during the interview process include the following:

Level 1 questions: Inquire about name, address, current and former occupation, former interpreting or translating experience, if any; language background and proficiency, educational background in the United States and in a foreign country, if applicable.

Level 2 questions: Inquire about travels outside the United States to encourage the discussion of economics or cultural differences, require the use of more sophisticated language to elicit control of precise vocabulary.

Level 3 questions: Place candidate in a hypothetical courtroom situation in which a problem is posed that requires candidates to state what they would do to remedy the situation. This allows the interviewer to hear candidates express themselves in non-egocentric language about a subject completely outside of themselves, in which candidates can no longer report on their own experiences but now must utilize language to hypothesize a solution to an imagined problem.

Level 4 questions: Inquire about the candidate's understanding of the United States form of government or of the United States judicial system. These technical and sophisticated content questions give the candidate an opportunity to perform at a level significantly higher than merely reporting on personal background or experience. The objective of the interviewer is not to judge the quality of the content, but to assess the English proficiency of the candidate during a discussion utilizing abstract concepts; in addition, the content may be an indication of the interpreter's legal knowledge. Obviously, the candidate who cannot reach Level 4 is to be considered suspect. It is doubtful that a candidate whose English proficiency is that limited would be successful at interpreting the highly technical language of the courtroom.

3.2. Biographical Sketch

The interviewer provides the candidate with a sheet of paper and asks the candidate to write a first-person narrative on personal background. This exercise requires no preparation or special knowledge on the part of the applicant, and deals with a subject on which everyone is an expert. This exercise provides the interviewer with insight into the candidate's sophistication in English by evaluating the variety of the vocabulary and syntactic structures employed. It also yields more information about the candidate's personal background.

3.3. Standardized Written Proficiency Examinations

Ideally, it would be preferable from a linguistic viewpoint to test for all language skills, including listening, speaking, reading, and writing, and all modes of interpreting, but the reality that confronts local courts in the selection of court interpreters makes this ideal impossible. At the very least, the supervisory interpreter can test for English proficiency by administering a written examination. The supervisory interpreter should rely upon available assessment tools that can be administered by a non-speaker of the language. Standardized written examinations are currently available through publishing houses, schools, and universities to test basic English and other major languages.

These materials are accompanied by answer keys, and many of the tests are multiple choice and easily scored. Disclosed forms of English tests such as the Test of English as a Foreign Language (TOEFL) are published in practice workbooks produced by companies such as Barron's, Educational Testing Service (ETS), and Newbury House. Additionally, tests such as the Scholastic Aptitude Test (SAT), the Advanced College Test (ACT), and the Graduate Record Examination (GRE) are available in a variety of practice workbooks. The use of this type of test gives the candidate the opportunity to demonstrate a command of English.

In addition to the use of standardized tests of written English proficiency, the interviewer may wish to utilize similar texts that are available for major languages. Tests in Spanish, German, French, Italian, and Russian are available from most colleges and universities, and may be available as well from the Educational Testing Service (ETS). For other languages in addition to Spanish, it may be possible to work with a university or college and borrow whatever instrument their faculties may have developed for their own use. The supervisor may also adapt an existing exam by using only appropriate portions. For instance, the TOEFL test is a three-part examination of a candidate's proficiency in listening, reading, and structure/vocabulary in English. The interviewer may wish to use only the structure/vocabulary section as a check on language.

Since the position of court interpreter is primarily one that relies on aural-oral skills, no selection procedure or assessment program for this position should depend solely on a written assessment. Any written form of testing should be used in conjunction with other assessments to make an ultimate decision as to the competence of a court interpreter candidate.

3.4. Shadowing

The interviewer places the candidate in a situation that utilizes a tape recorder, head phones, and a pre-recorded monologue. This might be one to two minutes of an opening or closing argument recorded at a moderate speed, 120 to 140 words per minute. The supervisor asks the candidate to listen to the monologue and simply to shadow the content of the tape, that is, to repeat the narrative simultaneously, word-for-word, in the same language as it is heard, in this case English. The supervisor follows a printed transcript of the tape and is able to assess the accuracy of the candidate's shadowing. This exercise closely parallels the simultaneous mode of interpretation but eliminates the transfer from one language to another. It provides evidence of the capacity to perform a function that is essential in simultaneous interpretation: the ability to listen to a speaker, process the information, and speak at the same time.

Assessing quality of performance on this exercise is relatively easy. First, the number of words in the exercise should be counted, because the criterion for measurement is the percentage rate of completion. The interviewer plays the pre-recorded passage and the candidate hears it on earphones. The interpreter candidate is then asked to shadow the passage simultaneously. The performance may be recorded on a second tape recorder for either subsequent scoring or to provide objective evidence should rejection of a candidate be followed by a challenge. The interviewer scores the performance by noting the words, phrases, clauses, or sentences the interpreter candidate omits or distorts. At the completion of the exercise, the interviewer computes the total number of words omitted or distorted. Then this sum is divided by the total number of words in the text to arrive at a percentage score for the candidate.

Whereas each supervisory interpreter will subjectively determine the rate of success that is acceptable for performing the function of a court interpreter in a particular court, the recommendation is that acceptable candidates should be able to shadow with at least eighty percent fidelity. The reason for this high standard is that shadowing tests only one component, albeit a critical one, of simultaneous interpretation. A candidate who is unable to shadow with the utmost precision would certainly be unable to cope with the complex semantic, syntactic, and terminological problems of actual simultaneous interpretation.

3.5. Memory Test

One of the salient indicators of interpreting skills is good short-term memory. Consecutive interpretation requires the interpreter to listen to a question or an answer of variable length and complexity and then interpret that utterance into the target language. A simple device to test for short-term memory is to read a question as it might be posed by an attorney and to ask the interpreter candidate to repeat as much of the question as possible. This exercise is a monolingual exercise and requires no interpretation. The only problem facing the candidate is to retain the content of the utterance long enough to deliver it back verbatim in the same language. This is in essence the consecutive interpretation counterpart to shadowing.

The following are examples of questions and answers that may be used in the memory exercise, with the scoring units underlined (scoring units are items that are representative of typical pitfalls and interpreting problems, that can be used to arrive at an objective assessment of the candidate's performance):

(1) Well, I don't know ... what I mean is, I'm not really sure, but it looks like the same .357.

(2) No, that's not true! I was not in the country on the 16th of February ... I didn't arrive here until March 28.

(3) Yes, I'm sure he's the one, because he has the same face, only the hair is different. It was much longer.

(4) I left my house at 7:15, walked over to 2nd Avenue and took the bus down to 177th.

(5) I saw two men get out of a 1988 white Toyota Corolla. They knocked on the door of the house across the street. Then the shorter of the two went around the back.

(6) I must remind you that you are under oath, Sir. I ask you again, did you see the deceased with the defendant on the day in question?

(7) Calling your attention to January 25, 1989, can you recall anything unusual that occurred during the morning in Apartment 721.

(8) You say they took the TV, two stereo speakers, a camera, and $175 in cash. Anything else?

(9) Are you now saying that he left the party before 11:30 p.m., because someone told you that or because you have an independent memory of his leaving at that hour?

(10) Is it a fair statement to say that you were at such a distance that you couldn't see their faces because of the poor lighting?

In scoring the memory test, the administrator focuses on the candidate's ability to recall the *scoring* units accurately, with no omissions or distortions. The objective of the memory exercise is to assess the candidate's ability to remember verbatim the questions and answers in the test tape. The examination tests memory/mimicry capability, not comprehension; therefore, exact words are required in the candidate's rendition. A candidate who begins to paraphrase should be reminded to repeat exactly what was heard.

The test administrator counts the number of items the candidate has correctly rendered. Missing half of the underlined items is tantamount to missing almost 50 percent of the significant features of the original message. If the interpreter cannot recall 50 percent of the message, it is doubtful that the person could interpret with even that degree of accuracy, since interpretation further taxes the memory. Any candidate who cannot recall a question of moderate length and complexity in English will most likely be unable to interpret the content of that question, or answer from a source language into a target language consecutively.

3.6. Back-Translation Technique

Without qualification, the most challenging task that the supervisory interpreter has in the assessment of interpreting skills is to determine the ability of the candidate to interpret into a language unknown to the test administrator. Not being able to determine what is being said, the test administrator is at a disadvantage. The utterances made might be gibberish, and the tester needs to discover what exactly those utterances mean.

One strategy that may be useful is to use the candidate's knowledge of the language as an aid in the assessment of performance. The test administrator can check the accuracy of the candidate's interpreting performance by not only requiring a candidate to interpret into the language, but also requiring the candidate to interpret her own rendition back into English. This strategy, termed back-translation, is analogous to the read-back memory feature used in computer communications systems.

This feature is used to verify the reception of correct data transmission from one computer system to another. The receiving computer system sends back the information received so that the originating system can verify the accuracy of the information by comparing the information in the confirmation signal with the original data. Brislin (1976) describes a project in which the work of Vietnamese translators was assessed using the back-translation technique, and notes that "the advantage of this technique is that a person who does not know the language from the middle of the sequence (Vietnamese, in this case) can gain some insight into the quality of the translation by comparing the two English versions" (p. 15).

The technique is simple. First, a set of ten questions and/or statements in English, similar to those that might be made by a witness at the stand or by an examining attorney, are pre-recorded by the test administrator. These questions and statements are discrete items and bear no relationship to each other in meaning or in context. Among the ten questions and statements are forty scoring items representing dates, times, places, precise or technical vocabulary, and certain grammatical structures that the test administrator will look for to verify the back-translation of the questions and statements. The testing tape should allow enough time provided between the utterances during which the candidate must complete the interpretation.

A sample set of questions and statements follows, with the scoring units underlined:

(1) Mr. Anderson, calling your attention to the morning of the 12th of May, 1988, did you on that date have the occasion to enter the downtown branch of the Bank of America to cash a check?

(2) Let me see if I get what you mean. Are you now saying that the man who was holding the gun on you that evening was the tall skinny one, the one wearing an earring?

(3) From the time you first saw the defendant running down the hallway until you heard the gunshot, how far do you estimate he had travelled?

(4) Are you now telling the jury that you were mistaken in your identification of the defendant and that you are now no longer sure that this is the man who robbed you in your jewelry store?

(5) Is your testimony, sir, that you were completely unaware that your travelling companion on flight 767 was carrying a coffee can full of cocaine in her suitcase?

(6) About 9:30, I walked into the park and waited for my friend by the brick wall. I was watching some tree trimmers when some plainclothes police officers stopped and arrested me.

(7) Well . . . as I've already told you, I tried on the coat, and then I got distracted because an old lady asked me to watch her packages. I didn't realize I had the coat on until I got outside the store.

(8) I was sitting by myself on the bus bench when that girl right there with the braids came and sat right next to me. She was very interested in my watch. Then she grabbed my purse and ran.

(9) He told me he was going to kill me. He then pulled out a long knife, and I believe he would have done it if those two women had not come by at that time.

(10) The man I saw was <u>blond</u>, about <u>as tall as you are</u> and wearing <u>blue jeans</u> and a <u>plaid shirt</u>.

One potential drawback to the back-translation technique is the possibility of distortion of the test results due to the candidate's reliance on memory of the original English questions and answers rather than interpreting back into English what was actually said and recorded during the initial phase of this technique. However, this potential problem can be minimized by separating the two phases—the initial interpretation of the questions and answers into the target language and the interpretation of what was originally recorded back into English—by a lapse of time. The passage of time contributes to the diminishing of memory. Therefore, we recommend that the first phase, the English-into-target-language portion, be conducted at the beginning of the assessment interview, and that the second phase, the back-translation into English, be the final task in the entire assessment process. This time lapse will reduce the potential for candidates to simply remember the original English statements and render them from memory, rather than from their own interpretation into the target language.

3.6.1. Procedure

The interpreter candidate is asked to listen through earphones to the questions and statements and to interpret them into the target language consecutively, as if interpreting at the stand. The candidate is allowed to take notes and a pad and pencil should be provided. During the examination, the candidate's performance should be recorded on a second tape recorder. When the candidate has completed the English-into-target-language portion, the newly recorded tape is set aside until the back-translation phase begins at the end of the entire assessment process. Additionally, any notes the candidate took during the examination should be collected and saved with the results of the assessment in case of challenges.

At the end of the entire assessment process, the back-translation portion begins. The test administrator rewinds the candidate's target language test tape and plays it back for the candidate, who listens to the recording through headphones. The test administrator instructs the candidate to interpret consecutively from the target language into English everything that is heard on the tape, without adding or omitting anything that is on the tape in the foreign language for each utterance. During the back-translation phase, the interpreter candidate should be provided with a clean note pad and pencil should the candidate wish to take notes. The test administrator should have a clean copy of the original script, and simply check the back-translation for omissions or distortions of the original test statements and questions, in particular of the underlined scorable items.

3.6.2. Scoring

In assessing the back-translation for completion, the test administrator should be mindful that the words will not always come back into their original English form. The test administrator should not confuse the substitution of words for a distortion of meaning. There is often more than one way to express the same thought with different words. The candidate should be given credit for a scoring unit if a concept has survived its transposition from one language to another and back intact, regardless of the specific word or words utilized in the original English. In item number 7, the words "I tried on" might very well be expressed by "I put on" or in item number 2, "holding the gun on you" may be expressed by "pointing the gun at you." In item number 5, the words "completely unaware" as well as "didn't know" are acceptable. Only if the concept is distorted or omitted should the scoring unit be counted wrong.

Out of forty scoring items, an interpreter candidate who gets twenty correct is only rendering half of the testimony or questions. If only thirty items are correct, the interpreter is rendering only 75 percent of the testimony or questions. The mathematics are plain, and it is up to the supervisory interpreter to determine what is an acceptable level of performance for the local court. As a point of comparison, candidates for Spanish/English Federal Court Interpreter Certification are expected to perform at the 78 percent level of accuracy in a forty-five minute examination in which 220 scoring items have been identified. At the very least, the final score of this back-translation procedure can be used as an objective comparison of the relative strengths of one interpreter candidate over another.

3.7. Other Assessment Possibilities

Because of the problems inherent in ascertaining the competency of prospective interpreters in languages for which no certification program exists, assessment strategies should be developed through collaborate efforts of federal, state, and local courts and institutions of higher learning. These entities could identify the languages of most critical need and cooperate in the utilization of human and fiscal resources, developing testing and training programs for interpreters who could be called upon to serve the various courts. Telephone assessments by language specialists and other such prepared and tape-recorded tests can be developed to aid the courts in this difficult task. This will be further discussed in Unit 7, Chapter 33. In the interim, some orderly and at least documentable procedure must be instituted to gauge, even crudely, the relative degree of skill of the interpreter who will be sent into court.

In the case of assessing untested Spanish interpreters, any local court system may communicate with the Administrative Office of the United States Courts (AO) to arrange an examination of a group of potential interpreters on a cost-reimbursement basis. The examinations utilized would be the Spanish/English Written Certification Examination and the Spanish-English Oral Interpreting Performance Test that have already been developed for certification of federal court interpreters.

The benefits to local courts of utilizing the Federal Court Interpreter Certification Examination are several: (1) It is a cost-efficient strategy which will eliminate the need for fiscal investment in the development of local certification programs. (2) The Federal Court Interpreter Certification Examination has a proven statistical history of reliability and has withstood legal challenge (Seltzer v. Foley, 1980). (3) Whereas the AO is disposed to cooperate with local jurisdictions in the administration of the court interpreter examination, it will not impose any federal standards of performance. Therefore, the local court or governmental agency may avail itself of an indisputably valid and reliable test, and establish its own standards of acceptable performance to conform to local need and complement any concomitant training program. This same kind of arrangement may also be possible with other agencies that have developed interpreter examinations, such as the Cooperative Personnel Services in California, or the State of New Jersey Administrative Office of the Courts. In this case, however, each state would have to conduct a linguistic analysis, set its own performance standard, and establish the external validity of the examination (see Unit 8, Chapter 36).

Chapter 16

Orientation, Training, and Monitoring of Interpreters

This chapter will examine the functions of the supervisor of court interpreter services with respect to the orientation of new interpreters, the ongoing training of all interpreters, and the day-to-day monitoring of interpreter performance to ensure that the highest standards of quality are maintained.

1. Orientation of New Interpreters

Once interpreter candidates have been recruited and assessed, another major responsibility the supervisory interpreter must undertake is the orientation of any interpreter who will provide services for the court. The supervisory interpreter is also responsible for any short-term training to prepare inexperienced interpreters to deliver quality language services.

Interpreters present themselves for court interpreting work in various states of preparedness. Therefore, it is incumbent upon the supervisor to assess what skills and knowledge potential interpreters possess regardless of the language involved. Some interpreters may be competent to interpret in two languages, but lack knowledge of legal procedure and terminology. Others may need to polish their basic English skills. The supervisory interpreter can devise an orientation program that will touch upon those areas of knowledge that novice interpreters generally are unfamiliar with. Before serving the court every person new to the profession would be required to attend a general orientation session presented by the supervisory interpreter.

Because most supervisory interpreters and administrators charged with the co-ordination and orientation of interpreters have time constraints, each court should consider developing videotapes to orient prospective interpreters to the courtroom. Creating a videotape is not beyond the abilities of court personnel; however, it may be more efficient to commission the production of this to a consultant who can produce the video with the advice of the interpreter. A videotape obviates the need to repeat the orientation procedure several times over a period of weeks and months, and provides an efficient and expeditious means of orientation in conjunction with other materials and discussions.

1.1. General Orientation Procedure

As the supervisory interpreter builds a roster of persons who have been interviewed and whose language competency has been assessed, it is necessary to prepare these persons for their first appearance in court by introducing them to courtroom procedures, ethics, protocol, legal terminology, and the role of the interpreter in the legal process.

Such an orientation would ideally be presented over a two-day period, but given the constraints of time and funding, a reasonable expectation would be to devote at least a half-day session to presenting the following information:

(1) The *roles and functions* of all the participants in the courtroom (see Unit VII, Chapter 1).

(2) The *logistics of the courtroom and the place of the interpreter* within the courtroom, including a discussion of where the interpreter sits and/or stands when interpreting for the defendant at counsel table, or for the witness at the stand, and the mode of interpretation utilized for each of these functions (see Unit 7, Chapter 29).

(3) *Principles of judicial interpreting,* touching upon issues such as conservation of the language and accuracy of interpretation (see Introduction and Unit 3, Chapter 12).

(4) *Introduction to judicial procedures,* including an overview of major hearings from arraignment to sentencing (see Unit 2 and Unit 7).

(5) *Interpreter ethics and protocol,* how and when to address the court, speaking to witnesses and jurors, and so on (see Unit 8).

(6) *Review of other related interpreter tasks and responsibilities,* such as jail, pre-trial, and lock-up interviews, translations of documents, and so on (see Unit 7).

(7) *Preparedness for the interpreting task,* carrying dictionaries and other reference materials, pad and pen, seeking information about the case assigned (see Unit 7).

(8) *Description of a sample procedure* such as an arraignment, from the moment the interpreter steps into the courtroom, indicating exactly what will take place, where the interpreter stands in relationship to the defendant and the attorney, what mode of interpretation is used, local protocol regarding the swearing in of the interpreter, or the identification of the interpreter on the record (see Unit 7).

(9) *Assignment of court observation,* to familiarize the prospective court interpreters with court proceedings. There is no better way to accomplish this objective than by direct observation. The novice interpreter should be assigned to observe a variety of court proceedings. Such observation can be monitored by providing the prospective interpreter with a hearings assignment signature form, such as the one suggested in the *Federal Court Interpreters Advisory Board: Report to the Director* (Administrative Office of the United States Courts, 1987). In this way, novices are able to have their attendance at various hearings verified by the signature of the court clerk. The supervisory interpreter can ask for the submission of this form within a particular period of time.

It is recommended that supervisory interpreters assign the reading of Units 2, 3, 7, and 8 of this book to supplement the general orientation process. It would also be advantageous for novice interpreters to be introduced to the *Los Angeles County Superior Court Interpreters Manual* (Almeida & Zahler, 1981) for ethics, legal procedures, and a set of glossaries of lexical domains most frequently encountered in court. Although the glossary is Spanish-English, the list of vocabulary items can be used by other-language interpreters for the creation of their own glossaries. Another valuable source for legal terminology is *Terms Most Often Used in Federal Court* (Administrative Office of the United States Courts, 1983).

1.2. Emergency Orientation Procedure

Many courthouses will experience emergency situations that will necessitate calling bilingual persons to interpret who are not certified and who have no interpreting experience in the courts. In this case, those responsible for the orientation of personnel used for emergency interpreting may have only a limited amount of time before the interpreters must perform their duties. The following is one recommended course of action for the court clerk or supervisory interpreter to follow:

(1) Describe the courtroom setting and present the interpreter with a diagram of the courtroom.

(2) Outline the procedure from the moment the interpreter steps into the courtroom, indicating exactly what will take place, for example:

(a) What type of hearing will the interpreter face? Will it be an arraignment or a preliminary hearing?

(b) What mode of interpretation will the interpreter be expected to use, simultaneous, consecutive, or both?

(c) What is the purpose and structure of the hearing?

(d) Will the defendant be pleading guilty? Will there be a probation department report that will need to be sight translated?

(e) Where is the interpreter to sit or stand?

(f) What is the pertinent protocol? Will the interpreter be called upon to identify herself or himself for the record?

(g) Will the interpreter be sworn in by the court clerk prior to the proceedings?

(h) If the interpreter does not understand the language of the witness or a particular word, how may the interpreter address the court or ask for clarification?

(i) Are there any individual practices or local customs of which the interpreter should be aware?

(3) Summarize for the interpreter the facts of the case and, if possible, allow the interpreter to read the complaint or other pertinent documents which will help the interpreter become familiar with the necessary vocabulary.

(4) Provide the interpreter with a stenographer's pad and sharpened pencil or pen.

(5) Inform the judge of the interpreter's qualifications and status.

(6) Provide the interpreter with an information packet. This packet should include:

(a) A map of the courthouse and courtroom, with the telephone number of the assignment office and the name of the supervisory interpreter, the clerk of court, and the judge.

(b) A paperback edition of *Black's* or *Gifis's* law dictionaries.

(c) The interpreter information card, for the interpreter to fill out and hand in to the supervisory interpreter or the clerk, i.e., name, address, telephone number, languages, and so on.

(d) Information regarding procedure for payment for services rendered, and the rate for half-day and full-day service.

(e) A copy of the *Terms Most Often Used in Federal Court* (Administrative Office of the United States Courts, 1983), if available, or a similar glossary.

(f) The assignment form.

(g) Any available information prepared specifically for the recipient of court interpreting services.

(h) Information on when to attend the next court interpreter general orientation seminar sponsored by the court.

(i) Information regarding the local or state court interpreter's association.

2. Short-Term and In-Service Training

In order to develop and maintain a professional level cadre of court interpreters, some local courts have assumed responsibility for the establishment of training programs designed to promote and improve the interpreters' skills. These programs have most frequently been successful when offered on Saturday mornings and announced as a mini-series of lectures and seminars.

The mini-series may include: (1) speakers from the public defender's office who might address interpreter problems and issues from the viewpoint of the defense; (2) attorneys representing the prosecutor's office who would similarly discuss interpreter problems as they are perceived by a prosecutor; (3) a judge speaking on judicial expectations of the court interpreter; (4) a law enforcement officer speaking on a particular area of information, such as driving under the influence, drug-related arrests, or weaponry nomenclature; (5) a senior court interpreter speaking on ethics and court protocol; (6) an attorney speaking on legal procedures and legal terminology; (7) an immigration officer speaking on immigration law, hearings, and regulations, illegal aliens, smuggling, and so forth; (8) a master interpreter teaching techniques of consecutive and simultaneous interpretation and sight translation using a mock-trial format and the electronic, simultaneous interpreting equipment used in courts for multi-defendant cases; or (9) a linguist or anthropologist speaking on comparative language or culture.

Prospective and regular per diem interpreters should be invited to attend and participate for the purposes of professional growth and improving their skills. The supervisory interpreter can be quite successful in encouraging interpreters to attend by judicious wording of the invitation, emphasizing the increased earning potential to be gained from enhancing skills and establishing a reputation as a serious professional. The visiting lecturers are often contracted and compensated for their services, representing the only expense for the court.

This training is particularly important for courts that are far removed from interpreter training programs sponsored by local colleges, universities, or professional organizations. By organizing and sponsoring interpreter training programs, such courts would be not only providing a service to interpreters but also improving the administration of justice.

An exemplary court-sponsored training program was offered by the Los Angeles Superior Court. It began the program for Spanish interpreters in anticipation of the advent of state certification, and then incorporated other languages, recognizing the need to upgrade the level of competence on the part of its interpreters.

This twenty-four-hour course of study was launched by the court in 1977 and was taught by three senior interpreters. It was the first formal course of study offered by a court for interpreter training in the United States. The following year, the program was expanded and offered on Saturdays by the California Court Interpreters Association. This collaboration between a court and a professional interpreting association resulted in a high rate of state interpreter certification, as well as a growing confidence in language services and the ability of the courts to serve the needs of the non-English-speaking witnesses and defendants. After reaching the conclusion that equal access to justice for limited- and non-English speakers is predicated upon the interpreting proficiency of the interpreters who serve the court, the Administrative Office of the New Jersey Courts set into motion the most comprehensive training and certification program undertaken by any state to date (New Jersey Supreme Court Task Force on Interpreter and Translation Services, 1985).

The state has not only developed a certification and testing program, but also sponsored a yearly interpreting conference and co-sponsored training programs in collaboration with the University of Arizona and Montclair State College, and sponsored through scholarship a number of staff interpreters at various institutions of higher learning, such as the John Jay College of Criminal Justice. Most recently, the New Jersey Consortium of Educators in Legal Interpretation and Translation published *Curricular Guidelines for the Development of Legal Interpreter Education* (1988), discussed in Unit 8, Chapter 35, of this text.

3. Long-Term Training

Whereas the primary responsibility for the acquisition and improvement of professional interpreting skills lies with the individual interpreter, some local courts have correctly seen the relationship between interpreting skills and the quality of justice. Accordingly, they have sponsored their interpreters' attendance at various summer and year-round programs in court interpreting, as well as seminars and conferences offered by professional organizations. Included are jurisdictions in Florida, California, Arizona, Nevada, Texas, New Jersey, New York, Washington, and other states. Recognizing that court interpreting is in its infancy, and that institutions of higher learning have not offered courses with sufficient breadth and consistency to produce qualified interpreters, courts have begun to institute their own competency standards. This will and should continue until such a time as the profession develops to maturity.

4. Monitoring of Interpreters

As part of the responsibilities of the office, the supervisory interpreter should observe the performance of interpreters in the courtroom. The obvious challenge for the supervisory interpreter is to monitor unfamiliar languages. But supervisory interpreters can observe the interpreter's manner and demeanor while in court, and if the person sits and stares off into space, oblivious to the proceedings in the courtroom, or if the person is sitting in the wrong place, or does not noticeably speak during a proceeding when expected to interpret in the simultaneous mode, the supervisory interpreter can take note of a staff or per diem interpreter's limitations and deficiencies. The interpreter at the stand is particularly observable; the individual's confidence or lack thereof while interpreting, timely and prompt interpretations, or, conversely, delayed reactions and labored delivery can be easily observed. The participation of the interpreter in unsanctioned conversation with the witness can be noted as evidence of the interpreter's unfamiliarity with court protocol. In short, even though the specific language may not be understood, much valuable information can be gleaned. When assessing the performance of the interpreters monitored in the courtroom, the supervisory interpreter should consider the following performance criteria required for due process as set forth by United States district court judges.

From November 29 through December 10, 1979, an author of this book, R. D. Gonzalez, participated in the first Federal Court Interpreter Certification Examination Development Panel, where she witnessed the original discussions by three federal judges, who explicated specific performance standards to the committee.

- Interpreters must be able to interpret every word of the original testimony of the witness, not omitting a single element, for that one element, as inconsequential as it may seem, could be an important factor in discovering the truth.

- Interpreters must be able to interpret a message as closely as possible to the manner in which the witness originally said it, so that the judge and the jury would be able to hear the "flavor" of the speaker's words and make judgments about the witness's credibility.

- Interpreters must be able to interpret a long response from the witness without interrupting the witness.

- Interpreters must be able to simultaneously interpret everything occurring in a proceeding in exactly the way it was said originally by the judge or attorney, so that important legal issues are not distorted when they are interpreted to the witness.

- Interpreters should understand the role of the interpreter, as distinguished from the role of an attorney, for example, and should confine themselves to interpreting rather than explaining or giving legal advice.

- Interpreters should have a comprehensive knowledge of both languages, from the formal usage of the court to the simple usage of the witnesses.

If the interpreting problems seem to stem from lack of training, the supervisory interpreter can call this to the interpreter's attention and utilize this assessment as the rationale for additional training. After apprising the interpreter of these shortcomings and establishing that the interpreter understands the nature of interpreting duties, the supervisory interpreter can check on progress on subsequent occasions.

If subsequent observations reveal that the interpreter is not performing according to the specified instructions, the supervisor can deduce with some validity that the interpreter may not have the language or interpreting competence necessary to perform the task. This would be grounds for discontinuing service. If the supervisory interpreter has grave doubt as to the precision and thoroughness of the interpreter's performance, the back-translation technique described in Chapter 15 of this unit could be used to provide further indication of accuracy.

In the case of monitoring the performance of an interpreter in a familiar language, the supervisory interpreter is in a position not only to observe but also to hear and understand the interpretation at the stand and check on accuracy and thoroughness. If there are flaws in the interpretation that distort meaning or that misrepresent the speaker's level of sophistication, the supervisory interpreter is justified in bringing this to the attention of the interpreter in private conversation. The job of monitoring performance and reporting constructively is not an easy task; it is one that requires great interpersonal skills. However, it is essential for maintaining high standards of performance. The monitoring and critique should be regarded as an integral part of the supervisory interpreter's job. Furthermore, the supervisory interpreter must strike a delicate balance between effective monitoring and overzealous supervision that would erode the interpreter's self-confidence.

One strategy that the supervisor can employ to document the ongoing monitoring of interpreter performance is to maintain a file of tape recordings of the in-court performance of regularly used interpreters, regardless of language. These tape recordings will form the basis for discussions in which the supervisor can assess the interpreter's performance and provide suggestions for improvement. This supervisor/ interpreter feedback is predicated, of course, on the supervisor's knowledge of the language recorded. If the supervisor does not know the language in question, the assistance of language experts can be sought to properly evaluate the interpreter's performance.

This procedure should be carried out in a spirit of cooperation; accordingly, the interpreter should be included in the planning and scheduling of the taping and the evaluation. At best, the taping of interpreter performance is stressful, and, at its very worst, threatening and intimidating. In order to minimize the negative factors inherent in the recording of the interpreter's performance, the supervisor should through words convey the idea of a mutual and cooperative effort, rather than a unilateral and judgmental approach. Notice the difference between "Marisa, we've got to cut an evaluation tape for you sometime next week. When do you think will be a good time?" and "I have a tape here, Marisa, that I recorded and I want to talk to you about some of the things you said." By being positive and non-threatening, and by making the interpreter feel included in the process, the supervisory interpreter can ensure that the interpreter will derive as much benefit as possible.

Chapter 17

Administrative Issues

This chapter provides some guidelines for managing administrative matters that fall within the purview of the director or supervisor of court interpreting services. It focuses specifically on assignment procedures, forms and records, fees, the use of electronic equipment, and the orientation of non-English speakers to the court system.

1. Assignment Procedures

When cases on the court's calendar have been identified in advance as requiring the services of a court interpreter, the assignment office has time to make telephone contact with interpreters to schedule them for the case or cases in question. Any number of interpreters in any number of languages may be needed for a particular day's calendar. Some days are trial dates that will require the long-term assignment of court interpreters to each case. Other calendars involve arraignments, which may require a large number of interpreters in one courtroom because of multiple defendants. Regardless of the specifics, the assignment office is able to anticipate needs and meet them.

In an ideal situation, the supervisory interpreter would have an unlimited number of full-time interpreters in every language that was ever requested. As the need arose, the assignment clerk or office would simply make the assignment from an ever-ready pool of staff interpreters whose full-time position would assure their availability everyday. This "utopian" situation is obviously a practical impossibility. Fiscal reality simply makes it unfeasible for a local court to hire a large number of full-time staff positions in an area where the demand for their services is unpredictable and fluctuates drastically from day to day. The practical solution to this problem is to develop and maintain a pool of available outside providers or per diem interpreters who will render service on an as-needed basis (see Chapter 15 for recruitment methods).

1.1. Availability Problems

Even when the language in question is a common one for which many interpreters are available—Spanish, for example—the assignment of appropriate interpreters is still a complex undertaking. Many interpreters work for several different courts and for many other government and private agencies. Some interpreters are available only certain days, or are only willing to work half days. Other complicating factors have to do with adhering to policies set by the assignment office, such as requiring an interpreter to remain on a trial from beginning to end, thus making the original assignment that much more difficult because of the time commitment. Often the request for interpreter services is imprecise, and delays result from the lack of information. Consider, for example, the assignment office being unable to proceed on a request for a Chinese interpreter until it is determined which dialect of Chinese is required. Similar problems are encountered with the dialects of Arabic and the languages spoken in the Philippines. Another factor in the difficulty of assigning interpreters is that some judges express a preference for certain interpreters who may be otherwise occupied. That fact notwithstanding, some judges go to the extent of issuing an order from the bench for a specific interpreter to return to that particular courtroom. Conversely, other judges give notice that certain interpreters, who might be available, are not to be assigned to their courtroom. These requests are to be taken very seriously.

1.2. Emergency Assignments

The most difficult and challenging task that confronts the supervisor comes about when the need for an interpreter has not been announced or discovered until the day of appearance. Unfortunately, this is a common occurrence. The problem may be simply the unavailability of a large number of interpreters in the same language. For example, the court may suddenly discover that it needs five Spanish interpreters at 4:00 P.M. on a Friday afternoon. Alternatively, it may be learned that a defendant with an English surname does not in fact speak English. In such instances, the case will have to be continued until the afternoon, or delayed even longer in order to give the supervisor the opportunity to locate an appropriate interpreter.

2. Forms and Records

Record-keeping will revolve around two main areas: (1) the history of language services and interpreter assignments, and (2) payroll or remuneration of per diem interpreters for services rendered.

2.1. Interpreter Assignments Master File

In most instances the interpreter supervisor will maintain a master log or file of requests for interpreter services. This file will contain all the pertinent data related to the specific request: case name and number, charges against the defendant, nature of the proceedings, interpreter assigned and language provided, courtroom location, and time and date of appearance.

2.2. Interpreter Assignment Sheet

When the individual assignment is made to a specific interpreter, it should be in the form of an assignment sheet containing all relevant and available information taken from the master file. The assignment sheet should contain the interpreter's name, and should provide space for statistical data as well as information regarding the disposition of the matter or possible continuance dates. Future assignments will depend on the information regarding continuance dates, and budgetary allocations may hinge on the accuracy of the data contained in these forms. These forms may also contain references to the type of language services provided: simultaneous or consecutive interpretation, services provided to prosecution or defense, and/or the amount of time spent. Any or all of these items may bear on the question of remuneration for services rendered or provide significant information for future reference.

2.3. Payroll Claim

Usually per diem interpreters' paychecks will be issued by a fiscal affairs or payroll office based on information provided by the interpreter assignment office. The data supplied to the supervisory interpreter by the per diem interpreters on their assignment sheets will be reflected in the interpreters' payroll claim forms. Per diem interpreters will claim a contract fee for each day worked, and the claim forms must be approved by the supervisor of interpreter services before being forwarded to the payroll office.

3. Fee Schedule

In the United States there is currently a great disparity in the schedule of fees paid to court interpreters, ranging from inappropriately low fees in some local courts to over $200 per day in the United States district courts, and even beyond that for professional conference interpreters. Five factors have contributed to this situation: (1) a lack of recognition of interpreting as a profession, (2) confusion as to the distinction between bilingualism and interpreting skills, (3) the prevalence of female interpreters, (4) bias against anything "foreign," and (5) the law of supply and demand. These factors will be discussed in detail in this section.

(1) *Lack of Recognition*: The field of court management does not recognize, for the most part, the existence of an interpreting profession. Unless a court administrator has attended an international conference where simultaneous interpretation is vital to communication, the role of the professional conference interpreter is unheard of and unknown. International relations, be they in the form of visiting dignitaries, formal meetings, or conferences would be quite difficult if not altogether impossible without the vital element of a language connection, the professional interpreter. The world of international business or trade would be equally hard pressed to conduct meetings or conferences without the function of the professional interpreter. Yet, the interpreting profession at its most competent levels is generally unknown to the court and to the court administrator.

(2) *Bilingualism and Interpreter Skills*: What is more familiar, and in many parts of our country, constitutes a part of the daily scene in and out of the courtroom, is people who speak a language other than English. Within the courthouse that bilingual person might be an attorney, a police officer, a custodian, or a clerk-typist. Perhaps a caveat is indicated here. When observing a bilingual person speak in both English and the non-English language, the court administrator generally tends to make two assumptions: first, that the bilingual person speaks the non-English language at least as well and to the same degree of proficiency as English (if the person is an English-dominant speaker); and second, that even if the bilingual person does not have a balanced facility in both languages, the fact that the person appears to speak two languages is indicative of the ability to interpret between the two languages. Neither of these assumptions is based on fact, and, more often than not, both will prove to

be false. The result is disappointment and often chaos within the courtroom. The stories are legion. Court personnel report the frightened, wide-eyed stare of bilingual individuals who are placed in the position of interpreter with no experience, background, or training in the field. Attorneys and judges complain of "interpreters" who engage the witness in heated questions and answers, only to report a simple "yes" or "no" for the record. Not unusual is the suspicion of omissions, distortions, and, in some instances, complete fabrication. The court administrator would be providing a service to the court by simply being fully cognizant of the fact that, while all interpreters are bilingual, not all bilinguals are interpreters.

(3) *The Prevalence of Female Interpreters*: The majority of court interpreters are women. This fact by itself could well be a factor in the lack of prestige attached to the profession, as reflected in the schedule of fees. Many women take advantage of this profession because of the opportunity to work part time as free-lancers with flexible hours. As a consequence of working part time, they are sometimes not taken seriously as professionals. This lack of professional regard is manifested in a reduced or depressed salary schedule or per diem fee. Many courts find it difficult to adequately reward a person whose skills are not recognized as truly professional. This phenomenon is certainly not without parallel in other fields of endeavor. Much has been written on the subject of the economic inequality of female-dominated professions such as teaching and nursing. Teachers and nurses, like court interpreters, possess a high level of skill and training, yet many feel compelled to leave their professions to seek higher levels of remuneration.

(4) *Bias against Anything "Foreign"*: The tradition in our country, despite its historical and cultural roots in many other lands, has been for immigrants to undergo a rapid process of "Americanization" and to assimilate into the mainstream, setting aside language and cultural ties. Those ethnic groups that are slow to Americanize or to divest themselves of the foreign language or other cultural characteristics are said to be clannish. Indeed, the very word "foreigner," with a certain inflection, can be used as a pejorative. Often the court interpreter may have an accent, revealing that English is a second language. The interpreter may even look "foreign," i.e., not Northern European, or may have been born in a country that is not on the United States politically preferred list at the moment. This interpreter is the object of negative bias. Those endeavors that attract foreigners are traditionally believed to be at the lower end of the economic ladder. Therefore, being considered "foreign" contributes to the low esteem accorded the court interpreting profession.

(5) *Supply and Demand*: In court interpreting, as in most other facets of our economic life, the law of supply and demand prevails. In those courts where the prerequisites or qualifications are low, or perhaps even non-existent—beyond an appropriate surname—there is an abundant supply of purportedly bilingual personnel on staff, or of candidates willing to do their best in a court of law regardless of language ability. Given the low requirements and the oversupply, court administrators see little reason to establish a professional-level schedule of fees. In many major cities, however, the court must compete not only with other higher-paying judicial systems but also with other government agencies for the services of the professional interpreter. These are full-time, free-lance professionals whose language abilities place them at the very top of their profession. Their competence has been established through examination by the AO, or by other examining agencies. In order to successfully compete for their services, the United States district courts have established a profes-

Table 1
1987 Court Interpreter Salaries and Per Diem Rates

Jurisdiction	Hourly Rate	Full Day	Half Day
AZ (Maricopa County)	—	$90	$65
AR (judicial dept.)	$17.50	—	—
CA (L.A. superior court)	—	$140	$100
CO	$30	—	—
CT	—	$50	—
Wash., D.C. (superior court)			
Sign language	$30	—	—
Fed. cert.	—	$210	$110
Uncertified	$20–$35	—	—
Exotic	—	$260	—
FL (Dade County)	$25 ($40 after 5 P.M.)	—	—
IL (Cook County)	—	$50	$35
MA (state courts)	$15	—	—
Sign language	$20	—	—
NJ	$25	$74	$46
NM			
State certified	$15	—	—
Uncertified	$10	—	—
NY (NY unified court system)	—	$80	—
PA (court of common pleas, Philadelphia)			
Romance languages	$33	—	—
All other languages	$40	—	—

sional schedule of interpreter fees. However, in at least two cities, Los Angeles and New York, the United States court has exceeded its own schedule for the half day (Los Angeles) and for the full day (New York), in order to equal the fees paid by other courts and/or agencies.

3.1. Comparisons of Fees

The question of remuneration for the court interpreter is one that has no easy solution. There is no one standard against which an interpreter might be measured in determining a fair salary or per diem rate. A recent study by the Administrative Office of the New Jersey Courts (1989), however, does provide insight into the complex issue. Generally, it documents the wide disparity of salaries and per diem rates of court interpreters and translators throughout the United States and Canada. A limited state-by-state comparison in Table 1 indicates that some states have a clearly defined

Table 1   *continued*

Jurisdiction	Hourly Rate	Full Day	Half Day
TX (El Paso)	$35	$150	—
United States courts			
Certified	—	$210	$110
Uncertified	—	$95	$50
WA	$6.75	—	—
WI (state courts)	—	—	$10 minimum

Note: The data in Table 1 are from *Compensating Interpreters and Translators: An International Survey of Wages Paid Salaried and Contracted Interpreters and Translators,* by Administrative Office of the New Jersey Courts, 1989, pp. 15-32. Adapted by permission.

per diem rate, while others prefer a per hour basis or a combined per hour and per diem rate (see Table 1).

A report from the Administrative Office of the New Jersey Courts (1989) reveals that in 1987:

1. The average starting salary for court interpreters ranges from a low of $15,262 in New Jersey to a high of $24,731 in United States courts. The highest average salary that can be reached by salaried staff court interpreters ranges from a low of $24,086 in New Jersey to a high of $50,342 in the United States courts.

2. The per diem rates range from a low of $50/day in the Connecticut, District of Columbia, and Massachusetts courts, to an average high of $113 in other states around the country [note that this does not include the fact that the United States courts pay certified interpreters the much higher daily rate of $210/day]. (p. 9)

The following tables, taken from the New Jersey study in whole or in part, will provide the court administrator with reference information regarding court interpreting rates and salaries for staff positions, as well as per diem rates.

Note: The data in Tables 2 through 6 are from *Compensating Interpreters and Translators: An International Survey of Wages Paid Salaried and Contracted Interpreters and Translators,* by Administrative Office of the New Jersey Courts, 1989, pp. 9-13. Adapted by permission.

3.2. **The California Example**

California is an example of the positive results, in terms of professional status, that can accrue from a state certification program. Certification provided a basis for increasing the per diem rate to a professional level. This was the culmination of efforts by many individuals and organizations within the legislative and judicial systems. One important leader in this movement was the interpreter's professional organization, the California Court Interpreters Association. The decade following state certification saw a steady and marked increase in the interpreter per diem rate commensurate with

Table 2

**Compensation of Interpreters and Translators
in the United States and Canada in 1987**

Jurisdiction	Staff Interpreters/Translators			
	Low Start	Avg. Low	Highest	Avg. Highest
NJ*	$ 9,538	$15,262	$39,993	$24,086
Neighboring states (NY & PA)*	$20,010	$22,124	$31,737	$28,075
Other states in region (DC, CT, & MA)*	$16,216	$20,366	$37,000	$28,584
Other U.S. jurisdictions*	$10,099	$17,991	$36,200	$26,059
U.S. federal courts*	$24,731**	—	$50,342**	—
Canadian courts (U.S. $)*	$22,495	—	$33,979	—
Sign language agencies	$14,000	$14,049	$24,600	$20,418
Other gov't. agencies	$12,500	$20,029	$74,336	$42,568
Canadian governments	$12,111	$15,929	$32,866	$35,274
Private agencies & individuals	$16,584	$20,769	$54,000	$36,216
Totals	$ 9,538	$17,365	$74,336	$31,043

* Court interpreting only.
** New federal GS grades 12–14 = $35,580 - $48,592; supervisory = $57,158.

increased perceptions of confidence in interpreter ability. As reflected in Table 7, the per diem rates in California are perhaps the highest in the nation (Mikkelson, 1989a, p. 5).

4. Management of the Use of Electronic Equipment

Multiple-defendant cases are a particular challenge for the supervisory interpreter of the court. Sometimes one interpreter is called upon to interpret simultaneously to a widely scattered group of non-English-speaking defendants interspersed among a larger group of English-speaking defendants. These may be defendants in custody and seated in a jury box, or they may be appearing in traffic court and seated in the audience. When the judge appears and begins to inform the defendants of their constitutional rights, the interpreter must speak to all the non-English speakers at once.

The results have been unsatisfactory for three reasons: (1) in order to be heard by all defendants, the interpreter must raise his or her voice to a level that is disruptive to the court. If the interpreter speaks softly so as not to disrupt the proceedings, not all defendants are able to hear the simultaneous interpretation being rendered *sotto voce*; (2) with one interpreter rendering for multiple defendants at counsel table, all

Table 3
Minimum Interpreting Rates Charged by Freelance Interpreters in 1987

Hourly Rate	No. of Persons Surveyed
$ 5	1
$ 8	2
$10	3
$12	1
$13	1
$14	1
$15	21
$16	1
$18	3
$20	35
$22	1
$24	1
$25	63
$28	1
$30	37
$35	19
$40	15
$45	8
$50	17
$52	1
$55	1
$60	2
$75	2
$100	3

Average hourly rate = $29.53

Per Case	No. of Persons Surveyed
$50	1

Per Day	No. of Persons Surveyed
$ 80	2
$200	1
$210	1
$220	1

Miscellaneous	No. of Persons Surveyed
$90 per 0–4 hrs.	1

Table 4
Minimum Interpreting Rates Charged by Interpreter Agencies in 1987

Hourly Rates	No. of Agencies Surveyed
$10	1
$20	3
$22	1
$25	4
$30	6
$35	6
$40	5
$45	2
$50	7
$55	2
$60	2
$95	1

Average hourly rate = $38.68

Per Half Day	No. of Agencies Surveyed
$140	1
$275	1

Miscellaneous	No. of Agencies Surveyed
$60 for first hour, $30 per hour thereafter	1
$75 for first hour, $15 per hour thereafter	1
$50 per hour for first two hours, $35 per hour thereafter	1

of the co-defendants are not able to communicate with their own attorneys and thereby assist in their defense during trial; (3) and finally, should any one of the defendants need to speak with the attorney, the simultaneous interpretation of the proceedings would be curtailed while the private communication took place between the attorney and the defendant.

This interruption of simultaneous interpretation has been found to violate the right to an interpreter as guaranteed by article 1, section 14 of the California Constitution (*People v. Resendes,* 1985; *People v. Rioz,* 1984). In *People v. Rioz* (1984) one interpreter translated the proceedings to four co-defendants, each of whom wore earphones to hear the interpreter. At one point in the proceedings the interpreter was "borrowed" to interpret for a witness at the stand. "Since the defendants were unable to communicate with their attorneys under this arrangement, the appellate court held that it violated each defendant's right to an interpreter" (Ilich, 1986, p. 7). These precedent-setting cases have resulted in the assignment of one interpreter for each

Table 5
Minimum Translating Rates Charged by Freelance Translators in 1987

Cents per Word	No. of Persons Surveyed
2	1
3	1
4	2
5	11
6	10
7	9
8	20
9	3
10	57
11	2
12	15
13	4
14	1
15	32
16	1
18	2
20	10
25	11
30	2
35	2
40	1
45	1
50	4
60	1
68	1
75	1
80	1

Average per word rate = 15.2 cents

Rate per Page	No. of Persons Surveyed
$20	4
$40	1
$70	1

Rate per Hour	No. of Persons Surveyed
$25	3

Rate per Chinese Character	No. of Persons Surveyed
$1.00	2

Table 6
Minimum Translating Rates Charged by Agencies in 1987

Cents per Word	No. of Agencies Surveyed
2	1
5	1
6	1
8	1
10	12
11	2
12	3
12.5	1
13	3
14	3
15	4
16	1
20	4
21	1
25	1
70	1

Average cents per word = 14.1

Rate per Page	No. of Agencies Surveyed
$ 5	1
$50	1

Miscellaneous	No. of Agencies Surveyed
20 cents per word for first 100 words, 10 cents per word thereafter	1
$50 per document	1

defendant in a multi-defendant case. In practice, however, the results have been ca-cophonous, with all interpreters interpreting at the same time.

Logistically, it is a good idea, in cases involving a single interpreter and more than one non-English speaker, to gather all clients into one area. Bailiffs can help group them closely, making it possible to interpret at close range and thereby minimize disruption of the proceedings. The interpreter should ask the bailiff(s) to group the non-English speakers either at the end of the rows of the jury box or in the front row of the jury box so that the simultaneous interpretation of constitutional rights may be rendered in a low voice audible to those non-English speakers but yet not so loud that it interferes with the comprehension of others.

In a traffic court situation, before proceedings begin, the interpreter may inquire in a loud voice if there are any non-English speakers in the audience who will need

Table 7
1989 California Court Interpreting Per Diem Rates

County	Half-Day	Full-Day
Alameda	$ 82	$164
Contra Costa	$ 75	$150
Los Angeles	$117	$171
Marin	$ 82	$164
Monterey	$ 60	$100
Orange	$117	$171
Riverside	$ 75	$115
Sacramento	$ 60	$120
San Benito	$ 60	$110
San Bernardino	$ 75	$115
San Diego	$ 82	$133
San Francisco	$ 75	$150
San Joaquin	$ 45	$ 90
San Mateo	$ 75	$150
Santa Clara	$ 82	$164
Santa Cruz	$ 60	$100

Note: The data in Table 7 are from "Court Interpreting Rates" by H. Mikkelson, 1989a, *The Polyglot*, 19 (2), p. 5. Adapted by permission.

the services of an interpreter. This inquiry will serve to (1) identify the non-English speakers so that the interpreter may secure the correct name and case number and be aware when the non-English speaker's name is called, and (2) identify those non-English speakers for the purpose of grouping them together physically so that they may hear the constitutional rights interpreted. In every instance the interpreter should strive to be heard by all non-English-speaking defendants yet not disrupt the court.

Infrared wireless communications systems are a new development that will allow one speaker to interpret for an unlimited number of listeners, provided each listener is wearing the headphone-receivers. Each headset is equipped with a photoelectric cell and a volume control that allows the wearer not only to hear the interpretation but also to adjust the volume for personal comfort. These headsets may be worn by a large number of non-English speakers during the arraignment procedure or by the defendants at trial. The judge may even grant the families of the accused the opportunity of hearing the proceedings in their own language while seated in the audience by allowing them to wear the receiver headsets.

Whatever the proceeding, but especially during a trial, the supervisory interpreter should assign two interpreters to interpret with the electronic equipment. Once the team of interpreters is assembled, a division of labor should be organized and a rotational duty schedule agreed upon. During trial, one interpreter interprets for the accused while the other stands by should there be a need for attorney-client communication. The interpreters should be instructed to switch roles every thirty minutes, thus giving the active interpreter a rest every half hour.

During the arraignment procedure one interpreter should be instructed to interpret the constitutional rights and the reading of the complaint if it is read from the bench. The second interpreter should be instructed to stand by the microphone or podium, if there is one, wherever the defendant is to enter a plea and to interpret aloud any and all responses of the defendant.

Court administrators may be hesitant to invest in a sophisticated system such as the one described above. The cost may seem prohibitive. In reality, the opposite is true. Several courts that have seen the demand for multiple interpreters grow report that the cost of the system has been more than offset by the savings garnered from the assignment of fewer interpreters in multiple-defendant cases.

5. Orientation of Non-English Speakers to the Courts

More often than not the defendant or witness entering the court system for the first time is confused and perhaps even frightened. This is particularly true of limited- or non-English speakers. Their lack of English is compounded by an equal, if not greater, lack of familiarity with the courtroom itself as well as the United States system of justice.

The result in many cases has been confusion for all involved, including the court. Some non-English-speaking defendants have erroneously assumed that the court-appointed interpreter at their side was a bilingual attorney, and have proceeded before the bench on the basis of that misassumption. Some non-English-speaking defendants have not understood the nature of the proceedings prior to the actual moment of appearance before the court. Witnesses at the stand have assumed incorrectly that the interpreter speaking their language was the examining attorney, and have even sat sideways at the witness stand in order to be more attentive. Their answers to the questions, accordingly, have often been directed away from the court and toward the interpreter.

The local court administrator can and should anticipate the most common problems facing the court with respect to the non-English speaker, with a view to insuring the orderly function of the legal process. Printed materials should be developed for distribution not just to limited- or non-English speakers, but to any individual who, due to a lack of education or legal sophistication, might benefit from an orientation to the courtroom or legal procedures prior to the actual appearance.

The development of printed materials, ideally by an agency specializing in the production of such brochures, cannot, of course, be undertaken in all languages. In most instances throughout the country, the language with the highest frequency of use in the courts is Spanish. Brochures developed in that language alone would expedite the legal process in many courtrooms. These brochures should minimally focus on two areas: (1) familiarizing the non-English speaker as well as the unsophisticated English speaker with the physical courtroom, and especially with the principals, i.e., "Who's Who in Court," and (2) explaining the role, responsibility, and limitation of the court interpreter with respect to non-English-speaking defendants and witnesses.

5.1. "Who's Who in Court"

Of primary importance in an efficient transition throughout the judicial process is an awareness of the physical courtroom and knowledge of who the officers of the court are. Many courts labor in the mistaken belief that all who enter the legal arena, regardless of language, know who the principal actors are. Many English speakers and non-English speakers alike are ignorant of who the various officers of the court are. Some come forward when their name is called but have little idea of the identity or position of the speaker who is addressing them. The development of a *Who's Who in Court* brochure with a diagram of the courtroom, patterned after one discussed in Unit 5, Chapter 22, would provide these individuals with information that many of us have absorbed after years of exposure to film and television.

5.2. The Role of the Court Interpreter

The following notice to non-English-speaking defendants and witnesses has been adapted from *The Use of Court Interpreters in New Mexico* (Valdés & Wilcox, 1986, p. 21). We also offer a Spanish translation for use by the local court for possible inclusion in a bilingual orientation brochure.

NOTICE TO DEFENDANTS

(1) An official court interpreter is going to help us in these proceedings and you should know what the interpreter can and cannot do. Basically, the court interpreter is here only to interpret between two languages. The interpreter is not a party in this case and is completely neutral. The interpreter is not working for the prosecution or the defense. The official court interpreter's sole responsibility is to interpret exactly and precisely what is said in court.

AVISO AL ACUSADO

(1) *Nos va a ayudar en este proceso un intérprete oficial del tribunal y debe saber Ud. lo que puede y lo que no puede hacer el intérprete. Básicamente, el intérprete del tribunal está aquí solamente para interpretar entre dos idiomas. El intérprete no tiene parte en este caso y es completamente imparcial. El intérprete no trabaja para la fiscalía ni para la defensa. La única responsabilidad del intérprete oficial del tribunal es de interpretar exacta y precisamente lo que se dice en el tribunal.*

(2) The court interpreter is not a lawyer and is prohibited from giving legal advice. The interpreter is solely to interpret. Please do not ask the court interpreter for legal advice.

(2) *El intérprete del tribunal no es abogado y se le prohibe dar consejos legales. El intérprete solamente debe de interpretar. Por favor, no le pida al intérprete que le dé consejos legales.*

(3) If you do not understand the court interpreter, please tell the judge. If you feel that the court interpreter is leaving out much of what is being said in court, please tell that to the judge, also.

(3) *Si Ud. no le entiende al intérprete del tribunal, favor de decírselo al juez. Si piensa que el intérprete está omitiendo mucho de lo que se dice en el tribunal, por favor dígaselo también al juez.*

(4) If you have any question as to the role or responsibility of the court interpreter, please ask the judge.

(4) *Si tiene Ud. alguna pregunta tocante al papel o a la responsabilidad del intérprete del tribunal favor de preguntárselo al juez.*

NOTICE TO WITNESS

(1) You will need to understand the role of the court interpreter. The court interpreter is here only to interpret the questions that an attorney or the judge asks you and to interpret your responses. The court interpreter will say only what you, the attorneys, or the judge say. The interpreter will not add words to your testimony, omit anything you say, or summarize what you say.

AVISO AL TESTIGO

(1) *Tendrá que tener Ud. un conocimiento en cuanto al papel del intérprete del tribunal. El intérprete está aquí sólo para interpretar las preguntas que le haga a Ud. un abogado o el juez, y también para interpretar las respuestas de Ud. El intérprete del tribunal dirá únicamente lo que diga Ud., el abogado o el juez. El intérprete no le añadirá palabras a su testimonio. No omitirá nada de lo que Ud. diga, ni dará solo un resumen de lo que Ud. diga.*

(2) If you do not understand the court interpreter, please inform the judge immediately.

(2) *Si no le entiende Ud. al intérprete del tribunal, infórmele al juez inmediatamente.*

(3) If you do not understand the question that is asked, please tell the person asking the question that you do not understand.

(3) *Si no entiende Ud. la pregunta que se le haga, infórmele a la persona haciéndole la pregunta que Ûd. no entiende.*

(4) Remember that you are giving testimony to the court and not to the court interpreter. Please speak directly to the attorney or to the judge. Do not speak directly to the court interpreter. Do not seek advice from or talk to the court interpreter.

(4) *Tenga presente que el testimonio que Ud. dará es para el tribunal y no para el intérprete. Al contestar, diríjale la palabra al abogado o al juez. No le hable directamente al intérprete del tribunal. No le pida consejos ni hable con el intérprete.*

(5) When you are at the stand, please speak clearly so that the entire court and not just the court interpreter can hear.

(5) *Mientras esté en el banquillo de los testigos, tenga la bondad de hablar claramente para que pueda oír todo el tribunal y no sólo el intérprete.*

(6) Please do not begin your answer to a question from an attorney or from the judge before you have heard the complete interpretation of the question in your language.

(6) *Favor de no comenzar su respuesta a una pregunta que le haga un abogado o el juez antes de que haya oído la interpretación de la pregunta en su idioma.*

(7) Finally, if you have any question as to the role or responsibilities of the court interpreter, please ask the judge.

(7) *Finalmente, si tiene Ud. cualquier pregunta en cuanto al papel o a la responsabilidad del intérprete del tribunal, favor de preguntárselo al juez.*

6. Interpreter's Oath

When the recruitment, preliminary assessment training, and orientation process is completed and the new interpreters are ready to enter the legal arena, they must be sworn in. Local custom will dictate whether they will take the oath but once in their career, every day they provide service, or on the record before each and every appearance. No matter the custom, the oath will be similar to the following one for a Spanish interpreter.

Do you solemnly swear that you will well and truly interpret Spanish into English and English into Spanish to the best of your ability in the cause(s) now pending before this court, so help you God?

The interpreter response, of course, is "I do." Local custom may dictate that the supervisor of court interpreters administer the oath and maintain a signed copy in each case file or in the courthouse.

Unit 5
Language and the Interpreter

Chapter 18

The Nature of Language

In this unit we outline general properties of language from a **linguistic perspective**, concentrating on those features which are of particular relevance to court interpretation. A linguistic perspective refers to an objective approach to language as contrasted to the prescriptive rules, or "dos and don'ts," traditionally associated with grammar. In reality, such rules are prescriptions of linguistic etiquette; that is, they prescribe or dictate how a person should speak and write in order to appear correct and educated.

Linguistic research, both theoretical and applied, has burgeoned over the past three decades, resulting in an expansion of knowledge about psychological, socio-cultural, and other aspects of language. This expansion is of great importance and potential benefit to translators and interpreters, as well as to those who use their services. Interpreters in particular can benefit from increasing their objective knowledge of language, because, being human, we tend to project our preconceived ideas, assumptions, and biases onto communicative interactions more than we realize. Indeed, the more complex the situation—such as that of interlingual communication requiring an intermediary for interpretation—the greater the potential for such projection and for misunderstanding. As a consequence, even when the interpreter has done everything possible to bridge the linguistic-cultural gap, communication can, and frequently will, break down.

In this chapter we seek to increase the interpreter's awareness of language features and their implications for interpretation through a summary description of the basic characteristics and subsystems of language. The relevance of these features of language to court interpretation will be shown through examples taken from testimony heard in courtrooms and other legal and quasi-legal settings.

1. Basic Characteristics and Subsystems of Language

Gardner (1983) classifies language capability as one of the multiple forms of human intelligence. In general, language is a highly complex system of human communication which is vocal-auditory in nature. ASL (American Sign Language) is a notable example of a natural language which is not vocal-auditory: rather it consists of "a system of manually produced visual signals analogous to words, taught to the deaf in the United States" (Akmajian, Demers, & Harnish, 1984, p. 517). Nida (1964) defines language as "words (or other units) which are organized according to 'rules of grammar' into various types of combinations" (p. 5). "Rules of grammar" refers to the inherent, underlying organizing principles of the language.

1.1. Langue vs. Parole

Saussure (1966) stressed the importance of distinguishing, within verbal communication, between the code or set of rules that is conventionally accepted by the community that uses a given language, and the everyday application of that code by the individuals in the community. *Langue* refers to the underlying rules of the language that govern it—these are the rules of syntax, grammar, and phonology. It is well defined and predictable, and changes slowly, only by convention. *Parole*, on the other hand, is the actual language spoken every day as it exists in its diverse varieties. It changes every day, in every situation, with every individual speaker.

1.2. Language Universals

The global term "language" includes all the many languages spoken in the world. Similar features among languages are called **language universals**. Some examples are the following: all languages contain **deep structures** (the underlying meaning of a sentence), **surface structures** (the outward manifestation of a sentence), and **transformations**, or formulas to convert, for example, a statement into a question. The same kinds of transformations will be found, no matter how different from English a language may appear to be, that is, deletion, addition, and rearrangement of constituent elements, or substitution of one form for another (Falk, 1978). There are ways to ask a question or to turn a positive statement into a negative one, or to qualify a noun. Also, all languages provide ways to make requests, ask questions, give orders, express disagreement or dissatisfaction or anger, or make assertions (Halliday, McIntosh, & Strevens, 1964). These **language functions** transcend grammatical forms and meaning. If one wishes for another person to close the window, any number of grammatical structures could be used to bring about the intended effect:

Would you please close the window?
(Yes-No question, polite request)

Don't you think it's cold in here (as the speaker shivers with cold)?
(Yes-No question, feigned opinion asking)

Shut the window!
(Command, using imperative form of the verb)

I wonder who left the window open?
(Embedded question)

Gee, I'm freezing!
(Declarative statement)

All of these structurally different language strings function in the same way—their social purpose is to make someone close the window. However, they are extremely different in **style** (the manner in which something is said) and **register** (the relative variety of language, as determined by the purpose of the communication and relationship between speakers). In court interpreting, conservation of style and register is of particular importance (see Unit 5, Chapter 21). Languages appear to be very different from one another, and on the surface they are. Yet on the phonetic level, we find that all languages draw their particular sounds from the same basic stock. Falk

(1978) notes that all sounds are the result of a very limited number of vocal tract activities. This means that, in theory, any human being can produce any sound from any language, and indeed utilize intuitive knowledge about language—what Chomsky (1965) called **linguistic competence**—along with cognitive, analytic, and mimetic or imitative skills to master other languages, given motivation, determination, and enough time. In terms of semantics, morphology, and syntax, languages that belong to the same general family show great similarities. For example, Navajo belongs to the Athabaskan language family and is closely interrelated to other Athabaskan languages such as Apache and Chipewyan (Young, 1988).

2. The Structure of Language

All languages are structured in the same manner, in the sense that all build by accretion, i.e., by gradual addition of new elements to form larger units of meaning. The process begins with **phonemes**, or basic elements of sounds (such as /p/ or /b/) which combine to form **morphemes**, the components of words; words in turn are arranged and rearranged in different patterns to form different types of **phrases** (a group of words with no subject or verb, for example, "on the street") and **sentences** (a complete thought with a subject and a verb, such as "I ran into him on the street"). Sentences combine to form a totality called **discourse**. Discourse refers to extended verbal expression in speech or writing. Courtroom discourse includes the monologues of judges and attorneys, and the questions and answers of attorneys and witnesses.

In this subsection we present an overview of the subsystems which comprise the overall structure of language: (1) **phonology**, (2) **morphology**, (3) **syntax**, (4) **semantics**, and (5) **pragmatics**.

2.1. Phonology

Phonology refers to language sounds and their patterning. The term refers to the abstract rules and principles which govern the distribution of sounds in a language, that is, what combination of sounds may occur in one language but not in another (Akmajian et al., 1984). Initial consonant clusters such as the /sk-/ sound in the word "school" are common in English, but do not occur in Spanish without a preceding vowel; thus the Spanish equivalent of "school" is *escuela*, and "spirit" is *espíritu*. The term **phonetics** usually refers to the production or articulation of sound by human beings (**articulatory phonetics**). When emphasis is on the properties of the speech sound waves, the subfield of study is called **acoustic phonetics**.

Of particular interest to interpreters is phonological variation as it occurs in different regions; for example, the fact that Spanish speakers from the Caribbean aspirate /s/ or drop /s/ in final position of both syllables and words is the single most important phonological feature of the Spanish of that area (Terrell & Salgués de Cargill, 1979). Aspiration, known in popular parlance as "swallowing the s" refers to a weak pharyngeal sound /h/ which is very similar to the sound of /h/ in English, the difference being that the English sound always occurs in syllable or word initial position—hot, hat—whereas aspiration occurs only in syllable or word final position in Spanish (Terrell & Salgués de Cargill, 1979). For example, the /s/ in *lástima* (syllable final) and in *los zapatos* (word final) is replaced by /h/ or often dropped in Caribbean Spanish and elsewhere, i.e., the latter becomes *loh sapatoh* or *lo sopato*.

This aspiration of syllable and word final /s/ makes it difficult at times for the unaccustomed ear to determine whether a noun or adjective is singular or plural, and consequently, the listener must rely more heavily on contextual cues. For the interpreter, such a situation represents an additional burden; therefore, every attempt should be made to train the ear to become more attuned to such phonological variation. This is particularly true in the case of Spanish interpreters with respect to the feature described here, since it is widespread in the Spanish-speaking world (Canfield, 1981).

The example given above is of a regional variation on the segmental, i.e., at the vocalic or consonantal level. Such variations also exist with respect to **suprasegmental** sound features such as stress, juncture, and pitch variations that work together to form the intonation or musical pattern of a sentence (Elgin, 1979).

2.2. Morphology

Morphology is the system of words and word building. A **morpheme** is considered the smallest significant unit of meaning. Morphemes are either **free** or **bound**. **Free morphemes** are words which can stand alone and include **content words** that are categorized as nouns, verbs, adjectives, and adverbs; and function words including articles, prepositions, demonstratives, and conjunctions.

Table 1
Selected Parts of Speech

Content Words	(English)	(French)	(Spanish)
Nouns	chair	*chaise*	*silla*
Verbs	to go	*aller*	*ir*
Adjectives	big	*grand(e)*	*grande*
Adverbs	rapidly	*rapidement*	*rápidamente*
Function Words			
Articles (Definite)	the	*le/la, les*	*el/la, los/las*
Articles (Indefinite)	a/an	*un/une*	*un/una*
Prepositions	to, from	*a, de*	*a, de*
Demonstratives	this/these	*ce/cette, ces*	*este/esta, estos/ estas*
Conjunctions	and	*et*	*y/e*

According to Akmajian et al. (1984), **bound morphemes** (morphemes which cannot function separately as words) include prefixes, suffixes, and bases or stems:

Word	Prefix	Stem	Suffix
Reduced	re-	duce	-d (indicates past tense)
Prescription	pre-	scrip	-tion

Morphemes contain a great deal of information and, therefore, meaning. A case in point, the Spanish verb system features **bound morphemes** which indicate *tense* or time as well as aspect, or the relation of action to the passage of time. For example, there are contrastive past tenses called the **preterite** and the **imperfect** that differentiate between an action which was completed at a point of reference in the past (preterite) and an action which was ongoing at that same point of reference. Thus the contrast between:

Completed action: *El me dijo que ellos **llegaron** anoche* (He told me that they *arrived* last night).

Ongoing action: *El me dijo que ellos **llegaban** anoche* (He told me that they *were arriving* last night).

Such a basic difference in form affects meaning profoundly. The bound morphemes which convey tense/aspect distinction are (a) *ron* and (b) *ban*. These suffixes also add information to show person and number, or third-person plural.

A knowledge of morphology in the source language (SL) and the target language (TL) is essential to the interpreter because morphology is the tool of lexical expansion. New words are created by combining pre-existing morphemes into combinations with new meanings to meet new needs. In Spanish new verbs are always created in the -AR classification, which is added to stems that denote the basic meaning, and any necessary prefixes to further refine the meaning of the new verb. Note the following:

alunizar (to land on the moon (*luna*))

amerizar (to land on the ocean (*mar*))

These verbs were coined in the last twenty years by analogy to the pre-existing verb *aterrizar* (to land on the ground/earth (*tierra*)).

Interpreters must also be aware of morphological variation in their working languages. In Haitian Creole, for instance, many frequently used verbs occur in both a basic and a shortened form. "To have" is *genyen*, or, more usually, *gen*; and the verb "to be able" may be pronounced *kapab*, *kap*, *kab*, or *ka* (Valdman & Rosemond, 1988, p. xiii). Spanish interpreters also need to be aware of the familiar pronoun *vos*, which exists in several national varieties of Latin American Spanish, and its corresponding verb forms.

2.3. Syntax

Syntax refers to the arrangement of words in a sentence to effect a particular meaning. According to the theory of linguistic competence (Chomsky, 1965), fluent speakers have intuitive knowledge of the finite set of procedures—the grammar—of their language. This knowledge makes linguistic **performance**, or production and comprehension of an infinite number of sentences, possible (Akmajian et al., 1984). This intuitive grasp of the language grammar causes the speaker to determine what usages "sound right" and which ones do not. In other words, the speaker will know when syntactic rules have been observed, and when they have been violated.

A native speaker of Spanish draws on linguistic competence to discern the grammaticality of the following utterances.

He became angry.   *Se puso enojado./Se enojó.*

He became crazy.	*Se volvió loco./Se enloqueció.*
He became famous. (by virtue of his deeds)	*Se hizo famoso.*
He became president. (by virtue of effort)	*Llegó a ser presidente.*
He became a Catholic.	*Se convirtió en católico.*

A native speaker would know which of these combinations to use in each context. Note that in English various contexts are handled by one verb, "became." In contrast, Spanish requires a different verb or verb phrase for each of the five contexts. A native speaker of Spanish would not use a verb inappropriate to the context; for example, *Se hizo enojado.*

A more general syntactic feature of Spanish and other languages, and one which has important implications for Spanish-English interpreters and translators, is described by Vásquez-Ayora (1977), who notes that Spanish-English translators experience the Spanish version as tending to be much longer than the English. This fact may be attributable to the aspects of syntactic structure which require amplification or "enlargement" when rendered into Spanish. Specifically, these include adverbs, verbs, adjectives, pronouns, demonstratives, and prepositions. Vásquez-Ayora (1977) offers some illustrations:

English: My aunt's car was behind the brick wall.

Spanish: *El coche de mi tía estaba detrás de la pared de ladrillo.*

English: In such cases, the person accompanying the deportee shall, if possible, escort him back to the deporting State.

Spanish: *En tales casos, la persona que acompaña al expulsado debe, si es posible, acompañarlo en su regreso al Estado de expulsión.* (p. 342)

These examples point out that the interpreter must routinely accommodate to the syntactic requirements of the TL.

Syntax, then, is both finite and infinite. It is finite in the sense that, as Lehmann (1983) observes, certain syntactic patterns such as questions and commands express a consistent meaning, and some sentences depend entirely upon syntactic clues for their meaning. Within the boundaries of the underlying rules, there is infinite potential through combining and recombining words into new phrases and sentences.

Because of the specific meanings of syntactic constructions, it is difficult to draw a sharp distinction between syntax and semantics. The two subsystems are both interrelated and distinct, and governed by their own sets of rules, as are the subfields of phonology and morphology. As was previously mentioned, these rules are descriptive rather than prescriptive; that is, they express generalizations and regularities about language as spoken by its native speakers.

2.4. Semantics

Semantics refers to the system of reference and meaning in a language. It is an area studied in both linguistics and in philosophy. In linguistics, semantics is generally considered to be the study of meaning and related notions in language (Akmajian et al., 1984).

Meaning is of two important types:

(1) *Linguistic meaning*: what the words really mean.
    Example: The sidewalk's not crowded.
    Meaning: There are few people on the sidewalk.

(2) *Speaker's meaning*: can be identical to the linguistic meaning, or it may differ. This depends on whether the speaker is speaking:

   (a) literally—simply observing that there are few people walking on the sidewalk, or

   (b) non-literally—through the use of such non-literal modes of speaking as:
      (1) sarcasm or irony
      (2) metaphor or metonymy
      (3) exaggeration.

If the speaker is a mother whose son is complaining because she is unable to pick him up from school and he will have to take the crowded school bus home, then the mother's statement "The sidewalk's not crowded" probably means "If you don't like the bus, walk home." The speaker's meaning is a non-literal one of sarcasm in this instance.

The speaker's meaning may also differ because of regional variations. For instance, in standard Spanish, the word *mueble* refers to any piece of furniture; in the border areas of the middle Rio Grande and lower Rio Grande Valley, however, *mueble* often refers to a vehicle. A water fountain in one part of the United States becomes a bubbler in certain parts of the Midwest; however, a bubbler in the West may mean the device used to water trees. Regular coffee in New York and other areas of the eastern seaboard is coffee with cream and sugar. Also, *tinto* in Colombia may refer to black coffee (*café tinto*), while in Spain one speaks of *vino tinto* (red wine).

In addition to regional differences in speakers' meanings, there can also be individual differences as well. Such differences may exist even among speakers of the same regional variety (Akmajian et al., 1984). Thus, a particular speaker may use an expression such as *tocar el piano* (to play the piano) to refer to the act of washing dishes after a family meal. Often such idiosyncratic usages arise from "insider references" in families and other close social groups.

2.4.1. Semantic Fields

Semantic fields are sets of words which are joined through shared or opposed semantic features. Classic semantic fields such as kinship, color, and cooking terms are comprised of words which are used to talk about the same general phenomena (Akmajian et al., 1984; Lehrer, 1974).

The notion of semantic field can be extended to any set of terms that are relevant to a concept or set of concepts. The court interpreter must develop both depth and breadth of vocabulary in order to cope with the infinite number of semantic fields that may comprise courtroom language. Therefore, the interpreter needs to develop as many areas of interest as possible, and build through reading and other life experiences a wide and profound lexicon for guidance through the many linguistically and conceptually difficult areas to be encountered. The interpreter is wise to collect or create glossaries in the following areas:

medical	animal and plants
anatomical	weaponry
legal	narcotics
traffic	automotive
forensic pathology	occupational
traffic	maritime
agricultural	dialectal variations

2.5. Discourse

2.5.1. Pragmatics/Speech Acts

The subsystems briefly described in this chapter are the building blocks of language. Beyond the basic level of phonology, morphology, syntax, and semantics lies the area of pragmatics, whose domain is that of "the properties of the world and of language users, when interacting with lexical and sentence semantics" (Falk, 1978, p. 240). Pragmatics governs the appropriate use of language for specific communicative intentions and the performance of particular speech acts for the purpose of fulfilling these intentions (Richards, 1978). The speaker's communicative intention in producing an utterance is often referred to as an illocutionary force. According to Falk (1978), types of illocutionary force include assertions, requests for action (imperatives), and requests for information (questions). In addition to illocutionary force, there are other pragmatic factors involving shared expectations about the conversation. These conversational principles include the following expectations:

(1) the speaker will be sincere and truthful,

(2) what is said will be relevant to the topic, the situation, the participant's relationship, and so on; and

(3) the amount of direct information conveyed will be the appropriate amount necessary for communication. Violation of any of these principles will result in disruption of communication. (Falk, 1978, p. 266)

Another aspect of meaning has to do with the participant's knowledge of the world and of situations. Speaking involves making assumptions about knowledge that we share with our listeners. Assumptions which affect our language use are called presuppositions, and are an important aspect of the performance and comprehension of speech acts (Falk, 1978).

The interpreter's role requires the ability to communicate the pragmatic aspects of SL discourse into TL. In order to do so, a high degree of communicative competence in both languages is essential. The term refers to both underlying knowledge about language and communicative language use, and skill in performing in actual communicative situations with this knowledge base (Omaggio, 1986).

In the model proposed by Canale and Swain (1980), there are four principal components of communicative competence: (1) grammatical, (2) sociolinguistic, (3) strategic, and (4) discourse. Grammatical competence means mastery of the linguistic code. Sociolinguistic competence involves knowing what style of language to use in a particular situational context with other speakers. Discourse competence refers to the ability to achieve cohesion in form and coherence in thought. Strategic competence has to do with the ability to compensate for communication breakdowns through the use of verbal and non-verbal communication strategies (Omaggio, 1986). For the interpreter, a high level of development in all of these areas of competence is essential in both SL and TL, as she must constantly draw on all four to perform her role in the courtroom.

Chapter 19

Aspects of Meaning

The purpose of this chapter is to outline aspects of meaning, including the nuances of words, the influence of culture, paralinguistics, and gestures. In addition, non-literal meaning, such as idioms and metaphor, will be examined. An important part of the chapter is language variation, including stylistic and regional variations, code-switching, jargon, and argot. Finally, there is a discussion of linguistic taboos. These aspects of meaning will be related to the work of the court interpreter through examples taken from courtroom language.

1. Nuances of Words

As we have noted in the preceding outline of some basic semantic concepts, there are two referential aspects of meaning: (1) denotation and (2) connotation. On the one hand there is semantic reference, or linguistic **denotation**, the standard definition of a word as it is found in a dictionary. The word "dog," for example, is defined as "a domesticated carnivorous mammal, *canis familiaris*, raised in a wide variety of breeds and probably originally derived from several wild species" (*American Heritage Dictionary*, 1973, p. 388).

People who have had contact with dogs, as most of us have at some time or other, will probably know that dogs are domesticated. Beyond that they will probably have their own ideas and feelings about the word/concept "dog." As Lehmann (1983) notes, "speakers also have their own conceptions of word meanings, as determined by their past experiences, their lifestyle, and their way of looking at things" (p. 144). These are word **connotations**, which vary from speaker to speaker.

For one speaker, the word dog may connote "loyal, loving, forgiving companion"; for another, whose past experience may have included a frightening encounter with a vicious dog, the word is likely to connote the opposite. Also, for a person who comes from a culture in which dogs are not held in high regard, as in parts of Latin America, the word will have a strong pejorative connotation. In Spanish, calling someone *peor que un perro* (worse than a dog) is a terrible insult. As Lehmann (1983) points out, the word for female dog has an unfavorable connotation in American culture, even though dogs in general are highly valued in Europe and North America (p. 8). The slang expression "It's a real dog of a . . . " (referring to a car, or anything else) is a pejorative connotative extension of the central meaning of dog.

The example discussed above represents the tip of the iceberg with respect to the extensive, ever-expanding knowledge the interpreter must have in order to function effectively in her role of conduit between SL and TL. With respect to linguistic denotation, the interpreter must amass knowledge of a large number of semantic fields. Other examples include special terminologies or jargons related to diverse professional groups and subgroups; these will be discussed under Varieties of Language in section 7. In addition to an extensive knowledge of linguistic denotations, the interpreter needs to be aware of how native speakers use certain words and syntactic structures in context, and what connotations certain words have to speakers from a particular region.

2. Usage

Usage issues may be very clear cut, as when a word is simply the wrong word or a non-word as in: "Her husband adored her and always put her up on a pedalstone" (rather than the correct word "pedestal"). Often, however, such issues are more subtle, as when a word or structure is not wrong but rather is used in a way that is unnatural for a native speaker. An example of this phenomenon is the use of the **passive** versus **active** constructions in English as opposed to Spanish. An **active** construction in English refers to the ACTOR-VERB-PATIENT pattern, while **passive** construction refers to the PATIENT-VERB-(by-AGENT) pattern:

Active: The embezzler forged the checks.

Passive: The checks were forged by the embezzler.

As Vásquez-Ayora (1977) observes, in Spanish there is a marked preference for active rather than passive verb constructions. English speakers, on the other hand, use the passive extensively, particularly in certain fields such as the legal profession. The passive construction is used widely in courtroom language because the agent of an action is often unknown or alleged. It is very common to hear sentences such as this: "Your honor, the defendant's name was sounded in the hallway, but no response was given." And in the questioning of witnesses, attorneys often rely heavily on the passive, as in these examples:

(1.)   Where were you when *you were approached by the man* with the smoke-stained mustache?

(1a.)   *¿Dónde estaba Ud. cuando se le acercó el hombre del bigote manchado de humo?*
(Literally, the above italicized portion states: himself to you approached the man.)

(2.)   You are charged with robbery under $300, which is a misdemeanor in the state of California.

(2a.)   *Se le acusa de (cometer) un robo de menos de $300, lo cual es un delito menor en el estado de California.*

Although the underlined phrases in the English sentences are syntactically very similar, Spanish usage dictates the use of different syntactic combinations in each case. Because of the Spanish preference for active constructions, the passive will often be conveyed by what the *Real Academia* calls the *pasiva refleja* (passive reflexsive), exemplified here in the underlined phrase of sentence 1a; as Vásquez-Ayora (1977) notes, this variant of the passive (which combines an active verb form with reflexive and objective pronoun forms) is an effective way to convey the passive meaning. Native speakers will instinctively know when this variant is appropriate, although they will probably not know why. Such is the instinct for native usage which the interpreter must continually seek to attain in the second language. These examples point to the fact that a category which may be single and invariable in one language may have more than one alternative in another language.

2.1. Lexico-Semantic Variation

Great care must be exercised not to overstep the boundaries of connotation in going from SL to TL. This issue can be classified as that of **lexico-semantic variation**. **Lexicon** refers to the corpus of words in a language, whereas **lexico-semantic variation** refers to differences in word meanings. In this regard, the problem of special concern to the interpreter is that of choosing the TL word which is closest in meaning to the SL word, where several alternatives may exist.

One word in the SL may have many independent meanings, necessitating several words in the TL to capture all the connotative differences. For instance, the Spanish verb *agarrar* has a number of meanings, among them to grasp, seize, grab, catch hold of, take, capture, catch, and so on. According to *Simon and Schuster's International Dictionary, English/Spanish Spanish/English* (1973), *agarrar* has six meanings as a **transitive verb** (a verb which can take an object), and three meanings as an **intransitive verb** (a verb which cannot take an object). *Agarrar* is a catch-all verb that can mean almost anything a speaker wishes it to. In certain areas in particular, such as South Texas border areas, the verb is widely used to mean "get" or "take," as in the following example:

(a) *Agarramos una casa.*
   (We got/bought a house.)

(b) *Agarramos a la niña y nos fuimos.*
   (We took the child and left.)

(c) *Me agarró la Inmigración.*
   (Immigration picked me up.)

(d) *Agarré las llaves del carro y salí de volada.*
   (I grabbed the car keys and took off in a hurry.)

In each of these examples, the English verbs represent varying degrees of forcefulness. Example (c), in particular, is an issue that arises often for interpreters. Let us suppose a defendant on the stand explains that during the commission of an alleged crime, he took some money that belonged to a co-defendant and later returned it because he felt ashamed and guilty. If the defendent uses *agarrar* in describing that action, the interpreter may render *agarré* as "I took" (the money). The effect in English will be more neutral than if the interpreter chooses "I grabbed the money," because for an English speaker, "grab" has a more active, assertive connotation than "take." In this scenario, the prosecuting attorney will very likely pick up on the verb—"Oh, so you grabbed the money that didn't belong to you" (in addition to committing the crime alleged). The effect of "grabbed" may be stronger than that of "took" and thus color the perception of the listeners who must judge the testimony of the witness.

Utterance by utterance, the interpreter must choose the best word(s) in seconds, on the basis of context; if the context is unclear, the interpreter should request rephrasing for specificity. Unless context clearly dictates otherwise, the most neutral choice is best in order to avoid over-interpretation. Of course if the context were different and physical violence were being described—*Me agarró del brazo y me lo torció* ("He grabbed my arm and twisted it"), the more neutral choice "took" would be inappropriate.

3. Cultural Meaning

Another significant area of variation in word connotations or nuances is that of cultural meaning. A word may have a cognate which on the surface appears to have the same basic meaning in SL and TL, but which may connote something quite different to speakers from different cultures. For example, the word "ranch" in American English usually connotes expansiveness, land, wealth, and livestock. In contrast, the cognate word *rancho* may refer to a small, humble structure when used by a Spanish-speaking ranch hand to refer to his living quarters.

Another example of differences in cultural meaning is seen in the word "formal." When applied to a person the Spanish word *formal* has a different and more complex meaning than the English cognate "formal," which is applied in a limited fashion to human beings. A person who is "formal" in English is "observant of conventional requirements of behavior, procedure, . . . ceremonies" (*The Random House Dictionary of the English Language*, 1987, p. 752). In Spanish, *una persona formal* is "serious, quiet, settled, correct, formal, sedate, reliable; punctual" (*Simon and Schuster*, 1973, p. 1227). This translation suggests a person who can be relied on to fulfill societal obligations and expectations. It is a word rich in cultural meaning for Spanish speakers in general.

Cultural meanings and connotations can be so complex that it is not possible to truly convey what the word means to a speaker from the culture in question. A case in point is the word-concept *voudou* as it relates to Haitian Creole. *Voudou* or *voodoo* is defined as "a religious cult of African origin practiced in the Western Hemisphere mainly by the Negroes of Haiti and characterized by a belief in sorcery and fetishes and rituals in which participants communicate by trance with ancestors, saints, or animistic deities" (*American Heritage*, 1973, p. 1437).

Voudou or *vodou* is a complex belief system which permeates Haitian culture in myriad ways (see d'Ans, 1987; Foster & Valdman, 1984; Laguerre, 1982). Because of this word's many connotations its cultural meaning cannot be adequately conveyed without expert explanation. In English "voodoo" tends to evoke negative stereotypical images of magic spells and zombies, without evoking the larger religious-historical-cultural context from which this belief system emerged and in which it operates.

Such a culturally loaded term has deep meaning far beyond its semantic reference. If it becomes important in a court case, an expert witness should be called to explain the meaning of the key term within the culture. To illustrate, a person of rural Haitian background was charged with a crime of violence in a state court in the United States. As his defense had to do with the compelling belief system of *vodou*, the attorney called an expert witness to testify as to the meaning of the word in the defendant's cultural context (B. Freeman, personal communication, June 9, 1989).

In a case such as the one described above, if an expert witness is not called, then the interpreter may be expected to explain cultural implications of an important word. The interpreter, however, should not take it upon herself to do so. According to the protocol described in Unit 8, Chapter 35, a conference with the attorney before the beginning of a trial may help forestall breakdowns in understanding, particularly those due to cultural meanings. As Figliulo (1984) notes, "trial preparation should both . . . disclose particular translation problems, which should be resolved before trial and any differences in attitude or culture that may hinder communication" (pp. 62-63). Communication blocks based on divergent cultural concepts, culture-bound terms, misperceptions of cultural concepts, and the like, should be anticipated and prepared for as much as possible.

3.1. Culturally Bound Terms

As is indicated in Unit 8, Professional Issues, terms with meanings highly dependent on a cultural context pose a particularly difficult dilemma for the interpreter. This is as true of all aspects of a language, from traditional kinship terms such as Spanish *compadre*, to current slang which may reflect usages drawn from the mass media, politics, sports, and other arenas. Interpreters for former President George Bush have had difficulty with such phrases as "blah blah," "read my lips," "stay tuned," "lighten up," "the vision thing," "the deployment thing," and "on the offense." His immediate predecessor also frustrated interpreters on occasion with his one-liners; for example, when asked once what he wanted Sandinista leaders of Nicaragua to do, he replied, "Cry uncle" (Seib, 1989).

Such slang is typical of courtroom language. Attorneys routinely use culture-bound terms along with a rich variety of idioms, metaphors, and folk sayings. The interpreter must keep abreast of current cultural allusions, slang, and new words, because they will be used in the courtroom, particularly when attorneys are attempting to persuade jurors through folksy, egalitarian rhetoric (see Chapter 20). For example, an attorney in a closing argument may accuse a defendant of "Leona-Helmsleyesque behavior, which is exceeded only by his Trump-like spending of the embezzled funds." The interpreter needs to be aware of the persons alluded to and their public images. Leona Helmsley was alleged to have conducted her business affairs without regard to the law while at the same time bragging about her improper conduct. Trump is a billionaire who is reportedly a lavish spender. A knowledge of current affairs would allow the interpreter to comprehend this statement and to formulate the TL equivalent.

The need for cultural-linguistic awareness is paramount in the interpreter's preparation, and indeed for all involved in the judicial process. Hansen et al. (1988) note the difficulty of translating the perspective that is conveyed by the language. This, in essence, is the ultimate challenge to the interpreter.

To a greater or lesser degree, people from different cultural-linguistic backgrounds are in the position of the protagonist of *The Gods Must Be Crazy* (Uys, 1980), a movie about a tribe of Bushmen whose seemingly idyllic existence is suddenly altered by a soda bottle that is thrown out of an airplane and lands in their midst. Having assumed that the bottle is a gift from the gods, the Bushmen are initially intrigued; however, disillusionment soon follows, for the "gift" is blamed for causing unhappiness among the group members. The leader, determined to return the unwanted gift to the gods, makes a long journey to throw the bottle off the end of the earth. At one point during his odyssey he gets hungry; upon seeing a goat he delightedly takes it, not knowing that he is stealing it. He knows nothing of theft, or private property. He is taken to court where, fortunately, he has for an interpreter a white man who has spent considerable time among the Bushmen and who is able to assist in convincing the authorities of the radical cultural differences leading to this grave misunderstanding. The Bushman is released to the custody of the interpreter's friend.

Unfortunately, in real life, solutions are not always so neat. Explaining abstract concepts such as due process of law to someone who may have nothing similar to relate to it may at the moment seem like an insurmountable problem (Hansen et al., 1988). There is also the matter of perception of a defendant because of cultural mannerisms. Figliulo (1984), in giving advice to attorneys who use interpreters for trial, notes that "for cross examination it may be important to know if the witness hesitates or qualifies responses in a manner only detectable by one conscious of mannerisms of a particular culture" (p. 63). For example, Spanish speakers often repeat the question before responding: "Where did I go? Well, I went. . . ." Understanding the witness's culturally influenced response behavior is invaluable for a judge or a jury who may, like others, believe that the witness is exhibiting flippant or sarcastic behavior. In anticipation of such culturally conditioned responses, Figliulo (1984) recommends that attorneys discuss any attitudinal or cultural differences that may hinder communication, and seek the interpreter's advice on how to overcome them.

4. Paralinguistic Features

Paralinguistic features of a language are audible gestures; paradoxically, as Hall (1959) elucidates in *Silent Language,* silence also has a linguistic function. However, as Bolinger and Sears (1981) observe, that silence is useful when one can use it to dominate the interaction and stave off "would-be interrupters." In order to avoid interruption while gathering their thoughts, speakers often use hesitation sounds, such as the English "uh" or Spanish *este.* Other examples of paralinguistic features are changes in intonation, as in drawls or sneers, or exaggerated emphasis or loudness.

Interpreters must be sensitive to these features in both their first and second languages. In addition, they should convey the closest equivalent to such features in SL when interpreting into TL. In this regard, they must walk a fine line between fidelity to the meaning of these sounds in the overall message, and either under- or over-interpreting. Under-interpretation entails disregarding the paralinguistic features in English, while over-interpretation would be the interpreter's drawing too much attention to her performance by being more highly expressive than the SL speaker. For example, an indignant French speaker says, *Qu'est-ce qu'il pensait ce type-là, que j'étais un voleur, moi?* (What did that guy think, that I was a <u>thief</u>?) and if the interpreter renders this as a flat statement, she will be under-interpreting; if, on the other hand, she raises her voice and exaggerates emphasis or stress, she will distort the meaning by over-interpreting. The tone she seeks to convey should be as faithful to the original as possible.

5. Gestures

In addition to audible gestures, communication entails visible gestures which are known as **kinesics.** Birdwhistell (1970) postulates that "body motion is a learned form of communication, which is patterned within a culture and which can be broken down into an ordered system of isolatable elements" (p. xi). As early as 1952, he developed a method for recording visible gestures (Bolinger & Sears, 1981). One of the many fascinating aspects of Birdwhistell's work in kinesics is the discovery that different ethnic groups display different kinesic behaviors. Fiorello La Guardia, for instance, spoke English, Yiddish, and Italian; observers who knew those cultures could tell which language he was speaking in newsreels without the sound (Birdwhistell, 1970).

On the other hand, cumulative research in parakinesic behavior indicates that, at least in Western European languages, there is also "a set of necessary and uniform body motion behaviors which are tied directly to linguistic structure" (Birdwhistell, 1970, pp. 102-3). There are two main types and four subtypes of audible and visible gestures which accompany ordinary speech (Bolinger & Sears, 1981).

5.1. Learned Gestures

These are acquired as part of a speaker's culture, as words are. They include:

(a) *Lexical gestures*: Visible gestures in this group include waving good-bye, shrugging the shoulders to mean "I don't know," the Spanish gesture of touching the outer corner of the eye with the index finger to tell a person to be careful; in speech this is called *tener mucho ojo* or simply ¡*ojo!* (eye).

(b) *Iconic gestures*: The speaker imitates an aspect of the thing signified (whissssshhh, bzzzzzzzz). Visible gestures would include pushing motions, throwing gestures (I threw the ball as hard as I could), and so on.

5.2. Instinctive Gestures

(a) *Voluntary*—cough to get attention; smile to please.

(b) *Involuntary*—cough or sneeze, blink or blush.

In time, Bolinger and Sears (1981) note, "all instinctive gestures acquire a social significance and take on local modifications, one reason why members of one culture may behave awkwardly when transplanted to another" (p. 67). Certain gestures from other cultures may create erroneous impressions, and the interpreter needs to be aware of this in order to foresee communication difficulties. For example, if a Chinese witness expresses anger merely by widening the eyes, and the jury does not know this gesture, how does it get interpreted? A judge or jury unfamiliar with this behavior may interpret it as fear or disbelief.

6. Non-Literal Language: Idioms and Metaphors

6.1. Idioms

Akmajian et al. (1984) note that idioms are expressions whose meaning is **noncompositional**. Their meaning is not a function of their individual component parts;

rather, idioms have a **unitary** meaning, as do proverbs. "In a flash" cannot be broken down into its component parts to decipher meaning.

As Makkai (1984, pp. v-vii) observes in *A Dictionary of American Idioms,* all known languages have idioms, American English being particularly rich in this respect. Idioms which correlate with basic parts of speech can be called lexemic idioms. Consider the following examples:

(a) Verbal: He thought he'd gotten away with it, but they found the weapon with his fingerprints on it (i.e., no one would know what he did).

(b) Nominal: The job only took two hours; it was a piece of cake (i.e., very easy).

(c) Adjectival: It was just a plain vanilla sort of house (i.e., ordinary, unadorned).

(d) Adverbial: The police were there in a flash (i.e., right away, immediately).

Other idioms are longer, phraseological idioms, or "turns of phrase." They are very common in American English. Some examples are: "to be up the creek" (in a predicament); "to fish or cut bait" (either do something or give it up); "to take the bull by the horns" (to face and deal with a problem directly); "to be between a rock and a hard place" (between two equally unpleasant alternatives). Still longer are sayings and proverbs, such as:

(a) "You can catch more flies with honey than with vinegar." (Peaceful means are more productive than aggressive ones.)

(b) "You can lead a horse to water, but you can't make him drink." (One can only influence another's behavior to a certain point.)

(c) "You can't judge a book by its cover." (Outer appearances can be deceiving.) (Makkai, 1984, p. vi)

As Falk (1978) points out, idioms, proverbs, and certain compound words (such as "greenhouse," "blackboard," "hot dog") must be entered into the lexicon of a grammar as if they were single units or morphemes; thus, it is not surprising that these items pose translation difficulties, because of the many ways in which concepts are expressed differently from one language to the next. What is expressed by one morpheme in one language may be expressed by several morphemes in another, or no idiomatic parallel may exist. Still, Falk (1978) notes:

> it is important to recognize that translation, even of idioms, is always possible. Although there may not be a word-by-word or morpheme-by-morpheme parallel between two languages, the concepts expressed in one can also be expressed in some way in the other. (p. 47)

6.2. The Interpreter and Idioms

The interpreter's task with respect to idioms is to find a way to express them accurately and intelligibly, so that speaker's meaning and intention is preserved at all times. Because they are embedded in longer discourse, which typically proceeds at a rapid pace, and because the possibilities of idiomatic expression—like that of all linguistic expression—are infinite, idioms challenge the interpreter's flexibility and resourcefulness to the maximum.

One example, the Spanish idiom *con las manos en la masa* (literally, "with one's hand in the dough") has a good English equivalent in "red-handed," as in "caught red-handed." This becomes an automatic response for the interpreter; thus when a defendant/witness says, *Me agarraron con las manos en la masa,* the interpreter can automatically render the sentence "I got caught red-handed," or "They caught me red-handed" if the identity of "they" is appropriate in the context. If not, the passive construction should be used; otherwise confusion may result from the questioner asking, "They? Who are they?" Therefore, if the antecedent has not been clearly established as "the police," the active construction should be avoided.

The interpreter needs as large a repertory as possible of both idiomatic and non-idiomatic equivalents, which can become automatic responses. Such idiomatic equivalents in German as *einen Narren an jemandem fressen* (literally, "a fool on somebody to devour") and its equivalent "to be crazy about somebody," and *das Kriegsbeil begraben* (literally, "the waraxe to bury") and its equivalent "to bury the hatchet," will be at her command (Falk, 1978, pp. 45-46). Thus, these idioms will not slow the interpreter down and interfere with the ability to maintain the flow of simultaneous or consecutive interpretation. Likewise a solid repertory of non-idiomatic equivalents, such as *sich übernehmen* (literally, "oneself to overexert") for "to bite off more than one can chew" (p. 46), will facilitate the interpreting process and free the interpreter to use resourcefulness in dealing with idioms which are more problematic in the TL.

When employing idioms that have no easily accessible equivalent in the TL, the interpreter must be able to quickly process the concepts being expressed, as well as to find an equivalent, intelligible phrase. Since the currently fashionable phrase "read my lips," used by George Bush in his 1988 presidential campaign, seems to have no ready equivalent in Spanish, one interpreter chose *mira lo que estoy diciendo* to convey this expression. A French interpreter chose the word *truc,* a vague term meaning roughly "something," when Mr. Bush refers to "the vision thing" or "the deployment thing." For "stay tuned," the Japanese translation became *daiyaru wo awase yoku-kiwo kete tsukete okinasai,* roughly, "put the dial in the right place and pay attention" (Seib, 1989, p. A8).

In the case of proverbs as with lexemic or phraseological idioms, the interpreter needs to build a storehouse of equivalents, be they proverbial or not. The greater the cultural differences between speakers of two languages, the greater the likelihood of having to understand the concept and express it in a non-proverbial way. In Haitian Creole one can find proverbial equivalents to such expressions as these found in Jeanty and Brown (1976):

(a) *Bon machè koute chè* (literally, "cheap things are expensive").
     "You get what you pay for."

(b) *Tou sa-k klèrè pa lò.*
     "All that glitters is not gold." (p. 91)

On the other hand, some sayings do not have familiar proverbial equivalents and therefore must be rendered in a way that conserves both meaning and intelligibility, such as the following: *Zè ki kalè trò bonè ti poul la pap viv* (literally, "egg which hatches too early the little chicken won't live"). A quasi-proverbial English equivalent of this saying is "fruit picked too soon won't ripen." Both the literal and non-literal quasi-proverbial versions convey the meaning in the absence of a true proverbial equivalent. Conveying the concept (even by literal translation) is the first priority.

6.3. Metaphor

Metaphor is another type of non-literal language use that frequently overlaps with idiomatic usage, as in the phrase "lame duck congressman," which is metaphorical in that a human being is implicitly compared with a lame duck; it is also idiomatic, because the individual meanings of the component words do not equal the total meaning of the phrase. According to Falk (1978), the difference between metaphors, idioms, and proverbs is that, "with a metaphor, it is always obvious that the expression is not intended in its literal meaning. . . . But idioms, proverbs, and compounds may have both a literal and a nonliteral meaning" (p. 44).

Metaphors are constantly being created. We "metaphorize" more than we realize and often our newly coined metaphors are ephemeral, because they refer to persons or events currently prominent in the news. "Watergate" has become a much-used metaphor for "scandal." Only time will tell if a particular metaphor will endure. The word "donnybrook" derives from Donnybrook Fair, an Irish festival noted for rioting and dissipation (*Random House Dictionary*, 1987, p. 583). The fair was discontinued in 1855, but the metaphor lives on as a noun meaning a brawl or contentious dispute.

7. Varieties of Language

Over the last three decades, sociolinguistics has become a major area in linguistic research. Fasold (1984) observes that the essence of sociolinguistics depends on two facts about language:

(1) Speakers of a language can say the same thing in more than one way. This phenomenon is called **variation**.

(2) Because language varies, speakers can simultaneously communicate information and define their own social situation, i.e., while transmitting ideas and information to others they are also making statements about who they are, what their group loyalties are, how they perceive their relationship to the listeners, and what the purpose of the communication is.

Because of this, Fasold (1984) concludes that "the study of the interplay between these two facts about language is exactly sociolinguistics" (pp. ix-x).

Sociolinguistic research has demonstrated that we all speak varieties of language rather than "a language" or "languages." Labov (1972) observed that there are no "single variety" speakers. Interpreters must deal with the language varieties of a wide range of speakers, from judges to witnesses, and their interpretations must accurately reflect these variations. This is precisely why the depth and breadth of their linguistic knowledge must be so extensive. In this section we outline the kinds of variation implicit in that knowledge.

7.1. Regional Varieties of Language

Akmajian et al. (1984) define **dialect** as "a distinct form of a language (or other communication system) that differs from other forms of that language in specific linguistic features (pronunciation, vocabulary, and/or grammar), possibly associated with some regional, social, or ethnic group, but that is nevertheless mutually intelligible with them" (p. 521). In popular usage, the term dialect often refers to a form of a language considered to be "substandard," "incorrect," or "corrupt," in contrast with the "standard," "correct," or "pure" form of the language. In linguistics, however, there are no such value judgments; dialect is simply a technical term used to refer to a distinct form of a language. However, because of the negative connotation associated with the term "dialect," we prefer to use the term **language variety**.

The ability to understand and interpret what we call a regional or language variety rests on the principle of **mutual intelligibility**. This principle makes it possible for Texans to communicate with New Yorkers, and Americans with Britishers, phonological, lexical, and grammatical differences notwithstanding. On the other hand, languages such as Mandarin and Cantonese have been traditionally regarded as "regional varieties" of Chinese, even though speakers from the North (Beijing or Mandarin dialect) cannot understand those from the South (Canton), and vice versa. This "regional variety" designation derives from the fact that they are related historically, are spoken in the same nation, and can use the same written language as a form of communication—hence the persistence of the term "dialect," despite the lack of mutual intelligibility (Akmajian et al., 1984).

Sometimes regional varieties are mutually intelligible, but for historical and political, rather than linguistic, reasons are considered languages rather than dialects. Such is the case with the American Indian languages of Tohono O'odham and Pima spoken by tribal groups living in Arizona and northern Mexico. The two languages are "extremely close phonologically and grammatically, with only minor linguistic differences in pronunciation and syntax . . . " (Akmajian et al., 1984, p. 290). However, because the two groups consider themselves to be distinct political entities, they consider their languages distinct as well. The examples above display how language is an inseparable part of a larger sociocultural-historical-political context. In countries throughout the world, "the standard national language is the dialect of the subculture with the most prestige and power" (p. 294).

The persons whom interpreters assist in court may be speakers of the standard or prestige dialect of their language, or they may not. They may be speakers of a variety of language which they themselves consider to be "inferior." They may be rural or urban, male or female, elderly, middle-aged, young, educated, or illiterate. They may also be monolingual or of limited bilingual ability; that is, they may speak or understand some English, but not have full control of the grammatical structures and lexicon of English and, therefore, feel the need for an interpreter in court.

7.2. Other Forms of Variation

All of the factors mentioned in the preceding paragraph combine to influence the speech style of the interpreter's client. Therefore, the interpreter must accept that client and surmount linguistic idiosyncrasies in order to successfully fulfill the interpreting function. To do this, the interpreter must remain aware of general patterns of regional variation in her languages; attune her ear to phonological variations by listening to native speakers, radio broadcasts, movies, tapes, and so on; build glossaries of lexical items which differ from dialect to dialect in an ever-widening number of semantic fields. In addition, the interpreter must be prepared to cope with such linguistic phenomena as code-switching. Most importantly, the interpreter must maintain a professional, non-judgmental attitude toward the varieties of languages encountered and the people who use them.

7.3. Code-Switching

Code-switching is the ability to switch back and forth among languages, varieties, and registers as the social situation or their own inner needs determine (Elgin, 1979). The example below of code-switching is common in the border areas of the United States, where Spanish and English are mixed and both languages influence each other because of the close proximity of two cultures. The speaker begins in Spanish, switches codes and inserts English, and then switches back into Spanish:

> *Yo no sabía qué pensar, me entiende, porque it was already ten-thirty, y ellos no me habían llamado todavía.*

> ("I didn't know what to think, you understand, because it was already ten-thirty, and they hadn't called me yet.")

Another frequent phenomenon in the courtroom is the incorporation of TL words in the SL with a strong SL accent. When this occurs, the interpreter should interpret the entire utterance, repeating the TL borrowed words verbatim. The possibility of switching is always present, particularly in semantic domains of occupation, place names, addresses, and so forth. Since these pieces will be imbedded in a longer flow of words, and are pronounced with an SL accent, they are sometimes more difficult to decipher, sometimes requiring a request for clarification. If a witness states, *Estaba trabajando pa' el "Jaga"* (I was working for Haggar), the interpreter may not recognize the referent *Jaga*. In this case, the interpreter simply repeats the item as phonologically close to what was heard as possible; it then falls to the judge or attorney to clarify. If the interpreter recognizes the item, then the English name is given—in this case, "Haggar." In these cases, the interpreter must adapt to the pronunciation of English words with the speaker's native accent superimposed.

7.4. Register, Language Style, and Level

Register refers to language level or style used in different settings. Joos (1967) theorizes that American English contains five styles used in differing situations by people, depending on the social context, the purpose of the discourse, and the relationship between the speakers. These five styles of formality, which he calls "the five clocks of English," are frozen, formal, consultative, casual, and intimate (pp. 24-36).

These variations within the same language require flexibility and resourcefulness of the interpreter, who must shift stylistic gears very quickly and without warning in the target language. Since this shifting of gears is at the very heart of court interpreting, given the depth and breadth of language with which court interpreters must deal, interpreters may anticipate that their resourcefulness will routinely be put to the test. Expanding their repertory, and linguistic resources is, therefore, a top priority. In the court setting, it is more likely that a shift in registers will occur in the speech of attorneys or judges.

Conservation of register is one of the greatest challenges of legal interpreting. It is the preservation of the way in which an idea was spoken in contrast to the bare sense of the message. Take, for example, the differences among these six statements:

His performance was on the uppermost regions of the normal curve.

She exhibits qualities of giftedness.

He is an intellectual.

She's a real genius.

He's a brain.

She's another Einstein.

Putting aside the possibly sarcastic underlying meanings each of these sentences could have and considering only the plain meaning, these six sentences basically have equivalent meanings. However, each of these represents a different style and therefore elicits very different reactions. Each sentence would most likely occur in very different settings, each appropriate to the subject at hand, the purpose of the communication, the intent of the speaker, the roles of the speakers, and the nature of their relationships.

The first example might be spoken by an expert witness in a formal explanation to the court, attesting to the intelligence of an individual. The second example might be found in the formal discourse of a school psychologist. The third sentence might be found in the speech of one colleague to another, discussing the qualities or shortcomings of a job applicant. The last three are examples of casual or intimate speech wherein the relationships between the speakers are closer and the situation is not formal. It is the duty of the interpreter to understand the situational context and the specific context the speaker refers to, in order to interpret correctly the style of the speaker. In this way, the interpreter can accurately conserve the *way* in which an idea was spoken in addition to its content and can achieve legal equivalence.

Conservation of register is the most essential element in the preservation of the "voice" of the speaker in combination with precise word choice and the maintenance of paralinguistic elements. For an in-depth discussion of register shift in legal language, see Chapter 21.

7.5. Repertory

Repertory refers to the spectrum of language varieties, such as semantic fields and registers that a speaker controls. A related term, **role**, refers to the relationship of speakers in conversational exchanges, and thus dictates the register or style of language used. A defendant appearing in court may assume a very different role from the more usual ones with family or friends, and the language used will reflect that difference to some degree. Even though the person may not have a wide repertory, the defendant will know to address the court differently than the defendant does friends. The defendant may not know exactly what words are appropriate forms of address, and if a Spanish speaker, the defendant may use *Su Majestad* (Your Majesty) instead of *Su Señoria* or *Señor Juez* (Your Honor). Nonetheless, the concept of contextual appropriateness will most likely not escape the defendant.

8. Varieties of Terminology

Matters that affect all aspects of life are encountered in court interpreting; consequently, everything is "grist for the interpreter's mill." In addition to the semantic fields to which we have referred previously, the court interpreter must acquire knowledge of a wide range of **terminologies** and **jargons**. Fields of specialized terminology include law, medicine, and chemistry, and are encountered in the testimony of chemists and pathologists who may appear in court. When the interpreter is frequently exposed to expert testimony from forensic chemists who routinely testify in narcotics cases, the interpreter will generally become familiar with the applicable terminology, with the goal of acquiring and compiling a glossary. When it is a matter of infrequent or one-time interpreting in an unusual case, the interpreter will need to prepare as fully as possible beforehand by researching as many of the specialized terms and learning the concepts or process by consulting reference books or experts in the field.

8.1. Jargons

Jargons are the technical, specialized vocabularies of a professional or "special interest" group; that is, they refer not only to the special terms used in certain professions, but also include the language of fishing enthusiasts, sports fans, music lovers, and so on. Jargons are not intentionally mystifying; however, for practical reasons, outsiders will not have had the time, opportunity, motivation, or schema (framework of related concepts or experiences) to learn them (Akmajian et al., 1984).

The most obvious jargon the court interpreter needs to learn is that of the law, or "legalese." An example of legalese is the verb phrase "to jump bail," meaning "to fail to appear in court while released on bond." Another is "to mirandize," meaning to read an arrested person the rights provided by the Miranda rule.

Law enforcement agencies have their own special jargons, which are intertwined with those of the legal profession. Often these terms are reduced to **acronyms**, or "word(s) formed from the initial letters or groups of letters of words in a set phrase or series of words" (*Random House Dictionary*, 1987, p. 18). These acronyms must be recognized by the interpreter. In federal courts, for example, CJA refers to Criminal Justice Act, and by extension to court-appointed attorneys. Immigration authorities typify agencies who rely heavily on the use of acronyms (EWI—Entry Without Inspection, VR—Voluntary Return, and so on.) Most criminal justice agencies refer frequently to a procedure known as "an NCIC check," NCIC being a computerized system of information, the National Crime Information Center. When acronyms are used in testimony, the interpreter will find that attorneys are careful to identify what the acronym stands for so that the jurors will understand, thereby providing the interpreter with the opportunity to interpret the concept or name for the listener at least once before the speaker reverts to the acronym. Law enforcement officers will describe their actions using their occupational jargon, as in this testimony from a typical drug case:

> We knew this thing was gearing up to happen. Right before it was going down, we prepared for the take down. We checked the layout of the roadside park, got suited up, then froze the situation.

A less jargony rendition would be:

We knew this drug deal was about to take place. Right before it was going to happen, we prepared to arrest the suspects. We checked the layout of the roadside park, put on protective gear and then ordered everyone to stay where they were.

In addition to the usual professional jargons that the interpreter hears on a daily basis in the courtroom, there is every conceivable kind of general occupational jargon which may be heard in witness testimony; in this sense, every witness is an expert on his or her own testimony, and will use certain terms which are peculiar to a particular field or occupation. The witness may be a farm worker engaged in "deroguing" and "detasseling" corn, for instance, or an oil field worker describing a "pressure bleed-off device," or a night club manager describing how "cashing out" is handled each evening at closing. In all cases, the interpreter will need to understand the concepts expressed and, if possible, learn some of the less familiar terminology beforehand. Since that is not always possible, the interpreter will develop the habit of taking notes and expanding personal glossaries by looking up terms during breaks and after proceedings, and consulting people who work in the field as to meanings which are unclear.

8.2. Argot

Another kind of specialized language is **argot**, the jargon of the criminal underworld (Akmajian et al., 1984). For example, "to front up" (money, vehicles, or any other goods necessary to carry out a criminal plan) means "to provide payment or necessary items beforehand." "To flash" is to show to the seller of illicit goods the cash one has on hand for the purchase of drugs, etc. **Taboo** words, such as obscenities and profanities, can occur at any time in the context of testimony in a criminal trial. The interpreter cannot, and must not, soften or in any way distort the meaning of the offensive word. If the witness uses more than a word or phrase in English, the interpreter should repeat it. As in all other instances, the principle of fidelity and accuracy obtains. It is important to note here that persons learning English as a second language will often acquire this jargon in English and use it in their speech.

From the foregoing discussion, we see that the interpreter is continuously engaged in learning new words as they arise in the course of interpreting. In addition to expanding vocabulary with respect to diverse semantic fields, technical terminology, and professional-occupational jargon, the interpreter also needs to keep abreast of new vocabulary. In this regard, the work of lexicographers is of interest. In books such as the *Longman Register of New Words* (Ayto, 1989), recently coined terms that have been culled from media usage are recorded, with contextual examples. Such tools as these are indispensable to the interpreter's growth. Equally important is the attitude of cultural sensitivity, linguistic impartiality, and the desire to continue learning and expanding the interpreter's knowledge.

Chapter 20

Characteristics of Legal Language

This chapter presents a brief overview of legal language with an emphasis on its historical evolution. The findings of legal scholar David Mellinkoff are considered and updated to reflect the language employed in courtrooms today.

1. Introduction

The task of the interpreter, to transfer a source message from one language to another, is further complicated by the language of the court. The interpreter must be concerned not only with the countless linguistic difficulties posed by the stunning diversity of modern-day criminal offenses, the argots of the *barrio* and law enforcement jargon, but also with the perplexing variety of language spoken and recited in the courtroom, commonly referred to as legal language. A complex species of English quite unlike any other, legal language has been protested for centuries. The great English author Jonathan Swift (1947) defined it as "a peculiar Cant and Jargon of their own, that no other Mortal can understand" (p. 297). Linguists and anthropologists have defined legal language in various ways: O'Barr (1982) defines it as a variety of English that can be distinguished from "ordinary English"; Charrow and Charrow (1979) describe it as a sublanguage; Gonzalez (1977, 1980) discusses it as a register in the Hallidayan (1964) sense. Whatever the terminology, most agree that legal language is a profession-specific, relatively antiquated, and anomalous category of English.

One of the most systematic and comprehensive studies of legal language was undertaken by the legal scholar David Mellinkoff (1963). In his definitive work *Language of the Law*, the origins of legal language are traced from its roots in Anglo-Saxon, Latin, and French, to its final emergence in pre-modern English. In addition to tracing its linguistic development, Mellinkoff identified several features occurring in legal language that render it relatively inaccessible to the layperson, calling it extraordinarily precise, yet ambiguous and equivocal. He characterized the language as wordy, unclear, pompous and dull and described the features that contribute to the uniqueness and complexity of this subcode. Examples of these aspects largely borrowed from Mellinkoff (Mellinkoff 1963, pp. 11-29) follow:

1. USE OF COMMON WORDS WITH SPECIALIZED LEGAL MEANINGS

Common Word	Specialized Legal Meaning
• action	lawsuit
• consideration	benefit to promisor or detriment to promisee
• counterpart	duplicate of a document
• covenant	sealed contract
• executed	signed and delivered
• instrument	legal document
• motion	formal request...
• party	person contracting or litigating

2. USE OF PROFESSIONAL JARGON

• alleged	• raise an issue
• argumentative	• reasonable man
• at issue	• reversed and remanded
• breaking and entering	• the case at bar
• cause of action	• without prejudice
• damages	

3. USE OF LATIN WORDS AND PHRASES

Latin Phrase	Specialized Legal Meaning
• *amicus curiae*	a friend of the court, a concerned citizen
• *corpus delicti*	the body of an offense
• *cui bono*	who benefits? in whose interest?
• *ex parte*	on one side only, done for one party
• *in propria persona*	on one's own behalf, without an attorney
• *nolo contendere*	not contested, not challenged
• *sui juris*	of his own right; not under legal disability to act for one's self

4. USE OF FRENCH WORDS NOT IN THE GENERAL ENGLISH VOCABULARY

French Word	Translation
• *alien*	to transfer
• *chose in action*	that which is the cause of suit
• *estoppel (estoppel in pais)*	to be stopped from making a claim
• *esquire*	attorney at law
• *fee simple, fee tail*	property inheritance categories

5. USE OF WORDS WITH AMBIGUOUS MEANING

- adequate remedy at law
- due process
- extreme cruelty
- obscene
- reasonable speed
- reputable
- satisfactory
- sound mind
- transaction
- undue influence
- undue interference
- undue restraint
- unreasonable
- unsound

6. USE OF TERMS OF ART

- alibi
- appeal
- bail
- *certiorari*
- defendant
- demurrer
- eminent domain
- felony
- garnishment
- habeas corpus
- injunction
- lessee
- negotiable instrument
- plaintiff
- *re judicatas*
- tort
- *voir dire*

7. ATTEMPTS AT EXTREME PRECISION

Use of absolutes:

none, never, all, unavoidable, irrevocable, impossible

Use of restrictions:

and no more, and no other purpose, shall not constitute a waiver, shall in no way

Use of delimiters:

including but not limited to, shall not be deemed to limit, nothing contained herein shall

8. FREQUENT USE OF FORMAL WORDS

In Court	In Affidavits
• hear ye, hear ye, hear ye	• being first duly sworn,
• Your Honor	deposes and says
• may it please the court	• further deponent saith not
	• before me, a notary public

In Contracts	In Oaths
• whereas	• I do solemnly swear . . . that I
• time is of the essence	will faithfully execute the
• be it remembered	Office of President of the
• know all men by these	United States;
present	

9. USE OF POMPOUS LANGUAGE

• anomalous result	• excluded in unmistakable
• can be no question	language
• cannot be doubted	• irrevocably concluded by
• cannot in reason be	• previous decisions
conceived	• made more manifest
• conclusive force . . .	• true and controlling
• dispose of the argument	principles

10. WORDINESS

For	Say
• annul	annul and set aside
• remove	entirely and completely
	remove
• will	last will and testament
• document	written document
• instrument	written instrument

Use of Noun Form	Rather Than
• to make application	to apply
• make investigations	investigate

Mellinkoff believed that much of the wordiness in legal language is caused by a heavy reliance on nouns. Although these features occur in everyday English, Mellinkoff rightly points out that they occur with higher frequency in the language of the law and mark the differences between legal and non-legal speech.

The layperson is further hindered from comprehending the language of the law by the legal shorthand frequently used by attorneys and judges. Mellinkoff (1963) observes that the legal code is largely incomprehensible to laypersons because the speaker truncates ideas to an almost symbolic form, as is shown in the following interchange:

First Lawyer: What did he say?

Witness: I told him I wouldn't and he insisted.

Second Lawyer: Move to strike for purposes of making an objection.

Judge: Granted. That may all go out as nonresponsive and a conclusion. Mr. Reporter, read the witness the question. [The question is read.]

Witness: He said that I'd better or ...

Second Lawyer: Objection. Extrajudicial statements not subject to cross.

First Lawyer: Offered only to show state of mind.

Judge: Overruled. Received for that limited purpose. (p. 18)

Interpreters must learn to recognize this legal shorthand and comprehend its cryptic code, since it is often used by lawyers to make objections and by judges to speak to the record.

Mellinkoff (1963) also calls legal language overcomplicated and unclear. In the following example a judge is delivering a message to jury members who are not legal professionals: "If Mrs. Smith's injury was caused partly by Mr. Jones's negligence and partly by her own negligence, she cannot recover" (p. 26). Rather than this straightforward and clear explanation, the jury is told the following:

You are instructed that contributory negligence in its legal significance is such an act or omission on the part of the plaintiff amounting to a want of ordinary care and prudence as occurring or co-operating with some negligent act of the defendant, was the proximate cause of the collision which resulted in the injuries or damages complained of. It may be described as such negligence on the part of the plaintiff, if found to exist, as helped to produce the injury or the damages complained of, and if you find from a preponderance of all the evidence in either of these cases that plaintiff in such case was guilty of any negligence that helped proximately to bring about or produce the injuries of which plaintiff complains, then and in such place the plaintiff cannot recover. (p. 26)

Distinguished jurists such as Thomas Jefferson (1943) and groups such as the Plain English Movement (Beardsley, 1941; Wydick, 1985) have worked diligently to change this wordy, overly complicated, and extremely formal speech style to relieve mystified laypersons and benumbed jurors; although significant progress has been made, the profession and its users have for the most part resisted change. From another perspective, it is understandable that a tradition so steeped in historical precedent would cling to the etiquette and antique flavor of its code (Gonzalez, 1980).

2. History and Major Influences

Courtroom language style is the end product of a series of historical incidents that have melded cultures, languages, and traditions into a unique communication code. Mellinkoff (1963) terms the product of this potpourri of languages, cultures, values, and rituals "a curious heirloom of another age" (p. 8) that is "not officially English." Although the beginnings of the tradition are difficult to pinpoint, the history of legal language parallels the history of England, and a variety of powerful historical and cultural forces as well as linguistic elements have left their imprint. Of those many influences, four will be briefly discussed here:

(1) Anglo-Saxon oral tradition and language

(2) The Catholic church

(3) The Norman conquest

(4) The rise of the guild

2.1. Anglo-Saxon Oral Tradition and Language

The largely illiterate Anglo-Saxon society relied on oral tradition for the propagation of knowledge and the functioning of its institutions, including the forum for settling disputes. All litigation was oral, and litigants used language that was designed to impress all those who listened, from neighbors to judges. Since nothing was written, all pleadings had to be committed to memory, giving rise to oratorical styles that aided memorization. This is manifest in the Anglo-Saxon literary tradition, exemplified by the epic poem *Beowulf,* which is replete with devices such as alliteration and the use of poetic meter, both of which facilitate the memorization of long pieces of discourse.

Besides making the language easier to memorize, these devices also made it easier for an audience to listen to, comprehend, and retain information. In the development of their legal tradition, the Anglo-Saxons naturally adopted these alliterative and rhythmical features, which still persist in the language of the law today, as is evident in the phrasing of familiar Anglo-Saxon oaths:

"... the truth, the whole truth, and nothing but the truth, so help me God."

"... for richer for poorer, in sickness and in health, until death do us part."

Vestiges of Old English are profuse in modern legal language. The jury is in the *box,* the witness takes the *stand,* the person who reports the verdict to the judge is the *foreman.* The Germanic method of compounding to form words with new meanings was a strong element of the Anglo-Saxon language. Such words are very much a part of modern legal language:

manslaughter

landlord

hearsay

aforesaid, forthwith

here words: hereafter, herein, hereof, heretofore, herewith

there words: thereabout, thereafter, thereat, thereby, therefore, therein, thereon, thereto

where words: whereas, whereby

witness, witnesseth

3. The Catholic Church

The church essentially shaped the common law of England and dominated the legal process for centuries (Mellinkoff, 1963). Before the early fourteenth century in England, lawyers and judges were priests. The *clerics* or *clergy* of the church became the *clerks* of the court. It was not until the late thirteenth century that the practice of law was secularized and regularized, and judges began to be selected from outside the church. One need only consider the similarities between a church hall and a court of justice to understand at least on a superficial level the influence of this religious institution. The correspondences are both fascinating and illuminating. Just as priests preside over a sacred altar, judges preside over a bench on a raised platform. Priests wear vestments and judges wear robes. British and Australian judges still wear red robes—the color of the robes of Roman Catholic cardinals. Priests refer to scripture in a sacred book and judges refer to a law within a code book. The pomp and circumstance and ceremony of the church have also left their mark on legal proceedings. Consider these parallels: The bar of justice is like the communion rail of the church, delineating the line between the audience and the sanctuary. Everyone rises when the judge enters the courtroom, just as everyone stands when the priest begins the entry procession. Both the mass of the church and a legal proceeding have a prescribed and predictable form. Judges, like priests, utter ritualized pronouncements that vary according to the ceremony or proceeding. And, in one instance, priests and judges, depending on the state, may perform the same function: namely, to unite a man and a woman in marriage.

These obvious parallels pale in comparison to the formidable impact the language of the church had on legal language in England during seven language periods, including Late Latin, Medieval Latin, Low Latin, Vulgar Latin, New Latin, and Law Latin. For at least 1,000 years legal codes and documents were written in Latin. In fact, 75 percent of the words common to formal English are Latin based. Words such as *ad hoc, affidavit, alias, alibi, bona fide, per capita, prima facie, pro forma, proviso,* and *quid pro quo* are just a few of the hundreds of words common both to everyday English and the law. In addition, legal language has plentiful non-Anglicized Latin phrases, such as those in Section 1 of this chapter, that legal practitioners and scholars have struggled to demystify for hundreds of years, to no avail.

4. The Norman Conquest

In 1066, when William the Conqueror took the throne of England, French became the official spoken language of the high legal courts, the royal court, and educated society. Latin remained the language of written legal documents while English continued to be spoken in the lower courts. French became the language of the legal system and contributed numerous legal terms of art that have never been replaced. Literally hundreds of French words, many of which are synonymous with English words and others that offer new conceptual distinctions, eventually were assimilated into English, such as "larceny" and "robbery," which are conceptually more specific than Old English "theft."

It was during this post-conquest period that a tremendous amount of borrowing took place from French into English. The French legal tradition became so deeply entrenched that barristers and other practitioners began to rely on French borrowings to express their legal ideas. This marked the beginning of doubling, where one term in French was linked side by side with a similar term in English (Mellinkoff, 1963, pp. 121-22).

French	or	English
devise		bequeath
infant		child
larceny		theft
marriage		wedding
property		goods
act		deed
memory		mind
novel		new
pardon		forgive
take possession		buy
purchase		buy
court		bench
evidence		witness

This doubling process became so commonplace that the process of pairing French words became habitual also:

French-Derived Synonyms

aid and abet	null and void
aid and comfort	pains and penalties
authorize and empower	cease and desist

Both the English-French and the French-French pairings are redundant. The interpreter must be cognizant of this redundancy and may render the meanings of these doublings with one word, instead of searching for two synonymous words (Gonzalez, 1983). For example, the Spanish interpreter can render "waive and give up" as *renunciar* and feel confident that the legal meaning has been conserved. This technique becomes necessary when synonyms are limited in the target language. When it is possible to render each word in redundant historical pairings, the interpreter must conserve them. Consider the following example:

English Triplet	Spanish Triplet
annoy, molest, harass	*molestar, estorbar, perturbar*

In this case, Spanish equivalents are plentiful; and if the interpreter can render them without a problem, they should be fully conserved. However, they may be rendered by one term because of time constraints or other necessities.

5. The Rise of the Guild

In the early period of the practice of law, before its regulation, guild interests prevailed. Two manifestations of this rising guild interest were: (1) the reliance on formbooks for formulaic instructions as to how to "sound" like a lawyer and (2) abuses of the system by clerks and lawyers such as padding.

5.1. Reliance on Formbooks

These legal "cookbooks" offered formulas for sounding "legal," and remnants of their prescriptions are still with us today. *The Pleader's Guide, A Didactic Poem* (Anstey, 1796) is a formbook written in verse that was used by clerks, scriveners, and real estate agents—not barristers—who studied the codes. This particular formbook was the origin of the appellations John Doe and Richard Roe, unidentified persons or persons to remain nameless in the proceeding which are still used today. Formbooks in general contained the following phrases still in current usage (Mellinkoff, 1963, pp. 12-23:

be it known present	in the premises
last will and testament	mutually agreed
party of the first part	party of the second part
aforesaid acts	false and untrue

5.2. Padding

Another characteristic of legal language is its excessive wordiness, a trait resulting from the fact that lawyers and clerks were paid according to the length of their documents. Therefore, they increased the size of documents, which in turn increased the fee. According to Mellinkoff (1963), there were a number of techniques used for padding:

(1) reciting unnecessary parts during the declaration and in the summoning of the jury;

(2) reciting allegations from counsel;

(3) adding words to any part of the document. (p. 22)

The "more is better" and "lose the syllable lose the cause" theories prevail. These linguistic mannerisms and characteristics have allowed lawyers to preserve a professional monopoly by locking up trade secrets in the safe of an unknown language. However, these code features have straightforward meanings, and interpreters can become familiar with them by investigating their origins and increasing their exposure to the use of such terms.

Thus, it is clear that legal usage constitutes a distinct domain of language. The interpreter should listen carefully to the language used by attorneys and judges in the courtroom to gain a full understanding of its many complexities and peculiarities. Although Latin is no longer a prerequisite of entrance into law school, there remain many terms of art and jargon which are directly traceable to the historical antecedents discussed in this chapter. Essentially, the interpreter must remain a diligent student of language to acquire these terms and keep abreast of the changing technology and incorporation of new terminology in the legal arena. The job of the interpreter is further complicated by the cross-cultural dimension of reconciling English legal language with Spanish legal concepts and terms (Franhenthaler & Zahler, 1984).

Chapter 21

Variation and Complexity of Legal Language

In the analysis of the features and historical context of legal language presented in the preceding chapter, no distinction was made between the written and spoken forms. However, the distinction has become very important to interdisciplinary scholars of legal language. This chapter will be primarily concerned with spoken courtroom language. It will examine legal language from the perspective of register characteristics and set forth the implications for court interpreters.

During the mid-1970s a group of scholars from various fields such as linguistics, sociology, anthropology, psychology, and the legal profession began to focus on legal language. Since then, increasing numbers of researchers (Berk-Seligson, 1987; Charrow, 1982; Charrow & Charrow, 1979; Charrow, Crandall, & Charrow, 1982; Danet, 1980; Elwork, Sales, & Alfini, 1982; Erickson, Lind, Johnson, & O'Barr, 1978; Gonzalez, 1977, 1980; O'Barr, 1982; O'Barr, Walker, Conley, Erickson, & Lind, 1976; Valdés, 1986) have addressed the broad question of how language relates to the law and the legal process. These studies explore the formal characteristics of legal language from a sociolinguistic point of view, both qualitatively—through ethnography—and quantitatively—through formal linguistic descriptive or statistical analyses. They investigate the form and function of socially patterned language variations, determine how it expresses power relationships, and measure the difficulties of comprehension.

Danet (1979) differentiates this research from discussions lawyers and jurists have had regarding language-related issues, by qualifying it as empirical rather than speculative, adding further that it emphasizes *law talk,* "the spoken language of legal professionals, their clients, and various others with whom they come into daily contact" (p. 367). Of particular importance for court interpreters are two categories of legal language studies, those that:

(1) examine the **register** of language—the variety of language used according to the setting and purpose of the communication and relationship of the speakers; and

(2) examine witness testimony and its effect on how the jury and judge perceive the credibility of the witness and the weighing of evidence. Included within this category is the subcategory of studies showing the consequences of interpretation on legal language.

This chapter will review the language of the courtroom from the first perspective, and Chapter 22 encompasses the latter distinction. Two studies of the register of courtroom language will be discussed here: the general conclusions of the significant and exhaustive research of the Duke Project (Erickson et al., 1978; Lind & O'Barr, 1979; O'Barr, 1982; O'Barr & Conley, 1976; O'Barr & Lind, 1981) and a study by

263

Gonzalez (1977). A common goal of these studies was to identify and describe the styles of language found in the courtroom.

1. The Duke Project

In an attempt to describe the major forms of stylistic variation in speech occurring in trials, four varieties of language were identified by O'Barr (1982) in the Duke Project: (1) formal spoken legal language, (2) formal standard English, (3) colloquial English, and (4) subcultural varieties. A description of his system (pp. 24-26) classifying courtroom language follows:

(1) **Formal spoken legal language**, popularly known as **legalese**, is described by O'Barr (1982) as the variety of spoken courtroom language that most resembles written legal language. The judge uses this mode to instruct jurors, pass judgment, and "speak to the record." Lawyers use this form less frequently than judges to address the court and make motions and requests. Linguistically, this form is characterized by lengthy sentences replete with professional jargon and complex syntax. This style actually accounts for only a small proportion of courtroom discourse and is generally termed **hypercorrect**. The hypercorrect forms "seventy-two hours," "not cognizant," and "determined" can be contrasted to the casual forms "three days," "didn't know," and "saw," respectively.

(2) **Formal standard English** is the language variety most typically used in the courtroom by lawyers and most witnesses. It generally is labeled **correct** English and closely corresponds to the grammar school English teacher's model for speaking. The lexicon is somewhat more formal than that of everyday speech. For example, the formal forms "opposite" and "able to be moved" (in the context of a medical emergency) can be contrasted to the casual forms "across from" and "not too bad off."

(3) **Colloquial English** is a form spoken by some witnesses. Most lawyers do not begin with this style, also referred to as casual English, but may move into it when interacting with witnesses who use it. It is lexically and syntactically similar to everyday English. This style is thus distinguished by such things as the use of contractions ("he doesn't know beans"), ellipses ("he left because I told him to (leave)"), a lexicon and syntax simpler than that of standard English or legalese, and certain phonological patterns ("I tol' him to quit buggin' me," versus "I advised him to refrain from harassing me").

(4) **Subcultural varieties** are spoken by segments of the society whose speech styles and mannerisms differ from the larger community, such as Black Vernacular English and the English spoken by the poorly educated. These varieties have their own syntactic, lexical, and phonological characteristics and are distinct from one another. As with colloquial English, lawyers may employ this style if they find it advantageous.

Duke Project observers noted that no one speaker used all four registers, although most speakers did shift among registers depending on what the situation seemed to require. Whether or not the choice is conscious, choosing to use one register over another can influence the level of power or powerlessness of speech in a legal proceeding. Both attorneys and witnesses have proved themselves adept at shifting among registers, whether or not they are aware of the social implications they are making in exercising this choice. This study supports the hypothesis that among legal professionals and laypersons there is a ranking of registers; as an informal rule, credibility, impact, and persuasiveness are functions of style (O'Barr et al., 1976).

The Duke Project found many instances of register manipulation in which lawyers not only varied their own linguistic style, but also tried to control the styles of witnesses. They found that a lawyer is likely to speak more informally to prospective jurors during *voir dire*, since speaking in a colloquial style may establish a solidarity with the jurors. On the other hand, a lawyer will likely distance him or herself from hostile witnesses by, for example, attempting to make colloquial or cultural varieties appear "stupid," or by suggesting that expert witnesses are using elevated speech to obscure simple matters. O'Barr et al. (1976) described an instance where a defense lawyer questioned a young man giving testimony in Black English. This man's testimony was critical for the lawyer's argument, and after each utterance the defense lawyer carefully restated in standard English what was said in Black English. The authors of the study add that it is not possible to know whether this was consciously or unconsciously motivated. With another witness whose testimony was unfavorable to his case the same lawyer was observed restating that witness's utterances in a casual, less correct form. According to O'Barr (1981):

> Degree of formality and other variations in presentational style in the courtroom have been described ethnographically by the Duke team and shown to be related to significant differences in the credibility, trustworthiness, competence, etc. of both witnesses and lawyers in simulations of the courtroom. (p. 396)

For the interpreter, therefore, **conservation** of register is a major component of producing a **legally equivalent interpretation**. Modifying, by lowering or raising the register, can alter the global impression the jury or judge has of the witness. In a Florida case a woman who testified in casual language replete with slang and profanities was made by the interpreter to sound like a gentle, grandmotherly senior citizen (Silva, 1981). According to the account, "The six jurors may have developed a more favorable impression of the old woman than they otherwise might have" (p. 2b). The accused was consequently convicted of rape and sentenced to life imprisonment. The case was subsequently overturned on the basis of poor interpretation. By not conserving the register the interpreter was unwittingly cloaking the "true" character of the witness as manifested by language.

2. The Gonzalez Study

Gonzalez conducted a study in 1977 to describe the register of courtroom language and ascertain the complexity of the speech of judges, attorneys, experts, and witnesses. The purpose of the study was to empirically devise indices of complexity that could be used as a set of constructs for a test of functional English proficiency. The test was designed to determine whether a Spanish-speaking person involved in the criminal justice system required the services of an interpreter. The results of this study later served as the complexity and register performance standards for the Federal Court Interpreter Certification Examination (Gonzalez, 1980, 1987b).

2.1. Register

Gonzalez's study of courtroom English, *The Register of Courtroom English* (1980), assumes a broad definition of register suggested by Halliday et al. (1964) to be "the variety [of language] according to use" (p. 77), which emanates from the Firthian concept of register as the relationship of language to social context (Firth, 1957). The study also utilizes Halliday's understanding of register as "the alignments and combinations of items or pattern" (Lyons, 1970, p. 29).

2.1.1. Register Determinants

Gonzalez examined three dimensions that must be considered in the description of any register, according to Joos (1967) and Halliday et al. (1964). These parameters are the following:

(1) *Field of discourse*: the purpose for which the speaker employs language, such as persuasion, discussion, and reporting.

(2) *Manner of discourse*: the relations among the participants in a language activity, which can be described according to the five styles designated by Joos (1967): frozen, formal, consultative, casual, and intimate (see Chapter 19).

(3) *Mode of discourse*: the medium of communication, primarily a distinction made between spoken and written language.

It is the product of these three dimensions that best defines register. Generally, Gonzalez's investigation revealed the existence of the five styles or registers of English as discussed by Joos (1967)—frozen, formal, consultative, casual, and intimate. This study is corroborated by a later investigation conducted by O'Barr and Lind (1981). One notable difference is O'Barr's (1982) conclusion that no one speaker used all styles. Gonzalez (1980) found that although no one speaker used all five styles, attorneys in opening statements would in their philosophical arguments turn from formal style and frozen definitions of law to consultative explanation and casual illustrations of the facts or issues for the jury. Judges also switched styles in jury instructions when they felt it necessary to give an example in plain, idiomatic language. The results of Gonzalez's analysis of the field, mode, and manner of courtroom discourse are briefly reported here:

2.1.1.1. Field of Discourse. In the case of courtroom language the field of discourse is generally technical because of the legal-issue basis and specific contextual domain, or the kind of case being tried, i.e., murder, robbery, illegal possession, use or sale of drugs, rape, burglary. The most significant variation within these specific fields of discourse is lexical, and even that variation is slight. The purpose of the discourse may be generally described as persuasive, interrogational, instructive, or informative. Attorneys are interrogational in cross-examination, persuasive in summary, and cajoling and accusatory in questioning. The expert witnesses are informative in their testimony. The judge is instructive when explaining points of law, directing the business of the court, or ruling on an objection. Predictably, judges are also judgmental, an intrinsic part of their role in the courtroom.

2.1.1.2. Manner of Discourse. The analysis of 10,000 words of transcript revealed that all five of the styles identified by Joos (1967) were present in courtroom language. The following findings resulted from the study of register parameters (Gonzalez, 1977):

(a) *Frozen*: The social roles and social attitudes within the court trial situation are formally defined and frozen. The judge's style of language is frozen, when citing from legal codes and procedural regulations in the instructions to the jury. These are formulas which cannot be changed. They are concretized and virtually immutable. Some examples are "This court is now open pursuant to adjournment," and "You will a true verdict render."

(b) *Formal*: When questioning a witness during an arraignment or speaking to attorneys and the jury, the judge uses formal language. Attorneys generally speak in the formal style when they address witnesses, the jury, and the judge. The language reflects this formality and permanency in matters of court etiquette, such as "You may approach the bench," and "The witness may step down." Formal language also serves to preserve the accuracy in matters of procedural techniques and announcements, and in matters of concretized phraseology which are generally standardized ways of avoiding verbal traps such as double meanings and misunderstandings.

(c) *Consultative*: Often attorneys use the consultative, or informative, style to explain legal definition within an opening or closing statement, or to offer an explication of an object or issue relevant to the case. An expert witness is consultative while explaining a point regarding the issues at hand in an informational style, as in: "This is a drug trafficking case arising out of a checkpoint stop."

(d) *Casual speech*: Witnesses generally speak in a casual or colloquial style. It is usually the language of insiders, in which there is presumed to be a significant amount of shared information. This speech is marked by a frequency of idiomatic expression, jargon, or argot, as in "They tried to bootstrap this case, the K-9 unit arrived and the dog alerted to the tail-gate area."

(e) *Intimate*: The speech of some witnesses may be so non-referential (ambiguous references and unclear antecedents because of no formal subjects) as to render it almost incomprehensible, for it is usually the kind of speech reserved for conversation between pairs. Idiosyncratic vocabulary terms are used, in addition to structures and syntax that is truncated and vague, as in the following:

> Well, you know, then he says, "Will I help him load this stuff, cause they're waiting."

Generally, the language of attorneys and judges is formal, yet both speak in colloquial or intimate style when using idiomatic or slang expressions to make a point. Judges tend to use the spectrum of registers in addressing attorneys and juries in some instances:

> Counselor, I'll entertain your motion and take judicial notice of the information you requested; but I'll tell you right now, you need to get your ducks in a row and get this matter settled before much longer.

Attorneys often mix frozen, formal, consultative, and casual language in the course of routine business. Attorneys addressing juries in opening and closing arguments typically mix styles, using a liberal sprinkling of appropriate idioms to make their point while establishing rapport with the jurors, as in this example:

> Ladies and gentlemen of the jury, through the evidence presented in this trial, we have shown that the defendant is guilty beyond a reasonable doubt, and that the defense has done nothing but put up a smoke screen and set out rabbit tracks to try to distract you from the truth.

2.1.1.3. Mode of Discourse.   Courtroom language is spoken both in spontaneous and non-spontaneous modes. In many instances the judge speaks spontaneously; however, when explaining a point of law while instructing the jury, the judge may read aloud from prepared material. Attorneys may question the defendant or the witnesses spontaneously, or they may recite questions they have laboriously prepared in advance. Attorneys may deliver memorized closing statements or may memorize an outline and spontaneously deliver the same speech. Witnesses may speak spontaneously or, in the case of expert witnesses, read a prepared report or description of an object or act.

2.2. Complexity Study

Complexity, in terms of comprehensibility of legal language, has been investigated by Charrow and Charrow (1979), Gustafsson (1975), Sales, Elwork, and Alfini (1977), Shuy (1978), and Shuy and Larkin (1978). They surveyed particular syntactic features of jury instructions and then tested ways of improving comprehension through manipulating them. Sales et al. (1977) scrutinized discourse features that cause comprehension problems, while Shuy and Larkin (1978) explored the language of insurance globally. It was clear from these studies that indices of complexity were not possible without in-depth linguistic or discourse analyses.

In order to discover features of complexity that could be used as indices of comparability, Gonzalez (1977) examined random samples of discourse from 10,000 words of court transcripts. Language samples were chosen from the spoken discourse of both prosecuting and defense attorneys, from judges, witnesses, and experts. The following features were inspected:

(1) *Readability*: An evaluation of the overall complexity of the structural, lexical, and conceptual load of the language, to determine the readability level.

(2) *Lexical*: A description of the characteristic features of the lexicon of courtroom language, comparing frequency of vocabulary in legal domain with that of ordinary English.

(3) *Structural*: The isolation of recurring patterns or combinations particular to the courtroom language situation.

(4) *Legal expression*: The examination of selected register-specific combinations and alignments. The results of these analyses are offered below.

2.2.1. Readability Assessment

Readability formulas are generally used to assess reading passages to select appropriate classroom material. Although the validity of readability formulas as determiners of linguistic complexity has been disputed (Charrow & Charrow 1979; Charrow & Crandall, 1978), Gonzalez (1977) used readability formulas in addition to other indices to measure conceptual load and to show *relative difficulty* of vocabulary and syntax. Redish (1979) contends that readability formulas only address issues of textual comprehensibility at a superficial level, while Charrow and Charrow (1979) allege that they overemphasize such features as word length and sentence length. In this study, readability was used in conjunction with four other measures of complexity and distinguishing register features; therefore, it represents only one perspective. The readability measure used in this study was the Yoakam formula; as it is particularly sensitive to vocabulary complexity, it was deemed an appropriate tool. As suggested by the Yoakam (1955) readability formula, passages of the court transcript were selected at random. The formula utilizes the Thorndike-Lorge Frequency List for determining the difficulty level (Thorndike & Lorge, 1959). Difficulty is expressed as grade levels five through fourteen.

The random passages measured by the Yoakam (1955) formula had an average difficulty level of grade 14. This exceeds the difficulty level of hearing the *New York Times* (grade 10) read aloud. The readability of most newspapers has been assessed to be in the range of sixth to eighth grade (Chall, 1958). The difficulty of the courtroom language sample was comparable to second-year college texts and approximated the complexity of Graduate Record Examinations. Other discourse and linguistic features also confirm this estimation of complexity.

2.2.2. Lexical Examination

Lexical items found in courtroom language are related legally construed concepts which are difficult, and often cannot be simplified (Charrow & Charrow, 1979). The Gonzalez lexical examination was based on an analysis of every fourth page of two separate case volumes concerning armed robbery and drug smuggling. These court transcripts were examined for the occurrence of words that occur relatively infrequently in common core English.

The Kucera and Francis (1970) *Computational Analysis of Present Day American English* is a computerized list of 1,014,234 words and served as a basis for comparison. The corpus of natural language texts—500 samples of continuous discourse—come from fifteen genres, including such categories as press reportage, *belles lettres*, biography, learned and scientific writings, and general fiction.

Words of a particular register are those occurring with significantly greater frequency in that domain than in "common core" language (White, 1974b). The assumption underlying the frequency list used in such studies is that the more often a word occurs in common language, the more likely any individual speaker of the language is to know that word. White (1974a, 1974b) and Chiu (1972) utilized the Kucera-Francis and Thorndike-Lorge word counts in determining lexical characteristics of register in the fields of administration and science, respectively.

Out of the 10,000-word sample, 210 were identified as specific to the register of the courtroom, meaning that they have a higher frequency of occurrence in the courtroom register than in the common core of the language (Gonzalez, 1980). Some words, such as "abetting," do not even appear on the Kucera-Francis list. Those words which form a part of the courtroom register had significantly higher frequencies or a specialized meaning. The following is an excerpt from this frequency list:

Table 1
Frequency Count of Courtroom Register Lexical Items:
A Sample

Lexical Items	Occurrence per 10,000 in Sample	Estimated Occurrence per Million Courtroom Register	Occurrence per Million Kucera
abet	2	200	no listing
accessory	6	600	1
acquittal	1	100	2
admission	7	700	33
circumstance	1	100	15

Note: The data in Table 1 is from *The Register of Courtroom English*, by R. D. Gonzalez, 1980, pp. 21-24.

Although the term "accessory," which occurred six times in 10,000 words, is shown to have appeared once in the common core, it is highly probable that it did not refer to an accomplice in a crime, but rather to a hat or glove or car feature such as a radio. In summary, vocabulary that appears in high frequency in courtroom usage appears in low frequency in common core English. Therefore, in terms of indices of complexity, the vocabulary one would expect to find in the courtroom is rarer and therefore conceptually more difficult.

2.2.3. Structural Study

The study of selected structures was based on randomly selected passages of court transcript. In this study, frequency of verbs and verb phrases was examined. The use of frequency studies is widespread; White (1974a, 1974b) and Chiu (1972), among others, have employed frequency studies for the purpose of defining specific registers.

Verb formation and use is key to a study of a language variety known for its convolutions and length. While length alone has not been found to be a significant determinant of comprehensibility (Charrow & Charrow 1979; Wearing, 1973), sentences containing embedded clauses have been found to be more difficult to remember and understand. In fact, embeddings have been found to be inversely related to comprehension (Fodor & Garrett, 1967). Gonzalez (1980) proposed that verb formation and frequency of finite versus non-finite verbs would be another measure of complexity that might serve as a predictor of difficulty, because of their relatedness to embedding and other sentence complicators.

Exactly 100 verb forms were identified from the corpus of 956 words. The following model adapted from White (1974a) was used in the analysis:

(a) *Identification and tabulation of finite verb groups with these categories*: simple one-item verbs ("might say"), complex forms of two words or more ("persuade to go," "expected to be"), verb strings, and passives.

(b) *Identification and tabulation of finite verb forms with these categories*: stems (more than one possible per verb group, including modals), *-s* (third-person singular marker), *-ed* (the past tense form of the verb), present tense forms of *to be* (am/is/are), past tense forms of *to be* (was/were).

(c) *Identification and tabulation of non-finite verb forms with these individual items specifically categorized*: *-ing* forms, *-en* past participle forms (with or without infinitive). (p. 406)

The greatest difference between the verbal profiles of the courtroom register and the "common core" occurs in the use of verb strings. The study revealed that fewer simple verb forms are used in the courtroom register than are used in the "common core." The greater number of verb strings occurring in the courtroom register reflects the procedure of questioning; the exactitude of expression in language that results from using modals such as "would," "could," "may," "might" as qualifiers; the number of causative constructions, such as verbs like "cause to be"; and emphasis added for dramatic effect. Nineteen percent of the finite verb groups are verb strings in the legal domain (Gonzalez, 1980), double that of the common core, using White's (1974a, 1974b) suggested figures for common core English.

Seventy percent of the finite non-to-be verb forms are past tense verbs (Gonzalez, 1980, p. 23). The large number of past tense finite verb forms found in the sample reflects the reporting of past events typical of examination and testimony. The language of the courtroom has a greater number of complex verbs and causative verbs in addition to fewer simple verbs. Therefore, legal language is denser than common core language. It has a greater number of verbs per sentence, resulting in more syntactical and semantic relationships to follow. This is one of the factors contributing to its general convolutedness.

2.2.4. Legal Expression

The language sample was informally examined for other idiosyncratic features:

Example 1:   "Did you wish to state your position as to why the evidence should be inadmissible?"

Analysis: "Did you wish," is an archaic formal use of past tense verb form, with subjunctive meaning, for exaggerated politeness. "To state your position" is a frozen legal expression, as is "the evidence is inadmissible." "As to" is a typical vague connective equivalent to "concerning" or "regarding."

Example 2:   "Please do not be misled if what I say will happen does not, in fact, happen."

Analysis: Of the sixteen words in this sentence, ten are integral parts of verb groups. Of the other six (please, if, what, I, in, fact), only three are essential—if, what, and I. This preponderance of verbals is typical of the courtroom register.

3. Implications for Court Interpreters

The features of courtroom language explored in studies reported in this chapter reveal that the language of the courtroom has a number of different varieties, depending on variables such as who is speaking to whom (judge to defendant, attorney to witness) and for what purpose (persuasive, admonitory, or instructional). The registers of the courtroom domain cover the entire gamut, from the formal, frozen legal formulas of jury instructions to the most casual, individually distinct speech of witness testimony.

In addition, legal language contains syntactic structures that are highly complex and not always understandable. It is characterized by a large number of words that do not occur frequently, if ever, in other domains; and by words that occur frequently in other domains but with different meanings. This variety of language contains bureaucratic jargon, shorthand, or code words that are difficult for the uninitiated to understand.

All of these aspects of courtroom discourse must be taken into consideration by the court interpreter, who has a duty to conserve not only the precise meaning of the SL message, but also the exact register, style, and tone. Thus, the interpreter faces a formidable task, first in deciphering the meaning of sometimes obscure, convoluted, or deliberately vague language, and secondly in conveying that message in exactly the same manner as it was spoken.

Chapter 22

Questioning Styles, Witness Testimony, and the Court Interpreter

1. Introduction

Two areas of legal language study are particularly relevant to work of interpreters: witness testimony and attorney questioning styles. If the interpreter understands the effect of the witness's language on the process, then he or she can be alert to the need to conserve the form and content of the witness's response or the attorney's question. A brief survey of pertinent research in this area will be followed by a cursory review of studies that consider the effect of witness testimony after the intervention of an interpreter.

2. Manipulating Testimony

Pivotal to the adversarial system of law is the presentation of testimony through direct examination and cross-examination of witnesses by attorneys (see Unit 2, Chapter 8). Many law schools offer trial advocacy classes as a part of their curricula (Mauet, 1988). It is well established that different modes of questioning and manipulation of witness's answering styles can be utilized for varying ends (Danet, 1979; Danet & Bogoch, 1979; Erickson, Lind, Johnson, & O'Barr, 1978; O'Barr, 1978, 1982; O'Barr & Conley, 1976; Parkinson, 1979; Philips, 1979). Lawyers exert significant control, or power, over the witnesses and therefore the flow of information. Attorneys can control this power in myriad ways—by asking a yes-no question (Is this the gun?) rather than a WH-question (Why were you there?), or framing questions that will elicit an answer in a desired style (Philips, 1985). In fact, Parkinson (1979) concludes that the outcome of a case can be predicted based on the question styles employed.

It is also assumed that language variation affects courtroom processes and thus has political significance. O'Barr et al. (1976) have explored this issue for many years. Their research proceeds from two axioms that are widely accepted in anthropological theory: (1) language variation in any setting is not random but socially patterned, and (2) a set of rules of successful tactics and strategies can be described for competitive arenas of all types, including courtrooms. In researching the connections between legal processes and the communication systems with which they are intertwined, many questions arise, such as: do participants consciously manipulate styles to affect outcomes?

Since linguistic variation is not neutral, we need to know more about the variations in the ways in which lawyers structure their questions and the ways in which such differences are perceived by witness, juror, and others in the courtroom. (p. 38)

3. Questioning Styles in the Courtroom

How do attorneys and judges manipulate the form of witnesses' or defendants' answers? Also, how much control is possible in different situations? Philips (1985) maintains that the role relationship determines the level of control possible:

> it is argued that the kind of role relationships which predominate in a procedure determine the extent to which courtroom speech is routinized, controlling and controlled as opposed to unplanned, egalitarian, and open-ended. In procedures like Changes of Plea or Trials, where speech is exchanged predominantly *between* [emphasis in original] "insiders," or officers of the court, such as a lawyer or judge who is knowledgeable of the law, and "outsiders," those being processed *by* [emphasis in original] the court, such as plaintiffs, defendants, and witnesses, questions by the insider will be highly routinized and controlling. The justification for the control from the point of view of members of the legal profession is their superior knowledge of the legal consequences of speech and their desire to protect those passing through the system from unwittingly damaging their own cases. (p. 4)

Philips concludes that response to question forms is regularly affected by the allocation of power in the courtroom. Thus, persons of less power and authority regularly provide answers that are more completely shaped by the form in which the speaker posed the question.

3.1. Yes-No and WH-Questions

In the study of cross-cultural-language use there are widespread patterns regarding language functions and the linguistic forms that carry out these functions. Often when both high and low varieties (socially accepted and unaccepted varieties) of a language exist, the features that distinguish each variety and the functions associated with them are quite similar among societies and languages that have been neither historically nor genetically related. Philips (1985) reports on recent studies that elaborate the cross-cultural similarities between uses of language and the forms for accomplishing these uses in such linguistic milieus as baby talk, politeness, and formal and informal interactions.

Patterns in the relation between function and form have also been suggested for interrogatives (Philips, 1985). It has been argued that a set of interrogatives, known in English as wh-words, and other sets in other languages, are multifunctional; that each question form can do more than question, they can direct or command. This is related to Lakoff's (1975) idea of powerful and powerless speech styles. She found that people of lower status tend to use a more indirect form (such as "Would you please close the door?" as opposed to "Close the door.") than when a person of higher or equal status directs another.

3.2. Implications for Interpreters

For interpreters, the conclusion to be drawn from all of these studies is that they must meticulously conserve the SL message. Altering the question from *yes-no* to *wh-* or vice versa, or to change the kind, form, or content of question asked of a witness may unwittingly shift the perceived distribution of power. While it may be a social goal to redistribute power, it is not the interpreter's role to influence the judicial process, alter the intent of counsel, or affect the perceptions of the trier of fact.

3.3. Testimony Styles: Narrative versus Fragmented Speech

It is useful to understand the different testimony styles of witnesses and defendants, since these styles are often what questioners may attempt to manipulate. Armed with the knowledge of what Berk-Seligson (1987) terms "linguistic pragmatics" (p. 1089), questioners, specifically lawyers, are able to manipulate witness testimony and thus influence judgments. Danet (1980) describes one case in which the alternate use of the words "baby" and "fetus" in an abortion trial was a central factor in judging the guilt or innocence of a physician. Witnesses as well as lawyers can use their knowledge of linguistic pragmatics to advantage, as Danet (1980) found in the Watergate hearings, wherein hedges were repeatedly used to blunt the force of testimony.

In the course of studying witness testimony in criminal trials, several scholars have isolated a number of recurring testimony styles that can be categorized as alternatively "narrative" or "fragmented" in style, and either "powerful" or "powerless." A narrative style contains full, elaborated answers, whereas fragmented testimony contains brief, incisive, non-elaborative responses. Basically, narrative and fragmentary styles are differentiated by the length of answers. Consider the following:

Narrative Style

Q. Now, calling your attention to the twenty-first day of November, a Saturday, what were your working hours that day?

A. Well, I was working from, uh, 7 A.M. to 3 P.M. I arrived at the store at 6:30 and opened the store at 7.

Fragmented Style

Q. Now, calling your attention to the twenty-first day of November, a Saturday, what were your working hours that day?

A. Well, I was working from 7 to 3.

Q. Was that 7 A.M.?

A. Yes.

Q. And what time that day did you arrive at the store?

A. 6:30

Q. 6:30. And did, uh, you open the store at 7 o'clock?

A. Yes, it has to be opened by then. (O'Barr, 1982, pp. 76-77)

O'Barr (1982) and Erickson et al. (1978) found that witnesses tended to use only one of these two styles in answering questions and the lawyer could control which style the witness used. This finding is corroborated by trial practice manuals that often state, based on implicit assumptions, that speakers of narrative answers are better perceived than those who speak in a fragmented style (Mauet, 1988).

4. Powerful versus Powerless Testimony

The notion of powerful and powerless speech is based on Lakoff's (1975) study of women's speech styles. Lakoff's conclusions have not gone unchallenged, but her characterization of what constitutes powerful and powerless speech is pertinent. After weeks of observation in trial court, O'Barr and his colleagues noticed that some witnesses were speaking in a manner that conformed quite closely to what Lakoff had described as the style typical of American women, also termed **powerless speech**. O'Barr (1982) summarizes Lakoff's (1975) conclusions that powerless speech is comprised of a constellation of several attributes, such as the use of (1) **intensifiers** (forms increasing the force of an assertion, such as "very" and "surely"); (2) **hedges** (forms reducing the force of an assertion, which allows a speaker to avoid making a strong commitment to an assertion, with words such as "sort of" and "a little"); (3) **hesitation forms** (fillers comprising pauses such as "uh," "um," and "let's see"); (4) **polite forms** such as "please," "thank you," and "ma'am" (used in addressing an attorney); (5) **witnesses asking the attorney questions** by using an interrogative rising intonation in normally declarative contexts (p. 67). Together these features constitute a powerless speech style, and as O'Barr found, persons of low social power use it in court. It is not necessarily only women who use this style, but rather lower-socio-economic status men and occupationally low-status women. Speech style characterized by an absence of this constellation of features is considered a powerful testimony style.

It has been consistently shown by social psychologists and linguists that aspects of a person's speech cause the hearer to form impressions of the speaker:

> ... the attribution of positive and negative evaluations of such characteristics as intelligence, honesty, and competence have been found to be a function of listeners' subjective reactions to a wide variety of linguistic and paralinguistic features. (Berk-Seligson, 1987, p. 1091)

Thus, testifying in a powerless fragmented versus a powerful narrative style can have a marked effect on the impressions the listener forms. In simulated courtroom studies, O'Barr (1982) measured attributes such as competence and social dynamism and found that simulated jurors attribute more positive qualities to witnesses who testify in powerful and narrative styles. The more fragmented the testimony, the lower the score in these areas; the more narrative the testimony, the higher the rating. Attribution of guilt did not show statistically significant correlation.

5. Powerful and Powerless Testimony: Implications for Court Interpreters

In an interpreted judicial proceeding, the interpreter is pivotal to the form in which testimony is eventually presented. This is to be expected, since the interpreter is the language intermediary who has final control over how the witness testimony is heard by the judge and the jury. An interpreter who abides by the principles of judicial interpretation and renders the legal equivalent truly serves the system and helps it function normally. However, the interpreter who distorts the testimony by not conserving—who adds words, hedges, hesitates, and omits—serves to impede the process by changing the original testimony style. Unfortunately, even unintentional tampering can seriously affect the outcome of the legal process for the defendant in question. As Danet (1979) indicates, to "sensitise members of the legal profession to the special problems of non-native speakers of the official language of any court... [there is a need] of research on multilingualism and its implications for the legal process" (p. 373).

This issue was first addressed in court interpreting by the specialists who developed the first Federal Court Interpreter Certification Examination (FCICE). The idea that the judicial context required exacting linguistic fidelity arose from an understanding of the requirements of this critical process. Studies by Astiz (1980, 1986), the Comptroller General of the United States (1977), and the Judicial Council of California (1977) found that interpreters—before certification in some state and federal courts, and after certification in state courts—were not conserving the meaning or form of the SL message. Gonzalez coined the term **conservation** in 1980 to sum up the testing standard an interpreter must meet to achieve the FCICE performance goal. This area has been studied by Berk-Seligson (1987).

6. The Berk-Seligson Study

Berk-Seligson's (1987) study confirms the suspicion that many interpreters are not rendering the legal equivalent of the original testimony into the TL. This study revealed that interpreters systematically alter the length of witnesses' testimony, and in the process tend to make that testimony powerless.

Because a number of one-word English constructions are translated as phrases of two or more words in Spanish, it is generally accepted that Spanish tends to be longer than English in translation (Vásquez-Ayora, 1977). After several months of courtroom observation, however, Berk-Seligson (1987) found that interpreters' English translations tended to be longer than the original Spanish testimony. She suggests that during the conversion from Spanish into English certain mechanisms appear systematically and result in features of a "powerless" testimony style. Berk-Seligson (1987) categorizes these mechanisms into the following: (1) hedges, (2) insertion of linguistic material that is perceived to be "understood" or underlying in the original utterances, (3) uncontracted forms, (4) rephrasing of what the interpreter himself has just said in the interpretation, (5) polite forms of speech, and (6) particles such as hesitation forms (p. 1107). Examples taken from Berk-Seligson (1987, pp. 1101-21) follow:

(1) *Hedges*: In this example, a case involving the transporting of illegal aliens, the witness is asked by the prosecuting attorney who else had accompanied him across the border.

Attorney:	Approximately how many?
Interpreter:	*¿Aproximadamente cuántos?*
Witness:	*Un promedio de veintiuno.*
Interpreter:	*Uh, probably* [emphasis in original] an average of twenty-one *people* [emphasis in original]. (p. 1107)

The witness actually said in Spanish "an average of twenty-one." Two elements were added by the interpreter, a hesitation form "uh," and a hedge "probably" (p. 1107). These two forms served to make the witness appear less sure, less definite, and less strongly committed to his affirmation. Thus, the English version of the witness's answer is weaker and less powerful than the original statement.

(2) *Insertion of substance considered to be "understood" in the meaning of utterances*: This is perhaps one of the most common ways that interpreters lengthen testimony as they translate from SL to TL. In the following example, the witness is asked if he ever had a conversation with the defendant, and he answers:

Witness:	*No, de ninguna manera.*
Interpreter:	No, in no way *did I ever have any conversation with him* [emphasis in original]. (p. 1109)

The italic portion of the interpreter's sentence may be "understood" by the English speaker to be underlying the answer. What the interpreter did was add an absolute, emphatic quality to the statement that was not conveyed by the witness's briefer and more accurate statement.

(3) *Uncontracted forms*: In this method of lengthening testimony, interpreters use uncontracted forms when English speakers would have normally used contracted forms. Most often this involves the "contraction of the auxiliaries 'be' and 'have,' the modal 'will,' and the full verb 'be' " (p. 1110). For example, when a speaker would normally say "I'll go," "they're here," or "she's seen it" (p. 1110), interpreters often opt for the hypercorrect form, such as "I will go," "they are here," and "she has seen it" (p. 1110).

Attorney:	Of what country are you a citizen?
Interpreter:	*¿De qué país es Ud. ciudadano?*
Witness:	*México.*
Interpreter:	*I am a citizen of* [emphasis in original] Mexico. (p. 1110)

The interpreter's hypercorrect translation is not faithful to the actual response of the witness. No stress was given to the subject pronoun or the verb by the witness, so there is no ostensive reason for the lack of the contraction of "I" and "am" by the interpreter. The translated answer is excessively formal and stilted and is typical of the hypercorrect grammar that O'Barr (1982) has found to produce negative estimations of witnesses.

(4) *Rephrasing and repeating interpretations*: In the course of interpreting an answer into English, interpreters return to and slightly refashion their interpretation,

even though the witness has not. Berk-Seligson (1987) suggests that this repetition is often an unconscious act, and occurs to give themselves time to formulate material they are about to present. However, repetition can be detrimental for the witness because jurors may be given the impression that the witness is hesitant or unsure. Sometimes, when problems of syntax arise, an interpreter rephrases for the sake of greater accuracy and fidelity. In the following example, the interpreter rephrases the interpretation in order to make the verb phrase active rather than passive. The question asked refers to the manner in which the witness and his companions were to be picked up by the defendant for the purpose of crossing the United States border.

> Witness: *Que pasaría pitando en el momento que era el carro que nos recogiera.*

> Interpreter: That the car would go by blowing its horn, when we were ready to be picked up, *or when he was ready to pick us up.* (p. 1112)

This type of change, from active voice to passive voice and vice versa, is common. Berk-Seligson (1987) remarks that such changes

> often result in the misassigning of agents to verbs, as in the case above. Such secondary errors seem to be related to the fact that the interpreter is focusing her attention on one aspect of the sentence, namely, the grammatical case of the verb, and it may be difficult for her to give as much attention to other elements in the sentence as she makes her syntactic adjustment. (p. 1112)

In this example, as in others, rephrasing nearly doubled the length of the witness's answer.

(5) *Politeness*: Another attribute in the constellation of features that comprise the powerless testimony style is politeness.

> Attorney: Did you last see him on Wednesday?

> Witness: *Sí, eso es cierto.*

> Interpreter: Yes, that's correct, sir.

In this example the interpreter transforms a curt reply into a polite one, creating a false impression of the witness. Polite forms have been found to influence juries, as witnesses who used them were judged more trustworthy and convincing than those who did not.

(6) *Particles and hesitation forms*: Interpretations should sound as sure or unsure in the TL as the speaker sounded in the SL. Interpreters frequently leave out what seem to them to be unimportant elements of discourse, omitting forms such as Spanish *ah* (uh), *este* (uhm or uh), and *pues* (well). Or, interpreters insert their own hesitation forms, since they arise easily as one is concentrating on interpreting. An interpreter's insertion of particles or hesitations can make a witness's testimony appear less certain and as a result less credible. Conversely, eliminating these forms from an original Spanish statement may give an inaccurate impression of certainty by the witness (Berk-Seligson, 1987, pp. 1115-16).

In the case of Spanish to English, interpreters tend to lengthen testimony and, in the process, make it powerless. This seems paradoxical: the shifting from a fragmented to a more narrative style has been found to make for a more powerful testimony style, yet an interpreter's lengthening does not. This is probably due to the interpreter's systematic incorporation of attributes of the powerless testimony constellation of features.

Far from being a neutral figure in the courtroom, Berk-Seligson (1987) concludes that court interpreters exert a "controlling force" (p. 1120) in the process, creating positive or negative impressions of the witness. This is, for the most part, an inadvertent control, and one that should be remedied by court interpreters. The interpreter should monitor his own language and behavior to minimize any distortion which might be introduced into the communication channel. This feat can only be accomplished if interpreters understand the interrelationship between language and the legal process. Her book, *The Bilingual Courtroom* (1990), further explores this curious sociolinguistic relationship among the interpreter, language, perception, and power.

Chapter 23

Categories of Interpreter Error: The University of Arizona Study

1. Introduction

After considering the nature of language, the critical role it plays in the legal process, and the extent to which the interpreter either impedes or facilitates the examination of witnesses, it is understandable why precision and accuracy are the *sine qua non* of the legal interpreter. However, interpreter error is inevitable. For interpreters whose language proficiency in the SL or TL is deficient or whose interpreting skills are undeveloped, error is frequent and consistent. For skilled interpreters, significant error is rare, although it tends to occur more often with fatigue. For both skilled and developing interpreters, unknown or seldom encountered conceptual fields impede comprehension and dramatically reduce accuracy.

Stylistic errors—such as the use of preferred meanings or grammatical forms—although abundant, are not the most dangerous of errors and are many times innocuous. However, errors that distort the meaning of the original or do not conserve the register or language level of a speaker have a serious adverse impact on the presentation of the facts and on the credibility of the witness.

The following categorization of interpreter errors is formed on the basis of ten years of formal descriptive analysis of the Spanish-English Federal Court Interpreter Certification oral examination performance tapes (Gonzalez, 1990b; Gonzalez & Arjona, 1989), training and testing experience with the University of Arizona Summer Institute for Court Interpretation, coupled with reviews of the relevant research by Berk-Seligson (1987), Astiz (1986), Belliveau, de la Bandera, and Lee (1988), and congressional testimony (Senate Bill Nos. 1724, 565, 1853), as well as a recent study of administrative hearings. Many of the following examples are gleaned from over 400 hours of recorded testimony in administrative proceedings, and nearly 2,000 hours of testing and student practice observation.

2. Error Categories

2.1. Literal Translation

Interpretation by language-deficient interpreters is marked by literal translation; interpreters focus not on the essential ideas but rather on the words, exchanging words between the SL and TL without converting or conserving the crucial concept. The meaning of the source message is generally lost, and is oftentimes so unidiomatic in the TL that it becomes absurd. In a legal setting, this feature robs testimony of its effect and accuracy, often making dramatic and crucially important testimony about a serious issue comedic, or so inane that it is immaterial to the listener.

Original:	*Trabajo en el empaque de limón.*
Interpreter:	I work in the package of lemons.
Should be:	I'm a lemon packer.

Original:	*Me sentía muy afligido.*
Interpreter:	I felt very afflicted.
Should be:	I felt very upset.

Original:	*Lo mataron con una arma.*
Interpreter:	They killed him with an arm.
Should be:	They killed him with a weapon.

Original:	*Es una inválida.*
Interpreter:	She is an invalid person.
Should be:	She is an invalid.

Sometimes these literal translations are decipherable after some analysis, and if they occur rarely in isolated segments, they may not drastically impede communication. However, a ceaseless stream of these combined with omissions and other distortions creates a language effect that short-circuits communication completely.

2.2. Inadequate Language Proficiency

The most frequent interpreter error is caused by the general lack of proficiency in the SL or TL or both. General lack of language fluency makes it impossible for an interpreter to comprehend text well enough to convert ideas fully and faithfully at the requisite speed into the TL without continual reliance on glossaries and dictionaries, and without faltering and communication breakdowns. Without language proficiency in place, the following specific processing problems arise and interfere with interpreting:

(1) The guessing or predicting skills that are requisite to pick up the correct cues for language processing are absent.

(2) The cognitive, linguistic, and causal association necessary for processing are thwarted by restricted wrong or hesitant choices of ambiguous cues.

(3) Attention span in the least developed language is limited because of the greater emphasis on comprehension and memory storage.

(4) Interference from one language to another is present at all levels (phono-logical, syntactic, morphological, lexical, discourse, and pragmatic).

Obviously, there is a correlation between speed and accuracy of interpretation and language proficiency. For example, Spanish-English interpreters who are unable to control verb tense formation and sequence, article usage, noun, adjective, and article number-and-gender concordance are obviously not highly proficient language users and therefore cannot be expected to interpret well. Language errors can be categorized into two major divisions: grammatical errors and lack of general and specific vocabulary.

2.2.1. Grammatical Errors

Often, the transformation of a present tense verb into a past tense verb, the subjunctive mood into the indicative mood, or a singular into a plural item radically affects the sense of a statement. Even credibility may be eroded by the inconsistency deriving from a tense or number shift, i.e., "Was it this year or last year?" "Didn't you say you had one brother and not two?" For instance, changing "couldn't" to "wouldn't" alters the motivation of the witness, and makes the witness seem bellig-erent and less trustworthy and sincere.

The following examples illustrate the negative impact tense errors have on the organization of facts over time:

Original: *Si hubiera tenido un familiar.* . . .

Interpreter: Maybe I had a relative there. . . .
               [Does this refer to a time in the past before another time in the past or to the present?

Should be: Maybe if I had had a relative there. . . .

Original: Were you afraid of the guerrillas?

Interpreter: *¿Teme Ud. a las guerrillas?*
               (Are you afraid of the guerrillas?)
               [Is the fear present or past?]

Should be: *¿Temía Ud. a las guerrillas?*
               (Were you afraid of the guerrillas?)

Original: *Si se dan cuenta que le han dado de alto allí nomás lo matan.*

Interpreter: If they noticed that I had been released, it would have been different.
               [Is the fear of their knowing present or past?]

Should be: If they find out that I was released, <u>they would kill me right on the</u> <u>spot</u>.

2.2.2. Lexical Errors

Other interpreters may control the two languages phonologically and grammatically, but make many errors because of a slim or inadequate grasp of both general and specialized vocabulary. Aspiring interpreters often possess a general vocabulary that is shallow in terms of synonyms and in differences in nuance and connotation, and underdeveloped in terms of shades of meaning, i.e., knowing the difference between "famous" and "notorious," knowing the difference between "spines," "quills," "stickers," "thorns," or the special meaning of "mule" as it relates to the drug world.

Accurate interpreting results from a combination of lexical precision and highly developed performance skills. One of the most frequently reported problems for aspiring interpreters who take the Federal Court Interpreter Certification Examination is a lack of general and specialized vocabulary. For example, 84 of the 222 failing performances in the 1989 Federal Court Interpreter Oral Examination (nearly 40 percent) could be attributed to an underdeveloped vocabulary or poor command of the language—either Spanish or English (Gonzalez, 1990b). Errors that indicate a lack of breadth occur whenever a somewhat technical subject is introduced, when the topic changes or when a new lexical domain unfamiliar to the interpreter is used. These examples illustrate this category:

Original: *Hoy en día muchas personas aparecen muertos.*

Interpreter: Nowendays [sic] a lot of people <u>reappear</u> dead.

Should be: Nowadays a lot of people <u>turn up</u> dead.

Original: *La vinieron a secuestrar.*

Interpreter: They came <u>to recruit</u> her.

Should be: They came to <u>kidnap</u> her.

It becomes very obvious when interpreters cannot deal with particular realms of language. They begin to paraphrase, define, invent, omit, guess, and very often lead the testimony into a web of confusion. Occasionally interpreters can successfully communicate by using paraphrasing or defining for vocabulary items that may not be in their active vocabulary.

However, more often than not, communication collapses totally, leaving many critical portions of testimony uninterpreted. An unskilled interpreter will have difficulty comprehending and converting jargon relating to crime such as fingerprinting, booking, sentencing, drugs, weaponry, medical, occupations, industrial, immigration, and other areas relevant to criminal justice. Because of their technical nature, these points are potentially the most crucial elements of evidence that judges must hear. For example, interpreters often have difficulty with a broad range of lexical items, such as oxen, hammer and sickle, massacre, shoe store, board of directors, sentry duty, firing squad, reinforcements, wick, common-law wife, inheritance, nicknames, badge, supervisor, polishing, reprisals, probation, shin, logistics, puppet, phone bank, and stash.

Language-deficient interpreters, like second-language learners, rely on false cognates, or invent words in order to express the meaning for which they have no lexicon available. Common false cognate errors are *actualmente* (at the present time) for actually (really); *defendiente* (a defender) for defendant (the one who is accused); *convicciones* (principles) for convictions (past proven crimes); *injuriar* (to insult) for injure (physical harm). In addition, interpreters will invent new words or phrases which have no validity in the TL, such as *esposa común* for common-law wife or *convictido* for convicted.

The following examples show how interpreting errors occur when attention is not given to the precise equivalents.

Original: *Ametrallaron la casa.*

Interpreter: They <u>shot</u> at the house.

Should be: They <u>machine-gunned</u> the house.

2.3. Errors in Register Conservation

A limited linguistic repertory does not allow the interpreter to closely reproduce the variety of styles that will occur in the court or legal hearing. The language of legal proceedings spans the entire spectrum, from very casual speech, to everyday colloquial, to the formal and frozen speech of judges and lawyers.

Witnesses may display casual, idiomatic, and linguistic varieties characteristic of their region or jargons specific to their jobs. A commonly held but mistaken belief is that persons of lower socioeconomic means, persons from rural backgrounds, or speakers of "broken English," such as second-language learners, use a very restricted code and therefore are "easy" to interpret for. Many Spanish speakers possess a very standard Spanish and use a broad range of vocabulary in spite of a lack of formal education. In truth, many uneducated or undereducated Latin Americans often have an eloquent high-register language that they use in a formal proceeding. This is also true, of course, for many other culture and language groups.

The conservation of register entails the ability to preserve erudite, frozen language as well as informal, casual language that is marked by heavy use of idiom and slang. For many interpreters who have not had experience with multiple registers, the varieties of speech styles found in court work can be problematic. Those who have learned the formal variety of language in school by studying literature find themselves at a loss with the informal varieties of casual speech used by individuals in friendly or intimate relationships. This is often the case with candidates of the Federal Court Interpreter Examination, who have trouble conserving the register of the speaker's extremely informal speech within the context of testimony or a police report. Slang and idioms are included on examination to test the comprehension of those items and evaluate the candidate's ability to render them in the same register as they were originally spoken.

English idioms such as "have the goods on," "jump the gun," "get ahead" are enigmatic for persons whose language knowledge is not comprehensive, just as are expressions such as *le costó mucho trabajo* (it took a lot of effort) and *¿qué le hace?*

(who cares?) are for non-proficient speakers of Spanish. Because testimony and the language of the court are replete with these casual everyday expressions that facilitate communication, these expressions often wreak havoc on interpreters going from English into Spanish. The problem is twofold: comprehending the idiom and formulating a culturally appropriate equivalent in the target language. Problems such as the following often occur:

Original: *...se la iban a pagar con mi familia.*

Interpreter: ...they would do something to my family.

Should be: They were going to take it out on my family.

Original: *...habían muchas orejas.*

Interpreter: ...people talked among each other.

Should be: There were many informants.

The report on the 1988 New Jersey screening test for interpreters demonstrates the problems interpreters have with certain idioms, such as "scared to death" within the context, "She's scared to death, can't sleep at night, and is always on edge," which only 28 percent of the 222 persons who took the examination interpreted correctly. Following are samples of the variety of candidate renditions:

She's afraid of death, she can't sleep at night, she's always on the, on the corner.

She's afraid of death, she can't sleep at night [rest omitted].

She, she is frightened, she can't sleep, to death, she can't sleep at night and she's always—at the point.

She is very afraid of her death because she feels, ummmmmm, threatened, she can't sleep at night, and she's always, ehmmmmm, she's always—irritated.

She's ah, she's afraid die, and she can't sleep at night and she's always—afraid. (Belliveau et al., 1988, pp. 10-11)

These renditions do not conserve the meaning of the concept and often absolutely misrepresent the sense of the original. A judge or jury hearing the interpretation would not have been afforded the opportunity to hear the speaker as he or she really expresses ideas.

Thirty-five of the 222 failing New Jersey candidates (nearly 16 percent) had particular problems conserving the language level of the speaker. These candidates seemed to have a good general command of the language, but did not demonstrate the linguistic flexibility and knowledge necessary to preserve different speech styles. In fact, for persons indisputably skilled in interpreting, conservation of register may be the single most difficult facet of the federal examination. *The Federal Court Interpreter Certification Examination Manual* is very clear about the importance of this aspect of interpretation and devotes two pages to the explanation of conservation (Gonzalez, 1986).

A speaker who sprinkles his speech with colorful idioms may have a very different effect on an audience than a speaker who uses plain language to describe an event. The use of idiomatic language and other varieties says much about a person's background, perspective, and may even suggest other attributes to a listener, as fair or unfair as these impressions may be. Therefore, an interpreter must have the ability to preserve these speech qualities.

2.4. Distortion

Mistranslation errors that distort the overall or partial meaning of the original message are quite prevalent among developing interpreters. These errors may stem from a lack of understanding that the ultimate goal of the interpreter is to conserve every idea and paralinguistic feature in the source message, whether or not these ideas "seem" consequential or "appropriate" to the formal setting, especially if they require profanities or sexually explicit language in order to render the true meaning.

Distortion may come about as a result of deficient language skills, memory, or interpreting skills. Distortion occurs most when testimony is lengthy (more than thirty-five words in one response). It can also occur when the SL discourse is short (less than fifteen words), or when discourse contains technical language, specific, previously unencountered data, emotional intensity, hedges, particles, false starts, unfinished sentences, temporally complex narration of events, and incoherent language. The following example shows how the interpreter significantly diminished the directness and impact of the speaker's statement.

Original: *Lo amenazaron, lo perseguían hasta que lo mataron.*

Interpreter: He had received some threats; all the time they were after him until he was killed.

Should be: They threatened him, they pursued him until they killed him.

(The correct rendition conserves the elements of fear, violence, and aggression that the interpreted version omitted.)

Original: Yo *no más* sentí *el gran golpe.*

Interpreter: I just felt a little punched.

Should be: I just felt the great blow.

Original: *Perdí un ojo andando combatiendo.*

Interpreter: I lost my eyesight when I was in combat.

Should be: I lost an eye in combat.

(The transformation of the loss of an eye to the loss of eyesight severely confuses the testimony and reduces its effect.)

Original: . . . los *apartan.*

Interpreter: . . . they take them apart.

Should be: . . . they take them <u>aside</u>.

Original: *Me <u>introdujo</u> a una oficina.*

Interpreter: He <u>introduced</u> me into an office.

Should be: He <u>took</u> me into an office.

2.5. Omission

Omitting words, such as definite articles, qualifiers, phrases, clauses, ideas, sentences, or large portions of discourse is also a frequent error. It often occurs as a result of fatigue, a factor which seriously diminishes the interpreter's ability to comprehend and process the information. For language-deficient interpreters, omission is the most often used strategy for handling technical terms, regional variants, conceptual ambiguities, or information overload. Those interpreters who cannot process information at the required rate or retain it in memory long enough are inclined to omit an idea or invent a substitute. In some cases, these interpreters would rather guess at an unknown term than ask permission of the court to inquire.

This dangerous practice leads to very confused witnesses who, having given a particular item of information in a previous response, cannot understand why they are asked the same or a similar question in the next response. They mistake the repetitious question as an invitation for further elaboration, which leads to confusion, frustration, and ultimately a failure to communicate. Often witness responses exceed forty-five words, and omission sometimes occurs when the interpreter is unable to handle this length of a response. In these instances language-deficient or developing interpreters omitted from five to fifteen propositions, or up to seventeen words—approximately two sentences.

Omissions can seriously vitiate a witness's story by robbing it of essential details, as in the following examples (words and phrases omitted by the interpreter are underlined):

Original: *Bueno, cuando ellos entraron dice que se asusto, ella quedó bien mal de los nervios. Cuando ella les preguntó qué pasó, se puso de frente, la apartaron, y allí la golpearon.*

Interpreter: She said that when they came in she got nervous, that she was very nervous. She asked what's happening, and when she asked that and got in front of them, they put her aside.

Should be: Well, when they entered, she says <u>she got scared</u> and became very nervous. When she asked them what was happening and faced them, <u>they took her aside and beat her up.</u>

Original: *Pues no lo mataron, sino <u>vivo</u> lo echaron allí.*

Interpreter: Well, they didn't kill him, they threw him in there.

Should be: Well, they didn't kill him, they threw him in there <u>alive</u>.

2.6. Added Information

When interpreters are unsure of the source message, they often add information, typically in the form of synonyms or other meanings. For the skilled interpreter, adding may be symptomatic of "thinking aloud" and may indicate that the interpreter does not have sufficient understanding of the context to make a decision about which meaning to assign the linguistic sign in question. It can also show a cautious attitude by the interpreter who does not want to restrict meaning for a phrase or word that has more than one possible meaning.

The developing or unskilled interpreter adds information when he or she cannot retain the ideas in the original source message. Many times, added information has been invented and bears little or no relationship to anything in the source message. Transforming a simple word or answer into a maze of guesses and possibilities strips the speaker's response of power. This lengthened speech is characteristic of "powerless" speech (Berk-Seligson, 1987). Examples of simple and forceful persuasive language being devitalized by pointless additions (underlined) abound:

Original: ... *que la mataron injustamente.*

Interpreter: ... <u>I believed</u> that they killed, and it was <u>an injustice what they did to her</u>.

Should be: ... that they killed her unjustly.

Original: I don't think you understand the situation right now. Now is the time to answer my questions.

Interpreter: <u>*Quiero decirle de que, no hay necesidad que Ud. use la quinta enmienda.*</u> (I want to tell you that it isn't necessary for you to claim the Fifth Amendment.) <u>*Este, le quisiera pedir que Ud. que contestara la pregunta.*</u> (Well, uh, I'd like to ask if you would answer the question.) *Ahora es el momento que Ud diga su testimonio.* (This is the time for you to say your testimony.)

Should be: *No creo que entiende Ud. lo que pasa ahorita. Este es el momento en que Ud. debe atestiguar.*

(I don't think you understand what is happening right now. This is the time to answer my questions.)

Original: *No sé.*

Interpreter: I have no idea.

Should be: I don't know.

(This not only lengthens the speaker's response, but shifts it into another attitude posture, which does not replicate stylistically the speaker's intention.)

2.7. Protocol, Procedure, and Ethics

Other problems stem from a general lack of professionalism and a misunderstanding of the role of the interpreter and can be classified as training issues. This area causes as much damage to effective communication as any linguistic issue. For example, interpreters do not understand their role as an objective medium. Instead of interpreting profanities and sexual references precisely, untrained interpreters tend to mask and generalize, thus distorting the actual record of events essential to fact gathering. In one case, a witness related that he had been verbally abused by a border patrol agent who called him a *¡Desgraciado maldito!* The interpreter rendered this as "You unworthy person. You're bad!" instead of "You damned bastard." The English version certainly would not have the same effect on a judge and a jury as the Spanish original had. In this case, the interpreter was operating on the assumption that profanities could not be introduced into a formal hearing. These and other issues of interpreter protocol often stem from a misunderstanding of their role.

For many interpreters, admitting error, correcting the record, inquiring with the witnesses, or consulting dictionaries and glossaries rarely occurs, thus contributing to the bewilderment of all parties concerned. Because of the interpreter's unwillingness to self-correct, there is a high potential that facts interpreted in error will be used against the witness, either in the examination of the evidence or in assessing the credibility of the witness.

This lack of understanding of the interpreter's role is also exhibited by some judges and attorneys. In one instance an attorney refused to allow an interpreter to examine trial documents that were not sealed, but pertinent to the case. The attorney assumed that a certified interpreter should not need to have any advance information concerning the nature of the case and specialized terminology involved in it. In fact, interpreters are obliged to prepare. In another setting, the judge asked witnesses to stop after four or five words so that the interpreter could more easily follow and keep up. This instruction severely obstructed the respondent's ability to complete a coherent thought and contributed to the inaccuracy of the interpretation because of the unnatural fragmentation since it is easier to perform a consecutive interpretation after a complete chunk of information has been uttered.

Some interpreters demonstrate a tremendous lack of professionalism by initiating conversations with witnesses, speaking to them in an inappropriate tone (commanding them to answer), summarizing for respondents or witnesses, guessing rather than inquiring, not taking notes for complex or long questions and responses, and denying their own mistakes when a mistake is noticed by an attorney or an interpretation challenged.

2.8. Non-Conservation of Paralinguistic Elements, Hedges, Fillers

Both language-deficient and developing interpreters often do not conserve the hesitation words, fillers, interrupted and incomplete sentences characteristic of real speech. Instead, these interpreters filter out all of these speech characteristics even though these particles are an important part of a witness's voice. For the judge and jury, lack of or inclusion of these fillers indicates something about the witness's veracity or lack thereof, his or her conviction, trustworthiness, etc. Summarily omitting these bits of language misrepresents the witness's testimony. Consider the following example:

Original: *Este, pues, no sé decirle. Es que cuando . . . no fíjese que sí fue así, pero comó le diré, a ver, a ver, vamos a ponerle que . . .*

Interpreter: Well, uh, because it is that way. Let's put it this way. . . .

Should be: Well, uh, I don't know how to say it. It's that when . . . no, of course it was that way, but how can I tell you? Let's see, let's see, let's put it this way. . . .

3. Conclusion

Many of these interpreting errors come about as a result of inadequate language knowledge, a deficient memory span, or inability to access prior information. However, some of these errors are the result of a misunderstanding of the role of the interpreter and lack of knowledge of protocol, ethics, and procedures. Error analysis is an area in court interpreting that demands scholarly attention. Out of this study can come not only a better understanding of the interpreting process, but also a clearer view of the path that training, testing, and in-service training of court interpreters should take.

Unit 6
Interpretation Theory and Practice

Chapter 24

Translation and Interpretation

The previous unit presented general linguistic theories and defined the terms used to describe linguistic phenomena. This unit, drawing on the theories and concepts discussed previously and presenting new ones, focuses specifically on the theoretical and practical aspects of translation and interpretation.

1. Chapter Overview

This chapter defines and distinguishes the terms **translation** and **interpretation**, as well as other related terms, and describes the complexities involved in these activities. It then examines the views of researchers and scholars in a variety of disciplines on language comprehension and interlingual communication, and applies the knowledge derived from this research to the particular domain of interpretation. Finally, there is a list of the specific problems posed by interlingual communication and a discussion of the strategies interpreters employ to solve those problems.

2. Definition of Terms

Translation: Catford (1965) defines translation as "the replacement of textual material in one language (SL) by the equivalent textual material in another language (TL)" (p. 20). Nida and Taber (1974) state that "Translating consists in reproducing in the receptor language the closest natural equivalent of the source-language message, first in terms of meaning and secondly in terms of style" (p. 12). The term **translation** is used in two different ways. First, it refers to the general process of converting a message from one language to another (Bathgate, 1985), and second, it refers to the written form of that process. In this chapter, translation will be used in the first, more general, sense.

Interpretation: This term denotes the oral form of the translation process. Seleskovitch (1978a) emphasizes the critical difference between translating written messages and interpreting oral messages by highlighting the interpreter's presence among those who use his services: the interpreter "is there with both speaker and listener. . . . He participates in a dialogue, his words are aimed at a listener whom he addresses directly and in whom he seeks to elicit a reaction . . . " (p. 2). Another important distinction between translation and interpretation is the difference time demand makes. Translators have time to reflect and craft their output, whereas interpreters must instantaneously arrive at a target language equivalent, while at the same time searching for further input.

As shown in the previous chapter, human language is a very complex system in which many different social, cultural, and psychological factors come to bear. Dealing with two such multifaceted systems at once compounds the complexity tremendously. Every day, professional translators and interpreters assist their clients in overcoming the language barrier by successfully converting written or oral messages from one language to another in a seemingly effortless operation. So successful are they that in many cases the reader/listener ceases to be aware that the person is not reading/hearing the original writer/speaker. In other words, the translator or interpreter does the job so well that the individual becomes invisible. Many people have written about this conversion operation from a variety of perspectives (Catford, 1965; Gerver & Sinaiko, 1978; Newmark, 1981; Nida, 1964; Nida & Taber, 1974; Seleskovitch, 1978a; Vásquez-Ayora, 1977; Wilss, 1982). Although all recognize the extreme difficulty of the task performed by the translator/interpreter, the intricate mental processes involved in this complex operation have never been fully explained. While machine translation has improved greatly, it has not yet been able to duplicate the powerful and extensive ability of the human mind to make lexical choices based on contextual, socioculturally bound meaning.

Language: From the perspective of the translator, Nida (1964) defines language as "words (or other units) which are organized, according 'to the rules of grammar,' into particular types of combinations" (p. 5). He points out that verbal language is just one of many communication codes, a code being "symbols organized into a system" (p. 7). Morse code and signal flags are examples of such systems; music and the pictorial arts can also be considered languages, as they are codes used to communicate. Human beings use these systems to convey ideas; but for the purposes of this chapter, **language** will denote verbal communication.

Source Language (SL): Source language is the language of the original message, the one being translated "out of." For example, when a witness answers questions in Spanish, and the interpreter renders them in English, Spanish is the **SL**.

Target Language (TL): The target language is the language into which the message is being translated. In the above illustration, English is the **TL**.

Unit of Translation: The unit of translation, also known as a unit of meaning or a chunk, is the smallest bit of information that cannot be further divided. It may be a single word or an entire phrase. Idioms are the most obvious example of units of translation: the translator or interpreter, faced with the sentence "You need to get to the bottom of this," or "You need to bite the bullet," or "I was caught in a jam," cannot simply find an equivalent in the TL for each word. A translator must find a conceptual equivalent and transfer the phrase as a whole; even one word may be used if it captures the meaning precisely. Units of translation are not necessarily idioms; they may be prepositional phrases or word affinity groups (words that commonly appear together in a given language for stylistic reasons). For example, in the sentence "She was in the kitchen washing dishes," the units of translation are "she was in the kitchen" and "washing dishes." The translator's choice of TL equivalents is dictated by the role each word plays in the unit. Thus, the equivalent of the verb "was" may be a verb in the TL that denotes location. If the TL requires a preposition, it will be dictated by the verb and the noun in the unit. The verb chosen for "washing" will be dictated by the word "dishes" (it may be that in the TL a different verb must be used depending on whether the item being washed is a car, a person, a place, and so forth). Lederer (1978) provides a definition of units of meaning that focuses specifically on simultaneous interpretation:

> Chunks of sense appear in interpretation whenever the interpreter has a clear understanding of a speaker's intended meaning.... Units of meaning are the synthesis of a number of words present in short-term memory associating with previous cognitive experiences or recollections; this merging into sense leaves a cognitive trace in the memory while the short-term memory is taking up and storing the ensuing words until a new synthesis occurs and a new cognitive unit adds up to those previously stored in the cognitive memory. (p. 330)

3. Oral Communication

Over the years, many scholars in a variety of fields, including philosophy, philology, sociology, linguistics, sociolinguistics, psycholinguistics, semantics, anthropology, cognitive psychology, and education have examined translation and interpretation from different perspectives. In their work, they have drawn on theories of oral communication devised by specialists in the field of linguistics.

3.1. Speaking Circuit

Many theories of translation and interpretation are based on the essential concepts developed by the linguist Ferdinand de Saussure (1966). Although Saussure did not study translation per se, he analyzed interpersonal communication and devised a model known as the **speaking circuit**.

In the speaking circuit posited by Saussure, two people, a source (S) and a receptor (R), are having a conversation. The opening of the circuit is in S's brain, where mental facts or concepts are associated with representations of linguistic sounds—primarily words, which Saussure termed "sound-images"—that are used to express these concepts. S thinks of a concept he wants to convey to R, and relates it immediately to a corresponding sound-image. A physiological process follows this psychological phenomenon: impulses corresponding to the images are transmitted from the brain to the body organs used to produce the sounds. The sound waves then travel from the mouth of S to the ear of R, in a purely physical process. The circuit continues in R, but the order is reversed; the physiological transmission of the sound-image is from the ear to the brain. In the brain, there is a psychological association of the sound-image with the corresponding concept. If the receptor decides to speak, the roles are transposed; correspondingly, the speaking circuit is reversed (see Figure 1).

> The physical form which the expression of concepts acquires (sound-images or words) is arbitrary. There is nothing intrinsic about an object—a chair, for example—that requires it be labeled "chair" or *silla* or "chaise." Any of those labels will be associated by the listener with the same underlying concept, assuming that he understands the language being used.

In fact, when R relates the sound-image to a concept, that physical form is shed. Seleskovitch (1978b) describes the process thus: "...as soon as a sentence has been understood, it loses any linguistic form ... we are conscious of our intent when speak-

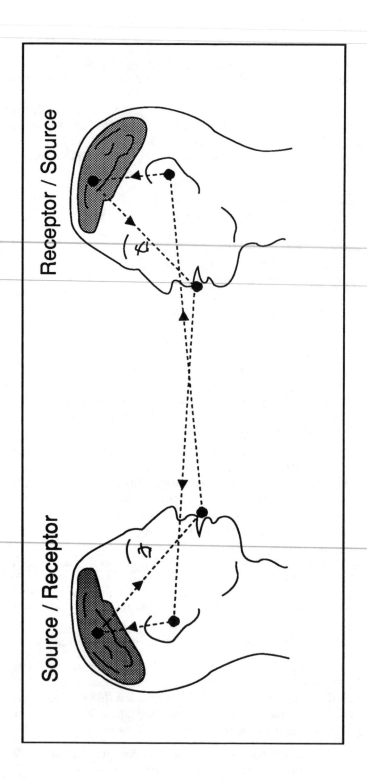

Figure 1. Roles of the source/receptor and receptor/source reverse when the speaker changes.

ing, of the sense we want to put across, not of the individual words or the grammar used to that effect and we listen to sense and grasp sense without paying attention to words" (p. 336).

Saussure (1966) developed the idea of the **linguistic sign,** which illustrates the link between concepts and their external form. "The linguistic sign unites, not a thing and a name, but a concept and a sound-image" (p. 66). The top half of the linguistic sign is the concept, and the bottom half is the external form (see Figure 2). The fact that the external form is arbitrary can be seen in the phenomenon of synonyms— two words that represent the same underlying concept (like "car" and "auto," "start" and "begin"); and homonyms—single words that represent multiple and unrelated concepts or objects ("bear" and "nut"), as depicted in Figure 3.

3.2. Oral Comprehension

Comprehension—the foundation of the communication process and, therefore, of interpretation—has changed significantly as psycholinguistics has grown as a field. Many traditional models of comprehension shared the basic features and assumptions of the one posited by Akmajian, Demers, and Harnish (1984, p. 435), as depicted in Figure 4.

This model of language comprehension is explained as follows:

It is generally assumed that the Speech Recognition Capacity identifies as much about the speech sounds as it can from the sound wave. Next, the Syntactic Parsing Capacity identifies the words by their sounds and analyzes the structure of the sentence, and the Semantic Interpretation Capacity puts the meaning of the words together in accordance with these syntactic relations. Finally, the

Figure 2. Visual of Saussure's linguistic sign; top half denotes the concept, and the bottom half the external form.

Pragmatic Interpretation Capacity selects a particular speech act as the most likely one the speaker is performing. If the hearer is right, communication is successful; if not, there has been a breakdown. (pp. 435-36)

In expounding this sequence of steps, Akmajian et al. (1984) note that the initial input is a continuous stream of sounds, and the hearer, if he or she understands the speaker's language, is able to "perceptually analyze a physical continuum into individual sounds" (p. 437). In other words, the hearer organizes the sounds into meaningful units.

In order to attach meaning to these sounds, the hearer must associate them with terms already present in his or her mental lexicon. It is known that humans are able to comprehend language at a rate of more than four words per second. Clearly such rapid processing would be impossible if the hearer searched randomly through his or her mental dictionary. Therefore, as Akmajian et al. (1984) hypothesize, there must be a "system for *accessing* [emphasis in original] the mental *lexicon* [emphasis in original]" (p. 438). They note that the mental lexicon is ordered by sounds, and that the ability to retrieve terms from it depends on recency of acquisition and frequency of use. They also point out that most words are ambiguous; that is, more than one connotation is possible. Some selection process is obviously involved in disambiguating the message. The authors cite research on this issue (Swinney, 1979; Tanenhaus, Leiman, & Seidenberg, 1979), and conclude that "... when we process sentences, all known meanings of the word are first automatically activated, then some as yet poorly understood process selects the most appropriate one based on various syntactic and semantic cues" (Akmajian et al., 1984, p. 439). They also cite findings by Lehiste

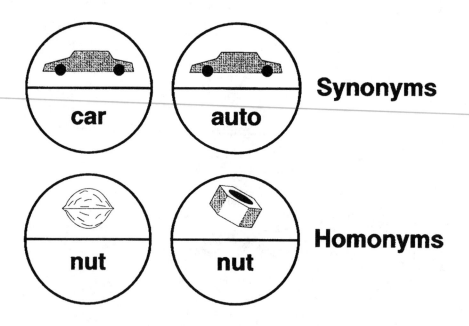

Figure 3. External form is arbitrary, as illustrated by synonyms and homonyms.

(1973) that indicate that the speaker's emphasis of certain words in an utterance aids the hearer in disambiguating the words.

Having assigned meaning to the individual words in the message, the hearer goes on to determine the meaning of the whole sentence based on the meanings of the constituent words and their syntactic relations. Bever (1970) proposes that in order to accomplish this task, the hearer employs certain strategies make intelligent guesses rather than investigating every possible syntactic structure. Fodor, Bever, and Garrett (1974), in their "click experiments," provided evidence that "...hearers process sentences in terms of major *clauses* [emphasis in original] of a sentence, and that these major constituents *resist interruption* [emphasis in original]" (Akmajian et al., 1984, p. 442). One can conclude from this that the major constituent structure is, in psychological terms, a "real basic unit of perception" (Akmajian et al., 1984, p. 442) for the hearer.

This model espouses a "bottom-up," physiological process rather than a conceptually based comprehension process. It does not account for top-down processing wherein we react conceptually to a language stimulus. The fact that we can understand a badly degraded sound signal if we know the language attests to the fact that language processing, more specifically, comprehension, is a "psycholinguistic guessing game." Goodman (1967) defines comprehension as "the ability to...anticipate that which has not been heard...in listening" (p. 16).

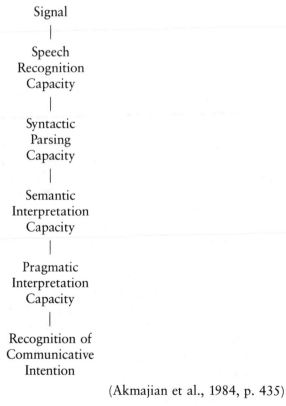

Signal
|
Speech
Recognition
Capacity
|
Syntactic
Parsing
Capacity
|
Semantic
Interpretation
Capacity
|
Pragmatic
Interpretation
Capacity
|
Recognition of
Communicative
Intention

(Akmajian et al., 1984, p. 435)

Figure 4. Early language comprehension model that ignores "top-down" and psycholinguistic processing.

Another important aspect of comprehension is schema theory—embodying the idea that any given language text does not carry meaning in and of itself. Rumelhart (1977) holds that schema is an abstract representation concept for an object, event, or situation. For example, everything we have learned about a topic is stored in a schema. The tango, for example, is a schema comprising men with fancy suits, ladies with the tight black skirts and spaghetti tops, passionate music, dancing with dips and curves, and stylized steps—all this is stored and can be activated by a tango rhythm or picture.

Comprehension, according to Ausubel (1978), is the process of relating the listener's or reader's background knowledge to new knowledge. It entails tapping all related scripts learned in previous experiences. Goodman (1967) hypothesizes that the listener constructs a message with background, cultural, and linguistic knowledge. The process of comprehending involves predicting or "guessing" the speaker's message by utilizing contextual, linguistic, and cultural cues. This is a departure from the "bottom-up" model presented above that implies a linear particle-to-larger idea movement.

As Omaggio (1986) contends, "Both bottom-up and top-down processing occur simultaneously in the comprehension process" (p. 102). Top-down processing accounts for not only background knowledge, but is conceptually driven and "helps the comprehender to resolve ambiguities and select among alternative interpretations of the data" (p. 102). In conclusion, although we are learning more about how we comprehend, the subject still requires more research to be fully understood. The research cited above deals with communication in just one language; the interlingual communication made possible by translators and interpreters is far more complex.

4. Interlingual Communication

In Section 3 we examined how humans communicate with one another by means of spoken messages. As Akmajian et al. (1984) point out, however, it is possible for communication to break down. To use Saussure's (1966) terms, there is an interruption in the speaking circuit for some reason. There may be outside interference (noise), and R cannot hear S; perhaps S uses a homonym such as "nut" and R does not associate it with the correct concept; or maybe S uses a code that R does not understand, and R is unable to make any associations between the sound-images and concepts. It is in the latter case that an interpreter is required to bridge the gap between the two speakers.

Even within a given language, no two speakers make the same psychological associations with the sound-images they perceive; when two separate languages are involved, the scenario becomes far more complex. Seleskovitch (1975) illustrates this point with the example of visitors viewing the host's slides of his vacation. For the host, the slides conjure up vivid memories of his experience, while the viewers merely see flat images of more or less identifiable objects on a screen. This example leads to the conclusion that:

> Any meaningful utterance is but the visible part of an iceberg, adequate to enable
> the intended recipient to work out the appropriate relationship between the visible
> and the invisible parts and, like the mariner who draws the right conclusions

and navigates on that basis, to apprehend the whole on the basis of the part. (p. 100)

The interpreter plays a dual role in the communication process; when S is speaking, the interpreter becomes R, and engages in all of the processes of the speaking circuit. Once having understood the SL message, the interpreter then becomes S, generating the equivalent message in the TL, and the TL listener becomes R. In Figure 5, Arjona (1978) shows what the speaking circuit looks like with the addition of the interpreter.

The interpreter faces all the same problems that any receptor encounters in the speaking circuit. Bell (1987) has adapted Saussure's concept of the linguistic sign, making it three-dimensional to illustrate the presence of other languages (see Figure 6). However, this model assumes a uniformity in conceptual structure across languages. Suppose there is no generic word for trees. For example, in English the word "corner" may be expressed in Spanish in at least two ways—*esquina* and *rincón*. The same problem exists for the word "you"; depending on how formal the context is, either *tú* or *usted* should be used.

4.1. Interpreting Process

With the intervention or mediation of the interpreter, the speaking circuit is connected, and communication takes place. As noted previously, the interpreter is both receptor and source, and goes through the same processes that monolingual receptors and sources undergo when generating and comprehending oral messages. The specific steps that the interpreter follows are described:

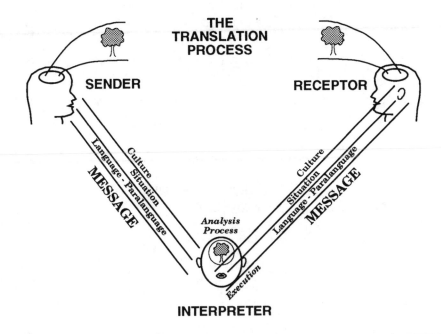

Figure 5. Speaking circuit after adding the interpreter.

(1) The interpreter, as receptor, hears the SL message and analyzes it for meaning or **decodes** it or reconstructs it, based on knowledge of the language, familiarity with the context, and personal experience. It is at this point that the interpreter, consciously or unconsciously, rejects any irrelevant or nonsensical potential meanings that might be attached to these particular phonemic structures. In the example cited by Seleskovitch (1978b, p. 334), when he hears the French sentence *la mer est forte*, he knows from the context that the meaning is "a heavy sea," not "a fat mother."

(2) The interpreter then breaks up the source message into workable chunks in a process that Kelly (1979) calls **segmentation**. In this process, he focuses on units of meaning, regardless of how many words they contain. The individual components (words) of a given unit of meaning may not be contiguous in the SL text. For example, in English it is common for verbs and prepositions to form a single unit of meaning, but the preposition does not always come right after the verb, especially in oral messages:

> He hosed his brand new car down.
> (hosed down)
>
> Be sure to turn all the lights off when you leave.
> (turn off)

The number of words in the unit of meaning will vary from one language to another. For example, the unit "to stay up all night" in English can be rendered with just one word in Spanish: *desvelarse*. An interpreter would be remiss in rendering "to stay up all night" as *quedarse despierto toda la noche*. In the legal context, for example, the

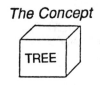

The Concept

TREE

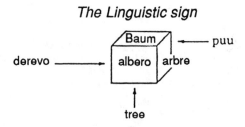

The Linguistic sign

Baum — puu

derevo → albero arbre

tree

Figure 6. Three-dimensional model of Saussure's circuit showing presence of other languages.

term **arraignment** does not have a direct equivalent in many other languages, and must be rendered as "the reading of the charges," or a similar phrase.

Thus, the interpreter sets aside the original form of the message and penetrates to the underlying meaning. However, as noted in other chapters in the discussion of **conservation**, the court interpreter cannot forget the original form entirely, because the external structure contains critical elements of the message (voice level, hesitation, false starts, and so on) that must be taken into consideration by the audience to determine credibility.

(3) In the next step the interpreter formulates the TL version and becomes the source in the speaking circuit. It is critical that the interpreter not only render accurately the content of the SL message but also make the TL version as close to a verbatim rendition of the SL as the TL allows. If, for example, the source says, "I observed the suspect exiting the vehicle," and the interpreter's TL version is "I saw the guy get out of the car," the meaning is reflected, but not the style of the original. If for some reason the TL does not allow the meaning to be conveyed with the same style as the SL version, and the interpreter is forced to choose between the two, priority should always be given to meaning over style. Thus, if the source uses the term *sancho* in Spanish, the interpreter must render it as "a man who slips in while the husband is away," because there is no equivalent slang expression in English. Legal jargon poses a similar problem. For example, in plea bargaining it is common to offer a "county lid," which means that the district attorney will recommend that the court limit the sentence to county jail. If there is no equivalent expression in the TL, the interpreter will have to describe the term in the TL.

(4) As the interpreter expresses the TL version of the message, he may receive some feedback from the receptor (a quizzical look, for example, indicating that communication is not taking place), and the interpreter may adapt his version accordingly, choosing more appropriate wording. Similarly, the interpreter is constantly self-monitoring, providing auto-feedback. He formulates a proposed TL version and then checks it against the SL message to make sure it is accurate before uttering it. Determining that it is incorrect, the interpreter will change the TL version. This loop of checking and self-correcting may occur several times before the TL rendition is expressed orally; it is a split-second process that is largely unconscious (see Chapter 27). On the other hand, the interpreter may begin the oral rendition of the TL message and realize that it is not correct, either because of feedback from the receptor or because it doesn't sound right, and will correct himself in mid-sentence.

Berk-Seligson (1987) has noted, however, that if the interpreter corrects the interpretation, the judge and jury will assume that the witness corrected the testimony, and it may detract from the witness's credibility. She cites evidence that "repetitions in a person's speech are associated with a lack of persuasiveness" (p. 1111) and gives this example:

Witness: *Que pasaría pitando en el momento que era el carro que nos recogiera.*

Interpreter: That the car would go by blowing its horn, when we were ready to be picked up, or when he was ready to pick us up. (p. 1112)

(In fact, the corrected version is also wrong, as the witness was referring to the car rather than the driver.) To avoid this problem, the interpreter should clearly label personal corrections as such: "When we were ready to be picked up—interpreter correction—when he was ready to pick us up."

4.2. Obstacles to Interlingual Communication

The addition of another language creates more potential barriers to communication. This section will discuss those obstacles, and the following section will present the problem-solving methods employed by interpreters to overcome them.

4.2.1. Ambiguity

As noted earlier, the external form taken by the expression of a concept is arbitrary, and one word or phrase may conceivably represent several different underlying concepts, depending on the context. The interpreter as R must clarify any ambiguities that arise. For example, here is a phrase that is fraught with ambiguity:

The police were ordered to stop smoking at midnight.

Several possible underlying meanings or **deep structures** could be intended here:

(1) The police received an order telling them to prohibit smoking by midnight.

(2) The police were told that they must quit smoking by midnight.

(3) At midnight the police received an order telling them to prohibit smoking.

(4) At midnight the police received an order telling them they must quit smoking.

(5) The police received an order telling them to keep people from smoking at midnight (but not at any other time).

(6) The police were told that they could not smoke at midnight (but they could at other times of the day).

Without any context, it is sometimes difficult for R to determine which deep structure S intends to convey. When S and R both speak the same language, some ambiguity may be tolerated without severely impeding communication. But when R is an interpreter who must transfer the message into the TL, clarifying any ambiguities becomes absolutely essential for communication to take place. For a further discussion of ambiguities in court interpreting, see Unit 8, Chapter 34, Section 1.4.1.

Sometimes, however, the interpreter may not be aware that a word has other possible meanings, because the context makes the intended meaning perfectly clear and irrelevant alternative meanings are automatically suppressed. Pergnier (1978) cites this example:

The French person who asks for 'une glace' in a restaurant will get his ice-cream without being, ever so transiently, conscious of the fact that, at the level of language-meaning, he has simultaneously asked for (and the waiter might in theory have understood that he has asked for) a looking-glass, a piece of ice, a window-pane, and many other things apart from an ice-cream. (pp. 201-2)

The court interpreter faced with ambiguity in the SL message is more constrained than translators and interpreters in other spheres of the profession, given the requirements of conservation and legal equivalence (Gonzalez, 1989c). Thus, when the unconscious execution described above does not take place and the ambiguity is not clarified, the interpreter must first attempt to retain the SL ambiguity in the TL. If that is impossible due to the syntactical or terminological limitations of the TL, the interpreter must stop the proceedings and ask for a clarification. If the interpreter were not in a formal court proceeding interpreting for the record, it would be permissible to clarify an ambiguity such as "you" in English, which could be either singular or plural, by offering both choices in the TL (e.g., *usted o ustedes* in Spanish). However, given the risks involved in making corrections or providing alternative word choices, as discussed by Berk-Seligson (1987) earlier in this chapter, the court interpreter dare not take such liberties. Therefore, it is imperative that the interpreter stop the proceedings and inform the court of the need to clarify the ambiguity. For a more detailed discussion of the problem of ambiguity, see Unit 8, Chapter 34, Section 1.4.1.

4.2.2. Different Semantic Area

The interpreter's job is further complicated by the fact that words do not have the same semantic area in the SL as in the TL. Thus, "glass" and *glace* are equivalents in French and English, and often can be used as direct translations of each other. Though each term has multiple referents, these referents may not be the same in the SL as in the TL. Their meanings may overlap, but they do not necessarily cover the same semantic area. To demonstrate the concept of semantic area, consider the English word "table," which has multiple meanings. It can denote (1) a piece of furniture, (2) the serving of food (as in "she sets a good table"), (3) a plateau, (4) a chart containing numbers, and (5) to delay (as in "they tabled the motion"). In French, the equivalent word table does represent concepts 1, 2, and 4, but not 3 and 5; in addition, it denotes other concepts not represented by the English equivalent, as illustrated in the expressions *aimer la table* (to enjoy the good life) and *faire table rase* (to wipe the slate clean, start from scratch).

Nida and Taber (1974) approach this concept another way by setting up a "chain of related meanings" for a word and looking at the equivalents of these terms in another language. For example, take the Spanish word *llave*, as depicted in Figure 7. The term *llave* corresponds to both "faucet" and "key" in English. The term "key" can be translated into Spanish as either *llave* or *clave*, depending on the context. *Clave*, in turn, can mean either "key" or "code," while the English term "code" corresponds to *código* in Spanish when used in the legal context.

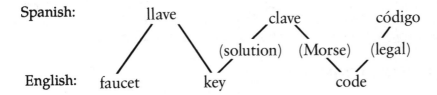

(p. 21)

Figure 7. Chain of related meanings for Spanish term *llave*.

In some cases, the court interpreter can solve the problem of different semantic areas by translating one word as two different words in the TL. For example, the English term "back" refers to both the upper and lower back, whereas for many Spanish speakers a distinction must be made between *espalda* (upper back) and *cintura* (lower back). The interpreter might translate the question "Did you injure your back?" as *¿Se lastimó Ud. de la espalda o cintura?* However, the dangers cited by Berk-Seligson (1987) must be taken into consideration by the court interpreter. For example, if a witness uses the term *camioneta* in Spanish, the interpreter who translated the term as "pickup truck," "station wagon," or "bus" (in Guatemala) would be misleading the jury into believing that the witness was not sure what kind of vehicle he saw. In such an instance, it is imperative that the interpreter stop the proceedings and request permission to clarify the term. For more discussion of this issue, see Unit 8, Chapter 34, Section 1.4.

4.2.3. Less Precision in TL

For cultural reasons, some languages lend themselves more easily to expressing certain concepts or certain types of material than do others. For example, Brislin (1978) and Whorf (1940) note that it is easier for Eskimos [and skiers] to convey more subtlety or precision in discussing the concept of snow; Arabic speakers have a wider variety of terms to choose from when discussing horses; and English speakers in the United States have a larger vocabulary available to them for talking about cars. Some culture groups have more terms available to them to describe subtleties that may not even be discerned by others. It is sometimes very difficult for an interpreter to cope with the paucity of terms in the TL. For example, English does not have an extensive set of kinship terms, and interpreters often have to make decisions about how important it is to convey the precise nature of a relationship. If a Spanish-speaking witness says, "I am working for my *concuñado*," in most cases the English term "brother-in-law" is sufficient to denote the relationship, even though the Spanish term is more specific. It refers to the spouse of one's own spouse's sibling; in English, the term brother-in-law covers the husband of one's sister, the brother of one's wife, or the husband of one's spouse's sister. In other cases, the term "in question" has no equivalent at all, and must be translated with a description. This is true of English automotive terms such as "hatchback" and "fastback." Conveying legal concepts in languages such as Navajo or Haitian Creole presents this same problem. For example, "jury" has no equivalent in Haitian Creole; therefore, the interpreter is forced to define the term as "the twelve men and women who will judge you." In Navajo, there is no semantic equivalent for "guilt," as the culture provides other ways of dealing with wrongdoing. Therefore, the closest culturally and linguistically appropriate equivalent for "Are you guilty?" is "Did you do it?," which may not be the most appropriate legal question since in English its use usually assumes guilt.

4.2.4. Different Perspectives

Another problem encountered by interpreters is the fact that *"languages do not choose the same set of words to point to the same objects or concepts so that speakers in individual languages do not use the same words to express the same ideas"* [emphasis in original] (Seleskovitch, 1978b, p. 337). Seleskovitch refers to this phenomenon as the keyhole principle, noting that English speakers focus on the relationship to the key when naming this object, while French speakers focus on the lock (*trou de serrure*, literally, "lock hole"). Spanish speakers call the same object *el ojo de la cerradura*, the "eye of the lock." When the languages and cultures involved are very dissimilar, the application of the "keyhole principle" becomes even more extreme. For example, in New Guinea the translation of "God forgives" is "God doesn't hang up jawbones." In the Sudan, what is known in English as the "Adam's apple" is "the thing that loves beer" (Nida & Rayburn, 1982).

For the court interpreter, the keyhole problem is really one of terminology. The interpreter must have a sufficient command of the TL to choose the appropriate term. The consequences of the improper translation of a term may range from the harmless (the TL version may sound quaint but understandable) to the disastrous (a complete misunderstanding of the intended meaning).

4.2.5. Idioms

Perhaps one of the most difficult elements for non-native speakers of a language, and for interpreters striving to achieve full command of their working languages, is the idiomatic aspect. Examples of idioms in English are "to shake hands" and "you're welcome." The Spanish equivalents of those idioms are *darse la mano* (literally, to give the hand), and *de nada* (literally, of [it's] nothing). Languages, being human creations, have certain inexplicable elements that are there for no discernible reason. There is no objective or logical reason why certain ideas are expressed the way they are or why certain words are associated with each other in a given language. As Nida and Taber (1974) suggest, "Each language has its own genius" (p. 3). Native speakers of a language have an "ear" for what sounds right and what sounds awkward, and the non-native speaker is recognized immediately, even if the speaker does not have an accent, because the person fails to observe these unwritten rules. For example, in English one often hears the phrase "flat denial." "Flat" and "denial" have an affinity for each other; they "go together." In Spanish, on the other hand, the adverb *tajantemente* (categorically, absolutely) comes to mind immediately when the verb *negar* (deny) is used.

As stated above, the problem of idioms for the court interpreter is one of mastery of the TL. It is essential that the TL version sound as natural and intelligible as the SL message. For this reason, the interpreter must continuously strive to improve the command of all working languages by using them in both oral and written form in as many contexts as possible.

4.2.6. Metaphors

Metaphors are another problematic area for interpreters and translators. Everyone has heard funny stories about newcomers to a language trying to express thoughts in terms of their own native tongue. There is the example of the English speaker attempting to comment on the inclement weather in newly acquired French: *Il est pleuvant chats et chiens*, thinking of the English expression, "It's raining cats and dogs." After gaining some experience with the French language, however, the speaker will know that the correct phrase is *Il pleut à verse* (literally, it is raining in a pouring fashion). In general, translators and interpreters strive to find an equivalent metaphor in the TL. If there is no equivalent, they translate the metaphor directly, if it makes sense to the TL audience. If a direct translation would not make sense in the TL, the translator or interpreter must use professional and linguistic judgment and expertise to devise an equivalent expression to convey the meaning and intent.

The court interpreter, who must provide a TL message that is as close as possible to a verbatim version of the SL message, must be very careful with metaphors. In many instances, the equivalent metaphor comes to mind immediately, and there is no question that it should be used (e.g., "that's a horse of a different color" for *eso es harina de otro costal*). Indeed, a literal translation would be unintelligible to the TL listener. On the other hand, some metaphors reflect the culture of the speaker, and translating them into an equivalent in the TL would strip the message of that cultural content. For example, if a Hispanic man testifies about how he is no longer able to *hacer uso de su mujer* since his car accident, the interpreter must make a decision. If he chooses the equivalent English euphemism "to have relations with his wife," he does not convey the cultural attitude reflected in the literal translation of the phrase, "to make use of his wife." In another example, if the witness says, *no tenía en donde caerme muerto*, the equivalent expression in English is "I didn't have a dime to my name," or the more vulgar "I didn't have a pot to piss in." Neither of these expressions conveys the desperation of the literal translation, "I didn't even have a place to fall down dead." In some cases, the interpreter may decide that the circumstances of the case merit a literal translation rather than an equivalent. This kind of split-second decision making is one of the many demands imposed on the court interpreter.

4.2.7. Syntax and Style

Some languages have a very rigid syntax, and word order is crucial in determining meaning. In other languages, the rules of syntax are more flexible. In English, for example, the subject must precede the verb in almost every instance, whereas in Spanish the subject may either precede or follow the verb. The style of a language is a more subtle but equally important aspect that must be taken into consideration by the interpreter. For example, it would sound odd to say, "He had a huge big spider on his arm." It sounds more natural to say "big huge." In Spanish, as is true of many languages, using the wrong word order can actually change the meaning of a sentence; in this example, *un hombre grande* (a big man) changes to *un gran hombre* (a great man). It cannot be overemphasized that the court interpreter must have a full command of all of his working languages in order to deal with both the overt and subtle features of the languages in faithfully conveying messages.

5. Techniques for Problem Solving

Faced with the obstacles inherent in oral communication in general, and interlingual communication in particular, interpreters employ a number of strategies or techniques to ensure the successful transfer of messages from the SL to the TL with no loss of meaning, tone, style, or intent. A number of translation theorists (Catford, 1965; Newmark, 1981; Nida, 1964; Nida & Taber, 1974; Vásquez-Ayora, 1977; Wilss, 1982, and others) have tried to identify and categorize these techniques in order to help translators develop their skills and improve their output. Although their emphasis has been almost exclusively on translation rather than interpretation, the techniques they identify can be adapted to court interpreting.

(1) The first option available to the interpreter is to translate the message **literally**, or verbatim, from SL to TL. If the two languages happen to approach this particular concept in the same way and their grammars are similar, this direct transfer poses no problems at all:

English : She is reading.

Spanish: *Ella está leyendo.*

(Vásquez-Ayora, 1977, p. 257)

But as we have seen before, serious problems can arise if an interpreter tries to find a direct equivalent in the TL:

English: I did not think much of him.

Spanish: *No he pensado mucho en él.*

(Vásquez-Ayora, 1977, p. 262)

The Spanish version actually means "I have not thought about him very much." The correct Spanish version would be *Tenía mala opinión de él* (I had a low opinion of him).

(2) Often the rules of grammar and style of the TL require a change in the parts of speech used, or a different word order. This process is known as **transposition**.

(a) Change in word order:

Spanish: *Va a llegar el lunes el envío de libros.*

(Will arrive Monday the shipment of books.)

English: The book shipment will arrive on Monday.

(b) Changing parts of speech (adjective to noun):

English: It was hard for her to keep quiet.

Spanish: *Ella tenía dificultad en guardar silencio.*

(She had difficulty in maintaining silence.)

(c) Changing parts of speech (verb to noun):

English: The farmer will lease the land to his neighbor.

Spanish: *El ranchero le dará el terreno a su vecino en arrendamiento.*

(The farmer will give the land to his neighbor in lease.)

(3) Sometimes it is necessary to make more drastic changes in the message to accommodate TL cultural norms. This is more difficult to achieve than transposition, because it is a subjective, intuitive process that does not rely on grammatical or stylistic rules. The primary consideration at all times, of course, is the conservation of meaning. The techniques described below have been identified as a means of helping people understand the process of translation, but the translator/interpreter should remember at all times that words are a means to an end, not the end itself. These changes should be made only when dictated by the nature of the TL.

(a) The first technique for solving the problem of cultural differences between the SL and the TL is **modulation,** in which the interpreter shifts point of view:

English: He cleared his throat.

French: *Il s'éclaircit la voix.*
           (He cleared his voice.)

Spanish: *Si mal no recuerdo.*
           (If I don't remember wrong.)

English: If I recall correctly.

(b) The second technique is known as **equivalence,** and it involves "the replacement of an SL situation by a communicatively comparable TL situation" (Wilss, 1982, p. 99):

English: Never mind about them!

Russian: *Bog s n'im'i!*
           (God with them!)
           (Catford, 1965, p. 26)

English: They are like two peas in a pod.

Spanish: *Se parecen como dos gotas de agua.*
           (They are as alike as two drops of water).
           (Vásquez-Ayora, 1977, p. 317)

(c) And finally, in extreme cases, the interpreter must utilize the technique of **adaptation** to compensate for sociocultural differences between the SL and TL communities. The example cited by Nida and Rayburn (1982) of "God forgives" being translated into "God doesn't hang up jawbones" in New Guinea illustrates this technique. Its use is limited in court interpretation, given the need for a verbatim rendition whenever possible. When terms with a high cultural content are used, sometimes it is preferable not to translate them at all. For example, the term *compadre* in Spanish is a kinship term that has no complete equivalent in English. In the courtroom setting, it is best to leave the term *compadre* as is in the English version, and let the attorney elucidate the meaning through follow-up questions of the witness. On the other hand, when translating from English to another language, sometimes it is preferable to retain an English term that has been "borrowed" by members of the immigrant community to express concepts that have no exact equivalent in their home countries. An example of this is the term probation. It is difficult to make this type of assumption, however; a recent immigrant may not be as familiar with these borrowed terms as someone who has resided in this country for several years. When in doubt, the interpreter should strive to find an equivalent in the TL.

(4) Another translation technique that is available to the interpreter is **amplification,** the expansion of the TL version to cover the entire scope of the SL message. It must be used with extreme caution in court interpreting.

English: They charged $2,000 for overhead.

Spanish: *Cobraron $2,000 por concepto de gastos generales.*

(They charged $2,000 for the item of general expenses.)

In this case, the native speaker feels the need to add words to clarify, or to be more idiomatic. Note that no information is added; the translator is just smoothing things over to make the message sound better.

(5) Another technique that must be used very conservatively and cautiously is known as **explicitation**, making explicit in the TL what was implicit in the SL:

English: To knock a place flat.

Spanish: *Derrumbarlo todo hasta dejarlo aplanado.*

(To knock everything down until it is left flattened.)

(Vásquez-Ayora, 1977, p. 358)

This technique becomes necessary when there is no direct equivalent in the TL, and the idea must be conveyed by **paraphrasing**. Another example of this is the term *mirandize*, which is commonly used by police officers. It must be translated as "to advise someone of her constitutional rights," or a similar phrase, because the concept does not exist in other countries. In such situations, the interpreter must decide whether the amplification or explicitation is an absolute necessity because of the grammar, style, or vocabulary limitations of the TL, or whether such a process is optional and the meaning could be conveyed adequately without it. The court interpreter should always avoid inserting any explanation that is not absolutely necessary from the linguistic point of view.

(6) Sometimes the TL is more efficient than the SL in expressing a given idea, and the translator is able to convey the meaning in fewer words. This technique has been identified by translation theorists as **omission** or **deletion**, but it is important to point out that not a single bit of meaning is left out when this technique is applied correctly. Perhaps a better term for our purposes would be **compression**. Again, this process should be undertaken only when it is required by the grammar or style of the TL; the interpreter should never edit the message to omit redundancies or elements which he feels are inappropriate:

English: The committee has failed to act.

Spanish: *La comisión no actuó.*

(The committee did not act.)

(Vásquez-Ayora, 1977, p. 362)

The interpreter would not convey an intelligible message to the Spanish-speaking listener if the sentence were rendered as *La comisión fracasó de actuar* [The commission failed (as in failed an examination or a course) to act]. Another situation in which compression may be appropriate is when a distinction is made in the SL that is not necessary in the TL. For example, in Spanish the letters *v* and *b* are pronounced the same in most instances, and they are usually distinguished in oral discourse (particularly when spelling words or names) by adding the words *chica* (small, for the letter *v*) and *grande* (large, for the letter *b*) to make sure the listener knows what letter is involved. When interpreting into English, the interpreter merely needs to pronounce the letters *v* and *b* clearly, and no further explicitation is necessary.

The interpreter must constantly make judgment calls as to whether it is proper to utilize the techniques of amplification, explicitation, or compression. In case of any doubt, it is preferable to stay closer to a direct translation of the SL message.

(7) Finally, another technique available to the interpreter is known as **compensation**. This means taking an element of the SL message and conveying it in a different form or at a different level of communication. For example, if a witness is testifying in Spanish and uses the familiar second-person pronoun *tú* to emphasize informality, *Mi patrón me dijo, "tú, vete para allá," muy despectivamente, y eso me ofendió*, the interpreter can compensate for the lack of a familiar pronoun in English by saying, "My boss said to me, '**Hey you**, get over there,' very rudely, and that offended me."

Another example of a term that requires compensation is the English adverbial phrase "at all," which conveys emphasis. If the attorney asks, "Did you have anything to drink at all that night?" the interpreter may have to convey that emphasis through tone of voice if there is no verbal equivalent in the TL. Again, this technique should be used with great caution, and at no time should the interpreter add any element of meaning that was not contained in the original message, or subtract anything from it.

6. Conclusion

The interpreter's goal in all cases is not only to achieve what Nida and Taber (1974) call **dynamic equivalence**, in which the TL receptor responds to the message exactly the way an SL receptor would, but to achieve **legal equivalence**. Thus, the interpreter is engaged in an ongoing process of problem solving and decision making. The more experienced the interpreter, the more automatic this process becomes. Sometimes the choices are not easy, and the problems are quite subtle. When faced with a phrase like "It's raining cats and dogs," it doesn't take much experience to recognize that a dynamic equivalent is required. The experienced interpreter would have no trouble recognizing a language situation that requires an equivalent expression for "The judge threw the book at him" in the TL, unless, of course, the context makes it clear that the judge literally threw a book at someone. On the other hand, if a witness says in Spanish, *Mi jefe me llamó la atención*, he or she may mean "My boss attracted my attention" (because the person was acting oddly or was dressed in a flashy manner, for example) or "My boss reprimanded me." Only the context can clarify that ambiguity. If there is insufficient context, experienced interpreters know that they must request more information before rendering the message into the TL.

The dilemmas posed by the translation process are difficult under any circumstances, but court interpreters face a greater challenge because of their legal and ethical responsibility to provide a verbatim rendition (meaning that no item of meaning is omitted, including non-verbal messages) or a legal equivalent of the utterance for the record. They are not allowed to make inferences or assumptions about the source's intentions, yet the very nature of interlingual communication requires that some intuitive leaps be made. Court interpreters must resist the overwhelming temptation to edit, improve, or make sense out of something that is seemingly illogical or unintelligible, but they must also make the TL message as intelligible to the TL receptor as it would be for an SL receptor.

Chapter 25

Theoretical Models of Interpretation

In the previous chapters, the features of human language have been defined and discussed and the interpreting process has been analyzed in detail from the standpoint of the raw material (SL message) and the end product (the TL version). In a sense, the interpretation has been regarded as a *fait accompli* to this point. The purpose of this chapter is to elucidate the intermediate steps in the process, in terms of the linguistic cognitive operations involved in transferring a message from one language to another.

1. Chapter Overview

The chapter will begin by presenting the models of translation and interpretation (T&I) that have been devised by theorists, most of whom are also practitioners of the profession. The strengths and weaknesses of these models and their ability to account for the full complexity of the interpreting process will be discussed, especially with respect to court interpreting. Then the classic model of human information processing (HIP) will be examined, and its implications for court interpreting will be explicated. Following that, two recent new models of automatic processing will be presented for the purpose of shedding more light on the interpreting process. And finally, a proposed model of Simultaneous Human Information Processing (SHIP), which has been devised by the authors of the book specifically from the standpoint of court interpreting, will be presented and discussed.

2. Models of Translation and Interpretation

2.1. Triangular Models

It has been demonstrated in previous chapters that in transferring a message from the TL to the SL, the interpreter must transcend the external form (the words) to get to the underlying meaning. The interpreter must then abandon the SL form and, working from the amorphous, abstract concept, attach a new TL form to it. Thus, the interpretation process can be viewed as triangular, rather than linear.

Figure 1 is a very simplified model of the interpreting process. In recent years, scholars have devised more complex models to illustrate this process. Seleskovitch (1975) and Lederer (1981) elaborate further on the triangular format, positing a "three-phase operation in which the first phase is verbal—incoming discourse, the

315

second is non-verbal, and the third is again verbal—the interpreter's reproduction of the message in the TL" (Mackintosh, 1985, p. 37).

Arjona (1978) and Wilss (1982) also use a modified triangular format in their depictions of the interpreting and translating process, respectively. The Arjona model is shown in Chapter 24 of this unit (Figure 5). The Wilss (1982, pp. 81-82) model is shown in Figures 2, 2.1, 2.2, 2.3, and 2.4, below:

The Wilss (1982) model is the first of these models to account for the necessary adaptation of the message to the demands of the TL. Thus, Figure 2 shows a completely balanced translation process. Here the form and content of the SL and those of the TL are reflected equally in the message ("M"). This is an illustration of true conservation of the meaning, style, intent, and tone of the original message. Figure 2.1 depicts a translation in which the message leans more heavily toward the content and style of the SL than those of the TL; in other words, the translation is not as understandable and stylistically correct as the original SL message. In Figure 2.2, the translator emphasizes the content and style of the TL to the detriment of those of the SL; that is, the TL version is stylistically correct but does not conserve the intent and tone of the SL message. Figure 2.3 shows the results of a translation that emphasizes form over content, and Figure 2.4 depicts a translation process in which "more weight is given in the TL to content, to the detriment of the SL text's stylistic perspective" (p. 82). All of the preceding models emphasize the fact that there is no direct connection between the SL and TL messages, that the interpreter mediates between the two and converts the message from concrete to abstract form, and then to concrete form in the TL.

2.2. Paralinguistic Models

The Cokely (1984) model (Figure 3) is a very complex visual representation of the complex set of operations that comprises interpretation. The value of his model is that it was one of the earliest comprehensive models. It takes into account both sociocultural and psycholinguistic factors, attempting to define interpretation from several different viewpoints.

Another innovation of Cokely's work is that he looks at miscues or errors in interpreting as an indication of how the process works. On a very fundamental level, errors do reflect the learning process, and pragmatically, an understanding of them allows interpreters to make constructive changes in their linguistic behavior. Also, miscues make it possible to study more closely how the mind works on a variety of levels, since they often result in dissonance between what we hear or say and what we know. Therefore, a model that includes the dimension of error is necessary to understand how humans learn and how they respond to error in general.

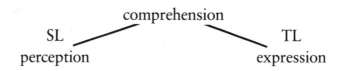

Figure 1. Rudimentary interpreting model.

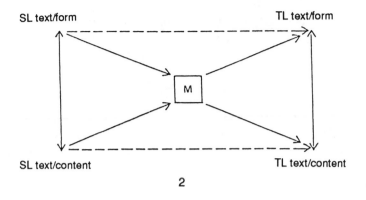

2

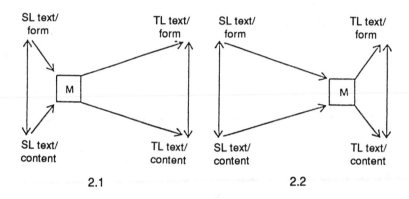

2.1   2.2

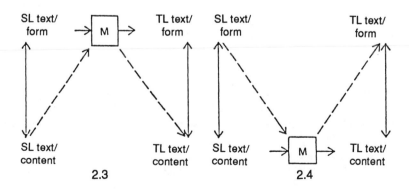

2.3   2.4

Figure 2. Examples of modified triangular models that depict the interpreting process.

Cokely (1984) elaborates further on contextual and situational cues in his model. According to Cokely (1984), whereas other models confine themselves to portraying the interpreter as a mediator between two languages, his model also stresses the mediation between two individuals and communities.

2.3. Information Processing Models

Two other models that are more comprehensive and draw more on recent research in cognitive psychology and information processing are the Gerver (1976) and Moser (1976, 1978) models. They are both derived from information processing research and focus exclusively on simultaneous interpretation (SI). The Gerver model posits two main aspects of the interpreting process:

(1) Permanent structural features such as the various types of memory systems. . . .

(2) Control processes which can be selected at the option of the interpreter, and which may also determine the distribution of attention to the different components of the task. (p. 191)

According to this model, "information may be acquired simultaneously in a buffer storage, while a running comparison can be carried out between output and previous input" (p. 193). The actual translation process is viewed in terms of decoding and encoding (see Figure 4, below):

In the flow chart the first instruction, decode and store, accesses a code book enabling the interpreter to decode the phonetic representation of each segment of the source language message, and understand it in terms of its underlying structure and meaning in relation to the context. The decoded message remains available both for encoding in the target language and for comparison with the resulting utterance. (pp. 196-97)

Gerver suggests that there is a loop in the process, as the interpreter checks the proposed output against the SL message stored in the buffer, and the interpreter may decide to delay the output if something does not match.

Moser's (1978) model is very similar to Gerver's, but it is more comprehensive in its description of the initial processing stages. It views the translation process in terms of decision making, and emphasizes the simultaneity of that process (see Figure 5):

The boxes represent STRUCTURAL COMPONENTS, describing the nature of the information stored at a given stage of processing, whereas the intermediate headings represent functional components, describing the individual operations performed at a particular stage of processing. Each diamond represents a decision point in the process; if the answer to a given question is YES, the process continues; if the answer is NO, this information is fed back to an earlier STRUCTURAL COMPONENT, from where a particular section of the process is iterated until a YES-reply allows the continuation of the process. Such an operation is carried out in a so-called rehearsal loop. At some decision points, however, such a rehearsal loop is initiated even if the decision furnished a YES-answer. This is because SI, as the term implies, involves a simultaneity of certain processing stages, i.e., attention is devoted to both the incoming message and to the operations involved in the target language output. (p. 354)

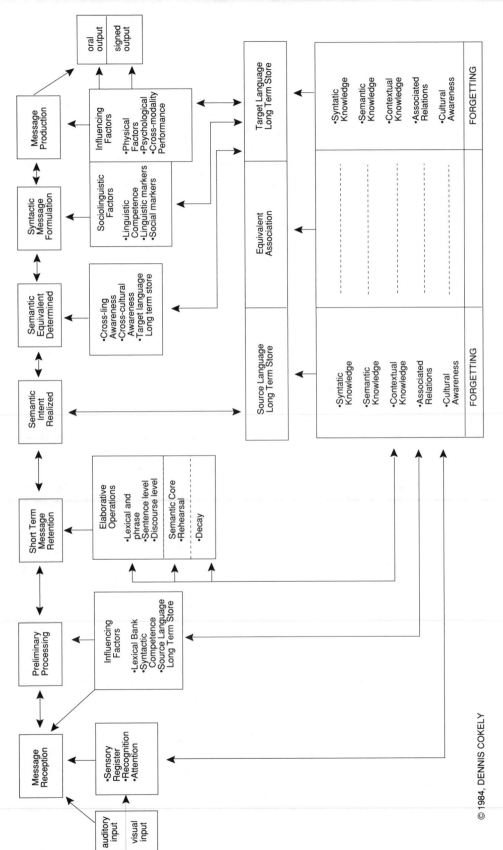

Figure 3. Model of interpreting that incorporates sociocultural and psycholinguistic factors.

© 1984, DENNIS COKELY

The Moser and Gerver models both represent great strides forward in efforts to account for the extreme complexity of the information processing involved in interpreting. They emphasize the demands that external factors such as background noise and speed of SL delivery place on the interpreter's processing capacity, and discuss strategies employed by interpreters for coping with these demands. They also provide for a rehearsal loop, which at least approaches an elucidation of the conservation and simultaneity elements that must be included in any model of court interpreting (see SHIP later in this chapter; and also Prideaux & Baker, 1984).

Another information and processing model of value is one forwarded by Colonomos (in press). This model is noteworthy in that it presents interpretation as a composing process. In this model, comprehension of the source message and production of the target language equivalent are affected by a bifurcated system of analysis and composition.

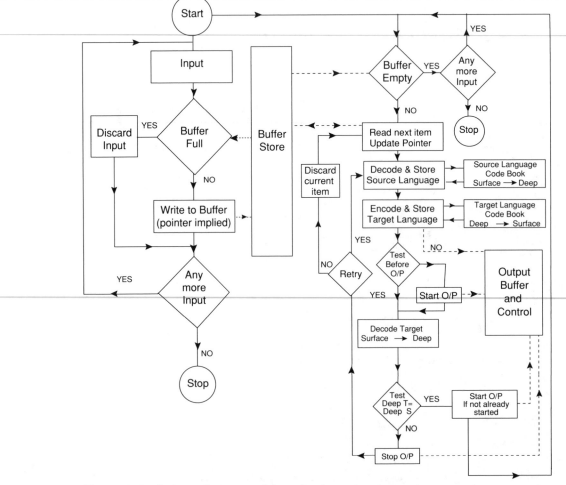

Figure 4. Early interpreting model explicitly incorporating human information processing theory.

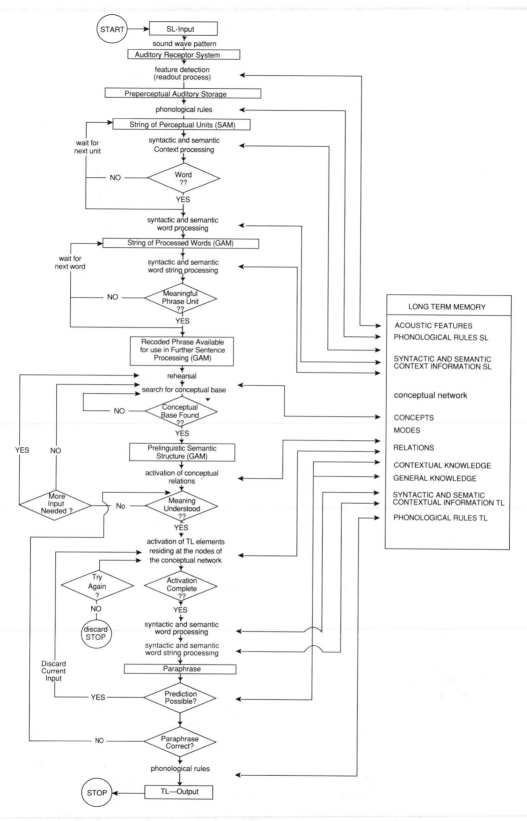

Figure 5. Interpreting model which emphasizes discrete structural components, simultaneity of the process, and human information processing theory.

Colonomos (in press) takes into account the situational content and the speaker and hypothesizes the factors that influence analysis to be (a) process and management skills, (b) linguistic and cultural competence, (c) knowledge of the world, (d) learning, and (e) knowledge of the environment. These help the interpreter comprehend and process the source message. Composing the equivalent target message is also influenced by those same competencies and skills.

The Colonomos (in press) model has recognized the creative processes involved in analyzing a source message and formulating a target message—an element that has heretofore been virtually unacknowledged. It also brings to light the cognitive aspects of information processing important to the comprehension or learning of new information. Colonomos acknowledges that the individual's general knowledge of the world, acquired through experience or learning, interacts with the source language message in order for analysis to occur. Viewed as a whole, this model comes closer than its predecessors to explaining the relationship of the interpreter's knowledge and experience to the successful analysis and construction of meaning.

2.4. Application to Court Interpreting

Most of the models presented here were developed specifically for conference interpretation, and others are limited to simultaneous interpretation as practiced by conference interpreters. The Wilss (1982) model focuses on translation, and the Colonomos (in press) and Cokely (1984) models were developed from the perspective of sign language interpreting. All of these variations—written, oral, and signed—of the translation process have many elements in common, and scholars, teachers, and students who are interested in translation and interpretation may find each of these models instructive. The models discussed in this chapter can, in combination, make a significant contribution to the understanding of the specific processes involved in court interpreting.

They do have their limitations, however. Court interpreters must adhere to certain legal standards that may not apply to any other type of interpreting or translating, and thus they are subject to unique demands. The most significant difference between the interpreting which is performed in the judicial setting and that which is carried out in the conference setting stems from the need for **conservation** of the intent, tone, style, and language level of the speaker, without adding, omitting, or deleting. In this context, conservation refers to the notion that, for the purposes of judging witness credibility and making a record of the proceedings, the interpreter is the voice of the witness. From a linguistic (but not legal) standpoint, the interpreter is the witness. In order for the judge and jury to hear exactly what the witness is saying, the interpreter must convey to the actors in the courtroom (and the readers of the transcript, in the case of an appeal) every element of the witness's message as if they were speakers of the SL and the interpreter were not there. This is what is known as a **legal language equivalent**, as delineated in the introduction of this volume.

In court interpretation, conservation of meaning takes precedence over all other considerations. The conference interpreter, in contrast, is given much more leeway to edit and alter the SL message in order to render it articulately, succinctly, and "naturally" in the TL. Indeed, the Federal Court Interpreters Advisory Board (Administrative Office of the United States Courts, 1987) reported on consultations with conference interpreters who had had some experience in the judicial setting, noting

Processed Transliteration

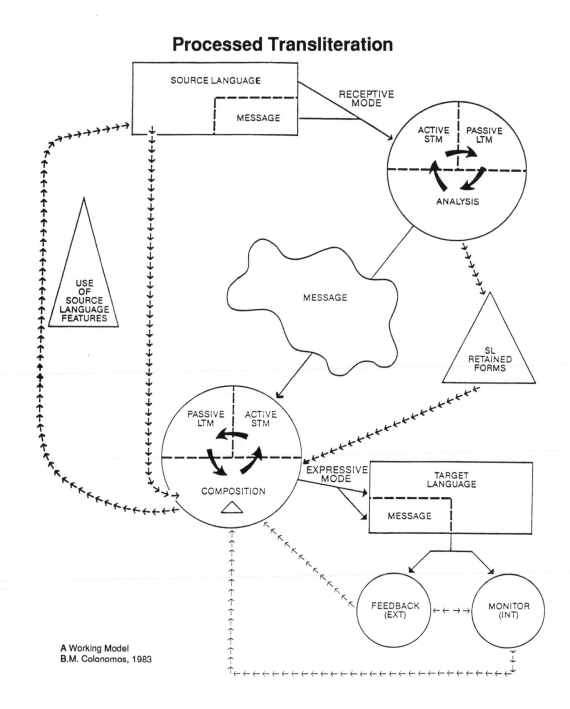

A Working Model
B.M. Colonomos, 1983

Figure 6. Interpreting model that presents interpreting as a psycholinguistic interactive process.

that they immediately recognized the significant differences between the two types of interpreting. These interpreters stated that in conference work, they were expected to:

> render the *meaning* [emphasis in original] in the target language without having to be fully *accurate* [emphasis in original] as to every word and nuance and, most importantly, they felt that often they could and even should embellish some portions of the speech that they were interpreting, without, of course, deviating from the overall meaning. They immediately understood that the preceding examples are totally unacceptable in court interpretation. (p. II-9)

Court interpreters must preserve elements of the message that conference interpreters would regard as non-essential, such as pauses, hedges, self-corrections, and so on. Consequently, court interpreters must retain the entire external, concrete form of the SL version (words, sentences) intact in memory for later reference, while at the same time reducing the message to an abstract form (images, concepts) for understanding, analysis, and processing. When they are ready to render the TL version, they refer back to the original structure of the SL message so that they can include the pauses, hedges, and other paralinguistic elements. Most of the models presented in this chapter, like other models of listening comprehension (Abbott, Greenwood, McKeating, & Wingard, 1981; Richards, 1983), provide for the intermediate step of abandoning the external form of the message and reducing it to an abstract form, but they fail to account for the conservation step that court interpreters must include. It is as if court interpreters make two copies of the SL message, one of which is retained intact and is used for inserting the paralinguistic elements into the TL version, after the other copy is abstracted in the manner suggested in these models.

Another deficiency of most of these models is their failure to explicate the cognitive processes involved in generating an interpretation from one language to another. Although a few of the models include short- and long-term memory components, these components alone do not fully explain the underlying cognitive and psycholinguistic processes in which the interpreter engages. Recent research on human information processing, though not focused specifically on interpretation, sheds some light on this point.

3. Human Information Processing

To better understand the limitations of the models of interpreting presented in this chapter, a review of the classic human information processing (HIP) model is essential. It is important to question the current interpreting models and the HIP model, on which many are based, before scholars attempt to develop a new paradigm powerful enough to explain the cognitive processes underlying interpretation. After an examination of the traditional HIP model, two recently proposed automatic processing models of HIP will be reviewed, insofar as they have major implications for court interpreting, and interpreting and translating in general.

3.1. Classic Human Information Processing Model

The widely accepted, classic HIP model represents a view of human information processing that is based on an analogy to computer information processing (Atkinson

& Shiffrin, 1968). Major features of this paradigm include sensory registers (SR) (McCloskey & Watkins, 1978), short-term memory (STM) (Bjork, 1970), and long-term memory (LTM) (Craik, 1973; Craik & Lockhart, 1972; Loftus & Loftus, 1980). According to this theory, information received from external environmental stimuli is briefly held in the five sensory registers, one for each modality: (1) hearing, (2) seeing, (3) touching, (4) smelling, and (5) tasting (Loftus, 1977; Paivio, 1971; Shepard, Kilpatric, & Cunningham, 1971; Sperling, 1963). Through the process of selective attention (Corteen & Wood, 1972), stimuli are then screened into STM as a function of their immediate relevance.

This model posits that STM, also referred to as active, working, or buffer memory, has extremely limited capacity for processing information (Miller, 1964; Schulman, 1970). Data are held in STM only as long as they are **rehearsed** (Adams, 1967; Horton & Mills, 1984). Rehearsal is the repetition or revisitation of information through visual, oral, or mental activities. Reinforcing the information by any of these means enables it to be **encoded** for a period of time long enough to bring it into awareness and thus render it viable for further processing (Wortman, Loftus, & Marshall, 1988). Encoding refers to the process involved in converting stimuli into forms that can be accessed by memory; common encoding strategies include naming and picturing objects. Additionally, Baddeley (1976, 1982) maintains that rehearsal stores items in STM phonemically; that is, the sound of words is repeated and retained. Thus, requisite to cognitive analysis is the manipulation (attention or rehearsal) of environmental stimuli.

According to classic HIP theory, the storage capacity of STM is limited in two ways: by time and by volume. Wortman et al. (1988) contend that information is lost from STM in about fifteen seconds unless it is encoded for long-term storage. Miller (1956) forwarded the idea that STM is limited to "seven plus or minus two" bits of information. Capacity can be expanded by increasing the size of those bits (Sperling, 1967). This is done by the process known as "chunking" (Ericsson, Chase, & Faloon, 1980). For example, if an interpreter is confronted with the question "On the night of the incident in question, Mr. Jones, what were you and the woman you say you are living with doing?" instead of trying to retain twenty-three words as separate bits of information, the interpreter organizes the words into units of meaning, or chunks. Thus, the interpreter divides the sentence into the following propositions:

on the night of the incident in question
Mr. Jones
what were you and the woman doing
you say you are living with her

Processes that are even more complex, such as learning and language production, would not be possible without long-term storage (Wortman et al., 1988). LTM, according to this view of human information processing, is the repository of all of our life experiences and knowledge. The capacity of long-term storage is unknown. Information is stored in LTM in the form of memories, and is classified in three ways: (1) **procedural** knowledge, (2) **semantic** knowledge, and (3) **episodic memories** (McKoon, Ratcliff, & Dell, 1986; Oakley, 1981; Tulving, 1972, 1985).

(1) **Procedural knowledge** encompasses learned associations which allow human beings to function in new situations by adapting old behaviors. (2) According to Wortman et al. (1988), **semantic** memories are mental representations of reality; in

other words, they are abstractions of objects, states, and qualities. (3) Finally, **episodic** memories are data stored in the form of personal experiences (Tulving, 1972). Traditional HIP theory also assumes that data are stored in LTM by an operation known as **deep processing**, that is, any activity encouraging further interaction with a word or idea in order to uncover or understand its meaning. Such activities include forming an image of the concept, rehearsing, drawing it, talking about it, and taking notes. According to Craik and Lockhart (1972), deep processing is essential to successful long-term storage. Correspondingly, it is thought that all of the activities undertaken to retain information in LTM also help to develop retrieval pathways that are essential for recalling the item at a later time (Klatzky, 1975).

HIP assumes that if stimuli make it past the primary memory or buffer zone, they proceed to STM which is the locus of higher order cognitive processing; all thinking takes place in this limited sphere (Kihlstrom, 1987; Wortman et al., 1988). Information stored in LTM is used in STM to facilitate the higher order cognitive processes involved in the organization and analysis of stimuli. Before information from LTM can be used in STM, it must first be retrieved. Two generally recognized operations that aid in retrieval are **feature detection** and **pattern recognition** (Hubel & Wiesel, 1965; Selfridge & Neisser 1960). In feature detection, distinguishing characteristics or qualities of the stimuli are identified to aid recall. Pattern recognition, on the other hand, matches the sounds, associated facts, and ideas of external stimuli with those of concepts already present in LTM. These retrieval mechanisms may account for the **tip-of-the-tongue phenomenon** wherein we can feel a word about to be verbalized but something is stopping us. Brown and McNeill (1966) and Reason and Mycielska (1982) report that information in LTM is stored by sounds, i.e., first letter usually, or by associated facts and meanings.

The **associated facts, ideas, and meanings** stored in LTM are referred to as **schema** (Bartlett, 1932), which are defined as interactive knowledge structures (Hastie, 1981; Rumelhart & Ortony, 1977) or "frameworks for the organization of knowledge about different domains" (Gerver, 1980). Schemata enable individuals to attach meaning to external stimuli based on prior experience. In this way, an individual can develop a set of expectations, select relevant information, and thus predict outcomes (Alba & Hasher, 1983; Anderson, 1977; Owens, Bower, & Black, 1979; Pichert & Anderson, 1977; Sanford 1985; Spiro, 1977).

Any discussion of memory is incomplete without taking into account the phenomenon of **forgetting**. Forgetting is attributed to the failure to store information successfully in STM and/or the inability to retrieve stored knowledge in LTM. Failure to store data in STM may be caused by interference of any kind (noise, sensory overload, language deficiency) or selective dismissal of information as irrelevant (Atkinson & Shiffrin, 1968; Bourne, Dominowski, & Loftus, 1979). Forgetting can also occur when memory pathways decay because they are not renewed periodically in LTM over time, or because of faulty retrieval procedures, or because memory is highly malleable and under constant change (Leippe, 1980; Yuille, 1980). Wortman et al. (1988) sum up the major causes of forgetting as: "decay of memory, interference from similar information that prompts confusion of memories, and the motivation to forget" (p. 171; also see Christiaansen, Sweeney, & Ochalek, 1983; Loftus, 1979; Powers, Andriks & Loftus, 1979).

Some of the interpreting models presented in this chapter feature memory as a major component, reflecting the influence of HIP research on translation and interpretation theory. Classic HIP, which is derived from psychological research on memory, is a linear model. This linear cognitive model assumes that information is processed in a sequential manner. Figure 7 depicts the Loftus model of human information processing.

Although classic HIP may shed some light on the dynamics of interpreting, it is clear that something much more complex is operating during the language conversion process. Gerver (1976) acknowledges the vast complexity of interpretation, and describes his own model as only "a first approximation" (p. 202) to a description of the processes involved in SI. Given the very limited capacity of STM and how little is known about LTM, HIP's ability to explicate the intricacies of converting one language into another is necessarily limited.

The HIP model further assumes a **central control center** called **working memory** that operates under a single set of rules and binds various perceptual-cognitive functions (such as listening, hearing, speaking) together in a unitary system (Wortman et al., 1988). The demands of court interpreting cast doubts on the ability of this prevailing model of HIP to explain how an interpreter can engage in multiple tasks, all in a linear sequence, and still have time to yield a product.

Finally, this model describes "unconscious" as those stimuli which are unattended to or unrehearsed and therefore either decay or are displaced before they can be encoded. As a result, conscious experiences such as thought and action are not believed to be influenced by any unconscious percepts or unretrieved/unretrievable memories. At best the "unconscious" is defined as pre-attentive perceptual processes such as feature detection and pattern recognition (Kihlstrom, 1987). Once the individual interacts with the stimulus, it is stored in LTM as a latent memory trace (Tulving, 1974; Tulving & Madigon, 1970). The failure to incorporate this element into the classic HIP model severely restricts its ability to explain how an interpreter can

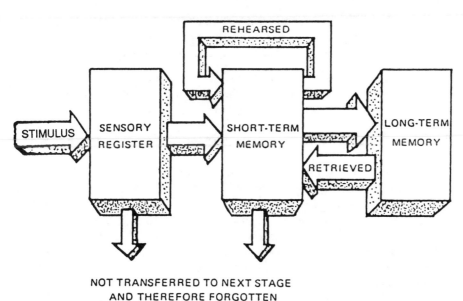

Figure 7. Loftus's classic model of human information processing.

unconsciously draw upon a wealth of sociocultural and sociolinguistic information, while at the same time making decisions about which word to select (Giles & St. Clair, 1979). Nonetheless, HIP theories and the components of the classic model have substantially increased our understanding of the processes involved in court interpreting. At the same time, these conventional models can help form the basis of new theoretical models designed to better explain the interpreting process.

Although many questions about how the mind accomplishes the operation of interpretation are not answered by the classic HIP model, two paradigms of automatic HIP developed in the field of cognitive sciences may offer some new insights. The most notable distinction between classic HIP and the recently developed automatic processing models is the assumption that many mental operations, such as introspection and perception, are outside conscious awareness (Kihlstrom, 1987, 1988). The two models that will be briefly presented are: J. R. Anderson's (1983) Adaptive Control of Thought (ACT*) [*denotes final version], and G. E. Hinton and J. A. Anderson's (1986) Parallel Distributed Processing (PDP). First the major features of these two models will be outlined, and then their implications will be discussed.

3.2. ACT* Model

Anderson (1983) describes ACT* as "a theory of *cognitive architecture* [emphasis in original]—that is, a theory of the basic principles of operation built into the cognitive system" (p. i). He assumes that memory is a single, unitary storage system rather than a binary system divided into STM and LTM. He refers to memory as consisting of both "temporary knowledge structures currently being attended and the active parts of long-term memory" (p. 119). According to this scheme, memory capacity is extensive. Anderson believes all stimuli that come into the production system enter three memories (p. 19):

(a) representations of the external environment (declarative),
(b) active goals which require processing (working), or
(c) pre-existing knowledge structures (production) (see Figure 8).

Anderson describes knowledge in the ACT* model in two ways: **declarative** and **procedural** (pp. 10-11). Declarative knowledge is general knowledge—most probably schema—and all specific facts, residing in LTM (pp. 23-25). ACT* concurs with the classic HIP model regarding the classification of information in that it views declarative knowledge as either **episodic** or **semantic** (pp. 70-71). Episodic information consists of primarily autobiographical memories in which the individual was an agent in an event. Characteristics of the event, such as distinct features of the environment and situational or contextual cues unique to the individual, are retained as memories of self as agent. The other large category of memory is semantic, also referred to as a mental lexicon; information is stored under its conceptual/abstract meaning, not by the circumstances under which the knowledge was acquired. Thus, all declarative knowledge is available to introspection, and we are aware and can actively remember processing this type of information once it is retrieved from LTM into working memory (pp. 10-11).

The second classification of knowledge is procedural. This knowledge encompasses the rules, skills, and strategies which help us to perform higher cognitive functions. **Procedural** information is stored in a "system of productions" (it can be

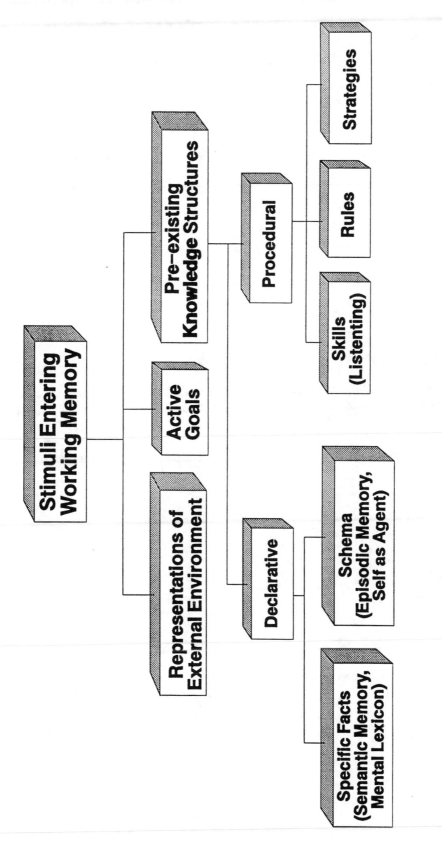

Figure 8. Flow chart of ACT* model [Author's conceptualization].

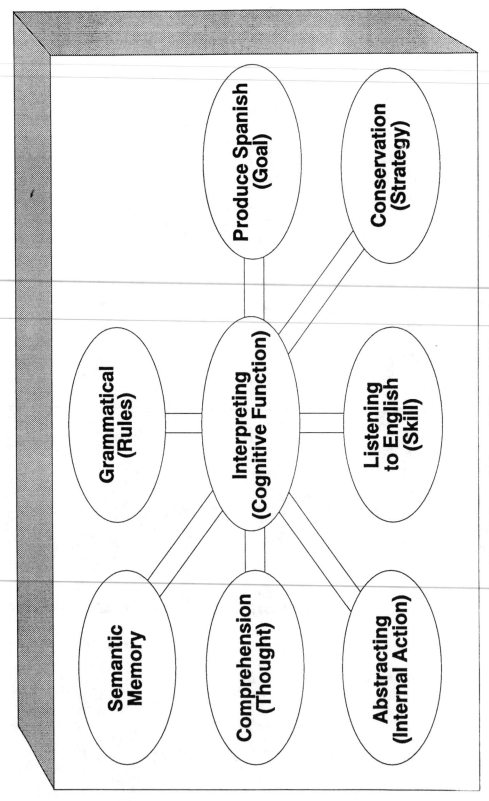

Figure 9. Procedural knowledge node from ACT* model [Author's conceptualization].

perceived as a constellation of nodes, see Figure 9) that reflect an individual's processing goals and the conditions under which some internal or external action will meet them.

Declarative knowledge is accessed through procedural knowledge nodes (Anderson, 1983, p. 76) that contain the operations of perception, memory, thought, and actions. Working memory employs both classes of knowledge during the performance of higher cognitive operations, many of which are assumed to be beyond conscious control. Like procedural knowledge, unconscious cognitive operations such as memory encoding and interpreting are believed to be unavailable to direct introspection. However, an individual can be aware of the goals, conditions, and products of procedural knowledge, though not the actual process or procedure he or she engages in. The product of these operations is then stored as declarative knowledge; the stronger the strength of a production node, then the more often a person must successfully practice (p. 30). And the more often a person practices, the faster the node will be available in the future. "The nodes of this network vary in strength with practice and with passage of time" (p. 208). For example, once an interpreter has used higher-order, unconscious cognitive processes to successfully convert the term "jury selection" into the target language, this term is then stored as declarative knowledge.

Working memory can be activated by either external perceptual processes or internal thought (p. 28). If one node of knowledge is stimulated by either form of activation, then all cognitive concepts that are linked together will also be activated through a system of associative links (p. 30). These associative links represent the connections among related concepts. Any procedural nodes that are linked with the external or internal stimuli are also stimulated. For example, if the word "arrest" is uttered, then the specific declarative knowledge node is activated and any other nodes that contain personal experiences or rules surrounding the concept of "arrest," such as jail, Miranda warnings, and police officers, will also be activated. Indeed, Anderson (1983) proposes an activation schema in which more familiar concepts spread more activation (more and more production modules are brought to bear on the problem). This theory has implications for interpreting. Anderson states: "There is considerable controversy about the basis for increased performance with practice, but Chapter 5 presents the evidence that increased capacity of working memory is a component of the improvement" (p. 29).

Although this model is similar to the classic HIP models in many respects, ACT* allows for one unitary working memory with highly structured knowledge nodes that are activated by both external and internal stimuli. Thus, ACT* can account for conscious as well as unconscious cognitive processes that operate independently or interactively, and chronologically or simultaneously. In a recent human information process model—Parallel Distributive Processing (PDP)—Hinton and Anderson (1986) challenge Anderson's (1983) ACT* system of productions and cognitive architecture scheme and attempt to attribute even greater importance to the role of the cognitive unconscious in explaining HIP.

3.3. Parallel Distributive Processing

The study of PDP models differs immensely from the classic HIP and ACT* theory, primarily because researchers in this area of cognitive science reject the computer analogy of information processing. PDP researchers acknowledge the physiology of the human brain and attempt to emulate its microstructural processes; specifically, models are designed after the synaptic connections of the neurons (McClelland, Rumelhart, & the PDP Group, 1986, pp. 10-11). PDP presupposes that there are a large number of processing units where information is stored, similar to ACT*'s knowledge nodes and production systems but composed primarily of simple units with simple tasks. According to this model, information is widely distributed in modules rather than localized in specific parts of the brain (pp. 33, 41). This wide distribution of information and processing units requires a massive and parallel processing component (p. 49). Hinton and Anderson (1986) propose that the brain operates using a similar parallel distributive processing system. Total activation time for their complex cognitive system is thought to be one-half second.

PDP theorists postulate that external or internal stimulation activate their models just as a brain would be because they strive to imitate the brain's structure (McClelland et al., 1986, p. 4). PDP models are likewise activated by external or internal stimulation (p. 15). Activation implies not only excitation of pertinent processing units but also inhibition of others which may not be needed for the stimuli being processed. For example, the authors of *Parallel Distributed Processing* (McClelland et al., 1986) posit that in language processing, syntax and semantics operate to mutually influence and constrain each other, and they tend to be reciprocal (1986, p. 6). The activation of individual processing units can vary continuously rather than discretely. Eventually the entire system reaches a steady state of activation in which pertinent information is called up or represented and is accessible to phenomenal awareness.

Each processing unit is devoted to specific and simple tasks (p. 47). Another postulate of this paradigm is that PDP allows for a large number of the processing units to work with each other simultaneously, so that analysis can proceed rapidly (p. 75). In fact, because of the great number of units influencing each other and the speed of information passing among the units, the rate of processing may exceed the span of conscious awareness. Because of the time factor, some modules may be accessible to awareness, and subsequently under conscious control. Hinton and Anderson (1986) claim that consciousness is a matter of time rather than stimulation or activation: "the clear implication of the PDP framework is that unconscious processing is fast and parallel, while conscious processing is slow and sequential" (Kihlstrom, 1987, p. 1446).

PDP configurations are distinct from the classic model in that various systems are thought to operate independently instead of under a central executive (p. 47). Furthermore, PDP posits that each independent system has a separate set of rules by which it abides. For example, PDP considers most information processing functions in memory, language, and thought to be unconscious (p. 75). During unconscious processing, concepts, ideas, or objects need not be fully activated in awareness before information in the processing units influences our experiences, thoughts, and actions. Therefore, information in the processing units that has not yet been consciously retrieved can still influence us.

Of particular interest to interpreters is the assumption of the PDP framework that if an ambiguity exists in the stimulus pattern, such as a miscue in hearing a word, then there will be a vacillation between alternatives (Kihlstrom, 1987). This would account for pauses and hedges while interpreters are considering alternatives to a word or phrase which are not immediately available to them while interpreting.

3.4. Implications of Unconscious Processes

According to Fodor (1983), the human nervous system is innately ready to accommodate domain-specific cognitive modules (language capability is one example) which are outside of consciousness and control. One implication of this assumption is that automatic processing by human beings demands little attention. However, it is commonly held that only a discrete amount of conscious attention span is available to humans; if there are too many demands on our limited attentional resources, then tasks carried on simultaneously (in awareness) will interfere with one another. Weaver (1972) notes that if too many stimuli are attended to at once, the energy devoted to such attending is dissipated. Wortman et al. (1988) report on a number of studies that have measured subjects' capacity for "selective attention," that is, their ability to screen out less important stimuli in order to conserve their attentional resources. They conclude from the findings of these studies that selective attention "is probably based on both physical *and* [emphasis in original] conceptual information" (p. 154); that is, listeners attend to both the physical characteristics and the content of a message.

Hirst, Neisser, and Spelke (1978) have found that HIP tasks—which are not innate and which take an enormous amount of our attention—may become routinized and unconscious as a result of practice. In their study, subjects were able to read difficult encyclopedia articles at a normal speed and level of comprehension while simultaneously hearing, transcribing, and understanding the meaning of dictated sentences related to what they read. The conclusion that can be drawn from this research is that after a skill has become routinized, if it is engaged by a specific stimulus, even unintentionally, then the routinized operation proceeds automatically. Therefore, any skill that once demanded much focused attention may become unconscious with practice. For example, novice court interpreters who take notes during consecutive interpretation are executing a cognitive procedure that can become routinized over time. With frequent practice, this skill will demand less and less conscious attention. After interpreters acquire the skill, it is difficult for them to describe what is actually happening. Conscious attention to the interpreting task thereafter may actually interfere with performance.

Unconscious processing has a number of implications for the interpreter. First, routinization may explain how a complex, multifaceted operation such as simultaneous interpretation can occur. Second, this concept strongly suggests that these complicated skills can be affected by training. Finally, skills that initially demanded extensive attentional resources can eventually, with practice, be performed automatically or unconsciously. Attentional resources that are freed up after routinization of a skill can then be channeled to other less developed or more demanding conscious functions, such as conservation of register or stylistic monitoring.

The classic HIP linear model purports to provide a description of how psycholinguistically complex information is processed by human beings. However, it does not account for the simultaneous functioning of a multiplicity of tasks that must converge in order for interpreting to take place. Thus, HIP theory does not begin to elucidate how an accurate, verbatim interpretation such as that expected in judicial proceedings can occur. Moreover, even the more powerful HIP paradigms—ACT* and PDP—individually cannot accurately describe the innumerable operations underlying the interpreting act. However, components of the classic HIP, ACT*, and PDP models each greatly contribute and offer insights into the structures and multifaceted systems of production that generate the conversion of one language to another.

3.5. Constraints of ACT* and PDP

Cognitive psychologists have not had the opportunity to apply the recent unconscious HIP models to an area as complex as interpreting. However, the need for legal equivalence in the courtroom (Gonzalez, 1989c) and the use of several languages in a set of complex cognitive operations challenges the completeness of the ACT* and PDP models. Most translation and interpretation scholars agree that to interpret a message accurately, the interpreter must transform it from concrete to abstract form, retaining both of those forms in memory. The message is processed multidimensionally, converted back from the abstract to the concrete (TL), and then checked against the concrete form of the original (SL) message. For example, if a police officer states in testimony, "I observed the subject convey himself to the vehicle in an ambulatory fashion," the interpreter will abstract that message, possibly to an image of a man walking over to a car. The abstract image is then converted to concrete form in the TL, but before uttering the TL version, the interpreter must compare it with the SL message and verify that it conserves the meaning and register. In this case, interpreting the testimony as "I saw the man walk over to the car," would be conserving the meaning but not the register. The interpreter would have to reject that version and formulate one at a higher register in the TL, within the bounds of intelligibility.

The existing human information processing models do not entirely account for the mind's ability to convert symbolic representations (words) into abstract concepts and to comprehend these concepts. Adding a second language to this set of processes exponentially increases the level of cognitive complexity. Fundamental operations of interpretation such as conservation and conversion are not addressed in most translation and interpretation or HIP models. Therefore, before a specific model of interpretation can be crafted, a general model of human information processing is called for.

Any newly devised model must not only be able to accommodate the unique cognitive operations involved in interpretation, but also take into account the constraints intrinsic to court interpretation: namely, the strict conservation of meaning with attention to the paralinguistic and extralinguistic qualities of the message. With this in mind, a model of simultaneous HIP is presented here.

The theoretical model proposed here is a hybrid of the currently proposed theories of HIP. This comprehensive model treats HIP and the interpreting act specifically from a communicative, cognitive, social, and linguistic perspective. It represents a more predictive, powerful, and explanatory tool for understanding the HIP phenomenon. Moreover, it is hoped that the enunciation of this model will spur interest in research on interpreting. Interpreters may be the single most important research resource for cognitive scientists who are interested in unconscious mental processes in human information processing.

4. Simultaneous Human Information Processing Model

Simultaneous Human Information Processing (SHIP) is a non-linear model of simultaneous information processing (see Figures 10 and 11). A description of its activation, configuration, components, assumptions, and limitations are comprehensively discussed in the subsections that follow. A "top-down" view of the model presented at the beginning of this chapter demonstrates how the model works in actual practice given the requirements and rigors of court interpretation. The chapter culminates with an example of SHIP's components in operation.

As with any new model, SHIP is a rough approximation of what might happen during human information processing. The primary reason for offering SHIP is to attempt to account for known phenomena with a model having the power and flexibility to explain and predict observed behaviors. One of the hardest concepts to understand about SHIP is that it is a three-dimensional model (see Figure 10 and Section 4.5, below). How SHIP operates is explained in the next section.

4.1. Description of SHIP's Operation

SHIP addresses the unique properties of court interpretation not accounted for by prior interpretation models. It is hoped that SHIP will spur interdisciplinary research into the area of the cognitive sciences and interpretation. To integrate complex human information processing with linguistic issues and interpretation demands a theory which will unify the knowledge of three fields.

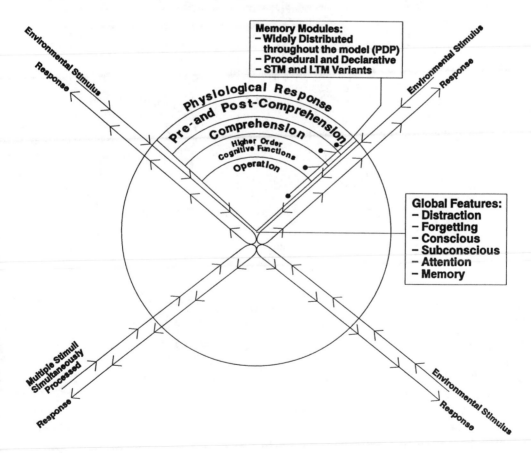

Figure 10. Simultaneous Human Information Processing (SHIP) model.

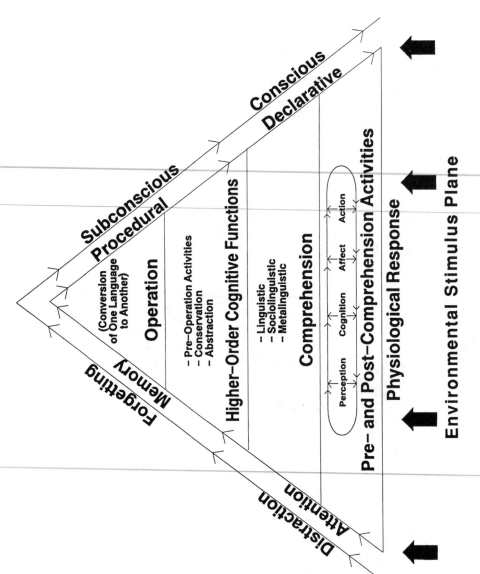

Figure 11. Cross-section of SHIP's cognitive hierarchy.

SHIP is modelled on the functions of neurons and synaptic connections in the mind. **Neurons**, widely distributed nerve cells, react to external stimuli which are received by nerve—or receptor—cells in the sense organs (eyes, ears, nose, mouth, skin). This stimulus becomes a biochemical electrical signal (Gurowitz, 1969) that is transferred to effector cells—the transmitters of these signals in the brain. The **synaptic connection** bridges the gap between neurons and synapses. A biochemical signal—or **neurotransmitter**—bridges the physical gap across the synapse to receptors on the individual neuron. Neuron transmitters bridge thousands of synapses, exciting and inhibiting neurons after receiving and reacting to a stimulus (Kolb & Whishaw, 1985; Milner, 1970; Ornstein & Thompson, 1984; Schwartz, 1973).

In SHIP, **activation** begins when a stimulus received by receptor cells produces **excitation** and **inhibition** of appropriate and inappropriate **declarative** or **procedural knowledge modules**. The **parallel distributive nature** of the neurons of the brain (Hinton & Anderson, 1986; Rumelhart, McClelland, the PDP Group, 1986), and the PDP network postulated in SHIP, then allows for simultaneous processing. Large numbers of memory modules work together rapidly and simultaneously to complete the myriad operations necessary to perform even a simple task such as listening. As long as the mind is active, therefore, the system is at a **minimally ready state**. In more demanding or motivating circumstances, the individual will necessarily use a larger number procedural and declarative knowledge modules or memory.

Figure 12 demonstrates how each component can be **simultaneously activated** (see Section 4.7, below). This figure is a different cross-section of the same globe as in Figures 10 and 11, above. The only difference is that the perspective of the model is now a globe sliced in half—the triangle or pyramid is then but a single slice of the entire global model of SHIP. The figure represents a snapshot in time of all the components activated simultaneously. While a linear model would have difficulty explaining multiple simultaneous activities, this paradigm easily accounts for progressively complex and numerous integrated operations.

This figure demonstrates the movement of a linguistic stimulus (**Has she been served?**) through the model. As the stimulus is processed by SHIP, it interacts with all the components, as is indicated by the arrows pointing toward the inputting channel. As the unit of meaning is acted upon by each component, it is changed, modified, or adapted by the information stored in each module. For example, **Has she been served?** undergoes processing by the linguistic, sociocultural, and sociolinguistic procedural or declarative modules (see Section 4.3.2, below), depending on the complexity of the operation, i.e., decoding "she" and tapping the schema for "process serving."

The stimulus is comprehended as a question, reformulated from passive to active, so that it is understood that the agent is not known and the pronoun refers to the **patient** (the object undergoing action in the sentence). **What** has been served becomes clear from the sociocultural context. It is implicit at this juncture in the legal process that the question refers to the serving of a subpoena to a woman. A sociocultural rule restricts the inappropriate schema, such as serving food in a restaurant or the fulfillment of a religious obligation to a female deity.

The interpreter consciously focuses on the effect a passive construction in the target language (*¿Ha sido citado?*) would have upon the comprehension for the listener. The interpreter is aware of the **pragmatic rules** governing the use of active and passive voice in both languages (see Section 4.2.2, Subsection (8), below) and has routinized

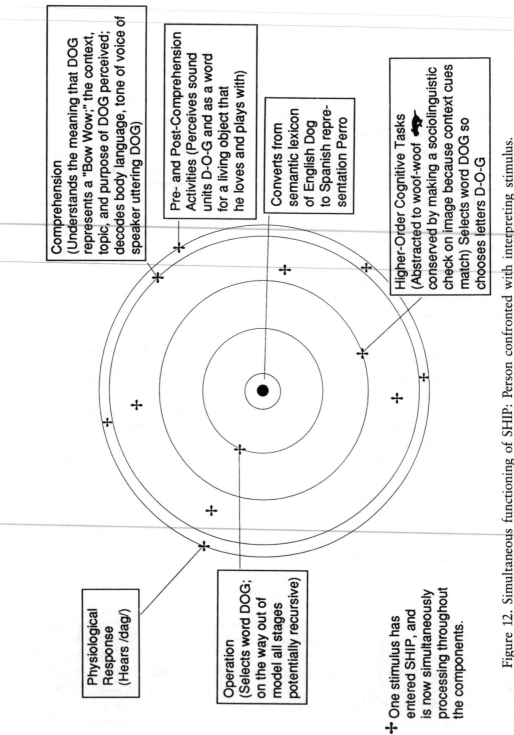

Comprehension
(Understands the meaning that DOG represents a "Bow Wow;" the context, topic, and purpose of DOG perceived; decodes body language, tone of voice of speaker uttering DOG)

Pre- and Post-Comprehension Activities (Perceives sound units D-O-G and as a word for a living object that he loves and plays with)

Converts from semantic lexicon of English Dog to Spanish representation Perro

Higher-Order Cognitive Tasks (Abstracts to woof-woof conserved by making a sociolinguistic check on image because context cues match) Selects word DOG so chooses letters D-O-G

Physiological Response (Hears /dag/)

Operation (Selects word DOG; on the way out of model all stages potentially recursive)

+ One stimulus has entered SHIP, and is now simultaneously processing throughout the components.

Figure 12. Simultaneous functioning of SHIP: Person confronted with interpreting stimulus.

the information after many years of manipulating these forms. Because the active string is more economical than the passive, and because Spanish tends to prefer the active over the passive, the interpreter (unconsciously) opts for the active construction. Once the final abstraction has been obtained—that is, of converting the "process serving" linguistic sign to "process serving" as an abstract concept in the SL, the conversion (finding the correct symbol in the TL) is initiated.

During conversion, in the schematic module of process serving, a search occurs and the appropriate target language response is retained (see Section 4.2.2, Subsection (10), below). At this point, reformulation into the TL begins. The "process serving predication" is acted upon by the **linguistic, sociocultural, pragmatic**, and **sociolinguistic components** (see Section 4.2.2, Subsection (8b), below). The interpreter may either consciously or unconsciously consider the problem of comprehensibility in the TL—whether to conserve the elliptical nature of the English stimulus or to add a phrase that would make the meaning more explicit. The interpreter contrasts the English and Spanish assumptions—English favors elliptical forms whereas Spanish does not. Conscious decision coupled with previous choice patterns results in a modified, non-elliptical form.

As the activated linguistic and sociolinguistic components guide the stimulus into the correct pathways, **conscious** and **unconscious processes** combine to complete higher-order cognitive functions (see Section 4.2.1, Subsection (3), below). The stimulus is abstracted to its TL meaning and form: *¿A él le han citado a comparecer?* [**Has he been served?**] Monitoring the proposed output, the interpreter matches the meaning and grammatical form with the original SL form and meaning held in **short-term memory** (see Sections 4.3.1 and 4.3.2, below). The interpreter realizes that the gender of the person has not been conserved in the SL. This is where the recursive nature of the model comes into play (see Section 4.6, below).

As this stimulus is processed, the information is checked in the conservation component and then reintroduced into the inputting channel until the correct abstraction and conversion occurs. At the second check (coming back down the TL side of the model, see Figure 14) in the conservation component, the meaning has been appropriately conserved and proceeds to pass through the physiological response component to become an expression in the target language. At any time that the stimulus is not clear, it can be checked and rechecked in one or more components.

Returning to our example, once interpreters discover the inaccuracy, they direct the stimuli (**he**) back into the linguistic component and the stimulus is modified according to pronoun gender rules in the morphological module (to *ella*). That abstraction is then incorporated into the stimulus that is held in short-term memory. Next, the phonological component superimposes question intonation, the sociolinguistic component modifies the stimulus for level of formality and the sociocultural/ pragmatics component rejects ellipsis because of contrasting Spanish-English rules. Lexical items are simultaneously being selected, and soon the higher order operation results in *¿A ella la han citado a comparecer?* (Has she been summoned to appear?, literally, to her she has been summoned to appear.) Notice that the *meaning* of the original SL unit has been retained.

The time lag between the perception, comprehension, conversion, conservation, and final interpretation of the stimulus can be as little as .25 seconds behind the SL utterance (Marslen-Wilson, 1973). As is evident from this simple example, the extensive number of decisions, judgments, selections, preferences, and other cognitive and physical activities debunks conscious processing as a plausible explanatory model. How then can the rapidity of the process be explained in light of the intricacy of the operations? SHIP postulates that **routinization** of the subskills (see Section 4.4, below) permits the **limited attentional span** (see Section 4.2.1, Subsections (5) and (6), below) of the interpreter to be freed to accomplish the interpreting tasks. Furthermore, the major skills of interpretation may also be routinized—after much practice—allowing the interpreter to pay more conscious attention to the task at hand, and facilitating accuracy and precision.

To fully grasp the functioning of SHIP, it is necessary to describe one final aspect: the inhibition of irrelevant modules. A key operating principle is that any perceived stimulus simultaneously inhibits and excites knowledge modules, as shown in Figure 13. The ambiguous phrase, **It's a right**, excites all relevant and irrelevant schemata. At the same time, a situational context is provided by the external environment—such as prior or subsequent utterances—and the schemata most likely to end in failure are suppressed.

Figure 13 hypothesizes an unconscious process guiding comprehension (designated by A, B, and C). This process may occur during the excitation and inhibition of knowledge modules. Individual schema, connected by associative links, are either excited or inhibited until the final abstract meaning is chosen. As is noted, since the external environment is a courtroom, the other possibilities cannot be rejected until additional stimuli supply enough context to allow for appropriate recognition, comprehension, and conservation. The same process simultaneously occurs in other knowledge modules as soon as a stimulus is perceived; because of the simultaneous nature of SHIP, simpler or more frequent concepts may be processed sooner than more complex or less well-known information. **Distraction, forgetting, inappropriate storage** (see Section 4.2.1, Subsection (6), below), and **limited attentional span** are examples of **perceptual distortions** which can interfere at the unconscious level with comprehension.

Now that a quick overview of SHIP has been offered, a closer inspection of the various components of the model is in order. The following section (depicted in Figure 11) presents the model's components. The reader should refer back to this figure as often as is needed. Following the presentation of the component parts, we offer a discussion of the major assumptions underlying the model.

4.2. Components of SHIP

Comprehending what each component of the model offers is essential to achieving an understanding of what affects information processing in interpreting. Figure 11 is a representation of SHIP's implied hierarchy. SHIP is composed of several internal layers, as well as external components. These arbitrary internal/external distinctions are made to help the reader comprehend how SHIP functions. As distinct from internal features, external features are global functions that can affect all other components of SHIP. For example, the conservation module within SHIP's comprehension level would not have as global an effect on memory as would forgetting a stimuli. The following discussion examines the external and internal features of SHIP.

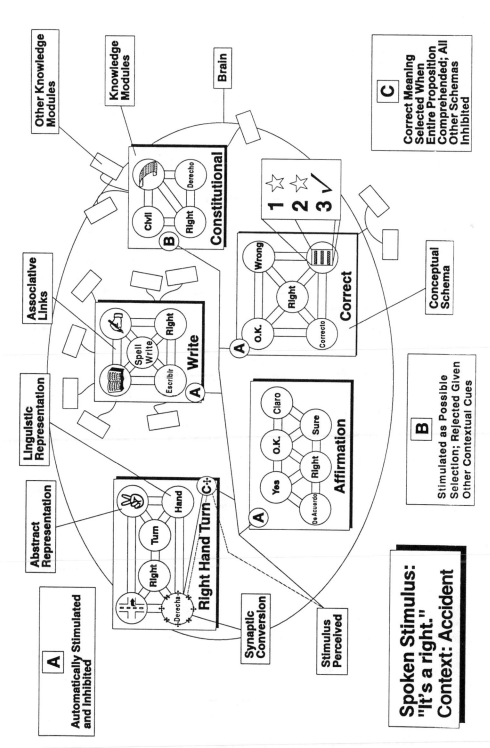

Figure 13. Model depicting excitation and inhibition of SHIP's knowledge modules.

4.2.1. External Features of SHIP

(1) **Environmental Stimulus Plane**: The first component is called the environmental stimulus plane. This level represents **everything outside of the human body**. The physical world is a constant source of stimuli of which human beings are consciously and unconsciously aware. As such, the environmental stimulus plane impinges on all of our senses. For interpreters, this level of SHIP is the source of all linguistic utterances.

(2) **Physiological Response**: The next level of SHIP is the physiological response. Essentially, this level encompasses the immediate reactions of the individual to stimuli received from the environmental plane. There is a physiological response in the ear when a person hears a sound from the environment. Similarly, when a person utters a sound, there is a physiological response; that is, the individual vibrates his or her vocal cords and hears his or her own voice. Any stimulus which enters or leaves the model can be evaluated, affected, and modified. This means that SHIP has interactive and recursive properties. In the case of the interpreter, listening to his own voice or that of others will result in particular changes. For example, if he thinks he is speaking too loudly while performing simultaneous interpretation at counsel table, he can lower his voice. Of course, if there are any physical handicaps, this may lead to sensory deficiency and will either contaminate stimuli or effectively eliminate it from processing (Yarmey, 1979).

(3) **Conscious and Unconscious Processes**: Modern human information processing has been viewed as primarily a conscious process (Kihlstrom, 1988). **Consciousness** is more than mere thought; it also includes memory, judgment, organization, decision making, and a host of other intellectual and even emotional skills. Consciousness has been, most commonly, thought to be cognition or awareness. The **subconscious** was traditionally thought to encompass ideas, impulses, and emotions that were beyond any type of intentional control. However, Kihlstrom (1988) believes that the **cognitive unconscious** can be subdivided into three categories: (a) procedural knowledge which is a strictly unconscious process (unavailable to introspection or awareness at all times); (b) preconscious declarative knowledge (not in consciousness at the time of processing, but accessible at a later time); and (c) subconscious processing (available to introspection but inaccessible to phenomenal awareness).

He posits that consciousness is not a perceptual-cognitive function (awareness) or focal attention, nor is it a process that resides in a cognitive staging area. As many language and learning scholars state, being aware of information even for sustained periods of time does not lead to it being encoded in memory (Stevick, 1976). Therefore, awareness is not necessarily consciousness. "Rather, **consciousness** [emphasis added] is an experiential quality that may, but need not, accompany even complex information processing activities . . . [it] requires that a link be forged between an activated mental representation of an event and an activated mental representation of oneself as the agent or experiencer of that event" (p. 9). SHIP assumes Kihlstrom's tripartite taxonomy in which the unconscious and subconscious are subdivisions of the cognitive unconscious.

SHIP explicitly recognizes the existence of both conscious and unconscious processes. However, rather than assuming that unconscious processes are not susceptible to any form of control, SHIP assumes not only that certain cognitive processes reside in the unconscious, but that through conscious effort and practice they can be shaped (see also Krashen, 1982; Lozanov, 1978). Simultaneous interpretation, long thought to be an innate talent that could not be learned, is in actuality a process consisting of various subskills (see Chapter 26).

It is recognized among some conference interpreters, translation scholars, and court interpreters that novices can acquire these skills and experienced interpreters can improve their performances by intensive practice. However, the notion that it is a higher-order cognitive skill that can be developed is relatively new (Gerver, 1971; Lambert, 1988); training and sustained educational programs for court interpreters are rare (Gonzalez, 1983). Simultaneous interpretation is an entirely unconscious process; nonetheless, the actual product (i.e., the TL version) can be analyzed by conscious processes, which means that the interpreter is aware of and can monitor his product (Krashen, 1985)—the interpretation.

(4) **Procedural and Declarative Knowledge**: All of the information stored in the brain can be classified as either procedural or declarative knowledge. An extensive review of these concepts can be found in the human information processing section of this chapter. An analogy which will clarify the differences between these two types can be seen by examining the word "trial." The word itself can be remembered as a discrete piece of information which refers to a formal hearing before a judge to decide the guilt or innocence of an alleged offender. The primary meaning attached to the word is an example of **declarative knowledge**.

Trial also has a **procedural** meaning which brings to mind a constellation of attendant situational contexts, cues, and objects related to the concept. For example, judge's bench, bailiff, jury, jury instructions, verdict, direct examination, testimony, witnesses, justice, and guilty or innocent will all be recalled when the word is mentioned. Word association networks evoke the pertinent vocabulary of a Spanish-English bilingual, such as trial, court, criminal, charges, *juicio* (trial), *acusación* (charge), *delito* (offense), *ley* (law), *procedimiento* (legal process), and so on.

(5) **Memory and Attention**: Attention refers to the cognitive process whereby the individual, either deliberately or in response to an environmental cue, focuses his or her perceptive capacities on a specific stimulus. **Selective attention** is an interpreter choosing to attend or listen to one particular speaker. An example of an environmental cue is a door slamming loudly in the courtroom, causing the interpreter to automatically turn his head and focus on the distracting stimulus. As explained above, focusing one's attention on a stimulus does not necessarily lead to that information being encoded in memory.

SHIP allows for extensive memory, that is, the ability of a person to retain information for either short or long periods of time. This global cognitive function allows the individual to keep declarative and procedural knowledge within easy access. **Schemata**, defined as large areas of procedural knowledge (Fiske & Linville, 1980), are integral components of the memory model proposed in SHIP. Through memory, particularly of schemata, the interpreter is able to predict what kind of language is required in a specific situational context. As soon as an interpreter has gained enough experience working in court, a schema around specific proceedings, such as an arraignment, can be developed. When the schema is in place, interpreters can rely upon their memory of the vocabulary, protocol, and procedural rules surrounding the arraignment proceeding. The more prototypic the stimuli, the faster it can be categorized (Hayes-Roth & Hayes-Roth, 1977; Reed, 1972). Various levels of categories are arranged hierarchically and can be used for different purposes (Rosch, Mervis,

Gray, Johnson, & Boyes-Braem, 1976). Thus, the more complex the categorization, the longer it takes to retrieve the pertinent information. The opposite would also be true: the simpler or more global the categorization, the faster it can be accessed.

(6) **Distraction and Forgetting**: On the other side of the cognitive "coin" of attention and memory are the functions of distraction and forgetting. Just as information can been coded for memorization, so too can it be **forgotten**, either selectively or in response to an environmental cue. Distraction typically is caused by the shifting of one's perceptual attention from a stimulus; an example would be overhearing a nearby whispered conversation in the middle of a boring speech. The result of distraction is forgetting. A deliberate decision to ignore a stimulus is an example of **selective forgetting**. As in the example cited in (5) above, a loud noise can cause the interpreter to be distracted from what is being said in the courtroom, and the decision to focus one's attention on whatever is causing the stimulus culminates in the original message being forgotten. Both of these global cognitive functions are a part of SHIP because they offer powerful explanations for observed phenomena.

4.2.2. Internal Features of SHIP

(7) **Pre- and Post-Comprehension Activities**: The internal features of SHIP have been ordered according to a cognitive hierarchy; those activities which are more complex are the least accessible to introspection. Four activities are prerequisite to comprehending any stimulus: perception, cognition, affect, and action—all of which can be analyzed in and of themselves or by their end products. **Perception** is distinguished from a purely physiological response by its intellectual or cognitive emphasis (Buckhout, 1974). In other words, the ear receiving sound waves that impinge upon its physical structure is different from an individual perceiving those sound waves to be words. **Cognition** is the systematic organization of information; it is commonly considered to be thought. Cognition in SHIP encompasses **recognition**, in the sense of being aware of something, and in its usual sense of perceiving a stimulus.

One highly recognized aspect of cognition is that the individual must become aware of stimulus in order for it to be **consciously** processed. SHIP accepts this narrow premise, along with Kihlstrom's (1988) contention that even stimulus of which one is unaware may be processed. Kihlstrom reaches this conclusion after reviewing the literature on persons who have amnesia, conversion disorders, or who have undergone hypnosis.

SHIP contends, as do most human information processing models, that **internal stimuli** is capable of being generated, and that it can also activate schema, procedural knowledge nodes, and declarative memory. Thought, therefore, in addition to physical stimuli, can animate SHIP. However, as mentioned above, this activity is accessible to phenomenal awareness and engages our limited attentional span. The classic example is of the daydreamer: the person possesses an internal world that seemingly does not affect the individual but which diverts his or her attention from the hustle and bustle of everyday life.

Affect is best conceptualized as the emotion attached to a word or a situation. It is believed that information is rarely stored in memory without affect (Bogoch, 1968). Consider the word "mom." Upon recognizing this word, the reader immediately experiences an emotional response. The affect of a word can influence how it is comprehended and eventually abstracted. Court interpreters, who must pay particular attention to conserving meaning in the TL, should be acquainted with the affect words carry with them.

Action can be both internal and external. External action is perceived by a person's senses as either specific behavioral acts (running) or procedural knowledge (how a trial is conducted). Internal action is the active thinking about a topic which does not necessarily attach to a physical act. For example, the term "abstracting meaning" succinctly defines the internal action (procedure) which may affect all stimuli perceived by the individual.

(8) **Comprehension**: Stimuli cannot be consciously comprehended unless the individual can apply his or her prior knowledge of the world, the language, and the sociocultural context to a situation. Essentially, comprehension is the construction (encoding) and reconstruction of meaning (decoding) based upon such knowledge.

A. Comprehending Stimuli

A.1. Comprehending Oral Language Stimuli

Oral language stimuli construction and reconstruction of meaning depends on: (a) **linguistic competence**—a knowledge of phonology (sound system), **morphology** (grammar system), **syntax** (word order and relationships), and **semantics** (meaning and lexicon); (b) **pragmatic/sociocultural competence** (the social rules that govern language use); (c) **discourse competence** (the relationship between sentences in larger pieces of discourse); and (d) **sociolinguistics** (language as it is used in a specific social and cultural context). These competencies reflect the communicative competence models of Canale and Swain (1980) combined with the theories of background knowledge (Ausubel, 1978) and the relevant contextual knowledge necessary for language comprehension. **Comprehension** takes place when communicative competencies act upon the stimulus, while simultaneously activating background/contextual knowledge, thus allowing the listener to reconstruct the speaker's meaning (see External Features of SHIP, 4.2.1).

A.2. Comprehending Written Language Stimuli

For written stimuli, the linguistic knowledge assumes an understanding of orthographic (written) symbols and their relationship to spoken language, the basic and complex syntactic arrangements of the language, and most of the linguistic elements necessary to understanding oral stimuli. In performing sight translation, for example, interpreters must be able to recognize the symbols on the page and convert them into mental "spoken words" or images. They must also be able to grasp the meaning of the words as they combine into phrases and sentences. They need to have a large lexicon in the SL as well as the TL, so they can choose the appropriate terms to render the TL version correctly.

A.3. Comprehending Non-Linguistic Stimuli

Although the examples cited here involve language stimuli, this component accounts for the comprehension of a variety of information. If the individual is confronted with a math problem, the information is processed in the same manner. Thus, if the problem is $3 + 4 = 7$, the individual perceives (hears or sees) the numerals, or symbols, and abstracts them to the concept of three of something, four of something, and so on. Knowledge of mathematical syntax enables the individual to understand what operation is referred to by the "+" sign, and thus to comprehend that if one adds three units of something to four units of something, the result is seven units of something.

B. Levels of Competence

B.1. Linguistic Competence

In court interpreting the comprehension process begins with the application of one's linguistic competence to language stimulus. The interpreter hears the SL message using **phonological** and **intonation rules**, captures the essence of the statement in the context of the **speech act**, perceives the situational and cultural context by using **discourse** and **sociolinguistic** and **sociocultural rules**, breaks the message down into units of meaning and their relationships (**syntax rules**), and finally into words (using **semantics** and the SL lexicon). All of these features of linguistic competence simultaneously act upon the message as it is being processed. Also affecting comprehension and construction of meaning are **paralinguistic** features of the message inherent in spoken communication, such as tone of voice, and non-verbal cues such as gestures.

B.2. Pragmatics/Sociocultural Competence

Pragmatics or the **sociocultural rules that govern linguistic interaction** impinge on the construction and reconstruction of meaning (Leech, 1983). These are the rules that **govern the appropriate use of language for specific communicative intentions**, or how context influences the way we comprehend sentences. How do speakers in a certain culture know what linguistic behavior is appropriate in a given situation? Speakers are guided by the rules they have assimilated through experience in that culture and language. For example, they know how to be polite in that culture, when to say **please, I would appreciate it greatly,** or **would you mind**. These rules govern all linguistic interactions in an infinite set of speech and topical circumstances, such as using cultural and linguistic cues to know when to initiate or end a conversation.

Script theory (Fiske & Taylor, 1984; Schank & Abelson, 1977) also contributes to our understanding of the comprehension process. A script is defined as "a structure that describes appropriate sequences of events in a particular context...a script is a predetermined, stereotyped sequence of actions that defines a well-known situation" (Shank & Abelson, 1977, p. 11). Scripts may be best understood as stored linguistic and social formulas. These important parts of our schema make it possible for us to comprehend an unfamiliar word in a familiar situation. Scripts would be stored in procedural knowledge modules as whole units.

B.3. Discourse Competence

Discourse competence is the ability to combine ideas into a coherent, cohesive set (Widdowson, 1978). A person who understands the discourse rules of a language will know how to use pronouns and grammatical connectors (i.e., conjunctions, adverbs, and transitional expressions, such as "then", "therefore", "well", "anyway", and "so after that"). Discourse competence also gives the speaker the ability to express sentences that meet the functional ends of his or her communicative intentions, such as knowing how to construct sentences and put them together in such a way as to effect persuasion, description, or comparison.

B.4. Sociolinguistic Competence

Sociolinguistic competence is the knowledge that dictates how issues of **register** (Firth, 1957) are perceived and acted upon by the individual (Halliday et al., 1964). In ascertaining a particular speech style, court interpreters draw on their familiarity with the present situation (courtroom, trial, testimony) and the topic at hand (armed robbery), as well as familiarity with the social and cultural elements that affect the speakers and their interaction—racism, poverty, religion, and so on. **Language attitude** (the negative or positive attitude toward a given language) or **language ego** (relative confidence in individual proficiency) also enters into this equation.

(9) **Higher-Order Cognitive Functions**: After stimuli are comprehended, a variety of unconscious procedures are triggered to prepare the stimuli for the ultimate cognitive **operation**. Most of these functions can be thought of as preparatory. For example, once a word has been comprehended, it may be abstracted to an image before being interpreted into another language. An additional higher-order cognitive function affecting the interpreter is the conservation of the word's abstracted meaning and its conversion into the appropriate symbol. For example, if the word "ring" is uttered, the interpreter must abstract to the image of a circular object. To further illustrate this point, more contextual cues would make it clear that a wedding ring was the object of interest, and the interpreter, while holding the image of a ring in mind, automatically and unconsciously continues searching for the more precise image of the wedding ring. Of course, not all words can be abstracted to an image, such as the concept "Americanism." The image evoked depends upon how that concept has been encoded by the individual: for some the image of a flag comes to mind, and for others, the idea of freedom.

(10) **Operation**: For interpreters, the conversion of a message from one language to another is the highest-order cognitive operation possible. For a mathematician, on the other hand, the highest order might be a complex algebraic equation. SHIP assumes that the nine components described above have operated simultaneously to prepare stimuli—which in this case are units of translation—for conversion. **Conversion is automatically executed when all the pre-operation activities or higher-order cognitive functions have been exhausted**, either by the conscious selection of predetermined pathways to the appropriate TL symbol (word), or by other unconscious means.

4.3. Assumptions

Generally, the parameters of SHIP differ significantly from existing interpreting models. SHIP rejects the linear HIP tradition in favor of a non-linear approach (see Non-linearity of SHIP, below). Although the linear aspect of classic HIP is rejected, individual components delineated by the classic model are invaluable to the understanding of observable human information processing phenomena; where appropriate,

SHIP incorporates systems such as STM and LTM for functional purposes. Rejecting the linear approach enables SHIP to adopt multiple functions that operate simultaneously and can explain observed phenomena. This model is based on the premise that skills and subskills that make up the function are routinized before the higher-order cognitive function can take place.

Because many of the definitions and concepts devised for HIP models help explain what occurs in the interpretation process, they have been adopted in SHIP. In the following presentation those definitions or assumptions of the model that are incorporated from previous conceptualizations will be distinguished from those that represent a divergence from conventional beliefs.

4.3.1. Assumptions about Memory

It has been estimated that 100 million pieces of information per second are received through our senses (Wortman et al., 1988); we are only remotely aware or conscious of a small percentage of that total. SHIP's non-linear nature, multiple modular memory capacity, and the assumption of numerous STM-like modules that operate simultaneously make the processing of large amounts of information possible. SHIP, like PDP, has unlimited memory (with both types of variants available), allowing multiple tasks to occur throughout the brain at the same time. Moreover, since SHIP is explicitly an unconscious operation model, the individual can never be aware of exactly how many pieces of information are being processed at once.

According to SHIP, memory is not a bipartite system, as in the classic HIP model (Figure 7 of this chapter), nor a global working memory as in ACT*. As suggested by the PDP model, memory may be better represented as multiple modules, consisting of perhaps hundreds, thousands, or millions of units throughout the mind. Unlike PDP, SHIP postulates that these memory modules include both STM and LTM components, such as those envisioned by the classic HIP theory. Essentially, numerous STM and LTM modules can operate simultaneously rather than successively. Consequently, classic HIP's linearity restricts the capacity for memory, whereas SHIP's non-linear nature allows for unlimited memory capacity. Due to the existence of these STM and LTM modules, it is probable that some cognitive functions may be linear within the modules itself. However, the global functioning of SHIP is not.

Unlimited memory can more reasonably account for the multiple and simultaneous tasks requisite to the rendering of an interpretation. Assuming the existence of multiple memory modules may be the key to understanding how an interpreter can hold several units of meaning in short-term memory—each a distinct abstraction—while at the same time searching for lexical items that match each representation, producing an utterance in a second language and simultaneously listening and initially processing the next unit. These complex, simultaneous activities are not as easily accounted for by the classic, linear HIP model.

Research stemming from the classic HIP model has led to the explication of the widely known seven-plus-or-minus-two phenomenon of memory (Miller, 1956), which delineates the supposed limitations of our memory span, based on the assumption that the interrelationship between STM and LTM is linear. That is, if we have only a limited capacity in STM, then a larger memory component for long-term—LTM—storage, must exist. However, this view raises critical questions. For example, must all the information resident in STM be processed—and eventually stored in LTM or forgotten—before the individual can acquire more information in STM and start the whole process over again? Even if many processes were occurring at an extraordinary speed, the amount of time necessary to perform several successive tasks and produce an interpretation into a second language would quickly exceed the time required for the completion of relatively simpler tasks like speaking in one's native language. Stevick (1976) reports on research that limits verbal STM is twenty to thirty seconds in length. Yet skilled interpreters are able to keep pace with even the fastest of speakers.

Because the working definition of classic HIP excludes unconscious processing, only observable memory phenomena are recognized and thought to be measurable. SHIP assumes that there is no limit to memory—STM or LTM—and for this reason, along with the assumption of non-linearity, can easily account for many memory phenomena, including the seven-plus-or-minus-two findings (Miller, 1956). The classic definition of the limits of STM did not account for the fact that human beings can remember significantly more than seven pieces of information; to explain the difference, the notion of "chunking" was developed. This obvious limitation of classic HIP led to the redefinition of "a piece of information" to "a unit of meaning." For example, a phone number can be remembered either as seven pieces of information, 7-9-8-6-1-5-1 or as two units of meaning, (798)-(6151). In this fashion, classic HIP accounted for an individual's ability to remember more than was originally thought possible. In spite of this definitional expansion, classic HIP is still limited by its conception of STM. STM still would not hold even a fraction of the voluminous information necessary in the interpreting process. Interpreters, for instance, often must hold whole paragraphs of information in STM before processing them consecutively at the witness stand.

4.3.2. Types of Memory

SHIP adopts the traditional classification of knowledge as either declarative or procedural (see ACT*, above; Taylor & Crocker, 1981). It also postulates that these memories are stored according to a preconceived schema after an external stimulus is observed and processed. Most schemata are posited to be organized into an interconnected network, much the same as has been theorized about schematic memory (Collins & Quillian, 1972; Tulving, 1972). The fact that a schema is called up during interpreting may account for the often-reported phenomenon of interpreters' ability to retrieve a word they did not believe was in their lexicon, without direct conscious attention to the task. This theory stipulates that procedural knowledge is stored in the classic LTM-type memory modules under distinct schemata. These LTM or schemata modules can vary in size and scope. Perhaps some are small schemata surrounding obscure topics, or even single concepts or words, and others encompass complex cognitive processes and vocabularies that are relatively large in size, or are part of a network of numerous, yet related, memory modules. These modules are connected by associative links, most probably biochemical pathways activated during the excitation and inhibition of pertinent memory modules.

In addition, the model concurs with Loftus's view that memory is influenced by expectations, stereotypes, and other variables or conditions (Loftus et al., 1978; Loftus & Palmer, 1974; Loftus, Schooler, & Wagenaar, 1985; Tousignant, Hall, & Loftus, 1986; Ward & Loftus, 1985). Because these variables affect memory, their influence can account for how information is correctly and incorrectly stored and retrieved in either declarative or procedural knowledge nodes. SHIP also recognizes and accepts the most widely held theories of how forgetting occurs (see Section 3.1, above). Forgetting may be a function of inappropriately classifying and storing specific facts, rules, or strategies under the wrong conceptual schema. Or, it may also be a consequence of allowing established memory pathways to fall into disuse and decay.

Both of these theories can explain an individual's inability to retrieve information. The implication for interpreters is that a training program integrating myriad concepts, skills, techniques, and operations may develop important storage schemas in memory. Repeated practice would help to establish and retain retrieval pathways. This advice seems contrary to that given by those who follow automatic processing models. Higgs and Clifford (1982), for example, assert that once automatic processes are learned they are difficult to suppress or alter:

> There appears to be a real danger of leading students too rapidly into the "creative aspects of language use," in that if successful communication is encouraged and rewarded for its own sake, the effect seems to be one of rewarding at the same time the incorrect communication strategies seized upon in attempting to deal with the communication situations presented. When these reinforced communication strategies fossilize prematurely, their subsequent modification or ultimate correction is rendered difficult to the point of impossibility. (p. 74)

Those who support automatic processing models such as grammatical approaches to language learning also do not take into account all of the affective and motivational purposes for learning. If their theories were to be followed to their logical conclusions, bad writers would always be bad writers no matter how much time they spend trying to restructure their writing schemata. However, experience tells us that even the worst writer can improve tremendously if global, holistic approaches to learning are incorporated (Anderson, 1982; Lord, Lepper, & Thompson, 1980), and students' motivations for wanting to become better writers are used to support their development. The same may be true of interpreters. With practical laboratory, holistic, motivationally based training, most interpreters can improve their individual skills and as a result their overall quality of interpretation. Gonzalez (1983), for example, reports an average 50 percent reduction in interpreter errors after three weeks of intensive, laboratory-based instruction.

Finally, as is often asked, where is the second language stored? Some subscribe to the theory that because the two lexicons may be acquired at different times, they must be stored in different memory modules. Others argue that there is one place where each concept is stored, and that all the vocabulary one learns surrounding that concept, whether it is in one or more languages, will also be stored at that location. In SHIP, when the particular procedural module is activated, appropriate concepts, words, and schemata that may be in a hundred different places in memory are automatically sought out; some of which may be stored alone, others together, and yet others will be stored as whole schemata. Because SHIP adopts the parallel distributive processing approach to human information processing, it is assumed that the proper memory modules (declarative and procedural) will be retrieved to accomplish the task, regardless of where the information actually resides in memory. Therefore, while some may desire the answer to the storage debate because of the implications for teaching/training, SHIP explicitly prefers a holistic approach. In its best form, words, their multiple meanings, and their appropriate use within a variety of contexts (i.e., the building of schemas) may be learned all at once. Practice calling up the knowledge structure and constant repetitions of the skills and subskills would work together to ensure the interpreter would somewhere in memory have the word, phrase, procedure, or rule in place and ready to recall.

4.3.3. Parallel Distributive Processing

Parallel distributive processing is a major feature of SHIP. It assumes that memory is not compartmentalized but rather widely distributed throughout the brain. Unlike classic HIP, which assumes that memory is under the direct control of an executive center, SHIP posits that **memory consists of multiple modules,** each able to function independently of the others without reliance upon a central memory center that directs cognitive traffic and attends to the most demanding stimuli.

Parallel distributive processing allows these multiple memory modules to work in a variety of ways: (1) collaboratively and simultaneously, (2) independently and simultaneously, or (3) some collaboratively and others independently. Information processing in memory, therefore, can take place in multiple locales. After a number of individual declarative memory modules work independently, separate procedural modules for syntax, morphology, and grammar can simultaneously piece together a sentence or larger linguistic unit once the individual modules are executed.

In the absence of a central executive (see Section 3.1, above), multiple stimuli can be processed utilizing various strategies, techniques, or pathways, depending on which tactics an individual favors and to the extent that skills have been routinized. Indeed, constructing a sentence in one's native language is accomplished by most people millions of times during their lives. Furthermore, individuals each have strong patterns of learning based on different cognitive abilities, i.e., aural (hearing), reading (written), oral memory, and so on. Therefore, the "central executive" function which is assumed to exist by traditional HIP scholars may simply be a construct developed to account for the multiplicity of functions necessary to produce a coherent end product.

The PDP feature permits **multiple processing functions** to take place **simultaneously.** Rejecting the linear model allows PDP to account for the simultaneous utilization of multiple planes of knowledge. Conscious as well as unconscious processes, conscious and unconscious memories, perceptions, thoughts, and actions, both old and new, constantly and simultaneously affect an individual's cognitive functions. Because memory is distributed in a parallel manner, even unretrieved (or what would appear to be unretrieved) memories, experiences, stereotypes, attitudes, customs, ideas, and competencies are constantly impinging upon cognitive operations and conscious experiences.

4.3.4. Non-Linearity of SHIP

SHIP attempts to closely simulate how the human mind processes information. Figures 10 and 11 contrast SHIP with the classic linear model shown in Figure 7. SHIP takes note of the fact that the brain receives stimuli through various modalities, and following that model, SHIP can also accommodate numerous sources of stimuli simultaneously. Figure 10 represents how large quantities of varied information can be processed without requiring prioritization; that is, one piece of information, or even a small number of tasks happening at the same time, need not be completely processed before the next piece of information is treated.

Figure 11, above, is a diagram of the various processing planes incorporated in SHIP. The triangular shape of the diagram and the existence of a variety of stages or components in the model make it appear linear. This potential ambiguity arises from the inability of a two-dimensional figure to represent a three-dimensional concept. SHIP is more appropriately represented by a hologram rather than a picture on a page. Comprehending this aspect of SHIP helps to dispel the idea that components of the model are arranged in order of importance or chronology. Below, in Configuration of SHIP in Space/Time, SHIP's shape is described in detail. In this configuration SHIP has been artificially ranked by cognitive complexity or by functions which are global to the model; this hierarchical ranking **does not imply linearity in processing.** The only relationship that SHIP assumes is that of introspection: the more internal, complex, or higher the cognitive function (such as interpreting), the less it will be accessible to introspection. Conversely, the less complex the cognitive function, the more accessible it is to conscious awareness and analysis. Moreover, most of the products of unconscious skills are also available to introspection (Bartol, 1983).

Examination of Figure 11 reveals that the first component of SHIP is the environmental stimulus plane. According to the cognitive complexity relationship stated above, the environmental stimulus dimension is accessible to introspection because it is external to the person. At the apex of the model is the actual operation of interpreting, which the model assumes to be entirely unconscious and internal, and therefore inaccessible to introspection. Abstraction, the ability to make cognitive associations with mental images or linguistic representations of reality in the brain, is closer to the top of the model. At present, we can only speculate how abstraction happens. It could be argued that abstraction is closer to an unconscious process, if not one itself. The components of the model are interchangeable and the ordering of the constituents as presented is arbitrary and does not reflect any assumptions regarding actual cognitive processing.

4.4. Routinization of Skills

Skills which are not innate, such as the ability to consecutively interpret, may be routinized and become unconscious operations. **Routinization** is the rehearsal, practice, and repetition of a complex skill until it becomes an unconscious response. After routinization of the task, the individual performing the function will no longer be conscious of the subskills involved. In the instance of consecutive interpretation, the amount of time and attention required for routinization is predicated upon the individual's linguistic and interpreting competence. The less proficient an individual is, the more time is required to routinize; perhaps even years of practice will be required.

Routinizing certain skills can be difficult. For example, consecutive interpretation consists of a multiple set of skills, including data storage, memory retrieval, and TL formulation, all of which occur simultaneously. Because each of these subskills is complex, any one of them that remains unroutinized will demand much conscious attention during the performance of interpretation (Pawley & Syder, 1983). Given that only a limited amount of conscious attention is available at any point in time (Wortman et al., 1988), multiple complex functions compete for this limited attention span and tend to interfere with one another. Therefore, if even one subfunction of consecutive interpretation is inadequately developed, the amount of concentration demanded by that subskill will seriously interfere with the ability of the individual to engage in the higher function.

For example, when an interpreter encounters a new use of a familiar word while consecutively interpreting in the courtroom: "Your Honor, defense counsel requests a testimonial *voir dire* of this expert witness." The novice interpreter would be distracted because the *voir dire* is usually done with the jury. While the interpreter is busy trying to decipher the new meaning of the word, time has elapsed. Even if the interpreter has retained much of what has gone on, there is, nonetheless, less attention span left to listen, comprehend, remember, and formulate information in the TL if the interpreter is distracted and must process other information.

In this case, routinization of a major function may be delayed, or never realized, until the deficient subskill(s) is enhanced. Once the subskills integral to simultaneous and consecutive interpretation are raised to a higher or unconscious level, consecutive and simultaneous interpretation must also be practiced intensively to become routinized. For interpreters, routinization of major interpreting skills allows them to concentrate their limited conscious attention span on matters of precision and the conservation of the intent, style, tone, and register of the original message. Routinization is most effectively and efficiently achieved when practice and repetition occur in a context that clearly approximates real conditions and challenges learners to integrate skills through the development of whole schemata.

4.5. Configuration of SHIP in Space/Time

Perhaps the best way to visualize SHIP is to imagine a globe (see Figure 10). An earth-like (globe) model captures the non-linear essence of SHIP, allows for a close inspection of the various dimensions necessary for human information processing, and illustrates the simultaneous and recursive nature of these planes.

Within the globe are strata-like cognitive dimensions analogous to the earth's crust: the magma, mantle, and core (see Figure 11, above). Additionally, the model contains a second level of stratification. Similar to the earth's atmosphere, cognitive dimensions surround the globe. Stratification of the cognitive dimensions does not imply ordering or linearity.

The analogy of the earth and its relationship to the atmosphere illustrates another aspect of SHIP: its recursive nature. The recursiveness of SHIP may best be understood by considering the movement of the earth and its atmosphere. The earth rotates in a clockwise manner while its atmosphere has the potential to rotate in a counter-clockwise direction. Consequently, the entire area of the earth's surface and every molecule of the atmosphere, theoretically, can interact with the surface of the globe. SHIP is assumed to operate in much the same way. An examination of Figure 12 reveals its multilevel interaction; every plane or dimension affects every other plane or level in the model.

The ability to rotate each layer of the model allows us to take into account both conscious and unconscious processes and the almost limitless memory which contains every piece of recalled and stored knowledge that simultaneously affects operational skills (procedural knowledge). Figure 11, a cross-section of the model, is similar to cross-sections of the earth's interior. Examination of an inner portion of the model facilitates a better understanding of how this proposed model functions.

4.6. Recursive Features of SHIP

Now that the individual components of SHIP have been more thoroughly described, the recursive nature of the model should be emphasized. Assume that Figure 14, below, is a three-dimensional object. Stimulus X_1 enters the processing channel, and all components of the model influence it as it progresses to the apex and exits. However, if there is interference at any point during the processing of the stimulus, it can return for further processing before exiting as a finished product, X_3. Even if X_2 exits and the social or environmental cues (e.g., a gasp or a quizzical look) indicate to the interpreter that an inappropriate response has been made, the stimulus can reenter the model for further processing until it exits as X_3. In other words, both internal thought and external environmental cues may activate the recursive feature of the model, and also demonstrates how the model is interactive between the language and the environment.

At any level of SHIP, there is the potential for breakdown. At the environmental level, for example, a new stimulus may appear, rendering the individual unable to perceive and categorize it properly. The person's inability to comprehend this unique stimulus would make abstraction impossible at the higher-order cognitive level.

Let us continue with the analogy of the stimulus entering an inputting channel to be comprehended. In order for that stimulus to culminate in a response, it must follow a similar path, interacting with all of the components. Again, all of the components and the numerous functions that are performed within them happen simultaneously and recursively. In addition, each and every component has the ability to influence the others.

4.7. Simultaneous Functioning

SHIP assumes that all levels and components of the model (discussed below) function simultaneously. "Simultaneously" is used here with the understanding that there is a time lag between the perception of an external stimulus and a response. For example, time passes between the perception of the fingers being on a hot surface and the initiation of motor activity to withdraw them from contact. According to the model, the stimulus is undergoing simultaneous processing in several memory modules to produce the resultant response. "Time lag" here encompasses the time required for information processing or the time between perception and response.

Like the PDP model, SHIP assumes that the time between activation and the attainment of a ready state is no longer than one-half second. It is commonly assumed that time is related to order in a linear fashion (chronology), but this is a misconception. Logically, it takes longer to process a longer utterance. Even if fifty modules are working at the same time, some relation to the linear nature of the input and output is inescapable. However, the time lag is related to complexity rather than to length of the utterance and is not, as has been long assumed, a classic linear relationship between length of utterance and time. The occurrence of these intervals of time, then, is not inconsistent with SHIP's non-linear assumption.

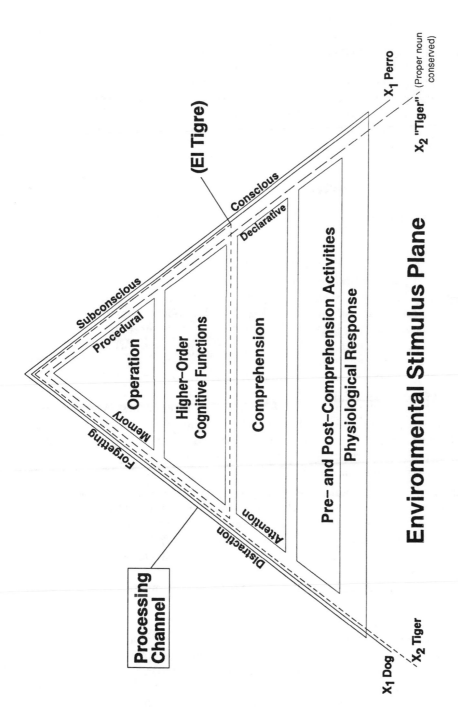

Figure 14. Recursive nature of SHIP.

It SHIP is accepted as a global explanation of how the mind works in relation to interpreting, and how it handles a multitude of tasks simultaneously, then true insight into the cognitive complexity of human beings can be gained. Imagine that all the components and aspects of SHIP were a model of what is happening in each and every schema module, and not just as a whole-brain function. Understanding this new level of complexity reinforces understanding of the vast capabilities of the mind. It also can help an interpreter to fathom the enormous undertaking of one of the most complex cognitive tasks known: the accurate transference of meaning from one language to another.

4.8. Application of SHIP

This section follows a linguistic stimulus as it moves through the various components of SHIP. Figure 15 illustrates the movement of a phrase *Es un burro* (literally, He's a donkey) through SHIP. In the **physiological component**, the interpreter hears and begins to phonologically process the sound waves, while at the same time screening out background noise and other irrelevant stimuli. At the **perceptual** level the interpreter begins deciphering this yet uncomprehended message and predicting that the stimulus has more to do with an idiomatic expression about common sense rather than an animal. At the **sociolinguistic competence** level, the perception is confirmed when the interpreter realizes that the topic of the conversation focuses on the defendant's character. The interpreter also processes the speaker's style of language to determine that *dummy* makes sense in that context. The interpreter also, based on the same evidence, rejects a higher register equivalent such as *dolt,* and a lower register, more vulgar, choice, *jackass.* In the course of the testimony the witness (a farmworker) is answering a question about the character of the defendant. Having listened to the tone of the question and the responses of the witness, the interpreter observes that the witness speaks very informally. Thus, the interpreter comprehends the message and makes a more refined prediction about meaning.

In the **higher-order cognitive skills** component, several important interpreting processes are unconsciously operating: abstraction, conservation, and other pre-operation activities. The interpreter **abstracts** the essential meaning of the message into the **highest indivisible pictorial (image) or semantic (word) representation.** In the example, the interpreter engages the consonant and vowel string of letters that represents the phrase *dummy* and the image of a donkey. This means the interpreter has used available situational cues to choose among potential meanings, while at the same time rejecting other possible meanings such as the *burro,* a Mexican dish made with a tortilla.

When comprehension is achieved, the interpreter also conserves the form and intent of the message. As the stimulus progresses through the **conservation** facet of the higher-order cognitive skill component, the interpreter focuses on retaining not only the semantic meaning of the entire utterance, but also the style and language level or register of the speaker. Krashen (1982) believes that conscious knowledge of [grammatical] rules are used for a "monitoring" function. Conservation, as practiced by court interpreters, requires familiarity with grammatical rules so that the TL message may be "matched," and edited if necessary, against the SL message. If the interpreter possesses such knowledge then he or she is free to focus on preserving the fidelity of the message between the SL and TL. In our example, the interpreter grasps

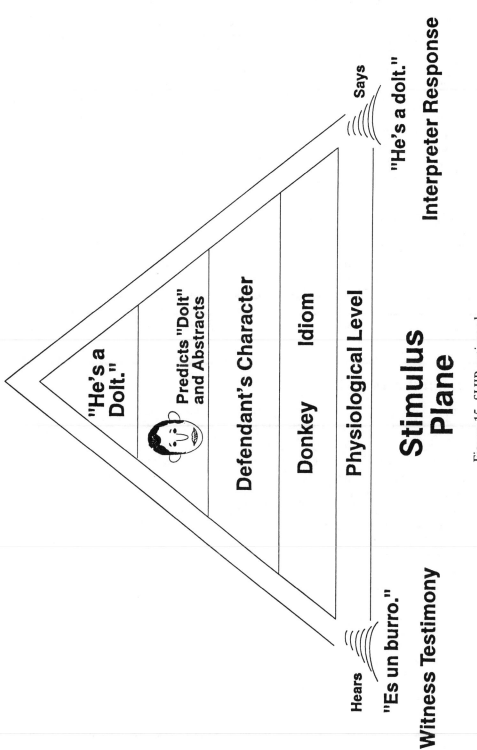

Figure 15. SHIP activated.

that the phrase to be interpreted is an idiomatic expression alluding to the defendant's lack of common sense or intelligence. The interpreter chooses the appropriate meaning—*dummy*.

In this pre-operation activities component, the message is being prepared by the interpreter to conserve the message, with all of its attendant grammatical structures, for the ultimate operation of conversion from the SL to the TL. At this point the interpreter, in response to the environmental cues of the courtroom, unconsciously retrieves from memory all of the pertinent vocabulary schemata, procedural knowledge, and interpreting processes that are needed to render an efficient interpretation. These pre-operation activities, depicted in Figure 15, are central to accomplishing the highest-order cognitive task of **converting** one language into another. *Es un burro* is converted into English in its **legal equivalent** form as *he's a dummy*, conserving the tone, style, intent, and register of the speaker.

The interpreting competency criteria set forth in this chapter are also very good objective measures of interpreter accuracy and skill level. The individual skills and strategies that help the interpreter produce a **legal equivalent** in the TL are the subject of other chapters in this book (see Chapters 2 and 5). Finally, in the application of SHIP to court interpreting, it is important to consider that throughout the process distortions such as forgetting, distractions, and the emotional affect of the interpreter's experience can bring about changes in meaning, comprehension, delay, and hesitation. If a competent, trained court interpreter's performance is affected by these phenomena, clearly an untrained, albeit highly proficient bilingual, would find it virtually impossible to produce a legal equivalent.

4.9. Limitations of SHIP

The most serious limitation of SHIP is that there is, as yet, no direct research verifying or challenging its validity. However, a plethora of anecdotal evidence and indirect research point to the cogency of SHIP. Of course, the model's primary assumption of unconscious processing necessarily forces speculation about the possibility of designing research to determine which processes are really at work. How can an unconscious process, which by definition is not accessible to awareness, ever be measured? For cognitive and linguistic researchers, SHIP poses the challenge of creating new ways of measuring seemingly untestable theories in order to verify or discredit their appropriateness. Fortunately, the field of interpretation contains a rich source of data and experimental subjects for interested scholars from a variety of disciplines to study how higher-order cognitive functions such as language, thought, action, and interpretation take place in the mind.

Chapter 26

Simultaneous Interpretation

This chapter will focus primarily on the simultaneous mode of interpreting as it is applied in the judicial setting, although research involving conference interpreters will be cited. The chapter will begin with a definition of simultaneous interpretation (SI), followed by a detailed description of the circumstances under which SI is employed by court interpreters, with specific emphasis on the rigorous demands of interpreting proceedings for criminal defendants. Next, the process of SI will be explicated in terms of the individual skills involved, and the research that has been conducted on SI will be discussed as it relates to court interpreting. Finally, training issues in SI are discussed, and exercises to improve interpreting skills are suggested.

1. Definition

Simultaneous interpretation refers to the technique whereby the interpreter speaks at the same time as the SL speaker. Historically, interpreting was performed consecutively with the interpreter waiting until the speaker had finished his or her utterance so that only one person would be talking at a time. After World War II, technological developments and the faster pace of life made SI both possible and necessary: the development of electronic equipment enabled one audience to hear an original speaker while another audience listened to the interpretation on a closed-circuit system. As cooperation among the international community increased, efficient communication became a priority. Although conference interpreters now enjoy great prestige for their artful mastery of SI at meetings sponsored by organizations such as the United Nations, the technique was originally introduced by court interpreters during the Nuremburg trials conducted after World War II (Ramler, 1988).

SI is widely recognized as a very difficult, complex mental task. Van Dam (1986) describes it as follows:

> [W]hile a speaker is delivering (orally) a message in a source language, the simultaneous interpreter transmits that message in a target language. . . . Unlike the translator, however, the interpreter does not have time to consult dictionaries or other sources: an acceptable solution must be found immediately; for the speaker, unaware that he may be creating problems for the interpreter, continues speaking. And thus the interpreter must continue interpreting. The interpreter listens for the message of the source language. While he concentrates on understanding the source language message, he conveys the message of the preceding passage in the target language. And while he concentrates on conveying the message stylistically and grammatically, he continues to listen for the next message of the source language. (pp. 443-44)

The term "simultaneous" implies that the interpreter is uttering the same message at the same time as the SL speaker, but the word is misleading. In fact, though the interpreter is speaking at the same time as the source, he is lagging behind the speaker at least one unit of thought as he interprets; he is hearing one idea while stating another. This time lag is known as *decalage* among interpreting experts. The length of the delay between the delivery of the SL message and that of the TL message depends on a number of variables, as will be explained in Section 4 later in this chapter. Regardless of the degree of *decalage,* interpreters must concentrate very intensely on both the SL message and their TL output. This concentration requirement places a great deal of pressure on interpreters.

Another source of pressure on the interpreter is the fact that he must produce the TL message just as quickly as the SL speaker, without the benefit of knowing what is to be said. Thus, he must keep up a steady pace while maintaining accuracy at all times. The stress inherent in this highly demanding and complex operation has been commented upon many times, most specifically in Parsons (1978), as well as others (Gerver, 1976; Moser, 1978; Moser-Mercer, 1985; Seleskovitch, 1978a).

2. Simultaneous in the Courtroom

Many people are familiar with the conference interpreters at the United Nations, who sit high above the General Assembly at the back of the hall in their booths, listening to the speeches through headphones and speaking into microphones wired to the delegates' earphones. The SI practiced by conference interpreters differs from the SI used by court interpreters, for while the conference interpreter has license to improve the SL message stylistically when converting it to the TL, the court interpreter cannot take such liberties. The conference interpreter, for example, may omit redundancies or pare down verbosity, but the court interpreter must retain every element of meaning, regardless of whether it is stylistically or grammatically correct, logical, or beneficial to the SL speaker's case (see the discussion of the terms "conservation" and "legal equivalence" in Chapter 1.)

Because in many jurisdictions non-English-speaking defendants are deemed to have a constitutional right to an interpreter any time they appear in court for any type of proceeding, SI is often used for jury selection, motions and objections by counsel, rulings by the court on such motions and objections, side-bar conferences between the attorneys and the judge, arguments before the jury, and jury instructions (for a more detailed discussion of this issue, refer to Unit 3).

SI is performed primarily from English to other languages, rather than vice versa. Occasionally SI will be used in proceedings where the interpreting goes in both directions. With the consent of the court, for example, it may be used to render testimony by witnesses, or statements by the defendant from counsel table. For more information on the use of SI in the courtroom see Unit 3, Chapter 13.

3. Process of Simultaneous Interpretation

Gerver (1976) notes the paucity of research that has been conducted on SI, and describes the complexity of the process from the standpoint of cognitive psychology:

[T]he task is extremely complex: though simultaneous listening and speaking rarely occurs in everyday verbal behavior, simultaneous interpreters manage not only to listen and speak simultaneously for reasonable lengths of time, but also to carry out complex transformations on the source-language message while uttering their translation in the target language. From the point of view of cognitive psychologists the task is a complex form of human information processing involving the perception, storage, retrieval, transformation, and transmission of verbal information. Furthermore, linguistic, motivational, situational, and a host of other factors cannot be ignored. (pp. 166-67)

Drawing on the models of interpreting and human information processing presented in Chapter 25 of this unit, the simultaneous interpreting task can be summed up as follows: The SL input is perceived and triggers a physiological response.

Once the stimulus, the SL message, is perceived, all of the operations of SHIP begin functioning at the same time. All of the relevant, appropriate information modules associated with the stimulus are excited, and the irrelevant, inappropriate modules are inhibited. Both conscious and unconscious operations are involved in this process (as in the example of *glace* cited in Chapter 24 of this unit, the interpreter is aware of selecting among certain alternatives, and is completely unaware of rejecting other alternatives that are totally inappropriate to the present situation). The more routinized the process and the more the interpreter has practiced SI, the more unconscious and automatic the process. Because the SHIP operations are recursive and interactive, the message continuously circulates through all the components as the interpreter, consciously or unconsciously, draws on schemata developed as a result of prior linguistic, cultural, and social experiences, as well as familiarity with the immediate context and setting. The end result is comprehension, the abstraction of the SL message into a lingual form.

As explained in the description of SHIP, the schema for the SL message includes all of the languages in which the interpreter has had the experience. The operation is non-linear; the interpreter does not first grasp the meaning of the SL message and retrieve the TL equivalent elsewhere in the brain; the TL equivalent is automatically called up with the schema. The preparation of the TL version, then, occurs simultaneously with the comprehension of the SL message.

Once interpreters have formulated the proposed TL version of the message, they compare it with the original version of the SL message retained intact in memory. At this point interpreters decide whether the two versions are identical in meaning, and if so, they proceed to utter the TL version, adding the pauses, self-corrections, and other paralinguistic elements from the SL message.

This complex process takes mere seconds to complete. In SI, of course, the speaker does not stop and wait for the interpreter, but moves on immediately to the next idea he or she wishes to express. Moser (1978) cites research showing that interpreters performing SI are both listening and speaking 60 to 75 percent of the time. Thus, the interpreter is not only engaging in the extremely complicated linguistic operations to process the speaker's first statement ((a) in Figure 1) and convert it to the TL but also attending to the speaker's next utterance (b) and processing it for comprehension, while simultaneously uttering the TL version (a'). Figure 1 is a graphic depiction of the SI process devised by van Hoof (1962). In this figure, the horizontal lines represent the passage of time, the top line being the SL message and the bottom line the TL

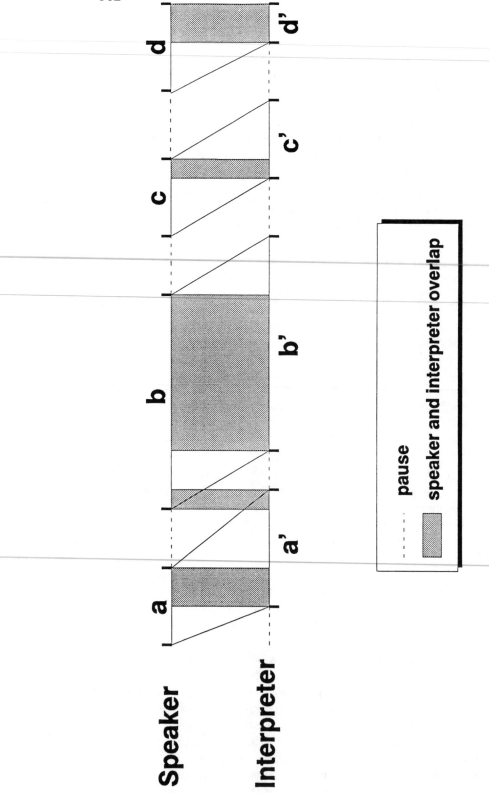

Figure 1. Van Hoof's (1962) depiction of simultaneous interpretation: Graphic depiction of time lag between SL and TL utterances.

message. The diagonal lines connecting the top and bottom lines delineate the units of meaning (a,b,c, etc., in the SL, and a',b',c', etc., in the TL), and the shaded portions represent overlapping speech (where no shading appears, only one person is speaking at a time). The dotted lines indicate pauses.

If the two versions are not identical at the end of SHIP, the interpreter must repeat these cognitive operations until satisfied that the SL and TL versions match. This accounts for the false starts and delays that occasionally occur in SI. If the interpreter begins processing the SL message before receiving enough contextual information, the interpreter may misunderstand the meaning (call up the wrong schema). Then the interpreter must waste time backtracking to begin again, falling further and further behind the speaker. The experienced interpreter is able to lag behind the speaker just enough to obtain sufficient information for accurate processing without falling so far behind that retaining the SL message in memory is impossible.

The more efficiently the interpreter is able to process the information, that is, the less time spent searching for equivalents, making false starts with insufficient information or unsatisfactory solutions, the more capacity the interpreter has available for attending new SL input and generating the appropriate TL version. Inexperienced interpreters who have not yet routinized the act of SI, or interpreters who have deficiencies in their linguistic knowledge, must devote more conscious effort to processing the SL message and formulating the TL version.

4. Strategies of SI

Experienced interpreters employ certain strategies to make efficient use of their processing capacity. A number of conference interpreters and researchers, whose findings will be presented here, have identified these strategies and elucidated them for the benefit of student interpreters.

4.1. Analysis

Foremost among these strategies is analysis, so essential to SI that it can be considered an intrinsic part of the process rather than an ancillary tactic; yet many novices fail to include this fundamental element in their attempts to render an SI of a message. They focus on finding word-for-word equivalents rather than penetrating the message to find the underlying meaning. The end result is the false starts and backtracking described above, or worse yet, an unknowing misinterpretation that is never corrected. As Le Ny (1978) points out, "the good simultaneous interpreter seems to be one who directly transforms the *organization* [emphasis in original] of information, simultaneously with comprehension" (p. 294). Seleskovitch (1978a) likens an interpreter performing SI to a sportscaster giving a running commentary on a soccer game: the sportscaster must analyze what is going on and convey it rapidly to the listeners, who cannot see the action. Like the interpreter, the sports announcer converts concepts from one medium to another, in this case from action to words. Although the court interpreter does not just provide a narrative to the defendant, but rather interprets every single unit of meaning that is uttered in the courtroom, the analogy is valuable in that it emphasizes the key role played by analysis in the interpreting process.

Lederer (1978), in her discussion of units of meaning, emphasizes that until the speaker has completed a thought, the interpreter is unable to process the words for comprehension. Only after "synthesizing" the meaning of a string of words can the interpreter associate them with previous cognitive experiences or recollections, leading to a "merging into sense" (p. 330). However, Lederer stresses that "Units of meaning are not a grammatical segmentation of language into syntactic units" (p. 330). This notion explains why sometimes it takes more words to express the same idea in one language than in another. Units of meaning have little to do with words per se; they are abstract ideas into which the interpreter reduces the SL message. As interpreters gain experience, they become more adept at analyzing the SL message and recognizing units of meaning.

Gerver (1976) reports on his own and others' research to demonstrate that interpreters use certain elements of the SL message to aid them in their analysis. One hypothesis tested was that "source-language pauses might delineate units of meaning for the interpreter, and thus assist with the segmentation of the almost continuous stream of source-language input." His conclusion is that "Source-language pauses do assist simultaneous interpreters in segmenting, decoding, and encoding of source-language messages" (pp. 179-80). Giles (1985) speaks of this analysis and output conflict as a balance.

4.2. Prediction

Another strategy identified by both Lederer (1978) and Moser (1978) is prediction, also known as syntactic anticipation. Prediction is a phenomenon that has also been described by researchers in connection with schemata (Rumelhart & Ortony, 1977) and foreign language comprehension (Abbott et al., 1981), and particularly with regard to reading comprehension in any language (Goodman, 1982). In the specific context of interpreting, prediction refers to the interpreter's ability to grasp the intent of a message before all of the words that comprise it have been uttered. Predictions are "guesstimates," or informed speculations about what is to occur, based on knowledge of the world, of the language and culture, and of the subject matter. The efficiency of information processing increases as a function of the interpreter's ability to predict the outcome of partially stated messages. Moser (1978) explains how this is possible:

> The question remains how the interpreter "knows" what will come in. The phenomenon must clearly be explained from the nature of the organization of semantic information in an interpreter. Extensive exposure to a particular language, or two or more languages, relevant syntactic knowledge, contextual knowledge (knowledge of the subject matter under discussion in a conference, as well as knowledge of the ongoing discussion in a conference) appear to be the prime candidates responsible for prediction. Within the context of this model I propose that predictability is a function of how fast and how many conceptual relations can be activated. To put it bluntly, the more the interpreter knows, the more he can predict, and the better his knowledge is of anything (i.e., the more relations have been established between concepts to form conceptual clusters or ideas), the faster he can predict. (pp. 359-60)

Similarly, Le Ny (1978) notes that the less new information is contained in the message, the less time it takes the interpreter to process it:

[T]he determining factor is not so much the formal rate of the speech, the loquaciousness of the speaker, but rather the rate at which *new* [emphasis in original] semantic information arrives, formal rate merely being an annoyance factor. The professional training of the interpreter undoubtedly helps greatly to progressively reduce the extent of this rate by decreasing the novelty of that which is heard. (p. 297)

The implications for training interpreters are clear. Because predicting relies on the interpreter's knowledge of the SL culture and language, including the typical syntactical and rhetorical arrangements and styles of sentences, paragraphs, and larger pieces of discourse, instructors and individuals wishing to improve their SI skills should use texts that represent major syntactical and rhetorical styles in their working languages. For example, understanding that English has basic expository patterns that include comparison, contrast, exemplification, generalization, description, analysis, classification, and formal argumentation will help the learner conduct the analysis necessary for the performance of SI. Familiarity with these patterns will increase the interpreter's ability to predict the outcome of oral messages.

Karmiloff-Smith (1978) draws on cognitive psychologists' research into schema and frameworks in her schematic representation of the interpreter's understanding process. She posits that:

The interpreter, while listening to a speaker, is constantly updating his mini-theory of the speaker's semantic intentions. Each speech act is not only the communication of new information, but the intricate interplay of new information and presuppositions based on the knowledge accumulated from the present discourse and on general extralinguistic knowledge. Thus, the content of each message unit enables the interpreter to form a temporary "knowledge framework" for the particular subject under discussion and to filter each new message through that framework. (p. 379)

Lederer (1978) identifies two types of prediction: (1) "language prediction," which is based on the interpreter's knowledge of the syntax and style of the SL and the TL, including word affinities, and (2) "sense expectation," which is based on the interpreter's familiarity with the speaker and the speaker's objectives, as well as the general situational context. The "sense expectation" aspect is highly dependent on the interpreter's general understanding and knowledge of the subject area. If the interpreter is well read and has a broad general knowledge—usually the kind of knowledge base engendered by formal education—the interpreter's prediction of the outcome of sentences and larger pieces of discourse will be more reliable, and simultaneous interpretation will be smoother, more efficient, and more accurate.

The court interpreter's familiarity with the languages involved, the subject matter of the testimony or argument, and the speaker's patterns of discourse contributes to the interpreter's ability to analyze the message and draw conclusions about its likely outcome. Of course, this strategy should be employed with great care, given the court interpreter's obligation to conserve all elements of the SL message with the utmost precision. However, the experienced interpreter can safely predict the noun that will follow the adjectives in this example: "Ladies and gentlemen of the jury, this is the most heinous, atrocious, grisly, and barbarous of all the crimes I have ever prosecuted." Knowledge of word affinity in English enables the interpreter to understand that the terms "heinous" and "grisly" are almost always accompanied by the word "crime."

Indeed, often the interpreter is forced to engage in prediction because of the syntactical demands of the TL; nouns must precede adjectives in Spanish, for example, and the verb usually comes at the end of the sentence in German.

4.3. Numerical Information

In connection with prediction, Moser-Mercer (1985) points out that numbers pose a particular problem to interpreters:

> From a language information processing point of view, the processing of numbers differs from that of continuous text in that numbers are largely unpredictable, i.e., one has to devote full attention to the incoming message, whereas...continuous text allows and even requires hypothesizing on the input. Thus, when numbers appear in a continuous text, the interpreter has to switch his processing procedures. (p. 97)

Numbers are of particular import to court interpreters, who must accurately convey penal code sections, serial numbers, court appearance dates, amounts of fines, years in prison, and other numerical information. When the text contains many facts and figures, interpreters tend to allow less *decalage* between the SL and TL messages. Many conference interpreters write down all the numbers that they encounter in SI, but for the court interpreter, who is often standing next to the defendant, such a strategy is not practical. One strategy is for court interpreters to become familiar with the most frequently mentioned penal code sections and the prevailing fines and sentences for common offenses, so that these figures will pose less of a problem to them.

4.4. Decalage

As mentioned earlier, one of the most important strategies employed by interpreters performing SI is to lag behind the speaker to a greater or lesser extent in order to gather sufficient information to comprehend the SL message and begin formulating the TL message. Indeed, like analysis, this lagging behind, or *decalage*, is an integral aspect of the SI process. Wilss (1978) points out that the amount of lag time depends on a number of objective factors (the nature of the SL text and the relations of equivalence between the SL and the TL) and subjective factors (the interpreter's knowledge and familiarity with the situation and speaker, fatigue, and simply individual preference). He also notes that "syntactic anticipation" (prediction) plays a key role in determining the amount of *decalage*. Wilss focuses on German-English SI which, because of the nature of German syntax, relies heavily on *decalage* and prediction. He states that the interpreter must "postpone the interpreting act" (i.e., lag behind the speaker) until hearing the verb, which comes at the end of the German sentence. This places a heavy burden on the interpreter's memory, and there is a danger that part of the message will decay in memory before she is able to formulate the corresponding TL message.

Interpreters must obviously increase their concentration ability and retention capacity to be able to retain large amounts of information, but they also have other tactics available to them. One such tactic is to reorganize the clauses in the message so that the partial information can be converted to the TL while the interpreter waits for more critical SL information. For example, if the speaker says, "I ask you, Ladies and Gentlemen of the jury, on this extremely important issue, to use your common sense," the interpreter translating into Spanish does not know whether to choose *pedir* or *preguntar* as the appropriate equivalent for "ask" until hearing the rest of sentence: "to use your common sense." When rendering the message in Spanish, therefore, the interpreter begins with *Damas y Caballeros del jurado, en este asunto tan importante,* before inserting the verb. Sometimes the interpreter may fall into the habit of using "neutral" or "non-committal" phrases to stall for time while waiting for the speaker to provide the needed information. Thus, when the speaker begins by saying, "Was there ever actually any participation on the part of my client in this case? I submit to you that there was not," the interpreter may begin with a neutral phrase in Spanish, *Hay que preguntarse si es que en realidad* (literally, "one must ask oneself whether in reality") before interpreting the rest of the sentence, *mi cliente tomó alguna parte en este caso, y yo les sugiero que no.* While this technique may be acceptable in conference interpreting, the court interpreter must be very cautious about inserting such phrases in order to avoid adding to the message or altering the register.

4.5. Queuing

Gerver (1976) focuses on the techniques employed by interpreters for coping with excessive speed of delivery of the SL message. He notes that 100 to 120 words per minute is a comfortable rate for interpretation, and that any deviation from that norm—either faster or slower—causes stress for the interpreter. Gerver identifies a number of strategies used by conference interpreters, but the only one that is appropriate for court interpreters is what is known as **queuing**. This term refers to the technique of lagging behind in the processing of information during heavy load periods (messages densely packed with information and delivered at a rapid speed) and catching up during periods when the rate of delivery is slower and the content of the message is not as dense. Gerver discusses the hypothesis that interpreters take advantage of pauses in the speaker's delivery to catch up, thus compensating for the so-called heavy load periods. He points out the limitations of this notion, citing evidence that the pauses are not nearly long or frequent enough to be useful to the interpreter. However, Richards (1983, p. 255) asserts that 30–50 percent of speaking time consists of pauses and hesitation, and the idea that interpreters may be able to utilize this time to their advantage bears further investigation.

4.6. Self-Monitoring

Finally, another strategy noted by several researchers is self-monitoring. From the standpoint of conservation of meaning, it can be said that the SL message must "run a gauntlet," with each phase of human information processing being a potential obstacle to understanding. After the interpreter has correctly comprehended the SL message and formulated an accurate TL equivalent message, one more hurdle remains: the delivery of that message. As indicated earlier, the interpreter is listening to one SL message while uttering her TL version of a previously stated SL message. If she does not also listen to her own speech, there is a great potential for "slip-of-the-tongue" errors, particularly as a result of interference from the incoming SL message.

Moser (1978) notes that the interpreter's processing of her own output should be "a function of the amount of capacity already taken up by the first (primarily attended) message" (p. 361). In other words, if interpreters have had difficulty processing the SL message, they will have little capacity available to monitor their own output, and they may mispronounce words, stumble over their delivery, or mistakenly use the wrong word (especially if a word they intend to use is very similar to one in the SL message they are attending). If interpreters hear themselves commit the error, they will correct it, but this, in turn, detracts from their capacity to process the SL input. When observing conference interpreters, Moser found that some errors in interpreter output were simply unnoticed and never corrected.

Gerver (1976) discusses the research that has been done on interpreter self-monitoring, and describes it as a testing process. Interpreters have stored the SL message for comparison with their proposed TL output, and when they are ready to utter the TL version, they run one final test, or match, to be sure their version is correct. Even after they have begun uttering the TL message, the testing process continues. If they are not satisfied, they may interrupt themselves and "loop through the routine again," or they may decide that "too much input will be lost if they attempt to correct their recent output or that the error is not critical" (p. 199). Gerver concludes that:

> Whether or not and to what extent testing and correction take place depend on the interpreter's criteria for adequate performance. When there is time, and when a high value is placed on accuracy, the criteria will be relatively high, but under stress, or when an interpreter does not value accuracy so highly (as is perhaps the case with minor slips), the criteria will be lower. (pp. 199-200)

In court interpreting, of course, the standard of accuracy is extremely high, and interpreter self-monitoring and self-correction are very important tasks. As Gerver indicates, "monitoring and possible revision and correction are an integral part of the process of simultaneous interpretation" (p. 202).

4.7. Graphic Depiction of SI Strategies

To show more clearly how the aforementioned SI strategies are implemented by interpreters, the diagrams developed by van Hoof (1962) are particularly useful. Illustrated here are examples of interpreting problems and their practical solutions. The horizontal lines represent the passage of time (from left to right), with each segment depicting a unit of meaning. The top line is the SL speaker and the bottom line is the interpreter's TL version. The shaded portions indicate times when the speaker and the interpreter are talking at the same time, and the dotted lines indicate pauses.

(1) Normal

<pre>
                              a
Speaker: /LADIES AND GENTLEMEN OF THE JURY, /WHAT WE
Interpreter: Damas y
         b   c
INTEND TO SHOW HERE / IS THAT OUR CLIENT IS NOT
     a'   b'
 Caballeros del Jurado, / lo que pensamos
</pre>

d
GUILTY / OF THESE MURDER CHARGES. /
                                      c'
demostrar aquí / es que nuestro cliente
                              d'
no es culpable / de estos cargos de asesinato.

Figure 2 and example (1) show how the interpreter waits until hearing a meaningful unit (a) from the SL speaker, and then begins interpreting it (a'). As the interpreter is uttering the TL version of (a), the speaker is going on to state (b), so the interpreter is uttering (a') while listening to (b). Then the interpreter goes on to interpret (b) while the speaker proceeds to idea (c). The interpreter utters (b') while processing (c), and so on.

(2) Units of Meaning: Variations in Length of Utterance
                                          a
Speaker: THE DEFENDANT WAS ARRAIGNED ON KIDNAPPING
                              b
CHARGES/ THREE MONTHS AGO,/ BUT IT WAS NOT
                                                    b'
Interpreter: *Hace tres meses/*
                  c
UNTIL THE DAY BEFORE YESTERDAY/ THAT HE SAW
                  a'
que al acusado le informaron de los cargos
                              d
HIS ATTORNEY FOR THE FIRST TIME.
                  c'
de secuestro,/ pero fue hasta anteayer/ que
                        d'
vio a su abogado por primera vez.

Figure 3 and example (2) show what happens when the number of words in a given unit of meaning varies from the SL to the TL. The interpreter may take less time to state the TL version than the original speaker did, or may require more time. The decalage between the interpreter and the speaker will fluctuate throughout the interpreting event.

(3) Prediction
                                          a
Speaker: THE COMMUNITY DEVELOPMENT AGENCIES / HAVE
                  Interpreter: *Las*
                              b
PLAYED AN UNEXPECTEDLY IMPORTANT—INDEED, I
                  a'
Agencias de Desarrollo Comunitario/ han
WOULD EVEN SAY CRUCIAL—ROLE / IN HELPING
                        b'
desempeñado un papel de inesperada importancia

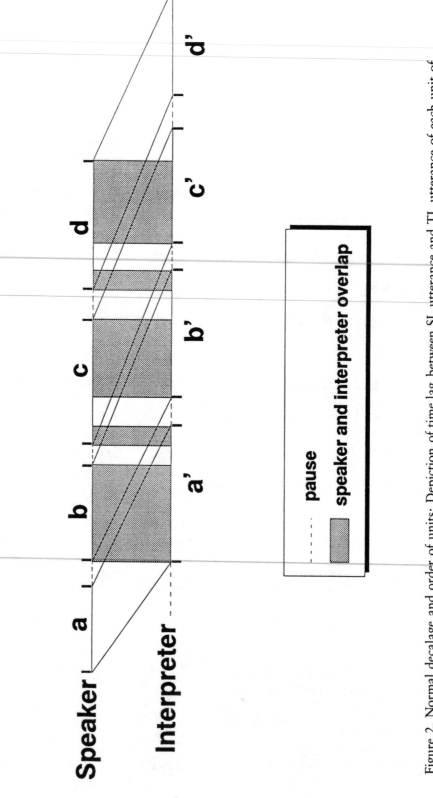

Figure 2. Normal decalage and order of units: Depiction of time lag between SL utterance and TL utterance of each unit of thought (van Hoof, 1962).

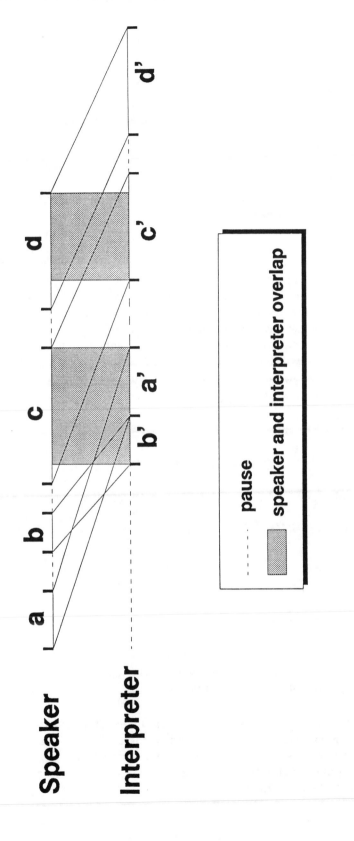

Figure 3. Fluctuating decalage: Illustration of variations in lag between speaker and interpreter, as dictated by length of TL utterance (van Hoof, 1962).

c   d

FORMER PRISON INMATES/ BECOME REINTEGRATED INTO SOCIETY.

b'

—efectivamente, de vital importancia, diría

c'   d'

yo—/al contribuir a que los ex-presos/ se reintegren a la sociedad.

Figure 4 and example (3) show that on occasion the interpreter must actually anticipate the speaker, stating part of the message before the speaker has actually said it. Here the interpreter begins to say the word *papel* seconds before the speaker says "role"; the interpreter was able to predict that the word "role" was coming, based on knowledge of the context and of word affinity in English. Having waited until the word "role" was uttered, the interpreter might have fallen too far behind to keep up with the speaker. As noted in the discussion of prediction earlier in this chapter, sometimes interpreters will make the decision to anticipate based on their knowledge of and experience with word affinities in the SL, while at other times this decision will be based on their familiarity with the context, the subject matter, and the speakers' styles. It should be pointed out that though prediction is a natural and unavoidable aspect of human communication, it entails certain risks when used as an interpreting technique. The more experienced and linguistically competent interpreters are, the less likely it is that they will jump to the wrong conclusion about what the speaker is saying. Clearly, though, this technique entails some risks, and should be used only when it is absolutely unavoidable.

(4) Split Units of Meaning

a   b

Speaker: *EL INGENIERO SANCHEZ,/ PRESIDENTE DE LA*

a'

Interpreter: Mr. Sanchez,/ the

c

COMPAÑIA,/ INFORMO AL PERSONAL/ QUE SERIA

b'   a'

president of the company,/ who is an engineer,/

d

NECESARIO DESOCUPAR A 50 DE ELLOS.

c'   d'

informed the staff/ that 50 of them would have to be laid off.

Sometimes, a unit of meaning must be distributed differently in the TL version than it was in the SL version, as shown in Figure 5. Interpreters will render as much as they can of a given unit of meaning in one utterance, and will have to fill in the rest of it later on.

Lederer (1978) reports on the results of a study she conducted at Paris University, in which she compared recorded speeches and their interpretation to determine exactly what the interpreter was hearing while speaking. Looking at the interpreting task this way provides some insight into the mental processes of the interpreter. Here is an excerpt from the Lederer study:

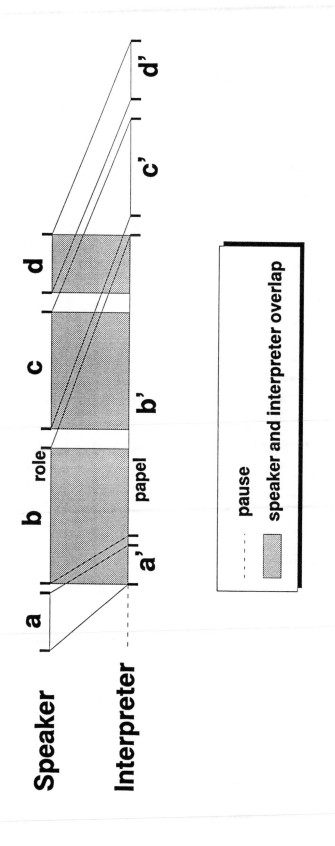

Figure 4. Prediction: The interpreter anticipates the word "role" (van Hoof, 1962).

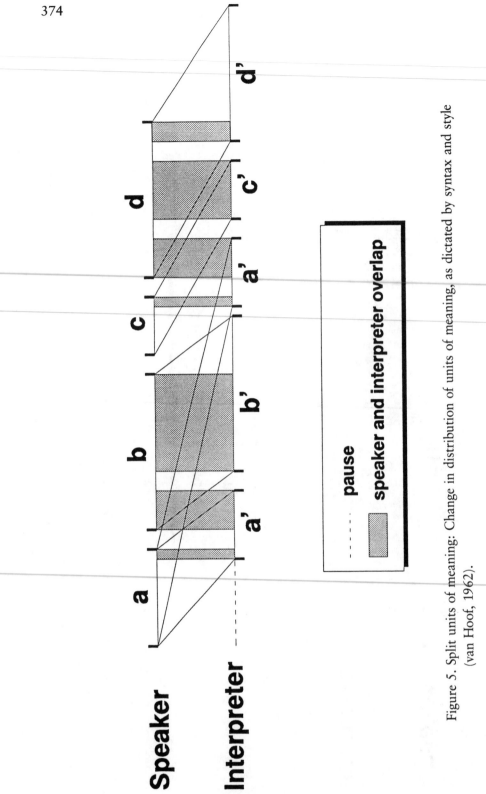

Figure 5. Split units of meaning: Change in distribution of units of meaning, as dictated by syntax and style (van Hoof, 1962).

APART FROM CERTAIN NECESSARY DEFENSIVE
Je crois que   le problème   est   extrêmement
WORK FROM SUCROSE   MANUFACTURERS
important.   A part certains travaux
AND   SUCROSE   USERS
nécessairement   défensifs
THERE   IS   A   REAL   NEED TO   IDENTIFY
de la part des fabricants et des industries utilisatrices de saccha-
WHERE,   WITHIN   THE   NORMAL SOCIETY
rose,   il   faut préciser
SUCROSE   AND   SIMILAR SUGARS   ARE
                        le
PLAYING IMPORTANT   POSITIVE ROLES.
                        rôle positif et important du sacccharose et autres sucres
DR. KINGSBURY'S   COMMENTS
chez les bien-portants.
WITH REGARD   TO   THE SPORTSMEN
Ce que Monsieur Kings-
ARE   PERTINENT.   HE   IS   RIGHT   ALSO
bury vient de nous dire à propos des sportifs est
TO IDENTIFY   THE POSSIBILITY
extrêmement pertinent. Il a aussi
OF OTHER   NEEDS   AT   OTHER   TIMES.
raison   de   dire qu'il y a
I DON'T THINK   THE   TOPIC   IS   A   SIMPLE ONE
d'autres besoins à certains moments au plutôt chez d'autres
WHEN   IT GETS   DOWN   TO   IT   . I.....
personnes. (pp. 325-26)

When the passage begins, the interpreter is still finishing the TL rendition of the speaker's previous utterance. At one point the interpreter deems it necessary to practice the technique of "explicitation" (see Chapter 24 in this unit): for the English "users" the interpreter states *industries utilisatrices,* because French style and usage dictate that more information be included. This is another illustration of how interpreters use their knowledge of the context and the languages involved to make decisions. The prevailing criterion here is what a speaker of the SL would understand on hearing the same words.

In another part of this passage, as the speaker is saying "... where, within the normal society,... " (Lederer, 1978) the interpreter slows down and then pauses, obviously confused about what "normal society" refers to. More information is needed before that particular idea can be rendered into the TL, so the interpreter "buys time" by changing the order of the sentence, skipping over "normal society" for the time being and working on "sucrose and similar sugars are playing important positive roles" (p. 326) (note the prediction of "roles": the interpreter's familiarity with word affinity in English clued the interpreter that "role" was likely to follow "playing important positive"). Then the interpreter suddenly realizes what "normal" referred to, and becomes aware that the French cognate *normale* does not convey the same information, and thus chooses the term *chez les bien-portants* (among people who enjoy good health). The interpreter speeds up slightly at this point to catch up with the speaker. Although the interpreter strives to maintain a steady pace so that the delivery will be pleasant to listen to, occasional pauses followed by bursts of speed are unavoidable.

These examples illustrate once again the importance of focusing on units of meaning rather than words. Before a unit of meaning or thought has been completed by the speaker, the interpreter has a mere string of words that make no sense. These words are stored in the interpreter's memory until enough information has been gathered to be meaningful. Then, "the words present in short-term memory seem to pull together and merge with the recollection of knowledge acquired [earlier]..., all of a sudden making sense" (Lederer, 1978, p. 330).

English legal discourse is full of examples of very long units of meaning which force the interpreter to wait before beginning to render them into the TL. Consider this question: "Are you now, or have you ever been at any time in the past, lawfully admitted to the United States for permanent residence?" Until the speaker says "admitted," the interpreter has little to work with. A skillful interpreter can engage in some mental gymnastics, changing the order of clauses in order to begin with a non-committal adverbial clause like "now or at any time in the past" before launching into the core of the message (assuming, of course, that the TL style and grammar permit this). At all times, however, the interpreter must take care not to alter the meaning of the original message when changing the order of the clauses.

5. Implications for Training in SI

Moser (1978), Moser-Mercer (1985), and van Dam (1986) have reported on methods for training students in SI based on the considerations discussed in this chapter. The basic principle governing the application of these methods is that isolating the individual tasks that comprise a skill creates controlled conditions for better problem solving, and thereby accelerates learning. Only one new exercise is presented at a time. Students practice the exercise repeatedly until they have reached the highest possible level of performance—that is, until the task has become routinized—and then move on to the next level of exercises. Moser (1978) divides the exercises into six categories: (1) abstraction of ideas (which develops analytical and listening skills), (2) paraphrasing (to further enhance analytical abilities), (3) probabilistic prognosis (in preparation for the prediction strategy discussed in this chapter), (4) decreasing reaction time (in preparation for the task of listening and speaking at the same time), (5) dual-task training (further enhancing the ability to deal with two different messages at once, one oral and the other written), and (6) shadowing (listening and speaking at the same time, within the same language).

The exercises described by Moser (1978), Moser-Mercer (1985), and van Dam (1986) were developed for the training of conference interpreters, but they can be adapted to meet the special needs of court interpreters. Since the various modes of interpretation involve many of the same mental tasks, the exercises recommended in the sight translation and consecutive interpretation chapters will contribute to the development of SI skills as well. The exercises in the sight translation chapter that are designed to develop analytical techniques are particularly applicable to SI, as are the memory-building exercises outlined in the consecutive chapter.

The following exercises, designed specifically to build the skills involved in SI, are divided into those that emphasize dual-tasking and those that emphasize input analysis. These exercises should be done in all of the interpreter's working languages, beginning with the native, or more dominant, language. They should be practiced daily, for about a half hour at a time, as SI skills must be acquired over time to allow for maximum routinization.

5.1. Dual-Tasking Exercises

(1) Have someone record passages from magazines or newspapers on tape, or record radio or television talk shows or interview programs (news broadcasts are not suitable for these exercises, because the pace is too fast and the content is too dense). The subject matter of these passages is irrelevant, but it should not be too technical or contain too many statistics and proper names. Essays and opinion columns are good sources of texts for recording. As you play back the tape, "shadow" the speaker: repeat everything the speaker says, verbatim. Try to stay further and further behind the speaker, until you are lagging at least one unit of meaning behind.

(2) Once you feel comfortable talking and listening at the same time, and are not leaving out too much, begin performing other tasks while shadowing. First, write the numerals from 1 to 100 on a piece of paper as you are repeating what the speaker says (make sure you are writing and speaking at the same time, not just writing during pauses). When you are able to do that successfully, write the numerals in reverse order, from 100 to 1. Then write them counting by 5's, by 3's, and so on. Note what happens whenever numbers appear in the text you are shadowing.

(3) When you are able to do exercise (2) with minimal errors, begin writing out words while shadowing. Begin with your name and address, written repeatedly. Then move on to a favorite poem or a passage, such as the preamble to the United States Constitution (always choose a passage in the same language as that which you are shadowing). When writing this text, you should copy from a piece of paper placed in front of you; do not try to write the passage from memory while shadowing the tape.

(4) While shadowing the tape as in the previous exercises, write down all the numbers and proper names you hear. Then play the tape back and check to see if you wrote them correctly.

The purpose of the above exercises is to accustom your mind to working on two "channels" at once, and to force you to lag behind the speaker. If you find yourself able to perform this exercise with no problem, move on to the next one; you should be taxing your mental capacities to the fullest at all times. On the other hand, if you are having difficulty keeping up with the speaker and are barely able to mumble a few words at a time, move back to the previous exercise until you are comfortable doing it. These exercises should be repeated as many times as necessary over a long period of time.

5.2. Analysis Exercises

(1) Using the same tapes you prepared for the above exercises (or with new ones, if you have grown tired of those), rephrase what the speaker says rather than simply

repeating it (see the example of the rephrasing exercise in the sight translation chapter). Stating the same message in different words forces you to lag behind the speaker, waiting until the person has said something meaningful for you to work with. In order to change the wording of the message without altering the meaning, you must thoroughly analyze and understand the original message. This exercise also develops your vocabulary, because you are constantly searching for synonyms and alternative ways of phrasing things. It is perfectly acceptable, and even advisable, for you to look up words and phrases in a dictionary or thesaurus before attempting to rephrase the passages on the tape. It does not matter how many times you go over the tape again; even if you have memorized the passages, you are still deriving benefit from the exercise. Rephrasing simulates mental processes required in SI, in that you must abandon the original wording and put the message into a different external form, while retaining all of its meaning.

(2) To develop your ability to predict the outcome of a message based on your knowledge of the SL's syntax and style and on your common sense and experience, do the following exercises with written passages from a magazine or newspaper:

(a) Cover up the latter half of a sentence, and try to predict the ending of it. Did certain key words provide important clues?

(b) Read the title of an entire article or essay, and try to predict the content. Confirm or reject your conclusion as you read the article.

(c) Read the article, paragraph by paragraph, predicting what will come next. Again, pick out key words that contain hints about the direction in which the author is heading.

(d) Repeat exercises (a) and (b) with oral input, having someone read the passages to you.

(e) Just as you increase your awareness of key words, learn to look for pitfalls that can lead you astray, such as embedded clauses and dangling participles. Develop your ability to skip over those distractions and get to the heart of a sentence or passage.

(3) Using all the techniques you have developed in the preceding exercises, begin interpreting from the SL to the TL. At first, use the tapes you have already recorded and worked on in the other exercises. Then make new tapes specifically for interpreting practice. You may want to choose texts related to law and the courts for this purpose, but do not make them too technical at first. When you feel you are ready, record some actual court proceedings for practice. Court reporting schools are a good source of professionally recorded tapes of law-related texts. Additional exercises and recommendations for improvement can be found in the *Federal Court Interpreter Certification Examination Manual* (Gonzalez, 1986).

Chapter 27

Consecutive Interpretation

This chapter begins with a definition of consecutive interpretation (CI), and then presents the skills required for CI and concludes with some recommendations for developing and improving those skills.

1. Definition

In CI the interpreter waits until the speaker has finished the SL message before rendering it into the TL. The SL message may last anywhere from a few seconds to several minutes, and the rate of speed and density of discourse vary with each speaker and subject matter. CI involves complex mental tasks of language perception, storage, retrieval, and generation, as described in the section on human information processing in Chapter 25 of this unit. Because of this complexity, many interpreters consider CI more difficult than simultaneous interpretation (SI). Seleskovitch (1978a) calls CI "perhaps the most noble of all types of interpretation" (p. vi).

Until the early 1940s CI was the only mode of interpreting used. Due to technological innovations, SI came into use after World War II, and CI has become less frequent in conference interpreting. Seleskovitch (1978a) cites statistics indicating that CI constitutes only 10 percent of the interpreting performed at international conferences, primarily those involving just two languages. Nevertheless, CI still has specific uses, particularly in court interpreting, but also in international gatherings as well. For more information on the use of CI in court interpretation, see Unit 3, Chapter 13. Weber (1984) states that CI is used in conferences whenever a high degree of accuracy is required, and "when participants in a meeting find it useful to have additional time for reflection during interpretation" (p. 34). This is because, as Seleskovitch (1978a) notes, in CI "the interpreter has the advantage of knowing the line of argument before he interprets," although she cautions that "few activities require such concentration or cause such fatigue" (p. 31).

As with SI, there is a major difference between the CI employed by court interpreters and that employed by conference interpreters. Conference interpreters generally wait until the speaker has gone on for up to twenty minutes, and do not render a verbatim version of the message in the TL. They often condense or edit the message, eliminating the kind of hedging cited above, and may actually make it sound more coherent, succinct, and smoother than the original. Court interpreters, however, must not omit a single element of meaning, whether verbal or non-verbal. In court interpreting, CI is used primarily for testimony given on the witness stand or in depositions, and for the questioning of the defendant by the judge (at arraignment, sentencing, or similar situations). A question is asked in English, the interpreter translates it into the TL, the witness gives an answer in the TL, the interpreter translates that answer into English, and so on. Because the interpreter represents the voice of the defendant to the court and vice versa, it is imperative for the interpreter to capture every element of the source language message and transfer it as wholly and faithfully as humanly possible. This is the difficulty of consecutive interpretation in the legal setting. Any distortion of style, meaning, disorganization, or nonfluency in delivery will negatively impact on the credibility of the witness and the effectiveness of the speaker (McCroskey & Mehrley, 1969; O'Barr, 1982).

2. Skills Required

Bowen and Bowen (1980) describe CI as having the following components: (1) discourse in the SL, (2) understanding and analyzing this discourse, and (3) reconstituting it in the TL. Thus, the interpreter perceives the SL message, processes it for meaning, and generates a TL version of the message, and, as Garretson (1981) points out, the "psychological" aspects of consecutive require the intensive use of memory. A number of specific skills are involved in this process: listening, prediction, memory, notetaking, and situational control.

2.1. Listening

To be able to process the SL message accurately, the interpreter must be able to listen effectively and attend to meaning. The term "attending" is often used to describe the type of listening that interpreters engage in. The difference is that hearing is a passive process involving an involuntary reaction of the senses and the nervous system, while listening is a voluntary, conscious effort to process the input selectively. Attending is the most alert, deliberate form of listening. It is no coincidence that we use the expression "to pay attention" in English. When we pay attention we are giving awareness, interest, and effort in order to receive information (or comfort or entertainment, depending on the setting). Active listening is hard work, which is why we do not give our attention indiscriminately.

Listening tends to be ignored or taken for granted, however, on the assumption that there is no need to devote any effort to it. In fact, we spend 45 percent of our time perceiving auditory input (Weaver, 1972). Recent research on listening comprehension reveals that three related levels of discourse processing are involved in listening: (1) propositional identification—that is, identifying units of meaning in the message, (2) interpretation of illocutionary force—determining the speaker's intention, and (3) activation of real world knowledge—calling up the appropriate scripts or schemas (Richards, 1983). Richards describes the processes involved in listening comprehension as follows:

(1) The type of interactional act or speech event in which the listener is involved is determined (e.g., conversation, lecture, discussion, debate).

(2) Scripts relevant to the particular situation are recalled.

(3) The goals of the speaker are inferred through reference to the situation, the script, and the sequential position of the utterance.

(4) The propositional meaning of the utterance is determined.

(5) An illocutionary meaning (the speaker's intention) is assigned to the message.

(6) This information is retained and acted upon, and the form in which it was originally received is deleted. (p. 223)

When this model is applied to court interpreting, in step 6 the interpreter does not entirely "delete" the form of the original message, but rather retains it in memory for comparison with the TL version to ensure conservation of every element of meaning. Richards (1983) also presents a taxonomy of listening skills which includes (among others) the following abilities:

- to retain chunks of language of different lengths for short periods
- to recognize the functions of stress and intonation to signal the information structure of utterances
- to detect key words (i.e., those which identify topics and propositions)
- to guess the meanings of words from the contexts in which they occur
- to recognize the communicative functions of utterances, according to situations, participants, goals
- to predict outcomes from events described
- to infer links and connections between events
- to deduce causes and effects from events
- to distinguish between literal and implied meanings
- to process speech at different rates
- to process speech containing pauses, errors, corrections
- to make use of facial, paralinguistic, and other clues to work out meanings (pp. 228-29)

Abbott et al. (1981) note that when people listen to a message in a language other than their native tongue, it takes them longer to process the information, they are more likely to make mistakes in comprehension, it is more difficult to predict outcome, and their memory is more heavily taxed and therefore works less efficiently. In a comprehensive review of the literature on listening, Dunkel (1985) reports research findings which suggest that subjects listening to messages in their second language have a shorter memory span and are, therefore, hindered in their processing capacity. Court interpreters must bear in mind all these factors when performing CI, as they will need to take extra precautions—more thorough notes or more concentrated listening—to compensate for these difficulties when the SL is not their dominant language.

2.2. **Prediction**

The notion of predicting outcome has been mentioned frequently by researchers who have studied listening comprehension, and those who have studied interpreting specifically (Lederer, 1978; Moser, 1978). One study (Abbott et al., 1981) emphasizes that:

our task is made easier by our ability to predict what is likely to come next and our ability to select which stretches of material we will pay maximum attention to and which we need not bother too much about. (p. 61)

Just as prediction plays a major role in the ability to perform accurate and efficient SI, it plays an accordingly significant role in CI.

The schema that is brought to bear in human information processing, as described in Chapter 25, also plays a role in prediction. As Le Ny (1978) states:

> The ordinary speaker selects the words he pronounces as a function of these preexisting schemata. The "natural" listener also usually interprets the words he hears as a function of them, and during the discourse he anticipates the words to come as a function of these schemata. (p. 291)

Redundancy is another critical factor in understanding messages. In the example cited by Abbott et al. (1981), "She put on her gloves to keep herself warm," the words "she," "her," and "herself" are redundancies; the listener could miss two of the three words and still understand the message (p. 68). During the course of a conversation, especially on the telephone, some individual words may be garbled or may not be heard, but the listener is able to understand the message anyway because of his or her knowledge of the context. The listener may not even be aware of having missed a word, for his or her mind automatically fills in the gap. For example, if you hear someone say, "I'm going to run out to the *smghf* to get some groceries," the message you will get is "I'm going to run out to the store to get some groceries" because that is what you expect to hear, based on prior experience.

Abbott et al. (1981) also emphasize how listeners pay particular attention to key words that link sentences and clauses together, and suggest what the next idea will be: "a reason (because), a contrasting statement (but, however), a result (so, therefore), an addition (also, not only that), a rephrasing (in other words, that is to say), or an example (for instance)" (p. 62). Another illustration of how listeners tend to predict outcome is cited by Rumelhart and Ortony (1977): "Mary heard the ice-cream man coming down the street. She remembered her birthday money and rushed into the house" (p. 113). The listener knows that Mary is a little girl, and she is going to get money to buy ice cream, even though nothing in these two sentences says that.

This kind of intuitive leap is very common in human information processing. Abbott et al. (1981) caution, however, that:

> efficient listeners and readers never switch off completely, because they have learnt that their predictions are occasionally wrong; the unexpected sometimes happens and we have to be prepared to modify our expectations in light of what we actually hear or read. (p. 62)

Thus, although prediction is a natural element of human communication, it poses obvious dangers to the accurate processing of messages. The individual's decision, whether conscious or unconscious, about what the message really was is affected by his or her own biases, expectations, and knowledge, and distortion can easily result. Court interpreters should be particularly aware of this phenomenon and make sure they interpret what they actually heard, not what they expected to hear.

2.3. Memory

All of the writings on CI that have been cited here (Bowen & Bowen, 1980; Seleskovitch, 1978a; Weber, 1984) emphasize the vital role played by memory. Indeed,

Seleskovitch (1978a) states that "memory and understanding are inseparable" (p. 34).

The function of memory in human information processing is discussed in detail in Chapter 25. To sum up that discussion briefly, the interpreter stores the SL message in memory and processes the message for comprehension by activating the relevant modules and schemata. These schemata contain the meanings associated with the SL terms in the message, and probably the appropriate TL terms as well. Once the interpreter has formulated a proposed TL version of the message, he or she checks it against the SL version originally stored in memory, and if the two versions match, the interpreter utters the TL version, inserting the paralinguistic elements where appropriate.

2.3.1. Strategies for Enhancing Retention

Some methods of increasing retention capacity are presented here. One of the most effective ways to improve retention and retrieval is to organize the incoming information to make it more manageable. This process of organizing is often referred to as "chunking," but some researchers (Kelly, 1979) call it "segmentation." Whatever it is called, the process involves dividing a message into meaningful units, possibly changing the sequence of ideas, to render it more understandable. Thus, to cite the example in Chapter 25 of this unit, the interpreter who hears the question, "On the night of the incident in question, Mr. Jones, what were you and the woman you say you are living with doing?" does not process the twenty-three words individually, but rather reduces them to four phrases or propositions, each of which can be remembered by means of a key word or visual image. In this way, interpreters limit the number of bits that have to be stored in memory, and relieve the burden on their limited retention capacity.

As noted earlier in this chapter, attentive listening is a key factor in this organization process. Another important element to consider is the nature of the input (coherence, density, speed of delivery, and so on). Baddeley (1976) notes that the storage of information in STM seems to rely on acoustic encoding (remembering the sounds of words), while storage in LTM relies on semantic encoding (analysis of meaning). Semantic encoding allows for a greater storage capacity than acoustic encoding does. Studies have shown that when the delivery of the sensory input is rapid and the content meaningless, subjects tend to employ acoustic encoding; they focus on individual words. When the message is meaningful, semantic encoding takes place, and the data are not easily forgotten (Baddeley, 1976). Bransford and Franks (1971) found in a study of subjects' ability to recall information that the subjects "did not store representations of particular sentences. Individual sentences lost their unique status in memory in favor of a more wholistic representation of semantic events" (p. 348). Le Ny (1978) hypothesizes that expert interpreters discard non-semantic information from their memory more quickly than non-interpreters, and that this rapid decay of non-semantic information facilitates the processing of semantic information. To maximize their memory capacity, therefore, interpreters must pay attention to the underlying meaning of the message rather than to the individual words that comprise it. As Atwater (1981) says, "Once you have begun paying attention to a verbal message, it is vital that you understand what you hear. For understanding is the key, to both listening and memory" (p. 93).

What makes the court interpreter's job much more difficult than that of the conference interpreter is that the court interpreter cannot entirely discard non-semantic information such as pauses and hedges because they must be included in the TL version in order to provide a legal equivalent of the SL message. Still, focusing on the semantic information—the underlying meaning—is a valid strategy for the court interpreter because it makes more storage capacity available for non-semantic information.

Assuming that memory is unlimited, the problem the interpreter faces is not storage capacity, but retrieval. Because so much data are stored in memory, it may take longer to find a given item. Memory is like a cross-referenced index card file: the more ways one has to index items or the more associations one has with items, the more easily they are retrieved. Or, looking at it from a different perspective, the more pathways that lead to an item, the more likely the individual will be able to take one and find what he or she is looking for. This is why it is so important for an interpreter to analyze a message as he or she hears it and to organize it into meaningful units (forming associations or pathways connecting things that are already stored in memory), rather than focusing on individual words.

Wortman et al. (1988) define this type of interaction with information as "deep processing." They postulate that memory is divided linearly into STM and LTM; information intended for long-term storage is processed differently than that which will be stored for a short time.

When people simply repeat something to themselves without considering its meaning (as they tend to do when they rehearse a telephone number), they may maintain that information in short-term memory effectively enough, but it may never become part of their long-term knowledge. In contrast, when people take a new piece of information and mentally process it—form an image of it, apply it to a problem, relate it to other things—it is more likely to be deposited in long-term storage. (p. 158)

Whether data will be successfully stored in memory depends on a number of subjective factors. People remember information better if they want to remember it, or if they know it is useful to them. For example, if an interpreter does not like seafood and does not use seafood terminology, he or she is more likely to forget these terms in his or her working languages. It is at this level that learning takes place. To ensure that newly learned information is stored in memory, full understanding must take place at the beginning. When an interpreter hears an unfamiliar word, for example, he or she should ask questions about how the word is used in various contexts and look it up in various references. After determining the meaning and usages of the term, the interpreter should record it in his or her personal glossary or make notes next to the entry in his or her dictionary. If learning a new concept, such as a legal proceeding or a technical procedure, the interpreter should organize the information into a logical sequence. It also helps to reinforce the storage by using the new concept or term whenever the opportunity arises.

It is important to point out that all of the senses, not just hearing, enter into the processing of spoken messages. Aural, visual, olfactory, tactile, and gustatory cues all play a role in memory, although the first three predominate. Moreover, individuals focus on different sensory stimuli, depending on their aptitudes. This is particularly true of visual and auditory perception; some people are "visualizers," and some are "verbalizers." Studies show, however, that although visualizers are more confident of their ability to retain and recall information, they perform the same as verbalizers on memory tests (Baddeley, 1976). Researchers have also found that visually recorded information takes longer to retrieve from memory, but also lasts longer. In addition, concrete information (facts and figures) is better retained with visual memory, while abstract information (concepts, principles, and ideas) is best remembered after being explained and understood in conversation (Atwater, 1981). For the court interpreter, it is useful to take notes (providing a visual record) of numbers and names, but copious note-taking may interfere with the understanding of more abstract information.

2.3.2. Forgetting

Just as important as the question of how we remember things is the question of how we forget. As mentioned earlier in this chapter, a variety of subjective and objective factors determine how data is stored in memory. Once information is stored there, another factor enters the picture: time. Over time, the memory "trace" or pathway may be gradually obliterated or masked by data that is stored subsequently, if the initial data is not strongly embedded (that is, if there are few associations with it, and therefore little reinforcement). In addition to the loss of memory due to subsequent input, which is known as "retroactive interference," forgetting can take place if data that is stored first makes a particularly strong impact and effectively blocks the storage of subsequent input. The latter process is known as "proactive interference." Whether a person remembers better what was heard first or last (the "recency effect") depends on how much time elapses before the person is required to recall the data, and on whether the individual has a chance to reinforce the storage of the data by "rehearsing" it or actively thinking about it. If recall is delayed and no rehearsal is possible, first-heard items are more likely to be remembered (Baddeley, 1976).

Another factor that determines whether a message is retained is the amount of new information it contains (Le Ny, 1978). If the interpreter has many associations with a particular item in memory (i.e., the person has heard the terminology many times before and is very familiar with the subject matter), retrieval is relatively easy and the interpreter's processing capacity is not overloaded. Wortman et al. (1988) stress that people tend to decide what is important and relevant, and therefore what should be stored in memory, on the basis of their schemata. Schemata also help people interpret the meaning of new information, and to elaborate on what they learn, enabling them to supply the necessary details according to their expectations. For example, during testimony about a burglary, the interpreter calls up a burglary schema in both the SL and the TL, which contains background knowledge of common situations that arise in burglaries, tools employed, methods of breaking in, and associated phrases such as "casing the joint" and "posting a lookout." As a result, upon hearing the term "safe," the interpreter will know without consciously thinking about it that the term refers to a box in which valuables are kept, not a state of being secure and free from harm. Similarly, upon hearing a new term, the interpreter will be better able to understand its meaning and to store it for future retrieval through associating it with other terms related to burglaries. Thus, the more knowledge and experience interpreters have in a wide range of subjects, the easier it is for them to retain and recall information.

In addition to the interference that can come from internal factors, extraneous factors can interfere with retention and recall. One of the most important of these is stress. The effect of stress on memory is a matter of degree, however. Studies have shown that moderate levels of stress or arousal can actually enhance performance, but after a certain point the impact becomes negative; people who are in a state of high physical or mental anxiety are unable to "pay adequate attention to important cues in their environment and thus may miss information that is crucial for accurate memory" (Loftus, 1980, p. 82). Thus, if an interpreter is flooded with stimuli unrelated to the SL message, such as physical cues signalling a headache, fatigue, or anxiety about possible challenges from attorneys, and so on, the interpreter is unable to attend exclusively to the SL message.

Other irrelevant stimuli that may interfere with the retention and recall of the SL message include visual cues (the witness may be wearing a particularly flashy tie, for instance) or auditory cues (people talking loudly in the hall, or perhaps an annoying speech mannerism of the witness). These factors can distract interpreters from the task at hand. Clearly, then, interpreters need to be in optimum physical condition so that such irrelevant stimuli can be kept to a minimum, and they need to be mentally alert and confident in order to concentrate all their energies on processing the SL message to generate a TL rendition.

In conclusion, we remember what is meaningful to us. For something to be meaningful, we must be able to associate it with prior experiences, emotions, linguistic knowledge, and so on. The more associations we have with something, the easier it is to remember. The key to remembering data is to analyze it as it comes in and organize it into a minimum number of "chunks." Acting on the input somehow (classifying it, visualizing it, taking notes on it, or experiencing an emotional reaction to it) helps us to retain it. As Seleskovitch (1978a) states:

> You only remember something if you have paid attention to it, if you relate the significance and meaning to your own experience; in short, if you reflect on it in such a way that you experience what is commonly known as "awareness." Memory is much more dependent on what you do with the information than on how your senses perceive it. (p. 37)

2.4. Notetaking

Perhaps the most common memory aid that people use in every aspect of life is notetaking. They jot down phone numbers, grocery lists, reminders about things to do, and so forth. Professionals in all fields use specialized notes to help them perform a variety of tasks, and interpreters are no exception. The notetaking system that has been devised by conference interpreters is discussed later on in this section.

Many researchers have investigated the function of notetaking in retention and recall (most in the context of students taking notes on university lectures, but some in the field of conference interpreting), and have identified a number of factors that determine the usefulness of notes. In a review of the literature, Dunkel (1985) indicates that the research findings are contradictory, with some studies suggesting that notetaking may interfere with listening comprehension while others conclude the opposite.

The speed of delivery may be a deciding factor; one of the studies cited revealed that "taking notes during a very rapid presentation may interfere with listening, while at slower speeds, it may enhance listening by increasing the concentration of the student" (p. 27). Efficiency of notetaking is another element that contributes to usefulness. Howe (1970), in particular, found a positive correlation between the "efficiency" of notetaking and the ability to recall information later. In other words, the fewer notes taken, the better the recall. This finding is corroborated by the empirical conclusions of the conference interpreters who have written about CI (Hebert, 1968; Rozan, 1956; Seleskovitch, 1975; van Hoof, 1962).

Researchers who have studied the effects of notetaking on retention and recall focus on two different aspects of the process: the act of taking notes and the notes themselves. For example, Mikkelson (1983) states that:

> The act of taking notes (deciding what to write and how to place it on the page) appears to aid in the analysis and processing of the information, and the interpreter is more likely to remember something that s/he has acted upon him/herself. (p. 6)

On the other hand, Dunkel (1985) cites a number of studies that "lent strong support to the external storage function of notes; the having and reviewing, rather than the taking per se of notes facilitated recall performance" (p. 22). Elsewhere in her review of the literature, Dunkel notes that "several researchers have concluded that the encoding benefit of notetaking actually accrues from having the opportunity to review notes and not from the mere act of notetaking itself" (p. 70). Lambert (1983), whose study dealt specifically with conference interpreters performing CI rather than students taking notes on lectures in the university setting, contends that both approaches are valid:

> The object of notes is to supplement memory efficiently, and individuals normally take notes with either or both of two aims in mind:
>
> (1) notes can be perceived as an external storage mechanism where the interpreter uses notes as a means of reproducing and storing knowledge for later consultation;
>
> (2) notes can also be examined via the note-taking process itself, where it is seen as an encoding mechanism that facilitates retention in that taking notes may contribute to the learner's acquisition of knowledge, in other words, his "learning," in a relatively direct manner. (p. 5)

2.4.1. Interpreter Notetaking System

A unique system of notetaking has been devised, analyzed, and explicated over the years by conference interpreters (Hebert, 1968; Rozan, 1956; Seleskovitch, 1975; van Hoof, 1962). This notetaking system can also be used in court interpreting, although due to the differences between court and conference interpreting mentioned at the beginning of this chapter, certain modifications must be made.

The underlying principle of the notes used by conference interpreters—commonly known as the "Rozan (1956) method," after Jean-François Rozan, who first recorded and analyzed the notetaking system he observed conference interpreters using—is that the SL message is abstracted into symbolic form to make it easier to convert into the

TL. It is important to remember that the notes are an aid to memory, not an end in themselves; interpreters concentrate on attending to and analyzing the SL message as they hear it, and try to keep the notes to a minimum. Very few words of the original message are written down, because interpreters focus on ideas, not words. They make very careful choices of what to write in their notes, selecting "key words" that will trigger their memory of an entire concept when they read the notes later. These key words may not even have been uttered in the SL message, but are representations that are meaningful to the interpreter. In addition to words, interpreters use a variety of other notations, as shown below. Each interpreter's notes are unique and personalized, and even another interpreter who knows the system may not be able to read them. Weber (1984) points out that "there are as many different note-taking systems as there are interpreters" (pp. 36–37), and that such a system cannot be imposed on another or learned by rote.

2.4.2. Techniques

The following techniques are used in the Rozan (1956) method to abstract ideas from the SL message:

(a) Placement of ideas on the page: indentation, verticalization.

(b) Abbreviation: common abbreviations such as atty, info, etc.; abbreviations from science (H_2O, Au, etc.); shorthand notations; and others.

(c) Symbols: mathematical and scientific symbols, Greek letters, arrows, punctuation marks, lines of negation, individualized symbols.

(d) Lines: negation, relationship, repetition, numbers, circles, underlining for emphasis.

2.4.3. Examples

Here are some examples of typical statements that an interpreter might take notes on, with sample notes provided in figure 1.

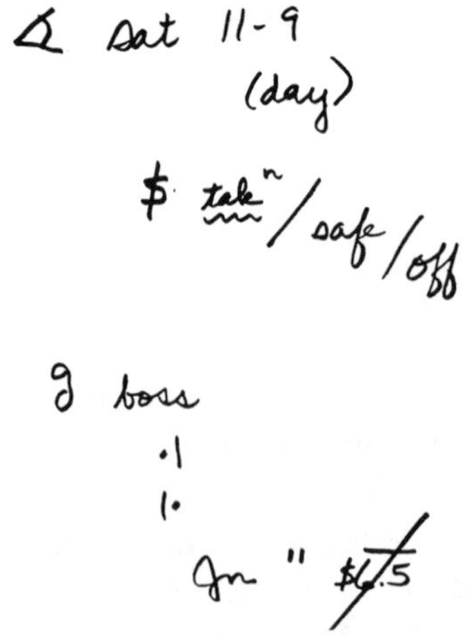

Figure 1. Sample "diagram" notetaking I.

(a) Now, drawing your attention to Saturday, November 9, the day of the incident, when the money was allegedly removed from the safe in the office, did you call your employer before or after John told you the $6,500 was missing?

Comments on figure 1: Note how few whole words are written down. The symbol ◁ is used to indicate focusing on, looking at, etc. The parentheses indicate an apposition or parenthetical remark that digresses from the subject a little or adds details. Note how the ideas are indented as the story progresses, with the most subordinate ideas being placed farthest to the left. It is clear that the interpreter is analyzing while listening, and establishing a hierarchy of ideas in logical progression. The next concept, about the money being removed from the safe, is brought out slightly to the right because it is more important than "the day of the incident," but still subordinate to the main idea of the question. The $ denotes money of any sort; "taken" is shorter than "removed" (an arrow might be used here as well), and the squiggly line underneath refers to the uncertainty of the statement ("allegedly"). The slash is a line of relationship (often representing a prepositional phrase), linking the money to the safe to the office (each of which is indented to show subordination). Then the g symbol, referring to telephone communication, is brought out all the way to the left to begin a new idea (the heart of the question). The word "boss" is used because it takes less time to write than "employer." The two symbols •| and |• are placed vertically, with a question mark at the side, to indicate that they are of equal hierarchy and that there is an alternative between them (the word "or" would serve just as well). And the last idea, a subordinate clause, begins with an abbreviation for John, the " symbol for talking, the line over $6.5 to denote thousand ($6.5 million would have two lines above, and so on), and the line of negation represents the concept of "missing."

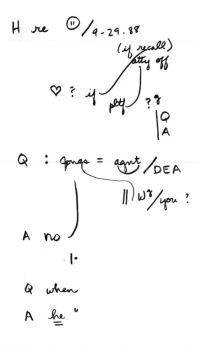

Figure 2. Sample "diagram" notetaking II.

(b) Mr. Hernandez, referring to the deposition you gave on September 29, 1988—if you recall giving that deposition in your attorney's office—I would like to ask you if you remember plaintiff's counsel asking you the following questions and you giving the following answers.

Question: Were you aware that Mr. Jones was an undercover agent of the Drug Enforcement Agency during the period that he worked for you?

Answer: No, I didn't know he was with the Drug Enforcement Agency at that time, not until later.

Question: When did you find out?

Answer: I found out when he told me himself.

Comments: The interpreter begins with an "H" as a reminder that the question begins with the witness's name; the interpreter already knows the name, and thus needs only a reminder. The "re" is a common abbreviation for regarding or referring to. The " with the circle around it indicates a formal speaking situation, such as a speech or deposition (the common abbreviation "depo" could also be used here). The slash relates the deposition to the date, and the "if recall" is placed in parentheses and indented to show that it is subordinate and a digression from the train of thought. The heart, brought out to the left to indicate that the main idea is being taken up again, refers to wanting or desiring. The question mark denotes "ask." The line after "if" goes back up to "recall" because the same idea is repeated and there is no need to write it twice. "Plaintiff's counsel" is abbreviated, and "asking" is represented by a question mark with the "g" to mark the gerund or participle (grammatical markers like "s" for plural, "n" for the "tion" suffix, etc., are elevated above the root to distinguish them). Q and A are common abbreviations for question and answer, and they are verticalized to indicate a list of items of equal importance. The first question is brought out to the left again, to indicate the beginning of a new main idea. The : symbol refers to mental or cognitive concepts (thought, knowledge, etc.). The = sign is used for the verb "to be," and related concepts. The line below "agent" denotes the prefix "under" (a line above would represent the prefix "over," as in oversee, overpayment, etc.). The slash indicates the genitive relationship ("of the"), and DEA is a commonly known abbreviation. The || symbol represents two things happening simultaneously or in parallel. The line to "Jones" indicates a repetition of the name. The "W" represents work or employment, with the elevated "d" denoting the past tense. The slash denotes the preposition "for" (another relationship). The answer begins at the left again, and a simple "no" with a line drawn up to the question (to indicate repetition) suffices to convey the idea, with the symbol |• indented underneath. The next question can be conveyed simply by "when," and the final answer shows the "he" underlined twice for emphasis ("himself"), with the " for the verb "told."

(c) Well, you see, I wanted to get downtown fast, you know, so I decided to hitchhike instead of walking. So this guy comes and picks me up on Main St., you know, and . . . I, uh, . . . well, you know, it had been raining the night before, and there was water all over the place, and his car stalled in the middle of a big puddle. So I ended up hoofing it after all, you know?

Comments: This text illustrates the difficulty of using notetaking in court interpreting. The interpreter must give a verbatim interpretation of the witness's answer, including

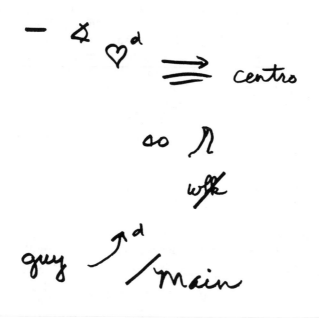

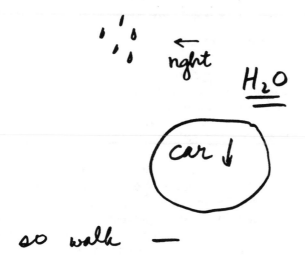

Figure 3. Sample "diagram" notetaking III.

the pauses and hedges. The horizontal lines throughout the notes show where there are hedges, but it is up to the interpreter to remember exactly what words were used.

The ◁ symbol is used once again for the concept of "see" (although this is really just a hedge, and should not be confused with the main idea). The heart represents "wanted," and an arrow (underlined for emphasis, "fast") denotes traveling or moving. The Spanish word *centro* is used for downtown, because it is more succinct. (Interpreters can take notes in whatever language or combination of languages they feel comfortable in, as long as they can understand the notes when it is time to read them back. If a particular term springs to mind and conveys the idea accurately, it does not matter if that word is from a language not involved in the proceedings.) A common error that must be guarded against is forgetting which language the notes must be rendered into, the SL or the TL. A generic symbol such as "Sp" or "Eng" at the beginning of the notes may suffice.

The "so" is an important word to include, because it shows the causal relationship between ideas (an arrow for causality or the ∗∗∗ symbol for "therefore" from mathematics would serve equally well). The interpreter then drew a little picture of a thumb to indicate "hitchhike," and drew a line of negation through the word "walk" to represent the idea "instead of" (the alternative not chosen). "Guy" begins the next idea out to the left, the upward arrow indicates "picks me up," and "Main" suffices to indicate the place. After a few hedges, the next idea is "rain," which the interpreter represented pictorially. The backward arrow above "nght" indicates the past. The abbreviation for water is underlined heavily to denote emphasis, "all over the place." The interpreter first wrote "car" and the downward arrow to indicate the stalling, and then drew a circle around it to portray the puddle pictorially. The final idea, brought out to the left to indicate its importance in the hierarchy, begins with "so" and then represents "hoofing it" with the more general word "walk." (The interpreter must remember the register of the term "hoofing it," and render it into the TL with an appropriately "slangy" term.)

2.4.4. Application to Court Interpreting

As noted above, the unique demands of court interpreting (conservation, legal equivalence) require some adaptation of this notetaking system. The emphasis of these notes is abstracting and symbolizing, and indeed that is the essence of the interpreting process. But court interpreters must first abandon the concrete structure of the message to penetrate to the underlying meaning, and then refer back to the SL structure, which they have retained in their STM, to make sure they reinsert such non-verbal elements as pauses, self-corrections, and hedges. Conference interpreters, in contrast, deliberately eliminate such elements from the TL message. Thus, court interpreters cannot allow a witness to go on for twenty minutes as conference interpreters do (nor would an attorney consent to such lengthy narrations), and must intervene when they know they cannot retain any more in their STM. Moreover, they must indicate the pauses and hedges in their notes to make sure they reinsert them in the process of giving the TL version.

In view of the rigorous standards of accuracy that interpreters must uphold in the judicial setting, many people wonder why court interpreters do not simply learn shorthand so that they can make a verbatim record and not have to rely on their memory. Weber (1984) points out that shorthand notes are word-oriented, and interpreters must focus on meaning rather than words. If interpreters did take down word-for-word everything the speaker said, they would then be faced with the task of sight translating shorthand notes, which is even more daunting a prospect than sight translating a plain typewritten text.

There is an inherent danger in notetaking that interpreters, court or conference, must guard against. It is all too easy to become excessively absorbed in the notes themselves, and forget to attend to the message as it is being uttered by the SL speaker. If interpreters do not look at the speaker, they will miss valuable non-verbal cues. Many novice interpreters make the mistake of scribbling away while the SL message is coming in, but then have trouble deciphering their notes afterward because they did not understand the overall meaning. They have an impressive list of facts (if they are fortunate enough to be able to read their own handwriting), but they cannot link them together in a meaningful way. In other words, they can't see the forest for the trees. It is important to remember that notes are merely a mnemonic aid.

Given the shorter length of the messages that interpreters deal with in the judicial setting, and given the limitations of the Rozan (1956) method of notetaking, one might question the usefulness of notetaking for the court interpreter. Indeed, there are many instances when the court interpreter does not need to take notes at all. A survey of interpreters who are certified to interpret in the federal courts (Mikkelson, Vasquez, & Gonzalez, 1989) revealed that most interpreters do not use notes for the storage and retrieval of every utterance in courtroom testimony. Of the interpreters who responded to the survey, 26 percent reported that they take notes during "every interpreting event," 26 percent said they do so "often," 31 percent said "sometimes," and 14 percent said "rarely." The majority of the interpreters reported that they take notes only on long questions and answers or those that contain specific data such as names, dates, numbers, and addresses.

Other factors that determine whether notes are taken, as indicated by the interpreters in the survey, include the nature of the proceedings or the event and the fatigue interpreters experience. Sixty-six percent of the respondents also indicated that they are more likely to rely on their memory (as opposed to only 11 percent who rely on their notes) to retain paralinguistic elements of the SL message such as pauses, hedges, and self-corrections. This survey did not investigate the language-dominance issue, but based on the findings reported by Abbott et al. (1981) and the research cited by Dunkel (1985) with regard to foreign language comprehension, it may be that interpreters are more likely to take notes when the SL is their "B" (foreign or acquired) language, but not when it is in their "A" (mother) language. This hypothesis should be the subject of further study. Clearly, court interpreters do not rely exclusively on notetaking to help them recall the SL message, but they do use notes extensively in certain situations. A great deal could be learned by conducting research on the factors that enter into the interpreter's decision as to whether or not to take notes.

2.4.5. Principles of Notetaking for Court Interpreting

The following general principles, based on the applicable features of the Rozan (1956) method and the specific demands of the judicial setting, can serve as a guide for notetaking by the court interpreter.

(a) Take only the notes you need. The majority of the questions and answers in typical witness testimony are short, and the interpreter may not need to take notes at all. If a short answer contains an address, interpreters may write down just an abbreviation of the address and nothing more. As interpreters gain experience, they will be able to gauge their memory capacity and will know how many notes they need to take, if any. Once interpreters decide to take notes, they should choose what to write judiciously, writing only words or symbols that will help them remember the message.

(b) Abbreviate, writing only what is meaningful to you. If the answer contains a description, such as "He had black hair, brown eyes, and a thick beard," the interpreter might take the following notes:

bl h

br ey

thk brd

Figure 4. Use of abbreviations for eyewitness description.

Abbreviations are very personalized and are based on the interpreter's own experience. If the interpreter has an extensive medical background, for example, "stat" may be used to mean "immediately, right away, quickly," whereas another interpreter would have to write more. If "def" is what the interpreter always uses to signify the defendant, those three letters are sufficient; but if he does not often use that abbreviation and fears he might confuse it with "definite" or "defer" or another similar word, he needs to use more letters of the word (e.g., "dfndt"). It is risky to invent "*ad hoc* abbreviations" or symbols that will mean nothing five minutes after they are written. In short, once the interpreter has made a judicious choice of what to write down, he should abbreviate as much as possible.

(c) Use pictures, diagrams, and relative position on the page. Some testimony lends itself to a graphic depiction, while other testimony may be more word oriented. If the witness gives an answer that can be easily visualized, the interpreter may choose to draw a picture rather than noting down words. For the descriptive answer given above, the interpreter might draw the picture presented in figure 5.

Figure 5. Graphic depiction of eyewitness description.

Notetaking is just one strategy that allows the interpreter to use the consecutive mode to its fullest potential. The following strategies permit the interpreter to exert considerable control over the situation without inhibiting the people who are trying to communicate.

2.5. Situational Control

In limited situations, and only rarely, is it wise to exert control over a speaker. The competent interpreter strives to be as unobtrusive as possible in the course of proceedings. However, even the most practiced interpreter may have a need to interrupt testimony, ask for repetition, or use physical proximity to slow speech. Overuse of these techniques, however, may indicate a need to work on the major or subskills of interpreting. Because non-verbal, visual cues (facial expressions, gestures, and so on) are just as important as verbal cues in the perception of messages, it is important for the interpreter to sit next to the witness, or to stand next to the defendant when the latter is being addressed by the judge, and be able to see the defendant's entire body. Since it is also important for other parties in the courtroom to be able to see the witness, interpreters should position themselves in such a way that they do not block anyone's view, particularly the jury's. Proper positioning is extremely important in CI and can forestall a situational control problem. For further discussion on the issue of the interpreter's position in the courtroom, see Units 7 and 8.

(1) Requesting a repetition: If for some reason interpreters feel they are unable to provide a precise interpretation (if they fail to hear a word or phrase, if the witness uses an unfamiliar term, or if they forget part of the answer), they must inform the court and request permission to inquire further. Under no circumstances should they bluff, gloss over the problem word, or try to guess what the answer was. Although the option of asking for a repetition of the answer is always available to interpreters, they should bear in mind that the witness is not likely to say exactly the same thing the second time around. Parts of the original answer may vanish without a trace. Moreover, by asking for a repetition of the answer, interpreters may inadvertently influence the witness's testimony by causing the person to think he or she said something wrong.

If the interpreter has missed only part of an answer, it is preferable to interpret the part the interpreter recalls before stopping and asking for a repetition or clarification. Thus, the interpreter might say, "I was walking down the street when suddenly I saw . . . Your Honor, the interpreter needs to have the last part of the answer repeated," or "Your Honor, the witness has used a term the interpreter is not familiar with." That way, at least the first part of the answer is in the record and the interpreter can eliminate it from the STM and concentrate on the remainder of the answer. On the other hand, if the problem lies at the beginning of the witness's response, or if the entire interpretation hinges on the meaning of the unknown term, then the interpreter must inform the court of the situation before interpreting any of the answer. Because asking for a repetition or definition of terms can cause these additional problems, it must be emphasized again that interpreters should develop their memory capacity and their vocabulary so that they need resort to this expedient only on rare occasions.

(2) Interruption and physical proximity: Interrupting the witness for the purpose of controlling the interpreting situation is a controversial issue that merits discussion here. The length of the utterance the interpreter must remember varies from a simple "yes" or "no" response to a rambling, disjointed answer from a witness to a long,

complex question from an attorney. A competent interpreter is able to process and interpret forty to sixty words of question-and-answer testimony without having to interrupt the speaker. In fact, the Federal Court Interpreter Certification Program regards this ability as a minimal performance standard in CI (see Unit 8, Chapter 36).

In the past, it has been standard practice for interpreters to interrupt the speaker in order to break up the speech into smaller segments. Administrative Order No. 85-002 (Superior Court of the State of Arizona, 1985), for example, lists the following among its standards of conduct:

> In interpreting in the consecutive mode, the interpreter may need to interrupt the discourse of the witness periodically to interpret or to review his notes. These interruptions should only create a pause during the witness's testimony and will not delete or stop parts of that testimony. The interpreter may arrange a system of signals with the witness before taking the stand, so as to facilitate this process. (Section vii.8)

Similarly, the San Diego Municipal Court's *General Information and Guidelines for Courtroom Interpreters* (1983) states that when it is obvious that an answer is too long and complex for the interpreter to render it fully in the TL, "the interpreter must interrupt the witness and break up his narrative into segments not greater than the interpreter's recall will allow for accurate translation. The essence or gist of a statement is not enough" (p. 7).

This practice has been abused, however, and, because of this tendency, should be avoided altogether. Because no limitations have been imposed with respect to the interruption of witnesses, some interpreters have developed a habit of cutting off the witness at every turn, relying on this technique to compensate for a deficient memory. These interpreters use hand signals to indicate when the witness should stop, and some even go to the extreme of placing their hand near the witness's mouth. When they have finished the interpretation of a segment of testimony, they use a beckoning gesture to signal the witness to continue. The result is a fragmented, staccato rendition that does not allow the actors in the courtroom to assess the witness's testimony adequately.

Thus, although some guidelines sanction the practice of interrupting the witness, it is not universally accepted. A standard principle of trial procedure is that the examining attorney is in charge of the examination process; even judges are reluctant to interfere with this vital means of presenting evidence. Generally speaking, examining attorneys try to maintain control over the testimony by discouraging witnesses from entering into long narratives. When an English-speaking witness does begin a narrative, the attorney may object and ask that the answer be stricken from the record. When the actors in the courtroom must wait for the interpretation, however, they do not have that ability to control the witness.

Faced with an extremely long answer by a witness, the interpreter has three options: (1) attempt to interpret it consecutively, relying on memory and notetaking, and run the risk of losing some of the paralinguistic elements of the answer; (2) switch to the simultaneous mode in order to give as complete an interpretation as possible; or (3) interrupt the witness and interpret the answer in smaller segments. The interpreter has an obligation to conserve every aspect of the witness's answer, and should make every effort to avoid summarizing. As for the second option, there are certain drawbacks to interpreting testimony simultaneously, as discussed in Chapter 26. The third option, interrupting the witness, should be regarded by the interpreter as a last resort.

A number of important factors must be taken into consideration by the interpreter when deciding whether it is appropriate to interrupt the speaker. The primary consideration, of course, is conservation of meaning. If, and only if, the SL message is so lengthy and complicated that the interpreter is unable to convey every element of meaning, even using notes, it is better to interrupt the speaker than to risk an incomplete interpretation. On the other hand, interpreters must bear in mind that they have an obligation to ensure that the communication process is as close as possible to that which would occur if there were no language barrier. Interrupting the train of thought of an attorney who is carefully formulating a question to elicit specific testimony, or of a witness who is trying to give a precise and complete answer to a question, adds another complication that would not be present if the speakers all understood the same language. A witness may find it intimidating to be interrupted in the middle of testimony, and may say less than he or she otherwise would. Moreover, as Berk-Seligson (1987), Erickson, Lind, Johnson, and O'Barr (1978), and O'Barr (1982) have made so evident in their research, the speech style of the witness plays a fundamental role in the jury's evaluation of that witness's credibility.

Thus, it is clear that interrupting witnesses or attorneys entails the risk of adversely affecting the communication process. Court interpreters must make every effort to develop their listening, notetaking, and memory skills sufficiently so that they will rarely have to interrupt attorneys or witnesses. Sometimes, however, interruptions are unavoidable, as attested by the survey of federally certified interpreters mentioned earlier in this chapter (Mikkelson, Vasquez, & Gonzalez, 1989). While only 3 percent of the interpreters stated that they interrupt a speaker "every interpreting event," 16 percent reported that they do so "often," and 49 percent indicated that they interrupt witnesses or attorneys "sometimes." Twenty-four percent of the interpreters reported interrupting the speaker "rarely," and 9 percent said they never interrupt.

When interpreters feel compelled to interrupt the speaker in order to ensure an accurate interpretation, they must do so with the least possible disruption of the flow of communication. First of all, interpreters must choose the right moment to intervene: If the witness or attorney is interrupted before having a chance to complete a thought, the interpretation may be misleading, because subsequent words might alter the meaning of the message. Moreover, a witness may lose his or her train of thought and be unable to complete the answer. And there is always the danger that the attorney will begin a follow-up question immediately after the interpretation, not realizing that the answer was not completed. On the other hand, if interpreters allow the witness to go on too long before intervening, they will be unable to give an accurate and complete interpretation. Therefore, it is important for interpreters to know the limits of their memory capacity and choose the appropriate point to interrupt before they have reached that limit. This technique is one that requires much practice and experience.

Interpreters must adapt to each new person for whom they interpret. If they establish a rapport with the witness, the two can develop a rhythm of turn-taking that will ensure a smooth flow of communication. When all of the actors in the courtroom are aware that the interpreter must occasionally interrupt the witness in order to ensure an accurate interpretation, there is less likelihood that the witness will alter his or her testimony or that the jury will be misled in evaluating the witness's credibility. If the witness is articulate and the testimony logical, the interpreter may not have to intervene at all, even for lengthy answers, because meaningful information can be retained more easily. On the other hand, if the witness pauses frequently, makes many self-corrections, and gives rambling, illogical answers, the interpreter will have to intervene more frequently to maintain accuracy. In addition, if interpreters are familiar with the subject matter (for example, if a witness is describing the operation of a machine and the interpreter has seen that machine in use), they can retain more information in memory and provide a more accurate interpretation.

3. Exercises for Improving Skills

Since CI involves the same public speaking and analytical aspects that other modes of interpretation require, these skills can be improved by doing the same exercises explained in the following chapter on sight translation. This section focuses on exercises that will help you develop your listening and memory skills.

3.1. Exercises to Enhance Listening/Attending Skills

(1) To increase your awareness of non-verbal cues, observe conversations you cannot hear (e.g., across a crowded room, outside your window, or on the television with the volume turned down). Pay attention to the individuals' facial expressions, eye gaze, posture, and gestures, as well as the distance they maintain from each other, and try to guess what the conversation is about. Do this exercise in all your working languages, if possible, and compare the differences.

(2) Another way to observe non-verbal cues is to listen to someone on the telephone (or in another situation in which you cannot see the person you are hearing) and to analyze the voice tone, volume, pitch, and noises such as tongue clicking and sighing, comparing them with the content of the message. Again, try to do this exercise in all your working languages and compare the difference.

(3) Go to a store with a friend, and ask the clerk about an item on the shelf or rack. Five minutes later, try to repeat to your friend exactly what the clerk said.

(4) When you are conversing with others, frequently ask, "What do you mean by that term?" to determine what other people mean when they talk and how they use words differently from you.

(5) Ask someone to give you directions to a place you know how to get to. Then ask someone to direct you to a place you could not find yourself. Compare what goes on in your mind in the two cases. Do you jump ahead or lose your train of thought?

(6) Analyze your listening errors. The next time you have a conversation with someone and miss part of what the person said, immediately analyze what went wrong. Were you daydreaming? Still handling something said earlier? Distracted by an unfamiliar or emotion-laden word? Was there physical interference?

(7) While listening to a speech or lecture, make an early evaluation of the speaker's intent or point, the solution being proposed, or the conclusion the person will reach. Make another evaluation at the end of the speech. How did your two assessments differ?

(8) Pay special attention to "linkage words" that determine the relationships of ideas (therefore, however, unless, and so forth, etc.). Make a list of such words, and listen to how they are used. Do this in all your working languages.

3.2. Memory-Building Exercises

(1) Pay attention to how your memory works. Are you a visualizer, a verbalizer, neither, or both? When you forget something you heard, try to analyze the type of interference that prevented you from storing or retrieving the information.

(2) To enhance your retention, have someone read a series of numbers (remember that the STM capacity may be limited to five to nine chunks, and how many numbers you will be able to recall depends on whether you can find patterns in them and organize them into chunks). As soon as you are able to give back seven numbers correctly, try the same exercise but say the numbers backward. You need to be capable of retaining the entire series of seven numbers in your STM in order to say them backward.

(3) To increase your analytical skills, read a newspaper or magazine and stop after each story; try to summarize the contents in one sentence. Do this in all your working languages.

(4) Repeat this exercise with an oral input (news magazine shows on television and talk shows on radio are a good source). During a commercial break, summarize the main idea in one sentence.

(5) Have someone record passages of newspaper or magazine articles for you to work with in the exercises listed below (in all your working languages). Try to choose texts about general subjects, without too much technical terminology or statistics. Alternatively, record radio and television talk shows or interview programs (choose programs in which the speakers are talking extemporaneously, not reading from a prepared script). In these exercises, you will not be translating, merely repeating the information in the same language. Gradually increase the length of the passages as you become more adept at the exercises:

(a) Listen to the passage without taking any notes, and try to repeat as much information as possible.

(b) Listen to the passage and take down "key words" that will help you remember the content. Then try to repeat as much information as possible. Compare the results you obtained by taking notes to those you obtained without any notes. This will give you an indication as to whether you need to take notes in the interpreting setting.

(c) Listen to the passage and try to repeat it verbatim (notetaking optional).

(d) As you listen to the passage, try to condense the information into a few meaningful units, bearing in mind your STM capacity for information. For example, if someone lists a series of jobs that have been held, you can group the jobs by location, type of product, etc. A string of numbers can be lumped into manageable chunks (e.g., people tend to state their social security numbers in groups, such as 348, 26, 9801 instead of 348269801). If the speaker lists all the parts of his or her body where he or she feels pain, you can rearrange them in logical order from head to toe. Note, however, that when interpreting actual testimony, the order of the speaker's words should not be changed except as required by the syntax of the TL.

(e) If the subject matter of the text is a controversial one about which you have a strong opinion, pay attention to your reaction while listening. Make sure your rendition reflects the opinion of the speaker, not your own.

(6) Obtain transcripts of question-and-answer testimony and perform a text analysis and chunking exercises, as described in the next chapter of this unit. Then, perform the prediction exercises described in the Simultaneous Interpretation, Chapter 26 of this unit. Finally, try to recall the questions and answers verbatim.

(7) Repeat the above exercises, but now translate between your working languages as you do so.

Note that improving your listening/attending and memory skills is an ongoing endeavor, which you can continue to refine with time and experience.

Chapter 28
Sight Translation

This chapter will begin with a definition of the technique of sight translation and an explanation of its uses. The different skills that comprise sight translation will then be isolated and explored. Next, the procedure of sight translating a given text will be analyzed step by step, and finally, exercises to improve sight translation skills will be presented.

1. Definition

Sight translation means the oral translation of a written document, a hybrid of translation and interpretation. This interpreting task relies on the comprehension of the written text and the instantaneous, oral translation of that text into the TL. As Weber (1984) describes it, sight translation is the transfer of a message "from the written medium (text) to the oral medium (interpretation)" (p. 3). The New Jersey Supreme Court Task Force on Interpreter and Translation Services (1985) further defines the task in the specific context of judicial interpreting:

> Here the court interpreter must bring to bear the requisite knowledge of the written word which characterizes the work of the legal translator, but must carry out the translation with the same rapidity of response which is required of court interpretation. (p. 64)

Sight translation is analogous to sight reading in music: the interpreter is given an SL document never seen before, and, with minimal preparation, the interpreter provides a complete oral translation of the document into the TL. Like accomplished musicians who play an apparently effortless version of a piece they have never laid eyes on, interpreters are actually drawing upon years of training and experience to perform this feat. The end product should be both faithful to the original text and pleasing to the ear (that is, in free-flowing, natural-sounding language).

2. Elements of Sight Translation

2.1. Conservation

Just as in every other aspect of judicial interpreting, the court interpreter must pay particular attention to conserving the register of the SL text. If the text to be sight translated is a complex legal document from another country, the interpreter must ensure that the TL version reflects the intricate, erudite style of the original. Similarly, if the text is a handwritten letter from a defendant with little education, the TL version must preserve the simple language and grammatical errors contained in the SL text. The users of interpreting services are generally unaware of the complexities of sight translation, which explains why they use phrases such as, "Will the interpreter read the document into the record?" Since sight translation appears to be a simple reading task, especially if it is performed well by a competent interpreter, they do not realize how demanding it is.

2.2. Written Language

Part of the complexity of sight translation lies with the nature of written language. Abbott et al. (1981), in their study of foreign language comprehension, point out that written material is usually more densely packed with information than spoken language. Furthermore, there are no pauses to allow the listener to catch up, and no intonation or stress to provide additional clues for comprehension. Although punctuation serves the function of intonation in most written documents, many handwritten documents that court interpreters are called upon to sight translate contain little or no punctuation, which further complicates their task.

2.3. Reading Comprehension

In order to perform the task of sight translation proficiently, interpreters must be adept at grasping the meaning of written texts, even those that are drafted in a complex, turgid style. To develop this ability, interpreters must read widely and voraciously. As the *Federal Court Interpreter Certification Manual* (Gonzalez, 1986) points out, "Many interpreters suggest that their expansive vocabularies have been developed through extensive and intensive reading of a wide variety of materials such as newspapers, journals, and literature in the respective languages over a period of years" (p. 5). This propensity to read is not just a preparatory exercise for becoming an interpreter; it should be a way of life. So vital is reading comprehension to the task of the court interpreter that the written portion of the Federal Court Interpreter Certification Examination includes a section that measures this skill. Gonzalez (1986) explains the reason for this part of the exam:

> Reading comprehension questions assess the examinee's ability to read keenly, to analyze a written passage from a variety of perspectives, including his or her understanding of not only explicit material but also of assumptions underlying such material and its implications. The length of the written passage creates a substantial context that enables the reader to examine a variety of relationships within the passage. In this way, the examinee can perceive the function of a single word as it relates to the passage more broadly, the interrelationships of ideas within the whole passage, and the author's relation to both the topic and the audience. (p. 16)

2.4. Prediction

One cognitive feature that sight translation shares with simultaneous interpretation is prediction. As discussed in Chapter 26 of this unit, prediction is a strategy interpreters must employ in order to process the SL message efficiently. Interpreters are able to predict the outcome of an incomplete message because of their knowledge of the SL syntax and style, as well as other sociolinguistic factors in the SL culture. In the case of sight translation, interpreters must be thoroughly versed in the various writing styles used in the SL (e.g., legal documents, personal letters, business correspondence, technical reports) so that they can be alert to common constructions that may pose translation problems. For example, legal documents in Spanish often begin sentences with a verb: *Comparecieron ante mí los subscribientes e hicieron constar lo siguiente.* English syntax requires that the subject precede the verb, so interpreters, recognizing that the initial verb is a common pitfall in translating from Spanish to English, must "predict" by reading ahead and finding the subject *los subscribientes* in order to render the following translation: "The undersigned appeared before me and declared the following." The importance of prediction as an interpreting skill is reflected in the fact that the written portion of the Federal Court Interpreter Certification Examination (Gonzalez, 1986) includes a section on sentence completion, which gauges the candidate's ability to "recognize words or phrases which best complete the meaning of a partial sentence, with reference to both logic and style" (p. 15).

3. Need for More Research

Little or no research has been done on sight translation; it is rarely mentioned in discussions of the skills required of interpreters and translators or of the mental processes involved in interpretation. Courses designed for the training of interpreters often devote less time to sight translation than to other modes of interpreting. Indeed, a model court interpreting curriculum presented in the journal *Meta* (Repa, 1981) makes absolutely no mention of sight translation. The New Jersey Task Force on Interpreter and Translation Services, in their final report of 1985, makes only one incidental reference to sight translation. Coughlin (1984) outlines the training that she believes interpreters should receive to prepare them to work in court, and she also fails to mention sight translation. One of the seminal works on research in interpreting, Gerver and Sinaiko's *Language Interpretation and Communication* (1978), contains no entry for sight translation in its index. Nor does Seleskovitch mention sight translation in her *Interpreting for International Conferences* (1978a). Only Weber (1984) discusses sight translation in any detail. He points out how important it is not only as a mode of interpretation, but also as a method of training interpreting students:

> Through sight translation, students learn how to conduct themselves in front of an audience. They also acquire the basic reflexes required to transpose a message into another language (assuming that they have not had any translation courses beforehand). Moreover, they develop a swift eye-brain-voice coordination, which becomes vital in the process of simultaneous interpretation of speeches that have been prepared beforehand and are read at top speed by the speaker. Finally, it is a little easier to analyze a message that is presented visually than one that is presented orally. (pp. 27-28)

4. Sight Translation in the Judicial Setting

Sight translation is a vital component of the court interpreter's work, as evidenced by the fact that it comprises one-third of the oral portion of the Federal Court Interpreter Certification Exam (Gonzalez, 1986). The New Jersey Supreme Court Task Force on Interpreting and Translation Services (1985) emphasizes the importance of making forms and documents available to non-English-speaking defendants, pointing out that it is "simply not feasible to publish a translated version of every court form in every language that will appear in the courts" (p. 46). The logical solution to that problem is for interpreters to provide sight translations of the documents in question.

As previously stated, there is a paucity of research data on sight translation in any setting, let alone in the courts. No known job analyses have been conducted to determine what percentage of their time court interpreters devote to sight translation. It can be asserted, however, that sight translation is frequently required of the court interpreter. The nature of the documents to be translated will vary depending on whether English is the TL or the SL.

4.1. English Documents

Perhaps the most frequent occasion for sight translation involves official documents such as waiver forms and probation and police reports to the defendant. In state agency hearings, one of the interpreter's pre-hearing duties is to sight translate the documents of the case file for the benefit of the claimant so that the latter may respond to them during the hearing. In all of these documents, the English tends to be a combination of ver _____ f___mal language at a high register and bureaucratic jargon, with occasional inforn_____ For example, a police report may contain the following ____ 'B in LN1 and observed suspect's veh _____ as a Caucasian male shouted out the _____ other aspect of court interpreting, in _____ ige or alter the content in any way t_____ it. On the other hand, interpreters m_____ iguage to enable them to understand _____ nts.

The jargon of s_____ vices, unemployment, and so on) is_____ lude many abbreviations. For exam_____ may contain the following notation:_____ /89, Er rept wages totaling $845 for r_____ as of 5/3/89." The interpreter who is_____ by the staff of the unemployment de_____ The claimant states he was laid off fo_____ on 5/30/89, but the employer reported wages totaling $845 _____ determination was done on 6/3/89, and the claimant was disqualified as of 5/3/89. When in doubt, the interpreter should ask the author of the report or an employee of the agency to explain the meaning of this "shop talk" (assuming such a person is available). If interpreters encounter a term they do not understand and no one is available to explain its meaning to them, they should inform the court or the hearing officer of this problem; they should not attempt to guess the meaning.

4.2. Non-English Documents

The court interpreter will be called upon to sight translate a wide variety of documents from other languages into English. These documents can be divided into two categories: informal and formal. The first includes affidavits and statements by witnesses or interested parties, letters to the judge or other court personnel, and other documents written by non-professionals who do not necessarily have a full command of their native tongue, or whose level of literacy makes their language difficult to comprehend. These documents may be written by hand, so in addition to the problems posed by poor grammar and spelling, run-on sentences, and non-standard usage, the interpreter may be faced with the task of deciphering illegible handwriting. Figure 1 illustrates the difficulties involved in sight translating handwritten documents.

The second category includes official documents from other countries: birth, death, and marriage certificates; school records; criminal records; medical reports; and the like. These documents are often written in very formal, technical language which is difficult to understand on the first reading. For example, the following sentence may take several readings to interpret properly:

> *Vista: La revocatoria interpuesta a fs. 1-2 contra el auto que abre esta causa a prueba. Fundándola, expresa el actor que se trata de un juicio por cobro de honorarios que debe tramitarse por el procedimiento de ejecucíon de sentencia (Artículo 23 de la Ley 123/78) y que por aplicación de los artículos 16 y siguientes del Código de Procedimientos, resultan inadmisibles las excepciones de inhabilidad de título y de compromiso opuestas; y a fs. 3-4 el demandado se opone a la revocatoria aduciendo que el procedimiento señalado no es aplicable cuando no se ejecutan honorarios contra la parte vencida, sino contra el patrocinado; que la circunstancia de haberse presentado un documento de donde surja un pago a cuenta que se presume una quita o remisión especial, es procedente la apertura a prueba y finalmente que unidos tales antecedentes con la circunstancia de haberse librado mandamiento por una suma mayor, alteran la ejecutoria, haciendo procedente la excepción de falsedad, de quita, pago y espera o remisión opuestas.*

The translation, rendered after careful scrutiny of the original text and based on an extensive knowledge of Spanish legal language, would resemble this version:

> Considering: The brief on pages 1-2 pursuing the revocation of the decree which summons the parties to produce their evidence in this cause. To substantiate such brief, Plaintiff states that the matter at hand concerns the collection of fees which must be pursued in accordance with the procedure for executing judgments (Article 23 of Law 123/78) and that, pursuant to Article 16 and successive articles of the Code of Procedure, the exceptions of invalidity of title and of compromise that have been raised are inadmissible. On pages 3-4 Defendant challenges such revocation, alleging that the aforementioned procedure is not applicable when the execution for fees is not directed against the losing party but against the client; that the circumstance of having submitted a document from which a payment on account emerges, which is presumed to be a quittance or special remission, does justify the summoning of the parties for production of evidence; and finally, that when such antecedents are added to the fact that a judicial order has been issued for a larger amount, the executory procedure is thus altered and

the exceptions of falsity, quittance, payment, and delay or remission which have been raised therefore become fit and proper.

If interpreters examine a document that is to be sight translated and determine that they need more time to research the terminology, they should so inform the court or

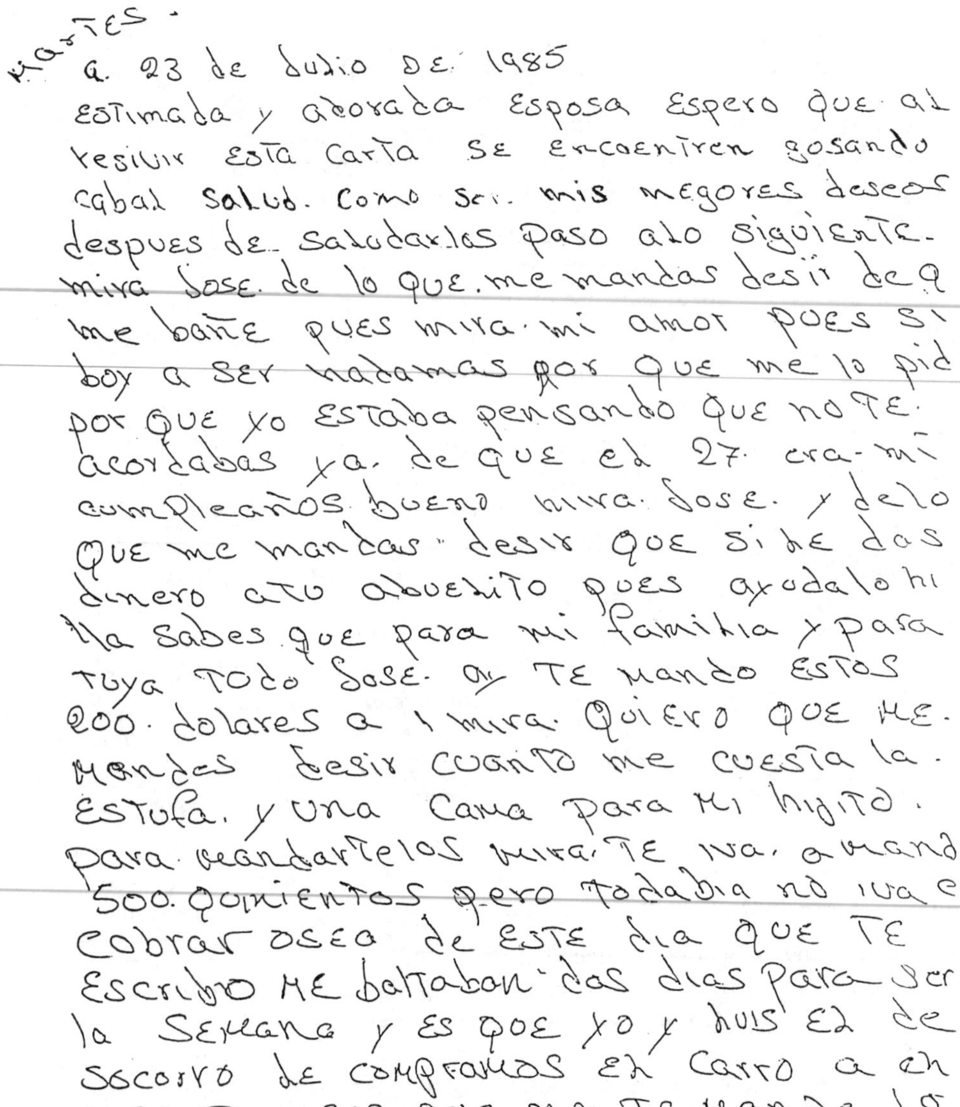

Martes.

a. 23 de Julio DE 1985
estimada y adorada esposa espero que al
resivir esta carta se encuentren gosando
cabal salud. como ser. mis megores deseos
despues de saludarlos paso alo siguiente.
mira Jose. de lo que me mandas desir de q
me bañe pues mira. mi amor pues si
boy a ser nadamas por que me lo pid
por que yo estaba pensando que no te.
acordabas ya. de que el 27. era mi
cumpleaños bueno mira. Jose. y delo
que me mandas desir que si le das
dinero a tu abuelito pues ayudalo hi
ya sabes que para mi familia y para
tuya todo Jose. oy te mando estos
200. dolares a 1 mira. Quiero que me.
mandes desir cuanto me cuesta la.
estufa. y una cama para mi hijito.
para mandartelos mira. te iva. a mand
500. quinientos pero todabia no iva e
cobrar oseo de este dia que te
escribo me faltaban dos dias para ser
la semana y es que yo y luis el de
socorro le compramos el carro a eh
y es por eso que no te mande lo.
400. es lo que te iva amandar pe
agarre 200, pero mira. este.
sabado te boy amandar. otros 10 c

Figure 1. Example of sight translation document.

the hearing officer. In some cases, all that is needed is an explanation of what the document is, or a summary of its contents. That assessment should be made by the court, however; interpreters should never decide on their own to summarize a document. If a translation of the entire document is required, interpreters should inform the court how long they think it will take to do the research. If they do not feel competent to translate the document at all, this should be made clear.

5. Skills Required

5.1. Full Command of Working Languages

It is clear, then, that court interpreters will encounter a very wide range of subject matters and registers in the documents they are called upon to sight translate. They must therefore have a full command of both the SL and the TL at all levels of usage so that they can render every aspect of meaning accurately.

5.2. Public Speaking

Another skill required for sight translation is public speaking: voice projection, clear enunciation, good posture, and smooth pacing. Coughlin (1984) states that the court interpreter "will...need to be heard distinctly and clearly and he will have to know how to protect his voice from becoming strained after several hours of work" (p. 420). When sight translation is done properly, it sounds as if the interpreter is simply reading a document written in the TL.

5.3. Mental Agility

As the interpreter is uttering the TL version of one segment of the SL document, he or she is also reading ahead in the document, analyzing the contents, and preparing what he or she will say next. In other words, his or her mind is working on two channels at once, and this requires a great deal of agility and flexibility. The most difficult aspect of sight translation is that the SL text is on paper, and it is therefore much easier to be constrained by the structure of the original. The interpreter must avoid being "hypnotized by the words," as Seleskovitch (1978a) emphasizes, concentrating instead on the underlying meaning:

> Words are actually a hindrance and not a help when one attempts to make sense out of a string of hundreds, if not thousands, of words. Taken in isolation, a word has a tendency to evoke all its current connotations and even its etymological meaning. The more evanescent, the more fleeting a word is, the easier it will be for the interpreter to discard it and retain only the meaning of the message; an accurate interpreter preserves meaning, not words. (p. 18)

As has been stressed repeatedly in this text, the interpreter must abandon the external structure of the SL message and penetrate to the underlying meaning.

6. Process of Sight Translation

These are the steps the interpreter follows when performing a typical sight translation, step by step: First, the interpreter takes a few moments to scan the document to determine the subject matter, context, style, and country of origin, and to discern the overall meaning of the text. An interpreter who is adept at sight translation will be able to grasp the meaning and intent of the document by immediately identifying the subject and predicate of each sentence. The interpreter is also alert to and makes a mental note of common pitfalls that are unique to the SL, such as dangling participles, and features such as parenthetical statements that can pose problems for sight translation in any language. Utilizing features such as punctuation (commas, parentheses, dashes), the interpreter skims passages quickly and identifies key features.

Then the interpreter begins translating sentence by sentence, focusing on one unit of meaning at a time. As the interpreter is uttering translation of one unit, the interpreter's eyes are scanning the next unit and he or she is analyzing its meaning in preparation for translating it. As we noted in Chapter 24, however, units of meaning are not always conveniently lined up one after another; they may be divided up. For example, in a typical criminal complaint, the interpreter will see a phrase like this: "did willfully, unlawfully and feloniously commit an assault. . . ." The verb in this sentence is "did commit an assault"; those four words are a single unit of meaning. The experienced interpreter will recognize that "did" is a past tense marker, will know that the words between it and the verb are adverbials, and will then search for the verb after the adverbials before attempting to translate the sentence.

It is important to maintain a steady pace when sight translating. One unit of meaning may be very easy to translate because it has a direct equivalent in the TL, while the next unit requires some mental gymnastics and takes a little longer. Interpreters should not hurry through the first one, only to be bogged down on the next. Rather, they should utter the TL rendition of the first unit slowly and evenly, buying time to concentrate on how they are going to handle the next unit.

7. Exercises

The novice interpreter can do a variety of exercises to build the skills required for sight translation. These exercises are grouped according to the particular skill that they emphasize. They should be performed in all of the interpreter's working languages.

7.1. Public Speaking Exercises

(1) *Reading aloud*: Take a magazine, newspaper, or book (a law textbook or legal form book would be helpful to practice reading legal language) and read passages aloud. It helps to have an audience, but if you do not have one, standing in front of a mirror is sufficient. Record yourself on audio- or videotape, and as you play back the tape, listen to yourself critically as if you were someone in the audience. Pay attention to your voice, posture, and speech mannerisms.

(2) *Controlling emotions*: Choose texts with a high emotional content (humor, anger, sadness) or with very controversial themes, and read them aloud as in Exercise (1). Practice controlling your emotions, making sure that you convey the emotion the author would have, not your personal reaction to the text.

(3) *Public speaking*: Look for opportunities to speak in public (school board meetings, city council meetings, church groups). Speaking before a group of people you know in a non-threatening situation helps you "break the ice" and gain confidence, so that speaking in an interpreting situation will no longer seem so intimidating.

7.2. Reading Ahead in Text

(1) *Extensive reading*: Build up your reading speed by reading as often as possible in a wide variety of fields (this also helps build vocabulary).

(2) *Analyzing*: After reading a text, analyze its content. Practice picking out the subject and verb of each sentence to find the basic kernels of meaning.

Example: Although less influential than in Argentina, migration from Europe in the late nineteenth and early twentieth centuries affected the development of Chilean political culture.

Subject: migration   Verb: affected

(3) *Identifying sentences and embedded sentences*: Read a text aloud, and as you are reading, break up long sentences into smaller, more manageable units.

Example: Juvenile delinquency, which is seen more often among minority youths in urban ghettos, nevertheless cannot be attributed to the urban environment alone, as it plagues the suburbs as well.

There are three embedded sentences in this complex sentence:

- (a) Juvenile delinquency is seen more often among minority youths in urban ghettos.
- (b) It cannot be attributed to the urban environment alone.
- (c) It plagues the suburbs as well.

(4) *Deciphering handwriting*: Obtain texts written by hand (e.g., letters), and practice deciphering the handwriting on the first oral reading.

7.3. Analytical Skills

(1) *Reading for content*: Read a text aloud to a friend, and afterward have the person ask you questions about its content.

(2) *Chunking*: Choose a text and mark off the units of meaning in it:

Example: I was getting ready to go out to lunch with my mother-in-law when all of a sudden I felt sick to my stomach. It occurred to me that it might be something psychosomatic, but I later found out that I was simply allergic to the perfume she always wore.

I was getting ready / to go out to lunch / with my mother-in-law / when all of a sudden / I felt sick to my stomach. / It occurred to me / that it might be something psychosomatic, / but I later found out / that I was simply allergic to the perfume / she always wore.

(3) *Using transcripts*: Perform the same task with transcripts of court proceedings (or any document with a question-and-answer format). Try to establish a hierarchy of importance of the units of meaning.

Example: Now, Mr. Jones, in your earlier testimony you mentioned that you had seen the defendant in that bar prior to the date of the incident. Can you tell us, or give us an approximation of, how long before the incident it was that you first saw the defendant in the El Camino bar?

Hierarchy of importance:

    (a) How long before the incident

    (b) You first saw the defendant

    (c) In the El Camino bar

    (d) Tell us, or give approximation

    (e) Had seen defendant prior to date of incident

    (f) Mentioned in earlier testimony

    (g) Mr. Jones

    (h) Now

(4) *Completing phrases*: Have a friend write a series of incomplete phrases. Complete the phrases and determine whether the resulting sentences convey the same idea the friend originally had in mind.

Example: After being reprimanded unfairly by her boss in front of her co-workers, the secretary tendered . . .

The judge determined that the defendant had strong ties to the community, and therefore released him . . .

As you do this exercise, take note of the errors you make and be aware of how susceptible we are to reaching false conclusions based on partial information.

(5) *Paraphrasing*: Read a text out loud, and rephrase it as you are going along, taking care not to change the meaning.

Example: Since political parties are found almost everywhere in Latin America, they would seem to be a common denominator in the region's political life. Yet this is not the case. Cultural, environmental, and historical influences on party development are so varied they challenge conventional notions. Most nations hold periodic elections, but, like parties, the implications of elections differ profoundly from those we assume from our own culture.

Rephrased: Because political parties can be found in just about every Latin American country, one might conclude that they are a common thread in the political life of this region. This is not so, however. There is such a great variety of cultural, environmental, and historical influences on the development of parties that commonly held ideas are contradicted. Elections are held periodically in the majority of countries, but the implications of these proceedings, like those of parties, are very different from the assumptions we can make in our own culture.

(6) *Expanding*: Read a text aloud, and expand it (that is, say the same thing in more words) as you are going along, again taking care not to change the meaning.

Example: In spite of what you may have heard, scientists are just like other people. A scientist walking down the street may look just like an insurance agent or a car salesman: no wild mane of hair, no white lab coat.

Expanded: Although you may have heard assertions to the contrary, there are no differences between scientists and people who are not in that profession. As a matter of fact, if you saw a scientist out for a stroll on the sidewalk, you might mistake him for a person who sells insurance, or an automobile dealer. Scientists don't all have wild manes of hair, and they don't always wear white laboratory coats.

(7) *Condensing*: Read a text aloud, and condense it (that is, say the same thing in fewer words) as you are going along, retaining the same meaning.

Example: The multiplicity of cues which are utilized in the categorizing and sorting of the environment into significant classes are reconstructed from the strategies and modes of coping with the problems presented to the subjects. In many situations, no certainty can be achieved; the varying trustworthiness and merely statistical validity of the cues frequently make inferences only probable.

Condensed: Many cues are used to classify the environment. They are reconstructed from the subjects' problem-solving strategies. Often, because the cues are not uniformly reliable and are only statistically valid, the results are not certain.

(8) *Manipulating the register*: Read a text aloud, and alter the register or language level as you go along, being careful not to stray from the original meaning.

Example: As I was driving to work in the morning, I noticed that the stop sign which used to be on the corner of Main and 1st had been removed.

Higher level: Upon transporting myself to my place of employment in a motor vehicle at some point in time prior to noon, I observed that the insignia which had formerly been stationed at the intersection of the thoroughfares known as Main and 1st to cause motorists to bring their vehicles to a stationary position, had been displaced.

Lower level: On my way to work in the morning I saw that they took out the stop sign that used to be at Main and 1st.

Note: These are learning exercises designed to build mental agility, linguistic flexibility, and analytical skills, and to heighten awareness of language usage. In actual sight translation, the interpreter does not paraphrase, summarize, or change the register of the original text.

Unit 7

Practical Considerations and Tasks

Chapter 29

Introduction to the Courtroom and Legal Actors

The previous units have provided an explanation of the need for interpretation in the courts and an overview of general criminal and legal procedure. Other units discuss the cognitive and linguistic complexity of the interpreting process, and the professional and ethical issues that guide the interpreter in practice.

In order to be successful, interpreters must enter the courtroom with a full command of the language, tools, and interpreting skills of their craft, and with a knowledge of courtroom procedure and pragmatics. In addition to excellent language and interpreting skills and an awareness of professional ethics, interpreters must have an understanding of their role in relation to other legal actors in the courtroom. This unit will introduce:

(1) the roles and functions of the all the participants in the courtroom;

(2) the logistics of the courtroom and place of the interpreter;

(3) an introduction to tape transcription and document translation; and

(4) language resources for the court interpreter.

It is safe to say that court interpreters beginning their career are typically entering the courtroom for the first time in their lives. The paradox is that interpreters are judged by others in the courtroom by how well they "appear" to know their responsibilities.

Historically, court interpreters have had no orientation to the physical courtroom prior to their first assignment. Yet a familiarity with the physical setting enables them to perform their function as language intermediaries in a confident and professional manner. The following section will discuss the physical courtroom and its participants.

1. The Physical Courtroom

A court is the place where legal matters are heard. It need not be a formal courtroom. For example, if a judge hears a matter in a hospital room, a jail, or any other location, that is where the "court" is. However, this section will focus on the formal courtroom with the traditional accouterments for the hearing of legal matters.

Although the architecture may vary or the relative location or style of the furnishings may change, the courtroom is the same, be it in a modern building with bleached oak courtrooms resembling a theater, or in an older, darker and more somber setting with noisy air conditioners and dark mahogany walls. The courtroom remains immutable: there is always a place for the audience, tables for counsel, the jury box, witness stand, and a judge's bench.

Immediately apparent upon walking into the courtroom is the audience seating area. Our system of justice incorporates the presence of the public. One has the right not only to a speedy trial but also a public one. Some sensational trials draw a large audience and the courtroom is filled to capacity with spectators. On the other hand, traffic courts with a single function, the arraignment of the accused, provide large seating areas only to accommodate a large number of people with traffic-related cases.

The interpreter will often interpret an arraignment for a defendant in the audience seating area. After rendering the statement of rights, the interpreter will often be called upon to read the complaint to the person in custody so that the defendant may be aware of the charges prior to entering the plea. If a defendant in custody has an attorney, the interpreter will be called upon to interpret in an attorney-client pre-plea conference. At all other times, the interpreter will usually be inside the railing.

The audience seating area is separated from the legal arena proper by a railing also known as the "bar of justice." It serves as a barrier and effectively maintains a physical division between the audience and the principal actors in the courtroom. It is sometimes a deterrent. Witnesses are not certain, despite being called forward, that they are to cross that line. New court interpreters are not yet confident as to their role or where they are to sit. The railing is a powerful and silent symbol of the power of the court.

2. The Legal Arena

Inside the railing is the legal arena—the sanctuary of the courtroom. This is where the accusation is made, all evidence presented, and all testimony heard. Here is where the court interpreter functions as a court attache in matters that involve the non-English-speaking defendant and/or witness. The configuration of the legal arena will change in accordance with the level of government, local preference, and architectural considerations.

2.1. Counsel Table

Closest in proximity to the railing in the arena are counsel tables. The main function of counsel tables is to provide a work area for both the prosecution and the defense. The tables are usually rectangular and face the judge's bench (see Figure 1).

The tables may be V-shaped with the apex away from the bench to allow the attorneys and the judge to face each other at a slight angle. The tables may even be half-round with the open end toward the judge's bench. In the United States district courts, the counsel tables usually face each other, with attorneys from each side sitting on the outside and facing the middle.

The counsel table is the place where interpreters most frequently work. Here they will interpret all of the proceedings for the benefit of the defendant, as well as interpreting for the judge, defense or prosecuting attorneys, and all witnesses. All verbal exchanges are interpreted for the defendant, be they objections, recitations of points and authorities, casual or formal comments between the judge and attorneys, or anything that an English-speaking defendant would hear.

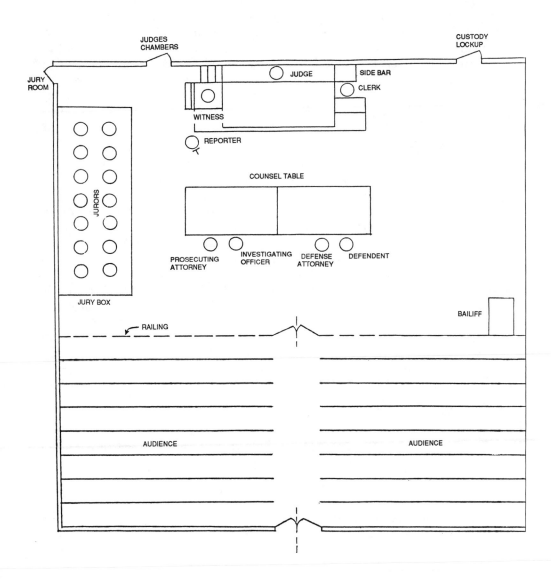

Figure 1. Typical configuration of courtroom at trial.

One of the most common proceedings in which the interpreter performs at counsel table is the arraignment. The defendant may either appear without benefit of counsel, in *propia persona* (or in *pro se*), or be represented by counsel. The defendant may be arraigned by either the judge or a prosecutor. In any case, the interpreter must stand next to the defendant and be prepared to interpret the arraignment procedure without any formal invitation by the judge. During this proceeding the interpreter stands at a right angle to the defendant so that the interpreter is speaking into the defendant's ear. Or the interpreter may choose to stand slightly behind the defendant in order to see the judge and have access to the defendant's ear at the same time (see Figure 2).

In all other proceedings, such as motions, trials, and preliminary hearings, where the defendant is at counsel table, the interpreter sits next to the defendant and interprets the proceedings simultaneously into the defendant's ear. It is advisable for the interpreter to position himself or herself in such a way that the defendant is situated between the interpreter and the witness at the stand. This will enable the interpreter to see and hear the witness at the same time. If the interpreter is sitting between the defendant and the attorney, the interpreter will be forced to interpret while looking away from a witness at the stand. The second benefit of this relative positioning is to put distance between the interpreter's voice and the defense attorney who might be distracted by the interpretation going on at his or her side. As in the arraignment procedure, the interpreter may choose to utilize the corner of the table to sit at a right angle to the defendant's ear, or elect to sit behind the defendant's shoulder for close accessibility to the defendant's ear. It is recommended that the interpreter choose one of these two positions so as to eliminate the strain of having to lean and interpret out of the side of his or her mouth (see Figure 3).

In the case of multiple non-English-speaking defendants, there are several options:

(1) one interpreter for all defendants, in which one person interprets for any number of defendants loud enough to be heard by all defendants, but not so loud as to disturb the court;

(2) one interpreter for each defendant, in which several people are interpreting for their respective defendants concurrently;

(3) the use of electronic equipment with headphones for each defendant, with one interpreter serving all defendants and a second interpreter standing by for any attorney-client conference that may be necessary. The second interpreter sits inside the railing, near the counsel table.

Each scenario has its relative merits as outlined in Unit 2.

2.2. Jury Box

The jury box may be either on the right or on the left, depending on the design of the courtroom. Its position, however, will determine which side of the room the prosecution will sit on. The prosecutor will always sit at counsel table nearest the jury and the defense will occupy the opposite end. The jury box will, in a criminal court, usually contain twelve chairs or seats for the jury. It is not unusual, however, for the jury box to contain fourteen seats to allow for the alternate jurors who might be called upon to take the place of any regular juror who may be unable to continue.

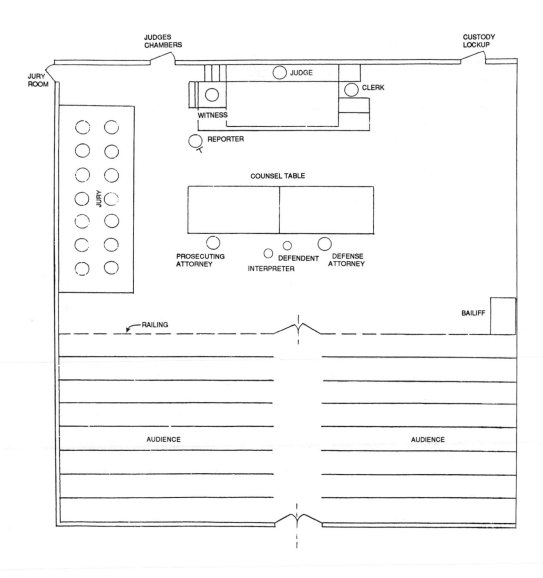

Figure 2. Position of interpreter during arraignment.

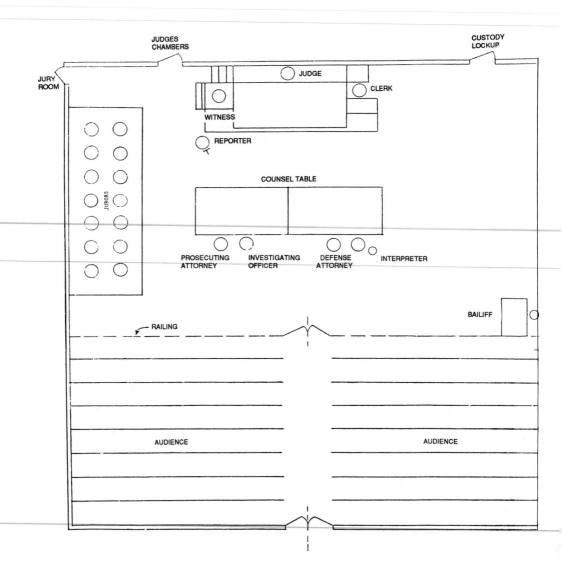

Figure 3. Placement of interpreter at counsel table.

Like the audience seating area, the jury box is frequently used to seat defendants who are in custody during arraignment. Some of those in custody speak no English, and it is here in the jury box that some court interpreters function as the linguistic link between the accused and the court (see Figure 4).

2.3. Witness Stand

Nearest the jury box is the witness stand. The jury not only needs to clearly hear the words of the witness but also must weigh the manner and comportment of the witness giving testimony. Close observation of a witness is an essential part of determining the credibility of that witness. It is at the witness stand that the interpreter becomes the most visible.

Traditionally, courtrooms have not been designed to accommodate interpreters at the witness stand. The court interpreter has been obliged to stand outside of the witness box and behind the witness so as to not obscure the view of the jurors. Often, the interpreter has to be positioned on the small steps that lead up to the witness stand (see Figure 5).

In some courtrooms the dimensions of the witness box allow a second chair to be placed behind or next to the witness. Some recently constructed courthouses have been planned to accommodate the interpreter by providing space in the witness stand and a second microphone for the interpreter. The provision of sufficient space for the interpreter lessens the fatigue experienced; reducing fatigue increases the fidelity of the interpretation and thus protects the accuracy of the record.

2.4. Judge's Bench

Generally, the judge's bench is the focal point of the courtroom and occupies the most elevated position. The judge presides from the bench close to the witness stand and the clerk's desk. The judge may enter from either side and will usually ascend to his or her seat from the same side. The judge's private office, which is behind the rear wall, is termed the judge's chambers. The judge may summon attorneys into chambers for conference, or attorneys may request to speak to the judge in chambers. The judge will conduct *in camera* inspections of evidence in chambers. During proceedings, the judge may also request attorneys to approach the bench and to speak to him or her at the **side bar**, which may be on either side of the bench. The **side bar conference** is usually on the record and as a consequence the court reporter joins the attorneys and judge at the side bar. However, since the conversation at the side bar is not audible to the defendant, interpretation is not required.

The court reporter is in close proximity to the judge's bench; the reporter usually sits immediately in front of the witness stand and may face in any direction (see Figure 5). As in the case of the interpreter, new courtrooms sometimes have a space built for the court reporter.

3. Lock-Up

Behind either the rear wall or one of the side walls there may be one or more temporary holding cells for those who are in custody waiting to appear in court.

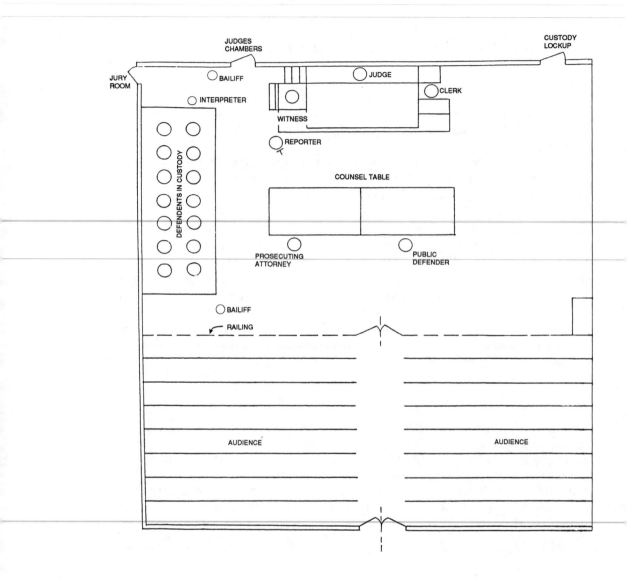

Figure 4. Position of interpreter during custody arraignment.

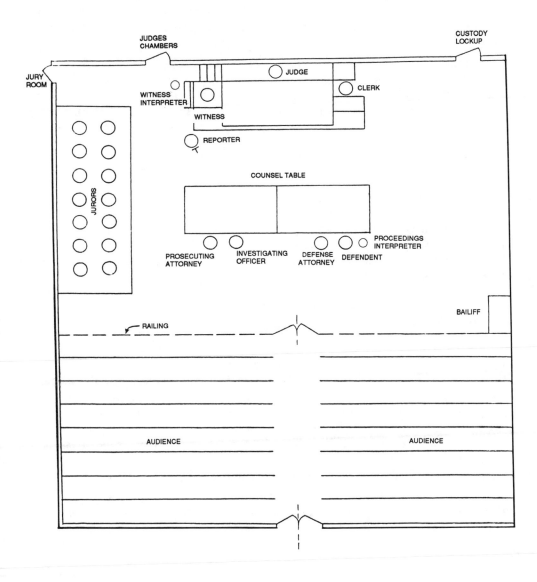

Figure 5. Placement of interpreter in the witness box.

These cells are called the **lock-up**. Those in police custody are transported daily from the jail to the courthouse and then transported back at the end of the day. The court interpreter is frequently called upon to assist in attorney-client interviews in the lock-up.

In large courthouses the lock-ups are large, roomy and provide for a glassed-in interview room under lock and key where the person in custody is observed at all times by the custodial agency. Smaller lock-ups have no such facilities and there is no other option but to speak to the defendant through the bars of the lock-up. There is always a temporary lock-up somewhere in the courthouse.

4. Legal Actors

Until now, the role of the interpreter has been an ambiguous one and neither the interpreter nor the other participants have had a clear understanding of the boundaries of and relationship to other legal actors. Much of these issues is discussed in the Professional Issues unit. It is imperative that the interpreter know all aspects of the other legal actors' functions.

4.1. The Judge

The judge is the presiding officer who oversees all legal matters and personnel in the courtroom. The judge makes all final determinations on motions, findings of fact, admission of evidence, and instructions of law. All comments by the judge, whatever their nature, are to be interpreted, with the exception of side bar conferences. Judges are greatly concerned that non-English speakers receive a true and accurate rendition of the proceedings. In the absence of a jury, the judge is the sole trier of fact, who alone determines the credibility of the witnesses and renders judgment. In the case of limited- and non-English speakers, judges depend upon an accurate interpretation of testimony free from additions, deletions, and modifications.

Finally, the judge is the ultimate arbiter of the record or court transcript. He or she may decide upon his or her own motion or upon motion of counsel to delete or modify the record. When the interpreter is aware of an interpretation error on the record, it is incumbent upon the interpreter to ask the judge to correct the record, with full confidence that the opportunity will be afforded. The judge relies upon the linguistic expertise of the interpreter, who has sworn to accurately interpret the testimony into English for the court record. That oath includes the correction of errors and the clarification of language ambiguities with non-English speakers. All problems that affect the interpreter's ability to interpret are to be referred to the judge for final resolution, as recommended in Unit 8, Professional Issues.

4.2. Clerk of Court

The clerk of court sits opposite the witness stand and is the business manager of the court. All matters that pertain to the court must be processed through the clerk, such as the filing of motions, appointments and requests to see the judge, and all fines that are paid directly to the court. In federal courts, and in some state courts, the management of language services falls within the purview of the clerk, who is responsible for planning and managing the court calendar. All parties, such as the prosecution, the defense, witnesses, the court reporter, the jurors, and the interpreter, report to the clerk of court to coordinate their participation and appearances.

The interpreter presents the court clerk with a business card and indicates the case to which the interpreter has been assigned or queries the clerk in the event that the interpreter does not know. In some jurisdictions, the clerk will have made the initial call to the interpreter to appear in court. Often the clerk not only has the authority to contract interpreters but may also be authorized to disburse payment, in the absence of a supervisory interpreter's office.

4.3. Court Reporter

The function of the court reporter is to provide an accurate, word-for-word transcript of the proceedings. It is imperative that the court reporter be aware of court interpreters' names and cases. Therefore, after presenting themselves to the clerk of the court, interpreters should identify themselves to the court reporter and also present a business card.

During the course of the interpreted proceedings, the court reporter frequently is unable to correctly spell non-English names, nicknames, and foreign geographic names that may come up in testimony. The court interpreter should be aware of this problem and should compile a list of these names for the court reporter as the proceeding progresses.

4.4. Bailiffs, Marshalls, and Sheriffs

Historically, there has always been an official in the courtroom whose duty is to maintain order. The bailiff is a peace officer and has power of arrest. Should there be any disruption in the courthouse, it is the bailiff's responsibility to quell the disturbance. Sheriffs, marshalls, or anyone appointed to maintain order may fulfill the capacity of bailiff. Who is appointed to serve as bailiff depends on the level of government and the local governmental organization. For example, in Los Angeles County, the Los Angeles County marshalls serve the function of bailiff in the various municipal courtrooms. The Los Angeles County sheriffs perform the same function in the superior courts. In United States district court many of the duties of the bailiff are performed by the United States federal marshalls.

One of the responsibilities of the bailiff is to contribute to the smooth functioning of the court by answering questions posed by the public. Bailiffs ensure that all participants, in particular defendants and witnesses, are in the right courtroom. They are usually in uniform; United States marshalls wear civilian attire with or without a badge displayed. Bailiffs, in their capacity as peace officers, have the power of arrest and may go into the field to serve subpoenas and/or arrest warrants. However, the primary responsibility of the bailiff is courtroom security. The bailiff may also be the temporary jailer of the in-custody defendants who are in the lock-up awaiting a court appearance. The bailiff is usually stationed just inside the courtroom railing, and acts as the buffer between the court and the audience. Should the court so order, the bailiff is also the officer who takes a defendant into custody. The baliff may also be charged with sequestering the jury, and is responsible for their isolation during deliberations.

4.5. Defense and Prosecution Attorneys

The prosecutor is the complaining party in a criminal action and represents the people of the governmental jurisdiction. If the prosecutor represents a municipality in a local court, such as a traffic court, he or she is a city attorney; at the state court level the prosecutor is the county district attorney; in the United States district court the prosecutor is the United States attorney. The prosecutor is referred to as "the People" in local and state courts, whereas in United States district courts he or she is termed "the Government." Prosecutors are charged with enforcing the law in their jurisdiction and are empowered to bring a criminal complaint against a person. If they are to secure a conviction by a judge or jury, they must meet the burden of proof. The prosecutor's office is empowered to amend the complaint and/or can enter into plea bargain agreements with the defense in exchange for a guilty plea by the defendant.

Often the prosecutor's case will depend on non-English-speaking witnesses, whose testimony must be interpreted in open court. In these instances the interpreter will be assigned to the prosecutor. Outside of the courtroom, the interpreter will help the prosecutor's office in the development of a case in pre-appearance witness interviews and with the translation of crucial evidentiary exhibits including documents, audio- and videotapes, letters, and records.

Because prosecutors have the burden of proof, they are given the privilege of sitting at counsel table closest to the jury and directly in front of the witness stand (see Figure 5), and of giving the first and last argument before the jury. Depending on the complexity of the case, the prosecutor may act alone or in concert with assistant prosecutors and/or an investigating officer of the law, such as a police officer, a DEA, FBI, INS, or CIA agent.

The defense attorney represents the person charged in a criminal complaint brought by the government, and may be a public defender, a private attorney appointed by the court at public expense, or an attorney privately hired by the defendant. The public defender is provided at public expense. In order to secure the services of a public defender, defendants must first file a financial affidavit with the court attesting to their indigent status. The judge then assigns an attorney from the public defender's office to the defendant. If the public defender's office is unable to provide defense counsel for an indigent defendant, the court may appoint a private attorney at public expense to defend a defendant. Those defendants who are able to afford their own attorney may hire any attorney of their choice.

All defense attorneys must be able to communicate with their clients and to interview prospective witnesses. Limited- or non-English-speaking defendants will only be able to communicate with their attorneys or participate in their own defense through an interpreter. Court interpreters are most frequently assigned to work with the defense. All written and oral communication between attorney and client is privileged and must not be divulged to anyone by the interpreter. Any such breach of confidence violates all interpreter codes of ethics and is punishable by law.

An interpreter working with the defense can interpret interviews in jail for defendants who are in custody. For defendants who are not in custody, i.e., out on their own recognizance or out on bail, the interpreter will assist in the attorney-client interview in the attorney's office, the courthouse, the lock-up, the attorney interview room, or even in the hall. Pre-appearance interviews with the witnesses can take place anywhere, even in a field setting, if necessary. In preparation for a court hearing, the interpreter will also translate for the defense any pertinent documents such as letters, birth and marriage certificates, and contracts.

During trial the interpreter, in addition to interpreting for the defendant at the counsel table, may also interpret at the stand for witnesses and/or the defendant, should the defendant elect to testify in his or her own defense. The defense counsel will sit at counsel table farthest from the jury box. In rare instances, defense counsel will be assisted by co-defense counsel. Frequently, a defendant may elect to act as his or her own attorney. When interpreting for the defendant in his or her capacity as a defendant, the interpreter sits at the counsel table as mentioned above. However, should the defendant elect to stand and address the judge or jury as his or her own defense counsel, the interpreter will then stand and interpret for the defendant regardless of location—at counsel table, at the podium, or in front of the jury.

4.6. The Jurors

The jury usually is composed of twelve jurors and two or more alternates. Prospective jurors are selected at random from a larger jury panel that is drawn from the community at large. The final selection of the jury takes place after *voir dire* examination by the judge, the prosecutor, and the defense attorney. The jurors act as triers of fact and render judgment in place of the judge in a jury trial. So great is the need for the impartiality of the jury that all officers of the court, including the interpreter, are enjoined from having any direct or indirect communication with the jury hearing a matter. Even casual conversations between the interpreter and a member of the jury—in a hallway or in an elevator—may give rise to the appearance of impropriety, which should be avoided at all costs. In order to weigh the non-English evidence presented, the jury—like the judge—depends upon the interpreter's precise rendition of the original testimony.

4.7. The Witnesses

In a criminal action the testimony of witnesses must not be tainted or influenced by the testimony of prior witnesses. To ensure that witnesses are not so affected, they are frequently ordered to wait in the hall or in a witness waiting room until they are called to render their testimony. Interpreters who are to interpret for a non-English-speaking witness should be aware that when the witness is called, the person may be confused and uncertain as to where to go. The interpreter should anticipate this by being at the stand and interpreting any court officer's direction to "please step forward, and be sworn." When the interpreter hears the defendant's name called as the next witness, the interpreter should guide or beckon the defendant to the witness stand. The interpreter should not wait for any direction to be given before doing this for the defendant. For this reason, the interpreter should be aware of who the non-English-speaking witnesses are prior to the commencement of the proceedings. This information can be obtained from the clerk of court, the prosecutor, the defense attorney, and from the reading of the complaint.

The interpreter should anticipate the need for interpreter services should a determination be made at the stand that a witness is limited- or non-English speaking. Upon such discovery, the interpreter should move to the stand without waiting for instruction. The ability of the interpreter to foresee the need for interpreting services, and make smooth transitions from one location to another within the courtroom, inspires the court's confidence and exemplifies professionalism. Like other officers of the court, interpreters take their cues from the sequence of events and knowledge of the legal process.

Interpreters are bound by their oath and professional codes of ethics to "well and truly" interpret from one language to another. This ethical obligation requires that interpreters be privy to all court documents that will facilitate the conceptual and linguistic understanding of the testimony. The interpreter's oath further demands that interpreters take the initiative to seek any and all information that will aid them to better serve the court. Interpreters should aggressively seek information from whatever source is available. For example, the complaint, transcripts from prior preliminary hearings, and police reports are all valuable resources for preparation of terminology. Prior to the commencement of the proceedings, interpreters should feel free to consult with attorneys about the nature of the proceedings, and identify names, places, and dates that will be important. Interpreters should not feel that they are excluded from the legal arena, and should move about the courtroom freely.

Chapter 30

Pragmatics of Judicial Proceedings and the Interpreter

Now that the logistics of the courtroom and its legal actors have been introduced, the pragmatics of a judicial proceeding as it relates to interpreters will be discussed. The following chronology will outline the actions of interpreters from arrival at the courthouse, through all of the phases of the trial, to its completion. It will also explain how interpreters communicate with the assignment office. For the purposes of this example, assume that the interpreter has been assigned to a particular trial by case name, case number, and courtroom. This scenario assumes that the defendant with whom the interpreter will be working has been arrested and arraigned, has entered a not-guilty plea, and elected to go to trial.

When interpreters are called by the assignment officer, they should obtain as much information as possible about the assignment including the type of proceeding, number of defendants, correct spelling of names, specific courtroom, and the street address of the courthouse. If possible, interpreters should procure and refer to a courthouse directory.

After ascertaining the nature of the case, the interpreter should obtain all pertinent reference materials. In particular, relevant glossaries and dictionaries should be taken to the court with the interpreter. The interpreter should be equipped with note pad, pen, and a good, lightweight bilingual dictionary. Some professional interpreters carry a briefcase with a small library of reference materials for easy access during proceedings. During the preparation period and when interpreting witness testimony at the stand, the interpreter will need to take notes, using the dictionary only to look up specialized or unfamiliar terminology. Some novice interpreters fear that carrying a dictionary might give the impression of poor language control, and that taking notes might suggest a poor memory. However, the opposite is true. Those who use reference materials actually demonstrate that they are precise in their use of words and are language lovers. Good consecutive interpretation techniques require note-taking, for even those who possess an excellent memory cannot remember each and every utterance. Rather than crutches, these implements should be regarded as vital tools of the craft.

At all costs, the universal nightmare of court interpreters should be avoided: that of being caught unprepared for the case at hand. Sometimes the interpreter is brought into a matter only after much time and effort has been expended trying to get along without an interpreter, or when it is belatedly discovered that the defendant or witness does not speak English. It may be that there has been prior testimony of which the newly assigned interpreter has no knowledge. The situation is obviously fraught with peril, but, happily, it is not the norm. The interpreter normally can and should prepare for the proceedings by making inquiries of counsel and by interviewing, if possible,

429

after attaining counsel's permission, the non-English speakers involved. This is especially true when the non-English speaker is to be a witness.

The efficient functioning of the court is dependent upon the timely arrival of all parties involved: attorneys, defendants, witnesses, the court reporter, and the interpreter. For this reason, the interpreter is well advised to arrive at the assigned courtroom in advance of the scheduled time. A morning assignment is typically for 9:00 A.M., although the courtroom is usually open a half hour before. Often the court calendar is posted outside of the courtroom. The interpreter should locate the correct courtroom and confirm the scheduling of the case.

The first responsibility of the interpreter upon entering the courtroom is to introduce himself or herself to the court clerk, the attorneys involved and the court reporter, providing them with a professional business card. He or she should inform them of the case to which he or she is assigned and inquire about the specific nature of the proceedings. The issue of identification of the court interpreter is so vital that some interpreters have attempted to solve the problem on their own by wearing name tags identifying themselves as court interpreters. In the United States Court, Central District of California, court interpreters wear photo identification cards and official identification badges issued by the federal court. The proper identification of court interpreters will allow them to move freely about the courtroom, in and about jails and lock-ups, and will prevent misunderstandings (e.g., mistaking the interpreter for an attorney).

Interpreters should inquire about the specific nature of the charges involved. They should begin thinking in terms of the topic, retrieving from memory terminology associated with the case, be it driving under the influence, rape, or the use of firearms.

In order to begin this preparation, the interpreter should make the following inquiries of defense counsel:

(1) I am _____ , the interpreter for the defense.
(2) Is there anything you can tell me that will help me interpret in this matter?
(3) Are you going to call any witnesses, and if so, what are their names?
(4) What are the witnesses going to say?
(5) Are there going to be any expert witnesses in this case?
(6) Is there anything that the expert has produced that I can read?
(7) What country is the defendant from?
(8) Is the defendant going to take the stand?
(9) May I interview your client to be able to hear if there are any language problems?
(10) Do you have any documents pertaining to the matter at hand that I could read, that are of particular interest to me, like a preliminary hearing transcript (see Unit 3, Chapter 14).

If prosecution witnesses are non-English speakers, the interpreter should interview the prosecutor to become familiar with any exhibits to be introduced into evidence. For example, the interpreter should inquire about the existence of tape transcripts, photographs, weapons, drug packages, and other evidence that is to be presented so as to be familiar with the terminology to be used at trial. The interpreter can ask: "Are you going to offer any physical exhibits?" If the exhibits are available, the interpreter should view them. For example, if the interpreter sees that one of the packages is wrapped in duct tape and will be described that way, the interpreter should refer to the dictionary in order to find out how "duct tape" is said in the other language. However, if the exhibits are not available to view, the interpreter should simply note the exhibits the prosecutor has enumerated.

The interpreter should also determine whether the prosecution will be calling any non-English-speaking or expert witnesses and the names of those witnesses. If an expert witness is to be used, it is predictable that the testimony will pertain strictly to the expert's profession. Equally predictable is the fact that such testimony will be extremely complex and replete with technical vocabulary. For example, if a fingerprint expert is called, then the interpreter can assume that a latent print was lifted from the scene of the crime and taken to an identification laboratory, that a fingerprint exemplar was taken from the defendant and a comparison made by an expert, resulting in a determination on the points of similarity between the prints. The expert's language may be predictable for an experienced interpreter, since it is so highly specialized. To a developing interpreter, the language of experts presents a sometimes overwhelming challenge.

The interpreter should also ask if there will be any other witnesses requiring interpreting services or if there will be a second interpreter. It should be obvious that prior to the proceedings, the interpreter may ask questions of any officer of the court, with the exception of the judge. Rarely will information be forthcoming if the interpreter does not take the initiative to ask for it. The roles of all the officers of the court have evolved over hundreds of years, and there is no doubt as to what the other actors in the legal arena may or may not do. All is defined and may even be part of statutory law. This is not true for court interpreters. Court interpreters are essentially establishing precedent in each courtroom where they practice. Thus, court interpreters should not be alarmed if they encounter resistance to their requests for information, but should be ready to elaborate on the reasons for the requests (see Unit 8, Chapter 34, Section 5.4).

The preparation phase can take place anywhere in the courtroom. The interpreter may sit in any unoccupied chair inside the railing or at counsel table and consult reference materials until the moment the case is called.

1. Jury Selection

During jury selection and prior to the commencement of the trial itself, the attorneys are seated at the counsel table and given an opportunity to examine each of the jury panel members. This examination is called *voir dire*. Each side has an opportunity to accept or reject any or all panel members. Defendants themselves may exercise this right and advise their attorney of their objections to any of the prospective jurors. The questions are repetitive and the jury selection process may be very lengthy, depending on local custom. When both sides are satisfied with the jury impaneled, the jury is sworn in. Throughout the entire process the interpreter interprets simultaneously to the defendant so that the individual may understand the jury selection process.

2. Pre-Trial Motion

Frequently, one or both parties may present a motion prior to the beginning of trial. A common pre-trial motion is one to suppress evidence on the grounds that certain portions of the evidence were obtained illegally and therefore should not be admitted. The argument is made by defense counsel and may be rebutted by the prosecution. Case law may be cited, technical questions may be raised by the judge, and points of authority may be raised by counsel. All of this interchange must be fully and simultaneously interpreted for the benefit of the defendant. The interpreter is to make no judgment as to the defendant's ability to understand the highly technical nature of the discourse, and should render a complete and accurate interpretation, conserving the formality of the source language. Anything less than a comprehensive interpretation will place the non-English-speaking defendant in a different legal position than a similarly situated English-speaking defendant. In this type of prepared legal argumentation, it is estimated that the speakers can reach upward of 180 words per minute. Counsel may quote or read portions of their legal briefs. At times the interchange can become heated and rhetorically complex.

3. The Trial Phase

The first order of business in all trials is the identification of the principals. The attorneys identify themselves for the record, as do interpreters. Should the interpreters forget to identify themselves, there will be no indication on the record of their appearance in that proceeding. If interpreters are interpreting for the defense, as soon as the defense attorney has identified him or her for the record, the interpreters should immediately greet the judge, identify themselves, and state the party for whom they are interpreting, such as, say: "Good morning, your honor, Jane Doe, interpreter for the defendant." It is at this time that the interpreter may also be sworn in on the record. This, however, will depend on local custom. If local protocol requires the interpreter to be sworn in on the record and if the court clerk and the judge should fail to swear in the interpreter, the interpreter should raise his or her hand and very succinctly ask to be sworn in: "Swear the interpreter, your honor?"

4. Opening Statement

Both the prosecution and the defense are afforded the opportunity to outline to the jury what they believe the evidence will show in the case. The prosecution will always say that the evidence will prove the defendant's guilt beyond a reasonable doubt. If the defense elects to address the jury, the comments will always indicate that the evidence will not prove the defendant's guilt beyond a reasonable doubt and may prove the defendant's innocence. The opening statements are a planned monologue that can be of any duration, depending on the complexity of the case. They are typically full of specific terminology and are sometimes delivered by attorneys who walk about the courtroom rather than standing at a podium; this often makes it difficult to hear. This narrative can be impassioned and delivered at a very fast pace. Depending on the speaker, the pace of these narratives may be deliberately slow or quite fast (120-220 words per minute). The interpreter simultaneously interprets the entire opening statement for the defendant, taking notes on names, places, dates, amounts, and so on. It is at this point that the interpreter gets the first detailed look at the evidence, and begins preparing accordingly. The pace, length, and complexity of the opening statement requires great concentration and stamina on the part of the interpreter.

5. English-Speaking-Witness Examination

The prosecution presents its case first. The first task facing the prosecution is to prove before the court that a crime has been committed; normally the first witness is a law enforcement officer who testifies to the circumstances surrounding his or her first exposure to the crime scene. This witness will probably mention dates, places, addresses, and descriptions, all of which will be repeated during the course of the trial. During the testimony of the prosecution's first witness, the interpreter interprets simultaneously to the defendant so that the defendant may follow the entire testimony.

As do both attorneys, the interpreter should take notes on the prosecution witnesses' testimony in order to be familiar with as many details of the case as possible. These will stand him or her in good stead should he or she be called upon to interpret for a subsequent witness. Since there is no language barrier between the prosecutor and the English-speaking witness, the exchange of questions and answers may be very quick. The testimony may proceed at a rate of up to 220 words per minute, requiring keen concentration on the part of the interpreter.

Once the prosecution has completed the direct examination, the defense attorney then has the opportunity to cross-examine the same witness. The interpreter should simultaneously interpret the cross-examination of the witness even if the very same ground is covered and the defendant has heard the answers to many of the questions already. The interpreter is not to edit them, or to make any determination as to which portions of the examination are to be interpreted. The interpreter must faithfully interpret the entire examination.

Frequently, the defendant will react to the testimony and address the interpreter with a comment, question, or protest. This comment or protest should be interpreted directly to the defense attorney. The interpreter should be aware of any communication that is required between the defendant and the attorney, or conversely between the attorney and the client. The interpreter is not to become a participant in the proceedings by making any independent observation, comment, or suggestion to the defense attorney about any question that should be asked of the witness. At the conclusion of defense counsel's examination, the prosecution may commence a redirect examination of the witness. Every time the prosecution elects to open a redirect examination, the defense will likewise have the opportunity to cross-examine.

At the conclusion of the first witness's testimony, the witness is thanked and asked to step down. There is frequently a question as to whether the witness may be "excused." There is a distinction between "stepping down" and "being excused." To step down allows the witness to leave the witness stand; however, the witness may not leave the courthouse. If the witness is "excused," he or she is then released as a witness and may leave the courtroom and the courthouse. The prosecution may call as many witnesses as necessary to prove that a crime has been committed and that the defendant is guilty. As stated before, the prosecution must prove guilt beyond a reasonable doubt. The defense, on the other hand, has no such burden and need not prove innocence. The defense may be vigorous and affirmative, or it may rely simply upon the argument that the prosecution has failed to prove its case.

If a witness for either the prosecution or the defense is called and the interpreter discovers that the witness does not speak English, and if there is no other interpreter for that witness, upon first mention of the witness's name the interpreter should immediately proceed to the witness stand to assist in the swearing in of the witness. The witness is asked to approach the stand, which is interpreted in a loud and clear voice audible throughout the courtroom. The witness is asked to raise his or her right hand and is sworn in by the court clerk. The oath is simultaneously interpreted quietly into the witness's ear and the witness's response is interpreted in a loud voice so that the court reporter can hear. The witness is then asked to sit at the witness stand and to state his or her full name for the record. The witness is frequently asked to spell his or her last name for the record. At times this presents a problem for the witness and the interpreter: many non-English-speaking persons of limited education have difficulty spelling their last names. Some interpreters feel that it is incumbent upon them to make the proceedings as expeditious as possible for the court and may bypass the witness's difficulty by unilaterally inserting the correct spelling of the family name. It may be a common practice, but it is ill advised, for this practice denies the court the opportunity to assess the witness's true demeanor and language level. The interpreter should allow the witness to spell his or her last name as correctly as possible. If there is a question as to a witness's true name, that question will be resolved by stipulation by the judge and attorneys involved.

6. Examination of a Non-English-Speaking Witness

At the earliest possible moment the interpreter should apprise the witness that the interpreter will be interpreting the attorneys' questions and that the witness should face and address the attorney directly, rather than facing the interpreter. If the interpreter has the opportunity to speak with witnesses prior to calling them to testify, these instructions should be given during that interview. Additionally, witnesses should be reminded never to directly address interpreters but rather to direct all comments back to the attorney. Interpreters should always utilize the first person and should never interpret into the third person ("I am not sure," rather than, "He says that he's not sure").

In contrast to the function at counsel table, where the interpreter interprets simultaneously into the defendant's ear, the interpreter now is the intermediary in a question-and-answer exchange, interpreting in the consecutive mode. As mentioned previously, the interpreter stands or sits next to the witness without blocking the view of the members of the jury. To weigh the testimony of the witness, the members of the jury must consider the witness's demeanor as the person answers questions posed by counsel. The questions posed by the examining attorney may be short and concise, or they may be long and involved. Interpreters at the stand may need to draw on their notetaking skills in order to render an accurate consecutive interpretation of the questions and answers by the witness. (For further discussion of notetaking, see Unit 6, Chapter 27.)

7. Closing Argument

After all the testimony has been presented and all the exhibits entered into evidence, when both sides have rested their cases, the prosecution and the defense are again afforded the opportunity to speak directly to the jury. The prosecution, bearing the burden of proof, is given two opportunities to speak to the jury. The prosecution will always speak to the jury about what it believes the evidence has shown and will assert that it has proven the defendant's guilt beyond a reasonable doubt. The defense will either argue that the evidence has not proven the guilt of the defendant or that it has proven the defendant's innocence.

Closing statements are called arguments and are intended to convince the jury. As a consequence they are forceful, lengthy, and possibly rapid (approximately 140 to 220 words per minute). They may include legal concepts, but they primarily consist of a summary of the testimony and evidence presented, and a persuasive argument. This is the last opportunity for counsel to sway the jury before it retires to deliberate. It is not uncommon for attorneys to wax poetic in their arguments, or to use literary references, quoting Shakespeare or the Bible to make their point. In their role as advocates, the attorneys are apt to speak at a pace that does not take into consideration the practical, critical problems faced by court interpreters and court reporters.

8. Instructions to the Jury

Before the jury retires to deliberate, specific instructions are given by the judge. These instructions always include legal definitions or quotations from codes or statutes, legal terminology, concepts of law, and philosophical discussions of the highest order. For example, if the charge is conspiracy to commit a particular crime, the judge defines the term "conspiracy." The instructions to the jury are a compilation of prepared forms that are agreed upon in advance by the attorneys and the judge. Interpreting jury instructions is extremely difficult and challenging for three reasons: (1) the procedure is lengthy, at least thirty minutes long, (2) it is read from a prepared text, and (3) its content is very dense. For these reasons the court interpreter should always request a copy of the jury instructions from the court clerk or the defense attorney. Even with the text the interpreter should be forewarned that the judge may depart from the prepared text and extemporize, using examples to illustrate a legal concept. Court interpreters should keep the instructions to the jury, study them, and make them part of their reference libraries.

9. The Verdict

After the instructions to the jury are completed, the judge excuses the jury to deliberate and reach a verdict. The jury may deliberate for as little as a few minutes or for days and weeks. When the jury returns with its finding, the judge asks the foreman of the jury to deliver the verdict to the bailiff. The bailiff gives the verdict form to the judge, who makes sure everything is in order. Then the clerk or the bailiff reads the verdict form aloud. Frequently the defendant is asked to stand and receive the verdict. At this point, the interpreter should stand alongside the defendant and simultaneously interpret the verdict.

10. Sentencing

At some point after the trial, the prosecution, the defendant, and defense counsel return to court for the imposition of sentence. In the interim the judge has received reports from various agencies, including but not limited to the probation department and the Immigration and Naturalization Service. The judge has read and considered these reports and imposes sentence, which may be time in custody, a fine, a period of probation, or any combination of these three.

The interpreter stands at the counsel table and interprets simultaneously everything that is said. This may include the attorney addressing the court, or the court addressing the defendant, and may even include an opportunity for the defendant to speak. Some jurisdictions allow the victim or the family of the victim to address the court prior to the imposition of sentence. The interpreter simultaneously interprets the statement made by the victim's family as well.

11. Communication with the Assignment Office

Should the trial proceed beyond one day, the interpreter must always inform the assignment office. The interpreter may be assigned to continue with the same case in progress or may be reassigned to another matter, in which case another interpreter would be assigned to the trial in progress. In any event it is incumbent upon the interpreter to keep the assignment office apprised of any continuance of a case in which interpreting services will be required. This is also true at the end of a trial if the case is continued for the imposition of sentence. If the case in progress is not adjourned to the following morning, the assignment office is not aware of the status unless the interpreter notifies the office. Once the assignment has been made, it is expected that it will continue until the end of the case; the responsibility rests with the interpreter, who should report back without any further notice, order, or subpoena. Communicating with the assignment office will better enable that office to serve the court by avoiding double assignments, failure to assign interpreters to a proceeding, and faulty payroll records.

All jurisdictions have a form to verify that interpreting services were provided that needs to be signed by some court official. Typically the person charged with this duty is the supervisory interpreter or court clerk. These signed documents, when filed, form the basis for the disbursement of funds to the interpreter.

This chronology of a typical trial involving a limited- or non-English-speaking defendant and/or witness has outlined the various areas where the court interpreter will function. This description has also pointed out various sources of vital information for court interpreters to gain insight critical to their craft, and has suggested specific techniques to be employed on specified occasions. The most important principle to be derived from this discussion is that, as the newest member of the legal cadre, the interpreter's role must be an assertive rather than a passive one. In addition to excellent bilingual proficiency and interpreting skills, interpreters must have an understanding of the legal context in which they work. Even assuming excellence of language skills, the interpreter must become a student of the legal process in order to fully grasp the role of the court interpreter. (For a more detailed discussion of legal procedures, see Units 2 and 3; for more information on the interpreting process, see Unit 6.)

Chapter 31

Tape Transcription and Document Translation

This chapter presents two ancillary tasks that court interpreters are often required to perform, tape transcription and document translation. The actual translation process involved in these tasks is similar to what the court interpreter ordinarily does in transferring a message from one language to another. Other aspects of tape transcription and document translation are quite task-specific, however, and certain procedures need to be followed. This chapter provides guidelines for interpreters who are called upon to carry out these tasks.

1. Tape Transcription

Frequently evidence presented in court will include exhibits based on tape recordings. Such evidence may be obtained by surveillance devices such as telephone bugs, planted microphones, microphones worn by undercover agents, and videotape cameras. Alternatively, tape recordings may be made overtly during interviews of witnesses or suspects by law enforcement officials. Tapes frequently play an important part in cases involving drugs, conspiracy, and all matters involving undocumented aliens. A given case may involve anywhere from a dozen to hundreds of tapes, depending upon the complexity of the case and the intensity of the surveillance. Review of the content of these tapes is impractical in their audio form, as it is excessively time consuming. Just as the most efficient way of reviewing the proceedings of a trial is to rely on a transcript, the most efficient way of re-examining the contents of the tapes is by means of a transcript. The transcript can be duplicated and distributed to all interested parties and can be easily referred to by page number.

Often these tapes will be in a language other than English and cannot be utilized by the prosecution as evidence in their original form. The tapes must first be transcribed and translated in order to be entered into evidence. In transcribed/translated form, the tapes may be used as evidence before the grand jury in order to seek an indictment; they may be utilized by any prosecuting agency at a preliminary hearing as proof of commission of a crime; and ultimately they can be used in a trial to prove the defendant guilty of a crime. Just as oral evidence in a language other than English must be interpreted by a certified court interpreter, tape transcription and translation must be performed by a certified court interpreter so that it will withstand challenges to its validity.

The quality of the recording on these tapes varies tremendously, depending on the conditions. For example, the questioning of a witness at police headquarters may be recorded on unsophisticated equipment, and a great deal of background noise

439

may make it difficult to hear everything that is said. Perhaps the most challenging tapes to transcribe and translate are those made by undercover agents under clandestine circumstances. The recording device is usually attached to the agent's body or secreted in his or her clothing, which makes for a poor quality recording. In addition to the noises made by the agent's clothing and movements, there tends to be a lot of background noise in the transactions being recorded (bar music, traffic, and so on). Moreover, the people involved in the transaction are not likely to speak loudly or enunciate clearly, given the nature of the business they are conducting.

For legal purposes, the transcript must exactly reflect the content of the original tape, including all hesitations and pauses, slang words, swear words, and even an indication of unintelligible words. Phonetic spelling is used to illustrate truncated expressions. It is similar in form to a legal transcript that identifies every utterance by speaker. A proper transcript should faithfully and accurately reflect every utterance of the speakers, as well as pauses. Grammatical errors and improper usage by the speakers should not be corrected, nor should incomplete phrases be completed. The transcript must also describe background noises and denote periods of silence. The transcriber/translator must observe the same strict standards of accuracy that govern the interpretation of oral testimony, bearing in mind that any mistranscription will result in an error in translation and ultimately will distort the evidence.

1.1. Transcription Equipment

It is very important to have the proper equipment for transcribing and translating audio tapes. The transcribing machine should have foot controls that allow the interpreter to listen to the tape while using a typewriter or word processor. Most tapes require extensive rewinding and repetition for proper transcription, and foot controls allow the transciber to save time. Because of the poor quality of most recordings, it is important to have sensitive, high fidelity headphones so that the transcribers can receive signals directly through the headphones, minimizing disturbances from the surroundings. The machine should also have manual controls that allow transcribers to adjust the volume, tone, and speed of the playback for optimum audibility and understanding.

It would be optimal if interpreters owned personal computers with word processing software, and high-quality printers. Because of the extensive editing that is required to produce an accurate, readable transcript and translation, a word processor is far more efficient than a typewriter. For more information on hardware and software, see Chapter 34. If interpreters have been contracted by a government agency, they should request that high-quality equipment be provided for the task. Translators or interpreters who wish to specialize in tape transcription would be wise to invest in professional tape-transcribing and word-processing equipment.

1.2. Transcription Procedure

The transcription of the tape is typically more arduous and time consuming than the translation, as it requires multiple playbacks of the tape under difficult listening conditions while simultaneously entering data into the word processor. The following steps are recommended for transcribing tapes:

(1) Listen to the entire tape to get an idea of the context and to become familiar with place names, nicknames, unusual word usages, and special circumstances that impinge on the case. Knowledge of the situation in which the conversation is taking place is essential to clarify any ambiguities. A major problem for the transcriber is distinguishing the different voices on the tape. During this initial playing, the transcriber is able to determine the number of speakers on the tape, and to become familiar with the individuals' voice characteristics and speaking styles. Only after transcribers have heard the entire tape can they successfully identify individual voices. This is an important issue, as there may be a dispute between the defense and prosecution as to who said what.

(2) Assign identities to the different speakers as Voice 1, Voice 2, etc. It is important to avoid naming the speakers, even if the names become clear from the context. Since translators were not there at the moment the words were spoken, they cannot attest to the identity of the speakers, but rather can only certify that certain words were uttered. It will be the task of others to identify the voices.

(3) Play a short portion of the tape and stop when you have reached the limit of what you can recall. These portions may involve an entire exchange between two or more people, or a set of greetings, a question and an answer, a joke, and a rebuttal. Type exactly what is said, including pauses, non-verbal utterances, and noises. If the transcriber is not certain of the meaning of any sound, the word "inaudible" or "unintelligible" in parentheses should be substituted for the sound in question. The transcriber should not hesitate to label even long passages as inaudible or unintelligible if there is any doubt; **guessing is inappropriate**. Sections of the tape that are blank or where there is electronic interference should be identified as such on the transcript, either by time or by position on the tape counter (e.g., "13 minutes of silence," or "electronic interference from #237 to #498"). In short, any and all sounds that are on the original tape should be described in the transcript, including squeaks, squawks, steps on gravel, doors slamming, music, traffic noises, and bathroom noises. It should be possible for a party who has not heard the tape to envision the scenes that are taking place based solely on the transcript.

(4) If there is doubt as to what was said or which voice is speaking, play the tape again. Repeat it as many times as necessary until that determination can be made. There should be no omissions; every utterance on the tape is to be set down and ascribed to the various voices. In the case of multiple voices, on a given tape, the transcriber will be obliged to listen to the same portion many times in order to concentrate on one single voice. In the event that more than one voice is heard at the same time, multiple listenings will soon filter out the interfering voices at each playback and the transcriber will ultimately be able to identify all the utterances.

(5) Once the preliminary transcript has been completed, play the entire tape again to compare the written text with the content of the tape. Listening to the tape and reading the text, the transcriber edits and checks for omissions. Quite often the transcriber will find that certain utterances were perhaps ascribed to the wrong voice or that certain words muttered under the breath can now be distinguished. Likewise, sounds that were unrecognizable at first and were labeled "unintelligible" may be correctly identified on the final playback. If the transcriber realizes that an omission has been made, he or she should immediately stop the tape and insert the missing information. This process should be repeated as many times as necessary. Only when

the transcriber is satisfied that there are no omissions and errors is he or she ready to undertake the translation.

1.3. Transcript Translation

The translation based upon the transcript should faithfully conserve the style, tone, language level, and intent of the speakers. A translation of a tape transcript that will be entered into evidence should be prepared with the same care and diligence as if the words were being interpreted live in open court, adhering to the same strict standards of accuracy. That is, colloquial expressions, slang, improper grammar, and profanity should be translated to the English equivalent, without editing, so that a judge and jury will have a true impression of the linguistic and socioeconomic level of the speaker. Errors or misstatements should not be corrected in the translation, but should be rendered exactly as stated, marked with a "[sic]" if necessary. In some cases, it may be necessary to identify the language the speaker used, if the conversation is taking place in two languages.

Vague or ambiguous statements should be translated into equally vague or ambiguous expressions in English. One of the most difficult aspects of translating tape transcripts is the nature of the language that is typically spoken in clandestine situations such as drug trafficking and smuggling operations. Ambiguities, code words, and euphemisms are the rule in such communication, and the translator must strive to conserve those forms of expression. Failure to accomplish this will tend to misrepresent the evidence.

Good translators should have a reference library of dictionaries and glossaries at their disposal. For example, it is advisable to have a good glossary of drug terminology at hand before undertaking to transcribe and translate tapes in a drug conspiracy case. The translator may need to consult multiple glossaries to research different dialectical and regional usages. In addition, the translator should not hesitate to consult with colleagues in the field who, because of their background and experience, may easily solve the problem in question. Many terms used in spoken language, particularly the argot of certain subgroups of society such as drug users, have not yet found their way into written references, and only human resources can supply the terminologies. For more information on resources, see Chapter 33.

As the translator proceeds through the text, the meaning of any particular word will be determined not only by its dictionary definition but by the language level of the speakers and the context within which the words are spoken. The translation process in and of itself is one of constant decision making. The translator must always consider all alternatives and, based on good judgment and professional expertise, determine the best possibility within the specified context.

1.4. Translator's Notes

Just as there are occasions when the court interpreter needs to provide an explanation of a term when interpreting courtroom testimony, occasionally the translator will have to annotate the transcript of a tape. This is particularly true of terms with double meanings that are frequently encountered in drug cases, and of words that do not have an English equivalent. In these cases, the term should be retained in the original language and marked with an asterisk. At the bottom of the page, the translator can explain the problem. Terms with no equivalent in English are relatively easy to handle. For example, the phrase *La bogotada llega el miércoles* should be rendered "The *bogotada* will arrive on Wednesday." At the bottom of the page will be the following:

> Translator's note: The *-ada* ending in Spanish is an intensifier that enhances the root word or refers to a large quantity of something. Here the term refers to a large quantity of something from Bogotá.

Terms with double meanings pose a more difficult problem, however. In these cases, one meaning of the term may be perfectly innocuous, while the other meaning is extremely incriminating. This is especially true of drug slang, in which drugs are deliberately referred to with harmless sounding words such as "horse" and "grass." Another example is the term *perico*, which literally means "parakeet" in Spanish but is commonly used in the drug world to refer to cocaine. It would be wrong for the translator to translate the term as "cocaine" in the transcript, but it would be equally misleading simply to say "parakeet" without an explanation. Thus, the translator should leave the term in the original language and put note at the bottom of the page explaining both the literal meaning of the term and the common usage of it. It is up to the prosecution and the defense to persuade the jury, through expert witness testimony if necessary, to accept one meaning or the other. This approach to translation is in keeping with the ethical responsibility of translators to remain impartial and maintain accuracy. Translators must bear in mind at all times that they will have to declare under oath that the translation is accurate.

1.5. Format of Transcript

The transcript should be prepared in a manner that facilitates a line-by-line comparison of the transcript and the translation. The transcript and its translation should appear side by side on a two-columned page with the transcript in the left column and the translation in the right column as shown:

	Spanish	English
Voice 1:	... *y, ¿ Porqué 'tas tan escamado?*	... So why are you sweatin' it so much?
Voice 2:	*Pos, no ... este ... es que ...*	Well, No ... Uh ... It's (just) that ...
Voice 3:	*Mira, todo está listo ... yo mismo le dije a ...*	Look, everything's set up ... I myself told ...
Voice 2:	*'Ta suave, ... 'ta suave ... yo no-más ... este ...*	It's cool, ... it's cool ... I just ... uh ...
Voice 1:	*Betito, mira, yo no te voy a chingar ...*	Betito, look, I'm not going to screw you ...
Voice 2:	*Yo sé ... yo sé ... Pero yo no conozco a ese vatony ...*	I know ... I know ... but I don't know that dude and ...
Voice 1:	*¿Y qué? .... tú sabes que el lo-* ... *el loco* (unintelligible words) *allá con tú ruca.*	So what? ... you know that (unintelligible words) over at your old lady's.

| Voice 3: | (Inaudible) (Power lawnmower in background) . . . *¿Cuánto traes?* | (Inaudible) (Power lawnmower in background) . . . How much you got? |
| Voice 2: | Aquí traigo 2 kilos (unintelligible) . . . *yerba* . . . *La carga, este, la carga está en mi camioneta.* | I've got 2 kilos here (unintelligible) . . . grass . . . The load, uh, the load is in my *camioneta.* |

(Translator's note: the term *camioneta* may mean a station wagon, pickup truck, camper, or van; it is not clear from the context which type of vehicle is meant.)

| Voice 3: | *¿ Cuándo le dijistes que* (unintelligible)? *¿Hoy domingo o mañana martes?* | When did you tell (unintelligible)? Today Sunday or tomorrow Tuesday? [sic]? |

(Electronic interference from #123 to #148 on the tape counter.)

| Voice 1: | *Vámonos, pues.* | Well, let's get going. Let's go. |

Note that the transcript shows incomplete utterances, which are faithfully reflected in the translation, and that no attempt is made to improve the grammar or language level. Note also that the translator has rendered vague terms such as *yerba* and *carga*, which have specific meanings in the drug context, in an equally vague way in the English. The defense and the prosecution can elicit testimony from expert witnesses (including the transcriber/translator, if necessary) to clarify the meaning of those terms. On the other hand, the term *camioneta* cannot be translated vaguely, so a translator's note is required.

1.6. Certification of the Transcript

The final transcript and translation must be certified by the court and must have a signed and sworn statement by the translator that he is a certified court interpreter qualified to do this work. The signed statement should be attached and form part of the entire document. There are several ways to get a document certified. In state courts, the interpreter may have the document certified in the office of the clerk, or it may be certified through the assignment office, or the supervising interpreter may assume responsibility for obtaining the certification. Regardless of the form it takes, the certification attests to the accuracy of the document so that it can be used for official purposes. Should there be any question as to the accuracy of the transcript and/or translation, the transcriber/translator can and will be called to the stand to testify and to account for any particular aspect of the translation. See Unit 3, Chapter 12, for a discussion of the interpreter as an expert witness.

With every translation that will be entered into evidence there exists the possibility that the translator will be called as a witness to justify the product. When the transcriber/translator is called to testify in court about what the tapes say, he or she must be prepared to withstand challenges by the defense or the prosecution, each of whom will attempt to give a certain slant to the words on the tape. The translator should resist all attempts on the part of others to influence his or her decision as to specific meaning of words on the tape. Frequently, the defense or the prosecution will insist that certain sounds represent certain words. The transcriber can only testify as to how he or she perceives those same sounds, and should never take any other person's view.

2. Document Translation

Another task that court interpreters are frequently asked to perform is the translation of written documents. Although translation is considered an ancillary task and may be required of the court interpreter only occasionally, it is essential that each and every translation be done correctly. The translated document may be used as evidence and, therefore, the standard of accuracy is just as high as that which court interpreters must apply to the interpretation of testimony for the record. The New Jersey Supreme Court Task Force on Interpreter and Translation Services (1985) points out that, "The legal translator must apply the same level of sophistication with which the court interpreter conveys oral messages" (p. 63).

Nida (1964), Engelbert (1982), and the American Translators Association Code of Ethical Practices (New Jersey Supreme Court Task Force on Interpreter and Translation Services, 1984) agree that the main criterion for determining whether a translation of any text or document is true to the original is the effect it has on the reader: the translation should convey the same impression to the reader as the original source language text would. Engelbert (1982, p. 197) observes: "Correctly identifying the prime reader and keeping that person's responses constantly in mind are prime requisites for faithfulness in translation." If the "prime reader" is a court of law, faithfulness means conserving every single element of meaning and adhering to the structure of the original as closely as the TL allows. Roberts and Pergnier (1987) further discuss the importance of equivalence.

2.1. Types of Documents

The documents that the court interpreter may be required to translate into English include, but are not limited to, the following: birth, death, and marriage certificates, divorce decrees, wills, business and personal correspondence, leases, business contracts, autopsy reports, medical records, psychiatric case histories, ships' logs, and bidding specifications. In addition to these formal documents, there may also be handwritten letters or declarations by witnesses that require translation into English.

The court and other government agencies may require that standard forms and letters be translated from English into other languages. These documents include waiver forms, financial affidavits, policy statements, conditions of probation, application forms, instructions, and form letters.

Each type of document poses different problems and requires a different style and format. The purpose for which the document will be used dictates the precision with which the translation must be performed. For example, an affidavit is just like oral testimony, and must be translated just as precisely as testimony on the witness stand would be—as close to verbatim as the TL allows. On the other hand, a letter addressed to the judge, containing the same information and the same style of language, would be translated in a manner that does not cling so closely to the syntax of the original, because its purpose is persuasive rather than evidentiary. Moreover, documents that rely heavily on standard formulas—such as business letters and legal forms—must be reworked considerably to read smoothly in the target language. This does not mean that the translator can change the meaning of the document; it simply means that a verbatim rendition is not only unnecessary but possibly incorrect. In other words, more liberties must be taken with style because of the nature of the text.

It is important for translators to know when it is acceptable to make such stylistic changes, and when they must adhere closely to the wording of the SL text. The New Jersey Supreme Court Task Force on Interpreter and Translator Services (1985) points out the dichotomy between the need for accuracy and the requirements of comprehensibility in the TL. If the SL is emphasized, the translation contains every semantic and syntactic element of the original, but reads less fluently. In contrast, if the TL is emphasized, the text reads smoothly but some elements of meaning may not be conveyed fully:

> Given the significance attached to the preservation of meaning in the legal field, at first blush legal translating and interpreting would appear to fall squarely into the approach which emphasizes the source language. Yet, the resulting text or interpretation might be incomprehensible if the cultural and linguistic norms of the target language are not taken into account. (p. 64)

Engelbert (1982) states that the translator must take into consideration the characteristics of legal language:

> Legal discourse is a highly specialized use of language requiring a special set of habits. Obviously, translating legal texts requires painstaking attention to detail and sensitivity to the consequences of subtle contextual changes. This kind of writing is such a departure from our everyday use of language that it is worthwhile to consider some of the specific characteristics of legal language which the translator should keep in mind. (p. 228)

The characteristics of legal discourse which Engelbert (1982) enumerates include the following: It is highly formulaic, formal, and precise, with "painstaking attention to minute detail" (p. 230). It is also characterized by convoluted sentence structures. All of these features must be taken into consideration by the translator, and must be reproduced as closely as possible in the TL version.

In preparing a legal document such as a birth or marriage certificate, great care should be taken to account for every feature of the document. The translation should indicate the presence of photographs, fingerprints, signatures and initials, government stamps and seals, serial numbers, and so on. These indications should be in the same physical location in the translation as in the original document so that a side-by-side comparison of the two will make it apparent that every detail has been included. For example, in the upper left corner of a birth certificate the translator may write: "Seal of the Republic of Peru. Illegible Stamp. Fees Paid. Illegible initials." No detail is too small to be overlooked. If a word is obliterated by a brown stain in the original, for instance, the translation should contain a notation in brackets: [word obliterated by brown stain].

Correspondence, much of which may be poorly handwritten by writers of limited education and sophistication, may comprise a significant portion of the document translation work. It is extremely challenging for the translator to decipher the handwriting of people whose penmanship, spelling, grammar, and ability to express themselves are deficient. The translator may have difficulty understanding the document, not only because of the penmanship and the lack of punctuation, but also because of omitted words, misspellings, malapropisms, and awkward usage. Except for the poor penmanship, however, the translator must make the translation as easy or as difficult to understand as the original document. In other words, the poor grammar and usage must be retained in the TL version so that the reader will be able to assess the language level of the author. Under no circumstances should the translator attempt to make the document more eloquent or logical than the SL text.

2.2. Resources

The most important tool the court interpreter needs in order to translate documents that meet this high standard is a thorough knowledge of the written forms of both the SL and the TL. Another essential resource is a good reference library. Translators should have at their disposal the reference materials that will enable them to practice their craft. In addition to standard bilingual dictionaries, they should have access to dictionaries and glossaries of technical terms, particularly in the fields of law, medicine, and business. It should be noted that dictionaries are not the only sources of terminology. Primary sources (textbooks, journal articles, and other writings in the TL by experts in the field) are valuable tools for the translator. Translators should know how to obtain materials in other specialized areas such as fingerprint analysis, chemistry, firearms and ballistics, and maritime terminology, in all of their working languages. For a more detailed discussion of resources available to the court interpreter, see Chapter 33. Unit 8, Chapter 35, contains a list of standard references that court interpreters should acquire, and the books listed in the bibliography at the end of this chapter also contain recommendations of reference works available to translators.

Quite often regional or slang expressions are not familiar to the translator who is working on a particular document, but the translator may have a colleague who is better versed in that area of terminology. Fellow translators and interpreters can be one of the richest resources for translators. Other human resources available to the translator include experts in the fields in question: lawyers, judges, doctors, engineers, university professors, and many others. Translators should have no qualms about picking up the telephone and calling someone, whether an acquaintance or not, who will be able to help them solve a translation problem.

As mentioned above, many legal documents are similar in form and repetitive in vocabulary. Court interpreters should develop a repertory of standard expressions that are frequently found in legal documents ("in witness whereof," "therefore be it resolved"), in all of their working languages. It is also a good idea to photocopy the documents that have been translated and to file them, with a copy of the translated version, for future reference. The next time a similar document is given to the interpreter to be translated, he or she can look up the previous document and solve the translation problems much more quickly. If given a lease to translate from Spanish to English, for example, he or she can find another Spanish lease that was translated before and cull phrases that have been already translated. Even better, if he or she has previously translated an English lease into Spanish, he or she can find phrases in the original English document to use in the English translation of the lease he or she is now translating, assuming that they have some features in common. In this way, the translated version will be much more authentic.

2.3. Translation Process

The following steps are recommended for translating a document:

(1) Determine the purpose for which the document will be used: an exhibit in a trial, background information for sentencing, explaining procedures to the public, and so on.

(2) Read the document from beginning to end, focusing on the subject matter, language level, and style. Engelbert (1982) recommends that the translator make sure the copy is entirely legible and that no pages are missing or out of order. She goes on to say:

> This reading yields important insights about how the text works, how the various parts are related, and what preliminary research has to be done. Never begin the translation of a text until you thoroughly understand what you are reading. (p. 212)

(3) Check your files to see if you have a previously translated document that is similar to the one you are about to translate.

(4) Obtain the necessary reference materials you need, and do any preliminary research that may be required to familiarize yourself with the subject matter in general.

(5) Read the text through another time for the purpose of planning the translation. Pay particular attention to problem terms, passages that are unclear, and passages that will require extensive reworking in the TL for stylistic reasons.

(6) Produce a first draft of the translation. Make sure you do not omit any element of meaning, and that you maintain the style and tone of the original text. Always focus on the meaning of the original text, rather than the individual words, so that you will not be a slave to the syntax of the original.

(7) Proofread the draft, correcting any errors in grammar, spelling, or style. Make sure the draft is coherent and is true to the meaning of the SL text. It is helpful to read the translation aloud to make sure that it reads smoothly and naturally, as if it were originally written in the TL.

(8) Compare the corrected draft with the SL text to make sure that nothing has been inadvertently omitted or eliminated during the course of reworking and editing.

(9) Produce the final copy. This copy should be clean and legible, with no typographical errors or obvious corrections. In the case of legal documents, it should resemble the original document in appearance as closely as possible (New Jersey Supreme Court Task Force on Interpreter and Translation Services, 1985).

2.4. Certification and Notarization

Often the user of a translation will request that it be certified or notarized. In many countries, translators are required to be licensed or certified in a procedure similar to that which is required for court interpreters in the United States. Certified or sworn translators are entitled to use a stamp (similar to that of a notary public) that lends legal validity to their translations. In the United States, however, there is no such regulation of translators. The closest thing to certification for translators is accreditation by the American Translators Association (ATA), which is strictly voluntary. To become accredited, candidates must take a translation exam administered by the ATA. The ATA exam is quite rigorous, and earning accreditation lends greater validity to the translator's work. Unfortunately, however, there are still many translators in this country who are not accredited, and their clients have no way of knowing whether their work is of good quality. In the future, it would be good policy for government entities to require that translators be accredited or certified just as court interpreters are today. This would ensure that the highest standards of professionalism will prevail.

Even without official certification, translators can still validate their work by attaching a statement to it (documents designed specifically for this purpose can be obtained from the National Notary Association), attesting that it is a true and correct translation of the original. The statement should clearly identify the original document so that there can be no question about what is being translated. Translators may indicate their credentials (professional degrees, interpreter certification, ATA accreditation) in this statement. A typical translator certification would read as follows:

> I, _____ , certified by the Administrative Office of the United States Courts for Spanish-English court interpreting and accredited by the American Translators Association for Spanish-English translation, do hereby declare that the attached birth certificate, identified with serial number _____ , is a true and correct translation of the Spanish original.

Translators then sign the document, and may or may not have their signatures notarized, depending on what the user of the translation desires. Note that this certification and notarization are not required by law in the United States, but may be requested by the party for whom the translation is being made.

In conclusion, document translation is a difficult and demanding task that court interpreters cannot afford to take for granted. They must prepare themselves by ensuring that they have a full command of the languages involved and access to the appropriate written reference works. Finally, they must make every effort to conserve the meaning, style, and form of the original document in their translated versions.

Chapter 32

Using Language Resources and References

The *Federal Court Interpreter Certification Manual* (Gonzalez, 1986) states that:

> The basic tool of the court interpreter is an extensive vocabulary in both languages: a vocabulary that spans the entire spectrum of possible language from jargon, argot, or slang to everyday colloquial and from technical language of a wide range of areas to formal and frozen language of legal instruments and codes. (p. 5)

This section discusses the different types of language resources, in printed, electronic, and oral form, that are available to court interpreters to help them develop this "basic tool." First, printed reference works will be discussed, and ways of obtaining and using them will be described. Then, the concept of terminology will be defined, with suggestions of ways to compile and maintain glossaries. Finally, human resources will be treated.

1. Printed Resources

1.1. Locating Reference Books and Materials

Court interpreters have a wealth of resources available to them in researching terminology, language usage, and legal concepts. The public library is the most obvious resource; it contains a trove of periodicals, works of fiction and non-fiction, reference books, and pamphlets, all of which can be of use to the interpreter in one way or another. For example, if the interpreter hears about a new drug that is being used on the streets and is curious about all of its implications, he or she can go to the public library and look in the *Reader's Guide to Periodical Literature* and find out if the drug has been mentioned in articles in the press, or in professional journals in the fields of psychology, sociology, criminology, medicine, education, and so on. The reference librarian can help the interpreter find local newspaper articles about the impact the drug is having on the community. Or the interpreter can find a textbook on pharmacology or toxicology, or a book on drug abuse for parents and school counselors, and investigate the matter further.

The next most obvious resource for the court interpreter is the law library. Most courthouses have law libraries that are open to the public, at least during certain hours of the day. Although it may not be possible to check out references, they can be consulted in the library and photocopied if need be. For instance, the interpreter may want to look up the jury instructions that will be read at the assigned trial in order to be prepared for the terminology in advance. Or the interpreter may want to consult form books to get an idea of the terminology used in a divorce decree or a will. A complete law library (such as may be found in the main courthouse of a large city or at a university law school) will also contain reference works on comparative law; these will help the interpreter research the most accurate possible translation for technical terms.

Libraries are not the only resources available to the interpreter. All public agencies have free pamphlets containing explanations of concepts or procedures that the interpreter may have to understand, as well as definitions of the technical jargon used by the agencies. Some agencies even have translations of these pamphlets in the languages of the major non-English-speaking communities that they serve. They also may publish glossaries of terms that have specific usages in their setting, with definitions in English and translations into major target languages. The interpreter who is interested in obtaining such materials should contact the state or federal headquarters of these agencies to inquire about them.

As far as languages other than English are concerned, the best source of materials is the country or countries where the language in question is spoken. Even if interpreters cannot travel to the country, they can subscribe to periodicals or order books by mail; embassies are often good sources of information as well. Many communities in the United States where large populations of speakers of other languages reside have materials in those languages in the public library. In addition, local newspapers are often published in such languages. If there is a large population that speaks a language other than English, there are probably stores that sell books, magazines, and newspapers written in that language. If interpreters do have an opportunity to travel to the countries where their working languages are spoken, they should visit public agencies and collect as much material as possible (pamphlets, glossaries, public information) in areas related to their work.

Another valuable source of information related to court interpreting is the newsletters and journals published by the professional associations of language specialists (*The ATA Chronicle, The Polyglot, Meta, Babel,* etc.). These publications often contain news of free glossaries available from state, national, and international organizations. They also print reviews of dictionaries and other reference works of interest to those in the profession.

1.2. How to Use Dictionaries

The bilingual dictionary is the reference tool that first springs to mind when people think of translation and interpretation. It is indeed a helpful tool, but it should not be relied upon exclusively. The unsophisticated user of bilingual resources may encounter some pitfalls, such as choosing the first equivalent given without knowing whether it really means the same thing or is used in the same way as the source-language term. A good bilingual dictionary will indicate the field of knowledge in which a term is used (e.g., medicine, economics), and will contain some contextual information. This avoids errors such as the translation of "there was a drop in oil production" as *hubo una gota de la producción de petróleo.* If the translator of that phrase had used the *American Heritage-Larousse Spanish Dictionary* (1986), the following entry would have been found:

drop — I. s. (of a liquid) *gota*; (trace) *poco, pizca* —not a d. of pity — *ni una pizca de compasión*; (earring) *arete m, pendiente m*; (candy) *pastilla*; cough d. — *pastilla para la tos*; (fall) *bajada, caída*; (height of fall) *altura*; (difference in levels) *desnivel m*; (in prices) *baja*; (in value, quality) *disminución f*; (slope) *pendiente f, declive m*; (abyss) *precipicio*; (by parachute) *lanzamiento*; (for messages) *buzón m*; TEAT. *telón m*; ELECTRON. *conexión de terminal*.

This entry indicates that the term as used in sense I is a noun (s), and then gives various equivalents depending on context (liquid, trace, earring). Some phrases are provided for help with usage, and nouns whose gender is not obvious are marked masculine (m) or feminine (f). Specialized fields of knowledge are indicated in caps (TEAT, ELECTRON).

Even the best of bilingual resources is not sufficient, however. If interpreters have any doubt about the meaning or usage of a term, they should consult a monolingual dictionary for verification. Often obscure alternate meanings of words are listed in monolingual references (particularly unabridged ones) but are absent from bilingual dictionaries. Some technical terms are either absent from or not fully defined in general monolingual dictionaries, and the interpreter must consult a specialized source. Depending on the field, that source might be a dictionary or encyclopedia, a professional journal, a textbook, or a research paper. Such specialized works are the most reliable and often the most current sources of information on what terms mean and how they are used in context.

Interpreters should develop their own library of reference works related to the specific fields they work in and the types of translation and interpreting services they provide. Here is a list of basic references that are the most useful:

(1) Monolingual dictionaries in all working languages

(2) Books on grammar, usage, and style in all working languages

(3) A bilingual dictionary for each language combination (e.g., Spanish-English, Portuguese-English)

(4) Monolingual legal dictionaries or law textbooks in all working languages, such as *Law Dictionary* (Gifis, 1984).

(5) A bilingual legal dictionary for each language combination, such as Robb's *Dictionary of Legal Terms* (1955).

(6) Slang dictionaries or glossaries

(7) Monolingual specialized technical resources (manuals, textbooks, dictionaries, glossaries, catalogues, and so on) on the following subjects: medicine, motor vehicles, weaponry, occupations (e.g., maritime, agriculture), and others

(8) Bilingual technical dictionaries

In general, monolingual references tend to be more reliable than bilingual or multilingual ones. Specialized multilingual dictionaries tend to be very expensive and are not always reliable in every language, so they must be purchased with caution. In evaluating a reference for possible purchase, the interpreter should consider some of the following factors: date of publication (in some fields terms become obsolete more rapidly than in others), qualifications of author and publisher (whether or not they have expertise in the field in question), and methodology and presentation (ease of finding material, clarity of definitions, usage notes, illustrations, legible typeface). A prospective buyer should also beware of "padding"—the inclusion of terms in a technical source that could be found anywhere but are inserted to make the dictionary look more comprehensive. A good way to evaluate a reference book is to choose a few terms that are already known and look them up to verify the quality and accuracy of the entries.

1.3. The Media

It is important to note that language is a living, dynamic entity. This applies to written language as well as spoken, but it is particularly true of the vernacular usage commonly encountered by the court interpreter. Therefore, printed references such as dictionaries and encyclopedias become obsolete quickly, though they are never useless. The most up-to-date sources are periodicals, particularly daily newspapers. Newspapers published in foreign countries always contain coverage of matters of local, regional, and international interest for readers. The interpreter can gain insights into foreign affairs, and can learn specific vocabulary while keeping abreast of current language usage in that country.

Foreign printed newspapers and periodicals provide exposure to various registers. Court interpreters should focus on articles about subjects that are relevant to their work: law, the administration of justice, specific crimes (drug trafficking, for example), language usage (e.g., street slang), changing social customs and mores, and so on. In addition, cartoons and joke sections should be of interest to the court interpreter as well (one indication of comprehension is the ability to understand the subtle nuances of a language as expressed in its humor). The interpreter may wish to subscribe to these publications, or they may be made available in the waiting room of the courthouse as part of the reading material that interpreters peruse between assignments. These collections of publications may form the basis for compilations of glossaries. The crossword puzzles in these publications are of particular challenge and benefit to the professional court interpreter. Another excellent source of current vernacular usage is fiction, especially the "popular" novels that are written and published with a short-term perspective. The court interpreter should be aware and fully appreciate that the print media reflect language as it is currently being used by its speakers; they contain a wealth of vocabulary, idioms, and local expressions ranging from the highest index of social acceptance to usage that is considered non-standard.

A primary source of information for human beings has always been other humans in close proximity. With the advent of the electronic age, people in a limited-speech community are able to see and hear those who are at a physical and temporal distance. Being able to hear the foreign language is a great advantage, and the court interpreter has the opportunity to listen to many foreign languages by means of radio. New words are discovered in radio drama, in broadcasts of sports events, and in foreign language newscasts. With the advent of television has come the opportunity of not only hearing the foreign language, but also of seeing the speakers of the foreign language. The viewer as well has the opportunity of using the image provided by the medium to discover through pictorial cues the true meaning of words. For example, news coverage of the 1987 earthquake in Mexico City showed wide areas of devastation in the capital, and the Spanish word *escombros* was one of the most frequently used words in telecasts. The images on the screen made it apparent that the word meant rubble and debris.

Television and videotapes allow viewers the opportunity to see foreign films and hear actors speak in regional varieties different from their own. The court interpreter can acquire a new vocabulary and expressions simply by watching a Japanese, Spanish, Korean, Chinese, or other foreign language film, the plot of which may involve sophisticated and urban speech or that of a rural community. The introduction of videotape technology provides the court interpreter with a practically unlimited opportunity of hearing and seeing the foreign language in use.

2. Glossaries

2.1. Need for Personal Glossaries

As stressed at the beginning of this chapter, the primary tool of the interpreter is a "vocabulary that spans the entire spectrum of possible language" (Gonzalez, 1986, p. 5). Thus far the discussion has focused on the various existing resources that are available to the interpreter for researching terminology and legal concepts. However, as has been emphasized throughout this unit, language is constantly changing, even from one day to the next in some cases, and standard reference works cannot keep pace with such dynamism. Not only does language change over time, but it also varies by region. It is difficult for printed reference works to reflect all of the different usages that prevail in the various parts of the world where a given language is spoken. As a result, it may become necessary for interpreters to compile and maintain their own glossaries to reflect the usages that they encounter in their daily work. The breadth and depth of language mastery required of the court interpreter demands not only constant terminology research, but also an ongoing dedication to the creation of glossaries.

The best way to gather the raw material for the interpreter's personal glossaries, that is, the words and phrases that the interpreter wishes to record for future use, is to carry a small notebook at all times. Interpreters should constantly be alert to the usage of language, and should jot down everything they hear or read—in all of their working languages—that they think may be of use to them in their interpreting work. Regardless of where the term is used (on the witness stand, in conversation, radio commercial, or movie), interpreters should record it in their notebooks along with an indication of the source. Any terms that are derived from the interpreters' working notes in court should also be recorded in these notebooks. As soon as they return to their home or office, they should transfer the term to their permanent glossaries, be they notebooks, index cards, or a computerized term bank. This transfer should be made as soon as possible after the first encounter with the term so that it will still be fresh in the interpreter's memory.

2.2. Terminology Defined

Before describing the procedure for compiling a terminology glossary, a definition of terms is in order. Many people wonder why interpreters insist on speaking of "terminology" instead of "vocabulary." *The Random House Dictionary of the English*

Language (1987, 2nd ed.) defines vocabulary as "a list or collection of the words or phrases of a language, technical field, etc., usually arranged in alphabetical order and defined" (p. 2129). It defines terminology as "the system of terms belonging or peculiar to a science, art, or specialized subject" (p. 1959). The essential distinction here is that a vocabulary or lexicon merely lists words in alphabetical order and defines them, whereas the concept of terminology views terms within an overall system. In other words, it focuses on the range of usages depending on specific situations.

Christian Galinski (1988), an internationally renowned expert on terminology, further clarifies the distinction:

> The term "terminology" is somewhat infelicitous in that it would seem to suggest that this field of knowledge is exclusively concerned with "terms" (i.e., words or groups of words designating concepts). Were this in fact the case, one would have to agree with those who cannot see any essential difference between terminology and lexicography.
>
> Terminology, however, deals primarily with the content aspect of the terms, i.e., with the *concepts* [emphasis in original]—units of knowledge, which by their very nature *never* occur in isolation, but are always integrated within the context of a concept system, regardless of the fact that our knowledge may often be incomplete and contain many gaps. (p. 493)

Historically, the science of terminology evolved as specialized languages developed in various fields of knowledge and the need to standardize usage became apparent. As early as the fifteenth century, scholars and technical specialists began to describe new inventions, techniques, or concepts, in universally recognized terms. Ever since then, it has been common practice for a team of subject specialists to collaborate on the development of a compendium of terms which all specialists in a given field can use without fear of misunderstanding. As international cooperation has grown in a wide range of fields, thanks to improved communication, the need for standardization has become even more urgent. Accordingly, efforts to compile not only monolingual terminologies but also multilingual ones have accelerated. As Galinski (1988) points out, "New technical, scientific and industrial fields of specialization are emerging virtually every day, and more languages are entering the scene of international specialized communication. An exponential growth in the need for specialized translation can therefore be expected" (p. 491).

The advent of computerized data storage and retrieval has greatly contributed to these efforts to codify and standardize terminology. At present, the European Community Nations and Canada are in the vanguard with respect to the compilation of computerized terminology banks specifically geared to translators and interpreters. Unfortunately, the subject matters and the language combinations available through these term banks are not those that would be of greatest use to court interpreters in the United States. Very little work has been done to compile terms in Spanish or any of the other languages most frequently encountered in the United States system of justice. As these terminology systems become more sophisticated and widespread, however, other languages and subject matters will be added.

2.3. Compiling Glossaries

As has been emphasized repeatedly throughout this book, the meaning of a given term changes with the context, sometimes dramatically. The interpreter must strive to avoid merely making a one-to-one association when transferring a concept from one language to another. Accordingly, an interpreter who is sophisticated in the use of terminology resources will avoid simply looking up words in the dictionary and seizing the first definition or translation provided, a procedure which results in the sort of gaffes or "bloopers" that translators and interpreters often deride, such as the "drop" example cited in this chapter.

When a new term is entered in the glossary, enough data must be recorded to ensure that the interpreter does not misuse the term in the future. They must note not only the translation of the term, but also the context in which it was used and the subject matter to which it relates. Many other factors intervene to determine how a term should be used: physical setting (courtroom, factory, restaurant), the speaker's region of origin, level of education, social status, and so on. Interpreters may also need to make note of grammatical factors such as prepositions that are commonly used with the term, gender, irregular verb conjugations, and so forth. Ideally, an entry in a glossary should contain the following information:

(1) the SL term;

(2) a definition of the term in the SL, including a contextual example;

(3) the TL equivalent(s);

(4) the source (date, place, person or publication, situation, country of origin, etc.);

(5) the field of knowledge to which the term belongs;

(6) comments on the term (e.g., "vulgar usage, not for polite company");

(7) grammatical information; and

(8) synonyms and antonyms (optional).

The most rudimentary form a glossary can take is that of a loose-leaf notebook in which terms are written down in the order in which they are acquired. Although this method of recording terms is very simple and inexpensive, it is difficult to use: not only is it hard to find terms that are entered in random order, but it is impossible to add new information to previous entries. A slightly more useful format would be a notebook with alphabetized sections for easier reference. The interpreter may want to have separate notebooks for different subject matters (e.g., law, weapons, drugs). An even more useful, but still simple and inexpensive, type of terminology glossary consists of index cards—one card per term—stored in a cabinet or box of some sort. The advantage of this system is that it can be constantly expanded and updated while still maintaining its systematic order. Again, separate boxes can be used for the different fields of knowledge. Each index card contains sufficient room for all of the information listed above, as well as later additions, and the cards can also be cross-referenced.

Translators and interpreters have been operating with shoeboxes and notebooks for many years. With the advent of personal computers, however, they have a much more convenient, efficient, and versatile tool at their disposal. The advantage of a computerized glossary is that it can be updated with ease, and terms can be retrieved instantaneously. A variety of software packages specifically designed for multilingual terminology glossaries are now available on the market.

Regardless of whether the interpreter uses a notebook, an index card file, or a computerized lexical data base, the entries should look like the following examples:

Spanish: *pescuezo*

Definition: *cuello* — "*me duele el pescuezo*"

English: neck

Source: Mexican farm worker in doctor's office, 12/3/88

Field: medicine, folk terms

Comments: This term is generally used for animals in standard Spanish, but many rural people use animal terms to describe parts of their own bodies. Not for use with sophisticated individuals.

Grammatical notes:

Synonyms and antonyms: syn. — *cogote, nuca*

English: outplacement

Definition: finding jobs for employees of a given company who have been laid off permanently. "This corporation has its own outplacement department."

Spanish: *colocación externa*

Source: *San Francisco Chronicle* want ads, personal reference (John Doe at Glutco, Inc., phone inquiry on 6/7/89)

Field: business

Comments: corporate usage, apparently not used by the Unemployment Department. Spanish equivalent is an educated guess; I have not seen this term anywhere.

Grammatical notes: noun — I haven't seen "to outplace" yet.

Synonyms and antonyms:

Spanish: *zulo*

Definition: place to hide goods (drugs, weapons) or people, often underground. "*La policía encontró tres kilos de cocaína en un zulo detrás de la casa.*"

English: storeroom, cache, hideout, warehouse, stash house

Source: *El País*, Spain, article on cocaine trafficking, 11/13/87.

Field: drug trafficking, terrorism

Comments: This term does not appear in the dictionary; it may be of Basque origin. The article was accompanied by photographs of the place in question, depicting an underground tunnel.

Grammatical notes: masculine noun

Synonyms and antonyms: syn. — *escondite, reserva*

English: counsel

Definition: attorney, legal adviser. "You have the right to be represented by counsel." "Counsel, please approach the bench."

Spanish: *abogado, asesor legal, consejero, licenciado* (Mexico), *letrado* (Spain), *procurador* (Spain, Chile)

Source: *Robb's Dictionary of Legal Terms,* court decision from Spain (*letrado*), personal references (*procurador* —Fulano Sotano from Chile), article on Mexican criminal trial in *Excelsior.*

Field: law

Comments: Be careful with the term procurador — it can be either a prosecutor or a defense attorney, depending on the country. In Chile it is similar to a law clerk in the U.S. See entries under District Attorney, Prosecutor, Solicitor, Barrister, *Procurador, Licenciado, Letrado*

Grammatical notes: Counsel can be either singular or plural; can be either form of address or title. In Spanish, use with *representar, defender, dirigir* (in Spain, *el letrado dirige, el procurador representa*)

Synonyms and antonyms: attorney, counselor, lawyer

Spanish: *balance*

Definition: 1. [look these up in Moliner]

English: 1. balance sheet   2. annual report   3. balance   4. assessment

Source: 3. California, Texas, personal reference 4. Cuba, *Granma,* 8/29/87

Field: 1, 2. accounting, business, government   3. general   4. general

Comments: 3. anglicism   4. Cuban usage

Grammatical notes: masculine noun

Synonyms and antonyms: 2. *memoria*

English: balance

Definition: 1. equilibrium   2. remainder   3. scale

Spanish: 1. *equilíbrio; balance (de pagos); correlato (de fuerzas)*   2. *saldo, resto*   3. *balanza, bóscula*

Source: *American Heritage Dictionary*

Field: 1. general   2. accounting   3. general

Comments:

Grammatical notes:

Synonyms and antonyms:

Spanish: *orden*

Definition: 1. [find in Moliner]

English: 1. order, system; peace, harmony 2. order, command; religious order

Source: *Diccionario del Uso* (Moliner)

Field: general

Comments: **del** orden **de** — *on the order of, in the neighborhood of; de* **primer** orden — *first class, first rate; las fuerzas del orden* — *law enforcement agencies;* **por** orden **de**—*on orders from*

Grammatical notes: 1. masculine noun   2. feminine noun

Synonyms and antonyms:

The above examples give some idea of the sort of data that should be included in a terminology entry. Interpreters should set up an index card system, or a computerized data base, with a standard format or template. Then when they add a new term, they merely fill in the blanks. It may be necessary to cross-reference some terms if they have similar meanings, or are used in close association with each other. Such cross-references would be included in the comments section. It is also useful to make entries in all of the interpreter's working languages so that terms can be looked up regardless of the direction of translation.

If a glossary becomes too large, it is very cumbersome to use, whether it consists of a card file in a shoebox or a computer data base. The solution to this problem is to have separate glossaries for separate fields of knowledge or subject matters. For example, an interpreter who works in the courts of a large city might have the following glossaries: law terms, drug slang, regionalisms, and technical terms. An interpreter who primarily works at state agency hearings in a rural area might have the following glossaries: bureaucratic jargon, medical terms, employment terms, agricultural terms, and regionalisms. These separate glossaries should also be cross-referenced where necessary.

In conclusion, a glossary of terms should be set up in such a way that the interpreter has a clear idea of what the term means and how it is used in a variety of contexts and fields. Some data included in the entry may seem obvious at the time the term is entered, but it may be years before the interpreter comes across the term again. In the meantime, the interpreter may have added hundreds of new terms to his or her knowledge store, and these details will be harder to retrieve from memory. If the glossaries are properly formatted and cross-referenced, the interpreter will have little trouble finding terms and using them correctly. For more information about glossaries of terms, see the references cited in the reading list at the end of this chapter.

3. Human Resources as Language References

The language resources consulted by the court interpreter do not always have to involve cutting-edge technology. One of the most valuable references available to the court interpreter is fellow human beings. As noted previously, new words are constantly emerging and the professional interpreter cannot wait for them to appear in books, for they are used from the moment of inception. These words may come from humble people, a specific field of new technology, or politics. New creative uses of language also arise from advertising and sports. Since words begin with people, the basic source for them is the people who use them. Court interpreters are, by nature, seekers of words. For them, language is a way of life, and they never miss an opportunity to discover new words, phrases, or usages. They have a never-ending curiosity about language, and are constantly seeking better ways of translating concepts from one language to another. Very often a simple question during a chance encounter in an elevator or hallway will solve a particularly perplexing problem for the court interpreter. Although court interpreters will never command the totality of any language's lexicon, they must forever seek to increase their vocabulary. The acquisition of new vocabulary for court interpreters should be structured instead of haphazard.

The following strategies represent ways in which interpreters may utilize human resources to broaden their terminological data bases.

3.1. Use of the Witness as a Language Resource

The court interpreter should regard non-English-speaking witnesses and defendants as vast sources of words from diverse regions of the world and different levels of society. The court interpreter can study the language of fellow human beings without regard to their socioeconomic status. Different people—from farmers to bankers—contribute rich modes of expression that can only be ignored by court interpreters at the risk of limiting their linguistic competence.

Witnesses represent subcultures such as gang members, drug users, smugglers of illegal aliens, and members of law enforcement agencies. All are an invaluable source of jargon, argot, and non-standard language. Expert witnesses bring their own sets of specialized vocabulary and terms of art. Each witness must be viewed as a potential source of information, and an opportunity to add new terms to the interpreter's lexicon.

The interpreter should make a habit of jotting down unfamiliar terms while sitting at counsel table. Such notetaking can be done even while interpreting, as it does not interfere with that function once the skill of speaking and writing simultaneously has been acquired. The terms noted are for future reference, discussion, and/or further research. Not only should unknown words be recorded, but also new meanings and connotations of familiar words, as well as new idiomatic expressions.

3.2. Attending Court Proceedings

The court interpreter may attend the proceedings in a courtroom and sit in the audience for the sole purpose of gaining exposure to the legal process. A great amount of knowledge and information may be gained simply by observing the court in action. The sophisticated vocabulary of attorneys is of particular interest to the court interpreter. Much can be learned simply by listening.

The court interpreter can focus on the language of each of the actors, unencumbered by the responsibility of functioning as a court interpreter. He or she may even take the opportunity to ask questions during a recess if it is convenient for the attorneys, clerk, or bailiff. If the court interpreter has a serious desire to progress professionally, he or she will be willing to ask questions without reservation during appropriate moments.

If the assignment office has no objection, an interpreter may be allowed to attend a hearing whose subject matter is of particular interest, such as new criminal investigation technology, agribusiness, or the toxic effect of drugs. For example, if there is an opportunity to attend a trial in which there is testimony about the identification of suspects through DNA research, the astute interpreter will realize that DNA identification will someday make fingerprinting obsolete and will also introduce new terminology into the courtroom. Thus, the interpreter should regard the opportunity to observe the DNA case as a learning experience.

The interpreter waiting in court for the case to be called similarly takes advantage of the opportunity to observe and listen to other matters in progress. It is also extremely helpful to observe experienced interpreters at work to see how they conduct themselves and to gain insight into how they solve difficult interpreting problems.

3.3. Conferring with Colleagues

Fellow practitioners in the field of court interpretation are an incalculably valuable human resource. The interpreter should take advantage of every opportunity to compare notes. An exchange of information on a daily basis is a vehicle for augmenting vocabularies. Court interpreters may confer during lunch breaks, court recesses, between assignments, and while in the interpreter waiting room. In short, any occasion during the work day when the interpreter comes in contact with other interpreters is an excellent opportunity to share information.

The information is not always exchanged in the form of question and answer. Quite often interpreters will regard the information they have learned as a curiosity or a tidbit of information that might titillate their fellow interpreters. For example, the new interpreter in the Southwest may be taken aback to find out that the Spanish word *chiva* (female goat) in drug terminology refers to heroin, and will want to share this information with colleagues. Or she may want to report a new regionalism she has discovered. For instance, the interpreter might learn that the word *choclo,* known to her as an ear of corn, also means an article of footwear in another part of the world.

Information may be shared with colleagues in the form of a question or puzzle to be solved by quoting the words of a witness and asking other interpreters to guess the meaning of the new term. An interpreter may come into the waiting room and say, "I just overheard two police officers talking about 'cold plating' and 'hot plating.' Anyone care to guess what they mean?" After an amusing exchange, the interpreter can reveal that the terms refer to putting legitimately obtained license plates on stolen cars (cold plating) and putting stolen license plates on stolen cars (hot plating).

Sometimes the occasion may be one of urgency, in which the interpreter needs to find the meaning or translation of an unknown term during the recess when there may be no printed or human resources close at hand. There is always, however, a telephone, and the interpreter can call the supervising interpreter. If the word or expression in question is known by the supervising interpreter, the answer will be immediately forthcoming. If it is unknown, the supervising interpreter or an assistant may consult reference materials that are in the interpreters' reference library. It is the duty of the supervising interpreter to help the interpreters in the field, and the interpreter should not hesitate to make such calls.

In one interpreter waiting room the interpreters write needed words on a huge blackboard. Other interpreters seeing these words write their meaning or the word in the other language. The blackboard is a constant source of information for those passing through this room. Several interpreters may embark on a group project to organize and compile new terminology and may even make copies for those interpreters with whom they work. These lists of terms are frequently expanded by the interpreters who receive the lists, and in many cases these lists form the basis for serious efforts to compile glossaries for the benefit of members of a professional organization.

Court interpreting organizations may sponsor professional seminars where these glossaries are made available. At professional interpreter conferences the interpreter may attend seminars on many topics about particular subjects of personal or professional interest. In a seminar the interpreter comes in contact with other interpreters from diverse regions of the state or country who have similar interests. This geographic perspective affords the interpreter an unparalleled opportunity for sharing and solving language problems. In the seminars offered by the professional organization, specific regionalisms are shared. In the interpreter seminars the leader is always an expert whose background in the field presents a unique opportunity to gain information not normally available in the courthouse.

Interpreter training programs offered by colleges and universities are venues for networking with other interpreters. These training programs attract interpreters from every corner of the country. University-sponsored training programs offer the means to expand lexicons and broaden interpreting skills. They afford the working interpreter an opportunity for exposure to professionals in the field of interpreter training, as well as the occasion to interrelate with interpreters who have knowledge of other dialectical forms and expressions.

3.4. Contacting Experts

Some court interpreters work in relative professional isolation; some serve the court far removed from colleagues and personal contacts. In some instances there is only one interpreter serving an entire courthouse. Even in these situations the court interpreter may seek information from government offices such as the police and sheriff's departments, and from language instructors in local high schools, colleges, and state or private universities. Introducing oneself as a court interpreter will open many doors and will provide the opportunity for many invaluable contacts. For example, the interpreter may be unaware of the Spanish term for "money laundering" and no reference book in the professional library will help. In this case, a phone conversation with a bilingual undercover narcotics agent would provide the answer. There are many experts in many fields that are always available by phone.

In conclusion, interpreters should be aware of the vast resources available to them beyond the traditional dictionary. They should make full use of those resources, and should regard the maintenance and upgrading of language skills as an ongoing endeavor that they will pursue for the rest of their lives.

Chapter 33
Technical Aids

This chapter discusses three types of equipment that court interpreters will most likely encounter during the course of their work: wireless equipment for simultaneous interpretation, computers, word processors and other electronic office equipment, and videoscript machines.

1. Simultaneous Equipment

From the very earliest days, courts have considered the problem of the court interpreter as just that: a problem. The sound of the interpreter's simultaneous interpretation whispered or murmured into the ear of the defendant at the counsel table has been a distraction to the judge, the court reporter, and all actors in the legal arena. The tradition, over hundreds of years, has been that one and only one person speaks at a time in a court of law. With the advent of the position of court interpreter, there are two people speaking at the same time: the speaker on the record and the interpreter simultaneously interpreting every word. Countless judges have admonished court interpreters to lower their voices. Some judges have stated categorically that they do not want to hear the court interpreter. No one has been more painfully aware of this intrusion into the courtroom than have court interpreters. They have sought, with varying degrees of success, to mute their voices so as not to be audible in the courtroom.

In the past, the more sophisticated attempts to solve this problem involved a closed-circuit sound system between the interpreter and the defendant so that only the defendant could hear the court interpreter. All closed-circuit systems employed headphones for the defendant and a microphone for the court interpreter. Some systems have even had a muzzle for the court interpreter, with the microphone implanted inside. In this way, the interpreter's voice is wholly contained within the muzzle, yet audible to the defendant by means of a wire connecting the interpreter's microphone to an amplifier and then to the defendant's ears through a headset.

Many interpreters purchased wired, portable closed-circuit systems that were easily carried in a briefcase. The only limitation on the number of listeners was the number of output jacks in the amplifier. The smallest amplifier could accommodate but one listener, but in theory, by increasing the power of the amplifier and the number of output jacks, any desired number of listeners could be accommodated. The drawback of these systems was always the number of wires that would have to be strewn about the counsel table and the courtroom. In some situations the number of wires interfered with the physical movement of court personnel.

Improved models of closed-circuit systems were developed and abandoned, and other systems of sound amplification were devised, using radio transmission from a transformer of limited wattage that would transmit radio waves through the air to wireless headsets worn in the courtroom by defendants and even spectators. The drawback of radio transmission communication was that radio waves could penetrate walls, and the radio transmissions could be heard in adjoining courtrooms and even on other floors in the same courthouse. The newest solution to the problem has been a communication system that is wireless but utilizes infrared light as the vehicle for transmission. The transmitter is set up in the vicinity of the judge's bench, and when activated floods the courtroom with infrared light that is undetectable to the human eye. The court interpreter's microphone is a highly sensitive instrument and is connected to the transmitter by a long lead that allows the court interpreter a great degree of mobility. In this way, interpreters may position themselves in any area of the courtroom that will enable them to hear, without regard to their proximity to the defendant or to any listener of the interpretation. The defendant or defendants or any other listener utilizes a headset that is in effect a receiver with its own independent volume control. It is not dependent on proximity to either the transmitter or the court interpreter. Rather, it may receive the signal in any position in the courtroom, be it as close to the transmitter as the court reporter or as far away as the last row in the audience.

The sensitivity of the system is such that it will even detect the sounds of breathing and swallowing. It is a unidirectional system that transmits the interpreter's signals to the listeners; it does not allow for communication from the defendant to the interpreter. For this reason, there should be a second or backup interpreter, if possible, who sits inside the railing and in the vicinity of counsel table in case a defendant wishes to consult with the attorney or vice versa during the course of the proceedings. The presence of the second interpreter allows the simultaneous interpretation to proceed in an uninterrupted fashion even if there is lengthy communication between attorney and client. Since the number of listeners is for all practical purposes unlimited, provided that they are inside the courtroom, in many instances the judge has allowed interested members of the audience—for example, non-English-speaking wives and families of the defendant—to use the headphones so that they may follow the proceedings. Since the vehicle for transmission is lightwaves that are wholly contained within the confines of the courtroom, similar systems can be employed on every floor and in adjoining or neighboring courtrooms with no interference. The super sensitivity of the microphone allows the court interpreter to interpret *sotto voce*, in a whispered voice that is almost inaudible even to those closest to the interpreter.

However, the expense of the system is such that it is beyond the reach of the individual court interpreter and must be purchased by the court with public funds. This equipment has been in use for five to ten years in a few courts throughout the country, yet as of this writing it has not been widely adopted. The federal courts are using it increasingly throughout the country. The usefulness of this equipment during the trial procedure is obvious. What may not be readily apparent is the system's productivity when large numbers are to be arraigned and informed of their constitutional rights. The mere issuance of a lightweight headphone receiver to any non-English speaker will automatically enable that person to hear a simultaneous interpretation of the whole arraignment procedure. With a second interpreter at the defendant's side, he or she would even be able to respond to the court immediately, either to enter a plea or to seek counsel.

The interpreter utilizing this sophisticated equipment for the first time should not attempt to assemble the components without first being trained or receiving some instruction from interpreters with experience or someone trained in the use of this equipment. Much time will be saved by avoiding trial-and-error experimentation, and there will be no undue delays of the proceedings at hand. Interpreters who work with this equipment are responsible for securing all the related components of the system from the custodian of the property (clerk's office, supervising interpreter's office), and arriving in the courtroom prior to the beginning of proceedings to set up, connect, and test the equipment. One interpreter should actually don a pair of headphones and sit somewhere in the audience while the second interpreter tests the system by speaking into the microphone.

2. Computers and Word Processors

The advent of the personal computer, with associated software, has revolutionized the way language professionals perform their day-to-day tasks. Although machine translation of written documents is still in its infancy, the court interpreter can derive much benefit from the use of a computer. As with translators, the application of the computer to the compilation of terminology glossaries is especially relevant for court interpreters, who must constantly update their lists of terms. This section will explain the hardware and software that is available on the market today, with particular attention to the needs of the court interpreter.

2.1. Hardware

A typical translator's work station consists of the following pieces of equipment:

- monitor (the part of the computer system that looks like a TV screen)
- one or two floppy or micro-diskette drives
- hard disk (optional)—20-megabyte minimum capacity
- system unit containing the central processor, the system's main memory (RAM), expansion cards, and various other electronic components. The amount of system RAM a computer contains is an important consideration. A minimum of 256 kilobytes (256K) is sufficient for most word processing tasks; 640K is preferable. The system also generally (but not necessarily) houses the diskette and hard disk drives.
- keyboard
- printer

Types of printers include: dot matrix, generally the least expensive and least acceptable for business use; near-letter-quality, which is more expensive but approaches typewritten quality; daisy wheel, slightly more expensive than dot matrix, letter-quality output; and laser, the most expensive, fastest, and most flexible type of printer currently available. Translators must make sure that the printer they have can accommodate the alphabet or character set that is required for all of their target languages. Dot matrix and laser printers are physically capable of reproducing any character set, but only when provided with the necessary software drivers and fonts. Daisy wheel printers are limited to the characters physically present on a given daisy wheel (though multiple daisy wheels are available and are interchangeable). A near-letter-quality dot matrix printer should at least be considered for purchase by the professional interpreter.

When personal computers first appeared on the market, the consumer had to choose among different operating systems that were incompatible with one another. In recent years competition has narrowed the field, so that virtually all personal computers sold today (with the notable exception of Apple computers) are compatible with the PC-DOS/MS-DOS operating system used by IBM personal computers. When deciding what kind of system to buy, the translator/interpreter should consider not only the range of software that is available for that type of computer (i.e., IBM-compatible vs. Apple Macintosh vs. Apple II), but also the ease of transferring data from his or her system to that of the client.

In general, the range of software available for IBM-compatible systems (also known as PCs) and Macintosh systems is approximately equivalent, although very specific needs may dictate one system or the other. Far less business-oriented software is available for the Apple II family of computers, which should probably be avoided on that basis alone.

When one considers ease of data transfer, however, the balance is nowhere near so even. IBM compatibles are far more prevalent than Macintoshes in the business world. Although it is possible to transfer data (not programs) from an IBM-compatible to a Macintosh and vice versa, it is not easy. Therefore, unless the translator's specific software needs dictate the choice of a Macintosh, an IBM-compatible is probably a better choice.

Although the decision to commit to one or the other of the two current personal computer "worlds" (i.e., IBM-compatible vs. Macintosh) should not be taken lightly, it is reassuring to note that the software and hardware which facilitate communication between these two operating systems is readily available, and may eventually even make the decision inconsequential.

Other hardware that the translator/interpreter might want to acquire includes a modem for communicating with other computers (ideal for sending work back and forth to distant clients, and for gaining access to data banks all over the world), a facsimile ("fax") machine for sending hard copy back and forth, and an optical scanner for converting hard copy characters to machine-readable form. The interpreter who translates only occasionally will probably not think that investing in such accessories is justified.

2.2. Software

A word processing package is the basic software that is required for translating on a personal computer. There are many different word processing programs on the market, each tailored to different user needs. Some word processing packages, such as WorldWriter, were designed specifically for multilingual use. A translator whose target language is always English need not be concerned about such matters as whether diacritical marks or non-Roman characters appear on the screen just as they will be printed, or whether language-specific spell-check programs are available, but these features are especially important to translators who work in other languages. The main objective should be the efficient performance of the specific tasks required by the translator; user-friendliness may make a package appealing initially, but it may soon become more of a hindrance than a help. The newsletter of the American Translators Association, *The ATA Chronicle,* and other ATA publications contain useful information about computer software for the translator/ interpreter.

Other software packages that can be of use to the translator/interpreter include bookkeeping software for billing and keeping track of jobs, desktop publishing programs for producing typeset, camera-ready copy with graphics and other sophisticated features, and lexical data bases (on-line terminology glossaries).

Of these types of software, lexical data bases are the most relevant to the work of the court interpreter and the most likely to be tailored specifically to the needs of language professionals. They consist of terms and associated information (target-language equivalents, sources, definitions, grammar and usage notes, and contextual examples). They can be personal glossaries compiled and used by an individual translator/interpreter, as described earlier in this chapter, purchased computerized glossaries, or large-scale term banks maintained by organizations and used by many subscribers all over the world.

It is now possible to purchase data base management programs designed specifically for personal lexical data bases (AutoTerm and Mercury, for example). Most of these programs allow the translator to maintain a variety of glossaries to which the interpreter can add unlimited terms and make constant updates. If the glossary is on-line, the translator can gain access to it without leaving the word processing program (using a split screen). Reference-only software, an electronic dictionary that can be read but not altered by the user, is also increasingly available on the market.

As for large-scale term banks, there are several in Europe and two in Canada, as of this writing. Subscribers gain access to them via modem, or, as in the case of the Termium bank in Canada, they can purchase compact disks containing the data; updated disks are sent periodically to all subscribers.

3. Videoscript Machine

The videoscript machine is one of the newest technological aids of the courtroom. It is used by the court reporter for hearing-impaired witnesses. This machine translates the phonetic symbols of the court reporter's stenotype into standard written English. The "transcript" appears on a monitor wherever it is needed in the courtroom, typically at the defense counsel table for the use of hearing-impaired defendants so that they may follow and respond to the proceedings.

Because the videoscript machine allows for easy and quick accessibility to the record, other actors in the legal arena may wish to utilize this equipment to review recent testimony, even when a hearing-impaired defendant is not involved. As this equipment becomes more pervasive in our nation's courtrooms, interpreters may come to rely upon the use of the videoscript machine for reference in the same way they would rely on printed scripts of instructions to the jury or statements of constitutional rights. If court interpreters miss an important detail of the testimony, they may use the displayed transcript for immediate reference to help them compensate for any omission they may have made.

The danger here is that the interpreter could become completely dependent upon the display rather than upon what is heard. The interpreter might stop listening to the proceedings and just sight translate the display on the screen. Should there be any error in the record, it would be compounded by the court interpreter depending upon the printed word rather than on what was actually said. Further, should there ever be any negative consequences (reversal or sanctions) as a result of inaccuracies based upon the reading of the text rather than what was actually said in court, the interpreter could not blame the court reporter for the errors. At some point prior to the proceedings, the court interpreter has sworn to "well and truly interpret to the best of **his or her** ability," and no qualifications or allowances are made for the ability or inability of any third party. The purpose of this discussion is not to pass judgment on the merits of the work performed by the court reporter, but rather to point out that the responsibility of the court interpreter may not be shifted to anyone else.

Unit 8

Professional Issues

Chapter 34

Ethical Principles and Standards

This chapter focuses on court interpreting as a profession. It enumerates the ethical principles and standards that should guide the interpreter, and explains the practical implications as well as the legal, professional, and ethical reasons for these principles and standards.

Definition of Profession

Black's Law Dictionary (1979) defines a profession as "A vocation or occupation requiring special, usually advanced, education and skill; ... The labor and skill involved in a profession is predominantly mental or intellectual, rather than physical or manual" (p. 1089). The New Jersey Supreme Court Task Force on Interpreter and Translation Services (1984), after analyzing this and other definitions, reached the conclusion that professionals are individuals who not only possess specialized knowledge, but also adhere to a code of ethics, demonstrate their mastery of skills through a licensing or certification process, and serve the public interest in the performance of their services.

These definitions indicate that two major elements of professionalism are demonstrated mastery of specialized knowledge, and ethical behavior in the service of the public interest. The particular areas of knowledge that court interpreters must master have been covered in other chapters of this book. Continuing education will be discussed at the end of this chapter; the ethical standards that court interpreters must adhere to are presented below.

Code of Ethics

Like all professions, interpreting began informally, with no legal or ethical guidelines to govern the services provided by individual interpreters. Over the years, as problems and issues arose, individual interpreters resolved them on an *ad hoc* basis. There were many discrepancies in the way different interpreters handled similar situations. With the evolution of professional associations, interpreters began to thrash out these issues together and eventually arrived at standard solutions to common problems. In addition, the users of interpreters—in the case of court interpreting, the legal profession, and the judiciary—began examining these issues from their own perspective and developed guidelines as well. Gradually, a definition of the interpreter's role in the overall process has taken shape (see Units 1 and 2).

A code of ethics is essential because the legal process, being a human process, is not clear cut, and many dilemmas arise which interpreters must solve as part of their daily functioning. Frishberg (1986) points out that engaging an interpreter is an act of trust which places a heavy moral burden on the interpreter. Edwards (1988) also cites the tremendous power wielded by the interpreter because he or she may be the only one present who understands both languages involved. Edwards explains, "It is the function of a code of ethics to guide the interpreter on how to wield that power" (p. 22). This opinion is seconded by Neumann Solow (1981), who goes on to say that "a code of ethics protects the interpreter and lessens the arbitrariness of his or her decisions by providing guidelines and standards to follow" (p. 39). The introduction to the Canons of Ethics for Court Interpreters and Legal Translators proposed by the New Jersey Supreme Court Task Force on Interpreter and Translation Services (1985) states that the purpose of the canons is "to upgrade the professional quality of . . . services and, thereby, support the administration of justice and promote the public's confidence in the Judiciary's ability to adlinister [sic] justice for all persons" (Appendix, p. 26).

The adoption of a code of ethics is imperative for shaping a profession and distinguishing it from others. Since court interpreting is still a fledgling profession, there is not yet a single canon of ethics that regulates the actions of interpreters. The various professional organizations to which interpreters and translators belong have devised their own codes of ethics, and various judicial and administrative entities have drawn up guidelines. Appendix C contains the code of ethics that governs interpreters in the federal courts. Other useful codes include those developed by the California Court Interpreters Association, the New Jersey Supreme Court Task Force on Interpreter and Translation Services (1985), and the California State Court Judicial Rules for Court Interpreters (Appendix F). At present, as noted by the New Jersey Task Force on Interpreter and Translation Services (1985), "Court interpreters and legal translators who are members of professional associations pledge to honor the codes of ethics of the respective associations. . . . However, this is a strictly voluntary arrangement with limited enforcement" (p. 126). It is hoped that the code of ethics contained in this chapter will serve as a standard that court interpreters throughout the nation can use to guide their own actions and to educate the legal community.

A code of ethics should be a living, flexible document that helps steer practitioners through the shoals of everyday experience, rather than something immutable that is engraved in stone. In any profession, novices tend to start out following the rules of conduct rigidly and formally. Later, as they establish themselves in the profession and gain credibility among their peers and clients, they learn how to apply these rules in accordance with common sense and their intelligent assessment of the situation. One characteristic that distinguishes professionals from mere employees is that they are able to apply independent judgment and the benefit of experience to resolve difficult conflicts. Blind adherence to a rigid set of rules serves no one; Emerson's familiar "a foolish consistency is the hobgoblin of little minds" underscores this point. In short, interpreters must uphold the spirit of the canon of ethics, and must not become entangled in following the letter of the rules.

The following discussion of ethics and responsibilities contains some guidelines that are intended to help interpreters deal with difficulties that frequently arise in the courtroom. Interpreters must make an ethical judgment in each individual situation and behave consistently with their education, training, ethical principles, common sense, and responsibility to their clients. It is also important to remember that the judge is the final arbiter of what is appropriate in his or her courtroom, and that the interpreter must defer to the judge. There are also many local rules of protocol in every courtroom, and the interpreter has a duty to learn and adhere to them as well. We hope that the following ethical standards and responsibilities, which should be common to all codes of ethics in the interpreting profession, will serve as an aid in decision making. Each item will be followed by a detailed discussion of the protocol or standard procedure for dealing with specific situations.

Ethical Standards and Responsibilities

1. The interpreter shall render a complete and accurate interpretation.
2. The interpreter shall remain impartial.
3. The interpreter shall maintain confidentiality.
4. The interpreter shall confine himself or herself to the role of interpreting.
5. The interpreter shall be prepared for any type of proceeding or case.
6. The interpreter shall ensure that the duties of his or her office are carried out under working conditions that are in the best interest of the court.
7. The interpreter shall be familiar with and adhere to all of these ethical standards, and shall maintain high standards of personal and professional conduct to promote public confidence in the administration of justice.

Discussion

1. The interpreter shall render a complete and accurate interpretation.

At the beginning of any legal proceeding, the interpreter takes an oath swearing to "well and truly interpret" that proceeding, or words to that effect. This means that the interpreter has a duty to protect the record, to ensure that it reflects precisely what was stated in the source language. *The Federal Court Interpreter Certification Examination Manual* (Gonzalez, 1986) states that "the court interpreter is required to transfer the message into the other language exactly, or as close to exactly, as originally spoken" (p. 5). Article 7 of the Code of Professional Responsibility of the Official Interpreters of the United States Courts (cited in Administrative Office of the United States Courts, 1987, p. F3-1) states that official court interpreters "preserve the level of language used by the speaker, and preserve the ambiguities and nuances of the speaker, without any editing." The New Jersey Supreme Court Task Force on Interpreter and Translation Services (1985) declares that "the *sine qua non* of interpreting and translating is precision, accuracy and completeness" (p. 58).

The reason for this high standard of accuracy is that the interpreter is the voice of the non-English speaker. Tayler (1988) points out that the Court Interpreters Act of 1978, which provides for interpreting services in all criminal and civil actions in the federal district courts, "is designed to put non-English-speaking witnesses, defendants, and litigants on an equal footing with those who are English-speaking" (p.

57). She notes that because the law does not provide any means to preserve the original foreign language witness testimony or discussions at counsel table, the use of qualified, certified interpreters is the only way to ensure a true and correct interpretation. Thus, with no permanent record of the original testimony, the interpreter has the overriding obligation to ensure that the TL rendition meets the highest standards of accuracy. The interpreter is very often the only bilingual person present upon whom everyone must rely to convey the witness's testimony precisely and completely.

Moreover, in some respects the interpreter actually takes the place of the witness. Susan Berk-Seligson (1987) emphasizes that because the interpreter stands next to the witness and is the only one understood by the listeners, the interpreter receives more attention than the witness. Indeed, "For all intents and purposes, it is as if the foreign language testimony had never been uttered" (p. 1096). Thus, the judge and/ or jury will base their conclusions about the credibility of witnesses and the relative weight of testimony on what the interpreter does and says.

Another consideration is the question of an appeal. Since appeals are decided on the basis of transcripts, and the words of the interpreter are the only permanent record of what the witness or the defendant said, the quality of interpretation has an impact on how the case will be viewed by an appellate court. Tayler (1988) stresses that "in a court proceeding where the interpreter may be the only bilingual individual present, errors by the interpreter may never be discovered, leaving no basis for appeal on the grounds of inaccurate interpretation" (p. 57). It is clear, then, that the quality of the interpretation is critical to the outcome of the case. Therefore, the importance of rendering a complete and accurate interpretation cannot be overemphasized.

1.1. Verbatim Interpretation

In order to render a complete and accurate version of the SL message, the interpreter must conserve every single element of information that was contained in the original source language (SL) message. The following is an explication of the elements of the SL message that must be kept intact in the target language version:

1.1.1. Language Level or Register

The interpreter must never alter the language level of the SL message when rendering it into the TL for the purpose of enhancing understanding or avoiding offense.

Protocol: As an example, if the attorney asks, "If I were to ask you who was your treating physician in the intervening period prior to your second accident, what would your response be?" The interpreter should not say in the TL, "Who was your doctor before your second accident?" Interpreters should not try to lower the register of question down to the witness's level, nor should they intervene and say that they do not think the question is understandable to the witness. If the witness does not understand the question, the person will say so; it is not the interpreter's job to speak up for him or her. It is important to remember, when interpreting a witness's testimony before a jury, that the jury will draw certain conclusions regarding the witness's sophistication and intelligence, based on the person's word choice, style, tone, and so forth. The interpreter should make sure the jurors have as much information in that regard as a native speaker of the TL would have in order to judge the witness's credibility.

1.1.2. Word Choice

Nuances of meaning are critical in courtroom testimony. Loftus and Palmer (1974, p. 586) found that subtle changes in word choice significantly altered witness's recollections of events. When a key word in the question was changed ("About how fast were the cars going when they hit/smashed/collided/bumped/contacted each other?"), subjects who were asked the question that contained the term "smashed" tended to increase their estimate of the speed, and recalled seeing broken glass when in fact there was none. Thus, interpreters must be very careful in selecting TL terms to make sure that they accurately and precisely reflect the SL meaning.

1.1.3. Obscenities

If witnesses use foul language or say anything that might be damaging to the case, the interpreter should not edit out the offending terms and must interpret exactly what is heard, conserving the original meaning. Section 18.1a., Paragraph (8) of The Judicial Council of California (1979), clearly states: "All words, including slang, vulgarisms, and epithets, should be interpreted to convey the intended meaning." The interpreter must remember, once again, that the jurors will make judgments about the honesty and credibility of the witness on the basis of the witness's manner of testifying. They should not be at a disadvantage because they do not know the TL. For cultural reasons, obscenities are particularly difficult to translate directly; a word-for-word translation may be meaningless in the TL. Interpreters should look for the closest equivalent in the TL, striving to elicit the same reaction from TL listeners as the SL message would elicit from SL listeners.

1.1.4. Repetition

Repetition is another aspect of hesitation. The guidelines for courtroom interpreters adopted by the San Diego Municipal Court (1983) state that interpreters should not add or subtract any words for the sake of clarity or expediency: "If a witness says, 'Yes, yes, yes, it's true,' the interpreter has to translate, 'Yes, yes, yes, it's true,' and NOT 'Yes, it's true' " (p. 9). Redundancies should also be preserved in the TL version. For example, when a witness says, "I watched him and observed him take the object from the box," the interpreter should not omit the redundant verb in the TL version. The only exception is in simultaneous interpretation; if there is a historical doublet or triplet (see Chapter 20) such as stop, cease, and desist, it may be rendered as one concept (Gonzalez, 1977).

1.1.5. Self-Corrections

Many speakers, attorneys and witnesses alike, make false starts and then revise their statements. It is especially important in interpreted witness testimony that all such self-corrections be included in the TL version, so that the judge and jury can draw conclusions as to how certain the witness is about the testimony, or how precise the person is in choosing words. The interpreter should never correct any errors made by a speaker, no matter how unintentional they may be. The *Los Angeles Superior Court Interpreters Manual* (Almeida & Zahler, 1981) states, "The interpreter must never correct erroneous facts posed in questions to non-English speaking witnesses. Conversely, the interpreter must never correct the testimony of non-English speaking witnesses even if the errors are obvious" (p. 12).

Protocol: If the witness makes a slip of the tongue and says, "I was born in 1853," and the interpreter knows the witness was actually born in 1953, he or she must resist the temptation to correct the error. Similarly, if the witness misspells his or her own name, the interpreter should not correct the error. No matter how incorrect, illogical, incriminating, or non-responsive the statement, the interpreter must translate it unquestioningly, exactly as it was stated.

1.1.6. Third-Person References

It is common for people who use interpreters to preface their statements with phrases like "Tell him that..." and "Ask him if..." rather than addressing each other directly. If they do so, the interpreter must not edit out those phrases. The parties involved may become confused, however, and the transcript of the proceedings will be unclear if this third-person style is used. Section 18.1, Paragraph (b)(1) of the *Standards of Judicial Administration Recommended by the Judicial Council of California* (1979), recognizes this problem, and states, "All questions by counsel examining a non-English speaking witness should be directed to the witness and not to the interpreter. For example, do not say: 'Ask him if...' " (see Appendix F).

Protocol: To avoid confusion, therefore, the interpreter should make the following request to the judge: "Your Honor, would the Court please instruct counsel and the witness to address each other directly rather than using the third person?"

1.2. Embellishments, Clarifications, Editing

While on the one hand interpreters must preserve every element in the original SL message, on the other hand, they must never add anything or elaborate on the message they are conveying, not even for the sake of clarifying or smoothing over choppy delivery. The following is a survey of the most often committed "addition" errors made by interpreters, and the recommended policy for negotiating them.

1.2.1. Fragmentary Statements

Courtroom testimony does not always proceed logically as if following a script. Witnesses often speak unclearly because they have told their stories many times before and assume that everyone knows what they are talking about (e.g., "I went to the ...you know...and there was...it was there."). Such vague and ambiguous statements are difficult to translate to another language, because more information is needed to choose the proper pronouns, prepositions, and verbs. Nevertheless, the interpreter must render as fragmentary a version as the original was, without inserting any additional information to enhance the clarity of the message.

1.2.2. Lengthening Testimony

Because the courtroom is a formal setting, interpreters may feel compelled to behave very formally; indeed, they may be tempted to raise the level of the witness's testimony in their interpreted version, making it more polite or erudite. This temptation must, however, be resisted at all times, because the interpreter may inadvertently affect perception of the witness's credibility. Lind, Conley, Erickson, and O'Barr (1978) and Erickson, Lind, Johnson, and O'Barr (1978) found that the social status and attributions and the speaking style of witnesses affected the way their testimony was evaluated by listeners.

Another study specifically focusing on court interpreters (Berk-Seligson, 1987), found that interpreters tend to amplify the testimony of witnesses by (1) adding hedges (inserting phrases such as "I believe" and "probably" that were not in the original message), (2) inserting "linguistic material that is perceived to be underlying or 'understood' in the original utterances," (p. 1107) (saying "yes I did," for example, when the witness simply said "yes"), (3) using uncontracted forms (saying "I am" instead of "I'm," the normally contracted form in spoken English), (4) rephrasing their own TL rendition (interpreting *gafas* as "glasses or sunglasses"), (5) adding polite forms of address, and (6) adding particles and hesitation forms (beginning the answer with "well," adding "sort of," among others). They also tend to be "hypercorrect" in their language usage, employing grammatical forms that are not ordinarily heard in oral speech ("going to" instead of "gonna," for example). Amplifications such as these distort the witness's testimony, and the jury may reach false conclusions about the credibility of that person.

Similarly, adding polite forms to the attorney's questions ("Can you please tell us" instead of "tell us") would make the questions less compelling. Clearly the interpreter's rendition of the witness's testimony can have a great impact on a jury's perception of that person's credibility, and therefore great care must be taken in choosing the appropriate words and delivery style.

1.2.3. Nonsensical Testimony

It is particularly difficult to interpret the testimony of a person who is highly excited or has mental problems and does not necessarily make sense. Marcos (1979) emphasizes the problem of the interpreter's inclination to "normalize" mental patients' thought disorders and edit their responses so that they make sense. His study was conducted in the hospital setting, but his conclusions apply to courtroom testimony as well. Here is an example of the kind of interpreting problems he observed:

Clinician to Spanish-speaking patient: "What about worries, do you have many worries?"

Interpreter to patient: "Is there anything that bothers you?"

Patient's response: "I know, I know that God is with me, I'm not afraid, they cannot get me [pause] I'm wearing these new pants and I feel protected, I feel good, I don't get headaches anymore."

Interpreter to clinician: "He says that he is not afraid, he feels good, he doesn't have headaches anymore." (p. 173)

It is important for interpreters to make every effort to state exactly what the witness said, no matter how illogical or irrelevant it may be. Sometimes this is very difficult because of ambiguities or incomplete phrases uttered by the witness; in such cases, interpreters should inform the court that they need to clarify the witness's statement before proceeding to interpret it. But under no circumstances should they edit, omit, or add to what the witness stated.

1.2.4. Non-Responsive Testimony

The court interpreter has an obligation to render non-responsive answers by witnesses just as precisely and accurately as any other testimony. According to the New Jersey Supreme Court Task Force on Interpreter and Translation Services (1985), "When a witness" answer to a question does not respond to a question that was posed to the witness, the witness [sic] court interpreter shall render a consecutive verbatim court interpretation, leaving issues of admissibility of such response to the court and counsel" (Appendix, p. 19).

1.3. Non-Verbal Communication

As noted earlier, language communication involves many non-verbal elements in addition to words per se. In the category of what some call "body language," these elements include posture, proximity, facial expressions, and gestures. Voice characteristics and speech patterns also constitute non-verbal elements of communication. Interpreters should certainly pay attention to all of these elements, but they should bear in mind that some of them, particularly facial expressions and hand gestures, vary considerably from one culture to another. They should not blindly imitate whatever the witness did, but should make sure the TL listeners receive the same message that was transmitted in the SL. According to Frishberg (1986), "Accuracy also means giving the receiver the complete message, including the part carried by pauses, hesitations, or other silent or non-verbal signals. The interpreter transmits the full message, not merely the words" (p. 65).

The interpreter has an obligation to convey every aspect of the witness's testimony, not only words but also paralinguistic elements such as pauses, false starts, and tone of voice. The importance of these paralinguistic or non-verbal elements cannot be overemphasized. As Seleskovitch (1978a) states:

Since instant understanding is necessary, the spoken language contains—in addition to words—many elements which aid understanding: gestures, facial expressions, style of delivery, changes in volume, pauses, etc. . . . The content of the message must be understood at the very moment it is uttered; if not, it will vanish without trace—it will be as if it had never been uttered. (p. 14)

In the courtroom, more than any other setting where interpreting takes place, the interpreter has an obligation to be particularly cognizant of these non-verbal elements and to account for each and every one of them in the TL version in order to conserve the meaning of the original and provide a precise legal equivalent (Gonzalez, 1989c).

That is why the consecutive interpretation (CI) that is practiced in the judicial setting places such a heavy demand on the interpreter's memory capacity.

There is some controversy with regard to the question of conveying the witness's emotions. Some contend that only the interpreter can hear the subtleties in the voice that reveal the witness's attitude. There is also the belief that if interpreters hear fear, anxiety, sorrow, remorse, arrogance, anger, or lack of certainty, they are bound to convey these intangibles in the TL to the best of their ability. This school of thought would require the interpreter to whisper if the SL message is whispered and to yell if the SL message is shouted.

From the linguistic perspective, it is virtually impossible to render an accurate and meaningful interpretation free of paralinguistic elements. Without conservation of the paralinguistic elements, the discourse may be homogenized. In practice, when a message is stripped of its paralinguistic elements, members of the bar sometimes complain that the judge and jury are deprived of the opportunity to hear the emotional quality of the testimony and, therefore, only receive a selective impression. The second school regards any attempt to mimic the witness, whether it be the tone of voice, attitude, or a gesture, as improper for the interpreter and outside of the sphere of the interpreter's responsibility. The interpreter should render a precise interpretation free of any paralinguistic elements and focus only upon converting words from one language to another. Both arguments have merit; therefore, it is best to take the middle ground. The interpreter's rendition should mirror the SL message to the degree that it contains the linguistic and paralinguistic elements that convey meaning. It is possible that because the witness is non-English speaking, the judge and jury may miss the intent or tone of the testimony. The interpreter must remember that his or her voice is the only comprehensible voice the judge and jury will hear. If interpreters hear hesitations, pauses, repetitions, or sentence fragments in the original message, these elements must be present in the delivery. Consider the following example:

¿Cómo?.....¿Cuándo?....¿El domingo?.....Pues...eh...estuve en casa todo el día.

The tenor of the testimony is completely altered if the interpreter were to render the SL into the TL as:

"I was home all day."

The interpreter should say in the TL:

"What?...When?...Sunday?...Well...uh...I was home all day."

Just as in English, the hesitations might connote lack of certainty or perhaps even insincerity, and removing those hesitations from the utterance distorts its impact. Even such linguistic elements as stammering, stuttering, a trembling voice, or emotional qualities such as anger, doubt, arrogance, indignation, and surprise should be rendered in a conservative, *unexaggerated* manner.

For example, stuttering can be suggested in the interpretation by a slight stammer, reflecting the original source. Emotional qualities such as anger, exasperation, and fear can be denoted by the interpreter through the use of tone of voice and particular stress and intonation patterns. Obvious emotional states like weeping and laughing need not be mimicked by the interpreter because they are patently obvious to the observer.

1.3.1. Volume and Tone of Voice

As shown in the theory chapter, an oral message is conveyed by more than just words; voice characteristics are one of the many non-verbal factors that come into play when messages are transmitted and received. Studies (Pearce, 1971; Pearce & Brommel, 1972) have shown that the style of delivery of a message, including voice characteristics, affects the way people perceive that message and judge the credibility of the speaker. The interpreter has an obligation to reproduce the SL speaker's tone of voice precisely in order to convey the same degree of hesitancy or assertiveness, as the case may be, that was present in the original message.

1.3.2. Pauses, Hesitation

The absence of vocal cues is just as significant as vocal cues are in linguistic communication. Lebra (1987) emphasizes the importance of silence in intercultural communication between Japanese and English. The common phrases "a pregnant pause" and "a meaningful silence" reflect the importance of interruptions in speech, and the interpreter should conserve them in the TL rendition. Attorneys may pause just before a critical point in their argument in order to draw attention and build suspense. Witnesses may pause at various points throughout their testimony because they are unsure of their recollections. All of this must be faithfully retained by the interpreter.

1.3.3. Rate of Speech

Closely related to periodic pauses in speech is the pace at which the words are uttered. Some witnesses who want to be sure their listeners are following their line of reasoning will speak at a measured pace, while other witnesses who are very excited about the events they are recounting will speak rapidly. Again, the interpreter must convey these elements in the TL version.

1.3.4. Emotions

By the same token, the interpreter must convey precisely the emotions such as anger, fear, shame, or excitement that are expressed by the SL speaker. Thus, when an aggressive attorney is bearing down on a witness to try to intimidate the person, the interpreter should be equally forceful. And when the witness answers questions in a timid way, the interpreter should retain that timidity in every aspect of the TL rendition. However, as noted in the Code of Professional Responsibility of the Official Interpreters of the United States Courts (Administrative Office of the United States Courts, 1987), the interpreter should "reflect the decorum of the Court and act with dignity . . . " (p. V-5). This means that the interpreter may have to convey the emotions expressed by the witness in a slightly attenuated form. If the interpreter were to burst into tears or scream out loud exactly as the witness did, it would make a mockery of the judicial process. If a witness expresses emotions in such an overt way (and the manifestations of these emotions are the same in the SL and TL cultures), the judge and jury can observe the witness's behavior and draw their own conclusions from that; the interpreter need not *literally* mimic the witness.

1.3.5. Equivalence

Often a witness will use body language that is common to the SL and TL cultures. Body language includes not only gestures but also features of paralanguage such as hissing and tongue-clicking. In this instance, it is generally accepted that the interpreter should allow the judge and members of the jury to use their own judgment about the meaning of the symbol and should refrain from imitating or explaining it.

A problem arises, however, if there is no equivalence between the two languages for a particular behavior. There is considerable controversy over the issue of compensating for non-verbal elements of meaning by substituting verbal elements that will be reflected in the transcript of the proceedings. By doing so the interpreter presumably compensates for the transference of non-verbal elements from one language to another; however, great liberty is taken with the SL message.

For this reason, one school of thought argues that there should be no compensation for non-verbal messages and that the interpretation of such paralinguistic elements is best left to the attorney to point out to the trier of fact. The stem of the controversy is a legal one: whether or not the interpreter is tampering with the witness's credibility. By adding to the original SL message, the interpreter may affect the ultimate opinion the judge and jury have of the witness.

Another school contends that non-verbal elements are a vital part of the message and should be conserved. Bressan (1987) advocates using "lexical, syntactic, and stylistic devices" (p. 74) in Italian when interpreting emphatic shifts in English that are conveyed through intonational variation, an option not available to the Italian speaker. He gives examples of how important intonation is in the speech patterns of English, and cautions that "in a courtroom case, the misinterpretation of an utterance . . . as the above could have serious consequences for the reputation and social standing of a person named at a trial" (p. 33). The New Jersey Supreme Court Task Force on Interpreter and Translation Services (1985) cites the example of defendants who avert their eyes because in their culture it is impolite to look someone in the eye, while "in the Anglo-American culture, . . . he may be presumed to have something to hide. . . . Without cross-cultural awareness, such a sign of respect could be mistaken . . . for guilt or evasion" (p. 33). Proponents who advocate a compensation model suggest that an interpreter employ verbal devices to attempt to conserve this non-verbal element of meaning. For example, the interpreter could show respect through tone of voice and posture, and possibly use polite forms of address in the TL to convey the idea of respect that the witness is showing by avoiding eye contact.

Although proponents of compensation believe there is nothing added to the meaning of the message by adding the word "Sir," for example, the style of the speaker has been significantly altered and a new idea has been added to the original message. Clearly, the legal equivalence of the SL message has not been retained. Failing to retain the legal equivalence of the message would violate these prescriptions. Thus, interpreters should be aware of these elements of meaning and should use their best judgment in striving to convey them while remaining faithful to the style and content of the SL message and protecting the record.

There have been no formal empirical studies which conclude that adopting compensatory devices such as inserting formal language into the TL message will accurately preserve a witness's body language. Moreover, there are no studies which indicate whether or not the witness's credibility is affected by the use of these devices.

There is a very delicate balance between the need to convey all of a message, including non-verbal elements, and the need to avoid mischaracterizing a witness's testimony in any way. The fact that this issue is very difficult to resolve, even after careful reflection and consideration, is made clear in Berk-Seligson's 1987 study. Although the primary point of the study is that interpreters may alter the perception of witness testimony by changing the speech style, Berk-Seligson herself suggests substituting the English expletive "jeez!" for the hissing noise made by a Spanish-speaking witness:

> The parakinesic sound produced by the witness is an elongated hissing sound which serves as a commentary on what he has just said; it is an expression of disgust. It is similar in force and tone to the American English exclamation, "jeez!" or to certain clicking sounds that indicate exasperation or disgust. (Footnote 10, p. 1122)

Protocol: Because this issue is not resolved and because much is at stake for the individual defendant, the interpreter should exhibit extreme caution in using these compensatory devices. However, in a case in which there is equivalence between sociolinguistic features, the interpreter should allow the members of the jury to use their own judgment about the meaning of the gestures. In the case of contrasting sociolinguistic features, the interpreter should not use compensatory devices but should leave the issue of raising these culturally bound ambiguities to the attorney in the course of the proceedings.

Generally, the attorney is responsible for calling to the attention of the judge any feature of testimony which can cast doubt on the credibility of a witness. Because it is the duty of the judge to resolve any objections raised, the judge may call upon the interpreter as an expert witness to clarify any linguistic/cultural ambiguities. In this specific situation, the interpreter may properly offer clarifying information, and would be justified in substituting gestures or paralinguistic expressions for non-verbal elements of the message.

1.3.6. Hand Gestures

Pointing or gesturing by witnesses is another element of communication that interpreters sometimes have difficulty conveying. Unlike the issue of compensating for non-verbal elements of meaning, there is little disagreement on this matter. It is generally agreed that interpreters **should not** reproduce witnesses' physical movements, as there is a danger of mischaracterizing testimony, or misdirecting the attention of the judge and jury. Moreover, the judge and jury can see the witness themselves. The *Los Angeles Superior Court Interpreters Manual* (Almeida & Zahler, 1981) states, "The interpreter should not emulate the gestures made by the witness. Physical motions express different meanings in each language" (p. 11). Similarly, Administrative Order No. 85-002 of the Superior Court of the State of Arizona, County of Maricopa (1985), pronounces: "The interpreter shall not repeat gestures made by his subject, nor shall he extrapolate meaning from such gestures. It falls to the Court or counsel to state for the record the nature and intent of the witness's gesture" (Section VII.5).

Protocol: When the witness points to a part of his or her body to describe where an injury occurred or where pain is felt, the interpreter should simply interpret whatever the witness said (e.g., "She shot me here.") and let the other parties see where the witness is pointing. If the witness says, "Well, I was sort of, uh, . . . " and then uses a hand gesture to complete the answer, the interpreter should state exactly what the witness said *without* copying the gesture, putting its meaning into words, or describing it. The attorney who is questioning the witness will describe the gesture for the record, and may ask a follow-up question in case an explanation is warranted. Only if the court specifically requests that the interpreter provide an explanation should the interpreter do so (e.g., "This hand gesture is used to mean 'drunk' ").

1.4. Duty to Protect the Record

It has been repeatedly stated throughout this book that interpreters are the voice of the witness, and their rendition of the witness's testimony is the only permanent record of what that person said under oath. The reason this point is emphasized so often is that it is central to the role of the interpreter. The interpreter serves two equally important functions: to enable the non-English-speaking defendant to understand everything that is stated in the legal proceedings pertaining to the case, and to enable the court to understand witnesses who testify in languages other than English. The following are some guidelines to help the interpreter guarantee that the transcript reflects exactly what such witnesses state in their testimony.

1.4.1. Conservation or Clarification of Ambiguities

Rainof (1980) identifies various ambiguities, which he labels "polysemantic contextual shifts," noting that "Words…change meaning within given contexts" (p. 197). He emphasizes the importance of clarifying such ambiguities before interpreting the message. The Spanish pronoun *su*, for example, can be either feminine or masculine, and the interpreter must ascertain which meaning is intended before rendering the TL version—in English, which would be "his" or "her." Rainof suggests that attorneys avoid known ambiguities in the English language, such as gender-based ones (e.g., cousin, driver, teacher—terms that are not gender-specific).

Protocol: In case of such an ambiguity, the interpreter should state: "Your Honor, the question/answer is ambiguous and the interpreter cannot proceed without clarification."

For example, if the witness says he or she was driving a *camioneta*, the interpreter must find out whether the witness is referring to a pickup truck, a station wagon, or a van before rendering the answer into English. Simply saying "She was driving a vehicle" is not as specific as the witness was. If the interpreter says, "He was driving a pickup or station wagon," the TL version sounds uncertain, when the witness was very clear about what kind of a vehicle it was. We might note here that it is dangerous to rely on documents read prior to the trial in attempting to clear up ambiguities; even though the police report may have said the vehicle was a pickup truck, it may have been in error because the reporting officer misunderstood the original Spanish. When in doubt, the interpreter should always ask the court permission to inquire with the witness: "Your Honor, the word *camioneta* is ambiguous. May the interpreter inquire with the witness." The outcome of not clarifying an ambiguity is problematic, because if the interpreter chooses the wrong option the entire course of the attorney's examination can be misdirected.

A second example: English requires that a pronoun subject be stated in all cases, while in Spanish that pronoun may be omitted. Moreover, in the imperfect tense in

Spanish, the verb conjugations are the same for the first, second, and third persons. It is not uncommon, therefore, to have an answer such as *Me dijo que estaba ahí*, which could mean any of the following:

He/she told me that he was there.

He/she told me that it was there.

He/she told me that she was there.

He/she told me that you were there.

He/she told me that I was there.

You told me that he was there.

You told me that it was there.

You told me that she was there.

You told me that you were there.

You told me that I was there.

In this case, again, the interpreter must request permission to clarify the answer before proceeding to interpret it. The interpreter should not seize upon the opportunity to delve into a contrastive analysis of the two languages, but is occupied with avoiding misdirecting the testimony.

Ambiguities may be intentional, however, and the interpreter should strive to retain them if the TL allows. Bennett (1981) discusses how difficult it is to interpret during cross-examination when the examining attorney phrases his or her questions very carefully and often in a deliberately vague or ambiguous manner:

> To put these questions into another language without distorting them in some way (such as making some of them less ambiguous or less subtly nuanced) is a daunting task, especially as the interpreter probably does not know where the questions are leading. (p. 16)

It may be possible to interpret the question "Where did the car hit you?" into Spanish as *¿Dónde le pegó el carro?* without clarifying whether the questioner is referring to the location of the accident or the part of the witness's body. On the other hand, attorneys will often ask this deliberately ambiguous question: "Did you have anything to drink in the car?" But the TL may require that the interpreter say either "Did you drink anything in the car?" or "Was there anything to drink in the car?"

Protocol: If the interpreter cannot retain the ambiguity in the TL but the context makes it clear which meaning is intended, he or she should clarify it in rendition. But if the interpreter is not certain of the meaning or is aware that the ambiguity is deliberate, the court must be informed that the TL version cannot be rendered without clarification. It is not the interpreter's job, however, to correct the attorneys' questions. If a question is vague or compound, the witness's answer will be ambiguous, but the problem is the same whether the language is English or any other. Since the problem is not language related, the interpreter should not intervene. It is the duty of opposing counsel to object to the question; if there is no objection, the interpreter must render an interpretation.

Witness testimony may also contain deliberate ambiguities. In drug cases, for instance, words with double meanings are often used. The Spanish term *yerba* literally means "weed," but is often used to refer to marijuana. The interpreter is placed in a delicate position, as the prosecution will want the interpretation of the word to be "marijuana" and the defense will want the interpreter to say "weed." Both translations are correct, and the interpreter would be justified in using either one.

Protocol: In some courts, interpreters are instructed to translate such terms literally, while in other courts the standard practice is to translate the term as it is commonly used in the drug context. If interpreters have any doubt, they should call the matter to the court's attention by requesting a side-bar conference: "Your Honor, the interpreter requests that we go off the record to discuss an ambiguous term."

1.4.2. Vague Answers

If a witness gives a vague answer, the interpreter must strive to interpret as well as possible, as vaguely as the original. If more information is needed for rendering an accurate English version, however, the interpreter must inform the court that a clarification is necessary.

1.4.3. Requesting a Repetition

If for any reason the interpreter needs to hear a portion of the witness's testimony again, the interpreter must ask the court's permission to have the witness repeat the answer.

Protocol: The interpreter should say, "Your Honor, the interpreter would like to request that the witness be instructed to repeat the answer." This need may arise if the witness gives a very lengthy answer and the interpreter is unable to recall a portion of it, or if the interpreter does not hear part of a question or answer. Losing concentration because of distractions or fatigue is not egregious; on the other hand, constant requests for repetitions are obviously unacceptable and the interpreter should guard against overuse of this technique.

1.4.4. Conservation of English

Interpreters must bear in mind that they are rendering testimony for the written record, and the court reporter is listening only to them, not to the witness. Therefore, if the witness gives an answer in English or states a name that everyone can understand without needing any interpretation, the interpreter must still repeat it for the record.

1.4.5. Correction of Own Errors

If at any point interpreters realize that they have previously made an error in interpretation, they should correct the record at the earliest opportunity. Thus, if subsequent testimony indicates that a word with several meanings was misinterpreted the first time it came up, an interpreter should state as soon as possible: "Your Honor, may the interpreter correct the record?" [Pause for judge's permission.] "The term 'thunder' in the witness's earlier testimony should actually have been interpreted as 'gunshot.'" Although this may seem like a minor point, in terms of evidence it is critical. It could have led to a misunderstanding of the facts, and ultimately to a conviction.

The interpreter should wait for a natural break in the testimony, such as when someone has stopped asking a series of questions. An opportune occasion would be when counsel has paused to review notes. No matter how much time has elapsed, the interpreter is duty bound to make a correction on the record. After the judge grants permission to correct the record, the interpreter states the error in the fewest words possible and then gives the correction.

1.4.6. Correction of an Error Made by a Peer

If an interpreter hears a peer make an error of serious consequence, he or she should at the earliest possible moment confer with his or her fellow interpreter to apprise the colleague of the error, thus giving him or her the opportunity to make a correction on the record. However, the interpreter hearing the error should not take it upon himself or herself to offer a correction, nor should he or she make the error known to any other party prior to informing the colleague. The only instance in which an interpreter should inform the court of a colleague's error is when that colleague fails to correct the record after notice is given.

1.4.7. Explanations

It is important for the interpreter to know when it is appropriate to intervene in order to ensure that communication is taking place and the record of testimony is accurate. As a general rule, stepping out of the role of interpreter and taking on the role of expert should be regarded as a measure of last resort, to be undertaken with greatest caution. The interpreter should under no circumstances act as an expert on matters outside of the realm of interpreting; like any professional, the interpreter should refrain from commenting or intervening in matters that are not within his or her area of expertise. There are times, though, when the interpreter, because of linguistic knowledge, is the only one who knows something in the interchange is amiss. For example, if the witness uses the Spanish term *pie* (foot) to mean the entire leg, as is common among rural Latin Americans, the interpreter may step out of the interpreting role and say: "Your Honor, the interpreter would like to clarify that it is common for rural Latin Americans to use the word for 'foot' to designate the entire leg."

Protocol: If communication is breaking down and the interpreter can easily resolve the issue, and if the term in question is an essential part of an answer that others could not possibly understand without an explanation, then intervention is warranted. But if it is apparent that the attorney is able to clarify the situation through follow-up questions, the interpreter should not interfere.

1.4.8. Culturally Bound References

Certain "culture-bound" terms, that is, terms whose meanings are highly dependent on the culture associated with the language, pose a particularly difficult dilemma for the interpreter because it is hard to find words in the TL to convey the meaning. The New Jersey Supreme Court Task Force on Interpreter and Translation Services (1985) notes in its report that "the communicative distance between linguistic minorities and the English-speaking majority is further widened by numerous cultural influences. Culture often invests similar words with different nuances, structures conversations, and determines the non-verbal aspects of communication" (p. 36). Names of meals, kinship terms, units of measurement, and forms of address are examples of this phenomenon.

Protocol: If no direct equivalent of such a phrase is readily available in the TL, it is usually better for the interpreter to leave it in the SL without translating it or volunteering an explanation. If it is important that everyone understand the term, the attorney can elicit an explanation from the witness by means of a follow-up question. In many cases, the meaning of the term may not be relevant enough to warrant an explanation. If the interpreters use an SL word or phrase on the record, they should jot it down to provide for the court reporter afterward, since the court reporter is not likely to know how it is spelled. This also applies to non-English names.

Examples:

(A) Dates

Sometimes it is necessary for the interpreter to intervene with an explanation. Culturally significant dates are an example of a situation that may require an explanation. If someone says in the TL, "I couldn't contact anyone at the office in Mexico because it was September 16," the interpreter may need to explain if there is no follow-up question. The interpreter may state: "Your Honor, may the interpreter provide an explanation? September 16 is Mexican Independence Day." Another problem with dates is the way they are written in numerical form. In English, it is customary to write the number corresponding to the month, then the number of the day, then the last two numbers of the year. In many other countries, however, the day precedes the month, and both Arabic and Roman numerals are used to distinguish them further. Foreign-born witnesses may become confused with written dates, and the interpreter may have to clarify the situation.

(B) Illiteracy

In many countries the literacy rate is very low. For example, in Haiti it is estimated that only 10 percent of the population can read and write (Gonzalez, 1989a). This poses a problem in courtroom testimony, beginning with the spelling of the witness's name. Some languages do not have an alphabet, and it is difficult for witnesses to "spell" names in terms of the Western alphabet. Even if the witness is literate, **verbal spelling** may not be common in the witness's culture because literacy is rare and it is not customary to spell out common surnames. For instance, in Latin American countries and in Spain, if someone is asked to spell his or her name, the person will respond "Gonzalez with a Z." This problem can be solved by the attorney who has called the witness; the attorney can provide the court with the correct spelling of the name to avoid confusion. It should be noted that proper names should never be "translated" or anglicized.

Protocol: If it is apparent that the witness is unable to provide a spelling and no one else is able to solve the problem, the interpreter may have to ask the court's permission to clarify matters. One way to do that would be to inform the court of the standard spelling of that name: "Your Honor, may the interpreter inform the court of the correct standard spelling of the name?" Another solution would be to write the name down, show it to the witness to verify if it is correct, and then spell it out loud for the court. In many cases the best way to proceed is to request a side-bar conference in order to avoid offending the witness or prejudicing the jury. It is helpful for interpreters and judges to discuss such situations and arrive at an agreement before a proceeding begins.

(C) Addresses

In many Third World countries few government services are available. Paved, numbered, and named streets, for example, are non-existent in some areas. If an individual from such a country is asked to give his or her street address in the United States, the individual may answer with, "I live across the street from the Dairy Queen on the same side of the road as the school, which is about five blocks from my house." These individuals are not giving evasive answers, but are following cultural norms. They may not even know the name of the business which employs them because in their countries it is customary to call the employer simply *El Patrón* ("the boss") or Don Julio, using only his first name. Although in the United States it is the norm to work for a business, e.g., IBM, Eileen's Flowers, in other countries it is commonly assumed that one can only work for a person. Often the personal relationship of the defendant to the employer is more important than the business itself, and the individual will answer, "I work for my brother-in-law."

(D) Units of Measurement

Another universal linguistic problem for interpreters is the interpretation of metric measures of weight, length, height, and similar technical descriptions. In all cases, the interpreter should simply restate the figure in English. For example, if a witness says that something weighed *tres kilos*, the interpreter should say "three kilos" rather than converting the figure to the United States system. Often courts expect the interpreter to convert the measure, but the better practice is to retain the unit of measurement used by the witness and await the request to convert by counsel or the court. In this way, the issue of converting the measurement is properly left to the court and is not at the interpreter's discretion. This practice preserves the accuracy of the record and the testimony, allowing it to appear in the transcript for purposes of appeal.

Caution: It is important to emphasize that it is the attorney's function to clear up misunderstandings with follow-up questions, and the interpreter should not usurp that role. The only situation in which the interpreter should interrupt in order to provide an explanation is when communication breaks down and it is apparent from the questions and answers that false assumptions are being made due to cultural misunderstandings. In such cases, the interpreter is the only one who has the specialized knowledge and training to realize that a misunderstanding is taking place. In short, the interpreter should be very conservative about intervening in the judicial process.

(E) Culturally Bound Concepts

Perhaps the most challenging cultural issue for interpreters and the courts is the problem of culture-bound concepts. As human beings we are often aware only of our own environment and surroundings. The ability to live in, visit, or explore other cultures may be limited because we are monolingual and cannot read other languages, nor do we have the time or money to explore all the world's cultures. This makes us aware only of our own surroundings and own culture. Our speech is consequently also limited.

In most cases this limitation does not hamper communication. However, for non-English speakers who are testifying or listening to court proceedings, an idea expressed in United States cultural terms is often not understood. For example, if an attorney is questioning a Navajo about being guilty or innocent, the Navajo will not understand. In Navajo culture and language, there is no equivalent for the concept of "guilt." In Navajo, one commits an act, but being "guilty" of it does not enter into the cultural framework. Therefore, the equivalent is "Did you do it?" Understanding the Navajo concept of time is also crucial. For instance, verbs do not show tense; rather, there is a complex set of aspect verb manners that "serve to define the verbal action that is represented by the verb base" (Young & Morgan, 1987, p. 164). There are eleven primary categories of aspect and ten subaspects. For example, there is a different marker to signify a motion begun and a motion completed: "I'm beginning to eat [a meal]" versus "I'm finishing a meal."

These cultural and linguistic concepts pose tremendous problems for the interpreter, and there are many different ones, depending on the language. If the interpreter understands the meaning of the SL (English) and that there is no equivalent in the TL or culture (Navajo), then the interpreter must tell the judge that there is a problem expressing the idea in the Navajo language. The outcome of not clarifying an ambiguity is problematic, because if the interpreter chooses the wrong option the entire course of the attorney's examination can be misdirected.

(F) Customs

An interpreter is involved in a case in which an eighteen-year-old Spanish-speaking boy from a Latin American country takes a ladder to a girl's bedroom. She is sixteen years of age. The defendant abducts her and takes her to his house where he keeps her. There is an incidence of sexual intercourse. He is arrested and charged with kidnapping, rape, and false imprisonment. The interpreter believes he has some information about certain customs in some rural area in a Latin American country that would tend to mitigate the action of the defendant.

Protocol: Under no circumstances should the interpreter interrupt the proceedings to say anything. The most inappropriate behavior an interpreter could display in this situation would be to stand up and explain to the judge that in this boy's village in the hinterlands of Mexico this is an extremely acceptable way of taking a wife.

The interpreter may, at the earliest possible opportunity, communicate these suspicions to defense counsel and suggest seeking expert advice (e.g., call a cultural anthropologist as an expert witness). The interpreter should never volunteer to act as an expert witness on cultural matters unless the interpreter's particular cultural and educational experience would so qualify. The interpreter may wish to clarify such widely known cultural issues such as holidays, kinship terms, or other items of **common knowledge**.

If interpreters are called to the stand and questioned on facts at issue, they are to answer to the best of their ability and the court will determine what weight to give to that testimony. The interpreter may testify like any other witness, or may be called to testify as an expert witness. In the latter case, the interpreter will be subjected to a *voir dire* examination in order to qualify.

1.4.9. Leaving Terms in the SL

In many cases it is not necessary to go into an explanation, either because the term in question is not germane to the issue at hand or because many English speakers are familiar with the term. One example of a term that does not require an explanation is the kinship term *compadre* in Spanish, which denotes a social/religious relationship that can involve the parents of one's godchild, the godparents of one's own child, the best man at a wedding, a sponsor at confirmation, or simply a close friend. It is a complicated term, but it usually has no bearing on the witness's testimony. In most cases, the interpreter may leave the word in Spanish and let the attorney ask for an explanation if one is necessary.

1.4.10. Identification of Interpreter Statements

When the interpreter does intervene, it is important to pause when switching from the witness role to the interpreter role to make it clear that the person is now speaking as the interpreter and is no longer rendering the witness's testimony.

Protocol: Administrative Order No. 85-002 of the Superior Court of the State of Arizona, County of Maricopa (1985), states: "The interpreter shall refer to himself as 'The interpreter' when interpreting for the record to avoid confusion with the pronoun 'I,' which shall refer to the interpreter's subject" (Section VII.4). Thus, in formal courtroom proceedings, it is common practice for interpreters to refer to themselves in the third person so that it is clear in the written record that they are speaking for themselves and not translating the words of the witness. In less formal settings outside the courtroom (e.g., depositions), the interpreter can simply pause and change voice tone slightly, then speak in the first person: "I believe the witness was referring to...."

1.5. Guessing

Interpreters should never guess about terms they have never heard before, including technical terms, personal references, or idiosyncratic uses of a common term by witnesses. Should they have a dictionary handy, and if the word or phrase they do not know is a standard term, they should ask the court's permission to look it up. The standard protocol for doing so is to state, "Your Honor, the witness has used a term that the interpreter is not familiar with, and he requests permission to consult his dictionary." They should not, however, simply grab the first equivalent found in the dictionary and use it. Dictionaries are handy reference tools but should not be relied on exclusively. If none of the terms listed in the dictionary seems appropriate, the interpreter should ask the court's permission to inquire of the witness or whoever used the problematic term: "Your Honor, the witness has used a word unknown to the interpreter. May the interpreter inquire?"

Under no circumstances should the interpreter attempt to clarify the issue or speak directly to the witness without the judge's permission. One of the most common complaints made by judges about interpreters throughout the country has been this unauthorized interpreter-witness exchange. This exchange is lost to the record; frequently when asked to recount what the witness said, the interpreter is unable to do so. No officer of the court is allowed to have a private conversation with a witness at the stand.

1.6. Response to Challenges

Perhaps one of the greatest ordeals an interpreter must face is challenges from bilingual parties who disagree with the interpretation. As the New Jersey Supreme Court Task Force on Interpreter and Translation Services (1985) notes, "interpreting is an exacting profession and cannot be error-free" (Appendix, p. 15). Frequently the interpreter is not the only person in the room who knows both the SL and the TL, and it is easy for people who are not under the severe pressure of interpreting to pick out mistakes. Sometimes a challenge comes from an attorney who has prepared the witness and knows what the testimony ought to be. Or it may come from someone who hears a familiar word and thinks he or she understood the answer better than the interpreter.

Protocol: Courts vary in their preferred procedures for handling challenges. The New Jersey Supreme Court Task Force on Interpreter and Translation Services (1985) recommends the following procedure: when an alleged error is detected by someone other than the court interpreter, that person should, if testimony is still being taken from the stand, bring the allegation to the attention of the court.

> At that time the court will determine first whether the issue surrounding the allegedly inaccurate interpretation is substantial enough to warrant determination. If the court agrees that the error could be prejudicial, then the court shall hear evidence as to what the correct interpretation should be from experts submitted by both counsel, from the court interpreter (who is already an expert witness), and from any other expert selected by the judge. The judge shall make a final determination in view of the evidence as to the correct interpretation. If the determination is different from the original interpretation, then the court shall amend the record accordingly. (Appendix, pp. 15-16)

Regardless of the exact procedure followed, the interpreter must respond to the challenge in a professional manner and not regard it as a personal affront. Technically, any person in the courtroom can challenge the interpretation, so interpreters should not be shocked, dismayed, or angered by challenges even if they come from the audience. If interpreters agree with the correction because they were indeed wrong, then they should change the record. If the proposed correction is unacceptable to them, they should stand by their original version. They may explain their reasoning if necessary, but they should not be on the defensive. In the end, the judge has the final word and the interpreter must abide by it. If the interpreter is asked to participate in a side-bar conference to resolve a linguistic issue, it might resemble the following exchange: The attorney objects when the interpreter asked "Was the envelope sealed?" and used the Spanish word *cerrado*. The attorney correctly points out to the judge that the word *cerrado* means "closed" but not sealed. The interpreter holds that the word *cerrado* can also mean "sealed." The judge asks the attorney which word would be preferred and the attorney suggests *sellado*. The interpreter points out that *sellado* also means "stamped." The judge resolves the matter by asking the interpreter to suggest a word or phrase; the interpreter answers "closed with glue." So the issue is settled with *cerrado con pegadura*. The interpreter is to participate in any rational attempt to resolve a linguistic issue and should never take the challenge personally, resort to emotional argument, or seize upon the opportunity to enlighten the court as to the linguistic and historical evolutions of the language.

If interpreters are calm but assertive when they are in the right, and if they obligingly correct errors when they are wrong, they will retain the confidence of those who are using their services and will be subject to fewer challenges in the future. Because language is so subtle and subjective, there are no right or wrong answers, and challenges will remain a fact of life for court interpreters. Indeed, it is part of the attorney's function to object to testimony—or the interpretation thereof—that does not favor the party the attorney represents, and challenges of the interpretation are part of the normal course of events in the courtroom.

1.7. Duty to Witness

When interpreting for a non-defendant witness, the interpreter has the same obligation to interpret objections, arguments, and other statements outside the question-and-answer format as in the case of a defendant-witness. The Court Interpreters Act of 1978, P.L. 95-539, clearly states that an interpreter shall be provided for a witness if that person " . . . speaks only or primarily a language other than the English language . . . so as to inhibit such witness" comprehension of questions and the presentation of such testimony" (§ 1827(d)1-2). The Superior Court of the State of Arizona, County of Maricopa (1985), in Administrative Order No. 85-002, requires that the interpreter "interpret simultaneously to the witness all objections made as to his examination and all instructions made to him/her" (Section V 2.2).

2. The interpreter shall remain impartial.

According to the *Los Angeles Superior Court Interpreters Manual* (Almeida & Zahler, 1981):

> Court interpreters shall not only be impartial and devoted to the best interest of the court, but shall so act and conduct themselves, both inside and outside the court, as not to give occasion for distrust of their impartiality or of their devotion to the court's best interest. (p. 2)

Throughout this chapter the term "client" has been used to denote the people for whom the interpreter interprets. Perhaps a further definition of the term is in order here, to emphasize whom the interpreter serves. There are two basic reasons for having an interpreter present in a court case—to enable the defendant to understand the proceedings, and to enable the court to understand all non-English speakers who address the court. Therefore, the interpreter's "clients" are all of the protagonists in the court proceeding: the defendant and defense counsel, the prosecution, the judge, the clerk and other court personnel, and all witnesses who testify. No matter for whom interpreters are interpreting at a given moment, they are officers of the court, neutral participants in the process. They are not part of the defense "team" if they are interpreting for the defendant, or part of the prosecution "team" if they are interpreting for prosecution witnesses. This is an aspect often misunderstood by interpreters who report being influenced by the social environment (Anderson, 1976, 1978).

2.1. Role of the Interpreter

It is important for all parties involved to know what the interpreter can and cannot do for his clients. Astiz (1986) cautions against the "adaptation role," that is, intervening to explain to people what is going on. He emphasizes that the court interpreter should not give the non-English speaker any advantage over the English speaker: "If the criminal justice system interpreter is successful in the 'adaption role,' he or she would provide the non-English speaking individuals with services not available to English speaking defendants and witnesses of equivalent intelligence and education" (p. 34). The interpreter is not an advocate for non-English speakers, nor is it the interpreter's role to teach them how to behave. Furthermore, interpreters must not make value judgments about the language or demeanor of the parties they interpret for. If the witness uses incorrect grammar or vulgar speech, or if the witness wears inappropriate dress, the interpreter should render the testimony just as faithfully as that of any other witness. Interpreters should not display any verbal or non-verbal behavior to convey to others that they deem the testimony improper or untruthful.

2.2. Appearance of Neutrality

The Code of Professional Responsibility of the Official Interpreters of the United States Courts (Administrative Office of the United States Courts, 1987) states, "The official court interpreters fulfill a special duty to interpret accurately and faithfully without indicating any personal bias, avoiding even the appearance of partiality" (p. V-1). The notion of the appearance of impartiality is important, because as noted above, it is essential that everyone be aware of the interpreter's neutral role. It may be that the interpreter has no bias whatsoever, but if jurors or other parties feel that the interpreter is likely to color or taint a witness's testimony, that testimony will have less credibility. According to the New Jersey Supreme Court Task Force on Interpreter and Translation Services (1985), "The appearance of bias or lack of objectivity on the part of the court interpreter, just as actual bias or lack of objectivity, are inconsistent with the neutral role of the interpreter" (p. 75).

2.2.1. Protocol

The Code of Professional Responsibility (Administrative Office of the United States Courts, 1987) that governs federal court interpreter provides guidance in this regard: "The official court interpreters maintain impartiality by avoiding undue contact with witnesses, attorneys, and defendants and their families, and any contact with jurors. This should not limit, nevertheless, those appropriate contacts necessary to prepare adequately for their assignments" (p. V-1). This means that the interpreter should not have any independent conversations with the witness on the stand. Of course, with the permission of counsel, the interpreter may converse briefly with the witness before testimony to ascertain the witness's country of origin, dialect, and speech mannerisms. During breaks, the interpreter should be polite to all parties, but not excessively friendly with any of them. If anyone attempts to strike up a conversation with the interpreter, the interpreter should decline politely and say, "I'm sorry, but as the official court interpreter I'm not allowed to talk to anyone while a trial is in progress."

2.2.2. Parties in the Case

Conversations between an interpreter and someone who is involved in a case, such as a juror or a witness, are even more susceptible to misinterpretation. The New Jersey Supreme Court Task Force on Interpreter and Translation Services (1985) provides, in its Canons of Ethics, that "A court interpreter or legal translator shall, in any jury trial, disclose to the court and contending parties all instances in which he or she is acquainted with any juror and shall disclose the extent of such knowledge" (Canon 11, Appendix, p. 27). The same is true of any party in a case. It may be that the judge will decide that the nature of the relationship is not such that the interpreter will be biased, but it still must be brought to the court's attention. As for other court and law enforcement professionals with whom an interpreter may work everyday, even questions such as "How's it going?" or "Are you working for the defense in this case?" can pose problems. Therefore, it is imperative that the interpreter avoid talking with anyone involved in a pending case.

2.3. Conflict of Interest

According to the *Los Angeles Superior Court Interpreters Manual* (Almeida & Zahler, 1981), "Any condition which impinges on the objectivity of the interpreter or affects his professional independence constitutes a conflict of interest" (p. 7). The Canon of Ethics for Court Interpreters and Legal Translators established by the New Jersey Supreme Court Task Force on Interpreter and Translation Services (1985) states:

> No court interpreter or legal translator shall render services in any matter in which he or she is an associate, friend or relative of a contending party. Neither shall she or he serve in any matter in which one has a stake, financial or otherwise, in the outcome. Nor shall any court interpreter or legal translator serve in a matter where he or she has been involved in the choice of counsel. (Canon 6, Appendix, p. 27)

If the interpreter has any interest in the outcome of a case (if a company the person works for would benefit monetarily, for example), the interpreter should inform the court immediately. The judge can decide whether there is any conflict of interest and whether the interpreter should be disqualified for possible bias. If a conflict of interest is discovered at any time after the interpreter accepts an assignment, the interpreter damages not only individual professional reputation but also that of the guild.

2.3.1. Prior Services

An interpreter who has performed services for one party in a case should not subsequently perform services for another party during the same case. Thus, it is unacceptable for the same person to interpret for both the defendant and prosecution witnesses. If an interpreter were to do so, it would seriously undermine the relationship of trust that must exist between interpreter and client. The impropriety of an interpreter performing services for both the defendant and the victim in a rape case, for example, is readily apparent. In some jurisdictions, such as the California state courts, case law specifically prohibits the use of the same interpreter for both defense and prosecution. In other states, however, there is no law or statute governing this matter, and it is up to the interpreter to inform the court of the conflict of interest. Some jurisdictions have even stricter provisions; the Canon of Ethics devised by the New Jersey Supreme Court Task Force on Interpreter and Translation Services (1985) states that an interpreter who has performed any services for either side prior to the trial shall not act as interpreter during the trial (Canon 5). The reason for this extreme caution is our adversarial system of justice. Just as attorneys must disqualify themselves from cases in which they represent or have in the past represented a party who may have some interest in the outcome, interpreters should be equally prudent in avoiding potential conflicts of interest.

2.4. Unobtrusiveness

The interpreter must be mindful at all times that communication is the primary objective of the interpretation process. Interpreters are not there to show off their knowledge or to impress people with their abilities. They should not engage in theatrics, drawing more attention to themselves than to the witness by exaggerating the emotions expressed by the witness. In the words of the Standards for Interpreted Court Proceedings drawn up by the New Jersey Supreme Court Task Force on Interpreter and Translation Services (1985):

> Court interpreters shall maintain a low profile, speak at volumes appropriate to the context, and be as unobtrusive as possible. The manner of dress, the positioning in the courtroom, and the style of work shall all contribute to maintaining a natural atmosphere in the courtroom such as there would be if no language barrier existed. (Appendix, p. 17)

The interpreter should emulate the example set by attorneys, most of whom dress in a conservative, business-like manner when appearing in court. Frishberg (1986) explains why this is important, "When everything is working best, the interpreter is unobtrusive and the fiction maintained by the interpreter and the clients that the clients are directly interacting is comfortable for all" (p. 62).

2.5. Detachment

Many codes of ethics require the interpreter to behave in a professional manner with all clients. For example, Administrative Order No. 85-002 of Superior Court of the State of Arizona, County of Maricopa (1985), provides that "The interpreter shall maintain a professional relationship with his subject, and avoid a sympathetic, advocacy or personal rapport with such person" (Section VIII.3). The New Jersey Supreme Court Task Force on Interpreter and Translation Services (1985) warns that the interpreter should not feel that he has a special bond with the non-English speaker just because they speak the same language: "It is the court interpreter's duty to maintain an objective, detached relationship, avoiding personal displays of emotion, subjective involvement, or social conversation" (p. 74). While it is important for interpreters to establish a rapport with the people they are interpreting for, they should not become too involved with them.

Protocol: One way to convey this professional detachment is to call people by their surnames—Mr. Jones, Ms. Smith. If there is a formal form of address in the TL (e.g., *usted* in Spanish), it should be used at all times, regardless of the age or status of the witness or defendant. It is important to note that the interpreter should observe the cultural norms of the TL in maintaining this formal behavior. For example, it would be appropriate to address a child witness with the informal pronoun in Spanish, as the formal one is rarely used with children.

2.6. Gratuities

According to the Code of Professional Responsibility that governs federal court interpreters, "The official court interpreters accept no remuneration, gifts, gratuities or valuable consideration but their authorized compensation in the performance of their official interpreting duties" (Administrative Office of the United States Courts, 1987, p. V-1). In other words, the interpreter should never accept any compensation from the parties involved in a case other than professional fees. Under no circumstances should the interpreter appear to be accepting a "reward" for the performance in a given case. Canon 12 of the Ethics for Court Interpreters and Legal Translators devised by the New Jersey Supreme Court Task Force on Interpreter and Translation Services (1985) declares, "The fees and remuneration of a court interpreter or legal translator shall never be contingent upon the success or failure of the cause in which she or he has been engaged" (Appendix, p. 28).

2.7. Personal Emotions

Interpreters should keep their own emotions in check; the only emotional re-actions they should express are those of the witness for whom they are interpreting. This may be very difficult at times, such as when graphic photographs of crime scenes are shown to a witness, when a witness unintentionally says something funny, or when a witness is clearly lying. Nonetheless, interpreters should strive at all times to reflect only the reactions of the parties they are interpreting for, not their own. The jury should be judging the credibility of the witness, not that of the interpreter.

3. The interpreter shall maintain confidentiality.

All codes of ethics for court interpreters emphasize the importance of preserving the confidential nature of legal communication. For example, Article 11 of the Code of Professional Responsibility of the Official Interpreters of the United States Courts provides that "The official court interpreters, except upon Court order, shall not disclose any information of a confidential nature about court cases obtained while performing their interpreting duties" (Administrative Office of the United States Courts, 1987, p. V-2). Administrative Order No. 85-002 of Superior Court of the State of Arizona, County of Maricopa (1985), states:

> In communications in which there exists an attorney-client privilege, that privilege shall extend to those instances in which the interpreter is a party to said com-munication.... The interpreter shall not reveal the defendant's communications to any person other than the defendant's attorney, unless the defendant consents or the Court determines that the privilege is waived or does not apply to the communication. (Section II. 1.5)

The New Jersey Supreme Court Task Force on Interpreter and Translation Services (1985) emphasizes that "As a party who must be present in order to make communication possible, the court interpreter has the obligation of keeping confidential all matters interpreted except for information which is part of the public record" (p. 73). Interpreters must also refrain from revealing anything they know about the defendant from previous cases, e.g., prior convictions and like matters.

Protocol: If interpreters have any doubts about whether or not they should divulge some information, they should call the court's attention to the matter: "Your Honor, may we go off the record to discuss a matter that involves a potential confidentiality issue?"

3.1. The Public and the Media

Even when court is not in session, an interpreter should not discuss any pending case with anyone. Indeed, after the verdict has been handed down, if the case is under appeal, the interpreter is still bound not to discuss it until its final disposition. According to the Canons of Ethics set down by the New Jersey Supreme Court Task Force on Interpreter and Translation Services (1985):

> No court interpreter or legal translator shall comment or render an opinion on the propriety or impropriety of a verdict in any matter in which he or she has served. Nor shall any court interpreter or legal translator comment upon the conduct of such proceedings. (Canon 9, Appendix, p. 27)

Often people in the audience, members of the jury or media, and witnesses are curious when they see an interpreter working on a case, and they want to ask questions about the profession. The interpreter should avoid even such casual conversation, lest it be misconstrued by an observer.

Protocol: Interpreters should courteously but firmly indicate to the member of the public that interpreters are ethically bound not to speak to anyone during the proceedings. They should politely excuse themselves. Any collusion between any of the parties and any members of the jury is improper, for it destroys the impartiality of the jury. Any conversation with any member of the jury by any officer of the court, including a per diem interpreter, could be misconstrued as an attempt to unduly influence the jury. The interpreter is especially prohibited from discussing testimony with any (potential) witness in a case. To do so is to taint future testimony. The best policy is never to speak with witnesses at any time except in the official performance of duties. Outside the court, of course, interpreters are free to discuss any aspect of their work as long as they do not reveal details of a specific case. In the case of the media, the interpreter should not grant an interview or make any comment about the case to the media. If a statement is made, the interpreter has no control over the form that it will take in its publication, and the comments may form the basis, real or imagined, for controversy. There is nothing to gain in the interview and there is everything to lose. Should the reporter suggest that the interpreter simply restrict comments to the issue of court interpreting technique or the profession, the interpreter should cooperate by making an appointment to discuss those topics at a future date, after the conclusion of the case in progress. Or, the reporter can be referred to another court interpreter not currently associated with the case in progress, or to a professional court interpreting organization.

3.2. "Off-the-Record" Remarks

Another aspect of confidentiality is remarks made by participants that are not intended to be heard by others or entered into the record. The interpreter must sometimes decide what constitutes a confidential statement that should not be interpreted, and what is a legitimate part of the proceeding. For example, in administrative hearings—which are less formal than court proceedings—it is a common occurrence for a husband and wife to confer with each other before one of them answers a question, and they will conduct this "conference" right in the hearing room in everyone's presence. They apparently are operating on the assumption that because they are not speaking English, they might as well be outside the room or whispering confidentially. It may be difficult for the interpreter to know when the conference ends and when the testimony begins. While one might argue that non-English speakers should not be treated any differently from English speakers, and that any comment made in English would be taken down by the court reporter, it can also be argued that the assumption of non-comprehension converts the conversation into a confidential communication. If interpreters have any doubt about what to do in such a situation, they should call the matter to the attention of the judge.

The reverse problem is discussed by Frishberg (1986): "The classic dilemma for the interpreter has been what to do when one party in the interaction (especially one in authority) says, 'Now don't interpret this . . .' " (p. 68). This is a highly unethical practice, and interpreters should not be placed in such a difficult position. As Frishberg asserts, it is not the role of the interpreter to make a judgment about what needs to be interpreted and what does not. Anything and everything that is said in English during the course of a legal proceeding should be interpreted for the non-English-speaking participant.

4. The interpreter shall confine himself or herself to the role of interpreting.

At the beginning of this chapter it was noted that the lines that define the roles of the various actors in the legal process are sometimes blurred, and it may be difficult to determine where one person's function begins and ends. The guidelines listed here are intended to help all the parties involved categorize those functions so that the interpreter will not be asked to perform or be tempted to usurp the duties of other actors.

4.1. Legal Advice

Every code of ethics and standards designed for court interpreters recommends against interpreters imparting legal advice. For instance, the Code of Professional Responsibility which binds federal court interpreters pronounces that, "The official court interpreter refrain from giving advice of any kind to any party or individual" (Administrative Office of the United States Courts, 1987, p. V-1). Guidelines recommended by the Judicial Council of California (1979) specify that "no legal advice should be given to a party or witness. Legal questions should be referred to the attorney or to the court" (Section 18.1(a)(5)). Examples of such questions include:

"What should I do?" "How do you see my case?" "What will happen if I plead guilty?" "Should I ask for a jury or court trial?" Interpreters are to inform the defendant that the interpreter is not an attorney and that the defendant should consult with the attorney for legal advice. The interpreter should always strive to clarify the different roles of interpreter and attorney at the earliest possible moment so there is no confusion in the mind of the defendant as to whom to consult for advice. Failure to do so is unethical. If the defendant were to plead guilty based on the belief that the interpreter was acting as the defendant's attorney, that plea could be declared constitutionally invalid. Giving legal aid to a non-English speaker is not considered a friendly act, but rather is a severe infringement of the professional responsibilities of the members of the bar. Thus, the boundaries of the interpreter's role do not include the dispensing of legal advice or providing legal representation. These functions fall within the purview of the attorney, and perhaps the judge, but never the interpreter, whose sole responsibility is to serve as a medium of communication.

4.1.1. General Information

It is clear, then, that the court interpreter should refrain from usurping the role of the attorney. Nonetheless, the situation is not always clear cut; defendants often ask interpreters questions about proceedings during breaks or even in open court. If the defendant is speaking on the record, of course, the interpreter must simply interpret the question into English. But questions asked off the record pose a subtler dilemma. Sometimes there is a fine line between practicing law and defining words in linguistic terms, or simply giving information that any layperson might dispense. The *Los Angeles Superior Court Interpreters Manual* (Almeida & Zahler, 1981) provides the following guideline: "The interpreter may give general information to a non-English speaking person regarding the time, place and nature of court proceedings. However, in matters requiring legal judgment, the individual should be referred to an attorney" (p. 8). For instance, if a defendant wants to know what the charge of burglary means, the definition of such a complex legal concept is beyond the expertise of an interpreter and should be left to an attorney. On the other hand, if a non-English speaker asks the interpreter where the probation department is, the interpreter may answer that question. Thus, if interpreters feel confident that they can correctly answer a defendant's informational question, they may do so, but if they have any doubts at all that the questions have legal implications, they should refer the defendant to the attorney.

4.1.2. Referrals

If the defendant is not represented by counsel, the interpreter should not express any opinions about whether the defendant should get an attorney or who would be a good one. The *Los Angeles Superior Court Interpreters Manual* (Almeida & Zahler, 1981) cautions:

> The interpreter should never function as an individual referral service for any attorney or attorneys. This kind of activity has the appearance of impropriety and is forbidden by the attorneys' Canons of Ethics. When asked to refer a non-English speaking person to an attorney, the interpreter should refer such individual to the local county or city Attorney Referral Service in civil matters, or to the Public Defender's Office in criminal matters. (pp. 8-9)

4.2. Clerical Work

In general, court interpreters should perform only those functions that are directly related to interpreting. They should not engage in clerical work or other non-related duties. In busy courtrooms, however, especially during proceedings such as arraignments or traffic court where many cases are being processed at once, interpreters are sometimes asked to help distribute documents to non-English speakers, to help them fill out forms, or to direct people to other offices.

Protocol: If interpreters' superiors instruct them to perform such duties, they may have no choice but to comply, but they must beware of the perils involved. They should also inform the court administration of the problems inherent in this deviation from the strict function of interpreting. Among these potential problems are: (1) Interpreters will ultimately be held accountable for work that they are not qualified for and which is not within their function. This activity will distract from the optimum performance of their legitimate duties. (2) They may appear to have authority and training that they do not have, and people may jump to false conclusions about their function; interpreters are often mistaken for attorneys in such proceedings because they are seen addressing many defendants in an official manner, asking them questions about matters such as how they intend to plea. (3) There is a lesser danger that the interpreter may begin to accept this false role by not setting boundaries, and that would perpetuate the problem.

One way to avoid these problems is for interpreters to wear badges that clearly identify them as court interpreters (in all their working languages). Just as the other participants in the legal process should respect the role of interpreters and not place undue demands on them, interpreters must be careful not to usurp the roles of other officers of the court: the judge, the district attorney, the public defender, the bailiff, the probation officer, the court reporter, the court clerk. For further discussion on the related duties of interpreters, see Unit 7.

4.3. Cultural Expertise

It should be emphasized that the court interpreter is a language specialist, not an anthropologist, a linguist, or a psychologist, and therefore should not be considered an expert on the culture or language of the non-English-speaking defendant or witness. Accordingly, the court interpreter should not volunteer information or be called to the witness stand to testify about cultural practices referred to in testimony, or about whether a Spanish speaker is likely to have understood a police officer's questions in broken Spanish. Authorities in the related fields of knowledge should be consulted in such matters. Neumann Solow (1981) addresses this problem clearly with reference to sign language interpreters. She cautions sign language interpreters against considering themselves experts on deafness, and advises referring the interested party to people who are experts in the field in question:

> We are experts in communication and are able to answer many questions about the communication aspect of deafness, but we should avoid acting as experts in areas such as psychology as it relates to deafness or the education of deaf people. (p. 48)

This does not preclude interpreters from providing explanations of terms that they have knowledge of in their capacity as language specialists. For more information on the interpreter as expert witness, see Unit 3, Chapter 12, Section 3.

4.4. Instructions to Parties

It is helpful for all parties involved in a case, particularly those who have never used an interpreter before, to be given some guidelines so that they will be fully cognizant of the interpreter's functions and not overstep the bounds of that role. The New Jersey Supreme Court Task Force on Interpreter and Translation Services (1985) suggests standards for interpreted court proceedings. In Sections 1.2.8.2 through 1.2.10.2 the New Jersey Supreme Court Task Force on Interpreter and Translation Services (1985) supplies the following instructions for judges to read to the parties:

Notice to Defendants. . . .

We are going to have official court interpreters help us through these proceedings and you should know what they can do and what they cannot do. Basically, court interpreters are here only to help us in the proceedings. They are not a party in this case, have no interest in this case, and will be completely neutral. Accordingly, they are working for neither [party A] or [party B]. The official' court interpreters', [sic] sole responsibility is to bridge our communication barrier.

The official court interpreters are not lawyers and are prohibited from giving legal advice. They are not social workers and are prohibited from providing social assistance to you or anyone else. Their only job is to interpret, translate written documents and do sight translation. So please do not ask court interpreters for legal advice or social assistance.

If you do not understand the court interpreter, please let me know. If the court interpreter leaves out much of what is going on, tell me that as well.

Do you have any questions about the role or responsibilities of the court interpreter?. . . .

Notice to Witness. . . .

I want you to understand the role of the court interpreter. The court interpreter is here only to interpret the questions that an attorney or I ask you and to interpret your responses. The court interpreter will say only what we or you say and will not add to your testimony, omit anything you say, or merely summarize.

If you do not understand the court interpreter, please say so immediately.

If you do not understand the question that was asked, ask the person who posed the question for a clarification of the question.

Remember that you are giving testimony to this court, not to the court interpreter. Therefore please speak directly to the attorney or me. Do not address your replies to the court interpreter. Do not seek advice from or talk to the court interpreter.

Please speak in a loud, clear voice so that the entire court and not just the court interpreter can hear. . . .

Finally, please do not formulate your answer to a question from counsel or me before you have heard the complete court interpretation of the question in your language. Please await the full court interpretation of the English before you reply.

Do you have any questions about the role or responsibilities of the court interpreter? . . .

Notice to the Jurors. . . .

(A) The court interpreter is an expert witness [referring to New Jersey law]. Therefore you should treat the court interpretation rendered of the witness testimony as if the witness had spoken English and no court interpreter were present.

(B) Do not give any weight to the fact that testimony is given in a language other than English. Do not allow the witness' inability to speak English to affect your view of the witness' credibility.

(C) If any of you understand the language of the witness, disregard completely what the witness says in the other language. Consider as evidence *only* [emphasis in original] what is provided by the court interpreter in English.

(D) [When the defendant requires a court interpreter] Do not attribute any prejudice to the fact that the defendant requires a court interpreter. This court seeks a fair trial of everyone regardless of the language they may speak. We will not permit bias against persons because they do not speak English. . . . (Appendix, pp. 11-14)

4.4.1. The Use of Interpreters by Attorneys

Attorneys are also advised to be aware of the problems inherent in interlingual communication when they examine a witness through an interpreter. Tayler (1988) recommends that attorneys adjust the language in their questions to the witness. She points out that attorneys tend to be very conscious of language in the formulation of their questions, but advises that they should eschew many of the "artifices of language" and make their questions simple and straightforward. "In this manner, it is the attorney as speaker, and not the interpreter as intermediary, who retains control" (p. 58), she emphasizes, going on to say that colloquial and idiomatic expressions are to be avoided if at all possible.

4.5. Other Problems

Because the role of court interpreters within the overall context of the court proceeding is so difficult to delineate, interpreters are frequently called upon to make rapid decisions and judgments regarding their role throughout the proceeding. The following are some of the issues that must be addressed.

4.5.1. Questions from the Witness

Frequently a witness who does not understand the interpreted question will address a question to the interpreter to clarify the matter:

Attorney: When did you first meet him?

Interpreter: (in TL) When did you first meet him?

Witness: (in TL) When did I what?

Protocol: The interpreter should not take it upon himself to repeat the question on his own, but rather should state in English, "When did I what?" Any question asked of an interpreter by a witness, even if it is asked because the interpreter did not speak loudly enough or made a poor word choice, should simply be interpreted into English.

4.5.2. Request for Repetition by the Judge or Counsel

If the attorney asks the interpreter to repeat an answer, the interpreter should defer to the court reporter, who has a verbatim record of the English version.

Protocol: Generally the judge will intervene and ask the court reporter to read back the answer. If no officer of the court makes such a request, the interpreter should do so: "Your Honor, the interpreter is not able to repeat the answer verbatim; may the court reporter read back the answer?" This should be done even if the interpreter believes he or she can repeat exactly what has just been said.

4.5.3. Clarifications

It is important to remember that the interpreter should never engage in any independent conversation with a witness on the stand, as that would arouse the suspicions of those present who do not understand the language in question. Therefore, if interpreters need a clarification, they should always inform the court and obtain the judge's permission to clarify something with the witness.

Protocol: "Your Honor, the witness has made an ambiguous statement and the interpreter needs to clarify it before she can proceed." Similarly, interpreters should not address the attorney directly about a problem with the question; they should always communicate through the judge.

4.5.4. Documents

If a witness hands a document to the interpreter during the testimony, the interpreter should not read the document or describe it in any way; the interpreter should hand it to the witness's attorney. Generally, the attorney will describe the document for the record and return it to the witness.

4.5.5. Instructions Not to Interpret

The interpreter is asked by the defense attorney to dispense with interpreting the instructions to the jury to the defendant. The interpreter is aware that interpreters are to interpret *all* of the proceedings for a non-English speaker.

Protocol: The interpreter asks defense counsel to have the judge order on the record that the interpreter dispense with the interpretation. The interpreter may state: "Counsel, have the judge order me not to interpret on the record. I am duty bound to interpret everything unless ordered to the contrary." Any request by counsel to omit interpretation of any portion of the proceedings is to be referred to the presiding judge. The interpreter should never assume that the lack of interpretation would have the approval of the judge. Making the request on the record gives defendants an opportunity to be a party to the waiver of their personal right to hear all portions of the proceedings. Should there be any future question as to the propriety or impropriety of omitting any portion of the proceeding, it will be on the record.

5. The interpreter shall be prepared for any type of proceeding or case.

It is impossible to predict the subject matter that will be introduced during the course of a trial or other legal proceeding. In a single case there may be expert witness testimony regarding ballistics tests, autopsies, and blood types, while key witnesses from a variety of countries may testify in street slang, and attorneys quote Shakespeare in their oral arguments. It is imperative that interpreters have a solid grounding in every aspect of their working languages and that they give top priority to constantly upgrading their skills. The *Federal Court Interpreter Certification Examination Manual* (Gonzalez, 1986) asserts that the court interpreter's basic tool is a broad vocabulary in both languages. Not only must interpreters have the vocabulary to function effectively in a variety of subject matters, but they must also have a solid grasp of legal concepts and fully understand the proceeding in which they are interpreting. Edwards (1988) sums up the matter simply: "If the interpreter understands the case, the defendant will understand it" (p. 23).

5.1. Continuing Education

All of the codes of ethics and standards of conduct that govern the activities of court interpreters emphasize the importance of continuing education. The *Los Angeles Superior Court Interpreters Manual* (Almeida & Zahler, 1981) stipulates that "The interpreter should be responsible for engaging in continuing education to keep himself informed of matters which can improve his performance" (p. 10). Administrative Order No. 85-002 of Superior Court of the State of Arizona, County of Maricopa (1985), provides that "The interpreter should, through continuing education, maintain and improve his interpreting skills and knowledge of procedures. The interpreter should seek to elevate the standards of performance of the interpreting profession" (Section VIII.9). Collecting and compiling glossaries on a variety of subjects and reading specialized texts are integral parts of the duties of the court interpreter as preparing ahead of time ensures that interpreters can fulfill their primary responsibility, that of rendering a complete and accurate interpretation.

5.2. Technical Terminology

It is very difficult to retain highly technical terms that are rarely used, so interpreters should carry with them the specialized glossaries that they need. (The opening arguments in a trial indicate what subjects will come up, and thereafter the interpreters can bring to court the necessary reference materials.) Court interpreters should spend their spare time, during breaks in the proceedings, reviewing these materials to make sure they know the terms that might be used.

5.3. Jury Instructions

Jury instructions contain a great deal of frozen language, archaic usage, and terms of art and present highly technical and complex legal issues. All of these factors combine to make the interpretation of jury instructions one of the most formidable and taxing tasks to perform. Moreover, it is always more difficult to interpret someone who is reading from a prepared text rather than speaking extemporaneously, because the pace is faster, there are fewer pauses, and the intonation is not always natural. It is advisable for the interpreter to prepare ahead. Shortly before the end of a trial, the attorneys and judge will have agreed upon the jury instructions that will be read. At that point, interpreters should ask for a copy of the instructions so that they can read and utilize them as a reference during delivery. A caution to the interpreter—although judges may read jury instructions, they also may depart from these texts and give highly detailed and idiomatic examples extemporaneously.

5.4. Familiarity with the Case

For complete accuracy, it is helpful for interpreters to familiarize themselves with the facts involved in the case at hand before beginning to interpret. Administrative Order No. 85-002 of Superior Court of the State of Arizona, County of Maricopa (1985), recommends that defense counsel provide the interpreter with "any official or unprivileged documents" (Section II.1.6) that are available. Rainof (1980) also emphasizes the need for the interpreter to peruse documents such as police reports and transcripts of preliminary hearings. The realities of day-to-day courtroom activity (overcrowded dockets, unpredictable dispositions) may work against this ideal, but interpreters should stress to court personnel how important it is for them to prepare so that they can perform their duties adequately. They should ask permission to review documents such as reports and case files before the trial begins (in the case of a major trial, several days in advance so that they can obtain the appropriate technical references) in order to prepare for technical terminology and clarify ambiguous terms that are used.

Caution: There is some risk, however, that in reading documents interpreters will develop certain biases or preconceptions that will interfere with an accurate interpretation. For instance, if they read a police report based on an interview conducted with a poor interpreter, they may get an erroneous idea of what the facts are and misinterpret ambiguities in the testimony. In one industrial accident case in California, preliminary reports contained references to the claimant complaining of "nausea" before falling (the claimant's foreman interpreted for her in the initial investigation). In subsequent interviews, the claimant was quoted as complaining of "dizziness." The investigator doubted the claimant's credibility until a certified court interpreter pointed out that the term *mareado* in Spanish can mean either nauseated or dizzy, sometimes both. When the claimant was asked about this matter in more detail, she indicated that she had felt dizzy. The point to be made here is that an unwary interpreter who read the preliminary report first might automatically translate *mareado* as "nauseated" throughout the proceedings because he or she was influenced by the error of the first interpreter. Thus, it is always beneficial for interpreters to have access to any information that enables them to prepare better for their interpreting assignment, but they should use the information with extreme caution and interpret what they *hear* not what they *know*.

5.5. Pre-Testimony Interview

In the interest of ensuring complete accuracy, it is very helpful for the interpreter to have an opportunity to talk with the client before the proceeding begins. This practice is so important that it is recommended in most sources on court interpreting (Almeida & Zahler, 1981; Judicial Council of California, 1979; New Jersey Supreme Court Task Force on Interpreter and Translation Services, 1985; Rainof, 1980). It enables the interpreter to become accustomed to the witness's speech mannerisms and determine whether any unusual dialect, regionalisms, or technical terms will come up during testimony. The interpreter should not, however, discuss the pending proceedings outside the presence of the witness's counsel. This is also an opportunity for the interpreter to explain to the witness how the interpreting process works and establish a few ground rules (e.g., to listen only to the interpreted question, not the English; to answer in first person to the person questioning, and so on). If the judge does not read the instructions recommended in Section 4.4 of this chapter, the interpreter should review those guidelines with the witness. Moreover, the interpreter can use this opportunity to establish rapport with the witness and gain his or her trust, as long as the relationship of professional detachment discussed in Section 2 is maintained.

5.6. Disqualification

There are times when very technical terminology or obscure slang is used in a case. If there is a great deal of such language in a given case, as in the trial of a group of sailors in which nautical terminology and maritime jargon will pervade the testimony, interpreters who feel they are incapable of performing adequately without taking extra time to prepare or do research should request the time and resources they need. Similarly, if they discover that anyone for whom they have been called to interpret speaks a dialect they are not fluent in, interpreters should inform the court. In these cases, the *Los Angeles Superior Court Interpreters Manual* (Almeida & Zahler, 1981) recommends that the interpreter "critically assess his ability to perform and should disqualify himself if he is not fully capable of providing a high quality, professional interpretation" (pp. 9-10). The Professional Code for Court Interpreters Ethics and Practice, drawn up by the Court Interpreters and Translators Association, is even more specific in this regard. Paragraph D of that code announces that the interpreter "should feel no compunction about withdrawing from a case in which he feels he will be unable to function effectively, due to lack of proficiency, preparation or difficulty in understanding a witness or defendant" (New Jersey Supreme Court Task Force on Interpreter and Translation Services, 1984, p. 113). Disqualifying oneself is not something to be taken lightly; it should be considered only when the interpreter has doubts about having the linguistic expertise to perform adequately. Before offering interpreting services as a court interpreter, interpreters must be sure that they have a solid grasp of all aspects of their working languages so that they will not encounter difficulties.

Solution: The interpreter must notify the attorney and the clerk of court that the interpreter is disqualifying himself or herself and may assist the assignment office in seeking an interpreter who has experience with the particular dialect. For example, all Chilean speakers of Spanish do not necessarily understand all Dominican speakers of Spanish, just as some American speakers of English do not understand some varieties of British English.

6. The interpreter shall ensure that the duties of his or her office are carried out under working conditions that are in the best interest of the court.

In keeping with the interpreter's fundamental obligation to provide a complete, accurate rendition of witnesses' testimony and to inform the defendant of everything that is said in the trial, interpreters have a parallel obligation to see that they operate under optimum conditions. This responsibility does not rest exclusively with interpreters, however, the court itself must ensure that interpreters have the proper conditions for performing their duties. The New Jersey Supreme Court Task Force on Interpreter and Translation Services (1985) lists the following obligations of the court:

(A) Maintaining courtrooms that are as quiet as possible;

(B) Permitting only one person to speak at a time; and

(C) Speaking and regulating the speech of others at a rate of speed and volume of speech which can be accommodated by the court interpreter. (Appendix, p. 11)

To guarantee proper working conditions, and thus the best possible performance by the interpreter, the following guidelines should be observed.

6.1. Periodic Breaks

Because interpreting is such a demanding task, it is imperative that the interpreter remain mentally alert at all times. It is not uncommon for the interpreter to be compared to a machine because of the speed, precision, and objectivity required. Frishberg (1986) points out the flaw in this analogy: "the interpreter's human needs may be neglected. For example, a machine might be expected to give consistent performance over many hours of operation, while a human interpreter needs periodic pauses to refresh mental and physical alertness" (p. 60). Frequently judges will interrupt proceedings to give the court reporter a break, because they know that having an accurate record depends on having an alert reporter. They sometimes forget, however, that another important way to protect the record is to make sure the court interpreter is alert and comfortable as well. As Bennett (1981) notes, requiring the interpreter to work for long periods of time "is a doubtful practice, since physical fatigue will coincide with the intellectual and psychological fatigue of interpreting and inevitably will tend to impair the quality of the interpreter's work" (p. 15; also see Cooper & Cooper, 1983). Almost every source on court interpreting (Almeida & Zahler, 1981; Edwards, 1988; Frishberg, 1986; New Jersey Supreme Court Task Force on Interpreter and Translation Services, 1985) addresses the issue of interpreter fatigue, recommending that periodic breaks be requested and given. Another factor to be taken into consideration is that attorneys often take advantage of interruptions in the proceedings to confer with their clients and use the services of court interpreters. It is important for court personnel to realize that the court interpreter should not thus be deprived of a break and that additional time must be allowed for the interpreter to rest.

6.2. Team Interpreting

The most effective way to avoid interpreter fatigue without unduly prolonging the proceedings is to have a team of interpreters assigned to each case. It is common practice in the United States district courts to assign two interpreters to any case lasting more than two hours (New Jersey Supreme Court Task Force on Interpreter and Translation Services, 1984, Chapter II, note 7). Most guidelines for the use of interpreters (Edwards, 1988; New Jersey Supreme Court Task Force on Interpreter and Translation Services, 1985; Superior Court of the State of Arizona, County of Maricopa, 1985) recommend that in trials interpreters should work in teams and relieve each other periodically. In many federal courts, the interpreters relieve each other every thirty minutes, which is the period prescribed by the Association Internationale d'Interprètes de Conférence (AIIC), the professional association of conference interpreters. In Canada, the standard is to relieve the interpreter every twenty minutes (Bennett, 1981). It is important to note that the time limits apply to both consecutive and simultaneous interpreting. Contrary to common assumptions, both are equally taxing. Indeed, Edwards (1988) asserts that "Work on the witness stand is even more grueling than work at the defense table" (p. 24). Nevertheless, every effort should be made to avoid changing interpreters in the middle of a single witness's testimony. When interpreters work in teams, it is important for the interpreter who is "resting" at the moment to continue observing and listening in order to maintain familiarity with the context of the testimony.

6.3. Workload

In order to comply with the above guidelines for preventing interpreter fatigue, the number of cases to be interpreted per day and per week must be limited. Moreover, as prescribed by the New Jersey Supreme Court Task Force on Interpreter and Translation Services (1985), "Cases involving a court interpreter shall be heard according to the schedule that makes the most efficient use of interpreting resources without conflicting with other priorities" (Appendix, p. 44). In other words, every effort must be made to call interpreted cases in the appropriate order to minimize the need to go back and forth between courtrooms.

6.4. Audibility

One of the key links in the chain of communication is the interpreter's ability to hear everything in the courtroom. It is generally agreed that this is an indispensable working condition that must be guaranteed for the interpreter. Administrative Order No. 85-002 of the Superior Court of the State of Arizona, County of Maricopa (1985), states that "All reasonable efforts should be made to ensure that the interpreter is able to hear adequately the voices he is interpreting" (Section VII.1). If someone is speaking at a rate that precludes a good, in-depth interpretation, or is speaking too softly to hear, or if there is some interference such as a loud noise outside the courtroom, the interpreter should inform the court. If an attorney is addressing the jury, and has his or her back to the interpreter, for example, the interpreter should call the court's attention to the problem: "Your Honor, the interpreter cannot hear counsel."

6.4.1. Position

The interpreter also should be positioned in such a way as to be able to hear everyone in the courtroom. According to the New Jersey Supreme Court Task Force on Interpreter and Translation Services (1985), court interpreters should be positioned in such a way that they can see every person in the courtroom and be seen by everyone but should not block the view of the judge, jury, or counsel. The report goes on to say that court interpreters shall always be positioned so that the non-English speaker can hear everything they say, and so that the court interpreter can hear everything that is said during the proceedings. Because factors other than audibility intervene in the positioning of the court interpreter (ensuring that the jury has a clear view of the witness, or meeting the bailiff's security requirements), the interpreter should have a designated place in the courtroom agreed upon by all court personnel; when new courtrooms are constructed, the need to accommodate language services should be a primary consideration.

6.5. Special Equipment

To fulfill the interpreter's obligation to be in a position to hear and see everything that goes on in the courtroom, it may be necessary to provide the interpreter with special equipment. Many courts today have acquired wireless simultaneous equipment so that their interpreters can sit anywhere in the courtroom and communicate with anyone who is wearing earphones, merely by whispering into a microphone. If interpreters feel that simultaneous equipment would facilitate effective interpreting, they should bring this matter to the attention of the presiding judge.

7. The interpreter shall be familiar with and adhere to all of these ethical standards, and shall maintain high standards of personal and professional conduct to promote public confidence in the administration of justice.

Court interpreters have the responsibility of being aware of all ethical standards that apply to their profession, to consciously apply them to everyday practice, and to inform clients of these principles should questions arise. As members of a learned profession that is dedicated to public service, interpreters have a duty to act responsibly.

This means that interpreters should anticipate potential problems, and that through an understanding and practice of these principles, actively avoid potentially compromising situations.

7.1 Candor with the Tribunal

Interpreters should never engage in dishonesty, misrepresentation, or knowingly make false statements. This practice not only reflects adversely on the individual but, by association and generalization, on the interpreting profession. A failure to report information is also tantamount to being dishonest. For example when an interpreter fills out an employment application, it should be filled out completely, including any information about prior convictions if any. In addition, the interpreter should report an indictment, if any, even if that indictment did not result in a conviction. Failure to report convictions on employment applications is often a punishable offense and could lead to later embarrassment and adverse employment actions. The interpreter should always be completely candid with the court in all situations.

7.2 Personal Conduct

Like all officers of the court, interpreters have the special duty to maintain high professional standards as well as exemplary personal conduct. If an interpreter has any reason to believe that any of his or her current personal conduct may bring the profession or the judicial system into question, then that personal conduct should be avoided. By the same token, if the interpreter believes that any past personal conduct may reflect adversely on his or her professional role in the court, then this behavior should be disclosed to the court. Displaying professionalism in all relationships with other court personnel at all times is the ideal interpreters should try to achieve. Courts may have rules prohibiting or governing fraternization between co-workers, and these rules should be followed in the same manner as ethical standards.

7.3 Fiscal Propriety

The interpreter should never engage in illegal conduct such as fraud or failure to disclose fiscal interests in conflict with the aims of justice. These acts would call into question the overall ethical standards of the profession and destroy the public trust. Other prohibited personal actions include breach of the public trust by being influenced in any way to alter testimony. Official court interpreters cannot accept any remuneration, gifts, gratuities, or special consideration over and above authorized compensation for performing official interpreting duties. Whereas court interpreters may use the knowledge they obtain in the course of their work to share with other official interpreters, knowledge gained in the same capacity or as a result of access to court records, personnel, or facilities, should not be exploited for personal gain, or the gain of others.

7.4 Upholding the Public Trust

The public expects the court and its employees to exemplify the highest ethical standards, and for this reason, professions affiliated with the court must make exceptional efforts to maintain that public trust, otherwise known as upholding a fiduciary duty. Engaging in any of these types of behaviors is damaging to the public's perception of the interpreter's ability to carry out his or her professional responsibilities. There are higher expectations of personal comportment in the court setting because of the public belief that high moral character of legal personnel is essential to the proper administration of justice.

Chapter 35

Professional Conduct

This chapter further defines professional conduct for the court interpreter, focusing in particular on the attitudes the interpreter should have, relations with colleagues, the benefits of belonging to a professional organization, and the importance of continuing education.

1. Professional Attitude

As explained in the preceding chapter, a professional is someone with specialized training and knowledge who uses these skills to further the public interest. In the case of court interpreters, they place their expertise at the service of the justice system. Because the pursuit of justice is such an essential aspect of our society, it is important for court interpreters to have an awareness of their proper role and the attitudes they and others should have toward their profession. This section enumerates some of the attitudes that court interpreters must have in order to be regarded as professionals.

As mentioned earlier, it is important for interpreters to remain impartial and objective in legal proceedings. If they maintain what Neumann Solow (1981) calls "detached involvement" with their clients, treating everyone with equal courtesy, they will earn their trust and respect.

Another factor that will build trust is self-confidence. Court interpreters must take pride in the quality of their work, and this pride will enable them to be assertive in ensuring proper working conditions and responding to challenges from attorneys. Of course, this pride must be well founded, which means that interpreters must work constantly on self-improvement and continuing education.

Professionals subordinate their own egos and personal concerns to the higher objective of serving their clients and the profession. The *Los Angeles Superior Court Interpreters Manual* (Almeida & Zahler, 1981) correctly observed that interpreters should be responsible for elevating the standards of performance of the interpreting profession. Court interpreters must be aware that they are part of a larger process and have a certain degree of humility about their role in that process. It may seem a contradiction in terms to say that humility and self-confidence are equally important qualities, but they are not mutually exclusive. Interpreters must have just the right combination of these two qualities to do their job well. Humility means being able to admit that one does not know everything, either in court or with colleagues, and being willing to do whatever it takes to fill in the gaps in one's knowledge. It takes a great deal of self-confidence to be that humble. Thus, professional interpreters are not afraid to inform the court that they do not know a term, and they do so in a calm and assertive manner. Similarly, they are not afraid to ask their colleagues about terminology or to ask for their help in solving a problem.

515

1.1. Awareness of Role

As noted, interpreters are indeed part of a larger process. Accordingly, they should fit into that process unobtrusively and not disrupt it. Article 2 of the Code of Professional Responsibility of the Official Interpreters of the United States Courts says, "The official court interpreters reflect the decorum of the Court and act with dignity and respect for the Court and its personnel.... The official court interpreters work unobtrusively with full awareness of the nature of the proceedings" (Administrative Office of the United States Court, 1987, p. V-I). The practical implications of this stricture are specified in the *Los Angeles Superior Court Interpreters Manual* (Almeida & Zahler, 1981):

> The interpreter should appear on time and report, immediately upon arrival, to the court clerk or other designated official.... The interpreter should wear appropriate clothing for court and be well groomed.... The interpreter should not leave the courtroom until the proceedings are officially terminated or he is officially excused. (p. 10)

Although interpreters should in no way draw attention to themselves, they must always maintain an erect posture and speak loudly and clearly for the record. If they are interpreting simultaneously for the defendant, however, they should keep their voices as low as possible to avoid disturbing others.

1.2. Relations with Colleagues

Maintaining good relations with one's colleagues is also part of being a professional. According to Article 10 of the Code of Professional Responsibility that governs federal court interpreters, "The official court interpreters undertake to support other official court interpreters, sharing knowledge and expertise with them to the extent practicable in the interests of the Court" (Administrative Office of the United States Courts, 1987, p. V-2). This sharing of information takes place at two levels: within the professional association of interpreters, and in the day-to-day activities of interpreters who work in the same court. Edwards (1988) stresses the value of cooperating with one's colleagues when working together on a trial. It is important to note that interpreters should always regard fellow interpreters as colleagues, not rivals. Interpreters should refrain from maligning them, even if they do not approve of their conduct or work. They must make every effort to share their knowledge with them and to learn from them. Neumann Solow (1981) points out that an individual interpreter's actions reflect on other interpreters and on the profession as a whole. She goes on to emphasize that since interpreters usually operate unsupervised, "self-policing" is an important aspect of their work: "We are responsible for our personal growth, as well as for the growth of our profession" (p. 4).

1.3. Role of the Professional Organization

A good forum for such sharing and learning is the interpreters' association—an essential part of any profession. Joining and participating actively in an association of one's colleagues is a key element of professional conduct. Professional organizations can provide the following benefits:

(1) *Mutual support and solidarity:* Interpreters can meet with each other and commiserate about their problems, provide emotional support, and take action to solve problems. As noted at the beginning of this chapter, the code of ethics drawn up by the association can provide orientation for interpreters who must decide how to handle difficult situations.

(2) *Community education:* The organization as a whole can provide the most appropriate setting for teaching the users of interpreting services about the profession, informing them what interpreters can and cannot do. Many issues that the interpreter cannot effectively address individually in court, such as cultural misunderstandings, establishing the proper functions of the interpreter, and ensuring adequate working conditions for the interpreter (including special equipment for simultaneous interpretation), can be addressed by the professional association in workshops or seminars for the legal community. A delegation from the local chapter may approach the court administration to request facilities that might help interpreters do a better job in court, such as a better sound system or an interpreter waiting room.

(3) *Community services:* The best way to let the community know that the interpreters' association exists is to become active in local events. Volunteering interpreter services for charities or public services (making sure that no professional interpreter or translator would be displaced, of course), or participating in community activities (a booth at a fair) establishes a reserve of good will that can be drawn upon when the interpreters' associations need public support.

(4) *Dissemination of information:* The newsletter or journal of the professional association can keep interpreters abreast of the latest developments in the field, including legislation that affects the profession, dictionaries and other publications that become available, research, and dates of certification exams. It may also serve as a forum for discussing ethical issues and airing grievances, or it may publish terminology glossaries.

(5) *Lobbying:* On a state and national level, the interpreters' association can work to improve the professional and economic status of the profession by maintaining contacts with key representatives and testifying in hearings to ensure that legislation and regulations are favorable to interpreters.

(6) *Local negotiations:* The local chapter of the professional association can form a united front for negotiations with local court officials in efforts to improve the working conditions and compensation of court interpreters. One court interpreter group, the Los Angeles Chapter of the California Court Interpreters Association, has used the strategy of hiring a labor negotiator to represent the interpreters in contract negotiations with the court administration. Thus, it has been able to pool the resources of the entire membership to further the objectives of the profession.

(7) *Job exchange:* Meetings of the local chapter can be informal clearinghouses for jobs, at which free-lance interpreters trade assignments which they may be unable to accommodate in their schedules. Regular attendance at these meetings provides novice interpreters with an opportunity to meet more experienced colleagues and to demonstrate an interest in self-improvement. If the more active interpreters are impressed with a novice interpreter's sincerity and dedication, they may begin turning over excess assignments to the entrant interpreter.

(8) *Continuing education:* On a local, state, and national level, the interpreters' association is the best forum for the continuing education of its members. At annual

conferences, special seminars, or regular meetings of the local chapter, guest speakers who are experts in their fields can help interpreters improve their knowledge or skills in a wide variety of areas. Local chapter meetings can focus on terminology, exchanges of dictionaries and glossaries, and planning educational excursions.

1.4. Court Interpreting and Translating Organizations

The court interpreting profession is still in its infancy, and its professional associations are still striving to find an identity so that they can become permanent institutions. As in any fledgling profession, there are growing pains and instability. As of this writing, there are two national professional associations that are comprised exclusively of court interpreters: the California Court Interpreters Association (CCIA) and the National Association of Judiciary Interpreters and Translators (NAJIT). The CCIA was founded in 1971 and is the oldest organization of its kind. Although most of its members are in California, it also has members throughout the United States. NAJIT's predecessor, the Court Interpreters and Translators Association (CITA), was founded in 1978, and while it also attempted to reach out to translators and interpreters across the nation, its membership concentrated on the eastern seaboard. NAJIT has convened national meetings and begun a publication series (Palma, 1987, 1988, 1989). Both CCIA and NAJIT hold regular meetings and conferences, publish newsletters, and sponsor the publication of educational materials.

Other professional associations in related fields have members who are court interpreters and have contributed to furthering the profession's objectives. The Registry of Interpreters for the Deaf (RID), founded in 1964, trains and certifies sign language interpreters. It has a legal interpreting certificate that is designed specifically for court interpreters. Although the RID is oriented toward sign language interpreting, many of its activities can benefit spoken language interpreters as well. Another related organization is the American Translators Association (ATA). This professional association was founded in 1959 and now has approximately 1,500 members nationwide. It publishes a newsletter, the *ATA Chronicle,* which has many articles and items of interest to court interpreters—many ATA members are both translators and court interpreters. The ATA also accredits translators by administering a series of rigorous exams.

Another organization that is active in the field of interpreter education is the Conference of Interpreter Trainers (CIT). Founded in 1979, this organization is oriented primarily toward sign language interpreters, but it welcomes interpreters of all languages as members. It holds annual conferences at which interpreter trainers present and discuss methods of interpreter education. The Association Internationale d'Interprètes de Conférence (AIIC), The American Association of Language Specialists (TAALS), and the American Society of Interpreters (ASI) are other professional associations that can benefit court interpreters. A list of the professional organizations in the field of translation and interpretation, with addresses and phone numbers, is provided in Appendix E of this book.

2. Continuing Education

Because human language is dynamic and ever changing, it is extremely important for court interpreters to keep abreast of the latest changes in usage, both by the public at large and by the specialized groups for whom they interpret (the legal community, court personnel, immigrant communities, gangs, and so on). Moreover, interpreting skills themselves require constant honing. For this reason, continuing education is a vital part of the interpreter's professional activities.

The New Jersey Supreme Court Task Force on Interpreter and Translation Services (1985) found that the job of court interpreter is extremely demanding, requiring a broad range of skills and knowledge. It emphasizes in its report that being bilingual is not sufficient, and that in addition to mastering two languages, the court interpreter must be aware of "lexical, grammatical, and syntactic differences" and have full command of "dialect, educational level, register, geographic variation, specialized terminology, untranslatable words or phrases, and style" (p. 61). The New Jersey Supreme Court Task Force also stresses the importance of language level or register, which requires subtle distinctions in word choice. It recommends that court interpreters be familiar with the legal systems of the countries whose languages are being interpreted so that they can translate terms correctly. Finally, the report discusses the importance of mastering the techniques of interpreting.

2.1. Interpreter Training

The state and federal court interpreter certification processes that began in the 1970s revealed that there was an urgent need for interpreter training throughout the nation. It became clear that programs were needed both to train novice interpreters and to provide continuing education for working interpreters. A number of educational institutions have developed courses at a variety of levels to train court interpreters. These institutions include but are not limited to the Monterey Institute of International Studies (an M.A. program for conference interpreters and translators, and a summer course in court interpreting), the University of Arizona Summer Institute for Court Interpretation (an intensive summer course in continuous operation for eight years (Gonzalez, 1983)), the University of California Los Angeles Extension Division (a two-semester course in court interpreting), California State University (San Diego campus), the John Jay College of Law in New York, Florida International University in Miami, the Laurentian University School of Translators and Interpreters, and Vancouver Community College in British Columbia (certificate programs in court interpreting).The University of Arizona Summer Institute offered the first Trainers Program in the United States in 1984 (Gonzalez, 1985).

As the opportunities for employment in the field of court interpreting expand, so will the availability of training for interpreters. It is important to investigate such courses carefully to determine whether the instructors are qualified and the materials instructive. The stated goals of the course should be reasonable; a weekend workshop that is advertised as a sure way to pass certification examinations is suspect, to say the least.

For more information on the availability of court interpreter training, the interpreter should inquire with the professional associations listed here or with the Administrative Office of the United States Courts. The New Jersey Supreme Court Task Force on Interpreter and Translation Services (1985) Background Report #21 also contains a detailed list of interpreter training programs. Often the newsletters of the professional associations contain announcements of courses being offered in this field. In addition, in states where certification is required for court interpreters, information on training can be obtained at the state office in charge of such certification. (See Appendix E.)

It is generally recognized that these court interpreting courses and programs have made a major contribution to interpreter education, but they are not enough. Given the vast amount of knowledge and the highly technical skills that are required of court interpreters, ideally they should be trained in a one- or two-year postgraduate program, as are conference interpreters. The New Jersey Consortium of Educators in Legal Interpretation and Translation (1988) recommends just such a program, in addition to a variety of shorter-term courses at various levels to meet other professional needs. The history of professions such as law and medicine shows that society does not recognize professions as such, and does not accord them the commensurate status and legitimacy, until formal degree programs and academic credentials are developed to give the members of the profession a separate identity. Continuing efforts at understanding the special educational needs of the legal interpreter have been further explored by the Northeast Conference on Legal Interpretation (Aguirre, 1989).

2.2. Support from Court Administration

The onus of continuing education should not fall exclusively on the individual interpreter. The courts should recognize the need for training and facilitate it in every way. The New Jersey Supreme Court Task Force on Interpreter and Translation Services (1985) makes the following recommendation: "The Supreme Court should recognize the need for ongoing training and provide for the continuing professional education of current and future personnel who provide court interpreting, legal translation, bilingual and bilingual/multicultural court support services" (p. 185). Such facilitation should include paying part of the tuition for training courses and compensating interpreters for time spent engaging in these educational pursuits. At least one court system, the Los Angeles County courts, already provides such benefits for interpreters who work in that system.

Specialized court interpreter training is not the only source of continuing education for the court interpreter. Many courses offered at local community colleges, adult education facilities, or universities can be of great benefit to interpreters as a supplement to specialized training. For example, courses in public speaking, criminology or the administration of justice, law, languages and literature, political science, weapons, medical terminology, auto mechanics, United States and world history, and other technical fields may provide the interpreter with valuable information, in terms of both background knowledge and terminology. If the community for which interpretation services are provided is employed primarily in one occupation (agriculture or the garment industry), it behooves the interpreter to become familiar with the theoretical concepts and specialized terminology involved in that occupation. Community college courses may be a valuable resource in that regard as well.

2.3. Informal Educational Activities

Aside from formal classroom education, field trips provide first-hand knowledge of many of the subjects that court interpreters must be able to manipulate. These excursions may be arranged by groups, such as the local chapter of the interpreters' association, or individually. Many police forces offer ride-along programs, in which citizens may accompany police officers on routine patrols to find out how they perform their daily duties. In addition, it is vitally important for novice interpreters to go to court as often as possible in order to familiarize themselves with the language and procedures of the court. While there, they should obtain copies of the documents used in the courtroom (waiver forms, for instance), which they will be expected to sight translate when they are serving as interpreters. Almost all court proceedings are public, so it is not difficult to observe the courts in action. It is not necessary to observe only interpreted proceedings; the prospective interpreter needs above all to become familiar with the English that is spoken in the courtroom.

As mentioned above, interpreters also need to become familiar with the working environment of the non-English speakers for whom they will be interpreting. Testimony about the occupational setting comes up routinely in almost any type of legal proceeding, and it is difficult to interpret such testimony if the interpreter is unfamiliar with the occupation in question. For this reason, it is very helpful to see the job site in person. Although some employers are reluctant to allow public access to the workplace, others are very concerned about public relations and are happy to arrange tours. They may be particularly cooperative if they have many employees who do not speak English and it is explained to them that legal proceedings which affect their business (labor relations hearings, unemployment appeals hearings) will be conducted more efficiently and accurately if interpreters are familiar with the job setting. If it is impossible to arrange a tour, the local chapter of the interpreters' association may invite an official from one of these companies to speak to interpreters and explain some of the technical terminology and procedures.

Another way for interpreters to learn new concepts and terminology, and to stay abreast of new developments, is to read as much and as widely as possible in all their working languages—interpreters should never take their native language for granted. Current periodicals such as magazines and newspapers are the most reliable source of actual language usage as they are updated constantly. The interpreter should look for articles about crimes, the court system, or law enforcement, although reading about any subject matter is always useful. Another good source of current language usage is novels that contain a high proportion of dialogue; television soap operas are also valuable in this respect. In fact, there is no written material that cannot be of some use to the interpreter; it is a good idea to develop the habit of reading avidly during spare time. In court, interpreters may find that they have many idle moments between assignments which can be used to great advantage for reading. The *Federal Court Interpreter Certification Examination Manual* (Gonzalez, 1986) contains a list of recommended periodicals and reading materials suitable for interpreters or for anyone wishing to master the language. For more information on the resources available to interpreters, see the section on language resources and references in Unit 7, Chapter 33.

In general, interpreters should increase their language awareness. They should pay attention to how people use language at all levels and in all settings. They should not be afraid to ask questions about language usage; many people are flattered by such questions, and are delighted to explain the meaning of an idiomatic expression or a proverb.

Chapter 36
Federal Certification

This chapter provides a detailed analysis and explanation of the Federal Court Interpreter Certification Examination (FCICE). It begins with an examination of the development process that was initiated pursuant to the legislative mandate of the Court Interpreters Act of 1978, explaining how the first Spanish-English examination was designed and how scoring criteria were derived. Then the parameters of the written and oral components of the examination are described in detail, and the innovations in the assessment procedure are explained. The chapter then discusses the development of the Navajo and Haitian Creole certification examinations, explaining the particular test development problems of oral tradition languages. The chapter concludes with a presentation of the results of the various administrations of the examination and discusses the implications of those results.

1. Introduction

One of the essential characteristics of a profession is the standards of entrance and conduct that it upholds in order to control the quality of the services rendered by its members. When a profession lacks standard educational programs of study for its practitioners, a performance-based examination that measures a candidate's skills becomes especially important as a means of controlling admission to the profession, as is the case with any professional examination. This performance- or proficiency-based examination measures minimal or higher level of ability needed to perform the required tasks.

Sometimes professional examinations are controlled by employing agencies that grant teacher certification on the basis of educational credentials, and, in many states now, of proficiency-based examinations. When the 1978 Court Interpreters Act was passed, Congress delegated certification of the court interpreter to the employing agency, the Administrative Office of the United States Courts (AO). The AO thereafter created a performance-based, criterion-referenced examination, with performance standards set by the needs of the courts—the users of professional interpreters. A benefit to this approach is that the certifying authority resides in an impartial body such as the AO, which can then set minimum standards based on its objective needs and guard against guild-oriented interests that may bias a certification process.

2. Initial Development

The Spanish-English FCICE is a criterion-referenced functional test of interpreting that was created by the federal courts to test the competency of interpreters to serve the United States district courts. This examination has had four notable effects:

(1) It has guaranteed federal judges that the quality of the interpretation services meets the minimum standards necessary to facilitate communication in a federal court of law.

(2) It has reified the branch of interpreting known as court or judicial interpreting by publishing its assessment criteria and standards.

(3) It has moved the field of interpretation into functional performance testing, implementing methodologies to assess performance both objectively and subjectively.

(4) It has transformed court interpreting from a vocational activity to the professional status it currently enjoys in the federal courts.

The development and implementation of the Spanish-English certification examination has generated a theoretical testing model that may be applied to any language. This model utilizes a bifurcated, criterion-referenced assessment process: (1) a written Spanish-English language proficiency evaluation and (2) an oral interpreting performance exam.

The certification procedure evolved through the planning of the AO's specialist Jon A. Leeth, whose objective was to implement the mandates of the Federal Court Interpreters Act of 1978. He conducted a thorough needs assessment in consultation with federal judges, court interpreters, conference interpreters, linguists, and psychometricians. This needs assessment led to the establishment of a task force whose function was to decide on the format and content of a certification examination that would suit the courts' needs and reflect the inherent linguistic characteristics of the language heard in court (Gee, 1986). The meticulous development of the certification is chronicled in an article by Arjona (1985), in the testimony of Gonzalez in *Seltzer v. Foley* (1980) and the findings of that case as announced by Judge Milton Pollack.

The following steps were taken to ensure that the examination and performance standards that were established accurately measured the tasks involved in court interpreting:

(1) Analyses of courtroom language were used to ascertain the linguistic complexity of the language involved in interpreting tasks. Joos's (1967) five-clock analysis of the levels of formality of English was used as an essential testing criteria. That is, different parts of the examination came to reflect the various levels of formality in courtroom language. Gonzalez's courtroom language complexity study became the empirical basis for the linguistic complexity of the federal examination (Gonzalez, 1977).

(2) The combined experiences and knowledge of conference interpreters and court interpreters were brought to bear to describe the tasks that court interpreters are called upon to do. The role of the conference interpreter—as elaborated by such renowned professionals as the late Theodore Fagan, former Chief Interpreter of the United Nations—was to locate the interpreting tasks within the broader perspective of interpreting in general.

(3) The theoretical and psycholinguistic underpinnings of interpreting processes were taken into account by researchers, including the late David Gerver of the University of Stirling, Scotland. Issues such as the cognitive complexity involved in simultaneous and consecutive interpretation were explored and testing techniques were developed to measure these skills.

(4) The participation of three federal judges—the Honorable Jose Gonzalez of the Florida district courts, the Honorable Juan Perez Gimenez of the Puerto Rico district courts, and the Honorable Reinaldo Garza of the Texas district courts—was critical in the development of performance standards and the task analysis. Judicial requisites became the foundational constructs in the certification procedure. The judges' prescriptions included the following:

(a) Interpreters must be able to interpret every word of the original testimony of the witness, not omitting a single element; for that one element, as inconsequential as it may seem, could be an important factor in discovering the truth.

(b) Interpreters must be able to interpret a message as closely as possible to the manner in which the witness originally said it, so that the judge and the jury will be able to hear the "flavor" of the words of the speaker and make judgments about the witness's credibility.

(c) Interpreters must be able to interpret a long response from the witness **without interrupting the witness.**

(d) Interpreters must be able to simultaneously interpret everything occurring in a proceeding in exactly the way it was said originally by the judge or attorney so that important legal issues are not distorted when they are interpreted to the witness.

(e) Interpreters should understand the role of the interpreter, as distinguished from the role of an attorney, for example, and should confine themselves to interpreting rather than explaining or giving legal advice.

(f) Interpreters should have a comprehensive knowledge of both languages, from the formal usage of the court to the simple usage of the witnesses.

These important criteria became the central constructs of the two-part examination, and also defined in a formal manner the differences between judicial interpretation and all other types of interpreting, in particular, conference interpreting. Thus, the certification examination procedure took its performance standards from the expectations of the judiciary and the language studies of Gonzalez (1977) and Briere (1978). Since then the studies of O'Barr (1981, 1982) have corroborated some of the initial findings of Gonzalez (1977).

3. Parameters of the Written Exam

The written test assesses an individual's knowledge of the formal registers of both Spanish and English at the college level of comprehension. The examination strictly adheres to the testing guidelines of the American Psychological Association (1985). It is piloted, statistically evaluated, and equated so that it is without question a fair and reliable instrument (see Table 1).

Both language sections of the examination contain five parallel subsections: Reading Comprehension, Synonyms, Sentence Completion, Usage, and Antonyms. All sections are at grade level fourteen (14), and each section has a cut-off score of 80 percent. The Spanish and English sections contain 80 multiple-choice items each, for a total of 160 questions. Candidates are allotted two and one-half hours to complete the entire examination, and must pass both sections of the exam in the same sitting to be eligible for the oral.

The synonym subsection tests direct knowledge of college-level vocabulary and tests general, as well as fine, distinctions within that vocabulary. The antonym subsection also tests direct knowledge of a formal vocabulary, and it too requires general and fine distinctions between meanings. The sentence completion subsection tests recognition of words or phrases which best complete the meaning of a partial sentence, with reference to syntax, logic, and style. The usage subsection tests the candidate's understanding of idiomatic expressions and syntactical and grammatical properties of the language. Within this subsection, the written form of the language, including punctuation, is also tested. The reading comprehension subsection tests the examinee's ability to read keenly, and to analyze a written passage for explicit and implicit material, main ideas, assumptions, inferences, interrelationship of words and ideas to whole passages, reasoning, and rhetoric.

Passing scores for the written examination are determined from one examination administration to another by using a sophisticated equating process. This process ensures that all cut-off scores are standardized and that each version is of equal difficulty from year to year. Since 1979, 9,750 candidates have attempted the written portion of the certification process. Twenty-two percent, or 1,810 persons, slightly more than one in five persons, have passed the written examination (Gonzalez, 1989c).

The written portion has proven to be highly reliable, with an average rating over seven administrations of .955 on the English section and .970 on the Spanish section of the examination (Gonzalez & Mishra, 1989). Reliability is a term used to indicate consistency; a perfect reliability score would be 1.00. Therefore, the examination has been an extremely consistent indicator of language proficiency over the years.

Table 1
Written Examination Technical and Subsection Information

| | Subsections | | |
	Spanish	English	Total
No. of items	80	80	160
Subsections	5	5	10
Grade level	14th	14th	College
Time allowed	—	—	2 1/2 hrs.
Overall reliability	.970/1.00	.955/1.00	—
Passage in same year	Concurrent	Concurrent	Both req. prior to oral
Cut-off	80%	80%	Determined statistically each year*

*Item analysis and equating procedures used to maintain level of difficulty and original proficiency standards.

4. Parameters of the Oral Examination

After candidates pass the written examination, then they are eligible to take the oral exam component. It is a functional performance test of a candidate's ability to interpret in a simulated courtroom setting. This instrument is divided into three sections discussed below that represent the most common interpreting modes used in court—sight translation, simultaneous and consecutive interpretation (see Table 2).

(1) *Sight translation* (from English to Spanish and from Spanish to English). In this ten-minute section, candidates are given two documents such as a will, police report, or contract, to read silently and interpret orally. Candidates are allotted five minutes to render each document.

(2) *Simultaneous interpretation* (from English into Spanish). Candidates listen on headphones to a seven-minute pre-recorded opening or closing argument by an attorney and render an interpretation at the same time the speaker is speaking.

(3) *Consecutive and simultaneous.* Cross-examination (from English into Spanish and Spanish into English).

(a) *Consecutive*: This is a fifteen-minute live simulation of an attorney's examination of a witness. Candidates must interpret from the TL into the SL and vice versa.

(b) *Simultaneous*: This portion of the exam is a four-minute pre-recorded cross-examination of a witness by an attorney. Using headphones, candidates listen to the tape while at the same time interpreting everything they hear.

As Table 2 illustrates, the oral certification examination consists of an interview and three test sections, two of which consist of two parts. Each portion of the exam is evaluated according to both objective and subjective criteria. Objective criteria are discrete points that are externally established and can be measured uniformly and reliably. Once these discrete points have been identified, they are not susceptible to mutation of any kind. These objective criteria are not subject to the discretion of the individual rater. The subjective assessment, on the other hand, depends on the rater's global impressions of performance. Raters are instructed to consider specified constellations of behavior in order to arrive at a subjective score of 1 (unacceptable), 2 (acceptable), or 3 (superior).

The subjective assessment criteria comprises two general categories: (1) fluency and delivery and (2) adaptability. The fluency and delivery category includes the candidate's pacing, coherence, composure, and stamina. The adaptability category refers to how resourceful the examinee is in responding to variations in the content, register, or style of the passage (Gonzalez, 1986).

The subjective criteria are the same throughout the examination. The objective criteria ostensibly changes with each component of the examination. For example, in the sight translation component, the objective criteria focuses on the conservation of register. A form of slang, such as "she stood me up" would be one of the objective scoring units, and the raters would be instructed to count as correct any equivalent phrase in Spanish that conserves both the meaning and the register. Thus, if the candidate says *no cumplió con su obligación conmigo* or *no acudió a la cita,* the scoring unit would be marked as an error, because the register was elevated. The term *me dejo plantado* or *me dejo parado* would be counted as correct. Notably, all of these choices convey the **meaning** of the original phrase, but the former two **are not at the correct register**. Although the objective criteria vary with the nature of the text being interpreted, conservation of meaning is always the common denominator.

The candidate's performance is evaluated by a three-member panel consisting of a federally certified court interpreter, a conference interpreter, and a language expert. The panel uses their multi-disciplinary exercise to help assess the candidate's interpreting skills.

Part I is a sight translation test, from Spanish to English and from English to Spanish. The objective criteria for the Spanish sight translation section, Part I-A, assesses the candidate's ability to utilize formal and frozen Spanish vocabulary to conserve every element of meaning when translating into English. The objective criteria for English sight translation measures the examinee's knowledge of slang, idiomatic expressions, the breadth of his or her colloquial English vocabulary, and the conservation of slang and idiomatic English into Spanish. Part II involves the testing of simultaneous interpretation of English into Spanish. Pre-recorded tapes are played into headphones, during which the candidate simultaneously renders the material verbally. The source topics, recorded at **120 words per minute**, are opening and closing statements by defense or prosecution attorneys from criminal or civil trials. Thus, this section may cover subjects such as drugs, immigration, weapons seizure, illegal printing of government documents, and so on. Using the objective criteria, the raters

Table 2
Overview of Federal Court Interpreter Oral Examination
Technical Information

Examination Subsection	Language Tested	Interpreting Skill Tested	Duration of Section	# Units Tested
Interview	—	—-	3 min.	—
Instruction	—	—	6 min.	—
Part I-A	Spanish to English	Sight Trans.	5 min.	22
Part I-B	English to Spanish	Sight Trans.	5 min.	22
Part II	English to Spanish	Simultaneous (120 wpm)	7 min.	70
Part III-A	English to Spanish Spanish to English	Cross-Exam— Consecutive	15 min.	66
Part III-B	English to Spanish	Simultaneous Cross-Exam (160 wpm)	4 min.	40
		Totals:	45 min.	220

assess the examinee's simultaneous interpretation of frozen and formal language, technical language, persuasive language, idiomatic expressions, conservation of language level, and the breadth and depth of the examinee's vocabulary.

Part III, like Part I, has two components. In Part III-A, the candidate's consecutive interpretation of English to Spanish and Spanish to English is tested. This element of the examination represents a live cross-examination of two Spanish-speaking witnesses. One Spanish-speaking witness simulates a speaker of an informal register, or colloquial speech, and the other Spanish-speaking witness uses formal Spanish. The topic source may be any criminal or civil case brought into federal court, including expert and eyewitness testimony. The objective criteria of the candidate's consecutive interpretation include all levels of the language register, colloquialisms, slang, technical language, interrupted sentences, false starts, hesitations, omissions, dates, places, numbers, specific details, grammatical issues, and long statements. The candidate must be able to interpret utterances of approximately **sixty words in length** without interrupting the speaker.

Part III-B tests the candidate's ability to simultaneously interpret the cross-examination of a Spanish-speaking witness by an English-speaking attorney. This text is recorded at **160 words per minute**. Pre-recorded tapes played into headphones to the candidate are to be rendered back in Spanish while he or she continues to listen. The tapes are based on transcripts adapted from criminal or civil cases heard in federal court. The objective criteria of this section include interrupted discourse, dates, names, numbers, government exhibit numbers, technical jargon, addresses, grammatical issues, and so forth.

5. Assessment: Objective and Subjective

The unique feature of the oral examination is its bipartite rating system involving subjective and objective assessment, as described in the preceding section. Two hundred and twenty (220) objective scoring units, distributed throughout the examination, represent important interpreting pitfalls, such as commonly used legal phrases, specialized terminology, grammatical items, idiomatic expressions, jargon, rhetorically charged argumentative language, purposefully ambiguous or extremely precise language, dates, addresses, quantities, and exhibit numbers, among others.

These items in the various texts are scoreable units, and are marked by the raters according to how precisely the candidate **conserves**, as opposed to **distorts**, the meaning of the grammatical or vocabulary item, while **preserving** the register. The concepts of "conservation" and objective scoring units were developed by Gonzalez, and the subjective scoring procedure by Arjona (Gonzalez & Arjona, 1989) for the Federal Court Interpreter Certification Examination Panel. This team developed the original rating procedure with the advice and counsel of Jon A. Leeth, project director (Arjona, 1985; Gonzalez, 1987b).

6. Cut-Off Score

Court interpreting experts, federally certified interpreters, conference interpreters, and language and linguistic specialists set 80 percent, or forty-five to forty-seven errors, as the passing score. They arrived at this cut-off by independently identifying the highest number of errors that could be committed before the level of interpretation becomes so unacceptable that it affects the fairness of the hearing. The exam is criterion referenced, that is, the cut-off score is pre-determined and does not change with the population of examinees (Gonzalez, 1986). An analysis of test results demonstrates the careful steps taken to ensure reliability over administrations (Mishra & Gonzalez, 1988).

7. Standardization of Administration

The oral exam is standardized in each aspect of its development and administration; thus, candidates who are tested in 1991 receive the same treatment as candidates who were tested in 1987 or even 1979. The length, difficulty, and testing process are identical and consistent from one administration to the next, ensuring fairness to each candidate. Immediately prior to the oral examination tours, a four-day session is conducted to provide rater training and to increase inter-rater reliability. Equating and standardization procedures are also used to maintain the original testing guidelines and to control the level of difficulty of the written exam. For a full description of standardizing strategies, see Gonzalez (1987b, 1988).

8. Results of the Federal Certification Examination

Table 3 (Gonzalez, 1989c) illustrates the number of persons certified through the seven administrations of the oral examinations. As of September 1989, 388 interpreters have been federally certified in this testing process.

The written and oral examinations have an overall pass rate of 4 percent. However, passage of the oral examination by qualified written examination candidates is 16

Table 3

Pass Rates for the Federal Court Interpreter Certification Examination

Date	# Partic. Written Exam	# Passes	# Partic. Oral Exam	# Passes	Total Cert. Rate
3/80	1,370	435 (32%)	371	121 (33%)	8.8%
11/80	1,601	582 (36%)	484	75 (15%)	4.7%
3/82	1,402	276 (19%)	331	26 (8%)	1.9%
9/83	1,609	215 (13%)	362	41 (11%)	2.5%
6/85	1,196	166 (14%)	253	29 (11%)	2.4%
3/87	1,121	136 (12%)	249	15 (6%)	1.3%
3/89	1,451	206 (20.6%)	322	81 (25%)	2.4%
Totals:	9,750	2,015 (20.6%)	2,372	388 (16%)	3.9%

percent. The rigorous nature of the examination guarantees a pool of tested individuals who are able to perform the skills and tasks necessary to ensure justice. The examination has been legally challenged. After a trial on the validity of the examination in *Seltzer v. Foley* (1980), Federal Judge Milton Pollack of the United States District Court of the Southern District of New York held that: "The said tests ... bore a rational and proper relation to skills ... required for requisite precision interpretation by bilingual interpreters in courtroom settings ... " (p. 608).

9. Equating Studies and Trend Analyses

9.1 Written Examination

To ensure high reliability and validity of the federal written certification examination, a rigorous statistical process is undertaken during and after development of each written exam. The **validity** of a testing instrument is established when the content of the test reflects the particular skills that one is attempting to measure. The content validity of the written examination is assured by the Examination Development Committee, which is constituted of practicing court and conference interpreters and language and testing specialists. The test assesses an individual's knowledge of the formal registers and to some extent knowledge of the informal registers of English and Spanish. The written examination tests college-level language proficiency, indicated as appropriate by studies of courtroom language.

In order to determine the reliability and validity of test items, a lengthy version of the written examination is piloted to a small population. The data collected from the administration of the pilot examination are subjected to commonly used item-analysis procedures. The final version of the written examination is then produced based upon the statistical analysis of the pilot data. Reliability indices are obtained for each subsection of the examination. **Reliability** is the extent to which the same examination is consistent over different administrations. Theoretically, reliability ranges from .0, no consistency over time, to 1.00, perfect consistency over time. The average reliability of the written examination is .955 for the English section and .970 for the Spanish section. These reliability ratings are extremely high; perfect reliability is never achieved on any examination.

In order to ensure that all versions of the written exam are equally difficult from year to year, a highly rigorous statistical process called **equating** is conducted. The process of equating is simply establishing that scores have the same weight on different tests. More specifically, two scores, one from test X and one from test Y, are considered equivalent if X and Y measure the same trait with equal reliability and percentile ranks. The equating process establishes an index of consistency from one examination administration to another. As a result of this equating procedure, cut-off scores for each administration of the examination can be determined. This procedure also accounts for the variation in passing scores from year to year. Results of these analyses indicate that the written exams are of equal difficulty across testing years. In conclusion, the written examination is highly valid, reliable, and consistently measuring the same traits over time.

9.2 Oral Examination

Many of the FCICE's critics insist that the examination has become progressively more difficult and stringent since the first administration in 1980. Yet in a recent equating study conducted by David Marshall (1989) and commissioned by the Federal Court Interpreter Certification Project at the University of Arizona, it was found that the 1980 oral examination was slightly more complex structurally and cognitively than the examinations of all later years: 1981, 1983, 1985, 1987, and 1989. Marshall (1989) computed a complexity index by examining the structural density of the language and the number of idiomatic expressions and other metaphorical uses of language. This study corroborates the results of a systemic discourse analysis that compared the 1980 and 1983 oral examinations and found that the 1980 exam presented candidates with a somewhat more challenging set of tasks (Fries, 1986).

The Fries study revealed that the simultaneous portions of Sets I and II of the 1980 and 1983 oral examinations showed some differences in grammatical and rhetorical structures, with the 1980 exam leading in rhetorical complexity. A systemic and semantic analysis indicated, however, that all four texts expressed roughly an equal range of relationships, or that subordinate and coordinate clauses appeared with similar frequency and in similar relationship to each other. Both of these studies confirm the trend analysis conducted by the University of Arizona Federal Court Interpreter Certification Project. An analysis of several indices of central tendency (passing scores and pass rates) indicated that both sets of the 1983, 1985, and 1987 oral examinations showed that examinees displayed similar performance patterns over a six-year period. This finding confirmed that these three examinations have been testing for the same skills (Gonzalez, 1988-89). On the basis of these three independently conducted studies, it can be concluded that the oral federal certification examination is consistently testing over the years the same set of tasks, and that in fact it may have become somewhat less demanding since 1980, although not markedly so.

10. Navajo and Haitian Creole Certification Examinations

In August of 1988, Congress appropriated funds to certify interpreters in Haitian Creole and Navajo, two languages for which certification was deemed to be necessary. As discussed in Unit 1, Chapter 5, these two languages were recommended for certification by the Federal Court Interpreter Advisory Board (Administrative Office of the United States Courts, 1987).

Very different developmental and procedural problems were faced in creating certification models for Navajo and Haitian Creole than were encountered in the development of the Spanish certification model. Because of both groups' historical isolation and their limited contact with the social and legal institutions of the United States, the same processes that were developed for Spanish certification were inappropriate. The courts officially requested that the Administrative Office develop certification examinations that would assure them that the linguistic needs of Navajos and Haitian Creole speakers were met (Administrative Office of the United States Courts, 1987). Pre-development meetings were held in 1988 and 1989 to discuss the unique cultural and linguistic issues that would affect the development of the certification examinations.

10.1. Navajo

Numerous cultural issues affected the development of the Navajo-English interpreting examination. For example, the approximately 200,000 members of the Navajo Nation are much more familiar with their own tribal law system than with that of the United States. Nevertheless, when faced with any charge higher than a misdemeanor and committed on federal land, they must appear in federal courts due to the jurisdictional relationship between the United States government and Native American nations.

Among the many cultural and linguistic differences between Navajo and English is one that is central to the United States justice system. The Navajo culture has no concept of guilt, and its lexicon contains no equivalent to the word "guilt" since the Navajo world view stresses communal rather than individual responsibility. In United States law, by contrast, the determination of individual guilt or innocence is the purpose of most criminal proceedings. In most courtrooms, an individual is deemed guilty of committing a crime if two criteria can be proved: (1) *actus reus*, commission of the act, and (2) *mens rea*, intent to commit the act.

The linguistic and conceptual differences between Navajo and English render simultaneous interpretation as it is practiced in court by Spanish-English interpreters impossible. There is a lack of one-to-one equivalents on the semantic or word level, and certain ideas are impossible to express on the conceptual level, except through long explanations of items and ideas that do not exist linguistically or culturally in Navajo. Therefore, it may take a Navajo interpreter three or four sentences to render one sentence or even one question in Navajo for the witness. As a result, it was necessary to allow a running summary rather than a simultaneous, word-for-word, concept-by-concept interpretation. Consequently, it is unreasonable to expect a Navajo interpreter to transfer all of the meaning intact at the same time as someone is speaking English in court. For this reason, simultaneous interpretation is not required on the certification examination for Navajo interpreters. A "running summary" instead takes its place.

Additionally, it is geometrically much harder for a Navajo interpreter to render long responses during a consecutive interpretation by witnesses because the memory problem is compounded by the vast cultural and linguistic differences between Navajo and English. Therefore, the consecutive section is somewhat shorter in word length than it is in the Spanish-English examination. The sight translation section essentially remains the same, but requires only English into Navajo because the Navajo oral tradition makes testing Navajo into English impossible.

No written examination in Navajo will be developed. First, less than 5 percent cent of the Navajo Nation is literate in Navajo, and secondly, the Navajo interpreter would rarely be called upon to read Navajo. It would be unfair to test in a language for which standard orthography is relatively new and for which so few books are in print. The certification procedure consists of a written examination testing knowledge of written English, and an oral test in both Navajo and English. The differences in varieties are quite marked in Navajo between the young and the elderly, particularly between on-reservation and off-reservation populations. While there are virtually no dialectal differences in the traditional sense, there are essentially "social dialects," such as the discernible differences between the speech of members of the American Navajo Church and others (R. Yazzie, personal communication, March 31, 1989). Interpreting between these distinct speech communities is not only a matter of word choice, but a matter of understanding culturally what must be explained from one group to another because of a complete difference in perspective and experience.

Of course, the grammatical and syntactical differences between English and Navajo are so great that a transliteration may be necessary at times, rather than a straight conceptual translation, so that the judge and the jury can ascertain the cultural, behavioral, and moral differences. Concepts such as "identify," which is a frequently used term in the legal setting, is a difficult concept that can only be expressed in Navajo as "come to know," or essentially as "What is this?" (Yazzie & Yazzie, 1985, p. 90). The concept of "inconsistency" is also basically foreign in Navajo. Six words are necessary to express it: "if one thing is allowed to happen, another thing cannot be" (Yazzie & Yazzie, 1985, p. 15). Actions are viewed passively by the Navajo, so that a horse does not kick a man, but rather the man "lets the horse kick him." All of these semantic, cultural, grammatical, and syntactical differences affect how communication takes place between English and Navajo.

The test development committee was aided by Judge Robert Yazzie of the Navajo Nation District Court, Window Rock; Robert Young (Professor Emeritus, University of New Mexico) and William Morgan, lexicographers of the Navajo language; and Mary Havatone, Professor of Linguistics, University of New Mexico, Ms. Esther Yazzie, M.A. in Education; and Alice Nuendorf, Professor of Education, among others. The first Navajo FCICE was administered in the fall of 1991; a total of five Navajos have been certified as of this date.

10.2. Haitian Creole

Another regional language services problem for the federal courts was encountered in Florida, in particular in Miami, with the recent arrival of approximately 50,000 Haitians in that area. An oral examination identical in format to the Spanish examination has already been developed for Haitian Creole. The decision to test written Haitian Creole was made on the basis of the strong literacy campaign that has sprung up in the last ten years, although only 10 percent of the population is literate in Haitian Creole. Its orthography has been stabilized only in the last eight years, and the question of Haitian Creole as a legitimate language rather than a dialect existing in a diglossic situation with French has finally been resolved in the past three years—it is now a recognized language holding constitutional status in Haiti (Stewart, 1962; Valdman, 1984). Since there has been only a recently established orthography, and Haitian Creole publications are rare, it was decided not to test written Haitian Creole at this time.

To develop the Haitian Creole certification examination, the AO formed the Haitian Creole Pre-Development and Test Development committees, whose members included two linguists from the Center of Applied Linguistics in Haiti, Professors Yves Dejean and Yves Josef; the Reverend Roger Desir; Professor Marie Racine of the University of the District of Columbia; Albert Valdman, Professor of Linguistics at Indiana University; Jowel Laguerre, M.A., and Professor Bryant Freeman of the

University of Kansas; Vivanne Boulous, Haitian/English interpreter; Glen Smucker, a cultural anthropologist; and Dr. Linda Haughton, Spanish/English federally certified interpreter. These specialists were instrumental in carrying out the task of developing an oral performance examination identical to the one produced for English. Because there is a heavy French influence in Haitian, and literacy, when it occurs, is in French, the pre-development team was faced first with determining which languages to test.

At the pre-development meeting held in Washington, D.C., it was decided that only Haitian Creole would be tested and not French, even though some Haitians who are extremely well educated may require a French interpreter. The Haitian Creole Pre-Development Committee concluded that because 90 percent of the Haitian population speaks Haitian Creole, and only 10 percent of the population speaks French, the 90 percent who have no other language to rely on for communication should be served. Furthermore, most French speakers of Haiti are believed to have a working command of Haitian Creole.

The test development team had to take into consideration certain cultural and linguistic issues, the most important being the Haitians' lack of identifiable legal-judicial understanding. While it might be assumed that the Napoleonic Code would permeate the understanding of legal-judicial procedure in a French-speaking country, the political situation in Haiti has made most judicial-legal concepts inaccessible to the majority of its citizens. Both rural and urban Haitians' concept of the law is often quite limited, and the Haitian legal system is quite different from that of the United States. It is rare that any of these concepts are represented by a word or phrase. The word "jury," although derived from French, does not have an equivalent in Haitian Creole. The term may be borrowed intact from English, but it is not understood unless it is paraphrased as "a group of people who judge you." It was therefore concluded that the scoring criteria would measure how resourceful a Haitian-Creole interpreter was in rendering these commonly used legal terms in a culturally understandable way to Haitians.

The oral examination in Haitian Creole consists of consecutive and simultaneous interpretation and sight translation from English into Haitian Creole and Haitian Creole into English. In addition, candidates must first pass a written English examination in order to qualify for the oral. The first Haitian Creole FCICE was administered in the fall of 1991; a total of four Haitian Creole interpreters have been certified as of this date.

11. Implications

The documented high reliability of the FCICE attests to the careful and stringent development procedures that have guided the certification process. However, the 4-percent certification rate is disturbing to many, and rather than attributing the reasons for this low rate of certification to the unavailability of education, training, and language and interpreting programs for interested examination candidates, some interpreters and/or members of the general public have leveled criticism against the examination itself. Of course this "there's something wrong with the test" attitude does nothing but exacerbate the anxiety of interpreters who have not been able to satisfy the performance requirement on this examination. Sensationalist attitudes such as that recently reflected in a popular journal (Sanders, 1989) about the fact that "only 308 have passed the rigorous Spanish-only federal certification process—a cadre far too small to handle the 43,000 annual requests for interpreters in 60 languages" (p. 25), typifies the superficial knowledge many uninformed critics have of this demanding examination. This *Time* article implied that perhaps the standards should be changed so that more of the need can be met. Yet the underlying reasons for this lack of proficient interpreters are rarely examined and insightful questions, such as the following, are seldom, if ever, asked:

> Why is it that in a country in which Spanish-speakers are the largest language minority, it is difficult to find a cadre of persons proficient enough in Spanish to pass the Federal Certification Examination?

> Why is it that the federal government does not institute an official training program to cultivate or develop a pool of persons who could pass the examination?

The fact that several thousand individuals over the past nine years have unsuccessfully attempted to achieve federal certification suggests that the Spanish/English bilingual population in United States has not been encouraged to develop its language through formal education and study. Bilingual education is, at best, a controversial subject, and, even when it is supported, maintenance of the foreign language is not encouraged. Shortages of qualified and minimally competent interpreters to serve both the State Department and the federal and state courts are blamed on allegedly faulty testing devices rather than on the attitudes toward language and language learning we have fostered in our society (see Chapter 38, Section 1.3).

Many of the candidates who attempted the Federal Certification Examination are those who have been raised in bilingual homes, but who have never had an opportunity to receive formal education or training in Spanish. Therefore, they possess a "home" variety of the language, not expanded or developed to include other registers and semantic domains. There are also a number of examinees who have studied and learned Spanish in secondary and post-secondary schools, and some in graduate school. However, their learning has been confined to very narrow domains of language—the formal, frozen registers—with limited social interaction and, therefore, limited exposure to informal, colloquial Spanish and occupational and professional argot, jargon, and slang. They are the products of undergraduate and graduate Spanish language programs that teach only one variety of language—the written, formal, and frozen variety of literary texts. As has been the case for at least two decades, foreign language programs are lacking in vitality; their focus is the teaching of a great literary tradition and not the language as it currently exists in both spoken and written form. Students are not trained to "produce" language orally, nor are they necessarily knowledgeable in the linguistic aspects of language, such as register, for instance. These deficits in the United States educational system are the true obstacles.

A number of individuals who have failed the examination contend that interpreters who have been certified are trying to restrict entrance into a "limited society." Of course, familiarity with the objective scoring process of the oral examination makes it clear that it is virtually impossible to bias the assessment; the objective scoring mechanism and a three-person, interdisciplinary rating panel guarantees against this occurrence. An appropriate and inappropriate range of translation equivalents is pre-determined—the candidate's performance is measured against this standard. Also, raters are instructed to accept any rendition that conserves meaning but which may not appear on the equivalent list. The number of units a candidate renders appropriately or inappropriately is computed, and it is this score, in conjunction with the subjective assessment, which determines passage.

Some candidates have complained that the written examination is not content specific. These candidates object to this aspect of the examination, even though the written examination announces itself to be a test of general language proficiency in English and Spanish at the college level. It is also important to realize that the fourteenth grade level language standard is, in fact, the average of the range of language spoken by judges, attorneys, experts, and witnesses. Some of the misperceptions about court interpreting derive from the notion that it is a vocation and not a profession, that knowing some legal language and legal jargon may qualify one to interpret all of the intellectually and linguistically complex ideas that surround a legal issue.

The rigor of this bifurcated examination is based on the legal requirements of the court as delineated above. The Federal Certification Examination is merely an extension of those rudimentary performance standards that judges have identified as essential to the work of an interpreter and to the administration of justice. A certification examination does what it must do by definition: it certifies that a person can adequately perform a given set of tasks at a minimum prescribed level of competency. It ensures that any judge, federal or state, can rely on the ability of a Spanish/English interpreter whose written and oral performance has been objectively scrutinized by FCICE examiners.

Although education and training would be effective in helping candidates develop proficiency, this issue is rarely addressed. Candidates who have come extremely close to passing the Federal Court Interpreter Certification Examination would obviously benefit from training. Those who are likely to benefit from training include: (1) those who have taken the examination and are in a particularly high band of performance; (2) those who have been working for the courts on a per diem basis for a number of years and are close to passing; and (3) those who are in certain high-need areas.

One very positive consequence of the FCICE is that it has enhanced the prestige of the court interpreting profession by acknowledging the extreme difficulty of the tasks involved. Not only has the legal profession begun to recognize the rigors of court interpreting (Arjona, 1983), but court interpreters themselves have become more aware of the exigencies of their profession. As a result, they have developed a more professional attitude toward their work and, more importantly, they have made a greater effort toward self-improvement. Federal certification has come to be regarded as a pinnacle of achievement for court interpreters, and has garnered international acclaim for its objective testing format in a profession that was heretofore evaluated wholly on a subjective basis. Consequently, even as some complain about the exacting requirements for certification, court interpreters strive to attain that objective, not only because of the financial incentives, but also for reasons of prestige. In response to interpreters' increased demand for training to prepare for the FCICE, established court interpreting programs such as that of the Monterey Institute of International Studies have expanded their offerings, and workshops and courses geared to the FCICE have begun to proliferate throughout the ation. Even if all of these interpreters are not ultimately successful in passing the exam, the entire profession, the judicial system, and those who receive interpreting services will benefit from the interpreters' improved skills and knowledge.

12. Conclusion

In conclusion, the FCICE is the first interpreter qualification instrument to take into account all of the complexities of the tasks involved in court interpreting. Because of the examination, the awareness of the difficulty and importance of the court interpreter's role in the criminal justice system has been heightened, not just among judges, attorneys, and court administrators, but also among court interpreters themselves. The result has been a trend toward improved working conditions and continuing education for court interpreters.

Moreover, the FCICE has proven to be a highly reliable and valid instrument that has been designed and administered in accordance with rigorous scientific standards of objectivity and has performed consistently over many years. It has set a standard for other examinations administered at other levels of court and in other languages. Due in large part to this examination, the federal courts have been assured a cadre of court interpreters known to possess the skills and knowledge that will enable them to provide the highest quality of language services, and thereby ensure that justice is imparted to all on an equal basis, regardless of the language they speak. Moreover, the model established for Spanish-English has now been validly promulgated, after adapting it to the specific needs of the languages, to both Navajo and Haitian Creole.

Chapter 37

State Certification

As described in Unit 1, Chapter 6, of this volume, in the 60s and 70s the growing recognition of the problems faced by linguistic minorities in the criminal justice system encouraged several state legislatures to pass measures mandating the certification and use of interpreters for non-English speakers in legal proceedings. This chapter presents an overview of the procedures to qualify interpreters in three states—California, New Mexico, and New Jersey, and Washington—pursuant to legislative measures and efforts. New York, which also regulates court interpreters through administrative means, will also be discussed. Appendix E (Directory of Professional Organizations and Certifying Bodies) presents a list of professional organizations and government bodies that certify or test interpreters.

California was the first state to offer certification, beginning at the county level in 1977 and then on a state-wide basis beginning in 1979. Although New Mexico was the first state to enact a constitutional amendment on the issue in 1911, it did not pass a statute mandating certification of interpreters until 1985. Actual certification testing in New Mexico was not offered until July of 1986. California also recognized the right to an interpreter and passed a constitutional amendment to that effect in 1974 (California Constitution, article 1, section 7).

Pursuant to Assembly Bill 2400 (1978), the Judicial Council of California was instructed to "establish standards for the professional conduct of interpreters, for determining the need for an interpreter, for ensuring the interpreter's understanding of court terminology and procedures, and for periodically reviewing the interpreter's skills" (Probasco & McDonald, 1979, p. 1). Accordingly, the California State Personnel Board developed a certification process consisting of a written and oral examination.

1. California

1.1. History of Examination Administration

The California interpreter certification examinations were first administered in 1979 by Cooperative Personnel Services (CPS) under contract to the California State Personnel Board. The two-phase examination consisted of a written component, which was intended to screen out candidates who did not possess minimum language competence, and an oral component. The written component tested candidates' knowledge of Spanish and English grammar and usage, reading comprehension, legal terminology, and their understanding of the ethical issues involved in court interpretation. Candidates who passed the written component went on to take the oral examination, which tested their mastery of sight translation, consecutive interpretation, and/or simultaneous interpretation, depending on the type of certification sought. The law was interpreted to mean that two different types of certification were required: court interpreter certification and administrative hearing interpreter certification. Court interpreter certification is required for interpreters who appear in court in criminal matters.

Administrative hearing certification is required in California for interpreters who appear at hearings conducted by the various administrative agencies, such as the Department of Motor Vehicles, Workmen's Compensation Appeals Board, and the Unemployment Insurance Appeals Board, among others. For reasons which are unclear, it was decided that administrative hearing interpreters did not need to be able to interpret simultaneously, even though simultaneous interpretation is in fact performed in these hearings.

The administrative hearing certification examination required passage of the written exam, sight translation, and consecutive interpretation portions of the oral exam. The Court Interpreter Certification Examination required passage of all of these components plus the simultaneous interpretation portion. These components will be discussed in more detail in Section 1.3 of this chapter.

Because of the overwhelming demand for Spanish interpreters in the state courts, it was the first language tested. Soon thereafter, the administrative hearing certification exam was also developed for Arabic, Cantonese, Japanese, Korean, Portuguese, Tagalog, and Vietnamese, those being the languages most in demand determined by the State Personnel Board. Because the State Personnel Board found that these languages were used primarily in administrative hearings rather than criminal court proceedings, no court interpreter certification exam was developed for them. Thus, the only language for which court interpreter certification was required for interpreters appearing in criminal matters was Spanish. In practice, some courts required administrative hearing certification for interpreters in the other seven languages, but it was not legally mandated.

According to Veale (1989), the written and oral examinations for Arabic, Cantonese, Japanese, Korean, Portuguese, Tagalog, and Vietnamese were based on translations of the Spanish examinations. These translations were reviewed by language specialists, who also served as examiners as well, since no interpreters could be used as examiners until they themselves had been certified.

From 1979 to 1983, the Spanish examinations were administered once a year, while the frequency of the exams in the other languages fluctuated according to the number of applications submitted by candidates and the availability of examiners in each language. The practical result was very infrequent administration of the examinations in these seven languages. In 1983, in response to the pressure of increased demand for certified interpreters in the Spanish language, CPS began to offer that examination more frequently. The Spanish certification exams are now offered once a month in Los Angeles, where demand is greatest, and several times a year in other California cities on an as-needed basis (A. McMorine, personal communication, August 15, 1989).

In addition, CPS decided to eliminate the written portion of the certification examinations in 1988. Not only did the written component lengthen the process and reduce the frequency of examination administration, but it failed to serve the purpose for which it had been designed: to screen out candidates who did not meet a minimum standard of language competency. The pass rate was so high it became clear that the examination was not discriminating well between able and less able candidates.

1.1.1. Administrative Hearings

In 1988, Assembly Bill 1386 mandated that court interpreter certification be extended to the seven languages that had previously been limited to administrative hearing certification. Consequently, the appropriate exam was developed and administered, again using the Spanish exam as a point of departure. As with the administrative hearing certification examination, the frequency of administration of this examination varies with the number of applications received. In the case of Portuguese, for example, no candidates applied at all, so that examination was not administered in the first round (Veale, 1989).

1.2. The Original Examination

The California interpreter certification examinations were originally constructed on the basis of contributions from various sources, including bilingual attorneys and educators. Because of the methodology employed in the construction of the test, the first examinations were flawed. The written portion of the examination contained three types of errors: (1) content (serious grammatical and stylistic mistakes), (2) production (typographical errors), and (3) test design (for example, some items had more than one correct answer while others had no correct answer at all). The written exam gave no evidence of having been piloted or field tested to reveal and correct these major errors before actual administration. Standard testing procedures were ignored in the administration of the oral exam as well. Due to the lack of objective performance standards and criteria, each administration of the examination was unique. For example, the simultaneous test was administered live, which meant that the speed and intonation varied each time the text was read. Examiners were not given objective criteria to apply, so some candidates were judged more leniently than others. Thus, interpreters throughout the state were not measured against the same yardstick, and there was no valid, objective way of measuring competency.

From 1979 to 1983, according to Ann McMorine, program manager of the CPS Interpreter Program, the pass rate was 35 to 50 percent for the court interpreter certification examination. McMorine believes that performance standards were set "unrealistically low," and speculates that perhaps many interpreters certified during that period might not pass today (personal communication, August 15, 1989). She also suggests that a lack of psychometric expertise and a misunderstanding of the definition of "**minimal competency**" may have led the California State Personnel Board to establish standards that were not sufficiently rigorous. Minimal competency in the field of testing and measurement refers to those skills a person must possess in order to perform a task competently, at a pre-determined baseline. Therefore, the first four years of testing may have proved to be both unreliable and invalid according to widely accepted testing standards.

After the first administration of the Spanish examinations in 1979, numerous complaints about the deficiencies were lodged (see Unit 1, Chapter 6). In response to such criticism, CPS gradually improved the design and administration of the examinations. One of the first steps it took was to consult with professional court interpreters, now certified and therefore eligible to participate in test development, to make the examinations more relevant to the actual demands of court interpreting. CPS also provided rater training for its examiners (Veale, 1989), and began to apply more demanding and task-oriented standards for passing the exams.

1.3. Present Certification Examinations

In their present form, the California interpreter certification examinations require candidates to demonstrate minimal competency in the following knowledge areas, skills, and abilities:

(1) Extensive knowledge of legal and technical terminology.
(2) Accurate translation without adding, deleting, paraphrasing, or changing the meaning of the examination material.
(3) Correct use of grammar and syntax.
(4) Retention and recall of conversation with little or no need to have information repeated.
(5) Performance of oral translation without [lengthy] hesitation. (See Cooperative Personnel Services, 1987, p. 1)

The oral portion of the court interpreter certification examination consists of three parts: (1) simultaneous interpretation, (2) consecutive interpretation, and (3) sight translation. The oral portion of the administrative hearing certification examination contains two parts: (1) consecutive interpretation and (2) sight translation. Because the two examinations overlap, if a candidate applies for both types of certification, he or she is given the court interpreter certification exam. If successful in all three portions, the candidate is awarded both certifications; if the simultaneous portion is failed, then the candidate is awarded administrative hearing certification. This procedure has been questioned because the need for simultaneous interpretation in administrative hearings has been recognized. New testing procedures are under review. If the candidate fails the sight translation and/or consecutive interpretation portions, the candidate is not certified for any setting. To repeat the examination, the candidate must retake all three parts, not just the portion previously failed.

The simultaneous portion consists of a three-minute tape recorded at a speed of 140 words per minute. Texts for this section are typically arraignments, motions, or code sections (A. McMorine, personal communication, August 15, 1989). The candidate must demonstrate an ability to keep pace with the speaker and interpret every element of meaning, without omitting or editing, and without altering the register or level of language.

The consecutive component consists of a simulated examination of a witness by an attorney. This portion of the examination is ten to fifteen minutes long. The question-answer exchange is read from a script by members of the rating panel. In this portion of the examination, the candidate is required to demonstrate an ability to retain typical questions and answers without having to interrupt the speaker. The candidate may take notes and may ask for a limited number of repetitions. As in the simultaneous portion, the candidate must not omit or edit any information, and must remain true to the style and tone of the source language message.

The sight translation portion of the examination consists of a document in English that must be translated into the target language, usually a document that one might encounter in a legal proceeding, such as an affidavit, explanation of rights, or police report, and a document in the other language to be sight translated into English, generally a legal document such as a birth certificate, will, or divorce decree. The documents are approximately 110 to 140 words in length. In each case, the candidate is given a few moments to look over the document, and then is expected to provide an oral interpretation of its content. There is no specified time limit for completion of the sight translation component.

All portions of the oral examination are tape recorded, and candidates who are dissatisfied with the results of their examination may file appeals for review by a review committee. At least twenty Spanish-examination appeals per month are reviewed, and approximately 1 percent are adjudicated in favor of the appellant (A. McMorine, personal communication, August 15, 1989). The examination is rated by a panel of two interpreters and one representative of CPS, using a rating form developed by CPS. The scoring system is subjective and has no objective scoring units.

1.4. Remaining Problems

The California certification examination developers have had difficulty calibrating both the complexity level of the examination and the cut-off score. This may be a direct result of never having conducted a task analysis that included a linguistic study of the level of courtroom language required in state courts or administrative hearings. It might also be a result of not having worked with an interdisciplinary panel of experts, including court interpreters, language specialists, and testing experts. The combined knowledge of these experts and their research may have resulted in valid performance standards.

Currently, the pass rate is 10 to 13 percent for the Spanish court interpreter examination and 12 to 16 percent for the Spanish administrative hearing examination (A. McMorine, personal communication, August 15, 1989). This is an indication that the performance standards are beginning to reflect the demanding nature of the task. The pass rates for the other languages, reported after the first administration of the court interpreter certification examination in 1988, are indicated in Table 1 (Veale, 1989).

1.5. Los Angeles Superior Court Certification

Within the state of California, even after the state-wide certification program was implemented, many local courts recognized that they had special needs that were not being met by the state program. In particular, the courts wanted to be certain that their interpreters were able to communicate effectively with local subgroups of Spanish speakers whose language usage varied because of their countries of origin or occupations. As a result, individual courts began requiring interpreters to pass a separate exam in addition to the state certification examinations. These individual exams emphasized local usage and the special problems encountered in cases requiring interpreters. For example, the Monterey County exam contains a great deal of agricultural terminology and reflects the problems inherent in interpreting for unsophisticated farmworkers, while the Los Angeles County exam emphasizes drug and weapon terminology, which are more likely to be encountered in the criminal cases in an urban setting.

The Los Angeles Superior Court was a pioneer in the testing and training of court interpreters. Even before Assembly Bill 2400 was passed in 1978, the Los Angeles Superior Court was not only administering its own test to assure minimum competence of court interpreters, but also providing training to upgrade the skills of the interpreters it employed. In 1977, the Los Angeles Superior Court replaced its traditional translation examination with an interpreter performance test. It recognized that although the ability to translate is related to the ability to interpret, the two are distinctly different processes.

Throughout the debate and preparation of the legislation in the State Assembly, Los Angeles Superior Court interpreters—through their professional organization, the California Court Interpreters Association, and under the auspices of the superior court itself—played a key role in ensuring that the bill's language reflected the demands of court interpretation. Simultaneously, the Los Angeles Superior Court continued to refine its own testing process to make sure it could count on a corps of qualified professionals to meet its ever-growing language services needs. Indeed, until the state certification exams were upgraded in the mid-80s, the Los Angeles Superior Court examination was a more accurate reflection of the exigencies of court interpretation and thus more rigorous; consequently, the pass rate was lower than that of state examinations.

At present, the Los Angeles Superior Court has an extensive testing and training program designed to meet its language services needs. Interpreter candidates representing over fifty languages are given a comprehensive written examination in English (at the level of the Graduate Record Examinations) and are required to translate a legal document from English into the other language and vice versa. Those who pass that portion of the examination are then given the oral component, which tests their knowledge of legal terminology, their mastery of sight translation, and consecutive and simultaneous interpretation. In the case of Spanish, the rating panel is present in person to administer the oral examination. In the case of the other languages,

Table 1
Pass Rates for the California Court Interpreter Certification Exam: Languages Other Than Spanish

Language	Took Exam	Passed Admin.	%	Passed Court	%
Arabic	13	—	—	3	20
Cantonese	30	12	40	6	20
Japanese	15	—	—	—	0
Korean	23	8	34	3	13
Portuguese	0	—	—	—	—
Tagalog	8	3	37	1	12
Vietnamese	45	9	20	13	29

which are tested on an as-needed basis, tape recordings of the candidate's performance are sent to experts throughout the country who have agreed to serve as raters. In the case of very infrequently encountered languages for which no experts can be found to serve as raters, the candidates take only the written English examination.

In addition, all interpreters are required to attend a one-day orientation and training session. At this session, the interpreters are introduced to the criminal justice system and are oriented as to the role of the interpreter within that context. They are also given training in the techniques of sight translation and simultaneous and consecutive interpretation, and are provided with terminology glossaries.

According to Hanne Mintz, linguistics specialist of the Los Angeles Superior Court, "in the past five years the number of per-diem interpreters working for the Los Angeles Superior Court has grown from approximately 180 to 257 in the Spanish language and from 155 to 196 in other languages" (Mikkelson, 1989b, p. 5). Even so, the demand for certified interpreters has outstripped the supply because of the astronomical rise in the number of court appearances requiring interpreters. As a result, the Los Angeles Superior Court has proposed an internship program aimed at providing in-service training for interpreters and improving their skills so that they will be able to pass the certification exams. Although this program has been challenged on the grounds that the use of non-certified interns violates the provisions of Assembly Bill 2400, it represents one solution to the problem of low pass rates resulting from the necessary modification of certification examinations to reflect the real demands of court interpreting.

2. New Mexico

Upon passage of the Court Interpreters Act of 1985, H.B. 343, a certification process in New Mexico was developed that included a written examination and an oral performance test. The written examination measures knowledge of the New Mexico judicial system and rules and standards for interpreter conduct.

According to Valdés and Wilcox (1986), interpreters are expected to demonstrate a knowledge of:

(a) general guidelines for using interpreters in New Mexico;

(b) rules and standards which govern the behavior of interpreters;

(c) basic legal concepts covered in *The Use of Court Interpreters in New Mexico: A Handbook for Judges, Attorneys, and Interpreters* (Valdés & Wilcox, 1986);

(d) legal terminology and general vocabulary.

The written examination, for which a fee is charged, has a multiple-choice format. It is administered by the Administrative Office of the New Mexico Courts and the Testing Center of the University of New Mexico.

Persons who pass the written examination are eligible for the oral interpreting examination. The oral examination format varies for three testing populations: (1) interpreters for the hearing impaired, (2) interpreters for New Mexican Indian languages, and (3) Spanish interpreters.

2.1. Interpreters for New Mexican Indian Languages

An outstanding feature of the New Mexico certification bill is the attention paid to the traditional Indian cultures of the state. According to Valdés and Wilcox (1986), interpreting examinations for Indian languages has been delegated to designated tribal boards and committees. Interpreters must demonstrate "... their ability to interpret from the New Mexican Indian language to English and vice versa, within the legal context" (Valdés & Wilcox, 1986, p. 28).

Those persons who successfully demonstrate competence to the tribal boards and are recommended by them will be certified by the state of New Mexico. This practice by New Mexico is certainly understandable because of the singular ability of the tribal boards to test language proficiency. However, no mention is made of any collaboration between the state of New Mexico and the tribal boards to guarantee uniform performance standards and to establish a basic agreement as to the quality of judicial interpretation that must be assessed. A more uniform approach to testing Indian languages should be considered, in order to ensure that a language barrier is not perpetuated by the certifying agency itself. Tribal boards and the state of New Mexico could collaborate and create certification examinations that respect both the Native American language and culture and the complexities of the language of the courtroom.

2.2. Oral Examination for Spanish Interpreters

Spanish interpreters must demonstrate their "... capacity to interpret in both the simultaneous and consecutive modes fluently and accurately" (Valdés & Wilcox, 1986, p. 29). The following elements are assessed as a part of the global interpretation:

(a) Precision and comprehensiveness of vocabulary, and

(b) Familiarity with various styles and levels of language, including New Mexican Spanish, as well as other major varieties of Spanish, such as general Mexican Spanish and Cuban.

The Spanish-English oral performance test consists of three parts:

(a) *Sight translation*: This section includes one Spanish text to be translated into English and one English text to be translated into Spanish. These texts are typically short simulated police reports or letters attesting to character.

(b) *Simultaneous interpretation*: This portion is a five-minute pre-recorded opening statement or closing statement of an attorney, to be rendered simultaneously by the interpreter.

(c) *Consecutive interpretation*: This part consists of a five-minute simulation of an examination of a Spanish-speaking witness by an attorney.

The primary criterion on which performance is assessed is whether or not the candidate has distorted the meaning of the elements of a passage. No objective scoring mechanism has been devised; however, raters are instructed to assess how well candidates render highly technical and legal terms as they listen to the rendition of the entire passage. The oral examination is rated by a panel of three examiners who apply a subjective scoring scale of 1 to 5. A candidate's final score is computed by averaging the scores of the raters.

Since 1986, New Mexico has tested approximately seventy-five persons. One-third of those who have taken the certification examination have passed. Only one version of the New Mexico examination has been developed (S. Adelo, personal communication, August 24, 1989). No validity or reliability studies have been conducted. In addition, it is unclear how performance standards were reached and what they represent. Therefore, the certification standards and procedure may not guarantee that interpreters have either the language or interpreting capability required to ensure due process to limited- and non-English-speaking persons in New Mexico.

3. New York

The demographics of New York has necessitated the use of interpreters in the courts since the 1940s; however, little recognition of their professional status or importance to the fair administration of justice had been granted until 1980, when a civil service job analysis was conducted. Paradoxically, this civil service approach has rendered the qualifying examination process almost useless. That New York has not taken the lead in developing court interpretation policy is surprising, since no other state has had to accommodate as many diverse languages through the years.

Little or no attention has been paid to the need for quality interpretation. No movement toward legislation or certification procedures is reported, and the mechanism employed to qualify persons for the position of interpreter is questionable in its design and performance standards. New York State does offer a civil service examination for court interpreters, but the performance standards do not reflect the complexity of the multiple tasks inherent in interpreting. Consequently, the examination does not appear to discriminate between competent and incompetent interpreters (D. Fellmeth, personal communication, August 15, 1989; R. Olivera, personal communication, August 17, 1989). New York has historically offered a civil service exam that interpreters were required to pass; in 1980, examinations specifically for the position of court interpreter were developed for the New York State Unified Court System.

3.1. Written and Oral Certification Examination

The New York interpreting examination consists of two parts, a written and an oral. The written examination tests knowledge of legal procedure and language through a multiple-choice format. A portion of the written examination is a pre-recorded set of sentences for which the candidate must choose appropriate endings. This paper-and-pencil test assesses a mixture of listening comprehension and syntactic, semantic, and other aspects of language proficiency in both Spanish and English (D. Fellmeth, personal communication, August 15, 1989). Once an examinee passes the written examination, he or she becomes eligible for the oral. The oral examination consists of two parts:

(a) *Sight translation*: This portion consists of two sight translations, one from English into Spanish and another from Spanish into English. It is generally 100-150 words in length, and the English text is a highly formal and frozen legal passage. The Spanish text is a simulated police report or deposition written in colloquial Spanish. This exercise is not timed, but the raters may cut off the candidate if they believe that the rendering is too slow and labored.

(b) *Cross-examination*: This section of the examination is a videotaped reading of prepared scripts involving the examination of two Spanish-speaking witnesses by an attorney. This exercise takes approximately fifteen to twenty minutes. The curious aspect of this examination is that interpreters are instructed to render the interpretation either in the consecutive or simultaneous mode. Neither is prescribed; therefore, candidates could elect to do the entire examination in the consecutive mode and never have their ability to interpret in the simultaneous mode scrutinized.

According to one rater, Rosa Olivera, Chief Interpreter of the United States District Court, Eastern District of New York, the speakers' voices on the videotape are distorted because of heavy English accents of the actors reading the Spanish parts (personal communication, August 17, 1989). The questions and responses represent the typical length, but not the complexity, of what is usually heard in the courtroom; for this reason, they do not adequately challenge the skills of the interpreter.

Because it is a civil service examination, it is given as often as necessary to develop a pool of qualified interpreters. Examinees who pass the examination are then placed on a list. As staff openings become available, interpreters are assigned positions, regardless of their performance level on the examination, every three years as of this writing. Pass rates and scores were not available; however, pass rates have decreased significantly since 1980, when the examination became more reflective of actual court interpreting job duties.

3.2. Assessment of Interpreting Performance

The candidate's performance is recorded for assessment by a panel of three interpreters who rate the performance subjectively. The candidate is assessed according to the entire performance. The panel members are asked to make a mental note about items that were missed in the course of the translation and to account for those in the assessment.

3.3. Validity and Reliability of the Civil Service Exam

From a test development and administration perspective—and from the standpoint of justice and equal access—the examination is deficient in many ways. For example, there is no evidence of reliability or validity studies undertaken for the examination. In addition, the performance standards and examination seem inconsistent with the real demands of court interpreting. It is widely accepted that simultaneous and consecutive interpretation are of separate but equal importance, and both must therefore be tested.

Nonetheless, according to David Fellmeth, Senior Interpreter of the New York Superior Court, the Civil Service Commission test developers failed to distinguish between simultaneous and consecutive interpretation, and did not consider either one indicative of interpreting skill (personal communication, August 15, 1989). A test that does not adequately measure competent interpreting performance compromises the due process rights of limited- and non-English speakers. The tragedy is that both courts and defendants depend on the results of a test that bears little resemblance to the actual demands of interpreting in the courts. These testing deficiencies cast doubt on the validity of court interpreting examination in the state of New York.

4. New Jersey

The New Jersey Court Interpreter Testing Program is the product of the intensive work of the New Jersey Supreme Court Task Force on Translation and Interpreting (1985). This task force conducted a comprehensive study of current interpreting needs and practices in New Jersey courts. The data were synthesized into a comprehensive plan, including a language services system for testing and training. The plan was later implemented by the Administrative Office of the New Jersey Courts, Court Interpreting Section. The most significant finding of the task force was that "(83%) of persons who were interpreting in courts did not possess the requisite skills, knowledge and training" (Belliveau, de la Bandera, & Lee, 1988, p. 1). Among their many recommendations to resolve this problem is the appropriation of funds in order to carry out a certification and training program.

4.1. Judicial Mandate to Test Interpreters in the State of New Jersey

On October 28, 1987, pending legislative action on the certification of interpreters, the following directive was issued by the Administrative Office of the Courts of New Jersey:

> Effective October, 1987, for Middlesex/Union County interpreter position: it is the policy of the Judiciary that (1) every applicant for a full-time court interpreting position in the Superior or a Municipal Court must be tested and approved by the Administrative Office of the Courts (AO) before being considered for hiring; and (2) every other new employee anywhere in the Superior Court or a Municipal Court who is expected to interpret for Spanish-speaking litigants must be approved by the AOC before being allowed to interpret. The policy is not retroactive and does not affect existing employees of the courts who are interpreting as of October, 1987, unless a local court administrator wishes to have existing personnel evaluated. (Lee, 1987, p. 2)

4.2. The New Jersey Examination

This policy set into motion the empirical research and development that has culminated in an evaluative tool emulating the Federal Court Interpreter Certification Examination. The *Overview of the Efforts of the Administrative Office of the New Jersey Courts* (Administrative Office of the New Jersey Courts, 1987) offers a comprehensive analysis of the testing process and its major assumptions and conclusions as a result of pilot testing. In addition to offering a comprehensive overview of the New Jersey examination, this publication, along with the *Federal Court Interpreter Certification Manual* (Gonzalez, 1986), can serve as a guide for any federal or state court or agency to implement a certification plan in consultation with experts. The

New Jersey test consists of an oral performance instrument and does not test language proficiency through a written examination, although this addition is contemplated.

4.3. Structure of the Examination

The certification examination is an oral interpreting performance test that consists of three portions:

(a) *Simultaneous interpretation*: This portion is a pre-recorded opening or closing statement recorded at between **125 and 150 words per minute.**

(b) *Consecutive interpretation*: This section involves the simulated examination of a witness by an attorney. Statements are up to **37 words in length.**

(c) *Sight interpretation*: This portion includes two texts, one to be interpreted from English into Spanish, and one from Spanish into English.

The New Jersey interpreter examination is parallel to the federal examination in terms of format, content, and assessment. The exams differ in the performance standards imposed and the derivation of the cut-off score. However, in terms of tasks, the New Jersey test is conceptually similar to the federal exam. The one notable difference in content is the length of sight translation, simultaneous, and consecutive exercises and the number of scoring units. The federal examination is approximately three times the length of the New Jersey examination, and for this reason identifies a greater number of scoring units than does the New Jersey test. Because of these and other elements, the federal exam is a more challenging testing instrument.

Another striking difference between the federal and New Jersey examinations is the assessment standard. The New Jersey examination requires a 70 percent score on both the simultaneous and consecutive portions of the exam and 60 percent on the sight translation portion. In contrast, the federal exam requires an 80 percent score on the examination as a whole. It is the observation of the New Jersey Chief of Court Interpreting, Robert Joe Lee, that minimal competency must be demonstrated in both the simultaneous and consecutive modes (Lee, 1987).

4.4. Results of the Exam

Less than 5 percent of the examinees have passed the New Jersey test. *There Must Be Something Wrong with That Test!* (Belliveau et al., 1988) is a secured publication surveying the preliminary results of this certification test, and offers some explanation of its low pass rates and the fact that no court employee who has taken the test has passed it. This instructive report showed how the use of revealed discrete scoring units made the interpreting examination and scoring process more objective. Because the report also features a list of the inappropriate responses candidates offered for particular phrases, clauses, or words, it is not available to the general public.

The authors identify ten types of scoring units used in the New Jersey exam: "grammar/verbs; false cognates/linguistic interference; general vocabulary; legal/technical/uncommon vocabulary; idioms; register; numbers/names; markers/intensifiers/emphases/precision; embeddings/position; and slang/colloquialisms" (Belliveau et al., 1988, p. 7). The examination provides for a critical range (see Chapter 38 of this unit). Thus, candidates who received a failing score of 60 percent on the entire test and 50 percent on each of the parts of the test were permitted to be hired because they demonstrated potential. As of August 1988, 102 persons had taken the examination and 5 persons had passed. The average candidate interpreted about 41 percent of all scoring units correctly.

4.5. New Jersey as a State Model

New Jersey is to be admired for the interest it has shown in developing an examination with performance standards that meet the demands of its courts' needs. State officials have demonstrated concern for the quality of the administration of justice to limited- and non-English-speaking persons and for protecting the integrity of its legal system. In a state where interpreting services were of reportedly low quality and where court interpreters enjoyed little if any status for their important role in the judicial process, this extensive program of certification and training was imperative. Realistic performance standards grounded in the complex demands of the courtroom can be achieved with the aid of the training component included in this comprehensive approach. Table 2 illustrates both differences and similarities between these particular state examinations and the Federal Interpreter Certification Examination (Gonzalez, 1988, pp. 30-31).

What are the implications for those states that have created certification programs that cannot validly ensure interpreter competency, and for states that have not initiated any formal policy to guarantee to the court that the language services being rendered are of the quality required by the judicial process? State courts must first address the question: Are the interpreters in this court performing at the level of competency required to sufficiently guarantee due process? For states with certification examinations in place, an important question remains: Is the examination administered in this state validly meeting the needs of the state's language minorities? If the standards of the examination are based on unverified supposition rather than actual linguistic data, the answer is probably no. For those states considering certification, an in-depth language and interpreting task analysis is required prior to instituting any program.

Table 2
Analysis of Performance Standards of Federal and State Interpreter Examinations

	Federal	California*	New Mexico	New York	New Jersey	Washington State
Needs assessment & linguistic analysis	Yes	Needs Only	Needs Only	Needs Only	Needs Only	Yes
Content exam	No	No	Yes	No	Yes	Yes
Written language exam	Yes	No	No	No	No	Yes
Oral task performance	Yes	Yes	Yes	Yes	Yes	Yes
Multi-disciplinary examiners	Yes	Yes	Yes	Yes	No	No
Multi-disciplinary development teams	Yes	No	No	No	Yes	No

*Does not include county examinations.

A lesson learned from the federal certification experience is that a quality certification program that tests the correct level of complexity brings about the desired effects, effects that come about whether candidates eventually become certified or not. Specifically, interpreters begin to set goals for themselves, using the examination as a standard, and they embark on formal language and interpreting improvement programs, either through formal instruction or self-education. This is the real benefit to interpreters and to the courts: dedication to achieving a higher standard.

For states that wish to re-address the certification issue, it is also important to remember that improving language services depends not only on a quality examination, but also on in-service, pre-service, or post-certification educational programs.

5. Washington State

Shortly after the enabling court interpreter legislation was passed in 1989, the state of Washington embarked on the development of an interpreter certification process. The State of Washington Task Force on Court Interpreting specified that a panel of court interpreting and test development experts be assembled to develop the certification process and that the examinations assess actual interpreting performance in addition to language proficiency and other knowledge. A team of court interpreters working in conjunction with Ms. Joanne Moore, J.D., administrative head of the program, developed a two-part Spanish-English certification examination patterned after the federal certification examination. Although the test development team was not itself interdisciplinary, testing specialists were consulted in the process of development and administration and the validity of the examination was checked by an interpreting examination expert. A complexity analysis was conducted on randomly selected Washington state court transcripts of interpreted cases in order to determine performance standards and content for the two examinations.

5.1. The Written Examination

The written examination is an indirect test of Spanish and English language proficiency patterned after the federal examination in format and content and thus tests depth and breadth of vocabulary, reading comprehension, and usage. One major difference between the state of Washington test and the federal certification examination is the addition in the Washington examination of a content portion to test potential interpreters' knowledge of legal terminology, terms of art, and knowledge of legal procedure. An analysis of the pass rates reported after the initial administration of the Spanish-English written examination—approximately 50 percent—tends to reveal that the performance standards of the written may have been underestimated for the level of language proficiency required in Spanish and English.

5.2. The Oral Examination

However, the oral examination more adequately captures the rigors of interpreting in the judicial setting in terms of its content, format, and scoring methodology. Attempts to ensure rater reliability and uniformity in administration were made by developing uniform test administration procedures, by training raters, and by standardizing the scoring methodology of objective items and the global decision-making for the subjective assessment. As of this writing, the report on final certification numbers in the state of Washington has not yet been disclosed.

The state of Washington's efforts in developing valid, reliable instruments and performance criteria are impressive as were their efforts in orienting candidates to court interpreting modes to be tested. Weekend workshops sponsored by the Court Interpreter Task Force were conducted by court interpreting specialists.

5.3. Certification of Asian Languages

Under current legislation, the state of Washington must also certify Asian languages, and plans for these certification instruments are now under development. It has not been determined whether or not the written form of these Asian languages will be tested or whether only a performance test of interpreting will be developed and administered.

6. Certification Model for States

States in the process of establishing or revamping a certification program would be well advised to take advantage of the research and development model for the federal certification examination, which is widely considered a state-of-the-art interpreting examination. Gonzalez (1988) in *The Federal Court Interpreter Certification Examination: A Model for State Courts* offers helpful guidelines for state courts and other agencies:

(1) Base certification examinations on a needs assessment/task analysis. The task analysis should include the following questions: What level of language competency is required? What are the tasks interpreters must perform? To set the federal standards for certification, language research and task analyses were conducted. Studies revealed that college-level proficiency in both languages and a precise knowledge of informal to formal, general, and technical vocabulary were required, this in addition to the simultaneous, consecutive, and sight translation modes of interpretation.

(2) Set standards high enough to command the expected and necessary performance. Rather than lowering test standards, encourage individuals to upgrade their skills in order to meet the high standards. Compromising standards only encourages incompetence.

(3) Form multi-disciplinary teams of practicing court interpreters, conference interpreters, and language specialists to conduct initial analyses, develop examinations, set standards, and evaluate candidates. Tests must also incorporate the concerns and expectations of judges and other court personnel.

(4) Develop a language proficiency and performance test of interpreting skills—not a written translation test.

(5) Develop, pilot, validate, and administer examinations according to standard testing guidelines.

(6) Evaluate the performance of candidates by utilizing qualified experts, i.e., conference interpreters, Federally Certified Court Interpreters, Federal Interpreters

who are "otherwise qualified," and language specialists. Candidate performance should not be judged by judges, attorneys, or other interested parties, but by a combination of interpreters and out-of-field specialists.

(7) Implement a certification system which includes training and testing after standards are determined. For some individuals a tri-partite system may be called for which includes training, supervised practice, and testing or any combination thereof to produce the needed qualified court interpreter personnel for state court systems. (pp. 28-29)

It is extremely important for interpreting and language proficiency examinations to reflect the appropriate interpreting modes, requisite language proficiency, and sociolinguistic context of a particular interpreting setting, i.e., a state court, an administrative agency, or a police department.

Unit 9

Conclusion

Chapter 38

A Look to the Future

This volume has attempted to foster an awareness of the critical role that the court interpreter plays in providing limited- and non-English speakers the ability to participate in their own defense. It has explicated the standard of "legal equivalence" (Gonzalez, 1989c) and traced the legal and social forces that have forged the role of the court interpreter. Emanating from the United States Constitution's standard of fairness, the court interpreter has become an essential player in the judicial process. Only by continuing to open the doors to education, social services, and justice can we look forward to a prosperous and productive society in which each person, regardless of English language ability, may participate. Interpreters, in particular, court interpreters, are a significant resource in accomplishing this goal. This chapter is devoted to examining new developments and trends that will have an impact on court interpreting in the future. Some difficult legal and professional problems are considered, as well as the critical need for the extension of certified interpreters to other agencies at both the state and federal level.

1. Legal Issues

The great increase of limited- and non-English speakers in the criminal justice system and the concomitant demand for court interpreters has led to a number of unforeseen issues being resolved on an *ad hoc* basis by individual courts throughout the country. Some solutions have been imposed by court decisions, others by legislative measure. In the interest of guaranteeing uniform justice throughout the country, it is important that these issues be debated and resolved. This section presents the most significant of these issues and offers recommendations.

1.1. Multiple-Defendant Cases

Multiple-defendant cases are not a new development in the legal system, nor are they an unusual occurrence. Yet, the dramatic growth in drug-related crimes, not only possession but conspiracy charges of all types, has increased the incidence of multiple-defendant cases heard in court. All too often, several if not all of the defendants involved in such cases require an interpreter. Many courts, either for reasons of economy or simply due to the unavailability of a sufficient number of interpreters, have attempted to proceed with a single interpreter for a large number of defendants— with unsatisfactory results.

In order to solve the practical problem of numerous voices, California courts are exploring the benefits of closed-circuit wireless systems for simultaneous interpretation. For a detailed description of the wireless system and its use, see Unit 4, Chapter 17, and Unit 7, Chapter 33.

1.2. Proceedings Interpreters and Prosecution Interpreters

As the use of interpreters increases in United States courtrooms, a widespread scrutiny of customary practices will lead to innovations in protocol. Historically, much has been made of the neutrality or impartiality of the court interpreter. The practice of allowing a single court interpreter to provide services for both sides during a proceeding has been common practice. However, this policy is changing. Courts have begun to recognize that there is a possible conflict of interest on the part of interpreters who have worked with the defense and who then are called upon to interpret for the prosecution's witness or vice versa. Accordingly, California and some United States district courts require the defense to contract a defense interpreter, also known as a proceedings interpreter, whose exclusive duty is to provide a simultaneous interpretation for the defendant at counsel table. The defense team may or may not enlist the services of a second interpreter for defense witnesses. The prosecution is then required to contract a prosecution interpreter for its witnesses. Thus, the current trend in California is to avoid requiring the interpreter to perform a double duty during the same proceeding.

Courts have also recognized that borrowing the defendant's interpreter for a prosecution witness, or even a defense witness at the stand, deprives the defendant of the ability to communicate with the attorney at counsel table. This particular interpretation of the California constitutional right to an interpreter throughout the proceedings has been discussed in *People vs. Mata Aguilar* (1984). Use of multiple interpreters to protect the defendant's Sixth Amendment rights may, therefore, become a major issue in other jurisdictions as well. However, with budget cuts also on the rise, a resolution to the problem may not necessarily be in favor of the defendant.

1.3. "English-Only" Movement

A disturbing trend in the United States today is the "English-only" movement, which has successfully lobbied for ballot initiatives in several state elections. The heated arguments for and against the proposed English Language Amendments (ELA) have created a political climate and social tension that has been termed a veritable "powderkeg" (Marshall, 1986, p. 7).

The ultimate goal of the proponents of the "English-only" movement is to pass a constitutional amendment to make English the official language of the United States. As Gonzalez, Schott, and Vasquez (1988) point out, "A host of non-profit organizations have sprung up to marshal political and financial support for the ELA, each with its own set of claims, slogans, and titles" (p. 24). These groups base their arguments on three myths: (1) that linguistic diversity leads to political conflict, (2) that an official language would foster national unity, and (3) that providing services in other languages hinders the assimilation of linguistic minorities and deprives them of the opportunity to learn English. Several historians and scholars view this position as nothing less than "veiled hostility" toward minority language groups in general, and Hispanics and Asians in particular (Alatis, 1986; Heath & Krasner, 1986; Judd, 1987).

Thus far, ELA proponents have succeeded in passing initiatives to make English the official language of seventeen states ("Official English Claims," 1988, p. 1). Only one state, New Mexico, has voted down such an initiative. In another state, Arizona, the ELA was declared violative of First Amendment rights in federal court, after being in place for just over a year. Opponents of the ELA have been lulled into a false sense of security by the fact that nothing of significance has happened in the states where "English-only" ballot measures have been approved: bilingual education, translated ballots and government pamphlets, and court interpreter services are still intact. Moreover, court decisions such as *Gutierrez v. Municipal Court of the Southeast Judicial District* (1987) in which the United States district court ruled that the state constitutional ELA is subordinate to federal law and, therefore, cannot be used as grounds to impose "English-only" regulations in the workplace, are cited as evidence that initiatives at the state level are relatively harmless. It is commonly assumed, therefore, that the movement is merely a symbolic one that at worst gives vent to xenophobic impulses.

This attitude reflects a misunderstanding of the genuine intentions of ELA advocates (Gonzalez, 1990a). The reason no major changes have taken place in states with ELA measures in place is that the aforementioned services are guaranteed by federal statutes; under the supremacy clause of the United States Constitution, federal rights are unaffected by even state constitutional amendments. The ultimate goal of the "English-only" movement, as noted above, is passage of an amendment to the United States Constitution that will make voidable existing federal legislation. Many analysts contend that it is unlikely a constitutional amendment would ever be passed at the federal level because such an amendment would require approval by a two-thirds majority of the fifty states. In this connection, Gonzalez, Vasquez, and Bichsel (in press) point out that three conditions have engendered support for similar movements in the past: war or national crisis, massive immigration, and economic recession; and that "two of the three conditions exist today: high immigration and economic decline" (p. 16). Furthermore, seventeen states have already shown that they are amenable to such proposals. Once the ELA forces are assured of having at least thirty-four states in favor of their objectives, they will launch a drive to pass a federal constitutional amendment, which would have far-reaching consequences. All of the efforts that have been made over the past few decades to guarantee equal access and opportunity to previously excluded language minorities would be at risk.

Therefore, although there is no immediate threat to the provision of interpreter services for limited- and non-English speakers in courtrooms throughout the United States district courts and many state courts, the potential threat is very real. Court interpreters cannot afford to remain content with the status quo and assume that court interpreting services are guaranteed by unassailable federal statutes and constitutional rights. They must recognize that, contrary to the impression ELA proponents have succeeded in creating, the "English-only" movement is not a question of language rights—whether people can choose to speak a given language or not—but an issue of access to guarantees and privileges that should be afforded equally to all, regardless of race, creed, color, gender, or *language*. Consequently, they must work actively against ELA measures, for professional as well as ethical reasons, to make sure that these hard-won rights and guarantees are not effectively eradicated.

1.4. Malpractice

Interpreter malpractice is potentially an issue of great import to the court interpreting profession. Fortunately, there is no record to date of any court interpreter having been sued for damages arising out of incompetent or erroneous interpretation. Because there is generally no record kept of the interpretation, either by the court reporter or by electronic recording, it is difficult to detect interpreting errors. However, as recording equipment is introduced into the courtroom, and as the number of limited-English speakers increases, it is entirely possible that appeals on the basis of poor interpretation will increase, and that a civil action could arise out of such a case. Throughout this text the critical importance of upholding the standards of "conservation" and "legal equivalence" (Gonzalez, 1989c) has been emphasized from the standpoint of the fair administration of justice. The individual interpreter, however, has another important reason for observing these high standards: maintaining professional reputation and guarding against accusation of malpractice.

Ideally, to protect themselves against liability for erroneous interpretation, interpreters should take out an errors-and-omissions insurance policy. Unfortunately, though such policies are available for other professionals, insurance companies have been unwilling to write an errors-and-omissions policy for professional court interpreters because they are few in number and it would not be profitable. In the late 1970s, the American Translators Association attempted to obtain an errors-and-omissions policy for its members. It succeeded in finding an insurance carrier that was willing to write the policy, but after only one year the carrier declined to renew the policies. Since then the ATA has been searching for another underwriter, but to no avail.

2. Professional Issues

2.1. Recertification

This section addresses a number of issues that will shape the court interpreting profession in the years to come, and recommends some approaches and strategies in anticipation of these developments. It begins with a discussion of the controversial issue of recertification. The question of recertification of court interpreters, although perhaps premature given the embryonic stage of first-time certification programs among the various states, is nonetheless pertinent.

2.1.1. Arguments For and Against

Proponents for recertification contend that court interpretation is a performance skill that is based on language proficiency and interpreting ability. This proficiency is subject to fossilization or stagnation, and even deterioration or loss. For example, interpreters begin their careers with adequate language and interpreting skills that would enable them to perform satisfactorily in any situation. If their daily experiences, however, require them to deal with little more than predictable, routine matters such as arraignments, they have little opportunity to grow linguistically. These interpreters would be hard pressed to perform satisfactorily in a different court situation, such as a jury trial, which would require the ability to handle a wide range of vocabulary (expert witness testimony, legal arguments, and so on). The proponents of recertification also maintain that the legal environment requires that court interpreters constantly update their vocabulary relating to new laws that are enacted, such as the sentencing guidelines that were instituted in the federal courts in 1987 (United States Sentencing Commission, 1987); new developments in criminal behavior and ever-changing drug slang; new technology employed in criminal investigations (genetic identification based on unique features of DNA); and additional regional dialects heard more frequently in the United States as new immigrant groups arrive from different countries (Nicaraguans who have arrived in Miami, which in the past had been dominated by Cuban immigrants). Indeed, some proponents of recertification cast aspersion on the very validity of early certification programs that might have failed to distinguish between the competent and the incompetent (for a further discussion of this issue see Unit 8, Chapter 37).

On the other side of the issue, there is the opinion that the results of a well-designed, reliable certification examination should be valid over time and that no recertification process is necessary. Opponents of recertification refer to other professions that require examination prior to passage into membership, pointing out that recertification is not required of attorneys or medical doctors for permanent membership in those professions. Some interpreters maintain that the very skills that were tested are utilized everyday in their job experience. Those interpreters whose court-related job responsibilities are limited may feel that the recertification requirement would discriminate against them. They believe that any loss in skills or failure to keep abreast of new developments with regard to terminology and usage is job imposed. That is, the daily job responsibilities imposed upon them by the court require that they specialize and perform highly specific language tasks, for example, interpreting misdemeanor traffic court arraignments as a permanent assignment.

Some interpreters argue against recertification from the standpoint of fairness. They feel that recertification is tantamount to "double jeopardy," reasoning that interpreters who were certified took the examination in good faith, and should not have their careers placed in jeopardy on the grounds of an allegedly invalid examination. Yet the issue of re-evaluation is not without precedent. This is especially true in skills-related areas. Police officers must periodically demonstrate their marksmanship on the pistol range. The health and abilities of airline pilots must be regularly evaluated to ensure public safety. Many argue that, not unlike these other fiduciary relationships, court interpreters also should be required to demonstrate competence periodically to protect the public from those whose language and interpreting skills may have diminished.

2.1.2. Alternatives

Perhaps the resolution of this question lies in the growing administrative ranks of supervisory interpreter personnel. As the court interpreting profession develops, the courts will be able to rely upon a growing cadre of interpreters educated and skilled in the supervision of interpreter services and the evaluation of personnel. The responsibility for continued evaluation of the practicing interpreter would rest where it properly belongs, with the supervisor who observes the interpreter's performance on a regular basis. Uniform standards will need to be developed for implementation by these interpreter/administrators. See Unit 4, Chapter 16, for a discussion of the criteria that supervisors should apply when monitoring the interpreters under their direction.

With regard to interpreters who work on a free-lance basis in other judicial and quasi-judicial settings, such as depositions and administrative hearings, and who are not necessarily supervised by anyone, the forces of the free market will serve to encourage interpreters to uphold high professional standards of performance in order to ensure continued employment. One might hypothesize that an interpreter whose skills are consistently below the acceptable level in the marketplace will suffer professional and economic consequences. Unfortunately, market forces are not always reliable, and unqualified interpreters may continue to serve as faulty language mediators.

2.2. Certification of Translators

As mentioned in Unit 7, Chapter 32, court interpreters are often called upon to translate documents as part of their duties. The standard of accuracy and completeness that governs the court interpreter's work is applied just as rigorously to the output of the translator. It is imperative that the user of translation services has some assurance that the translator is a competent and conscientious professional. In many countries, the critical importance of dependable translation services is reflected by a requirement that translators undergo a licensing procedure similar to the certification required of court interpreters in the United States. Once they have demonstrated their abilities by passing a test, translators are issued a license and a stamp. In countries that have such a licensing process, no one may claim to be a translator or provide such services unless the person displays the appropriate license. These licensed translators are known as sworn translators or public translators.

In the United States, translation services have been provided in just as haphazard a way as interpreting services. As with the case of court interpreters, it has traditionally been assumed that anyone who knew two languages could automatically translate between them. In the past, clients have had no way of knowing whether the translators they hired were competent. Being unfamiliar with the language involved, they had to take a leap of faith and trust that the translator's version was correct. As a result of the lack of regulation, many serious misunderstandings and even tragedies occurred due to faulty translations. The American Translators Association (ATA), anxious to make a distinction between qualified professional translators and amateurs, and to give the lay public some standard to apply when seeking translation services, instituted its own accreditation program. Professional translators who pass the ATA accreditation exams, which are given in a wide range of language combinations, now have a valid means of assuring their clients of their expertise.

The ATA accreditation program is a very commendable effort that has alleviated the quality control problem for translation clients; however, it is strictly a voluntary program. No doubt government entities will have to repeat the same steps they have taken with respect to court interpreting, that is, to mandate a certification procedure that will leave no room for doubt about the qualifications of the professional translator.

2.3. Machine Translation and Interpretation

The computer revolution that has touched almost every human endeavor in the last decade has had a major impact on the translation profession. The notion of a machine that can provide an instantaneous interpretation into any language from any other language has long been a fixture of science fiction novels and movies; ever since the invention of the computer, scientists and linguists have been striving to make that fictitious machine a reality.

Interestingly, one of the programs, developed by Fujitsu, involves converting a message into an intermediate code known as "interlingual," from which the message can then be converted into a variety of languages (Hillenbrand, 1989; Hutchins, 1986). This procedure makes the process more efficient by reducing the number of dictionaries that programmers have to construct. Thus, dictionaries would be compiled for Japanese-interlingual, German-interlingual, Korean-interlingual, etc., but not Japanese-German or German-Korean. This intermediate code is analogous to the abstraction process that a human interpreter or translator goes through when converting a message from one language to another.

Whenever automation has been introduced in a field of endeavor, fears of massive unemployment have proven unfounded; automation has merely increased the productivity of the existing human labor force. The same is true of machine translation. Translators who have incorporated computer aids into their work have found that their productivity increases geometrically, and they are able to take more translation assignments and increase their earning power. A software package designed to perform machine translation on personal computers is now on the market (Vasconcellos, 1989), making this cutting-edge technology available to individual translators. The advent of machine translation will simply expand the volume that the individual translator/editor can process at one time. The result will be more materials translated into more languages than ever before.

The benefits of such a machine are obvious: large volumes of written or oral discourse could be converted to any number of languages in a short time, unimpeded by human frailties such as fatigue, memory failure, or typographical errors. However, a computer that can process voiced input and convert it to voiced output in another language is still a thing of the future. Interpreters, therefore, are in no danger of being replaced by a machine anytime soon. But scientists, particularly in Japan where there is widespread awareness of translation needs, have made great strides in developing machines that can produce crude translations. Human editors take the raw output of the computer and resolve ambiguities, correct stylistic errors, and generally polish it into readable text. In general, the more technical the subject matter, the more the text lends itself to machine translation.

This is because technical terms, by their very nature, are subject to a number of semantic restrictions that narrow their denotative meanings. For example, the word "byte" has only one concrete technical meaning—a unit of information consisting of bits. Another important consideration is that written language changes much less rapidly than spoken language. Moreover, the idiomatic language that characterizes courtroom testimony by definition has fewer semantic restrictions than the technical terms an engineer might use in bidding specifications. In contrast, "bite" in general witness testimony may refer to a physical assault, a sarcastic comment, a mouthful of food, or a significant chunk. Therefore, some words have almost infinite connotations that would defy the binary storage of data that is the essence of computerized information processing. Consequently, barring a major breakthrough in artificial intelligence or some other computer-related technology, it is unlikely that court interpretation will be performed by a computer in our lifetime.

2.4. A National Professional Organization

At present, court interpreters in the United States are fragmented organizationally; few organizations represent the professional interests of court interpreters alone. Notable among these organizations is the California Court Interpreters Association (CCIA), which successfully played a role in lobbying for state certification of court interpreters in California in the late seventies. It has succeeded in organizing court interpreters in local chapters throughout California, one of the largest states in the union. CCIA, in turn, is the largest organization of its kind in the nation. Since membership is not restricted to California interpreters, there are many members who reside outside that state.

There are smaller court interpreting organizations within certain states, such as New Jersey, Arizona, and New Mexico. On the eastern seaboard, the National Association of Judiciary Interpreters and Translators (NAJIT, formerly the Court Interpreters and Translators Association, CITA) represents many interpreters and translators in several states of that region. These organizations publish newsletters for their members and hold yearly conferences. They also offer seminars and workshops to enable their members to grow intellectually and improve their professional skills.

Preliminary contacts have been made among these organizations in the past with a view to unification and the creation of an umbrella organization, but no effort to date has borne fruit. The political and perhaps professional future of United States court interpreters will hinge, to a great degree, on the success of efforts to establish a link between existing organizations and ultimately the formation of a single national professional association.

2.4.1. Benefits of a National Organization

For the court interpreting profession, a national organization would provide a vehicle for networking and communication among court interpreters, and would also serve as a political instrument to lobbying for favorable legislation at the federal and state levels (Deleon, O'Keefe, Vandenbos & Kraut, 1982; Gonzalez, 1987a). The national organization would be the prime mover in the creation of court interpreter associations in each state. The profession would benefit from the publication not only of national and regional newsletters to keep members abreast of new developments of interest to the profession, but also of a professional journal that would contain scholarly writings and more in-depth coverage of court interpreting issues. Moreover, a national organization would be capable of generating sufficient revenues to establish a national headquarters and hire a professional staff. In this connection, court interpreters could follow the lead of the American Translators Association (ATA), which has developed to the point that it can afford a small paid staff and acquire property for its national headquarters.

Another very important function that a national organization could fulfill effectively is that of continuing education. Such a large organization would have the resources to sponsor conferences, seminars, and workshops in many parts of the country, thereby reaching out to court interpreters in relatively remote areas who until now have been unable to avail themselves of interpreter training offerings for reasons of time, distance, and money. Not only would such educational programs contribute to upgrading the services provided by court interpreters throughout the country, but also the substantial resources that a nationwide organization could marshal would ensure that the most talented and knowledgeable specialists in the country would be brought in to impart their knowledge to court interpreters.

Additionally, the public image of the court interpreting profession could be enhanced through the public relations efforts of a national organization. A nationwide organization could promulgate a uniform code of ethics to be upheld by court interpreters in all states, and it could impose sanctions on its members. Court administrations and other public agencies throughout the nation, knowing that all members of this association were required to observe the highest standards of professional conduct, might be willing to enter into agreements to employ only members of the organization as staff or per diem interpreters. Currently, this lack of national ethical guidelines is an obstacle to the professional recognition of interpreters by federal and state governments. Ultimately, the national organization might be able to control membership in its organization by assuming the responsibility for determining competence and certifying court interpreters, as do the Registry of Interpreters for the Deaf (RID) and the ATA. The benefits of a national umbrella organization are myriad, and the time has arrived for court interpreters to join forces to promote their profession.

2.5. Developing a Pool of Court Interpreters

The future of court interpreting calls for a modification of the traditional goals and objectives of foreign language education at all levels. It is widely acknowledged that there is a lack of vitality in foreign language education and that it is not an area of preferred study in the United States. One significant way to change the perception students have of foreign language study and to revitalize the methodologies is to introduce translation and interpretation as career opportunities and as a significant part of the formal curriculum. The assimilation of interpreting into the curriculum will provide: (1) practical objectives and motivation for the study of foreign language and (2) a cognitively challenging exercise that will bring learned linguistic competence to the fore.

Students at the Summer Institute for Court Interpretation (Gonzalez, 1983) have commented almost unanimously on the tremendous impetus this intensive program provided in their language expansion and maintenance. Teachers of Spanish and bilingual education have observed that interpreting forces them to use language structures, vocabulary, and pragmatic features that they were familiar with only in a passive sense. The interpreting exercise provided an urgency of communication that increased learning. These case studies show that interpreting is an exciting language teaching technique that needs further investigation and pilot testing. Sidney Acosta, a secondary Spanish teacher in the Tucson Unified School District, reports that her inclusion of interpreting and mock trials in her intermediate and advanced high school Spanish courses made a significant difference in the motivational level and proficiency gains of her students (personal communication, July 1984).

In addition to the improvement of foreign language education, bilinguals in this country should be encouraged through bilingual education programs that strive to improve, widen, and expand native language ability through a maintenance curriculum. These rich human resources of Spanish, Chinese, Vietnamese, Navajo, Russian, Italian, and other languages can be groomed into professional interpreting positions available not only in court interpreting but in other fields of interpreting and translation as well. With the proper educational attention, these native bilinguals can raise their language proficiency to the level required to serve the interests of justice, commerce, and the health and welfare of the nation.

2.5.1. Call for Research

When the court interpreting profession establishes a presence in the nation's universities as a legitimate field of study, it will come increasingly to the attention of researchers and scholars as a fertile ground for investigation. Psychologists have long recognized that interpreters represent a rich source of material for research, as attested by the early studies of Goldman-Eisler (1967, 1968), Barik (1969, 1971, 1972, 1973), and particularly Gerver (1969, 1971, 1972a, 1972b, 1974a, 1974b). These and other scholars have merely scratched the surface of this vast resource that holds many discoveries about how the human mind processes information and solves problems. Flores d'Arcais (1978) points out that much research remains to be done in the fields of experimental psychology, psycholinguistics, sociolinguistics, and language education. A cognitive psychologist, d'Arcais lists a number of studies that could be conducted using interpreters as subjects, with a view to shedding more light on human information processing.

Although psychologists have led the way in conducting research on interpretation, scholars in other fields are beginning to take an interest. For example, in the field of legal anthropology, O'Barr (1982) has conducted a number of studies indirectly related to court interpreting; and Berk-Seligson (1987, 1988), a linguist, has focused specifically on court interpreter performance in her work. Gile (1988) reviews the research that has been conducted on conference interpreting, and proposes that interpreters themselves conduct studies in their areas of expertise. In fact, a number of practicing interpreters have written doctoral dissertations on interpretation or interpreting-related matters: Moser (1978), a conference interpreter with a doctorate in psychology; Cokely (1984), a sign-language interpreter with a doctorate in sociolinguistics; and Arjona, a translator and interpreter whose dissertation focuses on language policy and implementation of the Federal Court Interpreters Act of 1978.

There are a number of research questions to answer: What are the personal, linguistic, and psychological characteristics of an interpreter capable of passing the federal court interpreter certification exam? What are the bilingual life experiences that lead to competent language and interpreting abilities? What are the full ramifications of not conserving the register, style, tone, and intent of the speaker's words on the receptor, in this case, the judge and the jury? All of these topics require further investigation. What are the effects of poor interpreting on the outcome of a case? In short, the field of interpretation in general and court interpretation in particular represents a vast reservoir of topics for research in a wide variety of fields. In the years to come, the scholarly journals of this country and others will reflect the increasing interest in this fascinating field of endeavor.

3. Administrative Hearings

The Immigration and Naturalization Service (INS) plays an important legal role in our society. It is charged with the implementation of the laws relating to immigration and naturalization—those laws that exclude or allow the admission of persons to the United States according to a legislatively predetermined set of statutory requirements (Immigration Amendments, 1988; Immigration and Nationality Act, 1952; Immigration Reform and Control Act, 1986). The INS is also concerned with the amnesty, refugee, and asylum claims of persons seeking to enter or remain legally within the borders of the United States.

The INS is not a judicial organization, but an administrative agency with powers of enforcement delegated by the executive branch. These powers include enforcing the deportation or exclusion of those who are in violation of immigration and naturalization laws, stopping persons from entering at the national borders, and hearing and granting applications for admission to the United States.

This agency has a significant caseload of clients who do not speak English, and the use of interpreters within the INS and its quasi-judicial arm, the Executive Office of Immigration Review (EOIR), is on the rise. The hearings conducted by EOIR are not formal court hearings and do not necessarily follow recognized court rules and procedures. The INS, being a federal administrative agency, generally follows the federal Administrative Procedure Act of 1976 (Administrative Procedure Act of 1946). More specifically, the Immigration Reform and Control Act (1986), more commonly known as the Simpson-Mazzoli bill, stipulates the procedural and substantive due process guarantees that any person appearing before the EOIR can claim.

The use of interpreters in this setting is not closely regulated. Although immigration hearings are quasi-legal in nature, the interpretation techniques should be the same as those used in the courtroom: sight translation, consecutive, and simultaneous interpretation. The observance of due process in this area should be no less than that in a judicial setting, as the rights at risk are of such importance that only the true linguistic and cognitive presence of the respondent can guarantee a fair hearing.

The use of untrained and untested interpreters in immigration proceedings has raised serious questions regarding a respondent's right to a fair hearing. Recently the quality of the interpreting services provided in EOIR administrative hearings has been called into question. A class-action suit has been brought in the United States district court against the EOIR, challenging:

> the present inadequate system of interpretation for non-English speaking individuals appearing in immigration court wherein the Executive Office for Immigration Review (EOIR) employs unqualified, untrained and uncertified personnel to interpret. The present practice results in hearings wherein non-English speaking individuals are deprived of the opportunity to understand and fully comprehend what is being said by the English-speaking participants in the proceedings (*El Rescate Legal Services, Inc. et al., v. Executive Office for Immigration Review et al.,* 1988, p. 3).

As of this writing, EOIR is in the process of reconsidering its language services policy and is contemplating initiating a testing and certification training program. If planned and executed correctly, this program could serve as a model for other state and federal administrative agencies that currently employ untested interpreters.

3.1. Bilingual Personnel in Government Agencies

Another language-related lawsuit involved employees of the Tucson Police Department who were expected to provide language services above and beyond their normal duties. An early study conducted in connection with this suit found that the police department was relying on its Spanish-speaking personnel to perform complex tasks such as translation and interpretation for which the employees had no specialized training; it was assumed that their ability to speak two languages automatically qualified them to perform these functions. In addition to the issue of discriminatory treatment of these bilingual employees, the lawsuit makes clear that the police department failed to take the non-English-speaking public into account in its services planning and decision making, and it sought to remedy the situation by incorporating *ad hoc* language services into the organizational hierarchy of the department (Gonzalez, in press). In another Arizona case, a Spanish-surnamed police officer was suspended for refusing to provide language services in a language he didn't speak proficiently—Spanish. These cases illustrate that there is growing dissatisfaction with the way language services are provided, or not provided, by public agencies (Latimer, 1983). Furthermore, it is clear that agencies cannot simply rely on bilingual employees to cover their language service needs. They must hire or specifically train Spanish-language personnel for interpreting and translating skills, and must compensate them for performance of those skills and responsibilities.

There is evidence that public agencies are beginning to respond to such criticism, either under court order or in an effort to avoid lawsuits. After threat of suit, the Texas Employment Commission in 1987 put into operation a comprehensive language services program to provide language interpreters for those segments of the public whose primary language is other than English, and to provide key written forms and instructional information in the Spanish language (Texas Employment Commission, 1985).

The operating plan for this program called for the creation of bilingual positions with specific duties and prerequisites. Some job descriptions specified that candidates were required to interpret in the consecutive and simultaneous modes and pass certification requirements. This agency invested $350,000 to examine, train, and certify its interpreters and bilingual specialists, in an effort to ensure due process for its non-English-speaking claimants statewide.

3.2. Bilingual Services Act—The California Case

Not all such actions have been taken in response to lawsuits. California, which has been recognized as a leader in the drive to ensure equal access to public services for all members of its population, regardless of native language, began to take vigorous action in this regard in the 1970s. The Dymally-Alatorre Bilingual Services Act of 1973 was a sweeping measure that required:

> state and local agencies which furnish information or render services by contact with a *substantial number* [emphasis in original] of non-English-speaking people to employ a *sufficient number* [emphasis in original] of qualified bilingual persons in public contact positions or as interpreters to assist those in such positions, in order to insure provision of information and services in the non-English language. (Blaine, 1974, p. 662)

This was the first act of its kind in the country, and it represents one of the finest access policies in the United States. Its effect was far reaching. When the interpreter certification program was instituted in 1978, the legislature mandated that certified interpreters be provided for in administrative hearings as well as criminal court proceedings. A report prepared for the Judicial Council of California in connection with the 1978 law reviewed the case law and stated, "...it seems reasonable to conclude that a constitutional argument of substantial merit may be made for the existence of the right to an interpreter in administrative hearings involving the deprivation of an important right" (Judicial Council of California, 1976a, pp. III 25-26). Some administrative law agencies, such as the Agricultural Labor Relations Board, require that interpreters take a separate examination in addition to the one required for administrative hearings in general and to demonstrate that they are well versed in the terminology, procedures, and scenarios that are unique to that agency. More recently, legislation has been introduced in the California State Assembly to institute a medical interpreter certification program to govern interpreters who provide services in hospitals and other medical settings.

The cases discussed here demonstrate that language services are an increasingly important public issue. This is especially true in view of the fact that by the year 2000, one out of every five Americans will hail from a non-English-speaking or other-culture home (National Center for Education Statistics, 1989). Clearly the need for high-quality language services provided by language specialists or interpreters whose performance skills have been objectively tested is not limited to the courts. As the American sense of social justice grows, and as non-English speakers become more aware of the rights guaranteed by statutes and the Constitution, the quality of available language services will come under closer public scrutiny. The obvious conclusion is that planning for the future of the United States must take into account the need for foreign language and interpreter services in all facets of our linguistically diverse society.

4. Conclusion

Fundamentals of Court Interpretation has addressed a wide scope of needs and concerns, and has endeavored to synthesize the ever-growing body of knowledge related to the field of court interpretation. Rather than presenting a compendium of facts and practices as they currently exist in the field, *Fundamentals* has suggested practical solutions to common problems, and has recommended procedures and policies consistent with the most current and enlightened theory, experience, and research.

Fundamentals has presented a look at the field from both a global and specific perspective of interpretation, focusing on the interpreter in court on both a theoretical and practical dimension, and with a historical perspective as well as a viewpoint that anticipates future developments. The authors have intended this work for a diverse audience: practicing and aspiring court interpreters; scholars in the fields of linguistics, law, anthropology, and psychology; teachers of court interpretation; members of the judiciary and the bar; officers of the court and court administrators whose responsibilities include the supervision of court interpreter services. The final aim is that *Fundamentals* will prompt a realization and appreciation of the fact that court interpreting is a *sine qua non* for ensuring fairness, social justice, and equal access to the administration of justice systems for all limited- and non-English speakers in the United States.

APPENDIX A:
The Court Interpreters Act of 1978

PUBLIC LAW 95-539—OCT. 28, 1978

     PUBLIC LAW 95-539—OCT. 28, 1978

Public Law 95–539
95th Congress

An Act

Oct. 28, 1978

[S. 1315]

Court
Interpreters Act.
28 USC 1 note.

To provide more effectively for the use of interpreters in courts of the United States, and for other purposes.

Be it enacted by the Senate and House of Representatives of the United States of America in Congress assembled, That this Act may be cited as the "Court Interpreters Act".

SEC. 2. (a) Chapter 119 of title 28, United States Code, is amended by adding at the end thereof the following new sections:

28 USC 1827.

"§ 1827. **Interpreters in courts of the United States**

"(a) The Director of the Administrative Office of the United States Courts shall establish a program to facilitate the use of interpreters in courts of the United States.

"(b) The Director shall prescribe, determine, and certify the qualifications of persons who may serve as certified interpreters in courts of the United States in bilingual proceedings and proceedings involving the hearing impaired (whether or not also speech impaired), and in so doing, the Director shall consider the education, training, and experience of those persons. The Director shall maintain a current master list of all interpreters certified by the Director and shall report annually on the frequency of requests for, and the use and effectiveness of, interpreters. The Director shall prescribe a schedule of fees for services rendered by interpreters.

Annual report.

Fee schedule.

"(c) Each United States district court shall maintain on file in the office of the clerk of court a list of all persons who have been certified as interpreters, including bilingual interpreters and oral or manual interpreters for the hearing impaired (whether or not also speech impaired), by the Director of the Administrative Office of the United States Courts in accordance with the certification program established pursuant to subsection (b) of this section.

"(d) The presiding judicial officer, with the assistance of the Director of the Administrative Office of the United States Courts, shall utilize the services of the most available certified interpreter, or when no certified interpreter is reasonably available, as determined by the presiding judicial officer, the services

571

of an otherwise competent interpreter, in any criminal or civil action initiated by the United States in a United States district court (including a petition for a writ of habeas corpus initiated in the name of the United States by a relator), if the presiding judicial officer determines on such officer's own motion or on the motion of a party that such party (including a defendant in a criminal case), or a witness who may present testimony in such action

"(1) speaks only or primarily a language other than the English language; or

"(2) suffers from a hearing impairment (whether or not suffering also from a speech impairment) so as to inhibit such party's comprehension of the proceedings or communication with counsel or the presiding judicial officer, or so as to inhibit such witness' comprehension of questions and the presentation of such testimony.

92 STAT. 2041

"(e) (1) If any interpreter is unable to communicate effectively with the presiding judicial officer, the United States attorney, a party (including a defendant in a criminal case), or a witness, the presiding judicial officer shall dismiss such interpreter and obtain the services of another interpreter in accordance with this section.

"(2) In any criminal or civil action in a United States district court, if the presiding judicial officer does not appoint an interpreter under subsection (d) of this section, an individual requiring the services of an interpreter may seek assistance of the clerk of court or the Director of the Administrative Office of the United States Courts in obtaining the assistance of a certified interpreter.

Waiver, approval, and consultation.

"(f) (1) Any individual other than a witness who is entitled to interpretation under subsection (d) of this section may waive such interpretation in whole or in part. Such a waiver shall be effective only if approved by the presiding judicial officer and made expressly by such individual on the record after opportunity to consult with counsel and after the presiding judicial officer has explained to such individual, utilizing the services of the most available certified interpreter, or when no certified interpreter is reasonably available, as determined by the presiding judicial officer, the services of an otherwise competent interpreter, the nature and effect of the waiver.

"(2) An individual who waives under paragraph (1) of this subsection the right to an interpreter may utilize the services of a non-certified interpreter of such individual's choice whose fees, expenses, and costs shall be paid in the manner provided for the payment of such fees, expenses, and costs of an interpreter appointed under subsection (d) of this section.

Salaries, fees, and expenses
Post, p. 2042.

"(g) (1) Except as otherwise provided in this subsection or section 1828 of this title, the salaries, fees, expenses, and costs incident to providing the services of interpreters under subsection (d) of this section shall be paid by the Director of the Administrative Office of the United States Courts from sums appropriated to the Federal judiciary.

"(2) Such salaries, fees, expenses, and costs that are incurred with respect to Government witnesses shall, unless direction is made under paragraph (3) of this subsection, be paid by the Attorney General from sums appropriated to the Department of Justice.

"(3) The presiding judicial officer may in such officer's discretion direct that all or part of such salaries, fees, expenses, and costs shall be apportioned between or among the parties or shall be taxed as costs in a civil action.

"(4) Any moneys collected under this subsection may be used to reimburse the appropriations obligated and disbursed in payment for such services.

"(h) In any action in a court of the United States where the presiding judicial officer establishes, fixes, or approves the compensation and expenses payable to an interpreter from funds appropriated to the Federal judiciary, the presiding judicial officer shall not establish, fix, or approve compensation and expenses in excess of the maximum allowable under the schedule of fees for services prescribed pursuant to subsection (b) of this section.

"Presiding judicial officer."

"(i) The term 'presiding judicial officer' as used in this section and section 1828 of this title includes a judge of a United States district court, a United States magistrate, and a referee in bankruptcy.

92 STAT. 2042
"United States district court."
Infra.

"(j) The term 'United States district court' as used in this section and section 1828 of this title includes any court created by Act of Congress in a territory which is invested with any jurisdiction of a district court of the United States established by section 132 of this title.

28 USC 132.

"(k) The interpretation provided by certified interpreters pursuant to this section shall be in the consecutive mode except that the presiding judicial officer, with the approval of all interested parties, may authorize a simultaneous or summary interpretation when such officer determines that such interpretation will aid in the efficient administration of justice. The presiding judicial officer on such officer's motion or on the motion of a party may order that special interpretation services as authorized in section 1828 of this title be provided if such officer determines that provision of such services will aid in the efficient administration of justice.

28 USC 1828.
Program
establishment.

"§ 1828. Special interpretation services

"(a) The Director of the Administrative Office of the United States Courts shall establish a program for the provision of special interpretation services in criminal actions and in civil actions initiated by the United States (including petitions for writs of habeas corpus initiated in the name of the United States by relators) in a United States district court. The program shall provide a capacity for simultaneous interpretation services in multidefendant criminal actions and multidefendant civil actions.

"(b) Upon the request of any person in any action for which special interpretation services established pursuant to subsection (a) are not otherwise provided, the Director, with the approval of the presiding judicial officer, may make such services available to the person requesting the services on a reimbursable basis at rates established in conformity with section 501 of the Act of August 31, 1951 (ch. 376, title 5, 65 Stat. 290; 31 U.S.C. 483a), but the Director may require the prepayment of the estimated expenses of providing the services by the person requesting them.

Expenses.

"(c) Except as otherwise provided in this subsection, the expenses incident to providing services under subsection (a) of this section shall be paid by the Director from sums appropriated to the Federal judiciary. A presiding judicial officer, in such officer's discretion, may order that all or part of the expenses shall be apportioned between or among the parties or shall be taxed as costs in a civil action, and any moneys collected as a result of such order may be used to reimburse the appropriations obligated and disbursed in payment for such services.

"(d) Appropriations available to the Director shall be available to provide services in accordance with subsection (b) of this section, and moneys collected by the Director under that subsection may be used to reimburse the appropriations charged for such services. A presiding judicial officer, in such officer's discretion, may order that all or part of the expenses shall be apportioned between or among the parties or shall be taxed as costs in the action."

(b) The table of sections for chapter 119 of title 28, United States Code, is amended by adding at the end thereof the following:

"1827. Interpreters in courts of the United States.
"1828. Special interpretation services."

92 STAT. 2043

SEC. 3. Section 604(a) of title 28, United States Code, is amended—

(a) by striking out paragraph (10) and inserting in lieu thereof:

"(10) (A) Purchase, exchange, transfer, distribute, and assign the custody of lawbooks, equipment, supplies, and other personal property for the judicial branch of Government (except the Supreme Court unless otherwise provided pursuant to paragraph (17)); (B) provide or make available readily to each court appropriate equipment for the interpretation of proceedings in accordance with section 1828 of this title; and (C) enter into and perform contracts and other transactions upon such terms as the Director may deem appropriate as may be necessary to the conduct of the work of the judicial branch of Government (except the Supreme Court unless otherwise provided pursuant to paragraph (17)), and contracts for nonpersonal services for pretrial services agencies, for the interpretation of proceedings, and for the provision of special interpretation services pursuant to section 1828 of this title may be awarded without regard to section 3709 of the Revised Statutes of the United States (41 U.S.C. 5);"

Ante, p. 2042.

(b) by redesignating paragraph (13) as paragraph (17); and

(c) by inserting after paragraph (12) the following new paragraphs:

Interpreter programs, establishment.
Ante, p. 2040.

"(13) Pursuant to section 1827 of this title, establish a program for the certification and utilization of interpreters in courts of the United States;

"(14) Pursuant to section 1828 of this title, establish a program for the provision of special interpretation services in courts of the United States;

"(15) (A) In those districts where the Director considers it advisable based on the need for interpreters, authorize the full-time or part-time employment by the court of certified interpreters; (B) where the Director considers it advisable based on the need for interpreters, appoint certified interpreters on a full-time or part-time basis, for services in various courts when he determines that such appointments will result in the economical provision of interpretation services; and (C) pay out of moneys appropriated for the judiciary interpreters' salaries, fees, and expenses, and other costs which may accrue in accordance with the provisions of sections 1827 and 1828 of this title;

"(16) In the Director's discretion, (A) accept and utilize voluntary and uncompensated (gratuitous) services, including services as authorized by section 3102 of title 5, United States Code; and (B) accept, hold, administer, and utilize gifts and bequests of personal property for the purpose of aiding or facilitating the work of the judicial branch of Government, but gifts or bequests of money shall be covered into the Treasury;".

SEC. 4. Section 604 of title 28, United States Code, is amended further by inserting after subsection (e) the following new subsections:

Conduct standards, rules regulations. Publication in Federal Register.

"(f) The Director may make, promulgate, issue, rescind, and amend rules and regulations (including regulations prescribing standards of conduct for Administrative Office employees) as may be necessary to carry out the Director's functions, powers, duties, and authority. The Director may publish in the Federal Register such rules, regulations, and notices for the judicial branch of Government as the Director determines to be of public interest; and the Director of the Federal Register hereby is authorized to accept and shall publish such materials.

Exchanges or sales, evidence.

"(g) (1) When authorized to exchange personal property, the Director may exchange or sell similar items and may apply the exchange allowance or proceeds of sale in such cases in whole or in part payment for the property acquired, but any transaction carried out under the authority of this subsection shall be evidenced in writing.

Contracts.

"(2) The Director hereby is authorized to enter into contracts for public utility services and related terminal equipment for periods not exceeding ten years.".

SEC. 5. Section 602 of title 28, United States Code, is amended to read as follows:

Compensation.

5 USC 5101 et seq., 5331.

Ante, p. 2043.

"§ 602. Employees.

"(a) The Director shall appoint and fix the compensation of necessary employees of the Administrative Office in accordance with the provisions of chapter 51 and subchapter III of chapter 53 of title 5, relating to classification and General Schedule pay rates.

"(b) Notwithstanding any other law, the Director may appoint certified interpreters in accordance with section 604(a)(15)(B) of this title without regard to the provisions of chapter 51 and subchapter III of chapter 53 of title 5, relating to classification and General Schedule pay rates, but the compensation of any person appointed under this subsection shall not exceed the appropriate equivalent of the highest rate of pay payable for the highest grade established in the General Schedule, section 5332 of title 5.

"(c) The Director may obtain personal services as authorized by section 3109 of title 5, at rates not to exceed the appropriate equivalent of the highest rate of pay payable for the highest grade established in the General Schedule, section 5332 of title 5.

Authority delegations.

"(d) All functions of other officers and employees of the Administrative Office and all functions of organizational units of the Administrative Office are vested in the Director. The Director may delegate any of the Director's functions, powers, duties, and authority (except the authority to promulgate rules and regulations) to such officers and employees of the judicial branch of government as the Director may designate, and subject to such terms and conditions as the Director may consider appropriate; and may authorize the successive redelegation of such functions, powers, duties, and authority as the Director may deem desirable. All official acts performed by such officers and employees shall have the same force and effect as though performed by the Director in person.".

SEC. 6. Section 603 of title 28, United States Code, is amended by striking out the second paragraph thereof.

Taxation of costs.

SEC. 7. Section 1920 of title 28, United States Code, is amended by striking out the period at the end of paragraph (5) and inserting a semicolon in lieu thereof and by inserting after paragraph (5) the following new paragraph:

"(6) Compensation of court appointed experts, compensation of interpreters, and salaries, fees, expenses, and costs of special interpretation services under section 1828 of this title.".

Repeal.
28 USC 602 note.

SEC. 8. Section 5 (b) of the Act of September 23, 1959 (Public Law 86-370, 73 Stat. 652), is repealed.

92 STAT. 2045
Appropriation
authorization.

SEC. 9. There are authorized to be appropriated to the judicial branch of Government such sums as may be necessary to carry out the amendments made by this Act.

Effective dates.
28 USC 602 note.

SEC. 10. (a) Except as provided in subsection (b), this Act shall take effect on the date of the enactment of this Act.

(b) Section 2 of this Act shall take effect ninety days after the date of the enactment of this Act.

28 USC 692 note.

SEC. 11. Any contracts entered into under this Act or any of the amendments made by this act shall be limited to such extent or in such amounts as are provided in advance in appropriation Acts.

Approved October 28, 1978.

LEGISLATIVE HISTORY:

HOUSE REPORT No. 95-1687 accompanying H.R. 14030 (Comm. on the Judiciary).

SENATE REPORT No. 95-569 (Comm. on the Judiciary).

CONGRESSIONAL RECORD:
 Vol. 123 (1977): Nov. 4, considered and passed Senate.
 Vol. 124 (1978): Oct. 10, H.R. 14030 considered and passed House; passage
      vacated and S. 1315, amended, passed in lieu.
   Oct. 13, Senate concurred in House amendment.

APPENDIX B:
Interim Regulations for
Federal Court Interpreters

INTERIM REGULATIONS OF THE
DIRECTOR OF THE ADMINISTRATIVE OFFICE
OF THE UNITED STATES COURTS
IMPLEMENTING
THE COURT INTERPRETERS AMENDMENTS ACT OF 1988

Part I—General

§ 1. Authority

The Director of the Administrative Office of the United States Courts promulgates these regulations pursuant to authority of the Court Interpreters Amendments Act, Pub.L. 100-702, Title VII, § 703, 102 Stat. 4654 (1988) (codified at 28 U.S.C. § 1827(b)(1)).

§ 2. Definitions

In these regulations—

a. "Act" means the Court Interpreters Act of 1988 as amended, Pub.L. No. 95-539, 92 Stat. 2040 (1978), and Court Interpreter Amendments Act, Pub.L. No. 100-702, 102 Stat. 4654-4657 (1988) (codified at 28 U.S.C. §§ 604(a)14, 604(a)(15), 604(f), 1827 and 1828).

b. "Clerk" means the clerk of the district court, the clerk of the bankruptcy court, the district court executive or other court employee designated by the chief judge to implement the Act.

c. "Director" means the Director of the Administrative Office of the United States Courts or the Director's designee.

d. "Presiding judicial officer" means a United States district judge, a bankruptcy judge, or a United States magistrate, and in the case of a grand jury proceeding conducted under the auspices of a United States attorney, a United States attorney.

e. "Special audio equipment" means specially constructed interpreter booths in the courtroom. It does not include small, portable equipment, including headphones, for one or more defendants for simultaneous translation.

Part II—Certification

§ 3. Requirements in General

A candidate for certification shall be certified as an interpreter upon successful completion of a criterion-referenced performance examination which shall be administered under the supervision of the Court Administration Division. A criterion referenced performance examination is one in which the grade required for certification is based on an absolute standard rather than on the relative performance of examinees as measured against each other. The examination shall consist of written and oral parts.

§ 4. Languages for Which Certification is Required.

Certification has been established for the languages set forth in Appendix 1.

§ 5. Requirements for Certification in Sign Language.

In the case of sign language, certification is recognized for interpreters who hold a Legal Specialist Certificate from the Registry of Interpreters for the Deaf, Inc.

§ 6. List of Interpreters

Upon successful completion of the certification examination set forth in § 3, the Director shall issue a certification evidencing that the person named therein has qualified as a certified court interpreter for a specific language. The Director shall maintain a current master list of all certified interpreters and provide it to the courts.

Part III—Otherwise Qualified Interpreters

§ 7. In General

When a certified interpreter is not reasonably available, the court may use the services of an "otherwise qualified interpreter." The Director shall maintain a current master list of otherwise qualified interpreters and shall provide this list to the courts upon request.

Otherwise qualified interpreters consist of the following two categories: "professionally qualified" interpreters and "language skilled" interpreters.

§ 8. Professionally Qualified Interpreters

a. To qualify as a professionally qualified interpreter, an interpreter must demonstrate either:

  i. Prior existing employment as a conference or seminar interpreter (staff or contractual) for the Office of Language Services of the United States Department of State, for the United Nations, or for related agencies for which examinations are a condition of employment; or

  ii. Membership in good standing in a professional interpreters association whose by-laws and practices at a minimum require as follows:

  A. An application specifying a minimum of 50 hours of conference experience in the native language(s) of expertise; and

  B. The sponsorship of three active members in good standing who have been members of the same association for at least two years, whose language(s) of expertise are the same as the applicant's, and who attest to having witnessed the performance of the applicant, as well as to the accuracy of the statements on the application.

b. An interpreter who wishes to be included on the master list of professionally qualified shall submit to the Court Administration Division a resume detailing education, training, experience, current telephone number and mailing address, and when applicable, membership accreditation.

c. Interpreters of languages for which there is a certification by the Director cannot be considered as professionally qualified interpreters.

§ 9. Language Skilled Interpreters

An interpreter who does not qualify as a professionally qualified interpreter, but who can demonstrate to the satisfaction of the court the ability to interpret court proceedings from English to a designated language and from that language to English will be classified as a language skilled interpreter. The clerk will transmit to the Director the names of local interpreters determined to be language skilled by the court. Upon receipt of notification from the clerk, the name of the interpreter will be placed on the master list as a language skilled interpreter.

Part IV—Proceedings Requiring Appointment

§ 10. Criminal and Civil Actions Initiated by the United States

In judicial proceedings instituted by the United States, an interpreter will be appointed by the presiding judicial officer as required by 28 U.S.C. § 1827(d)(1). In bankruptcy courts, the presiding judicial officer will appoint an interpreter only if the United States initiates the proceeding. In accordance with 28 U.S.C. § 1827(g), the cost of court appointed interpreters will be paid by the United States from appropriations available to the judiciary.

Part V—Responsibilities of the Clerk

§ 11. Local Roster of Interpreters

In addition to the lists of interpreters furnished by the Director, the clerk shall maintain a local roster of certified, professionally qualified and language skilled interpreters.

§ 12. Locating Interpreters

When the presiding judicial officer determines that the Act requires the appointment of an interpreter:

a. The clerk shall consider first the designation of an available court-employee interpreter certified by the Director. If no certified court-employee interpreter is available, the clerk shall determine whether an individual from the roster of certified interpreters is available locally.

b. If no certified interpreter is available locally, the clerk shall:

i. Seek the services of a certified interpreter from another district. The clerk shall contact other districts, especially metropolitan courts with staff interpreters, for recommendations as to certified interpreters who may be available; and

ii. If necessary, communicate with the Court Administration Division for assistance.

c. The court may pay travel and subsistence costs when necessary to assure that certified interpreters are available.

d. If after taking the steps set forth above, no certified interpreter is reasonably available, the court may use the services of a professionally qualified interpreter.

e. A language skilled interpreter shall not be used if a professionally qualified interpreter is reasonably available.

§ 13. Assistance to Litigants

Where the Act does not require the appointment of an interpreter at the expense of the United States:

a. The clerk shall provide assistance to the parties in locating an available interpreter. The local roster of certified and otherwise qualified interpreters shall be made available for inspection during the normal business hours of clerks' offices.

b. The clerk shall, where possible, make available the services of an interpreter on a cost-reimbursable basis upon the request of any person in any action, if the presiding judicial officer approves the request. The presiding judicial officer also may require that the requesting party pay the estimated expenses of providing such services prior to the provision of the services.

§ 14. Multiple Interpreter Cases and Special Audio Equipment

a. The presiding judicial officer may use the services of multiple interpreters where necessary to aid interpretation of court proceedings. Generally, two or more interpreters should be designated to work in lengthy or multi-defendant trials in order to assure that the quality of interpretation does not decrease due to interpreter fatigue.

b. The presiding judicial officer may order the use of special audio equipment if necessary to aid in interpretation of court proceedings. The parties shall give timely notice to the clerk to facilitate arrangements for locating, borrowing or renting, and installing appropriate equipment.

§ 15. Provision of Interpreters for the Hearing Impaired

a. If interpreting services for the hearing impaired are required, the presiding judicial officer shall seek the services of an individual who holds a Legal Specialist Certificate from the Registry of Interpreters for the Deaf, Inc.

b. If no person with a Legal Specialist Certificate is reasonably available, the presiding judicial officer is responsible under the Act for ascertaining the competency of a proposed interpreter for the hearing impaired, preferably an individual possessing a Comprehensive Skills Certificate from the Registry of Interpreters for the Deaf.

§ 16. Prior Contact with Case, Qualification on the Record and Interpreter's Oath

a. Before being sworn to serve in a case, an interpreter shall be required to disclose to the court and to the parties any prior involvement with the case or with any party or witness involved therein.

b. Unless stipulated by all parties, the interpreter shall be qualified as an expert in accordance with Rule 604 of the Federal Rules of Evidence.

c. The presiding judicial officer is responsible for administering the oath in accordance with Rule 604 of the Federal Rules of Evidence.

d. The name of the interpreter serving during any court proceeding shall be noted on the docket and in the record of the case.

Part VI—Compensation and Expenses of Independent Contractors

§ 17. Contractual Status of Interpreters

a. A presiding judicial officer's selection of a person to serve as an interpreter does not constitute an appointment of that person as an employee of the United States, except in respect to an interpreter who otherwise is an employee of the United States by prior appointment. The interpreter's relationship to the United States is that of independent contractor.

b. Income taxes or social security taxes shall not be deducted from a contract interpreter's compensation. Social security benefits for the contract interpreter shall be based entirely on the interpreter's contributions as a self-employed individual, and the Government shall make no contribution as an employer.

c. The clerk shall prepare and transmit annually to each contract interpreter an Internal Revenue Service Form 1099-G.

§ 18. Contracts with Government Employees or Employee Controlled Concerns

a. The court shall not select an employee of the Government (as defined in 5 U.S.C. § 2105), other than a staff interpreter, to serve as an interpreter during that employees's assigned work period.

b. The court shall not select as an interpreter any person provided by a business substantially owned or controlled by a Government employee.

c. If a presiding judicial officer believes that an exception to paragraphs (a) or (b) should be made for reasons of exigent circumstances, approval shall be obtained from the Court Administration Division.

§ 19. Schedule of Fees

a. An interpreter shall be paid fees for services on the basis of full days and half days. The rates shall be set by the Director, subject to periodic review pursuant to the Act.

b. Fees for certified interpreters and professionally qualified interpreters shall be set at the same rate.

c. Fees for language skilled interpreters shall be set at a lesser rate than that set for certified and professionally qualified interpreters.

d. An interpreter shall be paid fees for services on the basis of days and half days. More than four hours and up to eight hours, excluding normal meal periods, constitutes a full day of service. Four hours or less shall constitute a half day's service. An interpreter who is called to and appears at the courthouse and is not used shall be compensated for a minimum of a half day. These rates are set forth in Appendix 2.

e. If an interpreter's services are required for more than eight hours in one day, e.g., for a protracted trial or jury deliberation, the court may fix the fees to be paid to the interpreter for the period exceeding eight hours, excluding a normal break, at a rate to be set by the Director. These rates are set forth in Appendix 2. Due to the nature and requirements of the work, overtime should be avoided unless more than one interpreter is working. No interpreter may receive a daily or cumulative biweekly fee that would exceed the gross daily or biweekly salary payable at the maximum pay cap for the Judiciary Salary Plan salary schedule.

f. If the court cannot locate an interpreter in a non-certified language at the above rates of pay, the clerk shall seek permission from the Court Administration Division to exceed such rates.

g. Compensation rates and expenses shall be explained and established before services are rendered, unless the circumstances of a particular situation preclude advance arrangements.

§ 20. Termination for Convenience

The presiding judicial officer may terminate a contract with an interpreter, in whole or in part, when it is in the best interest of the court. Payment shall be made to the interpreter only for the services rendered satisfactorily prior to the date of the termination. If the contract is terminated prior to the start of an assignment, a late cancellation payment may be required pursuant to § 21.

§ 21. Payment on Late Cancellation

If the interpreter is not notified by the court of the cancellation at least 24 hours prior to the start of an assignment, the interpreter shall be paid compensation for at least a half day's services and, if applicable, per diem travel expenses in accordance with the Judiciary Travel Regulations, unless otherwise agreed in advance.

Part VII—Reporting Requirements

§ 22. Interpreter Statistical Reporting

By March 31 of each year, the clerk shall provide the Court Administration with a calendar year report containing a summary, by language and by type of interpreter, of the number of docketed events for which interpreters were provided. The report is necessary for preparation of the Director's annual report to Congress.

APPENDIX 1

Languages For Which Certification Has Been Established*:

Spanish

APPENDIX 2

Fee Rates to Be Paid to Interpreters

The following rates have been set by the Director:

Certified and Professionally Qualified Interpreters:

Full Day:	$210**
Half Day:	$110
Overtime:	$30 per hour or part thereof

Language Skilled Interpreters:

Full Day:	$95
Half Day:	$55
Overtime:	$15.00 per hour or part thereof

*Author's Notes: As of Fall, 1990, both Navajo and Haitian Creole have been added to this list.

**As of March 1991, the daily fee for certified interpreters is $250 for a full day and $135 for a half day.

APPENDIX C:
Code of Professional Responsibility
of the Official Interpreters
of the United States Courts

Code of Professional Responsibility

Certified court interpreters are highly skilled professionals who fulfill an essential role in the administration of justice and in the protection of 4th and 6th Amendment rights for non-English speaking defendants. In their capacity as officers of the court, court interpreters are bound to a professional code of ethics to ensure due process of law. The Federal Court Interpreters Advisory Board developed a Code of Ethics and Professional Responsibility for all federal court interpreters. The Board adopted the following Cannons:

Cannon 1   Official court interpreters act strictly in the interests of the court they serve.

Cannon 2   Official court interpreters reflect proper court decorum and act with dignity and respect to the officials and staff of the court.

Cannon 3   Official court interpreters avoid professional or personal conduct which could discredit the court.

Cannon 4   Official court interpreters, except upon court order, shall not disclose any information of a confidential nature about court cases obtained while performing interpreting duties.

Cannon 5   Official court interpreters respect the restraints imposed by the need for confidentiality and secrecy as protected under applicable federal and state law. Interpreters shall disclose to the court, and to the parties in a case, any prior involvement with that case, or private involvement with the parties or others significantly involved in the case.

Cannon 6   Official court interpreters undertake to inform the court of any impediment in the observance of this Code or of any effort by another to cause this Code to be violated.

Cannon 7   Official court interpreters work unobtrusively with full awareness of the nature of the proceedings.

Cannon 8   Official court interpreters fulfill a special duty to interpret accurately and faithfully without indicating any personal bias, avoiding even the appearance of partiality.

Cannon 9   Official court interpreters maintain impartiality by avoiding undue contact with witnesses, attorneys, and defendants and their families, and any contact with jurors. This should not limit, however, those appropriate contacts necessary to prepare adequately for their assignment.

Cannon 10   Official court interpreters refrain from giving advice of any kind to any party or individual and from expressing personal opinion in a matter before the court.

Cannon 11   Official court interpreters perform to the best of their ability to assure due process for the parties, accurately state their professional qualifications and refuse any assignment for which they are not qualified or under conditions which substantially impair their effectiveness.

They preserve the level of language used, and the ambiguities and nuances of the speaker, without any editing. Implicit in the knowledge of their limitations is the duty to correct any error of interpretation, and demonstrate their professionalism by requesting clarification of ambiguous statements or unfamiliar vocabulary and to analyze objectively any challenge to their performance. Interpreters have the duty to call to the attention of the court any factors or conditions which adversely affect their ability to perform adequately.

Cannon 12   Official court interpreters accept no remuneration, gifts, gratuities, or valuable consideration in excess of their authorized compensation in the performance of their official interpreting duties. Additionally, they avoid conflict of interest or even the appearance thereof.

Cannon 13   Official court interpreters support other official court interpreters by sharing knowledge and expertise with them to the extent practicable in the interests of the court, and by never taking advantage of knowledge obtained in the performance of official duties, or by their access to court records, facilities, or privileges, for their own or another's personal gain.

Cannon 14   Official court interpreters of the United States courts willingly accept and agree to be bound by this code, and understand that appropriate sanctions may be imposed by the court for willful violations.

APPENDIX D:
The Court Interpreter
Amendments Act of 1988

TITLE VII—COURT INTERPRETERS AMENDMENTS

SEC. 701. SHORT TITLE.

This title may be cited as the "Court Interpreter Amendments Act of 1988."

SEC. 702. AUTHORITY OF THE DIRECTOR.

Section 1827(a) is amended to read as follows:

"(a) The Director of the Administrative Office of the United States Courts shall establish a program to facilitate the use of certified and otherwise qualified interpreters in judicial proceedings instituted by the United States."

SEC. 703. CERTIFICATION OF INTERPRETERS: OTHER QUALIFIED INTERPRETERS

Section 1827(b) is amended to read as follows:

"(b)(1) The Director shall prescribe, determine, and certify the qualifications of persons who may serve as certified interpreters, when the Director considers certification of interpreters to be merited, for the hearing impaired (whether or not also speech impaired) and persons who speak only or primarily a language other than the English language, in judicial proceedings instituted by the United States. The Director may certify interpreters for any language if the Director determines that there is a need for certified interpreters in that language. Upon the request of the Judicial Conference of the United States for certified interpreters in a language, the Director shall certify interpreters in that language. Upon such a request from the judicial council of a circuit and the approval of the Judicial Conference, the Director shall certify interpreters for that circuit in the language requested. The judicial council of a circuit shall identify and evaluate the needs of the districts within a circuit. The Director shall certify interpreters based on the results of criterion-referenced performance examinations. The Director shall issue regulations to carry out this paragraph within 1 year after the date of the enactment of the Judicial Improvements and Access to Justice Act.

"(2) Only in a case in which no certified interpreter is reasonably available as provided in subsection (d) of this section, including a case in which certification of interpreters is not provided under paragraph (1) in a particular language, may the services of otherwise qualified interpreters be used. The Director shall provide guidelines to the courts for the selection of otherwise qualified interpreters, in order to ensure that the highest standards of accuracy are maintained in all judicial proceedings subject to the provisions of this chapter.

"(3) The Director shall maintain a current master list of all certified interpreters and otherwise qualified interpreters and shall report periodically on the use and performance of both certified and otherwise qualified interpreters in judicial proceedings instituted by the United States and on the languages for which interpreters have been certified. The Director shall prescribe, subject to periodic review, a schedule of reasonable fees for services rendered by interpreters, certified or otherwise, used in proceedings instituted by the United States, and in doing so shall consider the prevailing rate of compensation for comparable service in other governmental entities.".

SEC. 704. LISTS OF INTERPRETERS: RESPONSIBILITY FOR SECURING SERVICES OF INTERPRETERS.

Section 1827(c) is amended to read as follows:

"(c)(1) Each United States district court shall maintain on file in the office of the clerk, and each United States attorney shall maintain on file, a list of all persons who have been certified as interpreters by the Director in accordance with subsection (b) of this section. The clerk shall make the list of certified interpreters for judicial proceeding available upon request.

"(2) The clerk of the court, or other court employee designated by the chief judge, shall be responsible for securing the services of certified interpreters and otherwise qualified interpreters required for proceedings initiated by the United States, except that the United States attorney is responsible for securing the services of such interpreters for governmental witnesses.".

SEC. 705. SOUND RECORDINGS.

Section 1827(d) is amended by—

(1) redesignating paragraphs (1) and (2) as subparagraphs (A) and (B), respectively;

(2) inserting "(1)" after "(d)"; and

(3) adding at the end thereof the following:

"(2) Upon the motion of a party, the presiding judicial officer shall determine whether to require the electronic sound recording of a judicial proceeding in which an interpreter is used under this section. In making this determination, the presiding judicial officer shall consider, among other things, the qualifications of the interpreter and prior experience in interpretation of court proceedings; whether the language to be interpreted is not one of the languages for which the Director has certified interpreters, and the complexity or length of the proceeding. In a grand jury proceeding, upon the motion of the accused, the presiding judicial officer shall require the electronic sound recording of the portion of the proceeding in which an interpreter is used.".

SEC. 706. AUTHORIZATION OF APPROPRIATIONS: PAYMENT FOR SERVICES OF INTERPRETERS.

Section 1827(g) is amended—

(a) by amending paragraphs (1), (2), and (3) to read as follows:

"(g)(1) There are authorized to be appropriated to the Federal judiciary, and to be paid by the Director of the Administrative Office of the United States Courts, such sums as may be necessary to establish a program to facilitate the use of certified and otherwise qualified interpreters, and otherwise fulfill the provisions of this section and the Judicial Improvements and Access to Justice Act, except as provided in paragraph (3).

"(2) Implementation of the provisions of this section is contingent upon the availability of appropriated funds to carry out the purposes of this section.

"(3) Such salaries, fees, expenses, and costs that are incurred with respect to Government witnesses (including for grand jury proceedings) shall, unless direction is made under paragraph (4), be paid by the Attorney General from sums appropriated to the Department of Justice.";

(b) by redesignating paragraph (4) as paragraph (5) and by inserting between paragraph (3) and paragraph (5) the following:

"(4) Upon the request of any person in any action for which interpreting services established pursuant to subsection (d) are not otherwise provided, the clerk of the court, or other court employee designated by the chief judge, upon the request of the presiding judicial officer, shall, where possible, make such services available to that person on a cost-reimbursable basis, but the judicial officer may also require the prepayment of the estimated expenses of providing such services.".

SEC. 707. APPROVAL OF COMPENSATION AND EXPENSES.

Section 1827(h) is amended to read as follows:

"(h) The presiding judicial officer shall approve the compensation and expenses payable to interpreters, pursuant to the schedule of fees prescribed by the Director under subsection (b)(3).".

SEC. 708. DEFINITIONS.

Subsections (i) and (j) of section 1827 are amended to read as follows:

"(i) The term 'presiding judicial officer' as used in this section refers to any judge of a United States district court, including a bankruptcy judge, a United States magistrate, and in the case of grand jury proceedings conducted under the auspices of the United States attorney, a United States attorney.

"(j) The term 'judicial proceedings instituted by the United States' as used in this section refers to all proceedings, whether criminal or civil, including pretrial and grand jury proceedings (as well as proceedings upon a petition for a writ of habeas corpus initiated in the name of the United States by a relator) conducted in, or pursuant to the lawful authority and jurisdiction of a United States district court. The term 'United States district court' as used in this subsection includes any court which is created by an Act of Congress in a territory and is invested with any jurisdiction of a district court established by chapter 5 of this title.".

SEC. 709. SIMULTANEOUS INTERPRETATION.

Section 1827(k) is amended to read as follows:

"(k) The interpretation provided by certified or otherwise qualified interpreters pursuant to this section shall be in the simultaneous mode for any party to a judicial proceeding instituted by the United States and in the consecutive mode for witnesses, except that the presiding judicial officer, sua sponte or on the motion of a party, may authorize a simultaneous, or consecutive interpretation when such officer determines after a hearing on the record that such interpretation will aid in the efficient administration of justice. The presiding judicial officer, on such officer's motion or on the motion of a party, may order that special interpretation services as authorized in section 1828 of this title be provided if such officer determines that the provision of such services will aid in the efficient administration of justice.".

SEC. 710. TECHNICAL AMENDMENTS.

(a) Section 1827(d) is amended—

(1) by striking out "competent" and inserting in lieu thereof "qualified";

(2) by striking out "any criminal" and all that follows through "relator)" and inserting in lieu thereof "judicial proceedings instituted by the United States"; and

(3) by striking out "such action" and inserting in lieu thereof "such judicial proceedings";

(b) 1827(e)(2) is amended by striking out "criminal or civil action in a United States district court" and inserting in lieu thereof "judicial proceedings instituted by the United States";

SEC. 711. IMPACT ON EXISTING PROGRAMS.

Nothing in this title shall be construed to terminate or diminish existing programs for the certification of interpreters.

SEC. 712. EFFECTIVE DATE.

This title shall become effective upon the date of enactment.

APPENDIX E:
Directory of Professional Organizations and Certifying Bodies

A. Translating and Interpreting Organizations

1. American Association of Interpreters (AAI)
   P.O. Box 9603
   Washington, DC 20016
   (703) 998-8636

2. The American Association of Language Specialists (TAALS)
   1000 Connecticut Avenue, NW
   Washington, DC 20036
   (202) 762-6174

3. Registry of Interpreters for the Deaf (RID)
   51 Monroe Street, Suite 1107
   Rockville, MD 20850
   (301) 279-0555

4. International Association of Conference Interpreters (AIIC)
   John Daniel Katz, Secretary General
   10 Avenue de Sechevon
   Ch-1202
   Geneva, Switzerland

5. American Translators Association (ATA)
   109 Croton Avenue
   Ossining, NY 10562
   (914) 941-1500

6. National Association of Judicial Interpreters and Translators (NAJIT)
   815 E. 14th Street, #6B
   Brooklyn, NY 11230

7. United Interpreters and Translators Association
   P.O. Box 390006
   San Diego, CA 92139
   (619) 475-8586

8. Mr. Henry Keleny
   Association of Legal Court Interpreters and Translators
   2114 Boulevard, St-Laurent
   Montreal, Quebec H2X 2T2
   Canada

9. American Society of Interpreters (ASI)
   P.O. Box 5558
   Washington, DC 20016

10. Arizona Court Interpreters Association (ACIA)
    P.O. Box 4283
    Phoenix, AZ 85030

11. California Court Interpreters Association (CCIA)
    and CCIA Publications
    P.O. Box 646
    Van Nuys, CA 91408
    (818) 995-3232

12. Court Interpreters Association of New Jersey
    5 Atlantic Street
    Hackensack, NJ 07601

13. Ms. Carmen Barros
    Association of Professional Court Legal Interpreters and Translators (APCLIT)
    P.O. Box 1389
    Ridgewood, NJ 07450
    (201) 447-1117

14. Ms. Jill Aubin
    Association of Legal Translators and Interpreters of Massachusetts (ALTIMA)
    John F. Kennedy Post Office
    Boston, MA 02114
    (617) 646-1163

B. Federal and State Administrative Programs

1. Mr. Rick McBride
   Chief, Court Reporting and Interpreting Section
   Court Administration Division
   Administrative Office of the United States Courts
   1120 Vermont Avenue, NW, Suite 1202
   Washington, DC 20544
   (202) 633-6151

2. Federal Court Interpreter Certification Project (FCICP)
   (Write or call for the free Federal Court Interpreter Certification Manual.)
   ML #67, Room 445
   The University of Arizona
   Tucson, AZ 85721
   (602) 621-3686; FAX: (602) 624-8130

3. Department of State
   Language Services Division
   Office of Interpreting
   2201 "C" Street, NW
   Washington, DC 20520
   (202) 647-3492

4. Department of Justice
   Executive Office for Immigration Review
   Office of Management and Administration
   5107 Leesburg Pike, Suite 2300
   Falls Church, VA 22041
   (703) 756-7134

5. California State Certification
   Cooperative Personnel Services
   California State Personnel Board
   Local Government Services Division
   909 12th Street, 1st Floor
   Sacramento, CA 95814
   (916) 322-2530

6. Mr. Robert Joe Lee
   Legal Translation and Bilingual Services Division
   Administrative Office of the New Jersey Courts
   CN 988, Warren and Market Street
   Trenton, NJ 08625
   (609) 984-5024

7. Interpreter/Translation Services
   County Clerk/Exec. Office
   111 N. Hill Street, Room 219
   Los Angeles, CA 90012
   (213) 974-5403

8. New York State Court Interpreting Examination
   Office of Court Administration, Room 1209
   270 Broadway
   New York, NY 10007
   (212) 417-5891

9. New Mexico Court Interpreter Certification
   Administrative Office of the Courts
   Supreme Court Building
   Santa Fe, NM 87503

10. Ms. Joanne Moore, J.D., Court Specialist
    Office of the Administrator for the Courts
    1206 S. Quince Street
    Olympia, WA 98504
    (206) 753-3365

11. Mr. Lee Hartman, Supervisor of Appeals
    Texas Employment Commission
    TEC Building
    Austin, TX 78778
    (512) 463-2803

12. Chief Interpreter
    Interpretation Services
    United Nations
    First Avenue
    New York, NY 10017
    (212) 754-8233

13. Ms. Betty Harnum, Coordinator of Legal Interpreting
    Government of the Northwest Territories
    Yellowknife, Northwest Territories X1A 2L9
    Canada
    (403) 920-6110; FAX: (403) 873-0106

APPENDIX F:
California State Court Judicial Rules for Court Interpreters

STANDARDS OF JUDICIAL ADMINISTRATION

SECTION 18. STANDARDS FOR DETERMINING THE NEED FOR A COURT INTERPRETER

(a) [**When an interpreter is needed**] An interpreter is needed if upon examination by the court a party or witness is unable to speak English so as to be understood directly by counsel, court, and jury, or if a party is unable to understand and speak English sufficiently to comprehend the proceedings and to assist counsel in the conduct of the case. Separate interpreters may be needed for each non-English speaking party. An additional interpreter may be needed to interpret witness testimony for the court.

(b) [**When an examination is required**] Upon request by a party or counsel, or whenever it appears that a party's or witness' primary language is not English or that a party or witness may not speak and understand English sufficiently to participate fully in the proceedings, the court should conduct an examination on the record to determine whether a court interpreter is needed. After the examination, the court should state its conclusion on the record, and the file in the case should be clearly marked to ensure that an interpreter will be present when needed in any subsequent proceeding.

(c) [**Examination of party or witness**] The examination of the party or witness to determine if an interpreter is needed should normally include questions on the following:

(1) Identification (for example: name, address, birthdate, age, place of birth);

(2) Active vocabulary in vernacular English (for example: "How did you come to the court today?" "What kind of work do you do?" "Where did you go to school?" "What was the highest grade you completed?" "Describe what you see in the court-room." "What have you eaten today?"). Questions should be phrased to avoid "yes-no" replies;

(3) The court proceedings (for example: the nature of the charge or the type of case before the court, the purpose of the proceedings and function of the court, the rights of a party or criminal defendant, and the responsibilities of a witness).

Adopted, eff. July 1, 1979.

SECTION 18.1 INTERPRETED PROCEEDINGS: INSTRUCTING PARTICIPANTS ON PROCEDURE

In interpreted proceedings the court should instruct the participants on the procedure to be followed. These instructions may be given in writing and should normally include:

(a) [**Instructions to interpreters**] The following instructions should be given to interpreters:

(1) A preappearance interview should be held with the party or witness to enable the interpreter to become familiar with speech patterns and linguistic traits and to

595

determine what technical or special terms may be used. Except when consent is given by counsel, the pending proceedings should not be discussed with the party unless the party's counsel is present or with a witness unless counsel for the party calling the witness is present.

(2) During the preappearance interview with a non-English speaking witness, the interpreter should give the following instructions on procedure:

(i) Speak in a loud, clear voice so that the entire court and not just the interpreter can hear.

(ii) All responses should be directed to the person asking the question, not to the interpreter.

(iii) Any question should be directed to counsel or to the court and not to the interpreter. Do not seek advice from or engage in discussion with the interpreter.

(3) During the preappearance interview with a non-English speaking party, the interpreter should give the following instructions on the procedure to be used when the party is not testifying:

(i) The interpreter will interpret all statements made in open court that are a part of the case.

(ii) Any questions should be directed to counsel. The interpreter will interpret all questions to counsel and the responses. Do not seek advice from or engage in discussion with the interpreter.

(4) Communications between counsel and client are not to be disclosed.

(5) No legal advice should be given to a party or witness. Legal questions should be referred to the attorney or to the court.

(6) All statements made by the witness should be interpreted including statements or questions to the interpreter. No summary of any testimony should be made except on instruction by the court.

(7) The court should be informed if the interpreter is unable to interpret a word, expression, or special terminology.

(8) All words, including slang, vulgarisms, and epithets, should be interpreted to convey the intended meaning.

(9) All statements made in the first person should be interpreted in the first person. For example, a statement or question should not be introduced with the words, "He says..."

(10) All inquiries or problems should be directed to the court and not to the witness or counsel. In unusual circumstances, the interpreter may request permission to approach the bench with counsel to discuss the problem.

(11) The interpreter should be positioned near the witness or party but should not block the view of the judge, jury, or counsel.

(12) The court should be informed if the interpreter becomes fatigued during the proceedings.

(13) An interpreter who is to interpret for a party at counsel table should speak loudly enough to be heard by the party or counsel but not so loudly as to interfere with the proceedings.

(b) [**Instructions to counsel**] The following instructions should be given to counsel:

(1) All questions by counsel examining a non-English speaking witness should be directed to the witness and not to the interpreter. For example do not say, "Ask him if..."

(2) If counsel understands both languages and disagrees with the interpretation, any objection should be directed to the court and not to the interpreter. Counsel should ask permission to approach the bench to discuss the problem.

(3) If counsel believes that a prospective interpreter lacks the qualifications necessary to serve as an interpreter in the matter before the court, counsel may be permitted to conduct a brief supplemental examination before the court decides whether to appoint the interpreter.

Adopted. eff. July 1, 1979.

SECTION 18.2 INTERPRETED PROCEEDINGS: INTERPRETER UNDERSTANDING OF TERMINOLOGY USED IN THE COURTS

Courts should use interpreters who can (a) understand terms generally used in the type of proceeding before the court, (b) explain these terms in English and the other language being used, and (c) interpret these terms into the other language being used. Interpreters recommended pursuant to section 68562 of the Government Code should meet these requirements. If no list of recommended interpreters is available, or if it appears an interpreter cannot understand and interpret the terms used in the proceeding, the judge should conduct a brief examination of the interpreter to determine if the interpreter is qualified to interpret in the proceeding. In conducting the examination the judge should, if possible, seek the assistance of an interpreter whose qualifications have been established.

Adopted, eff. July 1, 1979.

SECTION 18.3 STANDARDS OF PROFESSIONAL CONDUCT FOR COURT INTERPRETERS

(a) [**Accurate interpretation**] A court interpreter's best skills and judgment should be used to interpret accurately without embellishing, omitting, or editing.

(b) [**Conflicts of interest**] A court interpreter should disclose to the judge and to all parties any actual or apparent conflict of interest. Any condition that interferes with the objectivity of an interpreter constitutes a conflict of interest. A conflict may exist if the interpreter is acquainted with or related to any witness or party to the action or if the interpreter has an interest in the outcome of the case. An interpreter should not engage in conduct creating the appearance of bias, prejudice, or partiality.

(c) [**Confidentiality**] A court interpreter should not disclose privileged communications between counsel and client. A court interpreter should not make statements about the merits of the case during the proceeding.

(d) [**Giving legal advice**] A court interpreter should not give legal advice to parties and witnesses, nor recommend specific attorneys or law firms.

(e) [**Professional relationships**] A court interpreter should maintain a professional relationship with court officers, parties, witnesses, and attorneys. A court interpreter should strive for professional detachment.

(f) [**Continuing education and duty to the profession**] A court interpreter should, through continuing education, maintain and improve his or her interpreting skills and knowledge of procedures used by the courts. A court interpreter should seek to elevate the standards of performance of the interpreting profession.

Adopted, eff. July 1, 1979.

Bibliography

Abbott, G., Greenwood, J., McKeating, D., & Wingard, P. (1981). *The teaching of English as an international language: A practical guide.* London: Collins.

Abril, M. (1987). *Cross-cultural communication in health care: How to use interpreters' services (Facilitator's guide).* (Available from Biomedical Communications, Health Sciences Center, University of Arizona, Tucson, 85721).

Acuña, R. (1972). *Occupied America: The Chicano's struggle toward liberation.* San Francisco: Canfield Press.

Adams, C. F. (1973). Comments: "Citado a comparecer." ["Cited to appear."]: Language barriers and due process—Is mailed notice in English constitutionally sufficient? *California Law Review, 61*(6), 1395-1421.

Adams, J. A. (1967). *Human memory.* New York: McGraw-Hill.

Adelo, A. S. (1986a, May 28). Los intérpretes en las cortes de NM [Interpreters in the courts of NM]. *The New Mexican,* p. A-6.

Adelo, A. S. (1986b, October 19). Judges recognize the importance of interpreters. *The New Mexican,* p. A-5.

Adelo, A. S. (1989, February 27). The role of the interpreter in legal proceedings. *The New Mexico Lawyer,* p. 12.

Administrative Office of the New Jersey Courts. (1987). *Overview of efforts of the administrative office of the New Jersey courts to screen applicants for staff court interpreting positions.* (Confidential internal document). Trenton: Author, Court Interpreting, Legal Translating & Bilingual Services Section.

Administrative Office of the New Jersey Courts. (1989). *Compensating interpreters and translators: An international survey of wages paid salaried and contracted interpreters and translators.* Trenton: Author, Court Interpreting, Legal Translating & Bilingual Services Section.

Administrative Office of the New Jersey Courts. *Assembly Bill No. 2089,* Court Interpreters Act, pending legislation 1988 session, second printing. (Available from Author, Court Interpreting, Legal Translating & Bilingual Services Section of the Administrative Office of the Courts, CN-988, Trenton, NJ 08625).

Administrative Office of the United States Courts. (1983). *Terms most often used in federal court.* (Available from Author, 811 Vermont Ave., NW, Washington, DC 20544).

Administrative Office of the United States Courts. (1987, November). *Federal court interpreters advisory board: Report to the director.* (Available from Author, 811 Vermont Ave., NW, Washington, DC 20544).

Administrative Office of the United States Courts. (1990, September). *Federal court interpreters manual: Policies and procedures.* (Available from Author, 811 Vermont Ave., NW, Washington, DC 20544).

Administrative Office of the United States Courts. (1988). Draft regulations: Subsection 1.62, challenges to interpretation. (Available from Author, 811 Vermont Ave., NW, Washington, DC 20544).

Administrative Office of the United States Courts. (1989a). *Court interpreter statistics.* (Available from Author, 811 Vermont Ave., NW, Washington, DC 20544).

Administrative Office of the United States Courts. (1989b). *Interim court interpreter regulations.* (Available from Author, 811 Vermont Ave., NW, Washington, DC 20544).

Administrative Procedure Act of 1946, Pub. L. 404, 60 Stat. §§ 237-244; as amended by Pub. L. 89-554, 80 Stat. 378 (5 U.S.C. § 101 et seq., 1966) (contained in W. Gellhorn, C. Byse, P. L. Strauss, T. Rakoff, & R. A. Schotland (1987), *Administrative law: Cases and comments* (8th ed.)). New York: Foundation Press.

Aguirre, A. M. (Ed.) (1989). *Northeast conference on legal interpretation and translation.* Wayne, NJ: The Consortium of Educators in Legal Interpretation and Translation at Jersey City State College.

Akmajian, A., Demers, R. A., & Harnish, R. (1984). *Linguistics: An introduction to language and communication* (2nd ed.). Cambridge: MIT Press.

Alatis, J. E. (1986). Comment: The question of language policy. *International Journal of the Sociology of Language, 60,* 197-200.

Alba, J. W., & Hasher, L. (1983). Is memory schematic? *Psychological Bulletin, 93*(2), 203-31.

Allen v. U.S., 164 U.S. 492 (1896).

Almeida, F. M., & Zahler, S. (Eds.). (1981). *Los Angeles superior court interpreters manual.* Los Angeles: Los Angeles Superior Court.

The American Heritage dictionary of the English language. (1973). Boston: American Heritage Publishing & Houghton Mifflin.

American Heritage-Larousse Spanish dictionary. (1986). Boston: Houghton Mifflin.

American Psychological Association. (1985). *Standards for educational and psychological tests.* Washington, DC: Author.

Amory v. Fellowes, 5 Mass. 219 (1809).

Anderson, C. A. (1982). Inoculation and counterexplanation: Debiasing techniques in the perseverance of social theories. *Social Cognition, 1*(2), 126-39.

Anderson, J. R. (1983). *The architecture of cognition.* Cambridge, MA: Harvard University Press.

Anderson, R. B. (1976). Perspectives on the role of the interpreter. In R. W. Brislin (Ed.), *Translation: Applications and research* (pp. 208-28). New York: Gardner Press.

Anderson, R. B. (1978). Interpreter roles and interpretation situations: Cross-cutting typologies. In D. Gerver & H. W. Sinaiko (Eds.), *Language interpretation and communication* (pp. 217-30). New York: Plenum.

Anderson, R. C. (1977). The notion of schemata and the educational enterprise: General discussion of the conference. In R. C. Anderson, R. J. Spiro, & W. E. Montague (Eds.), *Schooling and the acquisition of knowledge* (pp. 415-31). Hillsdale, NJ: Lawrence Erlbaum Associates.

Anstey, J. (1796). *The pleader's guide, a didactic poem.* London: T. Cadell & W. Davies.

Arizona rules of court: State and federal. (1988). St. Paul, MN: West Publishing.

Arizona v. Natividad, 111 Ariz. 191, 526 P.2d 730 (1974).

Arjona, E. (1978). Intercultural communication and the training of interpreters at the Monterey Institute of Foreign Studies. In D. Gerver & H. W. Sinaiko (Eds.), *Language interpretation and communication* (pp. 35-44). New York: Plenum.

Arjona, E. (1983, February). Language planning in the judicial system: A look at the implementation of the U.S. Court Interpreters Act. *Language Planning Newsletter, 9*(1), 1-6.

Arjona, E. (1985). The court interpreters certification test design. In L. Elías-Olivares, E. A. Leone, R. Cisneros, & J. R. Gutiérrez (Eds.), *Spanish language use and public life in the United States* (pp. 181-200). Berlin: Mouton de Gruyter.

Arredondo, L., & Tapia, D. (1971-72). El Chicano y the Constitution: The legacy of *Hernandez v. Texas*—Grand jury discrimination. *University of San Francisco Law Review*, 6, 129-46.

Assembly Bill No. 2400, A.B. 86 Cal. State. 1973, c. 1182 (Gov't. Code Sec. 68560-68564) (1978).

Assembly Bill No. 1386, California (1988).

Astiz, C. (1980, July). *Language barriers in the criminal justice system: A look at the federal judiciary*. Paper presented at the National Hispanic Conference on Law Enforcement and Criminal Justice, Washington, DC.

Astiz, C. (1986). But they don't speak the language: Achieving quality control of translation in criminal courts. *The Judges' Journal*, 25(2), 32-35, 56.

Atkinson, R. C., & Shiffrin, R. M. (1968). Human memory: A proposed system and its control processes. In K. Spence & J. Spence (Eds.), *The psychology of learning and motivation: Advances in research and theory* (Vol. 2) (pp. 89-195). New York: Academic Press.

Atwater, E. (1981). *"I hear you": Listening skills to make you a better manager*. Englewood Cliffs: Prentice-Hall.

Auerbach, C. A., Hurst, W., Garrison, L. K., & Mermin, S. (1985). *The legal process: An introduction to decision making by judicial, legislative, executive, and administrative agencies*. San Francisco: Chandler Publishing.

Ausubel, D. (1978). *Educational psychology: A cognitive view* (2nd ed.). New York: Holt, Rinehart, & Winston.

Ayto, J. (Ed.). (1989). *Longman register of new words*. Avon, England: Bath Press.

Baddeley, A. D. (1976). *The psychology of memory*. New York: Basic Books.

Baddeley, A. D. (1982). *Your memory: A user's guide*. New York: Macmillan.

Barik, H. C. (1969). *A study of simultaneous interpretation*. Unpublished doctoral dissertation, University of North Carolina.

Barik, H. C. (1971). A description of various types of omissions, additions and errors of translation encountered in simultaneous interpretation. *Meta*, 16(4), 199-210.

Barik, H. C. (1972). *Simultaneous interpretation: Temporal and quantitative data*. Chapel Hill: University of North Carolina, L. L. Thurstone Laboratory.

Barik, H. C. (1973). *Simultaneous interpretation: Qualitative and linguistic data*. Chapel Hill: University of North Carolina, L. L. Thurstone Laboratory.

Bartlett, F. C. (1932). *Remembering: A study in experimental and social psychology*. London: Cambridge University Press.

Bartol, C. R. [with A. M. Bartol]. (1983). *Psychology and American law*. Belmont, CA: Wadsworth Publishing.

Bathgate, R. H. (1985). Studies of translation models 3: An interactive model of the translation process. *Meta*, 30(2), 129-38.

Baum, L. (1986). *American courts*. Boston: Houghton Mifflin.

Bayley, C. J. (1973). *Manual del traductor público [Manual for the public translator]*. Buenos Aires, Argentina: Author.

Beardsley, C. A. (1941, March). Beware of, eschew and avoid pompous prolixity and platitudinous epistles! *California State Bar Journal*, 16(3), 65-69.

Bell, R. T. (1987). Translation theory: Where are we going? *Meta*, 32(4), 403-15.

Belliveau, G., de la Bandera, E., & Lee, R. J. (1988). *There must be something wrong with that test! A glance at New Jersey's screening test for court interpreters.* (Confidential internal document). Trenton: Administrative Office of the New Jersey Courts, Court Interpreting, Legal Translation, and Bilingual Services Section.

Bennett, J. (1981). The role of court interpreting and the work of court interpreters. In R. P. Roberts (Ed.), *L'Interprétation auprès des tribunaux [Interpretation in the courts]* (pp. 11-18). Canada: University of Ottawa Press.

Bergenfield, G. (1978). Trying non-English conversant defendants: The use of an interpreter. *Oregon Law Review, 57,* 549-65.

Berger, M. J., Mitchell, J. B., & Clark, R. H. (1989). *Trial advocacy: Planning, analysis, and strategy.* Boston: Little, Brown.

Berk-Seligson, S. (1987). The intersection of testimony styles in interpreted judicial proceedings: Pragmatic alterations in Spanish testimony. *Linguistics, 25*(292), 1087-1125.

Berk-Seligson, S. (1988). The need for quality interpreting services in the courtroom. *The Court Manager, 3*(2), 10-14.

Berk-Seligson, S. (1990). *The bilingual courtroom: Court interpreters in the judicial process.* Chicago: The University of Chicago Press.

Berreby, D. (1982, December 20). Interpreters on call for more cases. *The National Law Journal,* pp. 1, 24-25.

Bever, T. (1970). The cognitive basis for linguistic structures. In J. Hayes (Ed.), *Cognition and the development of language.* New York: Wiley.

Bilby, R. A. (1983, June). Speech given at Summer Institute for Court Interpretation, University of Arizona, Tucson, AZ.

Bilingual Education Act of 1968, embodied in the Educational Amendments Act of 1984, Pub. L. 98-511, 98 Stat. 2366 (codified at 20 U.S.C. § 880b et seq. (1984)).

Birdwhistell, R. L. (1970). *Kinesics and context: Essays on body motion communication.* Philadelphia: University of Pennsylvania Press.

Biscaye, E., & Howard, P. G. (1987, May). *Aboriginal language translating and interpreting in the Northwest Territories.* Paper presented at the International Conference for Translators & Interpreters, Vancouver, British Columbia.

Bjork, R. A. (1970). Repetition and rehearsal mechanisms in models for STM. In D. A. Norman (Ed.), *Models of human memory.* New York: Academic Press.

Black's Law dictionary (5th ed.). (1979). St. Paul, MN: West Publishing.

Blaine, C. P. (1974). Breaking the language barrier: New rights for California's linguistic minorities. *Pacific Law Journal, 5*(2), 648-74.

Blanco, G. (1978). The implementation of bilingual/bicultural education programs in the United States. In B. Spolsky & R. Cooper (Eds.), *Case studies in bilingual education* (pp. 454-99). Rowley, MA: Newbury House.

Bogoch, S. (1968). *The biochemistry of memory, with an inquiry into the function of the brain mucoids.* England: Oxford University Press.

Bolinger, D., & Sears, D. A. (1981). *Aspects of language* (3rd ed.). New York: Harcourt Brace Jovanovich.

Bourne, L. E., Dominowski, R. L., & Loftus, E. (1979). *Cognitive processes.* Englewood Cliffs, NJ: Prentice-Hall.

Bowen, D., & Bowen, M. (1980). *Steps to consecutive interpretation.* Washington, DC: Pen & Booth.

Bransford, J. D., & Franks, J. J. (1971). The abstraction of linguistic ideas. *Cognitive Psychology, 2*(4), 331-50.

Bressan, D. (1987). Emphatic devices in English-Italian translation. *Multilingua, 6*(1), 69-75.

Briere, E. J. (1978). Limited English speakers and the Miranda rights. *TESOL Quarterly, 12*(3), 3-5.

Brislin, R. W. (1976). *Translation applications and research.* New York: Gardner Press.

Brislin, R. W. (1978). Contributions of cross-cultural orientation programs and power analysis to translation/interpretation. In D. Gerver & H. W. Sinaiko (Ed.), *Language interpretation and communication* (pp. 205-16). New York: Plenum.

Brown, R., & McNeill, D. (1966). The "tip of the tongue" phenomenon. *Journal of Verbal Learning and Verbal Behavior, 5*(4), 325-37.

Buckhout, R. (1974). Eyewitness testimony. *Scientific American, 231*(6), 23-31.

California Code of Civil Procedures § 1884 (cited in *People v. Young*, 108 Cal. 8, 41 Pac. 281 (1895)).

California Constitution, Article 1, Section 14. (1974).

Callejo, R. A. (1968, October/November). The case for the Spanish speaking. *Trial*, pp. 52-53.

Canadian Charter of Rights and Freedoms. Part One of the Constitution Act, Schedule B of the Canada Act (U.K.), 1982, C.11.

Canale, M., & Swain, M. (1980). Theoretical bases of communicative approaches to second language teaching and testing. *Applied Linguistics, 1,* 1-47.

Canfield, D. L. (1981). *Spanish pronunciation in the Americas.* Chicago: University of Chicago Press.

Carr, J. G. (1989). *Criminal procedure handbook.* New York: Clark Boardman.

Carr, S. E. (Ed.). (1984). *Manual for court interpreters* (Vols. 1-4). Vancouver: Vancouver Community College.

Carr, S. E. (1988). Towards a court interpreting system in a multi-cultural society: English-speaking British Columbia. In D. L. Hammond (Ed.), *American translators association conference 1988* (pp. 417-22). Medford, NJ: Learned Information.

Cataldo, B. F., Kempin, F. G., Jr., Stockton, J. M., & Weber, C. M. (1980). *Introduction to law and the legal process* (3rd ed.). New York: John Wiley & Sons.

Catford, J. C. (1965). *A linguistic theory of translation.* London: Oxford University Press.

Cervantes v. Cox, 350 F.2d 855 (1965).

Chall, J. S. (1958). *Readability: An appraisal of research and application.* Columbus: Ohio State University Press.

Chang, W. B., & Araujo, M. U. (1975). Interpreters for the defense: Due process for the non-English-speaking defendant. *California Law Review, 63*(3), 801-23.

Charrow, V. (1982). Linguistic theory and the study of legal and bureaucratic language. In L. K. Obler & L. Menn (Eds.), *Exceptional language and linguistics* (pp. 81-101). New York: Academic Press.

Charrow, V., & Charrow, R. (1979). Characteristics of the language of jury instructions. In J. Alatis & G. R. Tucker (Eds.), *Georgetown University round table on languages and linguistics* (pp. 163-85). Washington, DC: Georgetown University Press.

Charrow, V., & Crandall, J. (1978). *Legal language: What is it and what can we do about it?* Unpublished manuscript, American Institutes for Research and Center for Applied Linguistics, Arlington, VA.

Charrow, V., Crandall, J., & Charrow, R. (1982). Characteristics and functions of legal language. In R. Kittredge & J. Lehrberger (Eds.), *Sublanguage: Studies of language in restricted semantic domains* (pp. 175-90). Berlin: Mouton de Gruyter.

Chiu, R. K. (1972). Measuring register characteristics: A prerequisite for preparing advanced level TESOL programs. *TESOL Quarterly* (2), 6, 129-41.

Chomsky, N. (1965). *Aspects of the theory of syntax.* Cambridge: MIT Press.

Christiaansen, R. E., Sweeney, J. D., & Ochalek, K. (1983). Influencing eyewitness descriptions. *Law and Human Behavior,* 7(1), 59-65.

Civil Rights Act of 1964, Pub. L. 88-352, 78 Stat. 241 (as amended at 42 U.S.C. §§ 2000a to 2000h-6 (1982)).

Cleary, E. W. (Ed.). (1984). *McCormick on evidence* (3rd ed.). St. Paul, MN: West Publishing.

Cokely, D. (1984). *Towards a sociolinguistic model of the interpreting process: Focus on ASL and English.* Unpublished doctoral dissertation, Georgetown University, Washington, DC.

Collins, A. M., & Quillian, M. R. (1972). How to make a language user. In E. Tulving & W. Donaldson (Eds.), *Organization of memory* (pp. 309-51). New York: Academic Press.

Colonomos, B. (in press). The development of a model and its application to the teaching of interpretation. (Available from Author, The Bicultural Center, 5506 Kenilworth Ave., Ste. 105, Lower Level, Riverdale, MD 20737).

Combs, M. C., & Trasviña, J. (1986). Legal implications of the English language movement. In M. C. Combs (Ed.), *The English only movement: An agenda for discrimination* (pp. 24-31). Washington, DC: League of United Latin American Citizens (LULAC).

Commission on Bilingualism and Biculturalism. (1970). *The law of languages in Canada.* Ottawa: Royal Commission.

Comprehensive Crime Control Act of 1984, Pub. L. 98-473, 98 Stat. 1837; Title I, Bail Reform Act, 18 U.S.C. §3146 et seq.; Title II, Sentencing Reform Act, 18 U.S.C. §3551 et seq.; United States Sentencing Commission, 28 U.S.C. §991 et seq.

Comptroller General of the United States. (1977). *Use of interpreters for language-disabled persons involved in federal, state, and local judicial proceedings* (No. GGD-77-68). Washington, DC: U.S. GPO.

Congressional Record Senate 12445-12446. (Daily ed. 14 July 1975a).

Congressional Record House 6821. (Daily ed. 15 July 1975b).

Conley, J. M. (1979, September). Language in the courtroom. *Trial,* pp. 32-36.

Cooper, C. L., & Cooper, R. D. (1983). Occupational stress among international interpreters. *Journal of Occupational Medicine,* 25(12), 889-95.

Cooperative Personnel Services—Interpreter Program. (No date). *State personnel board qualifying examination for administrative hearing and court interpreter.* (Available from Author, 1820 Tribute Road, Suite A, Sacramento, CA 95815).

Cooperative Personnel Services—Interpreter Program. (1987). *State Personnel Board qualifying examination for administrative hearing interpreter.* (Available from Author, 1820 Tribute Road, Suite A, Sacramento, CA 95815).

Corpus Juris Secundum. (1988). 24A C.J.S. 1770(3), Criminal law, sufficiency of transcripts (p. 282, note 30). St. Paul, MN: West Publishing.

Corteen, R. S., & Wood, B. (1972). Automatic responses to shock-associated words in an unattended channel. *Journal of Experimental Psychology,* 94, 308-13.

Coughlin, J. (1984). Should court interpreters and conference interpreters be trained in separate academic programs? *Meta,* 29(4), 420-21.

Court Interpreter Amendments Act of 1988, Pub. L. 100-702, 102 Stat. 4654 (codified at 28 U.S.C. § 1827(b)(1) (1988)).

Court Interpreter Task Force of the State of Washington. (1986). *Initial report & recommendations of the court interpreter task force.* Olympia, WA: Office of the Administrator for the Courts.

Court Interpreters Act of 1978, Pub. L. 95-539, 92 Stat. 2040 (codified at 28 U.S.C. §1827 (1978)).

Court Interpreters Act of 1985, N.M. Stat. Ann. 38-10-1 (1985).

The Court Manager. (1988). 3(2).

Craik, F. I. (1973). Levels of analysis view of memory. In P. Pliner, L. Krames, & T. Alloway (Eds.), *Communication and affect: Language and thought* (pp. 45-65). New York: Academic Press.

Craik, F. I., & Lockhart, R. S. (1972). Levels of processing: A framework for memory research. *Journal of Verbal Learning and Verbal Behavior, 11*(6), 671-84.

Crawford, J. (1989). *Bilingual education: History, politics, theory, and practice.* Trenton: Crane Publishing.

Criminal code, title 13 (1988). In J. Shumway (Iss.), *Arizona revised statutes.* Secretary of State.

Criminal Justice Act of 1964, Pub. L. 88-455, 78 Stat. 552 (18 U.S.C. §3006A et seq.).

Cronheim, A. J., & Schwartz, A. H. (1976). Non-English-speaking persons in the criminal justice system: Current state of the law. *Cornell Law Review, 61*(2), 289-311.

Cummins, J. (1976). The influence of bilingualism on cognitive growth: A synthesis of research findings and explanatory hypothesis. *Working Papers on Bilingualism, 9*, 1-43.

Cummins, J. (1989). *Empowering minority students.* Sacramento: Santillana Publishing.

Cunliffe, I. G. (1984, April). *Interpreter usage in the legal system.* Paper presented at the Law Week Seminar of the Steering Committee. (Available from Ethnic Affairs Commission of New South Wales, 189 Kent St., Sydney 2000).

Danet, B. (1979). Language in the courtroom. In H. Giles, W. P. Robinson, & P. M. Smith (Eds.), *Language: Social psychological perspectives* (pp. 367-76). New York: Pergamon Press.

Danet, B. (1980). Language in the legal process. *Law and Society Review, 14*(3), 445-564.

Danet, B., & Bogoch, B. (1979, September). *Fixed fight or free-for-all? An empirical study of combativeness in the adversary system of justice.* Paper presented at the Conference on the Sociology of Law, International Sociological Association, Cagliari, Sardinia.

d'Ans, A. (1987). *Haiti: Paysage et société. [Landscape and society.]* Paris: Karthala.

Davis, J. (1980). Transcripts of *U.S. v. Hanigan*, No. CR-79-206-TUC-RMB. (Available from Official Court Reporter, United States District Court, P.O. Box 142, Tucson 85702).

Deitch, J. (1985, November 3). Court translation held lax. *The New York Times*, pp. 1, 15.

Deleon, P. H., O'Keefe, A. M., Vandenbos, G. R., & Kraut, A. (1982). How to influence public policy: A blueprint for activism. *American Psychologist, 37*(5), 476-85.

Devine, M. (1983). *Analysis of the Dene language: Information review.* Yellowknife, Northwest Territories, Canada: Government of the Northwest Territories, Department of Information.

District Judges Association, Committee on Pattern Jury Instructions. (1985a). *Pattern jury instructions: Civil cases.* St. Paul: West.

District Judges Association, Committee on Pattern Jury Instructions. (1985b). *Pattern jury instructions: Criminal cases with annotations and comments.* St. Paul: West.

Doucette v. State, 463 A.2d 741 (Me. 1983).

Dunkel, P. G. (1985). *The immediate recall of English lecture information by native and non-native speakers of English as a function of notetaking.* Unpublished doctoral dissertation, University of Arizona, Tucson.

Dusky v. United States, 271 F.2d 385 (8th Cir.), *reversed (per curiam)*, 362 U.S. 402 (1960).

Dymally-Alatorre Bilingual Services Act of 1973, A.B. 86 Cal. Stats. Ch. 1182, §7290 et seq. (1973).

Edwards, A. B. (1988). Ethical conduct for the court interpreter. *The Court Manager, 3*(2), 22-25.

Ehrmann, H. W. (1976). *Comparative legal cultures.* Englewood Cliffs, NJ: Prentice-Hall.

El Rescate Legal Services, Inc. et al., v. Executive Office for Immigration Review et al., United States District Court for the Central District of Los Angeles, Case No. 88-01201-WPG, Class Action (1988).

Elgin, S. H. (1979), *What is linguistics?* (2nd ed.). Englewood Cliffs, NJ: Prentice-Hall.

Elwork, A., Sales, B. D., & Alfini, J. (1982). *Making jury instructions understandable.* Charlottesville, VA: Michie.

Engelbert, J. (1982). Translating for legal personnel. In M. R. Frankenthaler (Ed.), *Skills for bilingual legal personnel* (pp. 191-282). Cincinnati, OH: South-Western Publishing.

Equal Employment Opportunity Act of 1972, Pub. L. 92-261, 86 Stat. 103 (codified at 42 U.S.C. §2000e et seq.).

Erickson, B., Lind, E. A., Johnson, B. C., & O'Barr, W. M. (1978). Speech style and impression formation in a court setting: The effects of "powerful" and "powerless" speech. *Journal of Experimental Social Psychology, 14*(3), 266-79.

Ericsson, K. A., Chase, W. G., & Faloon, S. (1980). Acquisition of a memory skill. *Science, 208*, 1181-82.

Escobar v. State, 30 Ariz. 159, 245 P. 356 (1926).

Esparza, M. (Producer), & Young, R. M. (Director). (1983). *The ballad of Gregorio Cortez* [Film]. Los Angeles: Embassy Home Entertainment.

Ewell, M., & Schrieberg, D. (1989, December 17). How court interpreters distort justice. *San Jose Mercury News*, p. 1A.

Falk, J. S. (1978). *Linguistics and language: A survey of basic concepts and implications* (2nd ed.). New York: John Wiley & Sons.

Farar v. Warfield, 8 Mart. (N.S.) 695 (1830). [Louisiana Reports].

Farmer, M. W. (1983, June 27). Outcome of case may depend on court interpreter's language skills. *The Christian Science Monitor*, p. 14.

Fasold, R. (1984). *The sociolinguistics of society.* Oxford: Basil Blackwell.

Federal civil judicial procedure and rules. (1989 ed.). St. Paul, MN: West Publishing.

Federal criminal code and rules. (1989 ed.). St. Paul, MN: West Publishing.

Federal Judicial Center. (1989, June). *Court interpreter qualification process amended, Navajo and Haitian Creole certification planned* (1989-241-150-00006). *The Third Branch: Bulletin of the Federal Courts, 21*(6), 7. Washington, DC: U.S. GPO.

Federal rules of civil procedure and appellate procedure. (1968). St. Paul, MN: West Publishing.

Federal rules of civil-appellate criminal procedure. (1968). St. Paul, MN: West Publishing.

Federal rules of evidence for United States courts and magistrates with amendments. (1966). St. Paul, MN: West Publishing.

Ferrara, P., & Minter, M. W. (1986). *Development and validation of written examinations for court interpreter.* New York: New York State Unified Court System, Office of Court Administration.

Figliulo, J. R. (1984). Breaking the language barrier. *Litigation, 10*(2), 32-33, 62-63.

Firth, J. R. (1957). *Papers in linguistics.* London: Oxford University Press.

Fishman, J., Nahirny, V. C., Hofman, J. E., & Hayden, R. G. (1966). *Language loyalty in the United States: The maintenance and perpetuation of non-English mother tongues by American ethnic and religious groups*. The Hague: Mouton.

Fiske, S. T., & Linville, P. W. (1980). What does the schema concept buy us? *Personality and Social Psychology Bulletin, 6*(4), 543-57.

Fiske, S. T., & Taylor, S. E. (1984). *Social cognition*. Reading, MA: Addison-Wesley Publishing.

Flaherty, F. J. (1983, March 14). The struggle continues. *The National Law Journal*, pp. 1, 20-21.

Flores d'Arcais, G. B. (1978). The contribution of cognitive psychology to the study of interpretation. In D. Gerver & H. W. Sinaiko (Eds.), *Language interpretation and communication* (pp. 385-402). New York: Plenum.

Fodor, J. A. (1983). *The modularity of mind*. Cambridge, MA: MIT/Bradford.

Fodor, J. A., Bever, T., & Garrett, M. (1974). *The psychology of language*. New York: McGraw-Hill.

Fodor, J. A., & Garrett, M. (1967). Some syntactic determinants of sentential complexity. *Perception and Psychophysics, 2*(7), 289-96.

Foster, C. R., & Valdman, A. (1984). *Haiti—today and tomorrow: An interdisciplinary study*. New York: University Press of America.

Frankenthaler, M. R. (1980). Spanish translation in the courtroom. *Social Action & the Law, 6*(4), 51-62.

Frankenthaler, M. R., & McCarter, H. L. (1978, Summer). A call for legislative action: The case for a New Jersey court interpreters act. *Seton Hall Legislative Journal, 3*(2), 125-65.

Frankenthaler, M. R., & Zahler, S. (1984). Las características del lenguaje jurídico: Comunicación en el ámbito legal [The characteristics of legal language communication in the legal setting]. *Revista de Lengua I Dret, 2*, 77-88.

Fries, P. (1986). *A systemic analysis of the 1980 and 1983 oral federal court interpreter Spanish certification examination*. (Confidential internal document). Tucson: University of Arizona, Federal Court Interpreter Certification Project.

Frishberg, N. (1986). *Interpreting: An introduction*. Silver Spring, MD: Registry of the Interpreters of the Deaf.

Furcolo, F. (1977). *"Law for you": Law for the layman*. Washington, DC: Acropolis Books.

Galinski, C. (1988). Terminology and information/knowledge management. In D. L. Hammond (Ed.), *Language at crossroads: Proceedings of the 29th annual conference* (pp. 485-92). Medford, NJ: Learned Information.

Gardiana v. Small Claims Court in and for San Leandro-Haya, 59 Cal. App. 3d 412, 130 Cal. Rptr. 675 (1976).

Gardner, H. (1983). *Frames of mind: The theory of multiple intelligences*. New York: Basic Books.

Garland, S. (1981a, December 7). Hispanic court cases: The verdict is all in the translation. *The Christian Science Monitor*, p. 23.

Garland, S. (1981b, December 9). Easing the plight of non-English-speaking defendants. *The Christian Science Monitor*, p. 18.

Garretson, D. A. (1981). A psychological approach to consecutive interpretation. *Meta, 26*(3), 244-54.

Gee Long v. State, 33 Ariz. 420, 265 P. 622 (1928).

Gee, T. G. (1986). Prepared statement on behalf of the United States Judicial Conference. In *Court interpreter's improvement act of 1985: Hearing before the subcommittee on the judiciary United States Senate.* 99th Cong., 2nd Session, S. 1853. Washington, DC: U.S. GPO.

Gerver, D. (1969). The effects of source language presentation rate on the performance of simultaneous conference interpreters. In F. Foulke (Ed.), *Proceedings of the 2nd Louisville Conference on rate and/or frequency controlled speech* (pp. 162-84). Louisville: University of Louisville.

Gerver, D. (1971). *Simultaneous interpretation and human information processing.* Unpublished doctoral dissertation, Oxford University.

Gerver, D. (1972a). A.S.P.A.—Automatic speech-pause analyzer. *Behavioral Research Methods and Instrumentation, 4,* 265-70.

Gerver, D. (1972b). *Simultaneous and consecutive interpretation and human information processing* (Research Report, HR 566/1). London: Social Science Research Council.

Gerver, D. (1974a). The effects of noise on the performance of simultaneous interpreters: Accuracy of performance. *Acta Psychologica, 38*(3), 159-67.

Gerver, D. (1974b). Simultaneous listening and speaking and retention of prose. *Quarterly Journal of Experimental Psychology, 26*(3), 337-41.

Gerver, D. (1976). Empirical studies of simultaneous interpretation: A review and a model. In R. W. Brislin (Ed.), *Translation: Applications and research* (pp. 165-207). New York: Gardner Press.

Gerver, D. (1980). *Conference interpretation: A review of recent theory and research.* Unpublished manuscript.

Gerver, D., & Sinaiko, H. W. (Eds.). (1978). *Language interpretation and communication.* New York: Plenum.

Gifis, S. H. (1984). *Law dictionary* (2nd ed.). Woodbury, NY: Barron's Educational Series.

Gile, D. (1985). Le modèle d'efforts et l'équilibre d'interprétation en interprétation simultanée [The efforts model and balanced interpretation in simultaneous interpretation]. *Meta, 30,* 44-48.

Gile, D. (1988). An overview of conference interpretation research and theory. In D. L. Hammond (Ed.), *Language at a crossroads: Proceedings of the 29th annual conference* (pp. 363-71). Medford, NJ: Learned Information.

Giles, H., & St. Clair, R. N. (Eds.). (1979). *Language and social psychology.* Oxford: Basil Blackwell.

Gish, S. (1988, May). *The health care interpreter: A specialized mental and medical health training program for sign language interpreters.* Paper presented at the International Conference for Translators and Interpreters, Crystal City, VA.

Glendon, M. S., Gordon, M. W., & Osakwe, C. (1982). *Comparative legal traditions in a nutshell.* St. Paul, MN: West Publishing.

Goldman-Eisler, F. (1967). Sequential temporal patterns and cognitive processes in speech. *Language and Speech, 10*(1), 122-32.

Goldman-Eisler, F. (1968). *Psycholinguistics: Experiments in spontaneous speech.* London: Academic Press.

Goldner, D. (1987a, May 4). Mistrial in Miami. *Miami Review,* pp. 1, 4, 9.

Goldner, D. (1987b, May 5). Mistrial in Miami. *Miami Review,* pp. 1, 4.

Goldner, D. (1987c, May 6). Mistrial in Miami. *Miami Review,* pp. 1, 4, 5.

Gonzales v. State, 372 A.2d 191 (Del. Supr. 1977).

Gonzalez, R. D. (1976). *English language handicap diagnostic instrument no. 1.* Tucson: Pima County Superior Court, Justice Interpreters Model Development. (Available from Author, University of Arizona, ML #67, Rm. 445, 85721).

Gonzalez, R. D. (1977). *The design and validation of an evaluative procedure to diagnose the English aural-oral competency of a Spanish-speaking-person in the justice system.* Unpublished doctoral dissertation, University of Arizona, Tucson.

Gonzalez, R. D. (1980). *The register of courtroom English.* [Monograph]. (Available from Administrative Office of the United States Courts, 811 Vermont Ave., NW, Washington, DC 20544).

Gonzalez, R. D. (Ed.). (1983). *Summer institute for court interpretation: A description and evaluation of a pilot training model.* Unpublished report to the Agnese Lindley Foundation. Tucson: Summer Institute for Court Interpretation, University of Arizona.

Gonzalez, R. D. (1985). *A description and evaluation of a pilot training model: The training of trainers of court interpreters.* Unpublished report to the Agnese Lindley Foundation. Tucson: Summer Institute of Court Interpretation, University of Arizona.

Gonzalez, R. D. (1986, December). *Federal court interpreter certification examination manual.* (Available from the Federal Court Interpreter Certification Project, ML #67, Rm. 445, University of Arizona, Tucson 85721).

Gonzalez, R. D. (1987a, September). *How to make your professional organization work for you.* Paper presented at the Arizona Court Interpreter Association Conference. (Available from Author, University of Arizona, ML #67, Rm. 445, Tucson 85721).

Gonzalez, R. D. (1987b, March). *Test specifications for the federal court interpreter certification examination.* (Confidential internal document). Tucson: University of Arizona, Federal Court Interpreter Certification Project.

Gonzalez, R. D. (1988, April). *The federal court interpreter certification examination: A model for state courts.* Tucson: University of Arizona, Federal Court Interpreter Certification Project.

Gonzalez, R. D. (1988-89). *A comparative analysis of the 1985 and 1987 federal oral certification examination.* (Confidential internal document). Tucson: University of Arizona, Federal Court Interpreter Certification Project.

Gonzalez, R. D. (1989a). *Cultural and linguistic issues affecting the design and implementation of a Haitian Creole federal court interpreter certification examination.* Tucson: University of Arizona, Federal Court Interpreter Certification Project.

Gonzalez, R. D. (1989b). *Cultural and linguistic issues affecting the design and implementation of a Navajo federal court interpreter certification examination.* Tucson: University of Arizona, Federal Court Interpreter Certification Project.

Gonzalez, R. D. (1989c). *Test specifications for the federal court interpreter certification examination.* (Confidential internal document). Tucson: University of Arizona, Federal Court Interpreter Certification Project.

Gonzalez, R. D. (1990a). In the aftermath of the ELA: Stripping language minorities of their rights. In S. Daniels (Ed.), *English Yes: Only No!* Urbana IL: National Council Teachers of English.

Gonzalez, R. D. (1990b). *Rater comments from the 1985, 1987, and 1989 federal court interpreter oral certification examinations.* (Confidential internal document). Tucson: University of Arizona, Federal Court Interpreter Certification Project.

Gonzalez, R. D. (1990c). When minority becomes majority: The changing face of the English classroom. *English Journal, 79 (1),* 16-23.

Gonzalez, R. D. (in press). Bilingual interactions in a formal setting: A pilot study of Hispanic employees of the City of Tucson. *Renato Rosaldo Monograph Series,* University of Arizona, Tucson.

Gonzalez, R. D., & Arjona, E. (1989). *Federal court interpreter certification examination oral proficiency rater training manual.* (Confidential internal document). Tucson: University of Arizona, Federal Court Interpreter Certification Project.

Gonzalez, R. D., & Mishra, S. (1989). *Statistical analysis of the 1989 federal court interpreter Spanish/English written certification examination.* (Confidential internal document). Tucson: University of Arizona, Federal Court Interpreter Certification Project.

Gonzalez, R. D., Schott, A. A., & Vasquez, V. F. (1988). The English language amendment: Examining myths. *English Journal, 77*(3), 24-30.

Gonzalez, R. D., & Vasquez, V. F. (1990). *Structural and linguistic analysis of the Navajo and Haitian Creole certification instruments: Recommendations for amending and editing certification development and testing methods and techniques.* (Confidential internal document). Tucson: University of Arizona, Federal Court Interpreter Certification Project.

Gonzalez, R. D., Vasquez, V. F., & Bichsel, J. (1992) Language rights and the Mexican Americans: Much ado about nothing. *Perspectives in Mexican American Studies, 3.* (Available from the Mexican American Studies and Research Center. Tucson: University of Arizona 85721).

Gonzalez v. People of Virgin Islands, 109 F.2d 215 (3d Cir. 1940).

Goodman, K. S. (1967). Reading: A psycholinguistic guessing game. *Journal of Reading Specialist, 6*(1), 126-35.

Goodman, K. S. (1982). What is universal about the reading process. In F. V. Gollasch (Ed.), *Language & literacy: The selected writings of Kenneth S. Goodman* (Vol. 1) (pp. 71-76). Boston: Routledge & Kegan Paul.

Grabau, C. M., & Williamson, D. R. (1985). Language barriers in our trial courts: The use of court interpreters in Massachusetts. *Massachusetts Law Review, 70*(3), 108-14.

Groisser, D. S. (1981). A right to translation assistance in administrative proceedings. *Columbia Journal of Law and Social Problems, 16*(4), 469-520.

Grusky, L. (1988). Using a new technique for witness stand interpreting. *The ATA Chronicle, 18,* 12-13.

Gurowitz, E. M. (1969).*The molecular basis of memory.* New York: Prentice-Hall.

Gustafsson, M. (1975). *Some syntactic properties of English law language.* Turku, Finland: University of Turku, Department of English.

Gutierrez v. Municipal Court of the Southeast Judicial District, County of Los Angeles. No. CV-2171-RG, slip op. at 1033 (9th Cir., Feb. 5, 1987).

Hahn, P. H. (1984). *The juvenile offender and the law* (3rd ed.). Cincinnati: Anderson Publishing.

Hakuta, K. (1986). *Mirror of language: The debate on bilingualism.* New York: Basic Books.

Hall, E. T. (1959). *The silent language.* New York: Doubleday.

Halliday, M. A., McIntosh, A., & Strevens, P. (1964). *The linguistic sciences and language teaching.* London: Longmans.

Hansen, R. C., Dator, J. A., Frye, H. M., Nudelman, S. A., & O'Neill, R. M. (1988). The changing face of America—how will demographic trends affect the courts? *Judicature, 72*(2), 125-32.

Harris, P. (1984). *An introduction to law* (2nd ed.). Littleton, CO: Fred B. Rothman.

Hastie, R. (1981). Schematic principles in human memory. In E. T. Higgins, C. P. Herman, & M. P. Zauna (Eds.), *Social Cognition: The Ontario symposium* (Vol. 1). Hillsdale, NJ: Erlbaum.

Hay, P. (1976). *An introduction to United States law.* New York: North-Holland Publishing.

Hayes-Roth, B., & Hayes-Roth, F. (1977). Concept learning and the recognition and classification of exemplars. *Journal of Verbal Learning and Verbal Behavior, 16,* 321-38.

Heath, S. B. (1977). Language and politics in the United States. In M. Saville-Troike (Ed.), *Georgetown University round table on language and linguistics* (pp. 267-96). Washington, DC: Georgetown University Press.

Heath, S. B. (1981). English in our language heritage. In C. A. Ferguson & S. B. Heath (Eds.), *Language in the U.S.A.* (pp. 6-20). Cambridge: University Press.

Heath, S. B., & Krasner, L. (1986). Comment. *International Journal of the Sociology of Language, 60,* 157-62.

Hebert, J. (1968). *The interpreter's handbook: How to become a conference interpreter* (2nd ed.). Geneva: Librairie de l'Université [The University Bookstore].

Henshaw, J. (1986, February 27). Court service for minorities under review. *Tucson Citizen,* pp. 1B, 4B.

Higgs, T. V., & Clifford, R. (1982). The push toward communication. In T. V. Higgs (Ed.), *Curriculum, competence, and the foreign language teacher* (pp. 57-79). ACTFL Foreign Language Education Series, Vol. 13. Lincolnwood, IL: National Textbook.

Hillenbrand, B. (1989, July 24). Trying to decipher Babel. *Time,* p. 62.

Hinton, G. E., & Anderson, J. A. (Eds.). (1986). *Parallel models of associative memory.* Hillsdale, NJ: Erlbaum.

Hippchen, L. J. (1977). Development of a plan for bilingual interpreters in the criminal courts of New Jersey. *The Justice System Journal, 2*(3), 258-69.

Hirst, W., Neisser, U., & Spelke, E. (1978). Divided attention. *Human Nature, 1*(6) 54-61.

Horton, D. L., & Mills, C. B. (1984). Human learning and memory. *Annual Review of Psychology, 35,* 361-94.

Howe, M. J. (1970). Using students' notes to examine the role of the individual learner in acquiring meaningful subject matter. *The Journal of Educational Research, 64*(2), 61-63.

Hubel, D. H., & Wiesel, T. N. (1965). Receptive fields and functional architecture in two nonstraite visual areas (18 and 19) of the cat. *Journal of Neurophysiology, 28*(2), 229-89.

Hutchins, W. J. (1986). *Machine translation: Past, present, future.* Chichester, England: Ellis Horwood Limited.

Ilich, D. M. (1986, May 2). A review of case and statutory law on court interpreters and translators. *Daily Journal Report,* pp. 3-9.

Immigration Amendments of 1988, Pub. L. 100-658, 102 Stat. 3908 (codified at 8 U.S.C. § 1101 et seq.). [Simpson-Mazzoli Act].

Immigration and Nationality Act of 1952, Pub. L. 82-414, 82nd Cong., 2nd Sess., June 27, 1952 (recodified at 8 U.S.C. § 274 & § 287 (a)(3)).

Immigration Reform and Control Act of 1986, Pub. L. 99-603, 100 Stat. 3359 (codified at 8 U.S.C. § 1101 et seq.).

In re Gault, 387 U.S. 1, 18 L. Ed. 2d 527, 87 S. Ct. 1428 (1967).

In re Muraviov, 192 Cal. App. 2d 604, 13 Cal. Rptr. 466 (Cal. App. 2d Dist. 1961).

In re Norberg, 4 Mass. 81 (1808).

Jara v. Municipal Court for San Antonio Judicial Dist. of Los Angeles City, 578 P.2d 94, 21 Cal. 3d 181, 145 Cal. Rptr. 847 (Cal. Sup. 1978).

Jeanty, E. A., & Brown, O. C. (1976). *Parol granmoun [Words of the elders]: 999 Haitian proverbs in Creole and English.* Editions Learning Center: Port-au-Prince, Haiti.

Jefferson, T. (1943). S. K. Padover (Ed.). *The complete Jefferson.* New York: Duell, Sloan & Pearce.

Joos, M. (1967). *The five clocks* (3rd ed.). Bloomington: Indiana University Press.

Judd, E. L. (1987). The English language amendment: A case study on language and politics. *TESOL Quarterly, 21*(1), 113-33.

Judicial Conference of the United States. (1988). *Pattern criminal jury instructions.* Washington, DC: Author.

Judicial Council of California. (1976a). *A report to the judicial council on the language needs of non-English-speaking persons in relation to the state's justice system, phase 1 report: Analysis of language needs and problems.* Sacramento: Arthur Young & Company.

Judicial Council of California. (1976b, May). *A report to the judicial council on the language needs of non-English-speaking persons in relation to the state's justice system, Vol. 2: Phase 2 report: Provision of court interpreting services: An overview, and interim report of the advisory committee.* Sacramento: Arthur Young & Company.

Judicial Council of California. (1977). *A report to the judicial council on the language needs of non-English-speaking persons in relation to the state's justice system, Vol. 3: Phase 3 report: Results of court interpreter demonstration project, and final study recommendations.* Sacramento: Arthur Young & Company.

Judicial Council of California. (1979). *Standards of judicial administration.* Sacramento: Author.

Kamisar, Y., LaFave, W. R., & Israel, J. H. (1986). *Basic criminal procedure* (6th ed.). St. Paul, MN: West Publishing.

Karmiloff-Smith, A. (1978). Adult simultaneous interpretation: A functional analysis of linguistic categories and a comparison with child development. In D. Gerver & H. W. Sinaiko (Eds.), *Language interpretation and communication* (pp. 369-83). New York: Plenum.

Karst, K. L. (1986). Paths to belonging: The constitution and cultural identity. *North Carolina Law Review, 64*(2), 303-77.

Kay v. State, 260 Ark. 681, 543 S.W.2d 479 (1976).

Keefe, W. J., & Ogul, M. S. (1981). *The American legislative process: Congress and the states* (5th ed.). Englewood Cliffs, NJ: Prentice-Hall.

Kelly, L. G. (1979). *The true interpreter: A history of translation theory and practice in the West.* New York: St. Martin's Press.

Kihlstrom, J. F. (1987). The cognitive unconscious. *Science, 237,* 1445-52.

Kihlstrom, J. F. (1988). Cognition, unconscious processes. *Neurosciences year: The yearbook of the encyclopedia of neuroscience.* Boston: Berkhauser Boston.

Klatzky, R. L. (1975). *Human memory: Structures and processes.* San Francisco: W. H. Freeman.

Kolb, B., & Whishaw, F. Q. (1985). *Fundamentals of human neuropsychology* (2nd ed.). San Francisco: W. H. Freeman.

Krashen, S. D. (1982). *Principles and practice in second language acquisition.* New York: Pergamon Press.

Krashen, S. D. (1985). *The input hypothesis: Issues and implications.* New York: Longman.

Kucera, H., & Francis, W. N. (1970). *Computational analysis of present day American English.* Rhode Island: Brown University Press.

Labov, W. (1972). *Sociolinguistic patterns.* Philadelphia: University of Pennsylvania Press.

LaFave, W. R., & Israel, J. H. (1985). *Criminal procedure.* St. Paul, MN: West Publishing.

Laguerre, M. S. (1982). *Urban life in the Caribbean: A study of Haitian urban community.* Cambridge, MA: Schenkman.

Lakoff, R. (1975). *Language and woman's place.* New York: Harper & Row.

Lambert, R. D. (1987). The case for a national foreign language center: An editorial. *The Modern Language Journal, 71*(1), 1-11.

Lambert, S. M. (1983). *Recall and recognition among conference interpreters.* Unpublished doctoral dissertation, University of Stirling, Scotland.

Lambert, S. M. (1988, October). A human information processing and cognitive approach to the training of simultaneous interpreters. In D. L. Hammond (Ed.), *Language at crossroads: Proceeding of the 29th annual conference of the American Translators Association* (pp. 379-87). Medford, NJ: Learned Information.

Landers, J. M., Martin, J. A., & Yeazell, S. C. (1988). *Federal rules of civil procedure with selected statutes.* Boston: Little, Brown.

Latimer, L. Y. (1983, July 5). Translators play growing role in area police departments. *The Washington Post,* pp. B1, B7.

Lau v. Nichols, 414 U.S. 563 (1974).

Le Ny, J. (1978). Psychosemantics and simultaneous interpretation. In D. Gerver & H. W. Sinaiko (Eds.), *Language interpretation and communication* (pp. 289-98). New York: Plenum.

Lebra, T. S. (1987). The cultural significance of silence in Japanese communication. *Multilingua,* 6(4), 343-57.

Lederer, M. (1978). Simultaneous interpretation: Units of meaning and other features. In D. Gerver & H. W. Sinaiko (Eds.), *Language interpretation and communication* (pp. 323-32). New York: Plenum.

Lederer, M. (1981). *La traduction simultanée-expérience et théorie [Simultaneous translation-experience and theory].* Thése [Thesis] d'Etat, Paris, Minard Lettres Modernes [Modern Language].

Lee, R. J. (1987, November). *Overview to the screening test for applicants for county court interpreting positions, developed and administered by the Administrative Office of the Courts.* Trenton, NJ: Administrative Office of the Courts.

Leech, G. N. (1983). *Principles of pragmatics.* London: Longman.

Leeth, J. (1985). *Keynote address.* Paper presented at the University of Arizona Summer Institute for Court Interpretation at Montclair State College, Montclair, NJ. (Available from Summer Institute for Court Interpretation, ML #67, Rm. 445, University of Arizona, Tucson 85721).

Legal Aid Commission of New South Wales. (1984). *¿Tiene un problema legal? [Do you have a legal problem?].* New South Wales: Author.

Legal Aid Commission of New South Wales. (1987). *¿Quién es quien en los tribunales? [Who's who in the courts?].* New South Wales: Author.

Legal Services Commission of New South Wales and the Law Society of New South Wales. (1984). *Interpreters in the legal system.* New South Wales: Author.

Lehiste, I. (1973). Phonetic disambiguation of syntactic ambiguity. *Glossa,* 7(2), 107-22.

Lehmann, W. P. (1983). *Language: An introduction.* New York: Random House.

Lehrer, A. (1974). *Semantic fields and lexical structure.* Amsterdam: North Holland.

Leippe, M. R. (1980). Effects of integrative memorial and cognitive processes on the correspondence of eyewitness accuracy and confidence. *Law and Human Behavior, 4,* 261-74.

Lewis v. United States, 146 U.S. 370 (1892).

Liebesny, H. J. (1981). *Foreign legal systems: A comparative analysis* (4th ed.). Washington, DC: George Washington University, National Law Center.

Lilly, G. C. (1978). *An introduction to the law of evidence.* St. Paul, MN: West Publishing.

Lind, E. A., Conley, J., Erickson, B. E., & O'Barr, W. M. (1978). Social attributions and conversation style in trial testimony. *Journal of Personality and Social Psychology, 36*(12), 1558-67.

Lind, E. A., & O'Barr, M. W. (1979). The social significance of speech in the courtroom. In H. Giles & R. St. Clair (Eds.), *Language and social psychology* (pp. 66-87). Oxford: Basil Blackwell.

Loftus, E. F. (1977). Shifting human color memory. *Memory and Cognition, 5,* 696-99.

Loftus, E. F. (1979). *Eyewitness testimony.* Cambridge, MA: Harvard University Press.

Loftus, E. F. (1980). *Memory.* Reading, MA: Addison-Wesley.

Loftus, E. F., & Loftus, G. R. (1980). On the permanence of stored information in the human brain. *American Psychologist, 35*(5), 409-20.

Loftus, E. F., Miller, D. G., & Burns, H. J. (1978). Semantic integration of verbal information into a visual memory. *Journal of Experimental Psychology: Human Learning and Memory, 4*(1), 19-31.

Loftus, E. F., & Palmer, J. C. (1974). Reconstruction of automobile destruction: An example of the interaction between language and memory. *Journal of Verbal Learning and Verbal Behavior, 13*(5), 585-89.

Loftus, E. F., Schooler, J. W., & Wagenaar, W. (1985). The fate of memory: Comment on McCloskey and Zaragoza. *Journal of Experimental Psychology: General, 114*(3), 375-80.

Lopez, P. S. (1973). *The plight of the language handicapped in judicial proceedings.* Unpublished manuscript.

Lopez, P. S. (1975). *Final report on the justice system interpreter model development project.* Tucson: Pima County Superior Court.

Lord, C. G., Lepper, M. R., & Thompson, W. C. (1980, September). Inhibiting biased assimilation in the consideration of new evidence on social policy issues. Paper presented at the meeting of the American Psychological Association, Montreal, Canada.

Lozanov, G. (1978). *Suggestology and outlines of suggestopedy.* New York: Gordon & Breach.

Lyons, J. (Ed.). (1970). *New horizons in linguistics.* Harmondsworth: Penguin.

Macías, R. F. (1979). Language choice and human rights in the United States. In J. E. Alatis & G. R. Tucker (Eds.), *Georgetown University round table on language and linguistics 1979* (pp. 86-101). Washington, DC: Georgetown University Press.

Mackintosh, J. (1985). The Kintsch and Van Dijk model of discourse comprehension and production applied to the interpretation process. *Meta, 30*(1), 37-43.

Madrid, A. (1986). Testimony on Proposition 63 delivered to the Joint Legislative Committee of the California State Legislature, September 29, 1986.

Makkai, A. (1984). What is an idiom? In M. T. Boatner & J. E. Gates (Eds.), *A dictionary of American idioms* (pp. iv-ix). Woodbury, NY: Barron's Educational Series.

Marcos, L. R. (1979). Effect of interpreters on the evaluation of psychopathology in non-English-speaking patients. *American Journal of Psychiatry, 136*(2), 171-74.

Marcos, L. R. (1980). The psychiatric evaluation and psychotherapy of the Hispanic bilingual patient. *Research Bulletin, 3*(2), 1-7.

Marshall, D. F. (1986). The question of an official language: Language rights and the English language amendment. *International Journal of Sociology of Language, 60,* 7-75.

Marshall, D. F. (1989). *Comparison of language complexity in federal court interpreter examination, 1980, 1983, 1985, and 1987.* (Confidential internal document). Tucson: University of Arizona, Federal Court Interpreter Certification Project.

Marslen-Wilson, W. D. (1973). Linguistic structure and speech shadowing at very short latencies. *Nature, 244,* 522-23.

Mauet, T. (1988). *Fundamentals of trial techniques* (2nd ed.). Boston: Little, Brown.

Mayagoitia, A. (1976). *A layman's guide to Mexican law.* Albuquerque: University of New Mexico Press.

McClelland, J. L., Rumelhart, D. E., & the PDP Research Group. (1986). *Parallel distributed processing: Explorations in the microstructure of cognition* (Vol. 2, Psychological and biological models). Cambridge, MA: MIT Press.

McCloskey, M., & Watkins, M. J. (1978). The seeing-more-than-is-there phenomenon: Implications for the locus of iconic storage. *Journal of Experimental Psychology, 4,* 553-65.

McCroskey, J. C., & Mehrley, R. S. (1969). The effects of disorganization and nonfluency on attitude change and source credibility. *Speech Monographs, 36*(1), 13-21.

McKoon, G., Ratcliff, R., & Dell, G. S. (1986). A critical evaluation of the semantic-episodic distinction. *Journal of Experimental Psychology: Learning, Memory and Cognition, 12*(2), 295-306.

Mellinkoff, D. (1963). *The language of the law.* Boston: Little, Brown.

Mermin, S. (1982). *Law and the legal system: An introduction* (2nd ed.). Boston: Little, Brown.

Meyer v. Foster, 16 Wis. 294 (1862).

Meyer v. Nebraska, 262 U.S. 390 (1923).

Mikkelson, H. (1983). Consecutive interpretation. *The Reflector, a Journal for Sign Language Teachers and Interpreters, 6,* 5-9.

Mikkelson, H. (1984). *Task analysis of court interpreting.* (Available from the Summer Institute for Court Interpretation, ML #67, Rm. 445, University of Arizona, Tucson, AZ 85721).

Mikkelson, H. (1989a, June). Court interpreting rates. *The Polyglot, 19*(2), 5.

Mikkelson, H. (1989b, June). Interpreter internship program to begin in L.A. *The Polyglot, 19*(2), 7, 11.

Mikkelson, H., Vasquez, V. F., & Gonzalez, R. D. (1989). Survey of federally certified interpreters' uses of interpreting techniques. Tucson: University of Arizona, Summer Institute for Court Interpretation.

Miller, G. A. (1956). The magical number seven, plus or minus two: Some limits on our capacity for processing information. *Psychological Review, 63*(2), 81-97.

Miller, G. A. (1964). Language and psychology. In E. H. Lennenberg (Ed.), *New directions in the study of language* (pp. 89-107). Cambridge, MA: MIT Press.

Miller, T. (1981). *On the border: Portraits of America's southwestern frontier.* Tucson: University of Arizona Press.

Milner, P. M. (1970). *Physiological psychology.* New York: Holt, Rinehart, & Winston.

Mishra, S., & Gonzalez, R. D. (1988). *Statistical analysis of the 1987 federal court interpreter Spanish-English written certification examination.* (Available from the Court Administration Division of the Administrative Office of the United States Courts, 811 Vermont Ave., NW, Washington, DC 20544).

Montoya, J. (1973). *The Bilingual Courts Act.* Hearings before the subcommittee on improvement in jucidial machinery of the committee on the judiciary, United States Senate. 93rd Cong., 2nd Sess. on S. 1724. October 10, 1973, & February 5, 1974.

Morris, B. G. (1967, July). The sixth amendment's right of confrontation and the non-English speaking accused. *Florida Bar Journal, 41*(7), 475-82.

Moser, B. (1976). *Simultaneous translation: Linguistic psycholinguistic and human information processing aspects.* Unpublished doctoral dissertation, University of Innsbruck.

Moser, B. (1978). Simultaneous interpretation: A hypothetical model and its practical application. In D. Gerver & H. W. Sinaiko (Eds.), *Language interpretation and communication* (pp. 353-68). New York: Plenum.

Moser-Mercer, B. (1985). Screening potential interpreters. *Meta, 30*(1), 97-100.

National Accreditation Authority for Translators and Interpreters. (1978). *Levels of accreditation for translators and interpreters.* Canberra, Australia: Australian Government Publishing Service.

National Accreditation Authority for Translators and Interpreters. (1987). *NAATI tests: Information (Candidates' manual).* Canberra, Australia: Author.

National Center for Education Statistics. (1989). *Minority student issues: Racial/ethnic data collected by the National Center for Education Statistics since 1969.* Washington, DC: U.S. Department of Education, Office of Educational Research and Improvement.

Negri, S. (1984, May 28). Multiple meanings. *Arizona Republic,* pp. D6-D7.

Neumann Solow, S. (1981). *Sign language interpreting: A basic resource book.* Silver Spring, MD: National Association of the Deaf.

New Jersey Consortium of Educators in Legal Interpretation and Translation. (1988). *Curricular guidelines for the development of legal interpreter education.* Upper Montclair: New Jersey Department of Higher Education, Project on Legal Interpretation, Montclair State College.

New Jersey Supreme Court Task Force on Interpreter and Translation Services. (1984). *Interpreting and translating as professions* (Background report #21). Trenton, NJ: Administrative Office of the Courts.

New Jersey Supreme Court Task Force on Interpreter and Translation Services. (1985, May). *Equal access to the courts for linguistic minorities* (Final report). Trenton, NJ: Administrative Office of the Courts.

New South Wales Attorney General's Department. (No date). *Information about local courts.* New South Wales: (Available from the New South Wales Attorney General's Department, Public Relations Unit on (02) 228 7777).

New York Laws of 1869, c. 249 (cited in *People v. Adams,* 89 Hun. 284, 35 N.Y. Supp. 648 (Sup. Ct. Dept. 2, 1895)).

Newmark, P. (1981). *Approaches to translation.* Oxford: Pergamon Press.

Nida, E. A. (1964). *Toward a science of translating.* New York: American Bible Society.

Nida, E. A. (1976). A framework for the analysis and evaluation of theories of translation. In R. W. Brislin (Ed.), *Translation: Applications and research* (pp. 47-91). New York: Gardner Press.

Nida, E. A., & Rayburn, W. D. (1982). *Meaning across cultures.* Maryknoll, New York: Orbis Books.

Nida, E. A., & Taber, C. P. (1974). *The theory and practice of translation.* New York: American Bible Society.

North Carolina v. Alford, 400 U.S. 25, 27 L. Ed. 2d 162, 91 S. Ct. 160 (1970).

Northwest Territories Department of Justice (1987). *Breaking the silence: A special report on interpreting in the Northwest Territories Courts.* Yellowknife, Northwest Territories, Canada: Government of the Northwest Territories, The Language Bureau, Department of Culture and Communications.

Oakley, D. A. (1981). Brain mechanisms of mammalian memory. *British Medical Bulletin, 37*(2), 175-80.

O'Barr, W. M. (1978). Legal assumptions about language. In L. N. Massery, II (Ed.), *Psychology and persuasion in advocacy* (pp. 384-403). Washington, DC: Association of Trial Lawyers of America, National College of Advocacy.

O'Barr, W. M. (1981). The language of the law. In C. A. Ferguson & S. B. Heath (Eds.), *Language in the USA* (pp. 386-406). England: Cambridge University Press.

O'Barr, W. M. (1982). *Linguistic evidence: Language, power, and strategy in the courtroom.* New York: Academic Press.

O'Barr, W. M., & Conley, E. A. (1976, Summer). When a juror watches a lawyer. *Barrister, 3,* pp. 8-11, 33.

O'Barr, W. M., & Lind, E. A. (1981). Ethnography and experimentation-partners in legal research. In B. D. Sales (Ed.), *The trial process* (pp. 181-207). New York: Plenum.

O'Barr, W. M., Walker, L., Conley J., Erickson, B., & Lind, A. (1976). Political aspects of speech styles in American trial courtroom. *Working Papers in Culture and Communication, 1,* 27-40.

Official English claims victory in 3 more states. (1988). *U.S. English Update,* p. 1.

Official Languages Act of 1969, R.S.C. 1970, C.O-2.

Omaggio, A. C. (1986). *Teaching language in context: Proficiency-oriented instruction.* Boston: Heinle & Heinle.

Ordinance to recognize and provide for the use of the aboriginal languages and to establish the official languages of the Northwest Territories, Counsel of the Northwest Territories, 2nd Session, 1984, assented to June 28, 1984 (Bill 9-84(2)).

Ornstein, R., & Thompson, R. F. (1984). *The amazing brain.* Boston: Houghton Mifflin.

Ortiz, A. (Ed.). (1983). *Handbook of North American Indians, Volume 10.* Washington, DC: Smithsonian Institution.

Owens, J., Bower, G. H., & Black, J. B. (1979). The "soap-opera" effect in story recall. *Memory and Cognition, 7,* 185-91.

Paivio, A. (1971). *Imagery and verbal processes.* New York: Holt, Rinehart & Winston.

Palma, J. (1987). *Introduction to judiciary interpreting.* New York: National Association of Judiciary Interpreters and Translators.

Palma, J. (1988). *Primer for judiciary interpreters.* New York: National Association of Judiciary Interpreters and Translators.

Palma, J. (1989). *Handbook for the legal profession: Working with interpreters.* New York: National Association of Judiciary Interpreters and Translators.

Paredes, A. (1958). The legend of Gregorio Cortez. From *"With his pistol in his hand": A border ballad and its hero.* Austin: University of Texas Press.

Parkinson, M. (1979, July). *Language behavior and courtroom success.* Paper presented at the International Conference on Language and Social Psychology, University of Bristol, England.

Parsons, H. M. (1978). Human factors to simultaneous interpretation. In D. Gerver & H. W. Sinaiko (Eds.), *Language interpretation and communication* (pp. 315-41). New York: Plenum.

Pawley, A., & Syder, F. H. (1983). Two puzzles for linguistic theory: Nativelike selection and nativelike fluency. In J. C. Richards & R. W. Schmidt (Eds.), *Language and communication* (pp. 117-55). New York: Longman.

Pearce, W. B. (1971). The effect of vocal cues on credibility and attitude change. *Western Speech, 35*(3), 176-84.

Pearce, W. B., & Brommel, B. J. (1972). Vocalic communication in persuasion. *Quarterly Journal of Speech, 58,* 298-306.

Pearce, W. B., & Conklin, F. (1971). Nonverbal vocalic communication and perceptions of a speaker. *Speech Monographs, 38*(3), 235-41.

Pennsylvania Act of March 27, 1865 (cited in *Commonwealth v. Sanson,* 67 Pa. St. (17 P. F. Smith) 322).

People v. Annett, 251 Cal. App. 2d 858, 59 Cal. Rptr. 888 (Cal. App. 2d Dist., 1967), *cert. denied,* 390 U.S. 1029 (1968).

People v. Chavez, 124 Cal. App. 3d 215, 177 Cal. Rptr. 306 (Cal. App. Dist. 1, 1981).

People v. Estany, 210 Cal. App. 2d 609, 26 Cal. Rptr. 757 (Cal. App. 2d Dist. 2, 1962).

People v. Hernandez, 8 N.Y. 2d 345, 170 N.E. 2d 673 (1960).

People v. Mata Aguilar, 35 Cal. 3d 785, 200 Cal. Rptr. 908 (Cal. 1984).

People v. Nguyen, Santa Clara County Superior Court, Department 2, September 26-27, 1989. In Ewell, M. (1989, December 17). Lost in translation: What jury heard was not what was said. *San Jose Mercury News,* p. 6A.

People v. Ramos, 26 N.Y. 2d 272, 258 N.E. 2d 197 (1970).

People v. Resendes, 164 Cal. App. 3d 812, 210 Cal. Rptr. 609 (Cal. App. 3d Dist. 5, 1985).

People v. Rioz, 161 Cal. App. 3d 905, 207 Cal. Rptr. 903 (Cal. App. 3d Dist. 5, 1984).

Pergnier, M. (1978). Language meaning and message meaning: Towards a sociolinguistic approach to translation. In D. Gerver & H. W. Sinaiko (Eds.), *Language interpretation and communication* (pp. 199-204). New York: Plenum.

Perovich v. United States, 205 U.S. 86 (1907).

Philbrick, F. A. (1949). *Language and the law: The semantics of forensic English.* New York: Macmillan.

Philips, S. U. (1979, July). *Syntactic variation in judges' use of language in the courtroom.* Paper presented at the International Conference on Language and Social Psychology, University of Bristol, England.

Philips, S. U. (1985). On the use of wh questions in American courtroom discourse: A study of the relation between form and language function. In L. Kedar (Ed.), *Language and power.* Norwood, NJ: Ablex Publishing.

Pichert, J. W., & Anderson, R. C. (1977). Taking different perspectives on a story. *Journal of Educational Psychology, 69,* 309-15.

Pointer v. Texas, 380 U.S. 400 (1965).

Pousada, A. (1979). Interpreting for language minorities in the courts. In J. E. Alatis & G. R. Tucker (Eds.), *Georgetown University round table on languages and linguistics* (pp. 186-208). Washington, DC: Georgetown University Press.

Powers, P. A., Andriks, J. L., & Loftus, E. F. (1979). Eyewitness accounts of females and males. *Journal of Applied Psychology, 64*(3), 339-47.

Prideaux, G. D., & Baker, W. J. (1984). An integrated perspective on cognitive strategies in language processing. *Meta, 29*(1), 81-90.

Pritchett, C. H. (1977). *The American Constitution* (3rd ed.). New York: McGraw-Hill.

Probasco, D., & McDonald, P. P. (1979, June). *Court interpreter validation study and examination plan.* (Available from Cooperative Personnel Services, First Floor, 909 12th Street, Sacramento, CA 95814).

Putsch, R. W. (1985, December 20). Cross-cultural communication: The special case of interpreters in health care. *JAMA,* pp. 3344-48.

Rainof, A. (1980, May). How best to use an interpreter in court. *California State Bar Journal, 55*(5), 196-200.

Ramler, S. (1988). Origins and challenges of simultaneous interpretation: The Nuremberg trial experience. In D. L. Hammond (Ed.), *Language at a crossroads: Proceedings of the 29th annual conference* (pp. 437-40). Medford, NJ: Learned Information.

The Random House Dictionary of the English language (2nd ed.). (1987). New York: Random House.

Real, M. L. (1973). *The Bilingual Courts Act.* Hearings before the subcommittee on improvements in judicial machinery of the committee on the judiciary, United States Senate. 93rd Cong., 2nd Sess. on S. 1724. October 10, 1973, & February 5, 1974.

Reason, J., & Mycielska, K. (1982). *Absent mind? The psychology of mental lapses and everyday errors*. Englewood Cliffs, NJ: Prentice-Hall.

Redish, J. C. (1979). Readability. In D. A. MacDonald (Ed.), *Drafting documents in plain language*. New York: Practising Law Institute.

Reed, S. K. (1972). Pattern recognition and categorization. *Cognitive Psychology, 3*, 382-407.

Reinhold, R. (1987, August 11). Need for translators is a costly burden for judicial system. *The New York Times*, pp. A1, D22.

Repa, J. (1981). A training program for court interpreters. *Meta, 26*(4), 394-96.

Repa, J. (1988). Professional status today and tomorrow: Case of court interpreters in Canada. In D. L. Hammond (Ed.), *American translators association conference* (pp. 441-49). Medford, NJ: Learned Information.

Richards, J. C. (1978). Models of language use and language learning. In J. C. Richards (Ed.), *Understanding second & foreign language learning: Issues & approaches* (pp. 94-116). Rowley, MA: Newbury House.

Richards, J. C. (1983). Listening comprehension: Approach, design, procedure. *TESOL Quarterly, 17*(2), 219-40.

Right to an interpreter [Note]. (1970-71). *Rutgers Law Review, 25*, 145-71.

Rivera-García, I. (1974). *Manual para la secretaria legal [Manual for the legal secretary]*. Orford, NH: Equity Publishing.

Robb, L. A. (1955). *Dictionary of legal terms, Spanish-English and English-Spanish*. New York: John Wiley & Sons.

Roberts, R. P. (Ed.). (1981). *L'interprétation auprès des tribunaux [Interpretation in the courts]*. Ottawa: Editions de l'Université d'Ottawa [Editions of the University of Ottawa].

Roberts, R. P., & Pergnier, M. (1987). L'Équivalence en traduction [Equivalence in translation]. *Meta, 32*, 392-402.

Rosch, E., Mervis, C. B., Gray, W., Johnson, D., & Boyes-Braem, P. (1976). Basic objects in natural categories. *Cognitive Psychology, 8*(3), 382-439.

Roy-Nicklen, L. (1988). Legal interpretation—Canada's northwest territories. In D. L. Hammond (Ed.), *American translators association conference* (pp. 429-35). Medford, NJ: Learned Information.

Rozan, J. F. (1956). *La prise de notes en interprétation consécutive [Note-taking in consecutive interpretation]*. Geneva: Georg.

Rubin, J. (1985). Spanish language planning in the United States. In L. Elías-Olivares, E. A. Leone, R. Cisneros, & J. R. Gutiérrez (Eds.), *Spanish language use and public life in the United States* (pp. 133-53). Berlin: Mouton de Gruyter.

Rumelhart, D. E. (1977). Understanding and summarizing brief stories. In D. Laberge & S. J. Sammuels (Eds.), *Basic processes in reading: Perception and comprehension* (pp. 265-303). Hillsdale, NJ: Lawrence Erlbaum Associates.

Rumelhart, D. E., McClelland, J. L., & the PDP Research Group. (1986). *Parallel distributed processing: Explorations in the microstructures of cognition* (Vol. 1, Foundations). Cambridge, MA: MIT Press.

Rumelhart, D. E., & Ortony, A. (1977). The representation of knowledge in memory. In R. C. Anderson, R. J. Spiro, & W. E. Montague (Eds.), *Schooling and the acquisition of knowledge* (pp. 99-135). Hillsdale, NJ: Lawrence Erlbaum Associates.

Rydstrom, J. F. (1971). Annotation: Right of accused to have evidence or court proceedings interpreted. *American Law Reports*, 3rd ed. (ALR), *36*, 276-312; 1989 Supplement pp. 32-43.

Safford, J. B. (1977). No comprendo [I don't understand]: The non-English-speaking defendant and the criminal process. *Journal of Criminal and Criminology, 68*(1), 15-30.

Sales, B. D., Elwork, A., & Alfini, J. (1977). Improving comprehension for jury instructions. In B. D. Sales (Ed.), *Perspectives in law and psychology: The criminal justice system* (Vol. 1, pp. 23-90). New York: Plenum.

San Diego Municipal Court (1983). *General information and 2 guidelines for courtroom interpreters.* San Diego: Author.

San Miguel, G. (1986). *One country, one language: A historical sketch of English language movements in the United States.* (Available from the Tomás Rivera Center, 710 North College Avenue, Claremont, CA 91711).

Sanders, A. L. (1989, May 29). Libertad and justicia for all [Liberty and justice for all]. *Time,* p. 25.

Sanford, A. J. (1985). *Cognition and cognitive psychology.* New York: Basic Books.

Saussure, F. (1966). W. Baskin (Trans.). C. Bally & A. Sechehaye (Eds. in collaboration with A. Riedlinger). *Course in general linguistics.* New York: McGraw-Hill.

Schank, R., & Abelson, R. (1977). *Scripts, plans, goals and understanding: An inquiry into human knowledge structures.* Hillsdale, NJ: Erlbaum.

Schrieberg, D. (1989, December 19). Interpreter problem runs beyond courtroom. *San Jose Mercury News,* p. 1A.

Schrieberg, D., & Ewell, M. (1989, December 18). State interpreting rules get lip service. *San Jose Mercury News,* p. 1A.

Schulman, H. G. (1970). Encoding and retention of semantic and phonemic information in short-term memory. *Journal of Verbal Learning and Verbal Behavior, 9*(5), 499-508.

Schwartz, B. (1984). *Administrative law* (2nd ed.). Boston: Little, Brown.

Schwartz, M. D. (1973). *Physiological psychology.* Englewood Cliffs, NJ: Prentice-Hall.

Schweda-Nicholson, N. (1985, May). Court interpreter training: A growing need. In *Proceedings of the Eastern Michigan University conference on languages for business and the professions,* Dearborn, MI (ERIC Document Reproduction Service No. ED 272 024).

Schweda-Nicholson, B. (1986). Language planning and policy development for court interpretation services in the United States. *Language Problems and Language Planning, 10*(2), 140-57.

Seib, G. F. (1989, June 21). Pardonnez-Moi [Pardon me], Mr. Bush: In French you make no sense: Foreign reporters wrestle with Bushtalk and lose: A bad case of the Blahs. *The Wall Street Journal,* pp. 1, A8.

Selected statutes, rules and standards on the legal profession (rev. ed.). (1989). St. Paul, MN: West Publishing.

Seleskovitch, D. (1975). *Langage, langues et mémoire: étude de la prise de notes en interprétation consécutive [Language usage, languages and memory: (A) Study of note-taking in consecutive interpretation].* Paris: Minard.

Seleskovitch, D. (1978a). *Interpreting for international conferences.* Washington, DC: Pen & Booth.

Seleskovitch, D. (1978b). Language and cognition. In D. Gerver & H. W. Sinaiko (Eds.), *Language interpretation and communication* (pp. 333-42). New York: Plenum.

Selfridge, O., & Neisser, U. (1960). Pattern recognition by machine. *Scientific American, 203*(2), 60-79.

Seltzer v. Foley, 502 F. Supp. 600 (1980).

Senate Bill No. 1724, Bilingual Courts Act. 93rd Cong., 2nd Sess. (1973).

Senate Bill No. 565, Bilingual Courts Act. 94th Cong., 1st Sess. (1974).

Senate Bill No. 1853, Amendments to the Court Interpreters Act, 1978, 99th Cong., 1st Sess. (1985).

Sentencing Act of 1987, Pub. L. 100-182, 100 Stat. 1266 (18 U.S.C. §3551 et seq.).

Shepard, R. N., Kilpatric, N. W., & Cunningham, J. P. (1971). The internal representation of numbers. *Cognitive Psychology, 7*(1), 82-138.

Shuy, R. W. (1978, May). *The consumer and insurance policy language.* Paper presented at the Conference on Consumers and Life Insurance—An Exchange of Views, Washington, DC.

Shuy, R. W., & Larkin, D. K. (1978). *Linguistic considerations in the simplification/clarification of insurance policy language.* Washington DC: Georgetown University and the Center for Applied Linguistics.

Siegel, L. J., & Senna, J. J. (1988). *Juvenile delinquency: Theory, practice, and law* (3rd ed.). St. Paul: West Publishing.

Silva, H. (1981, June 21). Interpreters can make difference. *The Miami Herald,* p. 2B.

Simon and Schuster's international dictionary: English/Spanish Spanish/English. (1973). New York: Simon & Schuster.

Snyder, W. H. (1988). Teaching language and translation today: Second language competence and translation skills. In D. L. Hammond (Ed.), *American translators association conference* (pp. 317-22). Medford, NJ: Learned Information.

Speedy Trial Act of 1974, Pub. L. 93-619, 88 Stat. 2076 (18 U.S.C. §3161 et seq.).

Sperling, G. (1963). A model for visual memory tests. *Human Factors, 5*(1), 19-31.

Sperling, G. (1967). Successive approximations to a model for short term memory. *Acta Psychologica* (Amsterdam), 285-92.

Spiro, R. J. (1977). Remembering information from text: The "state of schema" approach. In R. C. Anderson, R. J. Spiro, & W. E. Montague (Eds.), *Schooling and the acquisition of knowledge* (pp. 137-65). Hillsdale, NJ: Lawrence Erlbaum Associates.

State v. Burns, 78 N.W. 681 (1899).

State v. Kabinto, 106 Ariz. 575, 480 P. 2d 1 (1971).

State v. Sung J. Lee, 211 N.J. Super. 590 (App. Div. 1986).

State v. Vasquez, 101 Utah 444, 121 P. 2d 903 (1942).

Stevick, E. W. (1976). *Memory, meaning & method.* Rowley, MA: Newbury House.

Stewart, W. (1962). An outline of linguistic typology for describing multilingualism. In F. Rice (Ed.), *Study of the role of second languages in Asia, Africa, and Latin America* (pp. 15-25). Washington, DC: Center for Applied Linguistics.

Strength through wisdom: A critique of U.S. capacity. (1979). A report to the president from the president's commission on foreign language and internal studies. Washington, DC: U.S. GPO.

Suarez v. U.S., 309 F.2d 709 (5th Cir. 1962).

Substitute Senate Bill No. 5474, A bill relating to interpreters in legal proceedings. 51st Leg., 1989 Reg. Sess. Sec. 1-14. Washington (1989).

Superior Court of the State of Arizona. (1985). Maricopa County, *Administrative Order No. 85-002,* Phoenix.

Swift, J. (1947). *Gulliver's travels.* New York: Bonanza (Crown ed.) [First published 1727].

Swinney, D. (1979). Lexical access during sentence comprehension: (Re)consideration of context effects. *Journal of Verbal Learning and Verbal Behavior, 18*(6), 645-59.

Tanenhaus, M., Leiman, J., & Seidenberg, M. (1979). Evidence for multiple stages in the processing of ambiguous words in syntactic contexts. *Journal of Verbal Learning and Verbal Behavior, 18*(6), 427-40.

Task Force on Aboriginal Languages. (1986). *The report of the task force on aboriginal languages.* Northwest Territories: Government of the Northwest Territories.

Task Group on Court Interpreting in British Columbia. (1985, January). *Toward a court interpreting system in British Columbia.* Report presented to the Advisory Committee of the Program in Court Interpreting, Vancouver Community College. Victoria: Queen's Printer for British Columbia.

Tayler, M. R. (1988). Interpretation/translation assistance in immigration proceedings. *Immigration Journal, 11*(3), 57-61.

Taylor, S. E., & Crocker, J. (1981). Schematic bases of social information processing. In E. T. Higgins, C. P. Herman, & M. P. Zanna (Eds.), *Social cognition: The Ontario symposium* (Vol. 1). Hillsdale, NJ: Erlbaum.

Teitelbaum, H., & Hiller, R. J. (1977). *The legal perspective, bilingual education: Current perspectives* (Vol. 3). Arlington, VA: Center for Applied Linguistics.

Terrell, T. D., & Salgués de Cargill, M. (1979). *Lingüística aplicada a la enseñanza del español a anglohablantes [Linguistics applied to the teaching of Spanish to English speakers].* New York: John Wiley & Sons.

Terry v. State, 105 So. 386 (Ala. 1925).

Testimony of T. Kamiyama to the Grand Jury in the matter of the Rev. Sun Myoung Moon. (1981). In *Court interpreters improvement act of 1985: Hearing before the subcommittee on the judiciary United States Senate.* 99th Cong., 2nd Sess., S. 1853 (pp. 106-243). Washington, DC: U.S. GPO.

Texas Employment Commission. (1985). *Operating plan: Comprehensive language services program.* (Available from Author: TEC Building, Austin, Texas 78778).

Thorndike, E. L., & Lorge, I. (1959). *The teacher's word book of 30,000 words.* New York: Columbia University.

Torres v. U.S., 505 F. 2d 957 (1974).

Tousignant, J. P., Hall, D., & Loftus, E. P. (1986). Discrepancy detection and vulnerability to misleading postevent information. *Memory and Cognition, 14,* 329-38.

Treaty of Guadalupe Hidalgo, Mexico, signed 2 Feb. 1848. Treaties and Other International Acts (TIAS 207).

Tulving, E. (1972). Episodic and semantic memory. In E. Tulving & W. Donaldson (Eds.), *Organization of memory* (pp. 381-403). New York: Academic Press.

Tulving, E. (1974). Cue-dependent forgetting. *American Scientist, 62*(1), 74-82.

Tulving, E. (1985). How many memory systems are there? *American Psychologist, 40*(4), 385-98.

Tulving, E., & Madigon, S. A. (1970). Memory and verbal learning. *Annual Review of Psychology, 21,* 437-84.

Tunney, J. V. (1973). *The Bilingual Courts Act.* Hearings before the subcommittee on improvements in judicial machinery of the committee on the judiciary United States Senate. 93rd Cong., 2nd Sess. on S. 1724. October 10, 1973, & February 5, 1974.

U.S. ex rel. Ortiz v. Sielaff, 542 F.2d 377 (1976).

U.S. Senate Judiciary Committee. (1977). S. Rep. No. 569, 95th Cong., 1st Sess. 1 (1977).

U.S. v. Diharce-Estrada, 526 F.2d 637 (1976).

U.S. v. Pena, 542 F.2d 292 (1976).

U.S. v. Vera, 514 F.2d 102 (1975).

United States Commission on Civil Rights. (1970). *Mexican Americans and the administration of justice in the southwest.* Washington, DC: U.S. GPO.

United States ex rel. Negron v. New York, 434 F.2d 386 (2d Cir. 1970).

United States Sentencing Commission. (1987). *Sentencing guidelines and policy statements.* Washington, DC: Author.

United States v. Carrion, 488 F.2d 12 (1st Cir. 1973), *cert. denied,* 416 U.S. 907 (1974).

Uys, J. (Producer & Director). (1980). *The gods must be crazy* [Film]. South Africa: Mimosa/CAT Films Production/Panavision.

Valdés, G. (1982, October). *Language needs of Hispanic minorities in the criminal justice system: A research agenda.* Paper presented at El Español en Los Estados Unidos [Spanish in the United States] III: An Interdisciplinary Conference. Bloomington: Indiana University.

Valdés, G. (1986). Analyzing the demands that courtroom interaction makes upon speakers of ordinary English: Toward the development of a coherent descriptive framework. *Discourse Processes, 9*(3), 269-303.

Valdés, G., & Wilcox, P. (1986). *The use of court interpreters in New Mexico: A handbook for judges, attorneys, and interpreters.* Santa Fe: Administrative Office of the New Mexico Courts.

Valdman, A. (1984). The linguistic situation of Haiti. In C. R. Foster & A. Valdman (Eds.), *Haiti—today and tomorrow: An interdisciplinary study* (pp. 77-99). New York: University Press of America.

Valdman, A., & Rosemond, R. (1988). *Ann pale kreyòl [(Haitian) Creole is spoken]: An introductory course in Haitian Creole.* Bloomington: Indiana University, Creole Institute.

van Dam, I. M. (1986). Strategies of simultaneous interpretation: A methodology for the training of simultaneous interpreters. In K. Kummer (Ed.), *Building bridges: Proceedings of the 27th annual conference of the American translators association* (pp. 441-56). Medford, NJ: Learned Information.

van Hoof, H. (1962). *Théorie et practique de l'interprétation avec application particulière a l'anglais et au français [Theory and practice of interpretation with special application to English and French].* Munich: Hueber.

Vasconcellos, M. (1989, July). Technology corner: A visit to Bravice. *The ATA Chronicle, 18*(7), 12-13.

Vásquez-Ayora, G. (1977). *Introducción a la traductología. Curso básico de traducción [Introduction to translation (theory and practice). Fundamentals of translation].* Washington, DC: Georgetown University Press.

Veale, R. (1989, March). First state "exotic" language court interpreter exam. *The Polyglot, 19*(1), 1, 5, 7.

Vickovich, I. (1984, May). *Interpreting in the legal system.* Paper presented at the Law Week Seminar of the Steering Committee. (Available from Ethnic Affairs Commission of New South Wales, 189 Kent St., Sydney 2000).

Viliborghi v. State, 45 Ariz. 275, 43 P.2d 210 (1935).

Voting Rights Act Amendment of 1975, Pub. L. 98-110, 89 Stat. 400 (codified at 42 U.S.C. § 1973a et seq.; as amended § 1973aa-la (1982).

Voting Rights Act of 1965, Pub. L. 89-110, 79 Stat. 437 (codified at 42 U.S.C. § 1971-74).

Waggoner, D. (1988). Language minorities in the United States in the 1980s: The evidence from the 1980 census. In S. L. McKay & S. C. Wong (Eds.), *Language diversity: Problem or resource?* (pp. 69-108). Cambridge: Newbury House.

Walker, A. G. (1987). *Court reporters are interpreters too*. Paper presented at the Colloquium on Court Interpretation Issues, Montclair State College, New Jersey.

Waltz, J. R. (1983). *Introduction to criminal evidence* (2nd ed.). Chicago: Nelson-Hall.

Ward, R. A., & Loftus, E. F. (1985). Eyewitness performance in different psychological types. *The Journal of General Psychology, 112*(2), 191-200.

Wearing, A. J. (1973). The recall of sentences of varying length. *Australian Journal of Psychology, 25,* 155-61.

Weaver, C. H. (1972). *Human listening: Processes and behavior.* New York: Bobbs-Merrill.

Weber, W. K. (1984). *Training translators and conference interpreters.* Orlando, FL: Harcourt Brace Jovanovich.

Wells v. Kansas City Life Inc. Co. 46 F. Supp. 754 (D.N.D. 1942), *aff'd,* 133 F.2d 224 (8th Cir. 1943)).

Wexler, D. B. (1990). *Therapeutic jurisprudence: The law as a therapeutic agent.* Durham, NC: Carolina Academic Press.

White, R. V. (1974a, May). Communicative competence, registers, and second language teaching. *IRAL, 12*(1), 127-41.

White, R. V. (1974b, December). The concept of register and TESL. *TESOL Quarterly, 8*(4), 401-16.

Whorf, B. L. (1940). Science and linguistics. *Technology Review, 34,* 247-48.

Widdowson, H. G. (1978). *Teaching language as communication.* London: Oxford University Press.

Williams v. Florida, 399 U.S. 78 (1970).

Wilss, W. (1978). Syntactic anticipation in German-English simultaneous interpreting. In D. Gerver & H. W. Sinaiko (Eds.), *Language interpretation and communication* (pp. 343-52). New York: Plenum.

Wilss, W. (1982). *The science of translation: Problems and methods.* Tubingen, West Germany: Guntar Narr Verlag.

Wortman, C. B., Loftus, E. F., & Marshall, M. E. (1988). *Psychology* (3rd ed.). New York: Alfred A. Knopf.

Wydick, R. (1985). *Plain English for lawyers.* Durham, NC: Carolina Academic Press.

Yarmey, A. D. (1979). *The psychology of eyewitness testimony.* New York: The Free Press.

Yazzie, R., & Yazzie, E. D. (1985) *English/Navajo glossary of legal terms* (Vol. 1). Albuquerque: United States District Court of New Mexico. (Available from Administrative Office of the United States Courts, 811 Vermont Ave., NW, Washington, DC 20544).

Yoakam, G. A. (1955). *Basal reading instruction.* New York: McGraw-Hill.

Young, R. W. (1988). *An outline of Navajo morphology.* Albuquerque: University of New Mexico, Department of Humanities.

Young, R. W., & Morgan, W., Sr. (1987). *The Navajo language: A grammar and colloquial dictionary* (rev. ed.). Albuquerque: University of New Mexico Press.

Yuille, J. C. (1980). A critical examination of the psychological and practical implications of eyewitness research. *Law and Human Behavior, 4,* 335-46.

Zahler, S. (1984). Bail: Legal concepts and terminology. (Available from Author, Summer Institute for Court Interpretation, ML #67, Rm. 445, University of Arizona, Tucson 85721).

Zahler, S. (1989a, July). *Overview of the justice system in the United States.* Paper presented at the Summer Institute for Court Interpretation, University of Arizona, Tucson.

Zahler, S. (1989b, July). *Criminal procedure: Personnel, procedures, and practices.* Paper presented at the Summer Institute for Court Interpretation, University of Arizona, Tucson.

Zahler, S. (1989c, July). *The criminal trial.* Paper presented at the Summer Institute for Court Interpretation, University of Arizona, Tucson.

Zahler, S. (1989d, July). *Spanish for lawyers: What the interpreter should know.* Paper presented at the Summer Institute for Court Interpretation, University of Arizona, Tucson.

Zahler, S. (1989e, July). *Civil law: Procedures, practices, and terminology.* Paper presented at the Summer Institute for Court Interpretation, University of Arizona, Tucson.

Zahler, S. (1989f, July). *Civil law and common law legal systems: Comparisons and contrasts.* Paper presented at the Summer Institute for Court Interpretation, University of Arizona, Tucson.

Zavala, E. R. (1977). Testimony of Eleazar Ruelas Zavala in the matter of *State v. Hanigan.* Transcript of April 28, 1977. (Available from Summer Institute for Court Interpretation, ML #67, Rm. 445, University of Arizona, Tucson 85721).

Index of Legal Citations

Index of Names

Index of Subjects

Tables

Figures

About the Authors and Consultants

Roseann Dueñas González, Ph.D.

Roseann Dueñas González is Professor of English at the University of Arizona, where she has been a faculty member for the past nineteen years in the area of applied linguistics and English as a Second Language and an administrator of minority education programs. Her introduction to court interpreting issues began in 1976 when she was commissioned by Judge Ben Birdsall of the Superior Court of Arizona to study the register of courtroom English, the results of which ultimately became the standards for the Federal Court Interpreting Certification Examination. Professor González is the founder, developer, and director of the Summer Institute for Court Interpretation at the University of Arizona and the Training of Trainers of Court Interpreters established in 1983 and 1984, respectively. She has written and lectured extensively in the areas of language policy, judicial language policy, legal interpreter training, interpreter testing, language testing, minority education, and first and second language acquisition and instruction.

Professor González has served as the primary consultant on interpreter certification issues to the Administrative Office of the United States Courts for the past fourteen years and is a member of the Federal Court Interpreters Advisory Board. Additionally, she has consulted with several states and agencies, including the United States Department of Justice and the Texas Employment Commission, and has given numerous papers and lectures on judicial language policy and court interpreting training and certification. In addition, she has served as an expert witness on several foreign language and interpretation related matters and has testified before Congress on interpreter certification. As the former director of the Graduate Program in English as a Second Language at the University of Arizona from 1980 to 1990, she was instrumental in establishing the Second Language Acquisition and Teaching doctoral program there, which includes, among others, subareas of study in language education, testing and policy, including interpretation studies.

Victoria Félice Vásquez, J.D., M.A.

Victoria Félice Vásquez holds a Juris Doctorate with emphases in administrative, employment, criminal, and mental health law. She has completed her Masters Thesis and is continuing work toward a doctorate in the Psychology-Law and Policy Program under the auspices of the Law and Social Sciences interdisciplinary graduate program at the University of Arizona. Ms. Vásquez's research interest includes the legal, social, and policy issues that arise when the law attempts to regulate the use of language. Ms. Vásquez is the Assistant Director of the University of Arizona Summer Institute for Court Interpreting and has worked with this program and all its related programs since its inception in 1983. Ms. Vásquez has published in the area of language policy and has assisted with numerous research projects and co-authored research reports at the University of Arizona related to interpreter issues as well as minority education. In addition, as a member of expert witness teams, she has conducted applied research in the area of employment discrimination.

Holly Mikkelson, M.A.; FCCI; ATA accredited; CSC

Holly Mikkelson is Director of the Court Interpreting Program at the Monterey Institute of International Studies. She holds an M.A. in Intercultural Studies from the Monterey Institute of International Studies and is a Federally Certified Interpreter who is dedicated primarily to freelance translation and legal interpreting in state and federal courts and in administrative hearings for such entities as the California Unemployment Insurance Appeals Board, the Workmen's Compensation Appeals Board, the Agricultural Labor Relations Board, the California Department of Motor Vehicles, and many others. She has consulted with the Administrative Office of the United States Courts, the California Cooperative Personnel Services and other agencies on interpreter certification issues. In addition, she is a member of the California Judicial Council Advisory Committee on Court Interpreting.

Professor Mikkelson was a teaching associate with the Summer Institute for Court Interpretation at the University of Arizona Training of Trainers of Court Interpreters and has taught with the Summer Institute for Court Interpretation at the University of Arizona on other occasions. She has also taught at the University of California Extension in Santa Cruz; Montclair State College, and for the Federal Judicial Center. She has published in the area of court interpretation and has participated actively in court interpreter professional organizations and meetings and has through the years served the court interpreting profession through workshops, presentations, and seminars. Professor Mikkelson has been chapter chair of the CCIA, chair of the Continuing Education Committee, and is currently serving as editor of the *Polyglot*, the official newsletter of the California Court Interpreters Association.

Consultants

Sofia Zahler, J.D., FCCI

The late Sofia Zahler, a Federally Certified Spanish-English Interpreter, also interpreted in French, German, and Russian. A practicing attorney in Chile for thirty years, Dr. Zahler came to the United States and chose court interpretation as her second professional endeavor and became an exemplary practitioner and pioneer instructor in this area. Dr. Zahler was formerly Director of Court Interpreting Services at the United States District Court, Central District of California, Los Angeles, the federal court with the highest demand for language services in the United States. She was also chair of the Federal Court Interpreters Advisory Board, was a member of the core faculty of the Summer Institute for Court Interpretation at the University of Arizona since its inception and a faculty member of the Training of Trainers of Court Interpreters. In addition, Dr. Zahler served as a faculty member of the Court Interpreter Seminars at the National Judicial College in Reno, Nevada in 1981 and 1982 and was a featured lecturer at numerous staff interpreter workshops for the Administrative Office of the United States Courts. Her work lent direction to several state and federal agencies on interpreter certification matters. Dr. Zahler's early work in comparative legal systems, comparative legal terminology, and court interpreter ethics and procedure is seminal to the entire field of court interpretation in the United States.

Frank M. Almeida, FCCI

Frank M. Almeida is a Spanish-English Federally Certified Interpreter and the Director of Interpreter Services at the United States District Court, Central District of California, Los Angeles. He has been the lead faculty member of the Summer Institute for Court Interpretation at the University of Arizona since its establishment. A native of Los Angeles, Mr. Almeida was a master teacher for the Los Angeles Public Schools for thirty-four years and was a faculty member at the University of California at Los Angeles in the Bolivia Peace Corps Project from 1962 to 1963. His experience in court interpreting is extensive, and he has worked with the Los Angeles Superior court and the United States District Court in Los Angeles for the past twenty years. In 1977 he devised the first interpreting-performance testing program for the Los Angeles Superior Court. He became exemplar among court interpreting practitioners and was invited in 1979 by the California Court Interpreters Association to teach the first training program to court interpreters. His work with the late Ely Weinstein and the late Dr. Sofia Zahler represents the earliest efforts in court interpreter training and testing in the United States when he was a faculty member of the court interpreter seminars at the National Judicial College in Reno, Nevada in 1981 and 1982. Over the years he has worked closely with the Administrative Office of the United States Courts and other agencies on interpreter testing and certification issues.

Linda Haughton, Ph.D., FCCI, ATA Accredited

Linda Haughton is a Federally Certified Interpreter and a Staff Interpreter for the United States District Court in El Paso and has worked with the federal courts in two other Texas jurisdictions. Dr. Haughton holds a doctorate in Spanish language and literature and came to the world of court interpreting after having taught Spanish language, linguistics, and literature at the University of Arizona, the University of Wisconsin at Milwaukee, California State University at Los Angeles, and the University of Northern Colorado for a number of years.

She has been a member of the core faculty of the Summer Institute for Court Interpretation at the University of Arizona since 1986 and is now a lead faculty member. Over the years, she has consulted with the Administrative Office of the United States Courts, the United States Department of Justice, and several state agencies on interpreter certification and testing issues, including the states of New Jersey, Washington, and the Texas Employment Commission. She has given several papers and workshops on court interpreting and language. Dr. Haughton's meritorious work as a practitioner and a gifted teacher makes her an invaluable resource in the field of court interpreting.